DATE DUE

MY 8 '99			
NO 8 '99			
NO 16 '99			
DE 15 '99			
NO 21 '00			
NO 12 '02			
JE 8 '10			

DEMCO 38-296

The purpose of the Cambridge Edition is to offer translations of the best modern German edition of Kant's work in a uniform format suitable for Kant scholars. When complete (fourteen volumes are currently envisaged), the edition will include all of Kant's published writings and a generous selection from the unpublished writings such as the *Opus postumum, handschriftliche Nachlass,* lectures, and correspondence.

This volume contains the first translation into English of notes from Kant's lectures on metaphysics. These lectures, dating from the 1760s to the 1790s, touch on all the major topics and phases of Kant's philosophy. Most of these notes appeared only recently in the German Academy's edition; this translation offers many corrections of that edition.

As is standard in the volumes of the Cambridge Edition, there is substantial editorial apparatus. In this case, there are extensive explanatory and linguistic notes, a detailed subject index, glossaries of key terms, and a concordance that coordinates all of Kant's lectures on metaphysics with Baumgarten's *Metaphysics,* the textbook that Kant himself used.

THE CAMBRIDGE EDITION OF THE WORKS OF IMMANUEL KANT

IMMANUEL KANT

Lectures on metaphysics

THE CAMBRIDGE EDITION OF THE WORKS
OF IMMANUEL KANT

IMMANUEL KANT

Lectures on metaphysics

TRANSLATED AND EDITED BY

KARL AMERIKS

University of Notre Dame

AND

STEVE NARAGON

Manchester College

CAMBRIDGE
UNIVERSITY PRESS

CATE OF THE UNIVERSITY OF CAMBRIDGE
Street, Cambridge CB2 1RP, United Kingdom

CAMBRIDGE UNIVERSITY PRESS
The Edinburgh Building, Cambridge CB2 2RU, United Kingdom
40 West 20th Street, New York, NY 10011–4211, USA
10 Stamford Road, Oakleigh, Melbourne 3166, Australia

© Cambridge University Press 1997

First published 1997

Printed in the United States of America

Typeset in Ehrhardt

A catalog record for this book is available from the British Library.

Library of Congress Cataloging-in-Publication Data
Kant, Immanuel, 1724–1804.
[Lectures. English. Selections]
Lectures on metaphysics / Immanuel Kant; translated and edited by
Karl Ameriks and Steve Naragon.
p.   cm. – (The Cambridge edition of the works of Immanuel Kant)
Includes bibliographical references and indexes.
ISBN 0-521-36012-9
1. Metaphysics.   I. Ameriks, Karl, 1947–   .   II. Naragon, Steve.
III. Title.   IV. Series: Kant, Immanuel, 1724–1804.   Works.
English.   1992.
B2794.L432E5   1996
110 – dc20   96–8599
                            CIP

ISBN 0-521-36012-9 hardback

Contents

General editors' preface

Within a few years of the publication of his *Critique of Pure Reason* in 1781, Immanuel Kant (1724–1804) was recognized by his contemporaries as one of the seminal philosophers of modern times – indeed as one of the great philosophers of all time. This renown soon spread beyond German-speaking lands, and translations of Kant's work into English were published even before 1800. Since then, interpretations of Kant's views have come and gone and loyalty to his positions has waxed and waned, but his importance has not diminished. Generations of scholars have devoted their efforts to producing reliable translations of Kant into English as well as into other languages.

There are four main reasons for the present edition of Kant's writings:

1. Completeness. Although most of the works published in Kant's lifetime have been translated before, the most important ones more than once, only fragments of Kant's many important unpublished works have ever been translated. These include the *Opus postumum*, Kant's unfinished *magnum opus* on the transition from philosophy to physics; transcriptions of his classroom lectures; his correspondence; and his marginalia and other notes. One aim of this edition is to make a comprehensive sampling of these materials available in English for the first time.

2. Availability. Many English translations of Kant's works, especially those that have not individually played a large role in the subsequent development of philosophy, have long been inaccessible or out of print. Many of them, however, are crucial for the understanding of Kant's philosophical development, and the absence of some from English-language bibliographies may be responsible for erroneous or blinkered traditional interpretations of his doctrines by English-speaking philosophers.

3. Organization. Another aim of the present edition is to make all Kant's published work, both major and minor, available in comprehensive volumes organized both chronologically and topically, so as to facilitate the serious study of his philosophy by English-speaking readers.

4. Consistency of translation. Although many of Kant's major works have been translated by the most distinguished scholars of their day, some of these translations are now dated, and there is considerable terminological disparity among them. Our aim has been to enlist some of the most accomplished Kant scholars and translators to produce new translations, freeing readers from both the philosophical and literary preconceptions of previous generations and allowing them to approach texts, as far as possible, with the same directness as present-day readers of the German or Latin originals.

In pursuit of these goals, our editors and translators attempt to follow several fundamental principles:

1. As far as seems advisable, the edition employs a single general glossary, especially for Kant's technical terms. Although we have not attempted to restrict the prerogative of editors and translators in choice of terminology, we have maximized consistency by putting a single editor or editorial team in charge of each of the main groupings of Kant's writings, such as his work in practical philosophy, philosophy of religion, or natural science, so that there will be a high degree of terminological consistency, at least in dealing with the same subject matter.

2. Our translators try to avoid sacrificing literalness to readability. We hope to produce translations that approximate the originals in the sense that they leave as much of the interpretive work as possible to the reader.

3. The paragraph, and even more the sentence, is often Kant's unit of argument, and one can easily transform what Kant intends as a continuous argument into a mere series of assertions by breaking up a sentence so as to make it more readable. Therefore, we try to preserve Kant's own division of sentences and paragraphs wherever possible.

4. Earlier editions often attempted to improve Kant's texts on the basis of controversial conceptions about their proper interpretation. In our translations, emendation or improvement of the original edition is kept to the minimum necessary to correct obvious typographical errors.

5. Our editors and translators try to minimize interpretation in other ways as well, for example, by rigorously segregating Kant's own footnotes, the editors' purely linguistic notes, and their more explanatory or informational notes; notes in this last category are treated as endnotes rather than footnotes.

We have not attempted to standardize completely the format of individual volumes. Each, however, includes information about the context in which Kant wrote the translated works, an English-German glossary, an index, and other aids to comprehension. The general introduction to each volume includes an explanation of specific principles of translation and, where necessary, principles of selection of works included in that volume. The pagination of the standard German edition of Kant's works, *Kant's Gesammelte Schriften,* edited by the Royal Prussian (later German) Academy of Sciences (Berlin: Georg Reimer, later Walter de Gruyter & Co., 1900–), is indicated throughout by means of marginal numbers.

Our aim is to produce a comprehensive edition of Kant's writings, embodying and displaying the high standards attained by Kant scholarship in the English-speaking world during the second half of the twentieth century, and serving as both an instrument and a stimulus for the further development of Kant studies by English-speaking readers in the century to come. Because of our emphasis on literalness of translation and on information rather than interpretation in editorial practices, we hope our edition will continue to be usable despite the inevitable evolution and occasional revolutions in Kant scholarship.

PAUL GUYER
ALLEN W. WOOD

Acknowledgments

This project owes much to a number of institutions and individuals. The National Endowment for the Humanities granted essential support for the project through its translation and travel grants. At the University of Notre Dame, the Department of Philosophy and the Institute for Scholarship in the Liberal Arts also provided support; Michael Loux, Richard Foley, and Gary Gutting were instrumental in many ways. The Marburg Kant Archive, and in particular Reinhard Brandt and Werner Stark, was extraordinarily helpful at every stage; we are especially indebted to Dr. Stark for his unhesitating assistance in reading the manuscripts, as well as on many specific textual and historical points. We thank Dr. Podlaszewska of the Biblioteka Glowna, Universytetu Mikolaja Kopernika, of Torun (Poland) for kindly providing a microfilm of the *Metaphysik K₃* notes. The general editors of this series, Paul Guyer and Allen Wood, as well as Terry Moore at Cambridge University Press, were most encouraging and patient when the complications of this project delayed matters longer than we had expected. There are many other Kant scholars whose work and advice were also much appreciated at various points, but we are especially indebted for timely remarks by Manfred Kuehn, Michael Young, and Eric Watkins. Andy Dzida did the crucial work on the Latin translations in this volume, and his helpfulness went far beyond any reward we could offer. We would also like to thank Mitch Clearfield and Patrick Frierson for help in the final stages of the preparation of the text.

Translators' introduction

PRELIMINARY OVERVIEW

Kant was eloquent about the centrality of metaphysics in his view of philosophy: "Metaphysics is the spirit of philosophy. It is related to philosophy as the spirit of wine [*spiritus vini*] is to wine. It purifies our elementary concepts and thereby makes us capable of comprehending all sciences. In short, it is the greatest culture of the human understanding" (Ak. 29: 940).

These words are from the end of the *Metaphysik Mrongovius*, perhaps the most significant of the sets of student notes from Kant's lectures that are being translated here for the first time. Given the importance of metaphysics in Kant's system, it must seem remarkable that it has taken so long for his lectures on metaphysics to see the full light of day. Although notes from his lectures were widely used and distributed during his lifetime,[1] only parts of two sets of lectures on metaphysics were published (by Pölitz)[2] in the first half century after Kant's death. Parts of a few other sets were reproduced by other editors within the next hundred years,[3] and in

---

[1] Lehmann (1961, 15). Cf. Feldman (1936), and Heinze (1894, 656): "The lectures in L_2 and K_2 have been maintained in a thoroughly more understandable form than the Critical writings [and they provide] an excellent introduction to metaphysics in general as well as to the entirety of Kant's Critical philosophy."

[2] Pölitz (1821); cf. Castillo (1993).

[3] In chronological order, the publication history of the Metaphysics notes includes the following: 1843 – J. Tissot, translation into French of the Pölitz Metaphysics: *Leçons de métaphysique de Kant*, publiées par M. Poelitz, précédées d'une introduction où l'éditeur expose brèvement les principaux changements, survenus dans la métaphysique depuis Kant (Paris: Lagrange, 1843), xl, 446 pp.; 1889 – Carl du Prel (editor), partial reprint (pp. 125–261) of the Pölitz Metaphysics: *Immanuel Kants Vorlesungen über Psychologie*. Mit einer Einleitung: "Kants mystische Weltanschauung" (Leipzig: Ernst Günther, 1889), lxiv, 96 pp.; 1894 – Max Heinze, *Vorlesungen Kants über Metaphysik aus drei Semestern* (Leipzig: S. Hirzel, 1894), 248 pp., including the following fragments (1) *Rosenhagen/Korff* (Introduction), (2) *Rosenhagen/Korff/L₁* (discussion on space and time from the Ontology), (3) L_2 (Rational Psychology), (4) K_2 (Rational Psychology), and (5) K_2 (Natural Theology); 1901 – Otto Schlapp, *Kants Lehre vom Genie und die Entstehung der "Kritik der Urteilskraft"* (Göttingen: 1901), with fragments from K_2; 1911 – Paul Menzer, *Kants Lehre von der Entwicklung in Natur und Geschichte* (Berlin: Georg Reimer, 1911), 432 pp., with fragments of the *Herder;* 1924 – K. H. Schmidt (editor), new edition of the Pölitz Metaphysics: *Vorlesungen über die Metaphysik* (Rosswein: Pflugbeil, 1924), xv, 205 pp.; 1924 – Arnold Kowalewski (editor): *Die*

the 1920s philosophers such as Heinz Heimsoeth and Martin Heidegger made a strong case that Kant's traditional metaphysical concerns remained central even throughout his Critical period. Nonetheless, it was not until 1968 and 1970 that versions of these lectures appeared in the Academy edition of Kant's works, and they were seldom cited by scholars, let alone reviewed or discussed at length. Although Kant's work has become ever more popular, even in the Anglo-American world, it is his antimetaphysical statements and his ethical doctrines that have been drawing the most attention and sympathy recently.

In this situation, only a few years ago it was something of a risk for a scholar to invoke these lectures as backing for major interpretive claims.[4] But unexpected good fortune brought the discovery and publication in 1983 of two additional sets of Metaphysics lectures – *Mrongovius* and *Vigilantius (K_3)*. These especially detailed lectures have provided further confirmation of the general independence and reliability of the various sets of notes. We now have copious good notes from the 1760s, 1770s, 1780s, and 1790s. Taken together, these lectures (along with recently discovered ones on logic and ethics) provide surely the most striking addition to Kant literature in years. The scholarship of just the last few decades has finally given us a full picture of how, across the long range of his teaching career, Kant treated the central doctrines of philosophy. It is hard to imagine a more helpful extra background for understanding Kant's work than the lectures on metaphysics, which touch on all branches in the development of his Critical philosophy.

Despite their incomplete nature, the lectures are easy enough to compare, since they overlap at many points and all discuss common topics taken from Baumgarten's *Metaphysics* (the textbook Kant used in his metaphysics lectures). Just as in Kant's own published writings, there are important shifts in doctrine over the decades, but there are also clear and deep continuities. Of course, for any particular passage in the notes, it is not certain that what Kant said was transcribed correctly. The notes are often fragmentary, and their philosophical meaning is a matter of interpretation. Terms or doctrines are sometimes simply listed or juxtaposed, with no explicit indication of where Baumgarten's ideas are being merely repeated, or accepted, or meant to be corrected by Kant. Nonetheless, a

---

philosophischen Hauptvorlesungen Immanuel Kants. Nach den aufgefundenen Kolleghefien des Grafen Heinrich zu Dohna-Wundlacken (München and Leipzig: 1924), 633 pp., including the *Dohna;* 1964 – Hans Dietrich Irmscher (editor): *Aus den Vorlesungen der Jahre 1762 bis 1764. Auf Grund der Nachschrifien Johann Gottfried Herders,* edited by Hans Dietrich Irmscher (Köln: Kölner-Universitäts-Verlag, 1964), 178 pp. (Vol. 88 of the *Kant-Studien Ergänzungshefie*), including the *Herder.*

[4]See Ameriks (1982). Kant's lectures have also been used substantively in, e.g., Wood (1978b), Ritzel (1985), Guyer (1987), Brandt (1989), Carl (1989), Makkreel (1990), and Ameriks (1991).

philosophical reader with a general knowledge of Kant and of his era should be able to get fairly easily a good grasp of the spirit of the discussion and in this way determine in nearly all cases what very likely was meant. Repeated reading, especially of all the materials in this collection, and with an eye to comparing them with one another, can reveal a clear picture of Kant's own metaphysical "voice" as it maintains itself and develops through these lecture notes.

Our goal in this edition is to make such a reading now possible in English, with accuracy and yet a minimum of distraction. We have made a conscious effort to be literal and not to "clean up" the lectures.[5] We are presenting them in their raw form, and therefore many passages will appear incomplete and awkward, especially in translation. There was a natural temptation to rewrite the text in a smoother manner for the English-speaking reader, but it soon became apparent that the slightest adjustments can introduce controversial and difficult to monitor interpretive manipulations. Hence we tried to follow a policy of making (and indicating) changes only when it was felt that not doing so would be likely to result in a misreading of the text.

An unfortunate complication with these notes is that surprisingly many problems were found with the volumes of the Academy edition of Kant's works that are the primary basis of our translation. As is explained farther on, we had to depart in many places from the Academy text, but we did so only when we discovered a strong justification. In the future, a new German version of some of these materials may be prepared, but to wait until that day, or to attempt to anticipate such a critical edition ourselves, could have delayed this project until at least the next century. In any case, we already have reliable enough documents to believe that future adjustments will be minor.

Despite these complications, most of Kant's lectures are actually easier to grasp than many of his published works. His lectures on ethics have long functioned for students as an excellent introduction to his work, and his lectures on theology and logic have also developed a following among readers who can appreciate them to a large extent without getting into the intricacies of much of the Critical system. Kant's Metaphysics lectures were known to be his most abstract and difficult,[6] but even these are in some ways easier to follow than parts of his Critical writings. As time went on, Kant began to introduce his commentary with a helpful preliminary discussion of how, in general, his more epistemologically oriented procedure differed from the traditional approach of Baumgarten. By having to comment on Baumgarten, Kant was also forced to address traditional doctrines and to explain in a fairly detailed manner what his own views

[5]We have followed roughly the general procedure outlined in Young (1992, xxvii et seq.).
[6]Wood (1978a, 16). Cf. Kant's letter to Markus Herz, August 28, 1778 (Ak. 10: 240–42).

were. Many classical metaphysical topics that are neglected, or that seem to be simply replaced (almost with a kind of sleight of hand) by a "rule of experience" in the *Critique*, receive more direct discussion in the lectures.

Following Baumgarten, Kant's lectures were organized into a general introduction (Prolegomena) and Ontology, Cosmology, Psychology (Empirical and Rational), and Natural Theology sections (we capitalize these terms when referring to sections of the notes, as opposed to disciplines). We have ignored the Theology section because Kant's lectures on that topic are covered by other translators. Since space would not permit us to translate all of what remained, we decided on selections that would cover each of the other sections and that also would give a representation of lectures from each decade of Kant's mature career (see Table 1). In addition, because of the special importance of their extensive content and recent discovery, we have included the entirety of the *Vigilantius (K$_3$)* and *Mrongovius* notes, the latter being published here for the first time in proper order.

For different reasons, each of the Metaphysics lecture sets has great value for anyone trying to understand the core of Kant's philosophy. The 1760s are represented by only a sample of Herder's telegraphic notes, but their early date (and the fame of the note taker) provides interesting comparison with later works. We have focused on selections from the Cosmology, where Kant presents some arguments on idealism and interaction very close to those found in notes written thirty years later, and other passages reflect a position quite the opposite of his eventual Critical view. The 1770s are represented by a large selection from the set published long ago by Pölitz. The exact dating of this selection is the most controversial, but we have included all the evidence it provides of Kant's views on cosmology and psychology in this "silent decade" prior to the first *Critique*. There are especially striking passages here that still show a strong sympathy for rationalist arguments about the soul's substantiality, simplicity, and freedom. For the 1780s, we now have the *Metaphysik Mrongovius*. This is by far the longest text, and it gives us a rich new expression of Kant's thought at one of the most crucial times in his career. It dates from 1782–3 – right after the first edition of the first *Critique* and just before Kant published his *Prolegomena to Any Future Metaphysics*, his major practical works, and the second edition of the *Critique*. As a point of comparison for this decade, we also include the Rational Psychology portion of the much briefer *Volckmann* notes. From the 1790s, there are four selections: the *L$_2$*, available since the Pölitz edition and offered almost in its entirety; the *Dohna*, represented by all of its highly condensed Cosmology and Psychology sections; the Rational Psychology segment of *K$_2$*; and the complete *Vigilantius (K$_3$)*, which is written in a particularly smooth fashion and includes important remarks on aesthetics and ethics. These last two sets of notes are distinctive in the extent to which they depart from Baumgarten's order of topics, especially in the Ontology.

These selections are also designed to give broad coverage of all the topics of Kant's metaphysics. We have included all available versions of the Rational Psychology (after 1765), so that, in at least one area of metaphysics, readers can get complete evidence here of how much overlap and continuity there is between different periods and independent sources of Kant's work. We have not striven to eliminate all repetition, because it is important for readers to have examples of how closely related the various notes are, and to see the extent to which they confirm one another. We have also included most of the available treatments of Empirical Psychology and Cosmology, in order to give a good range of formulations of Kant's ideas on the many topics in these areas that are not developed in full detail in the *Critique*. Three versions of the Introduction and the Ontology are also provided, so that all aspects of Kant's metaphysics are covered by multiple presentations. In addition to the detailed Subject Index, the Concordance – which is keyed to the paragraph topics of Baumgarten's *Metaphysics* – should make it easy for scholars to compare Kant's discussion of specific issues.

To provide a quick overview of the relation between Baumgarten and Kant, we present here a synopsis of Baumgarten's *Metaphysics*,[7] followed by a listing (organized with an eye to Baumgarten) of some central topics and sections in Kant's *Critique of Pure Reason* and a correlation of them with the relevant subsections of Baumgarten that Kant discusses in the lectures:

Synopsis of Baumgarten's *Metaphysics*

1. Introduction (§§ 1–3)
2. Ontology (§§ 4–350)
   a) internal universal predicates: 1. possibility, 2. connection, 3. being (reality, essence, quality, and quantity), 4. unity, 5. truth, 6. perfection
   b) internal disjunctive predicates: 1. necessity, 2. mutability, 3. reality, 4. singularity, 5. wholeness, 6. substance (and accident and state), 7. simplicity, 8. finitude – and each of their opposites
   c) external and relative predicates: 1. sameness and difference, 2. simultaneity and succession, 3. types of cause, 4. sign and signified
3. Cosmology (§§ 351–500)
   a) the concept of a world: 1. positive, 2. negative
   b) parts of a world: 1. simples, in general and qua spirits, 2. composites, their genesis and nature
   c) perfection of a world: 1a. the idea of the best, b. interaction of substances (theories of explaining this), 2. the means: natural and supernatural

---

[7]For a slightly more detailed and hierarchically arranged synopsis as was printed in Baumgarten's text, see the reprint at Ak. 17: 19–23.

4. Psychology
   a) Empirical (§§ 504–739): 1. existence of soul, 2. faculties, a. cognitive (lower and higher), b. appetitive (in general, and lower and higher, qua spontaneous and free), 3. soul-body interaction
   b) Rational (§§ 740–99): 1. nature of the human soul, 2. systems explaining its interaction with the body, 3. its origin, 4. human immortality, 5. afterlife, 6. souls of brutes, 7. souls of nonhuman finite spirits
5. Theology (§§ 800–1000)
   a) concept of God: existence, intellect, will
   b) divine action: creation, its end, providence, decrees, revelation

Some Main Topics in Kant's *Critique of Pure Reason*

1. The idea of transcendental philosophy (Transcendental Analytic of Concepts): cf. Baumgarten 1, 2a1, 2a4–6
2. Quantity, space, and time (Transcendental Aesthetic, Axioms, First Antinomy): cf. Baumgarten 2a3, 2b2, 2b4, 2b8, 2c1–2, 3a, 3b2
3. Quality, simples (Anticipations, Second Paralogism, Second Antinomy): cf. Baumgarten, 2a3, 2b3,5,7, 3b1, 4b1; and substance (First Analogy, First and Third Paralogisms): cf. Baumgarten 2a3, 2b2, 2b6, 4a1, 4b1
4. Causality and community (Second and Third Analogies, Fourth Paralogism): cf. Baumgarten 2a2, 2b5–6, 2c2–3, 3a, 3b2, 3c1b, 4a3, 4b2–5
5. Spontaneity (Third Antinomy, Canon): cf. Baumgarten 2b6, 4a2b
6. Necessity (Postulates, Fourth Antinomy, Critique of Speculative Theology): cf. Baumgarten 2b1, 3a, 3c2, 5

A proper commentary on Kant's lectures here would obviously be tantamount to a discussion of nearly the whole of his philosophy. Because the Metaphysics lectures, especially the Introduction and Ontology sections, elucidate the basic concepts of Kant's entire philosophical system, each paragraph in them could be followed with references to many passages throughout his works. The exposition and interpretation of these lectures are, therefore, best left for another place.[8] Merely to begin to understand the lectures, however, some background information is certainly helpful and sometimes essential. The Academy edition includes an extensive set of endnotes to the text, prepared by Gerhard Lehmann. These endnotes are frequently hard to follow because of their scattered location, their highly abbreviated refer-

[8]For the beginning of an interpretation of the light that these lectures shed on Kant's ontology and aspects of the cosmology, see Ameriks (1992), and cf. Laywine (1993) and Watkins (1995). The relevance of the Metaphysics lectures for Kant's views on psychology, epistemology, and theology is explored in works cited in note 4.

ences and cross-references, and the many untranslated non-German terms. They do have a useful content, however, so, along with our own notes, we have included the great majority of them as Explanatory Notes at the end of the volume, after refashioning them so that they are intelligible on their own. Our guiding principle was that the English reader deserves historical assistance at least as much as the German reader does, and that this help should be made as accessible as it can be in a practical way.

Aside from Kant's own writings, the other most helpful background for these lectures is the Baumgarten text, which itself is highly dependent on Wolff and Leibniz. Extensive quotations and translations from Baumgarten are provided in the Explanatory Notes, and the basic structure of his work is repeated in the detailed headings of the Concordance, near the end of this volume.

KANT'S CAREER AS A LECTURER

Students aspiring to positions as teachers, pastors, or university professors typically supported themselves as private tutors after leaving the university until a post opened or, as in the case of would-be professors, until they had prepared materials sufficient for them to be appointed as docents – an unsalaried position that allowed one to offer lectures anywhere in the university. Kant matriculated as a student at the Albertus University in Königsberg on September 27, 1740, at the age of sixteen, and concluded his studies in 1746. After six years as a tutor to various families in the Königsberg area, he defended his Latin treatise "Concerning Fire" (*de igne*) on June 12, 1755, and was awarded the magister degree. On September 27 of the same year, he successfully defended a second Latin treatise, "A New Elucidation of the First Principles of Metaphysical Cognition," known as the "*nova dilucidatio*," after which he received the right to lecture as a docent.

The academic year was divided into winter (WS) and summer (SS) semesters, with Easter and the Feast of St. Michael (September 29) forming the beginning and end points. A new rector of the university was always elected on the first Sunday after each of these dates, and the official Catalog of Lectures offered for the following semester was to be posted eight days after the election of the rector, with classes beginning immediately thereafter (if the professors were diligent). Most classes met four times a week (Monday, Tuesday, Thursday, Friday) for one hour each (in reality, about forty minutes), leaving Wednesday and Saturday free for other academic affairs. So Kant's first lecture as a docent probably was given on Monday, October 13, 1755.[9] His first semester included

---

[9]An account of this first lecture is preserved for us in Borowski's biography of Kant (reprinted in Gross [1912, 85–7]). Ludwig Ernst Borowski (1740–1831) matriculated at the

courses on logic, metaphysics, mathematics, and physics, which were given in the home where he was living at the time (it was customary to lecture in one's own home or in a rented room). Kant apparently offered metaphysics twenty-five of his thirty semesters as a docent, although the records of this period are sketchy and not wholly reliable.[10]

Other professors and docents at the university were also lecturing on metaphysics, including the full professor of logic and metaphysics, who by virtue of his salaried position was required to give lectures on logic and metaphysics free of charge. This provided, no doubt, a certain competitive challenge among the docents, since only about three hundred students were currently enrolled at Königsberg,[11] and the only compensation for lecturing was the standard four thaler per student, paid by each student directly to the instructor at the end of the semester. Johann David Kypke (1692–1758) had held the logic and metaphysics chair since 1727. In 1758, it passed to Friedrich Johann Buck (1722–86), who passed it on to Kant in 1770, when the chair in mathematics, which Buck preferred, became vacant. So Kant became a full (*ordentlich*) professor of logic and metaphysics in 1770, which involved yet another public defense of a Latin treatise on August 21, 1770 – this time his inaugural dissertation, "Concerning the Form and Principles of the Sensible and Intelligible World" (*De mundi sensibilis atque intelligibilis forma et principiis*). The summer semester of 1770 was Kant's first as a full professor.[12] Because of his new obligation to give free lectures, Kant offered Logic in the summer and Metaphysics in the winter through SS 1796 (his last semester). He also lectured privately (for which students were still required to pay four thaler) on a variety of other courses, his two mainstays (after 1772) being Physical Geography (summer) and Anthropology (winter), both of which he taught Wednesdays and Saturdays (for two hours each day). He also taught courses entitled Moral Philosophy, Natural Law, Natural Theology, Theoretical Physics, Mathematics, Pedagogy, Philosophical Encyclopedia, Mineralogy (WS 1770 – 1), Mechanical Science (SS 1759, WS 1759–60, SS 1761), and possibly pyrotechnics.

university on March 20, 1754, attended Kant's lectures, and later became a close friend. He wrote the biography in 1792 and shared it with Kant for his corrections; but at Kant's request, publication was withheld until after Kant's death. Borowski was a well-known and popular figure with the government, and was eventually elevated to the rank of archbishop of the Evangelical Church (the only individual to have held such a rank in the history of Prussia). See Gause (1968, ii.257 and 1974, 26–7).

[10]For evidence concerning the history of Kant's Metaphysics lectures and the textbooks used, see Stark (1993, 323–6).

[11]Eulenberg (1904, 164, 260).

[12]Kant's letter of appointment (dated March 31, 1770) from Friedrich II and Minister von Fürst is reprinted at Ak. 10: 93–4. A fuller discussion of Kant's career as a university professor can be found in Stark (1995).

OVERVIEW OF THE METAPHYSICS NOTES

There are seventeen sets of student notes of Kant's Metaphysics lectures of whose existence we have at least mention. Seven of these sets are at least partially extant (*Herder, Mrongovius, Volckmann, von Schön I, von Schön II, L₂, Dohna*). Significant portions have been preserved of three of the remaining ten sets $(L_1, K_2, Vigilantius [K_3])$, minor fragments from three (*Korff, Rosenhagen, Willudovius*), and no text at all from the other four (*Nicolai, Motherby, Hippel, Reicke*). In Table 1, we indicate in schematic fashion those parts of the various notes that have been preserved (either as manuscript or as copy),[13] along with a likely date for the semester of lectures from which each originated, as well as where they are found in the Academy edition of Kant's writings and which of them have been translated for this volume. We also provide any other names by which the notes have been commonly cited in the literature (a.k.a.). The notes are arranged by their likely date of origin. We have made use of some of the names for the manuscripts suggested by Reinhard Brandt and Werner Stark of the Kant Archive in Marburg. The "L" and "K" designations were used by early scholars and stand for "Leipzig" and "Königsberg," respectively, and the "anon" (for instance, in "*anon-Hippel*") indicates that the name of the actual note taker is unknown; otherwise the name attached is that of the presumed author.

Two oddities should be noted. First, Max Heinze and others have offered excellent grounds for believing that *Korff, L₁,* and *Rosenhagen* all stem from some unknown fourth set of notes. Consequently, they are all given the same date, and there is also some overlap in where they appear in the Academy edition – here the text is simply labeled as L_1, but it was prepared by Heinze in such a way that it could serve equally well as a transcription from the other two sets of notes. We do not indicate a complete overlap with L_1, however, since Heinze – in comparing the texts – reported textual discrepancies between them only for the text as found at Ak. 28: 167–91. Second, *von Schön II*, which consists of twenty manuscript pages, has not been printed in the Academy edition.

HOW THE NOTES WERE WRITTEN

It is doubtful if any of the extant manuscripts were written in the lecture hall. Most of them have at least one of the following features: the handwriting is too regular, a straight-edge was used to make lines for writing the

---

[13]Many of the notes were destroyed, or in any event lost, during World War II and its aftermath. Fragments of some of these notes had been preserved by various prewar scholars, particularly Erdmann (1883, 1884), Heinze (1894), Schlapp (1901), and Arnoldt (1909, vols. iv, v).

Table 1: Kant's Metaphysics Lectures

Herder	a.k.a.	Manuscript	Copy	Date	Acad. Ed.	In this translation
Herder		complete	-	ca. 1762-4	28: 1-166, 839-962	C (28: 39-53)
anon-Korff	K$_1$	lost	I, fr.O	mid-1770s?	28: 167-91	-
anon-Rosenhagen	H	lost	I, fr.O	mid-1770s?	28: 167-91	-
anon-L$_1$	Pölitz	lost	Fr.O, rest complete?	mid-1770s?	28: 167-350	C, EP, RP (28: 195-301)
Nicolai				1775-6	-	-
Mrongovius		complete (I, O, C, EP, RP)	-	1782-3	29: 747-940	I, O, C, EP, RP (29: 747-940)
Volckmann		I, fr.O, RP, NT	-	1784-5	28: 351-459	RP (28: 440-50)
von Schön I		I, most of O	-	late 80s?	28: 461-524	-
von Schön II		fr.I, fr.O		?	-	-
anon-L$_2$	Pölitz	C, EP, RP, most of NT	I, O	1790-1?	28: 531-610	I, O, EP, RP (28: 531-94)
Dohna		complete (I, O, C, EP, RP, NT)	-	1792-3	28: 615-702	C, EP, RP (28: 656-90)
Motherby		lost	-	1792-3?		-
Willudovius	Marienstift	lost	fr.?	early 90s?	-	-
anon-K$_2$		lost	RP, NT, fr. of rest	early 90s?	28: 705-816	RP (28: 753-75)
Vigilantius	K$_3$, Arnoldt	lost	I, O, C, EP, RP	1794-5	29: 943-1040	I, O, C, EP, RP (29: 943-1040)
anon-Hippel		lost	-	?	-	-
anon-Reicke	Königsberg	lost	-	?	-	-

Abbreviations: I = Introduction, **O** = Ontology, **C** = Cosmology, **EP** = Empirical Psychology, **RP** = Rational Psychology, **NT** = Natural Theology, **fr** = fragments.

Publication Data for the Metaphysics Lectures: *Kant's gesammelte Schriften*, vol. 28, edited by Gerhard Lehmann, 1st half (Berlin: de Gruyter, 1968), pp. 1-524; vol. 28, 2nd half, 1st part (Berlin: de Gruyter, 1970), pp. 525-987; vol. 29, 1st half, 2nd part (Berlin: de Gruyter, 1983), pp. 743-1188.

headings (which are often written calligraphically or with various ornamentations), there are various characteristics typical of copying (e.g., words or entire lines are duplicated, or omitted and then inserted in the margin; or a blank space is left for inserting a word that the copyist apparently found illegible), or there is verbatim agreement with other notes (as is the case with L_1, Korff, and *Rosenhagen*). All the notes we have are written in ink, except some of the *Herder* notes, and it is probable that students used pencils in the lecture hall. The K_2 notes appear to be fairly similar to lecture-hall jottings but are probably a rewrite done at home. Those notes associated with a particular student are generally closer to the original set of notes. Some of the other notes may have been copied a number of times. As at other universities of the period, there was a lively trade in lecture notes: These were hand copied by poorer students and sold to their wealthier counterparts, who might then bring them to class and make additional notes in the (typically wide) margins (these added notes, of course, would derive from a later semester than the main body of notes).

As for material aspects of the notes: Most were in bound quarto volumes (with the exception of the *Volckmann* notes, which consisted of printer's sheets [*Bogen*] folded in the middle with most nested inside others). Some of the sets were bound in the same volume with other sets of notes (for instance, L_2 was bound with a set of notes from Kant's logic course). With regard to some of the notes, it is clear that more than one copyist was at work (the *Mrongovius* notes, for instance, show two separate handwritings). The darkness of the ink in each manuscript varies considerably. Typically it begins dark and grows paler on later pages, which is a result of the copyist's adding water to his ink to extend its life; after the ink grew too pale, he would add more powder to the solution to darken it (recall the likely poverty of these copyists).

THE LANGUAGE OF THE NOTES

Latin

Latin was quite common in the lectures of Kant's day and, although he lectured in German, his text (Baumgarten's *Metaphysics*) was in Latin, and various technical phrases in Latin had yet to find a commonly accepted German equivalent. In the Metaphysics notes, in particular, there are unusually many occurrences of Latin (both isolated terms and longer phrases), and these Latin terms and phrases are often important markers in the text, highlighting topics from Baumgarten. For these reasons, and to avoid interrupting the flow of the text by placing the translation either in footnotes or parenthetically, we provide the translation in the text, followed immediately by the original Latin between wedges (<>). For instance: "Philosophy in the scholastic sense <*in sensu scholastico*> is thus . . ."

Often the Latin appears mistranscribed or corrupt (many terms are constructed as a combination of German and Latin), but in general we do not engage in changing the Academy version unless there is a proper text that can be clearly identified as what the writer intended. Nonstandard spelling has not been corrected, although we have silently corrected the spelling of those terms that were abbreviated in the manuscript and that we feel were improperly expanded in the Academy edition. In texts like these it is often difficult to draw a clear line between what is Latin and what is German (the typography of the Academy edition makes no distinction). The status of many words was changing and ambiguous, as is illustrated both orthographically and typographically. For example, the spelling of "accident" shifts back and forth between *Accidenz* (the German spelling) and *accidens* (the Latin spelling), both in handwriting (where there are distinctly different letter shapes for Latin and German words) and in published works (where the typesetting alternates between "fraktur" for German text and "antiqua" for Latin); in Kant's *Critique of Pure Reason*, for instance, *accidens* is treated both as a Latin and as a German term, although *Accidenz* is always treated as German.

In the interest of reducing textual footnotes and typographical clutter, we adopted the following guidelines with respect to Latin and other foreign terms:

1. Non-German terms are translated, with the original following between wedges (as already mentioned).

2. If a Latin and a German term appear together in the text as equivalents, then the English translation will be followed by the wedged Latin and German terms, for example: "We have no innate concepts (<*notiones connatae;* G: *angebornen Begriffe*>) at all." In the original text, the Latin term was placed in parentheses after the German term.

3. As much as possible, we have treated terms as German rather than as non-German; to this end, words that were often written by the note takers (or later transcribers) as foreign (e.g., in the way the words were spelled or the kind of letters or type used) but have since been assimilated as cognates into the German vocabulary will be treated as German, and so do not appear between wedges as non-German text.[14]

4. *A priori* and *a posteriori* – adjectives meaning, roughly, that something is knowable or justifiable prior to experience or that it is not, respectively – are Latin terms that have become such a routine part of philosophical vocabulary that they are left italicized but untranslated (thus they do not appear between wedges except when part of a longer Latin phrase). Where these terms, or part of them, are emphasized in the

[14]For example, absolute, action, addition, adjective.

original (in the manuscript with underlining, in the Academy edition with spaced letters), the emphasis is mentioned in a footnote. There are a very few exceptions where other Latin terms appear outside of wedges, and these are noted if there is possible ambiguity.

Orthography

The reader who consults the German edition of the text should be alerted to the fact that there are shifts in orthography between eighteenth-century and modern German. Some are fairly common and innocuous (e.g., *th* to *t*, *i* to *j*), but others are potentially confusing (e.g., *wider* [against] is often spelled as *wieder* [again]). Capital letters are often not indicated in the manuscript, and Lehmann silently changes certain letters to capitals (those introducing either sentences or clauses following a colon). We have silently changed the cases to conform with standard English. Deviant spellings of Latin terms – such as a terminal *n* or *z* – have been retained, except that the rare *ß* has been replaced with *s* or *ss*.

Abbreviations

Many of the notes – such as *K₂*, *Dohna*, and *Mrongovius* – make extensive use of abbreviations, which suggests that they are probably not products of professional copyists. These abbreviations offer a challenge to transcribers because they are often ambiguous and inconsistently used. Their use also explains certain otherwise puzzling transcriptional errors in the Lehmann edition. For example, in one passage he misreads *logische* (logical) as *keine* (no); these words were commonly abbreviated as *L* and *K*, respectively, which have a similar appearance in the German script of the day. Signs for *nicht* (not) and *und* (and), if used at all, were used fairly consistently in a manuscript. The abbreviations are sometimes followed by a period, a colon, or a comma. Many words are abbreviated simply by omitting a vowel or ending (e.g., *d* = *der/die/das*; *abr* = *aber*; *odr* = *oder*). A passage from the *Mrongovius* notes gives some sense of the use of abbreviations:

die Praedicabil sind auch R. Verst Begr. abr aus den Catheg: hergeleitet dr Begr. ds ganzen ist ein praedicabile das unter dr Cath: dr Omnitudo steht, und so kenen wir viele Praedicab. untr diesr Cath. haben. Wenn man itzt von Cathgorien, Praedicamenten und predicabilibus redt so scheint man die alte scholastische Philosophie aufzuwärmen – . (sheet 45 of the *Mrongovius* notes [Ak. 29: 803_{12-18}])[15]

---

[15]This passage was singled out for comment in Zelazny and Stark (1987, 287–8). See also Blackall (1959), ch. 2, "The Language of Philosophy," and especially the sample from Wolff on page 32, which nicely illustrates the polyglot style of eighteenth-century German philosophical writers.

Filled out, this reads:

Die Praedicabilien sind auch reine Verstandesbegriffe, aber aus den Categorien hergeleitet; der Begriff des ganzen ist ein Praedicabile, das unter der Categorie der Omnitudo steht, und so kennen wir viele Praedicate unter dieser Categorie haben. Wenn man jetzt von Categorien, Praedicamenten und Praedicabilien redet, so scheint man die alte scholastische Philosophie aufzuwärmen.[16]

Apart from the abbreviations, the handwriting of the day often led to confusion among copyists and transcribers. For example, many of the letters are identical except in the number of spikes, so a series of spikes could potentially be any of several possible letter combinations (as delimited by the meaning of the surrounding text). Similarly, the capital *B* closely resembles the *L* and *K*, and so forth. The lower-case *u*, which otherwise is identical with an *n*, is identified by a dip or circle written above it, but occasionally this is inadvertently omitted.

Punctuation

We strove more for accuracy than for elegance, and we maintained the notelike character of the text. Much punctuation was added by Lehmann, the editor of the Academy edition; we retained most of the question marks he added, but we occasionally omitted periods that were wrongly added or that entered as typographical errors. We have added commas and semicolons occasionally but have not changed sentence and paragraph breaks without indication. We have also retained the frequent dashes, which are used in a variety of ways, such as to indicate conjunctions, inferences, and abrupt transitions. It should be kept in mind, however, that the punctuation in the lecture notes of a student is more fluid and haphazard than in Kant's own published writings, and in no literal sense do these various marks stem from Kant.

The notes often include lists that are enumerated using either numbers or letters (of either the Roman or the Greek alphabet). In the manuscript, the number or letter and the item following it are sometimes separated by a period, sometimes by a period and a right parenthesis, and sometimes by nothing at all. In none of the notes we examined is the number or letter

---

[16]Other frequently used abbreviations in the *Mrongovius* manuscript include the following: A = Autor (Author, i.e., Baumgarten); dh. = durch (through); Erf. = Erfahrung (experience); Erk. = Erkenntnis (cognition); h. (at the end of a word) = -heit (a common suffix); k. (at the end of a word) = – keit (a common suffix); K./k. = keine (no, none); Kenntnis (knowledge); L./l. = logisch (logical); M = Mensch/en (human/s); R = rein/en (pure), Regel (rule); s. = sein/e/er/en/em (his, its); sd = sind (are); SW = sinnliche Welt (sensible world); Θ (Greek theta) = Gott (God); trscdt = transcendent; trscdtal = transcendental; Urs = Ursprung (origin); v. = von (on, from, of); V = Vernunft (reason), Verstand (understanding), Vollkommenheit (perfection); Vern = Vernunft (reason); Verst = Verstand (understanding); w = weiter (further); W = Welt (world); Wissenschaft (science).

completely enclosed in parentheses. For the sake of clarity, however, we have silently enclosed all such numbers and letters in parentheses – for example, (1), (a) – when inside text and have followed them with periods when set off as lists.

Other aspects

We have tried to preserve emphasized words and phrases by placing them in italics. One exception is the word *Kritik* (Critique), which appears frequently in the notes. Although it often is used to describe a certain philosophical method, it occasionally appears to be a reference to Kant's book, *Kritik der reinen Vernunft* (*Critique of Pure Reason*). In these latter instances, we treat *Kritik* as a book title and accordingly italicize it in the translation, even though it is not emphasized in the original. This is done without a note.

Finally, we have introduced some uniformity into the appearance of chapter and section headings. In the manuscripts, these headings are generally *not* set off from the text with blank lines (as they appear in the Academy edition) but, rather, are underlined and followed by a period and are on a separate line written in the middle of the page. Some headings are written in *Schönschrift* (large ornamented letters). Chapter and section numbers are commonly on the same line as the title, and often without any punctuation or brackets separating them. We silently placed these chapter and section numbers on a line above the title (so as to avoid any ambiguities as to the meaning of the title) and added the word "Chapter" where appropriate. We also silently removed punctuation at the end of headings.

WHO WROTE THE NOTES?

Notes whose authorship is fairly certain are listed by their names: *Herder, Rosenhagen, Nicolai, Mrongovius, Volckmann, von Schön, Dohna, Motherby, Willudovius*, and *Vigilantius* (K_3). The rest are anonymous. The ages of the note takers are what one might expect of university students, many of whom matriculated at age 17 or 18 and remained at the university for two to four years.[17] The youngest note taker was Graf Dohna, who was 14 when he entered the university and 15 when he heard Kant's Metaphysics lectures, and the oldest was Vigilantius, a lawyer friend of Kant's whose notes were written when he was 37; but most of the others were from 18 to 22 years of age. Students typically sat through a year or two of courses offered by the philosophy faculty before moving on to studies in law,

---

[17]According to Eulenberg (1904, 144) students remained at German universities an average of two and one-third years in the second half of the eighteenth century. See also Stark (1995, 54).

medicine, or theology (the three "higher" faculties) – although notes and class schedules of some students show them attending Kant's lectures (as well as others in the philosophy faculty) throughout their academic career. A Logic course was generally taken before Metaphysics, and Kant is known to have encouraged students to take Poerschke's Logic course before taking his own.[18]

Brief biographical sketches of Herder, Mrongovius, Volckmann, Dohna, and Vigilantius are provided farther on, in the discussions of the individual sets of notes that were translated for this volume. Known authors of other sets of Metaphysics notes are the following: *Karl Ferdinand Nicolai* (c. 1753–1802) matriculated as a theology student on June 21, 1770, and went on to distinguish himself as a schoolteacher. He seems to have attended several of Kant's lectures, and his notes on Kant's Anthropology lectures from WS 1775–6 were possibly used by Otto Schlapp in 1900 before being lost during World War II. *William Motherby* (1776–1847) attended the Philanthropinum in Dessau before entering the university at Königsberg on March 8, 1792. His father, Robert Motherby, was Kant's friend and dinner companion, and his uncle the London physician George Motherby (1732–93) had introduced pox vaccines in England. William eventually graduated with a degree in medicine at Edinburgh, and then led the movement to inoculate against pox in Königsberg, opening the first vaccination clinic in the city quarter of Sackheim.[19] *Heinrich Theodor von Schön* (1773–1856) matriculated at Königsberg on October 25, 1788. He went on to become the *Oberpräsident* of Prussia and was a friend of Fichte's.[20] *Carl Gottfried Christian Rosenhagen* (variant spelling: *Rosenhayn*) matriculated at the university on May 1, 1788. Finally, *August Ludwig Bogislaus Willudovius* (in his memoirs he took the non-Latinized name "von Wildowski") matriculated at the university on March 14, 1791.

DATING THE NOTES

Determining the semester from which a set of notes originated is not as straightforward as has sometimes been assumed. Many of the manuscripts have dates on them (typically on a title page), but these dates need not refer to the semester of origin. In some cases, it is likely that they refer to when the notes were copied or acquired (such is likely with the *Rosenhagen* notes). Or a date might refer to when a student who had purchased a set

---

[18]Johann Christoph Mortzfeld, a physician in Königsberg, anonymously published a short biography of Kant's life in 1802 (*Fragmente aus Kants Leben. Ein biographischer Versuch*) in which he wrote, "Even among [Kant's] students the opinion had spread that his lectures were hard to grasp, for which reason most tended to begin with the lectures on physical geography or philosophical morals" (cited in Malter, 1990, 32).

[19]Gause (1968, ii. 232 and 1974, 42).

[20]Lehmann (1972, 1370); Gause (1968, ii. 323).

of notes actually heard Kant's lectures himself (perhaps the case with the K_2 notes). The contents of the lectures often provide clues to the dating, but seldom can they be taken at face value. For instance, the mention of an individual in the past tense – such as Crusius, who died in 1775 – might suggest that the lecture occurred sometime after that person's death, when in fact a later copyist merely changed the tense of a verb (this has been discovered in sets of notes where the date was already established).

Of the notes translated in this volume, the set most problematic for dating is the L_1. The dates for *Herder, Mrongovius, Volckmann, Dohna,* and *Vigilantius* are well established, and the content of the K_2 (which resembles the *Dohna* notes) clearly places it in the early 1790s, and the L_2 would seem to originate in the WS 1790–1. A closer discussion of the dates can be found in the following descriptions of the sets of notes.

HERDER

Johann Gottfried Herder (1744–1803) is perhaps Kant's best-known pupil and is said to have taken all of Kant's classes.[21] His notes are the only ones we have from any of Kant's lectures prior to 1770. He matriculated at the university on August 10, 1762, as a theology student and attended classes while supporting himself as an assistant teacher at the Collegium Fridericianum (the Latin school Kant had attended before going to a university). As a theology student, he read Rousseau two hours each day (or so it was marked out in his schedule).[22] After leaving the university in 1764, he taught and preached at Riga (1764–9) and served as the court preacher at Bückeburg (1771–6) and then as the general superintendent of the church district at Weimar (1776–1803). He was a close friend of Hamann's and an important critic of the German Enlightenment.

The *Herder* notes are spread over two locations in the Academy edition: 28: 1–166 and 28: 839–931 (these are printed in separate books); the second set was discovered after the first was ready to print. While these two sets do not overlap completely, much of them does, and in a way that is either verbatim or so close that the differences appear to be due to transcriptional errors rather than the original manuscripts themselves. The Cosmology section, which we have translated here, is found only in the first set of notes. There is much work yet to be done on the ordering and transcribing of these notes.

[21]Lehmann (1983, 1348). During Herder's time at the university, Kant lectured on the following subjects: Metaphysics, Logic, Moral Philosophy, Physical Geography, Theoretical Physics, and Mathematics (as reported in Arnoldt [1909,v]), and we have Herder's notes from each of these.
[22]Gause (1968, ii. 299).

$ANON$-L_1 AND $ANON$-L_2:
THE PÖLITZ METAPHYSICS

Karl Heinrich Ludwig Pölitz (1772–1838) studied at the university of Leipzig, held his first teaching post in the philosophy faculty there in 1794, and then changed teaching posts over the years until finally settling back in Leipzig as a professor of political science in 1820. Pölitz was an avid book collector from his earliest years, and a prolific writer as well. The "Pölitz Library," which he left to the Leipziger Stadtsbibliothek in his estate, included 13,360 works.

Pölitz bought several manuscripts from the estate of Friedrich Theodor Rink (1770–1811), one of Kant's early biographers. Rink had been a student of Kant's (matriculating at the university on April 1, 1789) as well as a dinner companion in later years, and Kant had allowed Rink to edit sets of student notes on his lectures on "Physical Geography" and "Education" for publication (1802 and 1803, respectively). Rink had been teaching at the Danzig gymnasium since 1792, first as a docent in theology, oriental languages, and Greek, being promoted in 1794 to assistant (*ausserordentliche*) professor of philosophy, and in 1798 to full professor of theology. From 1801 until his death in Leipzig ten years later, he served as pastor and director of the gymnasium.

The manuscripts purchased out of Rink's estate included a set of student notes on Kant's lectures on Natural Theology from the 1780s; these Pölitz published anonymously in 1817, followed in 1821 by a volume of notes from Kant's Metaphysics lectures – also coming, we assume, from the Rink estate.[23] As Pölitz indicates in his preface to the Metaphysics notes, the volume is a compilation of two sets of notes: from the older set of notes (L_1) he took the Cosmology, Psychology, and Natural Theology, and from the later set of notes (L_2) he took the Introduction and Ontology, as well as the Introduction (pp. 9–18) from the Logic notes that were bound together with the L_2. The order in his published volume followed the normal ordering of topics in Kant's lectures (except for the spurious Introduction from the Logic notes): (1) Introduction (Logic), (2) Introduction (Metaphysics), (3) Ontology, (4) Cosmology, (5) Psychology, and (6) Rational Theology. When he published the manuscripts, Pölitz claimed to have made no changes in the text other than correction of punctuation and occasional omission of

---

[23]Pölitz tells us in the preface to *Vorlesungen über die philosophische Religionslehre* (Leipzig, 1817), and also in the preface to the Metaphysics notes (1821), that he obtained the manuscript of the Religion lectures from a deceased former colleague of Kant's. Not until the preface of the second edition of the Religion notes (1830) does he identify Rink by name. (These three prefaces are reprinted at Ak. 28: 1511–18.) As for the origin of the Metaphysics notes, he simply says that they were "acquired through a lawful purchase" (Ak. 28: 1511), and we are left to assume that L_1 and L_2 actually came from Rink's estate.

superfluous words (such as "but," "or" and "thus"). He retained the various Germanized Latin terms (such as *necessitiren* and *Bonität*). Only a few phrases were omitted, where the note taker clearly had not understood Kant. Pölitz summed up the situation this way: "Thus the reader has in fact on every printed line the true Kant."[24] But Heinze, and later Stark, demonstrated that this is not quite true, and that Pölitz took far more liberties with the text than he indicated in his preface. For instance, Heinze noticed that all reference to Baumgarten is missing in L_1, which he believes was due to Pölitz's editing; we might add that the same is true of L_2, and that references to Baumgarten appear only in those portions of the notes not edited by Pölitz. (See, e.g., Ak. 28: 177 and 581.)

One of Pölitz's more egregious tamperings was the silent inclusion of nine pages of text from the Logic notes that are bound with L_2 (this is the section headed "*Einleitung*" with the subheadings "(1) *Von der Philosophie überhaupt*" and "(2) *Geschichte der Philosophie*" reprinted at Ak. 28: 531–40). Heinze had reported in 1894, in reviewing the notebook, that nine pages had been cut from the Logic manuscript (pp. 9–18). Seventy-two years later, while editing these notes for inclusion in Volume 24 of the Academy edition (1966), Lehmann indicated that he could not find this reported gap, and suggested that the only problem with the manuscript here was the pagination. Unfortunately, Lehmann was looking at the wrong point in the text for the gap; at Ak. 28: 507_{30} there is, as Lehmann suggests, no break in the text, but a careful reader *will* find a gap at 509_{28}, which is where the jump from page 8 to page 19 of the manuscript occurs. An examination of other sets of logic notes indicates that what is missing here is just the sort of text one finds at the beginning of the published Pölitz Metaphysics notes. So in reading the Pölitz Logic notes in Volume 24 of the Academy edition, one needs to insert Ak. 28: 531–40 at Ak. 24: 509_{28}.[25]

Pölitz believed that these notes (as well as the notes he had published on Natural Theology) were actually written down in Kant's lecture hall, as opposed to having been copied later. He understood the dates on the L_2 notes to mean that they were written down during Kant's 1788 lecture, with a second person making additions and amplifications during a later lecture in 1789 or 1790. The erroneous date 1798 appears on its title page. This date was crossed out, and "1789" is written in darker ink over it, possibly by a later user who realized that Kant was no longer lecturing in 1798 (perhaps assuming that the author had inadvertently reversed the digits). The Logic notes preceding the Metaphysics notes in the volume have written at their end the date 1790. This suggests the possibility that

---

[24]Pölitz (Ak. 28: 1512).
[25]Heinze (1894, 492, 503). For this discussion, we are indebted to Stark (1987, 156–7).

the Metaphysics followed the next semester (WS 1790–1), but the evidence is far from conclusive.[26]

As for dating L_1, Pölitz noted in his preface that this manuscript was older than the other manuscript – a conjecture based on the text itself, since the manuscript bears no date. Erdmann dated L_1 and *Korff* as stemming "certainly not before WS 1773–4 nor hardly much later."[27] Heinze effectively dismissed Erdmann's arguments, which amounted to finding textual features of the manuscripts that, it turns out, could just as easily have appeared in much later lectures (such as K_2). In general, Erdmann fastened on formulations that stem from the Baumgarten text and that Erdmann apparently assumed would disappear from the lectures after 1780; but as we know from the later notes, Kant engaged with and quoted the Baumgarten text throughout his teaching career.

Arnoldt argued that the texts of L_1 originated sometime after WS 1778–9, because near the end of the notes (ms, p. 396) there is a reference to Johann Georg Sulzer (1720–79) in the past tense, suggesting that the lecture occurred after Sulzer's death. And he argued that it originated sometime before 1784–5 because of a reference to water as elemental (ms, 168), suggesting that Kant would have learned of its composite nature no later than 1785, and perhaps as early as 1783 or 1784. Heinze found Arnoldt's "water argument" convincing but argued for an even earlier date as the latest possible year – namely 1779–80 – given the mention of an incomplete list of categories in the lectures. It struck Heinze as implausible that Kant would not have filled out the list to twelve once he had completed work on the *Critique of Pure Reason* (which he did sometime between December 1779 and November 1780). Also, Heinze was not convinced by Arnoldt's earlier date (based on the mention of Sulzer), but he does find in *Rosenhagen*, *Korff*, and L_1 two separate references to Crusius in the past tense. Since Crusius died October 18, 1775, he reasoned that the lecture on which these notes were based could not have been earlier than WS 1775–6. So Heinze dated the lecture as falling somewhere in the range WS 1775–6 – WS 1779–80. He also was able to compare the L_1 notes with the *Korff* and *Rosenhagen* and demonstrate that they are all copies of some unknown fourth set of notes. Menzer dated the lectures as just prior to 1781, thus either WS 1778–9 or 1779–80. He bases this on a possible reference to the "discovery" of the limits of reason made in the *Critique of Pure Reason* (published in 1781). Adickes agreed with Heinze's estimate of the early date (1775–6) but rejected his argument for the latter date, since he believed Kant had developed his table of categories as early as 1775–6 (which undermines Heinze's argument).

[26]Pölitz (Ak. 28: 1511), Heinze (1894, 486–7), Erdmann (1883, 135n), Lehmann (1972, 1339).
[27]Erdmann (1884, 65).

More recently, Wolfgang Carl proposed a date not before 1777–8 (arguing that the notes are dependent on Tetens's theory of the imagination, as expressed in 1777)[28] and not later than 1779–80.[29]

ANON-L$_I$: THE MANUSCRIPT

The L_I is a bound quarto volume of 157 pages. There is no title page. (The first page is blank.) On the spine: "P. Kants Metaphysik." Heinze notes that *Korff* and L_I may have been bound by the same bookbinder because their spines share the same gold decorations. Only the Ontology section is present. (The rest was removed during the preparation of Pölitz's edition.) Pages are unnumbered, with only the sheet number (*Bogenzahl*) indicated, and with wide, white margins; some of the pages are wholly or half blank, although nothing seems to be missing from the text at these points.

Various aspects of the text strongly indicate that it is a copy and not a set of original notes from the lecture hall. The handwriting is distinct, without abbreviations. As in *Korff*, lines have been drawn with a ruler under the headings, which are calligraphic and decorative. There are also blank spaces within lines where, apparently, the copyist was unable to read a word and so left a space for it to be inserted later. Occasionally an entire line is missing, or a word written twice – both common copy errors. This manuscript, once housed in the Leipzig Stadtsbibliothek, was lost during the war, and probably destroyed.[30]

ANON-L$_2$: THE MANUSCRIPT

The L_2 is in a quarto volume, bound together with a set of notes from Kant's Logic lectures (the so-called Pölitz logic notes) that precede it.[31] The logic notes comprise 136 pages; the Metaphysics, 54 pages. A title on the fly-leaf reads: "Logik und Metaphysik / von Kant / Ein Collegium ann. 1798 nachgeschrieben." The date "1789" is added in darker ink over the "1798." The title was written by a different hand than the notes themselves.

Those sections published by Pölitz (the Introduction and the Ontology)

---

[28]Johann Nikolaus Tetens (1736–1807), *Philosophischen Versuchen über die menschliche Natur und ihre Entwicklung* (Philosophical Essays on Human Nature and its Development) (Leipzig, 1777).
[29]Pölitz (Ak. 28: 1511), Arnoldt (1909, v. 58–62), Heinze (1894, 509–16), Menzer (1899, 65), Adickes (1970, 579), Lehmann (1972, 1345–7); Carl (1989, 117–18).
[30]Heinze (1894, 486–7); Adickes (Ak. 17: 570).
[31]The extant portion of this manuscript (the Cosmology, Psychology, and Natural Theology, as transcribed at Ak. 28: 581–609) is cataloged as Rep VI 42c at the university library in Leipzig.

are now missing, having apparently been lost at the printer's. The first part of the Cosmology is also missing, although this gap is probably only a single page, namely, the back of the last sheet of the Ontology. The pages have fairly wide margins in which occasional alterations or amplifications are written. These marginalia appear to be in a different hand, although Heinze surmises that they could be by the same author as the notes, but at a later date. The script is more hurried than in L_1, *Rosenhagen*, and *Korff*, but it is legible and includes scarcely any abbreviations. The text is not as detailed as in the other manuscripts; for instance, the Rational Psychology consists of only ten pages, whereas the corresponding L_1 text as published by Pölitz is roughly six times as long. The Ontology as published by Pölitz is the longest section of the manuscript but is about one-third shorter than the ontologies of L_1, *Rosenhagen*, and K_2.[32]

MRONGOVIUS

Christoph Coelestin Mrongovius was born July 19, 1764, in Hohenstein (Olsztynek). His father was a pastor who probably had also heard Kant's lectures while studying in Königsberg. Mrongovius matriculated on March 21, 1782. The summer semester began "eight days after the election of the Rector at the beginning of each semester,"[33] and the rector was elected "on the Sunday after Easter for the summer semester, and on the next Sunday after the Feast of St. Michael for the winter semester."[34] In 1782, Easter fell on March 31, and as we know from the diary of another student, Kant's first lecture that semester began right on schedule on Monday, April 15.[35] Assuming that Mrongovius actually began classes that semester, it was in his second semester that he attended Kant's course on Metaphysics (WS 1782–3). The following winter, in his fourth semester, he took Kant's Theology course (WS 1783–4), and then he took the Logic course (SS 1784) in his fifth semester. He attended Kant's Anthropology and Moral Philosophy lectures during WS 1784–5, and in his seventh semester he attended Kant's Physics lectures (SS 1785, the so-called *Danzig Physics* notes). After his university studies, he received a pastoral position at a protestant church in Danzig, where he also taught Polish at the local gymnasium (he had taught Polish and Greek at the Collegium Fridericianum while studying at Königsberg). Mrongovius went on to distinguish himself as a linguist and a student of the Masurian

---

[32]Heinze (1894, 502–4).
[33]Daniel Arnoldt (1746, i.199).
[34]From the statutes of the university, as reported in Daniel Arnoldt (1746, ii.87–8).
[35]From the diary of Christian Friedrich Puttlich (1763–1836), a theology student who matriculated two days after Mrongovius on March 23, 1782, and who attended Kant's Logic lectures, as well as his lectures on Physical Geography (which met Wednesdays and Saturdays). See Malter (1990, 186) and Gause (1968, ii.270).

and Kashubian cultures, also publishing one of the first German-Polish dictionaries.[36]

Mrongovius's Metaphysics notes (along with his others) were reported by Lehmann in 1972 as lost but were rediscovered in the late 1970s, and a transcription finally was published in 1983.[37] Lehmann did not have access to the manuscript itself while preparing his transcription, and most likely he worked from a set of photocopies.[38] Unfortunately, his transcription is unreliable in a variety of ways: (1) There are misplaced pages; (2) he failed to correct for later insertions within the manuscript; (3) he sometimes misread the text; and (4) he often changed word order, punctuation, and paragraph breaks without noting the change.[39] How we treat these errors is discussed in a later section of this introduction.

The manuscript is a worn, bound quarto volume containing 17 uncut printer's sheets (*Bogen*): 16 consist of 8 sheets, 1 (the last) of 4 sheets. The title page reads: "Metaphysic / vorgetragen / vom / Prof. Imanuel Kant. / nachgeschrieben / von / C. C: Mrongovius. 1783 d. 4. Febr." Many abbreviations are used. There is evidence of two hands, one of them probably being Mrongovius's. The notes clearly were not written in the lecture hall but may well be a fair copy made by Mrongovius shortly afterward. There are a few places where text was inadvertently omitted and then inserted with a sign. The paper is somewhat coarse, and the ink sometimes quite pale, making it difficult to read. The writing is uneven and often difficult to decipher. There are three sets of pagination: (1) in pencil, probably done by a librarian, is a complete pagination in the upper right corner; (2) in ink, pagination in the upper left corner, beginning on the back of the title page (the first page of text), ending with "39" on the back of sheet 20, starting again with "40" on the front of sheet 25, ending with "53" on the back of sheet 31; (3) four pages of text on the last sheets with writing (sheets 125 and 126) are paginated in ink from 17 to 20.[40]

VOLCKMANN

Johann Wilhelm Volckmann (1766–1836) matriculated at Königsberg as a theology student on August 13, 1782 (the same year as Mrongovius).

---

[36]Zelazny and Stark (1987, 279).

[37]See Lehmann (1972, 1339). Mrongovius's notes are housed at the Biblioteka Gdanska Polskiej Akademii Nauk in Gdansk (formerly Danzig). The Metaphysics notes have the call number "ms. 2214." A microfilm is available at the Kant Archive (Marburg) and with the translators.

[38]Lehmann's name is not on the sign-out record at the library in Gdansk; the last name prior to Werner Stark's, who first visited the archives in the mid-1980s, is that of Erich Adickes, who died in 1928.

[39]Much of this is treated in Zelazny and Stark (1987, 282–3).

[40]Zelazny and Stark (1987, 283).

Judging from the lecture notes he left behind, it appears he attended Kant's courses later in his academic career, beginning with Natural Theology in his third semester (WS 1783–4), Metaphysics in his fifth semester (WS 1784–5), and Physical Geography in his sixth (SS 1785). We also have a record of a set of Logic notes, but with no determined date.

The manuscript, with pages missing from the Ontology section, has 106 pages with a title page reading: "Metaphysische Vorlesungen des Herrn Prof: Kant nachgeschrieben im Jahr 1784 und 85 von J. W. Volckmann d. G.G. Be." It was written throughout with brown ink on laid paper with watermarks, is unpaginated, and consists of printer's sheets (*Bogen*) folded in the middle and nested inside the outermost. Of the four printer's sheets, three consist of four sheets and one of three sheets. Lehmann believes that it is in Volckmann's own handwriting, and that it is probably a fair copy made at home.[41]

DOHNA

Graf Heinrich Ludwig Adolph zu Dohna-Wundlacken (1777–1843) matriculated at Königsberg on June 15, 1791, having just turned fourteen the previous month. Dohna began his studies in WS 1791–2, at which time he studied logic with Poerschke,[42] Anthropology with Kant, and Modern European Political History with Mangelsdorff. In SS 1792, he attended two courses of Kant's (Logic[43] and Physical Geography), as well as Philosophical Encyclopedia with Kraus, and Ancient History and History of the Prussian-Brandenburg State with Mangelsdorff. In WS 1792–3, he attended Kant's Metaphysics lectures and Mangelsdorff's lectures on the History of the German Empire. There are no notes from SS 1793, Dohna's fourth semester of studies, possibly because of disruptions surrounding the death of his mother, which left Dohna an orphan (his father had died six years earlier). In WS 1793–4, he took German Law with Schmalz and General Statistics with Kraus. Presumably during SS 1794 he took Mechanical and Optical Sciences with Schulz and Institutions of the Roman Law with Schmalz, as well as Schmalz's Law Digest. Dohna left the university in 1795.[44]

Judging from the notes and from some of Professor Kraus's letters, Dohna was an exemplary student, and after his studies he passed examinations to work in the local government, eventually serving as a councilor overseeing the freeing of serfs in the area. In 1809, he was called to Berlin

---

[41]Lehmann (28: 1368–9).
[42]Kant typically encouraged students to take a course with Poerschke before attempting his own courses; whether such advice was the cause of Dohna's sequence of courses is unknown.
[43]These notes are translated in Young (1992, 425–516).
[44]Lehmann (1972, 1356–7); Kowalewski (1924, 11–13).

to serve as a state councilor, but with the coming of war he joined the military forces and distinguished himself with an Iron Cross. In 1831, in the midst of the revolution in Poland, Oberpräsident von Schön (another student of Kant's and author of a set of notes from the Metaphysics lectures) called Dohna back to Königsberg to serve as *Chefpräsident* there. In 1834, the king appointed him *Obermarschall* of Prussia, which he remained until his death in 1843.[45]

Dohna's Metaphysics manuscript[46] is easier to read than the *Mrongovius* and has fewer abbreviations. Being from a wealthy family (unlike Mrongovius), Dohna probably had either a professional copyist or his private tutor rewrite his notes. There are running entries of the lecture dates and hours throughout the notes.

ANON-K₂

This manuscript, which had been examined and (in part) copied by both Arnoldt and Heinze, was lost and probably destroyed in the bombing of Königsberg during World War II. (It had been housed in the Staats- und Universitätsbibliothek Königsberg as manuscript #1731.)[47] It was a bound quarto volume, with "Kants Metaphysik" written on the spine and a title and date ("im Winter 1794") written on the endpaper – all in the same hand as the notes themselves. The 294 pages were crowded and contained many abbreviations but were quite legible. Occasional amplifications were written in the wide margins.[48]

The notes probably stem from lectures given in the early 1790s. One would initially think the text stems from the Metaphysics lectures of WS 1794–5, since "Winter 1794" appears on its title page, and Kant is not reported as lecturing on metaphysics during the WS 1793–4 – this was Heinze's reasoning before seeing Arnoldt's account of *Vigilantius*, which almost certainly stems from WS 1794–5 and differs enough from K_2 to make a common origin for them implausible.[49] Hence Heinze sets the

---

[45]Kowalewski (1924, 15–25).

[46]This manuscript is currently in the private possession of the Dohna family. A microfilm is available at the Kant Archive (Marburg) and with the translators.

[47]The status of these manuscripts is still an open matter; see Komorowski (1980, 139–54).

[48]Arnoldt (1909, v.38–9): Heinze (1894, 506–7).

[49]The argument is difficult here. On the one hand, Arnoldt (1909, v.71–2) found K_2 and *Vigilantius* to stand in general agreement, so it seemed likely that K_2 truly did stem from the early 1790s. On the other hand, they differed in many particulars and, more important, in their form of expression and in their subject headings – all of which suggests that they originated in different semesters. Arnoldt also conjectured that K_2 was written out at home (as a "fair copy") and *Vigilantius* was written in the lecture hall; but we know that Arnoldt never saw the original *Vigilantius* (he worked from a copy made by Reicke), so much of the evidence that might decide the question of where the notes were composed was not available to him.

date at either 1791–2 or 1792–3. Arnoldt dates the text at 1793–4; Adickes, at the early 1790s.[50] The notes we have translated here (the Rational Psychology) come from the copy made by Heinze and reprinted at Ak. 28: 751–75.

VIGILANTIUS (K_3)

Johann Friedrich Vigilantius (1757–1823), a lawyer and Kant's legal adviser, was also an informal student of Kant's who apparently heard all of his lectures. He belonged to Kant's closest circle of dinner companions and, according to Wasianski, was present at Kant's death.[51] Along with the Metaphysics notes from WS 1794–5, we also have notes that are probably his from Kant's lectures on Physical Geography (SS 1793), Logic (SS 1793), and Moral Philosophy (WS 1793–4).

The original manuscript by Vigilantius was presumably destroyed during the bombing of Königsberg. The Metaphysics manuscript known as "*Vigilantius*" (also as "K_3" or "*Arnoldt*")[52] – which has been translated for the present volume – is a copy of Vigilantius's original notes prepared in 1883 by Rudolf Reicke, along with his eldest son, Johannes (called Hans), and his cousin Ida – hence the note written in pencil on sheet 12 verso: "collat. 5/i 83 mit Ida u. Hans zusammen. R."[53] Reicke had copied this manuscript perhaps in a manner similar to his copying of Kant's *Opus postumum* (preparatory to its publication); here Reicke copied those portions most difficult to read, his cousin Ida copied those portions least difficult to read, Johannes copied the rest, and the copies were carefully checked against the original.[54] Reicke presumably made the *Vigilantius* copy with the intention of publishing it. Several pages of this copy were lent to Arnoldt for his work, and it is assumed that these are the pages now missing. Lehmann, editor of the Academy transcription of these notes, was under the impression that this copy was prepared by Emil Arnoldt in the 1880s (thus Lehmann's erroneous designation "*Metaphysik Arnoldt*").[55]

[50]Arnoldt (1909, v.71–2); Heinze (1894, 591n); Adickes (1970, 579); Lehmann (1972, 1346).

[51]Lehmann (1979, 1045); Vorländer (ii, 301); Malter (1990, 514).

[52]The "K_3" designation comes from Max Heinze, and is used by Lehmann in the Academy edition. "Arnoldt" refers to Emil Arnoldt (1828–1905), an important Kant scholar who had access to many of the lecture notes.

[53]This copy, with the exception of a few missing pages (presumably those sent to Arnoldt), is housed at the Nikolaus Kopernikus Universität, Biblioteka Glowna, in Torun (Poland) under the call number "Rps 631." The original set of notes – lost during World War II – was part of the Gotthold collection at the Staats- und Universitätsbibliothek Königsberg. A microfilm is available at the Kant Archive (Marburg) and with the translators.

[54]See Arnoldt's letter to Kuno Fischer (June 20, 1884), excerpted in Arnoldt (1909, iv.379).

[55]Stark (1985, 331–2), Lehmann (1983, 1091–3). See also Schlapp (1901) and Malter (1977).

The Reicke copy lacks a title page. On the first page of notes is the heading "Bemerkungen über Metaphysic nach Baumgarten, aus dem Vortrage des HE. Prof. Kant pro 1794/95 / d. 13.t. Oktbr.," and at the end is "20t. Febr." The manuscript consists of 100 quarto sheets paginated in the upper right corner and contained in a brown envelope made of packing paper. These consist of 22 printer's sheets (*Bogen*), of which only the first 2 (sheets 1–12 and 13–22) are sewn together. Of the remaining loose printer's sheets there is no evidence of an earlier binding.[56] Sheet 100 is blank on both sides. There are four textual gaps, which are clearly accounted for by lost sheets. The writing is neat and in three different hands. Abbreviations and other features that probably existed in the original were omitted in the copy. There are also smaller notes interleaved with the manuscript. Marginal pagination occurs throughout (1a, 1b, 2a, 2b, etc.) marking the page breaks of the original *Vigilantius* manuscript. On the first few pages, there are vertical lines indicating the exact location of those page breaks. The sheets are numbered in the upper right corner of the front, but the numbers are often illegible and do not continue through the entire manuscript. (It appears that there may have been a different series of numbers for each of the three different copyists.) The marginal pagination (that is, the pagination of the original manuscript) is consequently the easiest way to refer to the text.

Arnoldt used some of these copied sheets for his "Excursus" – apparently not all of these sheets were returned, although some were – for example, the text printed at Ak. 29:1025 from the manuscript is also reproduced in Arnoldt (as reprinted at Ak. 28:830). Consequently there are several gaps in the marginal pagination. The manuscript as it now stands includes the following pages [^{R} = right-hand page; ^{L} = left-hand page]: (1) 1a^R–62a^L (partial, ending at Ak. 29: 1001$_2$), (2) 66b^R – 70a^L, (3) 161b^R–180a^L, (4) 203b^R–220a^L, (5) 279b^R–280^L. The notes end on page 280; the facing page is blank.

In his Academy transcription, Lehmann notes most (but not all) of this marginal pagination (though with a few errors) and most (but not all) of the other marginalia. Many of the other marginalia are preceded by what appears to be the words: "[Neben am Rand]." This is always in square brackets, sometimes with a period after "Rand," sometimes with a colon or no punctuation. This is clearly a note by the copyist indicating that the marginalia in the copy were also marginalia in the original. Some marginalia appear without this note. Occasionally, there are notes (again in square brackets) in the body of the text introducing longer marginalia. There are also a host of question marks in the margins, marks that resemble "cf.," and other marks of unknown significance. Lehmann notes much (but not all) of this editorial material introduced by the copyists.

---

[56]Stark (1985, 330–1).

Lehmann also suggests that the copyist (whom he mistakenly refers to as Arnoldt) added words to the text (either as marginalia that are not introduced with an editorial device or directly above a line). Lehmann does not preserve much of the indentation and spacing of the manuscript, other than the standard paragraph breaks. He generally adds blank lines around marginalia, which he inserts into the text (occasionally without note).[57]

THE LEHMANN TRANSCRIPTIONS IN THE ACADEMY EDITION

Gerhard Lehmann (1900–87) was involved with the Academy edition of Kant's writings since 1923, when, as a young scientist, he was employed by Artur Buchenau to help transcribe for publication Kant's *Opus postumum* (Vols. 21 [1936] and 22 [1938]).[58] In the early 1940s, he assumed the editorship of the "Vorlesungen" part of the Academy edition of Kant's works. With the help of an assistant, Lehmann transcribed several of these lecture notes for the Academy edition, though for certain notes the original manuscript was not available, in which case Lehmann reprinted already-published material (e.g., parts of L_1 and L_2 that had been printed by Pölitz and other fragments of those notes that had been preserved in published form by Heinze, parts of K_2 published by Heinze and Schlapp, and parts of *Korff* and *Rosenhagen* published by Heinze).[59] Some extant notes had previously published transcriptions (e.g., *Herder* and *Dohna*), but the *Mrongovius, von Schön, Volckmann,* and *Vigilantius* notes were transcribed and published by Lehmann for the first time.

Our translation is based on Lehmann's Academy-edition transcription as found in Volumes 28 and 29. In Volume 28, we found only minor errors. The transcriptions in Volume 29, however, are much less reliable, the Mrongovius notes being in the worst state – here there had been a mix-up in the pagination, as well as a host of transcriptional errors. Fortunately, we were able to check Lehmann's transcription against microfilms of the manuscripts for *Mrongovius, Vigilantius, Dohna,* and part of L_2, and we consulted these films whenever the meaning or spelling of the text appeared confused (and thus possibly mistranscribed), whenever Lehmann indicated making a change in the text, and whenever he reported that there were marginalia or other signs (as noted in the "Textänderungen und Lesarten" sections of his Academy volumes).

Problems with the Lehmann transcription are mentioned in the foot-

---

[57]Lehmann also draws on a few passages preserved in Arnoldt's "Excursus," which he added to the end of the Ontology section (see Ak. 29: 1005–9); these passages had already been printed (and with fewer errors) at Ak. 28: 825–9, and can be found in Arnoldt (1909, vol. 5).
[58]On the story behind this, see Förster (1993, xxiii) and Stark (1993, 158–84).
[59]Lehmann presents these as stemming from L_1, but they could just as easily be seen as stemming from *Korff* or *Rosenhagen* (Heinze provides variants of all three).

notes and include any erroneous additions or deletions of words or punctuation, as well as paragraph breaks or emphases (namely, underlining in
the manuscript). We do *not* note the following: (1) where Lehmann is
mistaken in his textual notes (the "Textänderungen und Lesarten") and
the mistake does not affect the translation; (2) where a word is crossed out
in the manuscript (and also absent from Lehmann's translation), where it
is crossed out and replaced, or where a word is *verbessert* (rewritten in
darker ink); (3) where inserted words or marginalia occur in paler or
darker ink or in a different hand; (4) abbreviations (Lehmann only sporadically notes these, suggesting that they are not common; in fact they are
quite common in the manuscripts); (5) where the ending of a word is
changed by Lehmann, but in a way that will not affect the translation; (6)
where a chapter or section heading is written in *schönschrift* (i.e., in large,
neatly written letters), and how it is placed on the page, (7) where letters
have been changed from lower to upper case. Readers consulting the
Metaphysics notes of the Academy edition should also be forewarned that
a fair number of Lehmann's page references to his transcription are
incorrect; since we have tried to correct these in our translations of Lehmann's notes, not all of the page numbers in our notes will match his.

BIBLIOGRAPHY

ADICKES, ERICH (1970). *German Kantian Bibliography* (New York: Burt Franklin; originally published 1893–6).

AMERIKS, KARL (1982). *Kant's Theory of Mind* (Oxford: Clarendon Press).

(1991). "Kant on Spontaneity: Some New Data," *Proceedings of the VII International Kant-
Kongress 1990* (Berlin: de Gruyter), pp. 436–46.

(1992). "The Critique of Metaphysics: Kant and Traditional Ontology" in *The Cambridge
Companion to Kant*, edited by Paul Guyer (Cambridge: Cambridge University Press),
pp. 249–79.

ARNOLDT, DANIEL HEINRICH (1746). *Ausführliche und mit Urkunden versehene Histo-
rie der königsbergischen Universität* (Königsberg: J. H. Hartung), two volumes and two
appendices.

ARNOLDT, EMIL (1909). "Characteristik von Kants Vorlesungen über Metaphysik und
möglichst vollständiges Verzeichnis aller von ihm gehaltenen oder auch nur angekün-
digten Vorlesungen," appendix to "Zur Beurteilung von Kants Kritik der reinen
Vernunft und Kants Prolegomena," *Altpreußischen Monatsschrift* (1892–3). Reprinted in
Arnoldt, *Gesammelte Schriften*, edited by Otto Schöndörffer, vol. 5: *Kritische Exkurse im
Gebiete der Kantforschung*, pt. 2 (Berlin: Bruno Cassirer).

BLACKALL, ERIC (1959). *The Emergence of German as a Literary Language, 1700–1775*
(Cambridge: Cambridge University Press).

BOROWSKI, LUDWIG ERNST VON (1804). *Darstellung des Lebens und Charakters Immanuel Kants* (Königsberg). Reprinted in Gross (1912).

BRANDT, REINHARD (1989). "Beobachtungen zur Anthropologie bei Kant (und He-
gel)" in *Psychologie und Anthropologie oder Philosophie des Geistes*, ed. Franz Hespet and

Burkhard Tuschling (Stuttgart-Bad Cannstatt: Frommann-Holzboog, 1991), pp. 75–106.

CARL, WOLFGANG (1989). *Der schweigende Kant: die Entwürfe zu einer Deduktion der Kategorien vor 1781* (Göttingen: Vandenhoeck & Reprecht).

CASTILLO, MONIQUE (1993). "Les 'Leçons' et la metaphysique," [Introduction to] *Immanuel Kant: Leçons de metaphysique* ["the Pölitz lectures"] (Paris: Librairie Générale Francaise), pp. 43–111.

ERDMANN, BENNO (1883). "Eine unbeachtet gebliebene Quelle zur Entwicklungsgeschichte Kant's," *Philosophische Monatshefte*, 19: 129–44.

(1884). "Mittheilungen über Kant's metaphysischen Standpunkt in der Zeit um 1774," *Philosophische Monatshefte*, 20: 65–97.

EULENBERG, FRANZ (1904). *Die Frequenz der deutschen Universitäten von ihrer Gründung bis zur Gegenwart*, vol. 24 (#2) of the *Abhandlungen der philologisch-historischen Klasse der königlich sächsischen Gesellschaft der Wissenschaften* (Leipzig: B. G. Teubner).

FELDMAN, ERICH (1936). "Die Geschichte der Philosophie in Kants Vorlesungen," *Philosophisches Jahrbuch*, 49: 167–98.

FÖRSTER, ECKART (1993). "Translator's Introduction" in Immanuel Kant, *Opus postumum*, translated by Eckart Förster and Michael Rosen (Cambridge: Cambridge University Press), pp. xv–lvii.

GAUSE, FRITZ (1968). *Die Geschichte der Stadt Königsberg in Preussen*, vol. 2: "Von der Königskrönung bis zum Ausbruch des ersten Weltkrieges" (Köln: Böhlau Verlag).

(1974). *Kant und Königsberg* (Leer, Ostfriesland: Verlag Gerhard Rautenberg).

GROSS, FELIX (ed.) (1912). *Immanuel Kant. Sein Leben in Darstellungen von Zeitgenossen. Die Biographien von L. E. Borowski, R. B. Jachmann und A. Ch. Wasianski* (Berlin).

GUYER, PAUL (1987). *Kant and the Claims of Knowledge* (Cambridge: Cambridge University Press).

HEINZE, MAX (1894). *Vorlesungen Kants über Metaphysik aus drei Semestern* (Lepzig: S. Hirzel).

KOMOROWSKI, WERNER (1980). "Das Schicksal der Staats- und Universitätsbibliothek Königsberg," *Bibliothek, Forschung und Praxis* (München), vol. 4, pp. 139–54.

KOWALEWSKI, ARNOLD (ed.) (1924). *Die philosophischen Hauptvorlesungen Immanuel Kants. Nach den aufgefundenen Kolleghefen des Grafen Heinrich zu Dohna-Wundlacken* (München and Leipzig).

LAYWINE, ALISON (1993). *Kant's Early Metaphysics and the Origins of the Critical Philosophy* (Atascadero: Ridgeview) (North American Kant Society Studies in Philosophy, vol. 3).

LEHMANN, GERHARD (1961). "Allgemeine Einleitung zu Kants Vorlesungen," *Immanuel Kant: Vorlesungen über Enzyklopädie und Logik*, Bd. 1: *Vorlesungen über Philosophische Enzyklopädie* (Berlin: Akademie Verlag). Published by the Deutsche Akademie der Wissenschaften zu Berlin.

(1972). "Einleitung: Kants Vorlesungen über Metaphysik und Rationaltheologie," *Kant's gesammelte Schriften*, vol. 28 (Berlin: de Gruyter), pp. 1338–72.

(1979). "Einleitung," *Kant's gesammelte Schriften*, vol. 27 (Berlin: de Gruyter), pp. 1037–68.

(1983). "Einleitung: Ergänzungen II," *Kant's gesammelte Schriften*, vol. 29 (Berlin: de Gruyter), pp. 1083–1103.

MAKKREEL, RUDOLF (1990). *Imagination and Interpretation in Kant* (Chicago: University of Chicago Press).

MALTER, RUDOLF (1977). "Die letzte überlieferte Metaphysik-Vorlesung Kants," *Kant-Studien*, 68: 464–7.

(1990). *Immanuel Kant in Rede und Gespräch* (Hamburg: Felix Meiner).

MENZER, PAUL (1899). "Der Entwicklungsgang der kantischen Ethik in den Jahren 1760–1785," *Kant-Studien*, 3: 41–104.

PÖLITZ, KARL HEINRICH LUDWIG (anonymous editor)

(1817). Vorlesungen über die philosophische Religionslehre (Leipzig: Carl Friedrich Franz). 2nd ed.: 1830.

(1821). *Immanuel Kants Vorlesungen über die Metaphysik. Zum Druck befördert von dem Herausgeber der Kantischen Vorlesungen über die philosophische Religionslehre* (Erfurt: Kaisers). (Reprint; Darmstadt: Wissenschaftliche Buchgesellschaft, 1975. References are to the reprint in the Academy edition, vol. 28, pp. 1511–14.)

RITZEL, WOLFGANG (1985). *Immanuel Kant: Eine Biographie* (Berlin: de Gruyter).

SCHLAPP, OTTO (1901). *Kants Lehre vom Genie und die Entstehung der "Kritik der Urteilskraft"* (Göttingen).

STARK, WERNER (1985). "Kantiana in Thorn," *Kant-Studien*, 76: 328–35.

(1993). *Nachforschungen zu Briefen und Handschriften Immanuel Kants* (Berlin: Akademie Verlag).

(1995). "Kant als akademischer Lehrer" in *Königsberg und Riga*, vol. 16 of the *Wolfenbütteler Studien zur Aufklärung*, edited by Heinz Ischreyt (Tübingen: Max Niemeyer Verlag), pp. 51–68.

VORLÄNDER, KARL (1924). *Immanuel Kant, der Mann und das Werk*, 2 vols. (Leipzig: Meiner).

WATKINS, ERIC (1995). "Kant's Theory of Physical Influx," *Archiv für Geschichte der Philosophie*, 77: 285–324.

WOOD, ALLEN (1978a). "Translator's Introduction" in Immanuel Kant, *Lectures on Philosophical Theology*, translated by Allen Wood and Gertrude Clark (Ithaca: Cornell University Press), pp. 9–18.

(1978b). *Kant's Rational Theology* (Ithaca: Cornell University Press).

YOUNG, J. MICHAEL (1992). "Translator's Introduction" in Immanuel Kant, *Lectures on Logic*, translated and edited by J. Michael Young (Cambridge: Cambridge University Press), pp. xv–xxxii.

ZELAZNY, MIROSLAW, AND WERNER STARK (1987). "Zu Krzysztof Celestyn Mrongovius und seinen Kollegheften nach Kants Vorlesungen," *Kant-Forschungen*, 1: 279–92.

Guide to abbreviations and
the translators' notes

We have adopted the following conventions and abbreviations to help minimize the number of explanatory notes in the text.

INDIVIDUALS FREQUENTLY MENTIONED IN THE TRANSLATORS' NOTES

Adickes, Erich (1866–1928). The editor of Kant's handwritten literary remains (vols. 14–23 of the Academy edition).

Arnoldt, Emil (1828–1905). A Kant scholar in whose *Gesammelte Schriften* is preserved considerable material regarding Kant's lecturing activity.

Baumgarten, Alexander Gottlieb (1714–62). A Wolffian philosopher teaching at Frankfurt/Oder. Kant used Baumgarten's *Metaphysica*, 4th ed. (Halle, 1757) as the official text in his Metaphysics lectures, and references in the text to "the author" are always to Baumgarten. The *Metaphysica* consists of 1,000 sections (§§), and is reprinted at Ak. 15: 3–54 (§§504–699) and Ak. 17: 7–226. We have relied on this Academy reprint in our translation.

Heinze, Max (1835–1909). Several of Kant's lectures were preserved in Heinze's *Vorlesungen Kants über Metaphysik aus drei Semestern*.

Lehmann, Gerhard (1900–87). The late editor of the most recent volumes of the Academy edition of Kant's *Gesammelte Schriften* (namely, vols. 20–29, excluding vols. 25–6 on anthropology and physical geography); the Metaphysics lectures are found in vols. 28–9. See our Introduction for a discussion of Lehmann's work on the edition.

Pölitz, Karl Heinrich Ludwig (1772–1838). An early publisher of Kant's lectures on Theology and Metaphysics. See the discussion of the L_1 and L_2 notes in the Introduction.

Reicke, Rudolph (1825–1905). A student of Karl Rosenkranz at Königsberg and later the university librarian, Reicke was founder and editor of the *Altpreussischen Monatsschrift*. He prepared the extant copy of *Metaphysik Vigilantius* (K_3) translated in this volume.

Wolff, Christian (1679–1754). A prolific philosopher writing in both Latin and German. Baumgarten's *Metaphysica* was based on Wolff's system, in particular his *Philosophia Prima Sive Ontologia* (Frankfurt, 1730), reprinted in *Gesammelte Werke,* edited by Jean Ecole (Hildesheim: Georg Olms Verlag, 1962), II Abteilung, Bd. 3. "Wolff's *Ontologia*" refers to this work.

APPENDIXES

English-German glossary and *German-English glossary:* In keeping with the other volumes in the Cambridge edition of Kant's works, we offer two brief glossaries of the more important terms found in the notes.

Latin-German equivalents occurring in the text: German was still developing as a philosophical language in the eighteenth century, and consequently Kant often provided pairs of Latin-German synonyms in his lectures (much as he did in his published writings). We have collected here such pairings as occur in the translated notes, and have also included occasional Greek and French equivalents.

Concordance of Baumgarten's Metaphysics *and Kant's Metaphysics lectures:* The concordance follows Baumgarten's sections and uses the headings listed in his "Synopsis" (reprinted at Ak. 17: 19–23). The subheadings are arranged by the topics that come from either Baumgarten or Kant. For equivalents of many of Baumgarten's Latin terms, we often followed Georg Friedrich Meier's German translation of Baumgarten's *Metaphysics*–2nd ed., edited by Johann August Eberhard (Halle: Carl Hermann Hemmerde, 1783). The concordance covers all the sets of notes translated for this volume, as well as page references to the *von Schön* notes, which were not translated. All references are to Volume 28 or 29 of the Academy edition, and those pages that have not been translated for the present volume appear between parentheses. Finally, a much more detailed cross-listing of the *Herder* notes with Baumgarten can be found at Ak. 28: 963–87.

NOTES

The reader will find two sets of notes: numbered explanatory notes are found at the end of the volume; lettered linguistic notes are found at the bottom of each page.

The linguistic notes include information on the following: (1) a German term or phrase that involves a pun or other nuance of meaning difficult to capture in English; (2) discrepancies between the manuscript and Lehmann's transcription, or where his interpretation of an abbreviation is questionable; (3) explanation of marginalia; (4) explanation of words, brackets, or punctuation added by the translators; (5) aspects of the manuscript that cannot be captured in the translated text, such as how a chapter heading is formed and written, where the handwriting changes to a different hand, lines drawn along the margin of the text (presumably for emphasis). A few of these footnotes stem from the original lecture notes, in which case each is introduced with an asterisk rather than a superscript letter.

The explanatory notes include information (largely from Lehmann) on the following: (1) historical references, titles of works, and so forth, (2) corresponding passages in Baumgarten's *Metaphysics;* and (3) occasional references to other passages dealing with the same topic as the passage noted (although this information is usually covered in the Concordance or the Subject Index). We silently introduced minor changes to Lehmann's notes for the sake of stylistic consistency, and we also corrected any misquotations of Baumgarten and added to the quotations where doing so would facilitate understanding. Significant additions to Lehmann's notes are indicated with square brackets. All works other than Kant's referred to in these notes are given full bibliographical citation. References to Kant's works, on the other hand, provide a short title (English, when available), with a fuller citation to be found in the Kant bibliography immediately after the notes. We were able to verify most of Lehmann's references, but the unavailability of various manuscripts and some published works precluded a complete verification.

INDEXES

Name index: The name index covers the translated lecture notes, as well as the Translators' Introduction.

Subject index: Given the wide-ranging, and occasionally repetitive nature of the lecture notes, it was important to develop a somewhat detailed cross-referenced subject index in order to provide a convenient basis for searching the notes for various topics.

ABBREVIATIONS USED IN THE TRANSLATORS' NOTES

Ak.   The standard edition of Kant's writings: *Kants gesammelte Schriften,* edited by the Königliche Preussischen Akademie der Wissenschaften (Berlin, 1900–   ). These are cited by volume, page, and line (where appropriate), all in arabic numerals, thus: Ak. 29: 506$_{21}$.

CrPR   Kant's *Critique of Pure Reason.* References to this use the standard A/B pagination of the first two editions.

Ms   Manuscript. When followed by page numbers (as in "ms, p. 3"), these refer to the manuscript itself, counting by *sheet* and designating the back of the sheet by an apostrophe (so 1 and 1' are the front and back, respectively, of the first sheet of the ms – what in a printed text would be pages 1 and 2). Lehmann uses "Opg" when referring to ms pagination, and generally does not use the system described here.

Refl. Kant's *Reflections*, printed in the Academy edition according to topic: Mathematics, Physics and Chemistry, and Physical Geography (Ak. 14); Anthropology (Ak. 15); Logic (Ak. 16); Metaphysics (Ak. 17–18); Moral Philosophy, Philosophy of Law, and Philosophy of Religion (Ak. 19). The number following refers to the reflection, and not to a page, thus: *Refl.* #111 (Ak. 15: 5).

BRACKETS AND TYPEFACES USED IN THE TEXT

[ ]   Text added by the translators.

[ ]^L   Text added by Lehmann and retained by the translators.

( )   Parentheses appearing in the manuscript (or at least in the Academy edition, in those cases where the manuscript was not available to check). We always noted when we added parentheses, except when using them to enclose numbers and letters in lists.

{ }   Text added in the margin of the manuscript. We insert the marginalia where indicated by the "insertion sign," if there is one; otherwise we insert them as close to where they are written as the main text allows. The location and status of the marginalia are described in the footnotes.

< >   Non-German – normally Latin, occasionally French or Greek. These non-German words and phrases are preceded by their English translation.

italics All foreign terms and all titles of books are placed in italics, as is all emphasized text (in the manuscript, underlined; in the Academy edition, set in spaced type). In those instances where a foreign term is *also* emphasized, we italicize the corresponding words in the English translation. For example: "The author says the *negative* nothing <*nihil negativum*> is . . ." – here *negativum* is underlined in the manuscript.

MARGINAL PAGINATION

The marginal pagination to the translation refers to Volumes 28 and 29 of the Academy edition.

PART I
Metaphysik Herder

1762–1764 (AK. 28: 39–53)

PART <*PARS*> II

§354. It is not necessary that the finitude of the world, which is yet to be proven, is brought into the definition.

The world is a *real whole* <*totum reale*>: all things in it stand in real connection <*in nexu reali*>.

The world is a whole which is not part of another <*totum quod non est pars alterius*>: otherwise this would be only a piece of the world.

The world is therefore a (real) whole of actual things, which is not part of another <*mundus ergo est totum (reale) actualium, quod non est pars alterius*>.

357. All things are in real connection <*in realnexu*>: they are connected in certain determinations, be they as they may.

358. (*In this world*) the world is present, of which I am a part. There is a reciprocal connection, either mediately or immediately <*(in hoc mundo) mundus praesens est, cujus sum pars ego. Est nexus mutuus vel mediate vel immediate*>.

361. (Cf. §354, as a proposition to be proven, should not be brought into the definition) As parts, all parts of the whole are in real connection <*in realnexu*> with one another as component parts <*compartibus*>: because they are grounds of the whole, and the whole cannot subsist without them. A part thus depends on some determinations of the others: consequently no part in the whole is independent – the whole [is] not independent – [but] contingent.

362. is an application of unity to the world: each world is a metaphysical One, because it is a whole: the more connection in it the more consequences flow from a single ground: the greater is the unity. But it is another question, whether aside from this one, still more worlds are possible. –

372. Is the world a mathematical infinity <*infinitum mathematicum*>, i.e., is it in comparison with unity greater than every number?

Take the distance of the sun, 22,000 earth diameters; the distance of the planets, which is 70,000 times farther: add yet a number, if it can be expressed by a number, then it is not larger than all numbers, even if this should be unknown to us. Is the world infinite in this way – is space infinite? Who can say? – God can indeed imagine an infinite without number, like eternity, but this concept is still difficult to conceive. Al-

3

though it is also difficult to imagine the boundary, because one thinks like Locke, that something would then have to be empty where one could as it were stretch out one's hand.

But is there only one *metaphysical world*? Not physical, for there are earth, moon, etc., many worlds. But rather metaphysical wholes, which are not parts of another *<tota, quae non sunt partes alterius>*. Cannot the existence of a thing be thought without connection *<nexus>*? Can there not be single things which are not at all conjoined *<connexa>* with these wholes *<tota>*? Can there not be wholes *<tota>* of series which stand in no connection *<nexu>* with this world? Perhaps the first grounds of connection through space and time are too unfamiliar. World *<mundus>* consists of parts grounded outside themselves *<partibus extra se positis>*: consequently simple, etc. A being cannot alone constitute a world: otherwise God would also be a world.

Section <Sectio> *II*

§380. Infinite progression *<progressus in infinitum>* is a hiding place of the human understanding: although one [thereby] immediately refutes oneself.[a] If all things are effects *<causata>*, then they are consequences, and are not posited unless something else has been posited *<rationata et non ponuntur, nisi posito alio>*. Thus there must necessarily be causes without qualification *<causae simpliciter talis>*.

Circular progression *<progressus curvilineus>*: would be, e.g., the Platonic year,[1] since after 72,000 years everything will be the same again, even the same human beings and their conduct here on earth. Presumably comes from the Chaldean astronomers, who noticed that every 72,000 years the course of the firmament would come round.

382. On *chance*: and destiny: the destiny of Spinoza,[2] which has perhaps not been rightly understood, belongs in natural theology *<theologia naturalis>*. Every ground determines its consequence necessarily: what is not necessary by a sufficient determinate ground is *chance*. = = No existence of things, such as the free actions of Crusius, [that] are pure chances *<casus puri>*. = = Here chance is contradistinguished with fate *<fato>*.

It is also called chance when one indeed knows grounds of an event, but does not have in view all the grounds of the event. – A new contrast *<contradistinction>* of chance to intended ends.

384. Regular *<ordinarius>* is everything that is in accord with the rules of some order. What is in accord with the rules of *good* order: is called ordered *<ordinatus>*.

Something absolutely beyond order *<extraordinarium absolutum>* is not at all to be thought, because God himself determined everything from sufficient grounds.

[a] We have added a period here (40₃₆).

Something relatively *beyond order* <*extraordinarium relativum*>, what is not in accord with the rules of a certain order. E.g., hypochondriacal laughter.

386. Example of a relative leap <*saltus respectivus*>: the transition of the godless into that perfect world – the transition from obscure to adequate concepts: often the teaching method of the author.

Leibniz built *a law of continuity* <*legem continuationis*> on the proposition that nothing happens in the world through a leap <*nil fit in mundo per saltum*>,[3] and it has not yet been in the proper light even for Maupertuis. There is a logical, mathematical, physical law.

(a) *Logical law*. Whatever applies in general to a certain magnitude that can become smaller, this also applies to it if it is vanishingly small. – All free actions are imputable – consequently the smallest degree of this, the natural actions, are also imputable.

b. *Mathematical law*, if a body is brought from rest into motion, then it goes through all of the smallest degrees of speed up to the highest degree of speed with which it has power, and if it is again brought to rest: then this happens through smaller degrees of speed. A light ray that reflects back from a mirror, reflects not all at once, but rather through the smallest degrees of deviation. 28:42

3. *Physical law*: the imperfect raises itself to the more perfect through the smallest degrees of perfection. E.g., the lifeless – plants, living plants, polyps, oysters, animals, until human beings. Maupertuis opines that a general flood tore many steps from this ladder, which the bones of unknown animals in excavations indicate, and thereby disturbed the connection for us.

388. E.g., the independent being <*ens independens*> – for if it belonged to the world as a part, it would be dependent upon it: thus it is a being beyond this world <*ens extramundanum*>, although it occupies no location outside the world.

389–91. Against Spinoza in natural theology <*theologia naturalis*>.

Chapter <Caput> II

Section <Sectio> I

392. 393. An egoist thinks that I, who am thinking here, am the only simple being, without connection <*nexu*> with others. [An] idealist, that there is merely a spiritual world. Origin of *idealism*, the truth that the body without thoughts constitutes no world. So Bishop Berkeley, in the treatise *On the Use of Tarwater for Our Body*, doubted whether there are any bodies at all.[4] He alleges that all bodies are mere appearances of bodies in our soul.[5] And that with much plausibility

1. for all sensation of bodies outside us is merely *in* us, e.g., beauty, ugliness, merely in our sensation, therefore the various judgments [on] color, not in the body, but rather merely in the refractions of the light rays,

as the prism teaches.[b] – It is foolish to recommend to him the proof of a beating, because he would also hold it to be lively appearances in him. The proof from experiences is ineffective, because he also holds them merely to be lively representations.

2. As in a dream, since one imagines things which nevertheless are not, far more lively than [when one is] awake: since an affection concerning absurdities is greater. And were dreams actually in mutual agreement, who would not hold them for occurring things? But could God not have so arranged it so that our life is a mutual dream, and that death would be only an awakening? In Locke's day an honest, learned man who had never lied passed himself off with all certainty as Socrates, who can refute this?[6] – – The weapons of truth, wisdom, goodness of God, are too dull against idealism, and even serve it. For would it not be a shorter way of wisdom, all the same, to effect by representations than by bodies?

28:43

Thus *logically* he cannot be refuted, but rather by the assent of other human beings and one's own conviction. – –

But since an idealist also sees nothing as body, then from him to egoism is only the smallest step, and that is much more damaging in natural theology <*theologia naturalis*>.

395. A material thing is that which is either matter, or a material element <*ens materiale, quod est vel materia, vel materiale elementum*>. Whoever maintains that all things in the world are matter, or elements of matter <*elementa materiae*>, is a materialist.

398. The author wants to prove it by the rule of identity: but since not everything that is required by an active power, and follows from a real ground, is clear through the rule of identity <*per regulam identitatis*>, then, etc.[7] The formal aspect of impenetrability is resistance. This is an action of an active power – has a real ground in real repugnance.

Every body – but not space – consists of simple parts.[c] The so-and-so part of a body is thus something that occupies the so-and-so part of space. But a simple part does not occupy a simple part of space, for the latter has none: and thus a body occupies space merely through the law of impenetrability <*per legem impenetrabilitatis*>.

399. Mathematical point <*punctum mathematicum*> is a location in space. Improperly called physical space, it is conceived as a simple place by abstracting from a place of space <*physicum spatium improprie dictum, abstrahendo a loco spatii concipitur ut locus simplex*>. Consequently the monad <*monas*> cannot be called a location, according to the author.

400. (Author)[8] The monads represent the universe; they are mirrors of the whole – but Leibniz went further: all simple substances represent the universe to themselves: they think. The inducement for this hypothesis is:

---

[b] We have added a period here (42_{30}).
[c] We have added a period here (43_{25}).

all that we think in a monad are outer relations – they are impenetrable to outer objects – they attract others – move – remain at rest – all outer relations. But now the monads must have, as simple substances without relations, posited alone <*solitario positae*>, an inner state: but what [other than] representations can one suppose as the basic inner powers of another being; thus the simple substances have a power that represents the universe <*vim repraesentationis universi*>. 28:44

Objection <*objectio*>: 1. How? Can a material element <*elementum materiae*> think: then matter also thinks? Response <*responsio*> that does not follow. A whole of many simple substances which are thinking, thinks only when all thoughts of each simple substance are unified in it. If each one of a hundred human beings learned by heart a verse from Virgil: would they then know the whole of Virgil by heart? Now, if not the latter, then matter also does not think.

> Objection <*objectio*> 2. We see no actions as consequences of thinking. –
> Response <*responsio*> 1. We also see no material elements <*elemente materiae*>, but rather merely the matter, but that does not prove that it thinks. 2. Not merely thoughts but also desires are required for actions, and they are not posited when one posits a power of representation <*vim repraesentativam*>.
> Objection <*objectio*> 3. These representations would of course have no use.[d]
> Response <*responsio*>: yes, from this inner state follows merely their outer state.
> Objection <*objectio*> 4. Could there not be besides the representation yet another inner state, which is unknown to us? Response <*responsio*>: thus this hypothesis remains merely probable: but it is this to a high degree.

§402. Everything in the wrong location.[9]

Section <Sectio> *II.* That in which *the extended* is posited absolutely, is space <*extensum in quo absolute posito, est spatium*>. A body is thus extended <*extensum*>, a monad <*monas*> not, because the monad occupies a space merely through its co-presence with others <*per compraesentiam cum aliis*>.

406. A thing consisting of monads is a real whole out of monads <*monadatum est totum reale ex monadibus*>, etc.

407. Any whole should be partially homogeneous <*totum quodlibet debet esse partialiter homogeneum*>. E.g.,[e] soul and body: not world and

---

[d] We have added a period here (44_{20}).

[e] Here and elsewhere in Herder's notes, we render "E." as "e.g." (44_{32}).

God – There can be wholes <*tota*> that are entirely heterogeneous <*heterogenea*> with others. E.g., other worlds opposed to ours.

408. Monads are in a reciprocal, real connection, that is, in reciprocal action and in real dependence <*monades sunt in nexu mutuo reali i.e. in actione mutua et dependentia reali*>. Real dependence shows itself merely from the effect: in the ocean all drops counteract against each other as component parts which are reciprocally joined to the whole <*compartes, quae mutuo sibi sunt connexa ad totum*>: with each whole <*toto*> there is a reciprocal connection <*nexus mutuus*> of the component parts <*compartium*>. In a real whole all parts necessarily must be in reciprocal action and reaction <*in mutua actione et reactione*>, i.e., in real connection <*in realnexu*>, because otherwise they do not constitute a whole. The parts of the sphere,^{f} of the world.

28:45

409–12. *In the universe* <*universo*> *no action is without counteraction*: for all substances stand in real connection <*in nexu reali*>; that is: they act and react. But the word reaction <*reactio*>, which the author uses here merely for reciprocal action <*mutuam actionem*>, implies the concept of the *against*, of real opposition, a consequence of which is privation <*privation*>. And this really opposed action is not general: for actions which are really <*realiter*> opposed must be homogeneous. Thoughts cannot be cancelled by motions: for motion is posited and cancelled merely by motive power and thus if the body reacted in this manner on the soul: then willing and moving would have to be the same – the powers of the one performing an action do not act, unless with an equal reaction <*vires agentis non agunt, nisi cum reactione aequali*>. E.g., a box on the ear hurts both with equal strength. Two balls which push against one another flatten each other equally.

A motion is an alteration of location; where there is no location, there is also no alteration. Now since a location is no absolute concept, §281, then motion is also a relative concept. A body moves merely with respect to some; in respect to others it is at rest, but one abstracts from these others because in such manner it would continue infinitely. Suppose two bodies moved at a distance of two inches apart: then they are at rest over against one another: in motion over against others. But one abstracts from all other objects and thus the motion is equal, because it is mutual, and the motive power is also equal. But now posit two equal powers against each other: the consequence of that is privation <*privation*> when two bodies thus move against one another with equal power: then the consequence is a comparative rest over against one another, because they both move equally quickly after the same kind of push: for one abstracts here from other objects with respect to which they still move. – Now since from the nature of motion it follows that a body does not move until it is pushed, and moves with motion

---

^{f} We are have added a comma here, where there is a gap in Lehmann (45$_4$).

proportional to the other: then a body has an inertia <*inertiam*>, but does it need a *power* of inertia <*vim inertiae*>? If a body is not pushed, then it does not move; if it is pushed, then it pushes back, this is no inertial power, but rather its pressure <*nisus*> toward motion, an actual motive power against the other that pushes, although it is at the same time at rest against the other things.Were the inertia a power, then it might also move before the push. Newton's law thus remains firm: a body remains in its own state of moving or resting unless an external power moves it <*corpus manet in statu suo movendi vel quiescendi, nisi externa vis eum moveat*>.

28:46

The use of that in psychology: is the soul bodily, i.e., does it not move until it is pushed?

A simple [element] of matter fills a space with respect to its connection <*nexus*> with others outside, for in space two different locations are present: consequently, in space an element is present, it fills a location in space: but merely through its co-presence <*per compraesentiam*>. But is there then a plurality in the co-presence? – Yes, but not a plurality in the parts, which again would have to be substances: – and thus they are on that account not extended, because they would have to occupy a space when posited alone <*solitarie posita*>. Now it merely fills a space merely [through] *presence* in space and indeed through its impenetrability <*praesentia in spatio et quidem per impenetrabilitatem*>: otherwise many substances could be in one space, but impenetrability is the power of counteraction against everything that wants to come into its space.

414. (Coherence) in the power of impenetrability is (definition) the power of repulsion <(*cohaerentia*) *in vi impenetrabilitatis est . . . vis repulsionis*>.[g] By its means, monads could never unify themselves to constitute a volume, but rather they would flee into infinity. Another power must thus maintain an equilibrium with impenetrability, this is the power of attraction <*vis attractiva*>. These two powers are in conflict <*in conflictu*> and determine space, that it is not larger due to impenetrability and not smaller due to cohesion.[h] Thus everything in nature is effective: a body contains its volume not by inertia but rather by action. From that arises cohesion. The author does not define it correctly,[10] for to every motion a third power is required; co-motion [of two objects] does not occur except by a third power; however, they cohere together by a third power greater than that which is required for the moving <*comotio fit non nisi per vim tertiam: cohaerent autem per vim tertiam, majorem ea, quae ad movendum requiritur*>. *Cohesion* is therefore attraction in contact <*cohaesio ergo est attractio in contactu*>.[i] *Contact* is immediate co-presence through the powers of impen-

---

[g] We have added a period here and a capital at the beginning of the sentence (46_{18-19}).

[h] We have changed a colon to a period here and in the next sentence, capitalizing the subsequent words ($46_{24, 25}$).

[i] We have added a period here (46_{30}).

etrability <*contactus est immediata compraesentia per vires impenetrabilitatis*>. But cannot a thing attract another without contact <*contactum*>? Newton maintained this. And thus there is attraction that is local or at a distance.

Concerning body we now have (1) presence in place <*praesentia in loco*>,ʲ (2) extension <*extensio*>, (3) impenetrability <*impenetrabilitas*>, (4) cohesion <*cohaesio*>, (5) inertia <*inertia*> (but not a power of inertia <*vis inertiae*>, also not tendency) since it never alters its state by itself, (6) mobility <*mobilitas*> (but not motive power <*vis motrix*>), every power moves until something resists it, which is opposed to inertia <*inertiae*>: but they do not move themselves, but rather have the ability to move when they are pushed. When a thing moves others, the power is merely impenetrability <*impenetrabilitas*>. But a body can never move itself through a motive power <*per vim motricem*>. Suppose a body in equilibrium <*in aequilibrio*> – a push happens – now if it moved itself, then it would immediately have to be in equilibrium <*in aequilibrio*> again.

28:47

415. But as for the alteration of a monad <*monas*> which does not belong to the composite world, does it not also happen by motion? The author's proof is uncertain,¹¹ but one's own experience almost shows that the thoughts of the soul are almost not without motion.

416. Power of representation <*vis repraesentationis*> not explained in accordance with Leibniz.¹²

417. Belongs in part to metaphysics and physics.

Motion and rest are relative concepts just like location: e.g., a ship moves: with respect to the ship one is at rest, with respect to the heavens one is moving.

Waning motion <*motus evanescens*> can be counted as rest.

418. With each body the parts are in conflict <*in conflictu*>. Through cohesion <*per cohaesionem*>: through impenetrability <*per impenetrabilitatem*>. The volume of a body, insofar as attraction and repulsion determine it, is equilibrium <*aequilibrium*>.

419. 20. Where extension is, that which is posited alone has parts. An element is a substance which is a simple part of matter <*qua extensum est, quod solitario positum, habet partes. Elementum est, substantia simplex pars materiae*>.

For otherwise not only will the simple parts be called elements, but rather also those that are not divisible further by the powers of nature. Thus the ancients had four elements: thus the little spheres out of which water consisted were the elements of water.

422. According to the author's meaning, every substance is immaterial.¹³ But elsewhere immaterial also means that which is not part of a whole. Thus there are simple substances, of which many taken together constitute a matter: others, which cannot constitute a matter. The former

---

ʲ We have changed a comma to a period here (46₃₄).

are material monads <*monades materiales*>; the latter, immaterial <*immateriales*>. It thus is asked in psychology: is a soul a material or immaterial monad <*monas materialis . . . immaterialis*>? Without this distinction, a simple soul still could be a monad <*monas*> of the body.

There is a fine distinction between body <*corpus*> and matter <*materia*>: matter is an impenetrable extension, determinable by reason of its form.[k] Body is an impenetrable extension, *determined* by reason of its form <*materia est extensum impenetrabile, ratione figurae determinabile. Corpus est extensum impenetrabile, ratione figurae determinatum*>.

According to common usage, immaterial and non-bodily are the same: but according to the previous distinction, immaterial is more.

423. Philosophy of the lazy, when one remains standing by the principled <*principiatis*> as principles <*principiis*>. E.g., when I assume something bodily as a simple substance. Those matters which are indivisible with respect to the powers of nature, are prime matters <*materiae primae*> (§420).

28:48

424. According to the author's definition, God is also an atom <*atomus*>, the monads also;

Atom <*Atomus*>: an element of matter which, in respect to those powers of nature which are usually divisive, is indivisible <*elementum materiae, quod respectu ad vires naturae habito dividentes, est indivisibile*>: e.g., gold dissolved in aqua regia, is transformed into its atoms.[14]

425. *Corpuscular philosophy* <*philosophia corpuscularis*>, e.g., the philosophy of Epicurus and Gassendi.

427. Something is *divisible* [(1)] metaphysically: insofar as a plurality is met in it: e.g., space. (2) Physically when its parts can be moved so that they are no longer parts <*cuius partes ita moveri possunt ut non amplius sint partes*>. E.g., all bodies.[l]

428. Matter is not absolutely divisible into infinity <*materia non est absolute divisibilis in infinitum*>. Matter consists of parts which will remain separated from all the rest. Composition is thus an accident; if all composition is suspended, simple substances still do remain. Thus matter consists of simple parts – consequently not divisible into infinity.

Space does not consist of simple parts. §240. 241.

(2) Is matter relatively divisible into infinity, i.e., does a body consist of infinitely many simple parts whose quantity is greater than every number? This is difficult to decide. One would have to prove that an infinite quantity is impossible. But can it not be possible, since quantity and number are not the same that there can be quantities which are too large for any number? Yet *probably* its parts are not infinitely many, because each element of matter occupies a space in the matter of which it is a part,

[k] We have added a period here (47_{34}).
[l] We have added a period here (48_{15}).

consequently every part would then have to occupy an infinite space, thus the matter must have finite parts, because it occupies a finite space; *what is a finite space?* That which has a relation to sensible space.

Most certainly this does not follow; however, it is also not as necessary to us as to those who believed: it is all the same whether a body is infinitely divisible or whether it has no simple parts at all. – A body still consists of simple parts: only they may be finite or infinite.

28:49   429. A material atom indivisible *in itself* is a contradiction in the predicate <*atomus materialis per se indivisibilis est contradictio in adjecto*>. The material atoms <*atomi materiales*> are merely indivisible in regard to the powers of nature <*indivisibiles ad vires naturae*>.

The atomistic philosophy can be true only if it very well <*prima*> acknowledges its ignorance.*[m]*

Section <Sectio> *III*

430. (Nature is quite often used improperly; but still never merely of concepts, thoughts: one does not assign a nature to, e.g., a triangle. It is thus used merely of such things which have a principle <*principium*> of effectiveness – and this is otherwise called *essence*.)

Essence concerns the logical concept, to which all others are subordinate, a feature which distinguishes the matter from all the rest. The essential concept is the determinate representation of a matter which distinguishes it from all others, from which one can derive all others, and which itself is derived from none. From the *nature* one can distinguish not merely the matter, but rather also give grounds of its alteration: consequently it concerns power and activity, the essential power is therefore the nature of the thing <*vis essentialis est ergo natura rei*>. E.g., the nature of quicksilver must contain the real ground of all of its consequences, i.e., the power, e.g., weight, fluidity, mobility. The author's definition comes to the same thing in a roundabout way.[15] For the principle of change is power <*mutationum principium est vis*>.*[n]*

431. Manner *of composition* <*modus compositionis*>. The consequence of the connectedness of the powers of all single parts. And these powers bring about the nature <*et hae vires efficiunt naturam*>: what is explained from the powers of the elements in conformity with their connection is explained from their nature. E.g., that all alterations of body as composite <*compositorum*> come by motion.

§432. Consequently all alteration according to laws of motion.*[o]*

433. According to the author's explanation, every body is a machine

---

[m] "*Agnoscirt,*" a Latin/German compound (49$_4$).

[n] We have added a period here (49$_{22}$).

[o] We have added a period here (49$_{28}$).

<*machina*>: but according to common usage, one makes machines from bodies, not machines from machines.

Therefore a machine [is] – – – a single thing according to particular laws <*machina ergo* – – – *secundum leges quasdam singula res*>.[16] For otherwise all bodies could rightly be called machines <*machinae*>, since they always have effective powers according to certain laws, are always in conflict by the power of attraction and the power of repulsion <*vi attractionis et repulsionis in conflictu*>.

Mechanism.[p] Whoever explains from the nature of a plant how it is that it always grows upwards, explains it mechanically <*per mechanismum*>.

434. A mechanical connection is a connection of bodies through which they act according to laws of motion <*nexus mechanicus est nexus corporum, quo secundum leges motus agunt*>.   28:50

435. E.g., if I explain desire and representation from the body. Maupertuis thinks one cannot mechanically explain the generation of that sort of thing.[17]

Physico-mechanistic fate <*fatum physicomechanicum*>: that things must happen by virtue of the law of motion: thus Newton explains the destruction of the world.[q]

Chapter <Caput> III

Section <Sectio> I

436. [The] author posits merely *what* a world must have as properties if it is the best, without deciding whether ours is the best.[18]

No perfection can be thought, even according to the common concept, without relation <*respectus*> to a thinking and rational being: a relation to rational beings is thus required of it (induction[r]): an uninhabited palace.

Objection <*objectio*> I. Should there be a most perfect world: then it would have to include within itself all possible things: nothing more could be posited to it, God could create no more. Response <*responsio*> quantity does not constitute perfection.

II. A most perfect world would be infinite, consequently God himself. But now a world is finite by force of definition <*vi definitionis*>, and if its perfections allow themselves to be infinitely enlarged, then a contradiction arises.

Response <*responsio*>: this most perfect world is not the most perfect being but rather merely the most perfect world: there remains an essential difference as heterogeneous <*heterogenea*>.

---

[p] We have added a period here and a capital at the beginning of the sentence (49_{36}).

[q] We have added a period here (50_8).

[r] "*induct:*"; we have read this as an abbreviation for "induction," and added a colon after the parentheses to indicate that the text is probably about the example of the palace (50_{15}).

438. The idealistic world is still more perfect than the egoistic world, because with the latter there is[s] always more possible. But the imperfection of the idealistic world is more difficult to prove, because bodies have no perfection in themselves except insofar as they are related to spirits. Now if spirits all could have representations without having bodies, then of course the idealistic world would be better, since the same ends are obtained by a shorter way. And the advantages of our world would have to be proved merely from the impossibility, that spirits without bodies could not have the same series of thoughts.

28:51   439. The materialistic world belongs in Psychology.[19]

440. Infinite (a) in the real sense, what has the greatest degree of perfection, (b) in the mathematical sense, what in comparison with unity is greater than all number. The world would be mathematically infinite if the quantity of mundane bodies were greater than all number. This mathematical infinity then would be successive <in successivis> if this series of things always would be continued. The world would be mathematically infinite simultaneously <in simultaneis> if the series of the coexisting bodies were greater than all number. This is indeed difficult for us to think because the number concepts are instruments of distinct cognitions for us: but since God needs no number with his representations, and the existence of one body could not hinder the other: therefore it does not appear to be absurd in itself.

The author confounds infinite <infinitum> and indefinite <indefinitum>:[20] the indefinite is that whose limits it is either not pleasing or not permitted to determine <indefinitum est, cuius limites determinare vel non placet, vel non licet>. Now were this the same as infinite <infinito>: then cheese, etc., would be infinite.

Section <Sectio> 2
Preparation. To the connection <nexu> of the things in the whole belong *not merely the existences of the things.* – It is always asked with this whether they constitute a whole <totum>, since each could exist alone. If they are many and coexistent, then they do not immediately have community on that account. Thus for a connection *something special, reciprocal action <mutua actio>*, is still required. For it is not possible for two substances without connection <nexu> to effect one another. – For without connection <nexu> nothing that takes place in A can have a consequence in B. Thus if a substance in its existence does not depend upon another: then substances could exist without connection: when two *substances effect each other: then A and B must necessarily depend upon C,*[t] otherwise nothing in existence could follow in B from A: but from that, that their existence depends upon a third:

---

[s] We have changed *sind* to *ist* (50₂₉).
[t] We have replaced a period with a comma here (51₂₈), but left in the string of colons.

it does not yet follow that they must be in connection <*in nexu*>: their *connection still requires a special ground: a special action still* of the creator, since he connected them. Thus *the state of diverse substances that each acts on and suffers from the others* (interaction <*commercium*>) has *a special ground in God,* who *willed that they should depend upon one another.*

If a substance suffers, then it must contain in *itself* by its own power the ground of the inherence of the accident, because otherwise the accident 28:52 would not inhere in it. But the ground of this must also be *in the efficient power of the substance,* because otherwise it would not act. Consequently the *powers of the substances are harmonious.* In relation to the powers of the others one contains the ground of the inherence of the accident. This body of doctrine is called established harmony <*harmonia stabilita*>, and since God willed it previously, preestablished <*praestabilita*>.

Synthetic preparation. Each subject in which *an accident inheres must itself contain a ground of its inherence.* For if, e.g., God could produce a thought in a soul merely by himself: then God, but not a soul, would have the thought: because there would be no connection <*nexus*> between them. Thus for the inherence of an accident in A its own power is required, and a merely external, not even a divine power, does not suffice. Otherwise I could also produce thoughts in a mere wooden post, if it were possible by a mere external power.

If two substances effect one another reciprocally <*mutuo*>: then the suffering, the *inherence of the accident,* happens *not merely by its own but rather also by external power:* for otherwise it would not be a *suffering.* E.g., I hear music: that requires the external power of the music, and the distinct representation of the notes requires one's own power of hearing.

An accident thus inheres by its own power, which contains the *sufficient inner ground* of it

yet also by *external* power, thus by *an outer ground* of inherence without which it would not have inhered. Now properly *no substance can contain the ground of the accident in the other, if it does not at the same time contain the ground of the substantial power and of the existence of the other:* I cannot become the ground of a thought in another if I am not at the same time the ground of the power that produces the thoughts: in this manner *God is the ground.* If two *substances are in interaction* <*in commercio*>, *the two depend on a third, so their powers are harmonious with one another: they stand in connection and relation, on account of the third substance which is the ground of both, and has willed a connection* <*nexus*>. E.g., the existence of the action of another does not depend simply on one action and one power. Thus all predicates must be produced by one's own power, but since an external power is also required exter- 28:53 nally:ᵘ then a third must have willed this harmony (established harmony

---

ᵘ "External power" translates *fremde Kraft*; "externally" translates *äusserlich* (53₁).

<harmonia stabilita>).*ᵛ* This connection *<nexus>* is between created beings, because the two in interaction *<in commercio>* must depend on a third.

If a substance is active by its own power under an outer condition, then it suffers.

450. If we want to conceive that one power suffers simply from the other, without its own power and thus without harmony, then that is called physical or real influence *<influxus physicus . . . realis>*. One commonly thinks: give me many things, I want something in the one, and something should follow in the other. But what explains this connection *<nexus>*? – Since one's own power to suffer is always required, this influence is impossible, even [for] God, because he can never produce the accident in another, except insofar as he is the ground of the power which produces the accident: e.g., regret in the soul.

ᵛ This period has been moved to the end of the parenthetical phrase (53₂).

PART II
Metaphysik L$_I$

MID-1770S (AK. 28: 195–301)

CONCEPT OF THE WORLD

Because cosmology borrows its principles not from experience, but rather from pure reason, it can be called *rational cosmology*. But because even the object as well, and not just the principles, is an object of pure reason and not experience, it is called transcendental cosmology <*cosmologia transscendentalis*>. In the Ontology we have already spoken of the limiting concepts, which constitute the limit in the series of cognitions. – In relation there were these three concepts: the relation of the substance to the accident; of the cause to the effect, and of the whole to the parts. – In all these cognitions we can think of a first and a last, through which a completeness <*completudo*> or totality arises in these cognitions. – In the relation of the substance to the accident, the substantial is that which is not an accident of another. – In the relation of the cause to the effect the first cause is the limiting concept, which is no effect of another <*causatum alterius*>. – In the third relation of the whole to the parts, the limiting concept is the whole which is not a part of another; and that is the concept of the *world*. This concept is a pure concept of reason,[a] and is not arbitrary, but rather is necessary to human reason. Our reason has a need that is not satisfied until it meets a completeness <*completudinem*> in the series of things, or until it can think a complete totality. – The world is a substantial whole <*totum substantiale*>; thus a whole of accidents is no world. Accidents also are not viewed as parts, not as component parts <*compartes*> of the whole. E.g., thoughts and movements do not belong to a human being; rather, these are parts of the state, but not of the whole. The world whole is thus not a whole of all states, but rather of all substances.

In the world whole we look at two aspects:

1. at *matter*, and that is the substances;
2. at *form*, that is the composition or the connection of many <*nexus plurium*>.

The connection can be twofold, *one-sided* or *reciprocal*. It is *one-sided* when the second depends on the first, but not the first on the second. It is

---

[a] We follow Lehmann in changing *Verstandesbegriff (concept of the understanding)* (in Pölitz) *to Vernunftbegriff* (195_{20}).

19

28:196

reciprocal when one determines the other. But substances constitute a whole not by one-sided, but rather by reciprocal connections and actions, and that is interaction <*commercium*>. An interaction <*commercium*> is thus necessary to the*ᵇ* substantial composite <*composito substantiali*>. The form of the substantial composite <*compositi substantialis*> thus rests on the interaction <*commercio*>. – God and the world therefore constitute no whole, because there is no interaction <*commercium*>, not a reciprocal but rather only a one-sided action; on the other hand the members of a political state constitute a whole because a reciprocal action is there; but the members do not constitute a whole with the regent because there the action is only one-sided. Accordingly all substances in the world stand in interaction <*commercio*>, and thereby constitute a whole. An aggregate is still not a whole; here only many things <*plura*> that stand in no reciprocal connection are thought. The difference of the world from every other composite <*composito*> is: that the world is a substantial whole which is not a part of another <*totum substantiale, quod non est pars alterius*>. – The plurality which is subordinated to none larger is the totality <*omnitudo*; G: *Allheit*>. Every composite <*compositum*> can be considered as a whole, e.g., an apple. The earth is a whole, but also at the same time a part of a still larger whole. But the world is also an absolute whole. The world whole is different from the whole of the states; states are in the world in all alterations, but the world is a substantial whole <*totum substantiale*>. We cannot represent the series of states wholly at once because they always pass away; but we can think the substances together, and then that is already a whole. I thus have a composite <*compositum*> which is no part of another; so this is the world. Substances are reckoned to the world, insofar as they stand in real connection <*in nexu reali*> and thus in interaction <*commercio*>. The aggregation of the substances in which there is no community still does not constitute a world. Reciprocal determination, the form of the world as a composite <*compositi*>, rests on the interaction <*commercio*>. If we thought substances without real connection <*absque nexu reali*> and without interaction <*commercium*>, where every substance would be in and for itself and they would have no community with one another, then that would indeed be a multitude <*multitudo*>, but still not a world.

Thus the connection <*nexus*> of substances that stand*ᶜ* in interaction <*commercio*> is the essential condition of the world.

With this there are clearly two questions to distinguish: "Is yet another world possible beyond this world? And, instead of this world, is another world possible?" – If one asked whether apart from one world yet other worlds were possible, then this does not contradict itself in and for itself.

28:197 The singularity of the world cannot be proven *a priori* from the concept

---

ᵇ We follow Lehmann in changing *im* (in the) in Pölitz to *zum* (to the)(196₂).

ᶜ We follow Lehmann in changing *bestehen* (subsist) in Pölitz to *stehen* (stand)(196₃₃).

of the world. For though we say the world is a substantial composite *<compositum substantiale>* where the substances stand in interaction *<in commercio>*, it clearly must then follow that this world constitutes a whole which is no part of another; but this does not refute that there could still be several such wholes in which an interaction *<commercium>* is to be met. – Thus the oneness of the world does not follow from its concept. But the oneness can be demonstrated from another ground, which is the following: if all things except one exist so that they all depend on the one, then it must follow that all existing substances except one are connected, and all together constitute a whole because they depend on one. It would thus *follow* from the communal [cause] and from *a highest cause that there is only one single world*, which will be demonstrated in the following. Thus in no way does the oneness of the world flow from its concept.

ON INFINITE PROGRESSION AND REGRESSION
<DE PROGRESSU ET REGRESSU IN INFINITUM>

Progression *<progressus>* is the continuation of a series when I distance myself from the limit *a priori <termino a priori>*. Regression *<regressus>* is when I approach the limit *a priori <termino a priori>*. The more I proceed in the series of subordinated things, the more I am in progression *<in progressu>*. But the farther I go back, the more I am in regression *<in regressu>*. – Our reason cannot make any representation of the possibility of things if a *first* cause is not assumed which is no effect of another *<causatum alterius>*. The cause must be complete and determinable. But if it is a subaltern cause *<causa subalterna>*, then it is not complete. We can have a first and a subaltern cause *<causam primam . . . subalternam>*. – Without a first cause *<causa prima>*, the series of subaltern causes *<causarum subalternarum>* is not determined sufficiently enough for reason to derive the effect *<causatum>*. It is thus not comprehensible to reason; that is: it cannot completely comprehend it, how the existence of a thing is possible insofar as it is grounded only in subaltern causes *<causis subalternis>*. – But although we cannot comprehend the infinite regression *<regressum in infinitum>* without assuming a first cause *<causam primam>*, we still also cannot say that such [a thing] is apodictically impossible; only that we cannot comprehend such [a thing] without assuming a first cause *<causam primam>*. In general when we ask: whether an infinite regression *<regressus in infinitum>* is possible, then this is something different than when we ask: does this series have no first cause? Infinite *<infinitum>* is a mathematical concept, and means a quantity which is larger than all number, thus that we must go back without end. But that does not mean[d] that there is no cause; this series can always depend on a cause. But because

28:198

---

[d] We follow Lehmann in omitting an *es* (in Pölitz) after *bedeutet* (198$_2$).

this series is larger than all number, we simply cannot come to the cause in going back. The difficulty thus lies in the question itself. One believes one comprehends the continuation in the series of the effects <*causatorum*>; one imagines the possibility of the infinite progression <*progressus in infinitum*>; but such a possibility is also with the regression <*regressus*>, for a quantity that is larger than all number is not impossible. – But an *infinite* quantity is impossible. We cannot comprehend infinity from the infinity in the series of causes <*in serie causarum*>, and from that we cannot infer a first cause <*causam primam*>; but rather from contingency: for the contingent has a cause that must be necessary and complete, thus a series of effects <*series causatorum*> has as its ground a first cause <*causam primam*>. – Thus if we ask: whether the world is *from eternity*? then that question is not the same [as]: whether it has no cause, but rather whether it has depended on a cause from eternity. Thus whether the regression <*regressus*> of the world is to infinity <*in infinitum*>, so that, if we go back, we do not come to the cause, although a cause is there. – Thus are confused the infinite regression in the series of causes <*regressus in infinitum in serie causarum*> without the first cause <*causa prima*>, and the impossibility in this series of successively subordinating effect to cause <*causatum causae*> and of coming to an end in it.

The proposition that we cannot successively come to the end in regressing <*in regrediendo*> was not seldom confused with the other: namely that the series has no cause; but these are *two matters*. – We cannot come to the end because the series is internal; but from that it does not follow that there is no cause. Of course, a human being cannot comprehend the smallest quantity, not even five strokes at once, except through repeated acts <*actus*> of positing. He must successively add one to one <*unum uni*>, but because this series is infinite, he never comes to an end in adding <*in addendo*>. From that it does not follow that such a series without cause is possible in itself. Intellectually I can comprehend how God could conceive eternity whole; for the highest cause is the complete cause of the series; thus it must cognize the whole series. But sensibly, that is, by means of time, I cannot comprehend this; for complete insight must happen through counting. But in counting I never come to an end. – Thus effects <*causata*> have a first cause <*causam primam*>; the under-

28:199 standing says this; thus the world has a cause; but this cause <*causa*> does not belong to the series, thus not to the world. Now this series subordinated to it may be finite or infinite, that is all the same; but the series of effects <*causatis*> still has a first cause <*causam primam*>. Thus if the question is raised: whether the world has a beginning, then the question must not be so viewed as if one asked: whether the world has a cause; for it must have a cause in any event; but rather, this means the boundary of the world from before <*a parte ante*>, when it had its beginning. But we cannot determine the boundaries of the world; not because we do not know how to determine them, but rather because they are undeterminable. There is a difficulty in thinking how a world could have been here from eternity; although it is also impossible to think how a series that has had a beginning can yet be infinite. But we find ourselves in the same quandary when it is asked: How can God have begun to act?

ON DESTINY AND CHANCE

Here are three propositions to notice:

1. all phenomena in the world do not exist by fate <*omnia phaenomena in mundo non existunt per fatum*>;
2. they do not come to be by chance <*non fiunt per casum*>;
3. they are not connected by a leap <*non connectuntur per saltum*>.

In the connection of things there are two sorts that are contrary to reason, and that is:

1. blind necessity, and
2. blind accident.

Blind means when one oneself cannot see; but also that through which one cannot see.*ᵉ* Blind necessity is thus that by means of which we can see nothing with the understanding. Blind necessity is *destiny*; blind accident is *chance*. Both are absurdities contrary to reason. Blind necessity means that which is not grounded either upon the essence of the matter itself, or upon some other cause. Blind accident is an event which is contingent, and indeed, that the contingency takes place in every regard. But something can be contingent in one regard and necessary in another regard; only that which is contingent in *every* regard is a blind accident. Blind necessity is opposed by a primordial being; but blind accident by a cause. Both are contrary to reason, because one thereby thinks of events that do not at all happen according to laws of the understanding and of reason. – If I assume a blind accident, something contingent absolutely and in every regard, then it is an exception to all laws and all grounds. If I assume a blind necessity, without an original necessity determined by a cause, then this necessity is a breach against the laws of the understanding and of reason. Thereby all right to judge is taken from us.*ᶠ* Thus both give no explanatory ground of events, and serve only as a cushion for ignorance, and deprive the understanding of all use. Opposed to both, chance as well as destiny, are *nature* and *freedom*. These are the two explanatory grounds

28:200

ᵉ For instance, *blindes Glas* is opaque glass – an example used in the *Metaphysik Mrongovius* (AK. 29: 923₁₈).

ᶠ We follow Lehmann in changing *ihr* (from it, i.e., from reason) in Pölitz to *uns* (from us)(200₇).

of the understanding, which are opposed to blind accident. Destiny is a blind necessity. If I oppose this blind necessity, then I derive the event from freedom. But if it is a necessity, then I derive it either from the absolute necessity, from the highest cause, or from hypothetical necessity, that is, from grounds of nature. – But the necessity of nature alone cannot be the explanatory ground of everything; the first ground of origination must happen through freedom, because nothing but freedom can furnish a ground of origination, of which more is said in the Rational Theology <theologia rationalis>. – Whoever excludes all freedom and assumes the necessity of nature, maintains strict fate <fatum strictum>. But whoever assumes absolute necessity, that everything is sheerly necessary, maintains Spinozistic fate <fatum spinozisticum>.

ON THE LEAP AND THE LAW OF CONTINUITY
<DE SALTU ET LEGE CONTINUITATIS>

A leap is a transition to a determination from a more distant ground in a connection of many members, without going through the intermediate members <membra intermedia>. The concept of a leap <saltu> concerns not merely events, but rather also things, and is opposed to continuity. Therefore we must speak first of continuity.

Every magnitude, or every whole as magnitude, can be considered as a continuous or discontinuous quantum <quantum continuum . . . discretum>. A continuum <continuum> is that in which a smallest is possible, but where one cannot determine in and for itself how many parts are in it. Continuity is thus the absolute indeterminability of the quantity of the parts in a whole. Thus where no smallest is possible, there is continuity; e.g., space and time are continuous quanta <quanta continua>. No smallest line is possible, for points are boundaries of the line. But between two boundaries there must always be a line; thus two points cannot be immediately next to one another, but rather there is always space between them. So it is as well with time; between two moments there is a time, just as between two points there is a line. All moments are positions in time, just as points [are] positions in space. All parts between points are themselves space, and all parts between moments are themselves parts of time. Accordingly the transition from one point to another cannot happen suddenly but rather continuously; that is: when one body transfers from one point to another, then it must go through infinitely many intermediate spaces, it must go through all intermediate locations lying between the one point in the line and the other. If something could transfer from one location to another without running through all intermediate locations, then this would be a change of place through a leap <mutatio loci per saltum>. But no thing goes immediately from one location to another except through all intermediate locations; it must go through the infinitely many parts of space. Further, no thing goes immediately from one state into another, i.e., through a leap <*per saltum*>, but rather the transition from one state to another happens [such]^L that the things must go though all intermediate states; thus one can say generally <*generaliter*>: all change <*mutatio*> is continuous <*continua*>. Every state has two limits <*terminos*>: from which <*a quo*> and to which <*ad quem*>. Each of these states is in a particular distinct moment. With each transition the thing is in two moments distinct from one another. The moment in which the thing is in the one state is distinct from the moment in which the thing arrives in the other state. But between two moments there is a time, just as between two points [there is] a space. Thus the transition happens in time; for in the moments in which it moves from A to B there is a time in which it is neither in A nor in B.^{g} But in this time it is in the mutation, in the transition. Thus a thing never goes immediately from one state into the other, but rather through all intermediate states, and thereby the alteration of the state of a thing is possible. The differences of the states all have a magnitude, and in this magnitude is continuity. The cause of the law of continuity is time. This law of continuity is no metaphysical whim, but rather a law that is spread through the whole of nature. E.g., the mind goes from obscure to clear representations not immediately, but rather through all the intermediate representations which are clearer than the first ones. This law of continuity is a proposition that *Leibniz* first set forth, but that until now only few have grasped. Thus in order to make it graspable, we want to consider it from another side, and then apply these cases to it. Every appearance is, as representation in the mind, under the form of inner sense, which is time. Every representation is so constituted that the mind goes through it in time; that is, the mind expounds the appearance; thus every appearance is expoundable. E.g., if the mind has a representation of a line, then it goes through all parts of the line, and expounds the appearance. We do not represent body other than by going through all its parts, and that is the exposition of the appearance. Thus we cannot be conscious of the object other than by expounding the object. The cause is that all our given representations happen in time. All objects of the senses are expoundable in our power of representation; that is: we can determine our mind gradually in time; one also calls that the going through of appearance, where one goes successively from one part to the other. From this it follows that there is no appearance and no part of a given appearance that could not be divided to infinity; thus there is nothing simple in appearance, neither in sequential appearance, nor where there is a manifold of appearance, for the present can be posited only to the extent that the mind goes through it and expounds the appearance.

28:202

---

^{g} We follow Lehmann in changing *im A noch im* (in Pölitz) to *in A noch in* (201$_{32}$).

Now it shall be shown that for this reason no appearance at all consists of simple parts. All appearance stands as one representation in time, and is expounded. A part of the whole appearance is expounded in a part of the whole time. Each part of the appearance thus lies in a part of time. But now no part of time is a moment, rather a part of time is itself a time; a moment is only the boundary of time, thus to every part of appearance belongs a part of time; accordingly, there is no part of appearance that is not in time. Now, just as time is divisible to infinity, so then too there is no part of the appearance that would not be divisible to infinity; for every part of the appearance is between two boundaries of time, between which it goes. This going through of a part of the appearance cannot happen in a moment; but what is enclosed between two boundaries itself has parts; for there is always a time between two moments. Therefore every part of the appearance can again be expounded; there is thus no simple appearance. Were there a simple appearance, then it would still have to be a part of a whole. But this series of appearances has a time, thus every part of the appearance also has a part of time. But now no part of time is simple, thus also no part of appearance is simple. – Now no transition from one location to another, from one state to another, is possible other than through infinitely many intermediate locations and intermediate states, of which the difference is smaller than the difference between the first and last. Thus two locations are not immediately next to one another, but rather find between themselves infinitely many intermediate locations. Likewise no body can alter immediately, rather it must go through all infinite intermediate alterations. There is no state immediately following another.[h] For if a body transfers from one state into another, then there must be a moment in which it goes out of the preceding state, and a moment in which it comes into the following state. Between these two moments is a time in which it is neither in the one nor in the other state, thus in an intermediate state, which is a ground why it transfers into the following state. Just as this is said of alterations, that they are continuous, so is it as well with velocity. No body moves immediately with velocity at once; rather it must go through infinitely many degrees of velocity which are ever larger, and come ever closer to the determined velocity.

This is the first law of nature, whose necessity can be comprehended *a priori*. Further, on this law rests: no body can go immediately from rest to motion, and from motion again into rest, without it going through the infinitely small degrees of motion and of rest. Further: no body alters its direction immediately without an intermediate rest, e.g., in a triangle. A point does not move immediately from one direction into another without an intermediate rest. Presence in one location through a time is rest. But that motion is interrupted between whose parts there is a rest, thus a body

28:203

28:204

---

[h] We follow Lehmann in changing *aufeinander* (in Pölitz) to *auf einen anderen* (203_{18}).

does not alter its direction immediately, except through an intermediate rest. But should its direction be altered without an intermediate rest, then it must alter its direction continuously, and this happens in a bent line, but not in an angle. It goes continuously through infinitely small degrees of deviation from the first direction to the other. – Further, one notes in physics: no light ray alters its direction suddenly (which *Newton* demonstrated), but rather continuously. The light ray which falls on a mirror refracts with an acute angle, but is in the mirror for a time; and then the same is true of it that was said earlier of a body in the movement of a triangle. Thus it rests in the mirror; but it would rest forever if a new power did not give it a new direction. – Accordingly every appearance has a magnitude; consequently nothing is simple. No part of appearance, neither of inner nor outer sense, neither in a series nor in an aggregate, is simple. All appearances are thus expoundable in time. Every part of the appearance receives a part of time in the exposition, as the entire appearance receives an entire time; for every part of time is itself a time, and every part of space is itself a space. No part in space and time is simple. There is indeed something simple, that is, a point in space and a moment in time; but those are not parts of space and of time; for otherwise one could think of them before space and time. But now I think a moment in time and a point in space; thus they are determinations and not parts. Now since nothing is simple in time, and every appearance receives a time, then likewise nothing is simple in appearance. Now since likewise nothing is simple in space, every body and every matter is infinitely divisible, for every part of the body stands between two boundaries of space, thus always occupies a space. But that which is infinitely divisible is a continuous quantum <*quantum continuum*>; every appearance is thus a continuous quantum <*quantum continuum*>.

But are substances nonetheless simple? Of course! But when I see bodies, then I see no substances, but rather appearances. I also cannot at all perceive the substances, for no being, other than the creator alone, can perceive the substances of another thing. Thus what is in space and in time is infinitely divisible; no part is the smallest, neither in space nor in time. The law of continuity thus rests on the continuity of space and of time. But that these are continuous quanta <*quanta continua*> is proved from this, because a point in space and a moment in time are not parts, but rather boundaries of space and of time. Although all experiences happen through the senses; thus, we can still anticipate appearances through the understanding, and comprehend *a priori* the conditions of objects. Continuity of forms <*continuitas formarum*> consists in this, that between a concept in genus and species <*in genere et specie*>, and also between one species and the other, there are infinitely many intermediate species, whose differences are ever smaller. E.g., between a scholar and a human being of common sense there are infinitely many degrees of schol-

28:205

arliness, which come ever nearer to a scholar. That is the continuity of kinds in the logical sense. The physical proposition of the continuity of the forms <*formarum*> is quite different from the logical. The physical [proposition] has indeed a great lustre in reason, but not in its execution. I do find a transition from the mineral kingdom into the plant kingdom, which is already a beginning of life; further from the plant kingdom into the animal kingdom, where there are also various small degrees of life; but the highest life is freedom, which I find with human beings. If I go still further, then I am already among thinking beings in the ideal world. Now it is asked whether this determines itself, or whether the series continues. If one says: God ends the series; then *Voltaire* correctly says: God does not belong to the series, rather he *maintains* the series; he is, according to his nature, wholly different from the series, and if the series could be continued to infinity, one still could not come upon beings who would be next to God, and [go] from this immediately to God. *Voltaire* says: human beings like to imagine such series; e.g., from the Pope down to the Capuchins.¹ But this would still not be a continuous quantum <*quantum continuum*>, but rather a discrete one <*discretum*>, whose parts are determinable in space. If creatures exist there still must be a space between one and the other creature, in which there is no infinite degree of intermediate creatures; thus the physical law of continuity is only *comparative*.²

ON THE PARTS OF THE UNIVERSE

It is very good to bring the dogmatist into motion, so that he does not believe: he is sure and his matter is certain. A certain kind of skeptical method is therefore necessary to form doubt, in order better to comprehend and discover the truth. Now which doubts are these? The first thing that is entirely certain is this: that I am; I feel myself, I know for certain that I am; but with just such certainty I do not know that other beings are outside me. I do see appearances (phenomena); but I am not certain that the same thing underlies these appearances; for in dreams I also have representations and appearances, and were the dreams only orderly, so that one would always begin to dream where one had left off, then one could always maintain that one was in the other world. Thus here I also cannot know what underlies the appearance. – Whoever maintains that nothing exists besides himself is an egoist. One cannot refute an egoist by demonstration, and indeed for this reason, that from the same effects <*causatis*> one cannot infer the cause. These appearances could indeed have many other causes underlying them, which produce just such effects. The possibility of two causes of the same effect thus makes it that one cannot prove it apodictically to the egoist.³

That appearances are, is certain; but that we cannot know *what* underlies the appearances comes from this, that our intuitions are not intellec-

28:206

tual, but rather sensuous. *We know nothing more of things than the manner in which we are affected by them; but not what is in the things.* – He who imagines that bodies have no reality,[i] but rather are only appearances, that there are no true objects of the senses, which actual beings underlie, who thus assumes mere spirits, and no substances underlying the body, he is an *idealist*.

Egoism and idealism can be taken in two ways in philosophy: *problematically* and *dogmatically*. *Problematically* it is only a skeptical trial for testing the strength of certainty, and indeed of egoism for the existence of other beings, and of idealism for the existence of corporeal beings outside of us. It is a skeptical test of the reliability of my senses. The reliability of inner sense is certain. I am, I feel that and intuit myself immediately. This proposition thus has a reliability of experience. But that something is *outside me*, of that the senses can provide no reliability; for the appearances can indeed be a play of my power of imagination. – Further the senses also cannot provide any reliability against idealism, for bodies could indeed be only the manner of the appearance, how we are affected by them. It is not proved yet that bodies are, just because I see; for such appearance can also always take place without the things, just as, e.g., color, warmth, the rainbow are not properties of bodies, but rather only the manner in which we are affected by objects. The senses prove only *the manner of the contact* by the appearances in me. Egoism and idealism are thus a skeptical trial *where one denies not the things, but rather takes away the reliability of the senses.* That the senses cannot give any proof (which is very good in philosophy) serves to distinguish the investigations. The understanding can indeed add something to the reliability of the senses, for if things are altered, then there must be in them a ground of the alteration. Thus egoism and idealism remain as problematic in philosophy.[j]

But *dogmatic egoism* is a hidden Spinozism.[4] *Spinoza* says: there is only one being, and all others are modifications of the one being. *Dogmatic idealism* is mystical, and can be called *Platonic idealism*. I myself intuit myself, but bodies only as they affect me. But this manner does not teach me the properties of things, e.g., wax held by a fire melts, and clay dries. Thus the difference lies here in the bodies, how they are affected. But bodies are pure appearances which something must underlie. So far I have philosophized correctly. But if I want to go further in the determinations, then I deteriorate into mystical idealism. *If I maintain thinking beings of which I have intellectual intuition, then that is mystical.* But intuition is only sensuous, for only the senses intuit; the understanding does not intuit, but rather reflects. Dogmatic egoism and idealism must be banned from

28:207

---

[i] We follow Lehmann in changing *Realitäten* (realities) in Pölitz to *Realität* (reality)(206_{26}).
[j] Pölitz reads *Idealismus als problematisch in der Philosphie*, which we follow; Lehmann omits *als* and moves *problematisch* (207_{17}).

philosophy because it is of no use. *Leibniz* was attached to Platonic idealism. He says: the world is an aggregate of monads, and their essential power is the power of representation <*vis repraesentativa*>. I cannot imagine any other power than the thinking power as essential in substances; all others are only modifications. Representation is thus the only one that I can cognize absolutely as an accident in substances. Accordingly, *Leibniz* thus says: all substances are monads or simple parts that have power of representation <*vim repraesentativam*>, and appear among all phenomena <*phaenomenis*>. But it was already just said: all appearance is continuous, and no part of the appearance is simple, thus bodies do not consist of simple parts or monads. However, if they are thought through the understanding the substantial composites <*composita substantialia*> consist of simple parts. But whether all substances <*substantialia*> have representative power <*vim repraesentativam*> cannot be decided here. Thus the proposition that leads us to the mystical and intelligible worlds <*mundo mystico . . . intelligibili*> is banned from philosophy.

28:208

Now we come to the transcendental concepts of bodies, and that is *impenetrability* and *extension*. Impenetrability means the resistance of the extended in space, insofar as it is impossible to occupy the space of the object other than by annihilation of the object, thus what can fill a space and resists the impossibility of sustaining its presence in space.

Mathematical points were already discussed above. Matter does [not]ᴸ consist of simple parts, thus not of points. Physical points <*puncta physica*> are a contradiction <*contradictio*>; they are supposed to mean appearance that is simple and immediate. All points are mathematical; they are not parts, but rather determinations.

The location of each thing is a point. If I want to know the location of a thing, e.g., of the moon, then I must search it until the center, and there no grain of sand can be the location; for otherwise one could ask, onᵏ which side of the grain of sand is the location? Rather the location is a point. Thus space does not consist of points, much less matter of simple parts.

ON THE GENESIS OF BODIES

The connection of substances constitutes what is essential in the concept of the world. Reciprocal action constitutes the form of the world. Reaction <*reactio*> is reaction.ˡ Reciprocal action is in the whole, and here a substance is acting <*agens*>; and so there must be a reciprocal action with every whole. Not every reaction is a counteraction. Counteraction is resistance <*resistentia*>; but not every reaction <*reactio*> is a resistance <*re-*

ᵏ We follow Lehmann in changing *von* (in Pölitz) to *auf* (208₂₆).
ˡ Here the Latin *reactio* is given its German equivalent, *Rückwirkung* (208₃₂). Related words in this passage are *Wechselwirkung* (reciprocal action) and *Gegenwirkung* (counteraction).

sistens>. Although this is a good proposition of physics,[m] and it is quite good to engage in such considerations, it still does not belong in transcendental cosmology. – The constituent parts *<partes constitutivae>* of the 28:209 universe as absolute first parts are simple parts or substances. – In matter as well as in the material world, we cannot assume any absolute first parts.[n] A whole of matter has no absolutely first constituent parts *<partes constitutivas absolute primas>*. One calls the first simple parts elements; thus matter has no elements. It is true that, comparatively speaking with respect to a division, we do call something in matter an element; but this is itself still an actual material, only it cannot be extended further, and these are physical elements which themselves are matter; but metaphysical elements are simple. Matter is possible only through this, that it fills space; thus every part of it must fill a space, because it is between two boundaries; and thus matter does not consist of simple parts. Matter is also no substance, but rather only a phenomenon of substance. That which remains in appearance, what underlies the manifold in body, we call substance. Now because we find in bodies substances that we call substances only by analogy *<per analogiam>*, we cannot infer that matter consists of simple parts, because it is considered not as substance, but rather only as phenomenon. I cognize no other substance and also have no other concept of substance than through intuition. Thus no metaphysical elements can be assumed in matter, but rather physical ones, which comparatively speaking are called elements, because they cannot be divided any further. The physical elements can be twofold: as elements according to species, and as elements according to unity. So the [alcoholic][L] part of beer is an element according to species, because it is composed of many kinds; but water cannot be sorted into diverse matter of diverse species.[5]

Sorting is what one calls the separating of species from one another; but dividing is when one separates something into diverse parts according to matter. – *Atom* is a part of matter that cannot be divided by any power of nature. Such atoms have been assumed by many; among the moderns *Descartes* was attached to this opinion. He said, if these primal bodies, or constitutive parts of all matter, could always be further divided, then no species would remain perdurable; then ashes could come from water. But now since every species consists of particular parts, there must be certain primal parts.

The mode of explanation of bodies rests on the properties of space, 28:210 time, and motion. The general properties of bodies are: impenetrability, connection, and shape. These general properties of bodies are the ground

---

[m] We do not follow Lehmann here in his changing *physischer* (in Pölitz) to *physikalischer* (208$_{36}$).
[n] We follow Lehmann in adding the negative to this sentence, which is missing in Pölitz (209$_3$).

of all physical explanation of body. If something is explained from these general properties of bodies by means of a communicated motion, then that is the *mechanical* mode of explanation. But when something is explained by the powers of nature, which we do not comprehend, but of which experience teaches us, then this is a physical or *dynamic* mode of explanation; e.g., citric acid dissolves crab's eye.[6] If I explain this by communicated atoms, then that is mechanical. – *Newton* was the first one who suspended the mechanical mode of explanation and attempted to explain by physical powers. He gave matter a power of *attraction*, which underlies it essentially and originally, but which does not at all depend on the shape of the matter. – However, the mechanical mode of explanation must always precede first; at first one must attempt mechanically, and seek to explain the communication of motion without an assumed power.

One must assume no basic power until it is not possible otherwise. *The assumption of special basic powers of phenomena is desperation in philosophy.*

One calls it a hidden quality <*qualitatem occultam*> when one assumes an original power without having a concept of it; e.g., when one asked in earlier times: why does water follow in the hollow of a bucket being pulled up? One said: the matter has an aversion to empty space. They called that: horror of the void <*horror vacui*>. Thus they attributed a *desire* to matter, and in this manner reason is often put off with a word, which it must accept instead of a ground. Before I do that, I rather seek to explain *mechanically*. Those who explain it *physically* assume basic powers; those who explain it *mechanically*[o] assume an initial motion and basic shape of a basic matter, and that is what *Epicurus* did. He imagined that these atoms are in a motion, that all fall downwards, and would in all eternity always fall downwards if they had not collided together. But so that this would happen, he assumed certain atoms that began the collisions; but how this came about, that he did not know. Since these began to collide together, then all atoms also fell together at the same time, until shapes, animals, human beings and everything came out of it. This is the origin of bodies.[p] Those who explained it mechanically, took motion or the parts as the ground. The best mode of explanation of all phenomena of bodies is the physico-mechanical. This is opposed to the *pneumatic*, which one must not use in the corporeal world without need.

28:211

ON THE NATURE OF BODIES

The first inner ground [of that][L] which belongs to the actuality of a thing is *nature*, but what belongs to the possibility and to the concept of the thing is *essence*. A triangle has no nature, for it is no actuality, but rather only shape,

[o] We follow Lehmann in changing *metaphysisch* (metaphysical) in Pölitz to *mechanisch* (210₃₂).
[p] We follow Lehmann in changing *Atomen* (atoms) in Pölitz to *Körper* (211₂).

thus in all of geometry there is no nature. Thus to the divine essence or concept, by which God distinguishes himself from all, would belong, e.g., the necessity of his nature, the unalterability, the impassibility. – The essence of body is that which belongs to its concept; but nature [is that] by which all phenomena can be explained. What is general in the nature of bodies, what contains the principle of all phenomena, is very little, namely impenetrability, connection, and shape. Thus even more[q] goes into the nature of the body than what can be derived from the concept, because here this cannot be applied so easily, as in physics.

ON THE PERFECTION OF THE WORLD

Here one cannot yet speak of the best world <*mundo optimo*>, for we do not yet have any concept of ends; but metaphysical perfection can surely be treated. Metaphysical perfection consists in reality. – Reality or thingness is that something is perfect as a thing. A real thing is something positive, where negations are as well. Metaphysical perfection thus consists in the degree of reality. The most perfect world is thus in the metaphysical sense that which has the highest degree of reality which can ever belong to a world, the highest that is ever possible for a world. If we think of all realities which can ever belong to the world, then we have the most perfect or most real world <*mundum perfectissimum . . . realissimum*>; but the most real world <*mundus realissimus*>[r] is not yet the most real being <*ens realissimum*>. – The world is a whole of substances, which are in reciprocal connection, and thereby constitute a unity, a whole; a whole of contingent substances, in that they reciprocally determine each other, thus that one limits the other. Accordingly the most perfect world of all is still only a whole of contingent substances; – the most perfect world is thus only a whole that has more perfection than any other thing can have.

28:212

ON THE INTERACTION <*COMMERCIO*> OF SUBSTANCES

The primordial being of the world stands indeed in connection with the things of the world, but not in union, as belonging to a whole, but rather it stands only in a connection of derivation;[s] accordingly the [primordial] being of the world does not belong to the world as to a whole, because in a whole there is a reciprocal determination, but the primordial being is indeterminable. – But in every whole there are connections and there

[q] We follow Lehmann in changing *nicht mehr* (no more) in Pölitz to *noch mehr* (211₁₉).
[r] We are reading *abermundus* as the German *aber* (but) and the Latin *mundus* (world)(211₃₄).
[s] Two different words are translated as "connection" here: the first is *Verknüpfung*, the second *Verbindung* (212₈₋₁₀).

are connections.¹ The substances of the world thus stand in reciprocal passive connection <*in nexu mutuo passivo*>, and this is interaction <*commercium*>, where the state of the one depends upon the state of the other, where one determines the other and is again determined by it. But between God and the world there is not such an interaction <*commercium*>, for God receives nothing back from the world.

But how is an interaction <*commercium*> in a whole even possible? This question is the same as the first, for where there is an aggregate of substances there is not yet a world, rather the interaction <*commercium*> of substances first constitutes a world. The mere existence of substances, however, does not constitute an interaction <*commercium*>, rather to the existence of substances another ground must be added through which an interaction <*commercium*> arises. – Suppose <*posito*>: if all substances were necessary, then they would not stand in any interaction <*commercio*>, for then each would so exist in and for itself as though no other were there.⁷ Its existence would be wholly independent of the existence of others, and then they would stand in no interaction <*commercio*>; accordingly absolutely necessary substances cannot stand in interaction <*commercio*>. Suppose <*posito*>: if there were two Gods, each of which created a world, then the world of the one would not be able to stand in interaction <*commercio*> with the world of the other, rather each would have to subsist for itself. No reference and no relation would be possible; for this reason there also cannot be two Gods. But one could say: we imagine all things in space; and then the things must stand in interaction <*in commercio*> with one another simply because they are in one space. But to exist in space is not merely to exist, rather to exist in space already means: to be in community; for space is a phenomenon of the general connection of the world, and we want to have precisely the ground of this connection through space. –

28:213

Interaction <*commercium*> can be either:

1. original <*originarium*>, or
2. derivative <*derivativum*>. –

It is original <*originarium*> when it grounds itself already on the existence of the substances. Now it is already shown that no interaction <*commercium*> can arise merely from existence. To maintain this connection of substances without any ground, merely because they are there, is that which the *Wolffian* philosophy called physical influence <*influxum physicum*>⁸ in a crude sense which could be better called blind <*caecum*>. – Space would clearly laugh at us if we were to ask it such; it would say: that is already so, that must already be so, but in itself it is not

---

¹ G: *eine Verknüpfung und ein Zusammenhang* (212₁₃₋₁₄).

necessary. Accordingly original interaction <*commercium originarium*> does not take place.

Derivative interaction <*commercium derivativum*> is when, besides the existence of the substances, yet a third ground is necessary. Derivative interaction <*commercium derivativum*> can be twofold: by physical and hyperphysical influence <*per influxum physicum et hyperphysicum*>. But we must here distinguish physical influence <*influxum physicum*> from the original physical influence in the crude sense <*influxu physico originario in sensu crassiori*>. The former is derivative influence <*influxus derivativus*>, which refers to the laws of nature; it may ground itself otherwise on whatever it wants. But hyperphysical influence <*influxus hyperphysicus*> is according to the laws that are posited by another being. – One could ask here: under which conditions would the substances originally <*originarie*> influence [one another][L]? Since an original influence of the substances happens without the mediation of a third, then no substance can influence another originally <*originarie*>, except for those of which it itself is a cause; e.g., the influence of God on the world, the influence of the creator on creatures, is thus possible only originally <*originarie*>. But for substances of which no other being is the cause, the influence cannot take place among one another originally <*originarie*>. Accordingly, as long as they do not depend on one another, substances can influence one another not originally <*originarie*>, but rather by means of a third substance, from which they are all produced;[u] for then their principles <*principia*> are grounded all on one principle <*principium*>.

But where there is an interaction <*commercium*>, there is not only an | 28:214
influence, but also a reciprocal influence, for one substance cannot influence the other originally <*originarie*>, because one cannot be reciprocally the author of the other, which is absurd. Now since there is interaction <*commercium*> in every world, this interaction <*commercium*> must be derivative <*derivativum*>. The interaction <*commercium*> of substances thus rests on that, that they are all there through one, and because of that the manifold of substances has a unity, and thereby they make a whole.

All necessary beings are *isolated* (not in space, such that each occupies a different space; for space already connects), rather in themselves. Interaction <*commercium*> is thus possible not through space, but rather only through this, that they all are through One and depend on One; for otherwise those that depend on another would not stand in interaction <*in commercio*> with each other. Every world thus presupposes a primordial being, for no interaction <*commercium*> is possible except insofar they are all[v] there through One. As phenomenon, space is the infinite connection of substances with each other. Through the understanding

---

[u] We follow Lehmann in changing *hergebracht* (in Pölitz) to *hervorgebracht* (213_{37}).
[v] We follow Lehmann in changing *also* (thus) in Pölitz to *alle* (214_{17}).

we comprehend only their connection, to the extent they all lie in the divine. This is the only ground for comprehending the connection of substances through the understanding, to the extent we intuit the substances as though they lay generally in the divine. If we imagine this connection *sensibly*, then it happens through space. Thus space is the highest condition of the *possibility* of the connection. Now if we sensibly represent the connection of substances, which consists in this, that God is present to all things, then we can say: *space is the phenomenon of the divine [omni]*L *presence.* – In order to comprehend better the systems of explaining interaction <*systemata commercii explicandi*>, one notes: that derivative interaction <*commercium derivativum*>, which rests on a third being, happens either by physical or hyperphysical influence <*per influxum physicum . . . hyperphysicum*>. Physical influence <*influxus physicus*> happens according to universal laws of the nature of things. Hyperphysical influence <*influxus hyperphysicus*> happens not according to universal laws, but rather according to universal determinations of the extramundane being <*entis extramundani*>. E.g., if all members in the human body move according to my will according to universal laws, then this is physical influence <*influxus physicus*>. But when a third being moves my foot when I want to move it, then this is hyperphysical influence <*influxus hyperphysicus*>. This influence <*influxus*> is again twofold: automatic <*automaticus*> or occasionalistic <*occasionalisticus*>.

28:215 Automatic harmony <*harmonia automatica*> (for then it is no longer interaction <*commercium*>, but rather harmony <*harmonia*>) is when for every single case the highest cause has to arrange an agreement; thus where the agreement rests not on universal laws, but rather on a primordial arrangement which God put in the machine of the world. E.g., if a machine that played the flute were arranged such that it could accompany only that piece that I played; but were I to play a new one, then a new arrangement would also have to be made. But if I say: the ground is not arranged in the beginning such that at every occasion God accomplished the effect continuously with the continuation of the world, then this would be occasionalistic hyperphysical influence <*influxus hyperphysicus occasionalisticus*>. Both are hyperphysical. – Automatic harmony <*harmoniam automaticum*> is also called preestablished harmony <*harmoniam praestabilitam*>, and [the nonautomatic]L occasionalistic harmony <*harmoniam occasionalisticam*>. *Leibniz* maintained the first system, *Descartes* the other. Both interactions <*commercia*>, insofar as they are hyperphysical, provide no other connection <*nexum*> than an ideal one, and the interaction <*commercium*> would be an ideal interaction <*commercium*>. But the world is a totality <*totum*>, therefore the interaction <*commercium*> must be a *real* one. Accordingly the system of explaining substantial interaction <*systema explicationis commercii substantialis*> is no other than that by influence <*per influxum*>. Only by

36

influence <*per influxum*> can the substances be in real connection <*in nexu reali*>. This influence <*influxus*> is physical <*physicus*>, and indeed derivative <*derivativus*>. This is the correct concept, that the substances, in that they are all through One, constitute a unity of substance and of the manifold of alteration. This is a relation according to necessary universal laws. Two points are thus to be noticed with this influence <*influxus*>: that it is neither a blind connection <*nexus caecus*>, nor a hyperphysical one <*hyperphysicus*>; further, that the actual representation of the connection of substances among one another consists in this: that they all *perdure*, in that they are all there through One. The concept of the unity of the world grounds itself thus on the unity of the primordial being. When this [unity] is comprehended in the natural theology <*theologia naturali*>, then the unity of the world will follow from it necessarily.

ON THE NATURAL AND SUPERNATURAL

Nature is the internal first ground of that which belongs to the actuality of a thing. But essence is the first principle of the possibility of a thing. All things, all substances have nature. Nature must be distinguished: in the particular nature of a thing, and in the entirety of nature. The particular nature is the first principle out of which arises that which belongs to the thing; e.g., the nature of the body is that which belongs to the body as body. There are as many natures as there are things. What belongs to the accidental aspect of substances is reckoned to nature. But essence deals with a logical predicate, what belongs to the concept of the thing. The diverse natures constitute the entirety of nature, the unity of the world. The entirety of nature is the nature of the world, which one also calls *nature in general*. But the sum of the particular natures alone, and the nature of all parts, does not yet constitute the entirety of nature; rather to that must also be added the *unification*.

28:216

Opposed to the natural is: the *contrary to nature, supernatural,* and *unnatural. – Natural* is what can be explained from the particular nature of the thing and also from the entirety of nature. – *Contrary to nature* is what does not flow from the determinate nature of the thing. – *Unnatural* is what contradicts the particular nature of a thing. – *Supernatural* is what cannot be explained from the entirety of nature, but rather where the ground must be sought in the extramundane being <*ente extramundano*>. The cause of the contrary to nature is sought in the entirety of nature. The course of nature is the series of the alterations of events. Order of nature is just this same series of alterations, but only to the extent they stand under a general rule. The course of nature is to be distinguished from the order of nature. *The course of nature can be cognized empirically; but the order through the understanding, because I perceive the rule.* The course of

37

nature is every time an order of nature, for as long as the events follow naturally, they have in the nature of things a principle from which they arise. Every nature has laws. The laws are general formulas through which the manifold is cognized from the general principle; *for the rule of order is a formula.* We can think that the course of nature can be interrupted if something supernatural is foisted on the multiple alterations which arise from the nature of the world. The supernatural in the series of order interrupts the course and the order of nature. –

Events take place in time. But time is in the world. The beginning of nature is only the condition under which the events in the world can happen. *Accordingly creation is not an event,* but rather is only that through which the events <*eventus*> happen. It is thus a supernatural action

28:217 <*actio supernaturalis*>, but does not belong to the course of the world; it belongs to the supernatural <*supernaturali*>, which interrupts the course of nature.

ON MIRACLES

An event in the world that does not happen according to the order of nature is a miracle. The word *miracle* is supposed to mean an event which does not happen in conformity with cognized nature, although it could be in conformity with a higher order. We are amazed[w] only when something happens that is not usual. If supernatural events were usual, then no one would be amazed by them. One is thus amazed only when something is contrary to the cognized order of nature. But here we are not taking into consideration the cognized order of nature, but rather are taking an event that is a miracle in and for itself. – Miracles are opposed to natural events. With miracles we notice that they can happen *from the powers of nature,* and that is the *matter* of the miracle. But that the event flows from these powers of nature [*not*]ᴸ *according to the order of things,* that is the *form* of the miracle. The cause of the miracle thus lies not merely in the matter, but rather also in the form. Miracles are accordingly twofold: material and formal miracles <*miracula materialia . . . formalia*>.

[Those miracles are] material in which the cause of the event is not natural <*materialia, in quibus causa eventus non est naturalis*>. [Those miracles are] formal in which the determination of the cause does not happen according to the order of nature <*formalia, in quibus determinatio causae non fit secundum ordinem naturae*>. A material miracle is an event in which even the cause is outside of nature. A formal miracle, where the cause is indeed in nature, but the determination of its action does not happen according to the order of nature. Material ones <*materialia*> are those for which the power is not met with in nature. Formal

---

[w] *Wir wundern uns;* this is closely related to the German term for miracle (*Wunder*).

ones <*formalia*> are [those] for which the powers do lie in nature, but the determination of the powers for the event does not happen according to the course of nature. Something can thus be grounded in nature with respect to the matter <*quoad materiam*>, but not with respect to the form <*quoad formam*>. The essence of the miracle thus rests on the form, on the determination of the order of nature. Through this much theological delusion is destroyed, if one takes the trouble to explain the miracles half-naturally, and to seek out the powers in nature. But the miracle does not become smaller thereby, for if it is supposed to be a miracle, then one is not to be at a loss with respect to the intermediate causes and put into God's hands a natural means; for the *determination* 28:218 of this natural means is still not in nature, and then it is just as much a miracle. E.g., if one explains the overthrow of Sennacherib[9] by means of an angel (every divine effect and execution of divine decrees is understood by means of an angel), by the deadly Samiel wind, then that is indeed how it stands with the wind, but it is just as much a miracle that the wind has to work on the army of Sennacherib exactly at that time. One likewise endeavors to explain the passage of the children of Israel through the Red Sea, in that one says: the wind so divested a part of the Red Sea of water that the children of Israel were able to go through. Here the cause lies indeed in nature, but it does not occur according to the order of nature that a wind had to blow then, when a people was oppressed and persecuted by a foreign king; thus a special direction is required here. – A formal miracle is as much a miracle as a material one. The formal miracles <*miracula formalia*> are classified further into preestablished <*praestabilita*> and occasional <*occasionalia*>. A preestablished miracle <*miraculum praestabilitum*> is: when already from the beginning on the arrangement of nature is made so that in particular cases the cause does not produce an effect according to universal laws. E.g., if already from the beginning God had made such an arrangement that the wind would have to blow in the single case of the passage of the children of Israel through the Red Sea, or if he had created it on the occasion of the passage. Thus the subterfuges of regarding miracles as formal <*formalia*> and preestablished <*praestabilita*> serve for nothing more than pasting shut one's eyes. Thereby the use of reason is interrupted even more than by the material miracles <*miracula materialia*>. The use of reason demands that we must think there is a nature, that is, a principle of the world, where the determinations of the world issue according to universal rules. Thus the use of reason takes place so far as nature and an order of nature is there. Order is thus the single condition of the use of reason. The understanding accepts this as a necessary hypothesis, that all appearances happen according to rules. Every interruption of nature is thus a disturbance of the understanding. – But miracles are not impossible in themselves, for we assume the order of the things as a necessary hypothesis, on account of the arrangement of the understanding and of reason. But miracles <*miracula*> cannot be assumed

28:219   *except in the greatest emergency. But the greatest emergency is that where we must suspend the use of our reason itself.* In that case miracles must be conceded only where we are authorized to hem in the use of reason in nature. – The condition under which it is allowed to assume miracles is this: the course of nature does not coincide with moral laws. Thus imperfection is in the course of nature; it does not agree with the conditions which should concur as motives for the moral laws. Miracles are possible in order to complement this imperfection. But because of that we do not need to assume miracles; indeed we can still hope that someday nature will agree with morality. But the highest morality is a union with the highest being. Now when a case is of the sort that cannot be cognized through the natural order, but it refers to the end of morality, in this case it is allowed to assume miracles. Now if the gospel of Christ has such ends, then it is allowed to assume miracles. Miracles <*miracula*> can be either strict <*rigorosa*> or comparative <*comparativa*>. – A strict miracle is a supernatural event, insofar as it interrupts the order of nature <*miraculum rigorosum est eventus supernaturalis, quatenus interrumpit ordinem naturae*>. – A comparative miracle <*miraculum comparativum*> is when an event is indeed natural in view of the entirety of nature, but cannot be cognized according to known nature. To that belongs everything that can be explained by the influence of spirits. This can indeed be possible according to the entirety of nature, but it goes beyond the limits of our understanding, in that we are acquainted just as little with the nature of spirits as with the nature of God. Accordingly for the maxims of reason it is the same thing if we assume something happens by spirits, or by the highest being itself, because we are unacquainted with the nature of either beings. And if we already want to assume miracles, then it is better to assume such miracles as can be brought about by the highest being and not by spirits.

   In general we are not authorized to do that; it is an audacity to go off the track that God has prescribed our understanding to use. We must investigate the causes, and not push[x] everything onto the direction of God. Who told us to assign everything immediately to God? Clearly it all terminates ultimately in that, but we should remain in the circle that is given to us. It is an audacity to want to discover the secrets of God. Accordingly

28:220   there is nothing devout about invoking miracles, rather something blamable and reprehensible.[y] – Miracles must be *seldom*; many try to maintain this, especially theologians; but the word *seldom* is indeterminate here, for one does not know whether miracles about every ten years are seldom or

---

[x] We follow Lehmann in changing *schreiben* (write) in Pölitz to *schieben* (219₃₅).

[y] This sentence (219₃₉–220₁) is not in Pölitz; Lehmann follows Heinze (*Vorlesungen Kants*, p. 535), adding it from *Metaphysik H* and/or *Metaphysik K₁*.

already a lot. Thus this cannot be proven objectively by the understanding; but according to subjective principles we want to assume miracles as seldom, for the understanding allows itself to be used according to rules. – Rules and propositions can be found through experience, if we see that certain events in certain relations are in general harmony with one another; therefore every exception of an event suspends the rule. Now if exceptions to the rules happen abundantly and often, then they suspend the use of the rules, consequently also the use of reason. – The exceptions are exceptions <*exceptiones*> of the rule. But exceptions <*exceptionen*> must not be more than cases of determination, for otherwise, if there are more exceptions <*exceptiones*>, then they suspend the rule, and then they are no longer exceptions <*exceptiones*>, but rather other rules must then be made from the exceptions <*exceptionen*>; accordingly exceptions <*exceptionen*> must be only seldom. Only because there is an order of nature, are there miracles; were there no order of nature, then it could not be interrupted. But miracles are events which interrupt the order of nature. Thus, for there to be order, events must agree in a certain relation according to general laws, and miracles must be assumed only as an exception from order and rule. But the exceptions are seldom. The cause for assuming miracles as seldom lies in the use of the understanding.

There are two sorts of minds with respect to miracles: some who indeed do not deny miracles but make them difficult; but others who are quite inclined to assume them. The cause lies in the use of reason. Whoever is accustomed to avail himself of his reason makes difficulties with respect to miracles; but whoever makes no use [of][L] reason assumes miracles quite gladly, for then he does not need to reflect, and is just as clever as the other. One is more inclined to attribute miracles to past times than to present times, although one cannot at all prove why miracles could not also happen now just as before. The cause of that is: what happened previously by miracles does not at all disturb the present use of reason. But we should also not believe of the ancients that they disturbed the use of their understanding by miracles; thus there likewise reigned at that time the principle not to assume that which makes the use of the understanding impossible with respect to the order of nature.[z] We thus cannot blame anyone if he *seeks* to give an explanation of miracles, namely when thereby nothing in morality is diminished.

28:221

---

[z] This clause ("there likewise reigned . . . ," 221$_{2-5}$) is not in Pölitz, which instead reads: "they must also have used it just as we do." Lehmann follows Heinze (*Vorlesungen Kants*, p. 535) in adding this clause from *Metaphysik H* and/or *Metaphysik K$_1$*.

(3) Psychology

INTRODUCTORY CONCEPTS

In the previous parts of metaphysics nature in general was treated, and objects were considered in general. In this respect nature means the summation of all inner principles and all of that which belongs to the existence of the thing. But when one speaks of nature generally <*generaliter*>, it is only according to the form, and then nature does not mean an object, but rather only the manner *in which* an object exists. – Nature is in existence what essence is in the concept. In the Cosmology the nature of each thing in general, the nature of the world, or nature in the general sense where this means the summation of all natures, was spoken of, and then nature is the summation of all objects of the senses. This cognition of the objects of senses is *physiology*. Now what is no object of the senses goes beyond nature and is hyperphysical. Accordingly the summation of all objects of the senses is nature, and the cognition of this nature is physiology. This cognition of nature or physiology can be twofold: *empirical* and *rational*. This classification of physiology applies only to the form. – *Empirical* physiology is the cognition of the objects of the senses insofar as it is obtained from principles of experience. *Rational* physiology is the cognition of objects insofar as it is obtained not from experience, but rather from a concept of reason. The *object* is always an object of the senses and experience; only the *cognition* of it can be attained through pure concepts of reason, for thereby physiology is distinguished from transcen-

28:222 dental philosophy, where the object is also borrowed not from experience, but rather from pure[a] reason. Thus to rational physiology <*physiologia rationalis*> will belong, e.g., that a body is infinitely divisible, for a whole of matter belongs to the concept of body. But matter occupies a space, and space is infinitely divisible, thus every appearance in space [is] as well. To matter belongs further a certain lifelessness (power of inertia <*vis inertiae*>), by which it is distinguished from thinking being. Accordingly matter cannot move otherwise than as driven by an external power. All of this belongs to rational physiology <*physiologia rationalis*>, and in general one can comprehend the entire doctrine of motion from the concept of body. But that bodies attract one another, that they are heavy, that bodies

---

[a] We follow Lehmann in changing *einer* (one) in Pölitz to *reiner* (222₁).

are fluid – all of that can be cognized only from experience; consequently, this belongs to empirical physiology <*physiologia empirica*>. But physiology also can be classified according to the object or the matter. Since physiology is a cognition of the objects of the senses, one easily can comprehend the *classification* when one notes that one has two sorts of sense, namely an *outer* and an *inner* sense. There is accordingly a physiology of objects of *outer*, and a physiology of objects of *inner* sense. The physiology of outer sense is *physics*, and the physiology of inner sense is *psychology*. According to the previous classification, both parts, physics as well as psychology, can be twofold according to the form: empirical and rational. There is accordingly an empirical and rational physics and psychology. The general determination of action, or the general character of the object of inner sense, is *thinking*; and the general character of the object of outer sense is *moving*. Thus in general psychology <*psychologia generalis*> thinking beings in general are treated, which is *pneumatology*. But in special psychology <*psychologia speciali*>, the thinking subject which we know, and that is *our soul*. In just the same manner the objects of outer sense, or bodies in general, are treated in the general physics <*physica generali*>, and the bodies which we are acquainted with in the special physics <*physica speciali*>. Empirical psychology <*psychologia empirica*> *is the cognition of the objects of inner sense insofar as it is obtained from experience.* Empirical physics <*physica empirica*> is the cognition of the objects of outer sense insofar as it is borrowed from experience. Rational psychology *is the cognition of the objects of inner sense insofar as it is borrowed from pure reason. – Empirical psychology belongs to metaphysics* no more than empirical physics does.[10] For the doctrine of experience of inner sense is the cognition of the appearances of inner sense, just as bodies are appearances of outer sense. Thus just the same happens in empirical psychology <*psychologia empirica*> as happens in empirical physics; only that the stuff in empirical psychology <*psychologia empirica*> is given through inner, and in empirical physics through outer, sense. Both are thus doctrines of experience.

28:223

Metaphysics distinguishes itself from physics and all doctrine of experience through this, that it is a science of pure reason, physics on the other hand borrows its principles <*principia*> from experience. It is quite proper to determine the boundaries of the sciences and to comprehend the ground of the classifications so that one has a system; for without this one is always an apprentice, and one does not know how the science, e.g., psychology, has come into metaphysics, and whether it would not be possible that various sciences could be brought in here. Accordingly one comprehends that rational psychology <*psychologia rationalis*> and rational physics <*physica rationalis*> indeed belong to metaphysics because their principles are borrowed from pure reason. But empirical psychology <*psychologia empirica*> and empirical physics <*physica empirica*> do not at all belong there.

The cause as to why empirical psychology <*psychologia empirica*> has been placed in metaphysics is clearly this: one never really knew what metaphysics is, although it was expounded on for so long. One did not know how to determine its boundaries, therefore one placed much in it that did not belong there; this rested on the definition, in that one defined it by "the first principles of human cognition." But nothing is determined by this at all, for in all fields there is always a first. The second cause was clearly this: the doctrine of experience of the appearances of the soul has not arrived at any system such that it could have constituted a separate academic discipline. Were it as large as empirical physics, then it would also have been separated from metaphysics by its vast extent. But because it is small and one did not want wholly to do away with it,[b] one pushed it into metaphysics with rational psychology, and the custom surely cannot be so quickly abolished. But now it has already become quite large, and it

28:224 will attain almost as great a magnitude as empirical physics. *It also deserves to be separately expounded, just as empirical physics does*; for the cognition of human beings is in no way inferior to the cognition of bodies; indeed, according to worth it is much to be preferred to the other. If it becomes an academic science, then it is in the position to attain its full magnitude, for in the sciences an academic teacher has more practice than a scholar on his own. The first sees more readily the gaps and what is indistinct through more frequent lectures on it, and has with every new lecture a new determination to improve this. *With time there will accordingly be trips undertaken in order to cognize human beings, such as have been undertaken to become acquainted with plants and animals.* Psychology is thus a physiology of inner sense or of thinking beings, just as physics is a physiology of outer sense or of corporeal beings. I consider thinking beings either merely from concepts, and this is rational psychology <*psychologia rationalis*>; or through experience, which in part happens internally in myself, or externally, where I perceive other natures, and cognize according to the analogy that they have with me; and that is empirical psychology <*psychologia empirica*>, where I consider thinking natures through experience. The substrate <*substratum*> which underlies and which expresses the consciousness of inner sense is the *concept of I*, which is merely a concept of empirical psychology. The proposition: *I am*, was assumed by *Descartes* as the first proposition of experience that is evident; for I could have representations of the body even if there were no bodies there; but I intuit myself, I am immediately conscious of myself. But I am not conscious of the existence of all things outside me, but rather only of the representation. But it does not follow that things also must always underlie such representations, they are only analogues <*analoga*> of experience; I infer existence from experience. This *I* can be taken in a twofold sense: *I as*

---

[b] We follow Lehmann in changing *weglassen* (to leave out) in Pölitz to *wegschaffen* (223₃₆).

human being, and *I as intelligence*. I, *as a human being*, am an object of *inner* and *outer* sense. I *as intelligence* am an object *of inner sense only*; I do not say: I am a body, but rather: what attaches to me is a body. This intelligence, which is connected with the body and constitutes a human being, is called *soul*; but *considered alone* without the body it is called intelligence. The soul is thus not merely thinking substance, but rather constitutes a unity inso-   28:225 far as it is connected with the body. Accordingly the alterations of the body are my alterations.

As soul, I am determined by the body, and stand with it in interaction <*commercio*>. As *intelligence*, I am at no location, for location is a relation of outer intuition, but as intelligence I am not an outer object which can be determined with respect to relation. My location in the world is thus determined by the location of my body in the world, for whatever is to appear and stand in outer relation must be a body. Thus I will not be able to determine my location immediately, but rather as soul I determine my location in the world through the body; but I cannot determine my location in the body, for then I would have to be able to intuit myself in an outer relation. The *location* that we represent to ourselves *of the soul in the brain* is only a consciousness of the closer dependence on that place of the body where the soul works most. It is an analogue <*analogon*> of location, but not its place. Mere consciousness already gives me the difference between soul and body, for the outer, what I see on me, is clearly to be distinguished from the thinking principle <*principio*> in me, and this thinking principle is again distinguished from all that which can be only an object of the outer senses.

A human being whose body has been split open can see his entrails and all his inner parts, thus *this* inner is merely a bodily being, and wholly different from the thinking being. A human being can lose many of his members, but for that he still remains and can say: I am. A foot belongs to him. But if it is sawed off, then he looks upon it just as upon any other matter which he can no longer use, like an old boot which he must throw away. But he himself always remains unaltered, and his thinking I loses nothing. Everyone easily comprehends this, even by the most common understanding, that he has a soul which is different from the body.

The mere concept of the I, which is unalterable, which one cannot at all describe any further so far as it expresses and distinguishes the object of inner sense, is the foundation of many other concepts. For this concept of the I expresses:

1. substantiality. – Substance is the first subject of all inhering accidents. But this I is an absolute subject, to which all accidents and predi-   28:226 cates can belong, and which cannot at all be a predicate of another thing. Thus the I expresses the substantial; for that substrate <*substratum*> in which all accidents inhere is the substantial. This is the only case where we can immediately intuit the substance. Of no thing can we intuit the

substrate <*substratum*> and the first subject; but in myself I intuit the substance immediately. The I thus expresses not only the substance, but rather also the substantial itself. Indeed, what is still more, from this I we have borrowed the concept which we have in general of all substances. This is the original concept of substances. This concept of the I expresses

2. *simplicity*, that the soul which thinks in me constitutes an absolute unity, a singular individual in the absolute sense <*singulare in sensu absoluto*>, and thus simplicity, for many substances together cannot constitute a soul. – A many can indeed not say: I; this is thus the strictest singular <*singularis*>. – Finally this concept of the I also expresses

3. *immateriality*. The cause that human beings thought of themselves as spiritual beings is the analysis of themselves. It happened through this analysis, what they thought when they represented themselves as objects of inner sense; for according to their consciousness it must have been obvious to them that this is no object of outer sense. But what is no object of outer sense is immaterial. – But something is *immaterial* if it is present in space without taking up a space, and without being impenetrable.

As intelligence, I am a being that thinks and that wills. *But thinking and willing cannot be intuited*; thus I am no object of outer^c intuition. But what is no object of outer intuition is immaterial. This works^d only insofar as this main category proves the consciousness of a subject, which is distinguished from the body, thus proves a soul; therefore we can already speak of a soul to that extent. I am conscious of two kinds of objects:

1. of my subject and my state;
2. of things outside me. –

28:227 My representation is directed either to objects or to myself. In the first case I am conscious of other cognitions; in the second case of my subject. E.g., a human being who is reckoning is conscious of numbers, but not at all of his subject during the time that he is reckoning. This is the logical consciousness <*conscientia logica*>, which is distinguished from the psychological consciousness <*conscientia psychologica*>, where one is conscious only of one's subject. *Objective* consciousness, or cognition with consciousness of objects, is a necessary condition for having a cognition of any objects. But *subjective* consciousness is a forcible state. It is an observing turned upon itself; it is not discursive, but rather intuitive. The healthiest state is the consciousness of outer objects. Yet the state of perception or of the consciousness of oneself is also necessary, and indeed necessary as a revision. Consciousness is a knowledge of that which belongs to me. It is a representation of my representations, it is a self-perception, perception. As concerns objective consciousness, those representations which

---

^c We follow Lehmann in changing *äusserlichen* (external) in Pölitz to *äusseren* (226₃₂).
^d We do not follow Lehmann in changing *dient* (in Pölitz) to *denkt* (thinks)(226₃₃).

we have of objects of which one is conscious are called *clear* representations; those of whose features one is also conscious, *distinct*; those of which one is not at all conscious, *obscure*. These distinctions properly belong in logic. As far as belongs to psychology, one notes here that there are obscure representations. *Leibniz* said: the greatest treasure of the soul consists in obscure representations, which become distinct only through the consciousness of the soul. If through a supernatural revelation we were to become immediately conscious of all our obscure representations and of the whole extent of the soul at once, then we might be astonished at ourselves and at the treasure in our soul, of what abundance it contains of cognitions in itself. When we cast our eyes through a telescope upon the furthest heavenly bodies, then the telescope does nothing more than awaken in us the consciousness of countless heavenly bodies which cannot be seen with the naked eye, but which already lay obscurely in our soul. Were a human being able to be conscious of all that which he perceives of bodies through microscopes, then he would have a great knowledge of bodies, which actually he already has now, only that he is not himself conscious of it. Further, everything that is taught in metaphysics and morality, every human being already knows; only he was not himself conscious of it; and he who explains and expounds this to us actually tells   28:228
us nothing new that we would not have already known, rather he only makes it that I become conscious of that which was already in me. Were God suddenly to bring light immediately into our soul, that we could be conscious of all our representations, then we would see all mundane bodies entirely clearly and distinctly, just as if we had them before our eyes. When, accordingly, in the future life our soul will become conscious of all its obscure representations, then the most learned will get no farther than the most unlearned; the only difference is that now the learned is already here conscious of something more. But if a light will go on in each soul, then they are both equally clear and distinct. There thus lies in the field of obscure representations a treasure which constitutes the deep abyss of human cognitions which we are unable to reach.

ON THE GENERAL CLASSIFICATION OF THE MENTAL FACULTIES

I feel myself either as *passive* or as *self-active*. What belongs to my faculty so far as I am passive belongs to my lower faculty. What belongs to my faculty so far as I am active belongs to my higher faculty.

Three things belong to my faculty:

1. *representations*;
2. *desires*, and
3. the *feeling of pleasure and displeasure*.

The *faculty of representations*, or the faculty of cognition, is either the *lower* faculty of cognition or the *higher* faculty of cognition. The *lower* faculty of cognition is a power to have representations so far as we are affected by objects. The *higher* faculty of cognition is a power to have representations from ourselves.

The *faculty of desire* is either a *higher* or a *lower* faculty of desire. The *lower* faculty of desire is a power to desire something so far as we are affected by objects. The *higher* faculty of desire is a power to desire something from ourselves independently of objects.

Likewise the *faculty of pleasure and displeasure* is also a *higher* or *lower* faculty. The *lower* faculty of pleasure and displeasure is a power to find satisfaction or dissatisfaction in the objects which affect us. The *higher* faculty of pleasure and displeasure is a power to sense a pleasure and displeasure in ourselves, independently of objects. All lower faculties constitute *sensibility* and all higher faculties constitute *intellectuality*. *Sensitivity* is a condition of objects for cognizing something so far as one is affected by objects; and for desiring something, or for having satisfaction or dissatisfaction, so far as one is affected by objects. – But *intellectuality* is a faculty of representation, of desires, or of the feeling of pleasure and displeasure, so far as one is wholly independent of objects. Sensible cognitions are sensible *not because* they are confused, but rather because they take place in the mind so far as it is affected by objects. The intellectual cognitions are again intellectual *not because* they are distinct but because they arise from ourselves. Accordingly intellectual representations can be confused and sensible ones distinct. Because something is intellectual, it is not yet [on that account] distinct, and because something is sensible, it is not yet [on that account] obscure. Thus there is sensible and intellectual distinctness. The sensible consists in intuition, the intellectual in concepts. Sensibility is the passive property of our faculty of cognition so far as we are affected by objects. But intellectuality is the spontaneity of our faculty so far as we ourselves either cognize or desire something or have satisfaction or dissatisfaction in something. – The reason why *Wolff* and others hold confused cognitions to be sensible is this: because cognition, before it is worked on by the understanding, has no distinctness, rather cognition is still logically confused, i.e., if it cannot be comprehended through concepts. But aesthetically confused is that which cannot be distinctly grasped through the senses. Now if cognition is confused, then the cause is not because it is sensible, but because it is logically confused, and the understanding has not yet worked on it. All cognitions that come from the senses are at first logically confused if they are not yet worked on by the understanding; but on that account, because they are still confused, they are not sensible; rather if they are taken from the senses, then they remain sensible according to their source, even when they are worked on by the understanding and become distinct. For distinct-

ness and obscurity are only forms, which belong as much to sensible as to 28:230
intellectual representations. But they are sensible and intellectual according to their source, be they distinct or confused.

ON THE SENSIBLE FACULTY OF COGNITION
IN PARTICULAR

The sensible faculty of cognition contains those representations that we
have of objects so far as we are affected by them.

But we differentiate the sensible faculty of cognition into: the faculty of
the senses themselves, and the imitated cognition of the senses. Sensible
cognition arises either entirely from the impression of the object, and then
this sensible cognition is a representation of the senses themselves, or
sensible cognition arises from the mind, but under the condition under
which the mind is affected by objects, and then sensible cognition is an
imitated representation of the senses. E.g., the representation of that which
I see; further the representation of the sour, sweet, etc., are representations
of the senses themselves. But if I make present to myself a house that I saw
earlier, then the representation arises now from the mind, but still under
the condition that the sense was previously affected by this object. Such
sensible cognitions which arise from the spontaneity of the mind are called:
cognitions of the formative power, and the cognitions which arise through the
impression of the object are called: *representations of the senses themselves*.

One can classify sensibility also in the following manner: all sensible
cognitions are either *given* or *made*. To the given we can reckon sense in
general, or the representation of the senses themselves. To the made we
reckon:[11]

1. fictive faculty <*facultatem fingendi*>;
2. faculty of composing <*facultatem componendi*>;
3. faculty of signifying <*facultatem signandi*>.

But to the fictive faculty <*facultas fingendi*> belong:

a. faculty of illustration <*facultas formandi*>,
b. faculty of imagining <*facultas imaginandi*>,
c. faculty of anticipation <*facultas praevidendi*>.

The representations of the formative power are thus classified:

1. into the formative power in itself, which is the genus <*genus*>;
2. into the illustrative power <*facultas formandi*; G: *Abbildungskraft*>, 28:231
3. into the imitative power <*facultas imaginandi*; G: *Nachbildungskraft*>,
4. in the anticipatory power <*facultas praevidendi*; G: *Vorbildungskraft*>.

These powers all belong to the formative power of the sensible faculty. This formative power which belongs to sensibility is distinguished from the thinking power, which belongs to the understanding.

ON THE REPRESENTATIONS OF
THE SENSES THEMSELVES

The representations of the senses themselves are possible insofar as we are affected by objects. But we can be affected by objects in diverse ways, that is: the representations of objects through which an impression arises are distinguished from one another, e.g., tasting is different from smelling. So far as the diverse senses have no similarity, we call them specific senses, of which we have five: seeing, hearing, smelling, tasting, and feeling. The cause that we have a certain number of senses is that we have a certain number of organs of the body through which we receive the impression of objects, and thus we classify the senses according to the classification of the organs of the body. But we also have other sensible sensations, for which we have no special organs, and which we thus also cannot distinguish, e.g., the feeling of cold and warm, of pressure,ᵉ etc., is extended over our entire body. Because we thus have no more than five organs, we also assume only five senses.

Some of these senses are objective, others subjective. The objective senses are at the same time connected with the subjective; thus the objective senses are not only objective, but also subjective. Either the objective is greater in the senses than the subjective, or the subjective is greater than the objective. E.g., with seeing, the objective is greater than the subjective, and with a strong sound that pierces the ears, the subjective is greater. But if we look not to the strength, but rather to the quality of the senses, then we notice that seeing, hearing, and feeling are senses more objective than subjective, but smelling and tasting are more subjective than objective. The subjective senses are senses of enjoyment,ᶠ the objective senses, on the other hand, are instructive senses. The instructive senses are either fine, if they act on us by means of fine material from a distance, or coarse, if they act on us and affect us by means of a coarse material. Thus the sense of sight is the finest because the material of light, by means of which objects affect us, is the finest. Hearing is somewhat coarser, but touch the coarsest. Sight and touch are completely objective representations. But touch is the fundamental one of the objective representations, for through touch I can perceive shapes when I can touch them from all sides, it is thus the interpretive art of shapes. Through sight I cognize only the surface of the object.

28:232

ᵉ We follow Lehmann in changing *Schallen* (sounding) in Pölitz to *Druckes* (231₂₂).
ᶠ We follow Lehmann in changing *Gewissens* (conscience) in Pölitz to *Genusses* (231₃₅).

We must not believe that all cognitions of the senses come from the senses; but rather also from the understanding, which reflects upon the objects which the senses offer us, through which we then obtain sensible cognitions. In such a way there arises with us a fallacy of subreption <*vitium subreptionis*>, in that because we have been accustomed since childhood to imagine everything through the senses, we do not notice the reflection of the understanding upon the senses, and take cognitions to be immediate intuitions of the senses.

The ancient philosophers, like Aristotle, and after him the Scholastics, said that all our concepts came from the senses, which they expressed by the proposition: nothing is in the intellect which was not first in the senses <*nihil est in intellectu, quod non antea fuerit in sensu*>. The understanding can cognize nothing that the senses have not previously experienced. In this Aristotle spoke contrary to *Plato*, who as a mystical philosopher maintained the opposite, and considered concepts not only as innate, but rather also as something left over from the prior intuition of God, from which the body now hinders us. – Epicurus again went too far and said: all our concepts are experiential concepts of the senses. In order to cognize this determinately and to comprehend how far the proposition of Aristotle can be allowed, one must limit the proposition somewhat, and say: as far as concerns the matter, nothing is in the intellect which was not first in the senses <*nihil est quoad materiam in intellectu, quod non antea fuit in sensu*>. The senses must give us the *matter* and the stuff, and this matter is worked on by the understanding. But what concerns the *form* of concepts, that is intellectual. The first source of cognition thus lies in matter, which the senses offer. The second source of cognition lies in the spontaneity of the understanding. If a human being only has stuff, then he can always make new representations. E.g., if he has already had the representation of color once, then through the transposition of colors he can form new representa- 28:233 tions which do not at all exist in nature. But one cannot at all imagine new senses because we lack the stuff for that. The senses are thus a necessary principle of cognition.

But we also have a principle of cognition through concepts which contain nothing at all from the senses, that is: we have cognitions of objects so far as we are not affected by the senses, and these are *intellectual* concepts. Thus there are sensuous and intellectual concepts. We can therefore say: there is nothing in the understanding with respect to matter that was not in the senses; but with respect to form there are cognitions, intellectual ones, which are not an object of the senses at all. E.g., in morality sensible cognitions provide the *a posteriori* basis, but understanding has the basic concepts. But one must mention this: that even the concepts of the understanding, although they are not drawn from the senses, do arise on the occasion of experience; e.g., no one would have the concept of cause and effect if he had not perceived causes through experience. No human being would have the concept of virtue if he were always among utter rogues. Accordingly the senses do constitute to this extent the ground of all cognitions, although not all cognitions have their origin in them. – Although they are no principle of being <*principium essendi*>, they are still a necessary condition <*conditio sine qua non*>.

But how do they come into the understanding? One must not assume them as innate and inborn, for that brings all investigation to a close, and is very unphilosophical. If they are inborn, then they are revelations. – *Crusius* had his head full of such wild fantasies,[12] and he was quite happy that he could think such. But concepts have arisen through the understanding, according to its nature, on the occasion of experience; for on the occasion of experience and the senses the understanding forms concepts which are not from the senses but rather drawn from the reflection on the senses. – *Locke* was badly mistaken here in that he believed *all* his concepts to be drawn from experience; for he did draw them from the reflection which is applied to the objects of the senses. Thus with respect to matter all arise from the senses; with respect to form from the understanding, but they are not inborn in the understanding, but rather come about through reflection on the occasion of experience. We practice this action of reflection as soon as we have impressions of the senses. This reflection becomes familiar to us by habit so that we do not notice that we reflect; and then we believe that it lies in sensible intuition.

28:234

Now we want to see how far concepts depend on reflection. In particular, we can have cognitions of objects of which we have no sensation at all through the senses. So the congenitally blind can have a cognition of light, just like someone sighted, which the understanding presents to him; only that he does not have the sensation, and of that we also cannot speak, for here each has his own sensation with the word light. Thus we can separate the impressions from the judgments. Cognition of the senses through the understanding is something other than cognition through impression. Now if we take the reflections on sensation to be impressions, then we commit an error of distinguishing. The objects of the senses induce us to judge. These judgments are experiences, so far as they are true; but if they are provisional judgments, then they are a seeming.[g] Seeming precedes experience, for it is a provisional judgment by the understanding on the object of the senses. Seeming is not true and also not false, for it is the inducement for a judgment from experience. Seeming must thus be distinguished from appearance. Appearance lies in the senses, but seeming is only the inducement for judging from the appearance. Perception applies as much to seeming as to actual objects of experience, e.g., the sun rises, it sets, refers to seeming. From the seeming of the objects arises an illusion,

---

[g] The German *Schein* is translated here as "seeming," and "appearance" (below) is the translation of *Erscheinung*, while *Illusion* is translated as "illusion."

and also a deception of the senses. Illusion is still no deception of the senses, it is a hasty judgment which the following one immediately contests. We love such illusions considerably, e.g., we are not deceived by an optical box, for we know that it is not so; but we are moved to a judgment which is immediately refuted by the understanding. Delusions are to be distinguished from the deceptions of the senses; with a delusion I discover the deception. Because the objects of the senses induce us to judge, the errors are assigned to the senses falsely, since they are properly attributable to the reflection on the senses. We note accordingly the proposition: the senses do not deceive <*sensus non fallunt*>. This happens not because they judge correctly, but rather because they do not judge at all, but in the senses lies the seeming. They mislead judgment, although they do not deceive. The proposition gives us opportunity to examine the grounds of   28:235
judgments and through their dissolution to discover the deceit. This proposition thus gives us occasion to see through the ground of the errors. General concepts arise not through the senses, but rather through the understanding.

Through the senses only singular judgments arise; thus through them we do not receive the concept of cause and effect, also not the concept of lack, for negation cannot affect the senses, and I cannot say: I have seen that no one is in the room, for I cannot see nothing.

After we have considered, with sensibility, the representations of the senses themselves, which also can be called the faculty of sensation, [thus] also of the senses[h] insofar as we obtain representations and cognitions to the extent that we are affected by objects (the cognitions are possible only so far as the objects have an influence on our senses); so now we want to consider the *imitated cognition of the senses*, which is also quite fittingly called the *formative power*, which is a faculty for making out of ourselves cognitions which in themselves nevertheless have the form according to which objects would affect our senses. This formative faculty[i] thus actually belongs to sensibility, it produces representations, either of the *present* time, or representations of the *past* time, or also representations of the *future* time. Accordingly the formative faculty consists:

1. of the faculty of *illustration* <*facultas formandi*; G: *Vermögen der Abbildung*>, whose representations are of present time;
2. of the faculty of *imitation* <*facultas imaginandi*; G: *Vermögen der Nachbildung*>, whose representations are of past time;
3. of the faculty of *anticipation* <*facultas praevidendi*; G: *Vermögen der Vorbildung*>, whose representations are of future time.

---

[h] We follow Lehmann in changing *Sinn* (sense) in Pölitz to *Sinne* (235_{13}).
[i] The common root *Bildung* (formation), as in *Bildungsvermögen* (formative faculty), is used below (235_{26-31}) in *Abbildung* (illustration), *Nachbildung* (imitation), and *Vorbildung* (anticipation).

My mind is always busy with forming the image of the manifold while it goes through [it].ᴸ E.g., when I see a city, the mind then forms an image of the object which it has before it while it runs through the manifold. Therefore if a human being comes into a room which is piled high with pictures*j* and decorations, then he can make no image of it, because his mind cannot run through the manifold. It does not know from which end

28:236   it should begin in order to illustrate the object. So it is reported that when a stranger enters St. Peter's church in Rome, he is wholly disconcerted on account of the manifold splendor. The cause is: his soul cannot go through the manifold in order to illustrate it. This illustrative*k* faculty is the formative faculty of intuition. The mind must undertake many observations in order to illustrate an object so that it illustrates the object differently from each side. E.g., a city appears differently from the east than from the west. There are thus many appearances of a matter according to the various sides and points of view. The mind must make an illustration from all these appearances by taking them all together.

The *second* faculty is the faculty of *imitation*, according to which my mind draws forth the representations of the senses from previous times, and connects them with the representations of the present. I reproduce the representations of past time through association, according to which one representation draws forth another, because it had been accompanying it. This is the faculty of reproductive imagination. Elsewhere it is falsely called the faculty of imagination,*l* which is however of a wholly different sort, for it is one thing when I imagine a palace that I have seen earlier and something else when I make *new* images. The latter is the faculty of imagination, of which there will be a report later.

The *third* faculty is the faculty of *anticipation*.*m* Although a future item makes no impression in me and thus no image, but rather only a present item does, one can still make in advance an image of future items, and imagine something in advance. E.g., one imagines the form in which one will be when one wants to give a speech. – But how is an anticipation of a future item possible? A present appearance has representations of the past and of the following time. But in my representations there is a series of the following representations, where the representations of the past relate to the present, just as the representations of the present relate to the future.

---

j *Bild* is translated here both as "picture" and as "image."

k *Abbildende* (illustrative) is based on *bildende* (formative), and *abbilden* can also be translated as "to form an image of," just as *sich einbilden* (236₂₇) can mean "to imagine" or "to make an image" (*sich ein Bild machen*).

l *Einbildungsvermögen* here is the standard German term for "imagination," which is contrasted with a more specific *reproductive* faculty designated in the previous sentence by the Latinate term *imagination*, and translated here as "reproductive imagination."

m The components of *Vorbildung* (anticipation) suggest setting up a "prior" (*vor*) "picture" (*Bild*).

Just as I can go from the present into the past, I can also go from the present into the future. Just as the present state follows on the past, so the future follows on the present. This happens according to laws of the reproductive imagination.

This differentiation of the formative power concerns time. But there is yet another difference, according to which we obtain two more faculties of the formative power. These faculties are the *faculty of imagination* and the *faculty of correlation.*" The faculty of *imagination* is the faculty for producing images from oneself, independent of the actuality of objects, where the images are not borrowed from experience. E.g., an architect pretends to build a house which he has not yet seen. One calls this faculty the faculty of *fantasy*, and [it] must not be confused with reproductive imagination.[13] The power of imagination is a sensible fictive power, although we also have a fictive power of the understanding. 28:237

The *faculty of correlation* is the faculty of characterization. Characterization is a correlation of another. Correlation is a means for producing the image of another thing. So words are correlates of things for conceiving representations of the things. Because it represents images, it therefore belongs to sensibility, although the images come from ourselves rather than through the influence of objects; but with respect to form it still belongs to sensibility.

Finally one could yet add a *faculty of cultivation.*° We have not only a faculty but also a drive to cultivate and to complete everything. So if things, stories, comedies or the like appear to us to be deficient, then without fail we endeavor to bring it to an end; one is annoyed that the thing is not whole. This presupposes a faculty for making an idea of the whole and for comparing objects with the idea of the whole.

All these acts <*actus*> of the formative power can happen *voluntarily* and also *involuntarily*. Insofar as they happen *involuntarily*, they belong wholly to sensibility; but so far as they happen *voluntarily*, they belong to the higher faculty of cognition. *Memory* is thus a faculty of voluntary reproductive imagination or imitation; thus between memory and the faculty of imitation there is no essential difference. So it is as well with other formative faculties. Hypochondriacal persons have involuntary imaginations. The voluntary imaginative faculty is the fictive faculty.*

Of the faculty of correlation or faculty of characterization <*facultate characteristica*> we must note something in yet more detail: a representa- 28:238

" The components of *Gegenbildung* (correlation) suggest setting a picture "against" (*gegen*) another.

° The components of *Ausbildung* (cultivation) suggest a building up of pictures, as well as education in general.

ᵖ Lehmann misreads *Dichtkunstvermögen* (in Pölitz) as *Deutungsvermögen*, and subsequently changes it to *Dichtungsvermögen* (237_{38}).

tion which serves as a means of reproduction by association is a *symbol* <*symbolum*>. The most symbolic representations occur with the cognition of God. These are altogether by analogy <*per analogiam*>, i.e., through an agreement of the relationships; e.g., with ancient peoples the sun was a symbol <*symbolum*>, a representation of divine perfection because present everywhere in the great cosmic system, it bestows much (light and warmth), without receiving.[14] So the human body can serve as a symbol of a republic in which all members constitute a whole. A cognition of the understanding which is indirectly <*indirecte*> intellectual and is cognized through the understanding, but is produced through an analogy of sensible cognition, is a symbolic cognition, which is opposed to logical cognition, just as the intuitive is to the discursive. The cognition of the understanding is symbolic[q] if it is indirectly <*indirecte*> intellectual and is produced through an analogy of sensible cognition, but is cognized through the understanding. The symbol <*symbolum*> is only a means to promote the intellection; it serves only the immediate cognition of the understanding, but with time it must fall away. The cognitions of all oriental nations are symbolic. Thus where intuition is not immediately allowed to us, there we must help ourselves by analogy <*per analogiam*> with symbolic cognition. We can also say: cognition is symbolic where the object is cognized in the sign, but with discursive cognition the signs are not symbols <*symbola*>, because I do not cognize the object in the sign but rather the sign produces only the representation of the object for me. E.g., the word table is no symbol, but rather only a means for producing the representation of the understanding through association.

ON THE HIGHER FACULTY OF COGNITION

After we have treated the lower faculty of cognition or of the representations which we have from objects so far as we are affected by them (thus conducting ourselves passively), we come now to the higher faculty of cognition, or to the representations which we have through voluntary practice, where we are the author of the representations.

28:239

General consideration of this:

The understanding is not only a faculty of rules, but rather its principle is also that all of our cognitions and objects must stand under a rule. All appearances stand under a rule, for all objects, so far as they *appear*, appear in relations of time and space. But so far as they are *thought*, they must stand under a rule, for otherwise they could not be thought. Thus whatever a rule makes impossible, that is contrary to the understanding.

---

[q] We follow Lehmann in changing *logisch* (logical) in Pölitz to *symbolisch* (238₁₆).

The maxim of the understanding is: everything that happens, happens according to rules, and all cognitions are under a rule. The more cognitions that can be derived *a priori* from a principle *<principio>*, the more unity the rule has. But how do the pure concepts of the understanding enter the head? We have cognitions of objects of intuition by virtue of the formative power, which is between the understanding and sensibility. If this formative power is in the abstract *<in abstracto>*, then it is the understanding. The conditions and actions of the formative power, taken in the abstract *<in abstracto>*, are pure concepts of the understanding and categories of the understanding. E.g., the pure concept of the understanding of substance and accident comes from the formative power in the following manner: the formative power must have something permanent underlying it, besides the manifold that alters, for were there nothing at the foundation of the formative power, then it also could change nothing. Now the permanent is the pure concept of substance, and the manifold of accident. All highest principles of the understanding *a priori* are general rules which express the conditions of the formative power in all appearances with which we can determine how the appearances are connected among themselves; for that which makes cognition possible, which is its condition, that is also the condition of things. We have *a priori* principles which base themselves upon the condition of intuition, e.g., all propositions of geometry. Likewise we have also ascertained *a priori* principles of thinking. What is the necessary condition of thinking belongs to the objective, and what is a necessary condition of intuition also belongs to things. Objects must conform to the conditions under which they can be cognized; that is the nature of the human understanding. Understanding *a priori* is thus the faculty for reflect- 28:240 ing on objects. The understanding does not go beyond the boundaries of the objects of the senses, but still *up to the boundary*: that is God and the future world. It is therefore called the higher faculty of cognition because spontaneity is considered in it, while passivity was in the lower faculty of cognition. The higher faculty of cognition is also called the understanding, in the general sense. In this meaning the understanding is the faculty of concepts, or also the faculty of judgments, but also the faculty of rules.' All three of these definitions are the same, for a concept is a cognition' which can serve as a predicate in a possible judgment. But a judgment' is a representation of the comparison with a general feature, and a concept is a general feature. But a judgment is also always a rule, for a rule gives the relation of the particular to the general. E.g., Cicero is learned, here the predicate *learned* serves for the judging of the actions of Cicero, thus it serves as a rule. Accordingly the three definitions converge into one. We

---

' We follow Lehmann in changing *Regel* (rule) in Pölitz to *Regeln* (240₉).
' We follow Lehmann in changing *Kenntniss* (acquaintance) in Pölitz to *Erkenntniss* (240₁₀).
' We follow Lehmann in changing *Begriff* (concept) in Pölitz to *Urtheil* (240₁₁).

can also say, the understanding is the faculty of general cognitions. As representations, general cognitions are concepts, and as comparison of representations, general cognitions are judgments; every general judgment is thus a rule. – Sensibility is a faculty of intuition. Parallel to[u] sensibility is the understanding as the faculty of concepts. Sensibility has original forms, but the understanding is a faculty of rules,[v] through which it is distinguished from sensibility, which consists only of forms. The senses are a faculty of perception, but the understanding of reflection. If one says: the understanding is a faculty of more distinct cognitions, then this is falsely defined, for sensibility still rests ultimately on consciousness. But consciousness is necessary for all cognitions and representations, accordingly sensible cognitions can also be distinct. But because consciousness is a necessary condition <conditio sine qua non> of cognitions, it is reckoned to the higher faculty of cognition. But distinctness is not a necessary condition of the cognitions of the understanding because there can also be a distinctness of intuition. The distinctness of concepts is, however, the distinctness of the understanding. – But when we define the understanding negatively, in opposition with sensibility, then the understanding is a faculty for cognizing things independently of the manner in which they appear to us.

28:241 But the understanding is the faculty for cognizing things as they are. It indeed appears that when I define the understanding as a faculty for cognizing things as they are, this is not negative; but when I consider it in opposition with sensibility, then I still do not know (namely, if sensibility cognizes things as they appear, but the understanding as they are) *how* the understanding cognizes them; I know only this much, *that it does not cognize them such as they appear.* This definition has its advantage in that it is general, and is directed not only at the human understanding but rather at understanding in general. – But how can I cognize things such as they are? Either through intuition or concepts. Human understanding is only a faculty for cognizing things such as they are through concepts and reflection, thus merely discursively. All our cognitions are only logical and discursive, but not ostensive and intuitive. But we can think of an understanding which cognizes things as they are, but through intuition. Such an understanding is intuitive. *There can be such an understanding, but the human understanding is not it.* This definition has given occasion to the *mystical representation of the understanding.* Namely, if we think of the human understanding as a faculty for cognizing through intuition things such as they are, then this is *a mystical understanding*, e.g., if we believe that there lies in the soul a faculty of intellectual intuitions, then this is a mystical understanding. We have a faculty for cognizing things such as they are, but not through intuition, but rather through concepts. If these concepts are pure concepts of the under-

---

[u] We follow Lehmann in changing *in* (in) in Pölitz to *zu* (240₂₂).
[v] We follow Lehmann in changing *Regel* (rule) in Pölitz to *Regeln* (240₂₄).

standing, then they are transcendental. But if they are applied to appearances, then they are empirical concepts, and the use of the understanding is an empirical use.

As we have considered the understanding up to now, it is opposed to sensibility and is called the higher faculty of cognition. This understanding, taken generally, and the higher faculty of cognition, is threefold: *understanding, power of judgment*, and *reason*. Here the understanding is taken strictly <*stricte*>, where it is a species of the general meaning of understanding and means the higher faculty of cognition. This higher faculty of cognition consists thus:

1. of a general judgment;
2. of a subsumption under this judgment, and
3. of a conclusion. –

The principle of the general judgment, or of the rule, is the *understand-*   28:242
ing taken strictly <*stricte*>. The principle of subsumption under this rule is the *power of judgment*, and the *a priori* principle <*principium a priori*> of the rule is *reason*. – What cannot be subsumed under any empirical judgment is an *a priori* judgment. The faculty of judgments that cannot be subsumed under any empirical judgment is reason. One can also say: reason is the faculty of *a priori* rules, or of *a priori* concepts.

I use my understanding in all respects, also in empirical cognitions, and that is the empirical use of the understanding. But we can also have an *a priori* use of the understanding, and this is reason. E.g., everything contingent has a cause; here the use of understanding is *a priori*, for no experience teaches me that. Understanding and reason are thus different only with respect to empirical and pure use. But we also have an intermediate faculty between the two, namely for subsuming under a general judgment and under a general rule, and that is the power of judgment. At first I ask: is the general rule *a priori* or *a posteriori*? And then: does the case belong under the rule? E.g., everything simple thinks, is an *a priori* rule. Now I see whether the soul of a human being belongs under this rule, and can be subsumed under it. This faculty for subsuming under rules is so separate from other faculties that human beings can indeed have a faculty of general rules, but wholly without having this faculty for subsuming under the rule and applying the rule concretely <*in concreto*>.

Understanding is the faculty for cognizing the particular from the general – the power of judgment, for cognizing the general from the particular – and reason, for cognizing *a priori* the general, and collecting rules from the multiple appearances. The particular is given here from which one has to make a general rule. But the power of judgment is the reverse; there a general rule is given from which the particular must be determined. Thus the power of judgment is necessary in order to know whether the particular belongs under the general rule. This has in it the peculiarity *that it cannot be learned through instruction*, but rather that one must acquire an aptitude in it through practice. The understanding can be instructed, but not the power of judgment. Reason is the faculty for cognizing general *a priori* rules wholly separated from experience. E.g., everything contingent must have a first cause; experience does not teach that.

28:243

The greatness of the understanding rests on two parts: on the faculty of concepts, and on the reference of general concepts to particular cases. The more the judgments have a reference to the particular cases, the more expansive and extensively clear is the understanding; and the more the understanding is connected with intuitions, the more expansive and brighter it is. Accordingly whoever can apply well the general rules in examples, comparisons, and particular cases of common life has an expansive understanding. The understanding is thus instructed in a twofold manner:

a. that one accustom it to general rules, or use it abstractly <*in abstracto*>, and
b. that one apply these general rules in experience, or use it concretely <*in concreto*>.

Here one must not believe that this is the same as the power of judgment, for the power of judgment is only a faculty for knowing whether a given case belongs under a rule, which is to be distinguished from the understanding, which is applied concretely <*in concreto*> to the experiential cases of life. Understanding concretely <*in concreto*> is only a faculty of memory of the general rule; but thereby one cannot yet distinguish whether the given case belongs under the rule. But the power of judgment is a faculty of differentiation.

The use of reason is also twofold:

a. a pure, and
b. an empirical use.

The pure use of reason is that which concerns objects which are not at all objects of senses. The empirical use is when I cognize something *a priori* which is confirmed *a posteriori*; e.g., in experimental physics. A pure use of reason is that where the rule is confirmed not through experience. But where the rule itself is taken from experience there is no use of reason.

We can further distinguish as *healthy* and *learned* faculties all three faculties that constitute the higher faculty of cognition. So we then have a healthy understanding,[w] a healthy power of judgment, and a healthy rea-

---

[w] G: *gesunde Verstand*; this is normally translated as "common sense," but we chose the more literal translation here because of the parallel with judgment and reason.

son; but also a speculative understanding, a speculative power of judgment, and reason. The healthy use of these faculties shows itself concretely *<in concreto>* in the cases where experience can provide the proof of the correctness of this power of cognition. If I use my understanding, my power of judgment, and reason, so that it can be discerned through experience that it is true, then I have a healthy understanding, a healthy power of judgment, and reason. If I go no further with my powers of cognition than only so far as experience can confirm, then that is a healthy use of the powers of cognition. The speculative use of the understanding and of reason is to use the rule without experience, so far as they have a faculty. The speculative power of judgment is where the ground of the correct use lies not in experience, but rather in general grounds. –

28:244

With respect to cognitions one distinguishes *temper* and *genius*. – Temper is an inclination for learning, but genius for finding cognitions that cannot at all be taught. A *mind* is a gift for cognitions. One distinguishes minds with respect to aptitude as fine and dull; with respect to objects, as mathematical and philosophical minds. This is treated in greater detail in anthropology.

Before we pass over to the faculty of pleasure and displeasure, we still must (as a transition of the higher faculty of cognition to the faculty of differentiation of objects according to feeling, pleasure and displeasure) treat of the *faculty for comparing*, and for cognizing objects in comparison. The formative faculty, or the faculty of cognition, are faculties for producing representations. But now we still also have a faculty for comparing representations, and that is *wit* and *acumen*. Wit (*<ingenium*; G: *Witz>*) is the faculty for comparing objects according to differences. The faculty of agreement or of sameness underlies our general concepts. In each judgment I cognize that something either belongs under the general concept or not; this is wit *<ingenium>*. E.g., whether foxes belong under the general concept of dog. Thus one can seek comparison and agreement in the whole of nature. But when I have a negative judgment, when I find that it does not belong to the general concept, but rather is different from it, then that is acumen (*<acumen*; G: *Scharfsinn>*). The expressions of acumen are those through which we guard our cognitions from error, and thus purify them, when we say what the things are not. But through wit *<ingenium>* we broaden our cognitions; wit *<ingenium>* is thus the first. At first I make all sorts of comparisons, but then acumen *<acumen>* comes and distinguishes one from the other. So at first human beings will have taken everything hard to be stones, according to wit *<ingenium>*, but after this are they gradually distinguished, one from the other. One does not rightly know to which faculties these can be properly reckoned, whether to the lower or the higher faculty of cognition. In general the higher faculty of cognition is applied to the lower. Thus they should belong to the higher faculty of cognition.

28:245

ON THE FACULTY OF PLEASURE AND
DISPLEASURE

The second faculty of the soul is the faculty for distinguishing things according to the feeling of pleasure and displeasure, or of satisfaction and dissatisfaction. The faculty of pleasure and displeasure is no faculty of cognition, but rather is wholly distinguished from it. The determinations of things with respect to which we manifest pleasure and displeasure are not determinations which belong simply to the objects, but rather ones which refer to the constitution of the subject. I cannot have representations of things through the faculty of cognition otherwise than according to the determination which would have been met with in them even if they had not been represented at all, e.g., I would cognize the round figure in a circle without the circle having been represented. But the determinations of good and evil, of beautiful and ugly, of agreeable and disagreeable, are determinations which could not at all have been perceived in things if these were not cognized through representation. Therefore those determinations which, without representation, cannot be cognized in things do not belong to the faculty of cognition, because this [faculty], even without representation of things, can cognize the determinations belonging to them; rather there must be a *special* faculty in us for perceiving these in them. They are thus not determinations which refer with respect to our faculty of cognition, but rather refer to a wholly other faculty, whose condition, to be sure, is the faculty of cognition, for without that I cannot have any pleasure and displeasure in an object; but it is a special faculty which is distinguished from the faculty of cognition. If I speak of an object insofar it is beautiful or ugly, agreeable or disagreeable, then I am acquainted not with the object in itself, as it is, but rather as it affects me. If *Euclid* speaks of a circle, then he does not describe it insofar as it is beautiful, but rather what it is in itself. But in order to cognize something as beautiful, etc., there is required for that a special faculty in us, but not in the object. If we take away the faculty of pleasure and displeasure from all rational beings, and enlarge their faculty of cognition however much, then they would cognize all objects without being moved by them; everything would be the same to them, for they would lack the faculty for being affected by objects. All pleasure and displeasure presupposes cognition of an object, either a cognition of sensation or of intuition, or of concepts; and just as one says: there is no desire for the unknown <*ignoti nulla cupido*>, so could one also say: there is no satisfaction in the unknown <*ignoti nulla complacentia*>. But it is not cognition in which pleasure is met, but rather *feeling*, for which cognition is the condition. – All predicates of things which express pleasure and displeasure are not predicates that belong to the object in and for itself, or predicates that stand in relation to our power of cognition; rather they are predicates of the faculty

28:246

in us for being affected by things. It has been said:[15] this faculty would be a cognition of the perfection and imperfection of objects, but perfection is not the feeling of the beautiful and agreeable; rather perfection is the completeness of the object. Now it is indeed true that all completeness pleases, and we have a faculty for applying the idea of completeness to everything, and for cultivating everything completely; but cognizing the completeness, i.e., the perfection of the object, that is not a cognition of pleasure; rather, in certain cases there is still a question whether it is connected with pleasure and displeasure. Granted that the object is an object of pleasure, then sometimes perfection pleases, and sometimes completeness is not required for pleasure. With pleasure and displeasure what matters is not the object, but rather *how* the object affects the mind. Pleasure and displeasure are faculties through which objects are distinguished, not [according to] what is met with in themselves, but rather [according to] how the representation of them makes an impression on our subject, and how our feeling is moved there by –

But what is a feeling? That is something hard to determine. We sense ourselves. Representations can be twofold: representations of the object and of the subject. Our representations can be compared, either with the objects or with the entire life of the subject. The subjective representation of the entire power of life for receiving or excluding objects is the relation of satisfaction or dissatisfaction. Thus feeling is the relation of the objects not to the representation, but rather to the entire power of the mind, for either most inwardly receiving them or excluding them. The receiving is the feeling of pleasure, and the excluding [is] of displeasure. *The beautiful is thus not the relation of cognition to the object, but rather to the subject.* More cannot be said of this here. Accordingly we have two perfections: *logical* and *aesthetic*. The first perfection is when my cognition comes to agree with the object, and the second perfection is when my cognition agrees with the subject. 28:247

We have an inner principle for acting from representations, and that is life. Now if a representation harmonizes with the entire power of the mind, with the principle of life, then this is *pleasure*. But if the representation is of the kind that resists the principle of life, then this relation of conflict in us is *displeasure*. Objects are accordingly beautiful, ugly, etc., not in and for themselves, but rather in reference to living beings. *But what takes place only in reference to living beings, of that the ground must be in the living being;* accordingly there must be a faculty in the living being for perceiving such properties in objects. Pleasure and displeasure is thus a faculty of the agreement or of the conflict of the principle of life with respect to certain representations or impressions of objects.

Life is the inner principle of self-activity. Living beings which act according to this inner principle must act according to representations. Now there can be a promotion, but also a hindrance to life. The feeling of the promotion of life is pleasure, and the feeling of the*ˣ* hindrance of life is displeasure. Pleasure is thus a ground of activity, and displeasure a hindrance of activity. Pleasure thus consists in desiring; displeasure, on the other hand, in abhorring. – Now we see what connection pleasure and displeasure have with thinking beings. Only active beings can have pleasure and displeasure. Subjects that are active according to representations 28:248 have pleasure and displeasure. Thus a creature that is not active according to representations has no faculty of pleasure and displeasure.

Life is threefold:[16]

1. *animal,*
2. *human,* and
3. *spiritual* life.

There is thus a threefold pleasure. *Animal pleasure* consists in the feeling of the private senses. *Human pleasure* is feeling according to a universal sense, by means of the sensible power of judgment; it is a middle thing and is cognized from sensibility through an idea. *Spiritual pleasure* is ideal, and is cognized from pure concepts of the understanding. Pleasure or displeasure, satisfaction or dissatisfaction, is either objective or subjective. If the ground of the satisfaction or dissatisfaction of the object agrees with the determined subject, then this is subjective satisfaction or dissatisfaction. This arises from the senses. Each particular sense is a ground of subjective satisfaction. Thus what satisfies or dissatisfies according to private grounds of the senses of a subject, that is subjective satisfaction or dissatisfaction. Satisfaction from private grounds of the senses of a subject is *gratification,* and the object is agreeable. Dissatisfaction from private grounds of the senses of a subject is *non-gratification* or *pain,* and the object is disagreeable. But if I say: something is agreeable or disagreeable, then that expresses only a subjective satisfaction or dissatisfaction from privately valid grounds of satisfaction or dissatisfaction. Because a certain object always seems agreeable or disagreeable [to me], it does not yet follow that it must seem so to everyone. One can therefore not dispute about this. *Objective* satisfaction or dissatisfaction consists in pleasure and displeasure in the object, not in a relation to particular conditions of the subject, but rather to a universal judgment that has a universal validity and is valid for everyone independent of the particular conditions of the subject. Thus what is a universal ground of the universally valid satisfaction or dissatisfaction, that is an *objective* satisfaction or dissatisfaction. This objective satisfaction or dissatisfaction is *twofold*: something pleases or displeases *either* according to universal sensibility *or* according to the

---

ˣ We follow Lehmann in changing *von der* (in Pölitz) to *von dem* (247₃₄).

universal[y] power of cognition. What pleases from agreement with the
universal sense, that is beautiful, and if it displeases from the same   28:249
ground, it is ugly. What pleases from the agreement of the general power
of cognition is *good*, and if it displeases from the same ground, then it is
evil.

That in which the sense of human beings agree is the *universal* sense.
But how can a human being pass a judgment according to the universal
sense, since he still considers the object according to his private sense?
The community among human beings constitutes a communal sense. Out
of the intercourse among human beings a communal sense arises which is
valid for everyone. Thus whoever does not come into a community has no
communal sense. – The beautiful and the ugly can be distinguished by
human beings only so far as they are in a community. Thus whomever
something pleases according to a communal and universally valid sense,
he has *taste*. Taste is therefore a faculty for judging through satisfaction or
dissatisfaction, according to the communal and universally valid sense.
But taste is still always only a judging through the relation of the senses,
and on that account this faculty is a faculty of pleasure and displeasure.
Objective satisfaction or dissatisfaction, or judging objects according to
universally valid grounds of the power of cognition, is the higher faculty of
pleasure and displeasure. This is the faculty for judging of an object
whether it pleases or displeases from cognition of the understanding
according to universally valid principles. If something is an object of
intellectual satisfaction, then it is good; if it is an object of intellectual
dissatisfaction, then it is evil. – Good is what must please everyone
necessarily. – But the beautiful does not please everyone necessarily,
rather the agreement of the judgment is contingent.[z] But *the* agreement of
the judgments of satisfaction or dissatisfaction by the understanding, according to which the object is either good or evil, is necessary. But how
can the good please, since it does not awaken any gratification? Were
virtues agreeable, then everyone would be virtuous; but now everyone
wishes, if feasible, to be virtuous only sometime. He comprehends that it
is good, but it does not gratify him. *Freedom* is the greatest degree of
activity and of life. Animal life has no spontaneity. Now if I feel that
something agrees with the highest degree of freedom, thus with the spiritual life, then that pleases me. This pleasure is intellectual pleasure. One   28:250
has a satisfaction with it, without its gratifying one. Such intellectual
pleasure is *only in morality*. But from where does morality get such plea-

---

[y] G: *allgemein*. This is translated in this section usually as "universal" and often as "general"
in others. Sometimes it can be translated as "common," and the root *gemein* is found in
allgemein, *gemeinschaftlich* (communal), and *Gemeinschaft* (community).
[z] Lehmann misreads *zufällig* (in Pölitz) as *zulässig* (249[29]), and then changes it to *zufällig* (see
Ak. 28: 1471).

sure? All morality is the harmony of freedom with itself. E.g., whoever lies does not agree with his freedom, because he is bound by the lie. *Whatever harmonizes with freedom agrees with the whole of life. Whatever agrees with the whole of life, pleases.* However, this is only a reflective pleasure; we find here no gratification, but rather approve of it through reflection. Virtue thus has no gratification, but instead approval, for a human being feels his spiritual life and the highest degree of his freedom.

Now we can make the following classification as well. Something is an object of pleasure in sensation, or an object of pleasure in intuition, or of the sensible universal power of judgment, i.e., an object of pleasure according to concepts of the understanding. If something pleases in sensation, then it *gratifies*, and the object is agreeable. What is an object of intuition or of the sensible power of judgment, that *pleases*, and the object is beautiful. What is an object of pleasure according to concepts of the understanding is *approved of*, and the object is good. In order to distinguish the agreeable and disagreeable we need feeling; in order to distinguish the beautiful and ugly, we need taste; in order to distinguish the evil and good, we need reason. In the investigation of the agreeable and disagreeable we have no communal standard, because it refers to the private sensation of the subject. Therefore one cannot engage in any dispute over the agreeable and disagreeable, for a dispute is an attempt to bring the other to consent to one's judgment. But because each[a] has his own private sensation here, no one can be required to accept the sensation of the other. But with the beautiful it is otherwise. There the beautiful is not that which pleases one, but rather what has the approval of all; it does please through sense as well, but through a universal sense. For the investigation of the beautiful and the ugly we thus have a communal standard; this is the communal sense. This communal sense arises thus: each private sensation is still not a wholly particular sensation, but rather the private sensation of the one must accord with the private sensation of the other, and through this agreement we receive a universal rule. This is the communal sense or *taste*. Whatever then agrees, is beautiful. Now this can indeed not please one private sense, but still please according to the universal rule. Whomever it does not please, whose private sense does not agree with the universal rule, has no taste. Taste is thus the power of judgment of the senses, through which it is cognized what agrees with the sense of others; it is thus a pleasure and displeasure in community with others. The universal agreement of sensibility is what constitutes the ground of satisfaction through taste. E.g., a house is beautiful not because it gratifies through intuition (for here a mess hall is perhaps more gratifying to many), but rather because it is an object of universal satisfaction; because thousands can have a gratification in one

28:251

---

[a] We follow Lehmann in changing *jedes* (in Pölitz) to *jeder* (250₂₉).

and the same object. It is also like this with music. Sight and hearing are accordingly senses of taste and communal. But smell and taste are only private senses of sensation. Agreeable is that which agrees with the private sense; but beautiful is that which agrees with the communal sense. One can dispute about the beautiful because the agreement of many human beings provides a judgment which can be set against a single judgment. Taste has its rule, for every universal agreement in a feature is the ground of rules. These rules are not *a priori*, and not in and for themselves, but rather they are empirical, and sensibility must be cognized *a posteriori*. Accordingly one can indeed dispute about an *a posteriori* rule, but not debate. For to debate is to contest the grounds of the other from principles of reason. It is false when one says: a human being has a wholly particular taste, for if he chooses that which displeases others, then he has no taste at all because taste must be judged according to the communal sense. If a human being were wholly alone on an island, then he would choose not according to taste but rather according to appetite. Thus only in the community of others does he have taste. Taste produces nothing new, rather it merely moderates what is produced, that it pleases all.

One could also say: that some rules of taste are *a priori*; but not immediately *a priori*, rather comparatively, so that these *a priori* rules are themselves grounded on universal rules of experience. E.g., order, proportion, symmetry, harmony in music are rules which I cognize *a priori* and comprehend that they please all; but they are again grounded on universal *a posteriori* rules. We could also maintain a necessary taste, e.g., everyone has taste for *Homer*, *Cicero*, *Virgil*, etc.

28:252

The good is an object of the understanding and is judged by the understanding. We call an object good *in itself*, and not in relation. If I say, a matter is *good*, then I say this without reference to other objects. But if I say a matter is *beautiful*, then I say only how I sense it, and how it appears to me. Thus the good must also please those beings who have no such sensibility like ours, but that does not hold with the agreeable and beautiful. Something is good either *mediately* or *immediately*. Something is good *mediately* if it agrees with something else, as a means to an end. *Immediately* good is what pleases in and for itself in a universal and necessary way.

In order to sum up briefly all that is to be said of pleasure and displeasure, one notes that all pleasure and displeasure is either sensible or intellectual. The lower faculty, or sensible pleasure and displeasure, rests on the representation of the object by sensibility. The higher faculty of pleasure and displeasure, or intellectual pleasure and displeasure, rests on the representations of the object by the understanding. Sensible pleasure and displeasure is twofold: either it rests on the relation of sensible sensation, or of sensible intuition. Pleasure is in relation to sensible sensation so far as it agrees with the state of the subject, so far as this is altered by the object. It*b* pleases sensibly, but subjectively, and there the object is agreeable. – Pleasure is in relation to sensible intuition so far as it agrees merely with the faculty of sensibility in general, i.e., it pleases sensibly and objectively, and then the object is beautiful. Thus on this rests the difference of the beautiful and agreeable, of sensible gratifications and gratifications according to taste. If the object agrees only with the state of the subject, then it cannot please universally, but rather according to the private satisfaction of the subject. But if the object agrees with the universal laws of sensibility in general, then it must also please universally. To the universal laws of sensibility belongs, e.g., that order, idea of the whole, etc., are perceived in the object. Now what is valid for everyone in relation to a universal judgment pleases objectively. But what is valid in relation to a private judgment pleases subjectively. Feeling is therefore not to be so cultivated as taste, because feeling is valid only for me, but taste universally. Intellectual pleasure is what pleases universally, but according to the universal laws of the understanding, not the universal laws of sensibility. The object of intellectual pleasure is good. The beautiful is also an object that pleases universally, but according to universal laws of sensibility, whereas the good [pleases] according to universal laws of the understanding. The good is independent of *how* the object appears to the senses; it must be taken as how it is in and for itself, e.g., truthfulness.

An object is indifferent as long as it is neither an object of pleasure nor of displeasure. One calls such objects *indifferent things <adiaphora>*.[17] Indifferent things *<adiaphora>* can be either aesthetic or logical; either according to laws of sensibility or of understanding. Aesthetically indifferent things *<adiaphora aesthetica>* are neither disagreeable nor agreeable, neither beautiful nor ugly. Logically indifferent things *<adiaphora logica>* are neither good nor evil. Some say that there are no indifferent things *<adiaphora>*. There clearly are no absolutely indifferent things *<adiaphora absoluta>*, where a thing is supposedly neither good nor evil in any relation, but in certain cases there still is such a thing, e.g., whether I should give alms to the poor with the right or the left hand, etc. But it would be most harmful if one wanted to reckon among the indifferent things *<adiaphora>* an action that belongs under a law of morality. Where there is a universally determined law, there no indifferent things *<adiaphora>* are valid; but where there is no universal law that determines something, there can be indifferent things *<adiaphora>*.

ON THE FACULTY OF DESIRE

The third faculty of our soul is the faculty of desire. The faculty of pleasure and displeasure was the relation of the object to our feeling of

b We follow Lehmann in changing *Es* (in Pölitz) to *Er* (252₂₉, and again at 252₃₂).

28:253

activity, either of the promotion or of the obstruction[c] of life. But insofar as the faculty of pleasure and displeasure is a faculty of certain activities and actions which are suitable to it, to that extent there is a *desire*. Desire is 28:254 thus *a pleasure insofar as it is a ground of an activity for determining certain representations of the object*. If the representation is a ground for determining us for the object, then we *desire* the object. Dissatisfaction in an object, insofar as it can be the cause of a representation, is *abhorrence*. The pleasure of the activity in the production of representation is twofold: either we determine this activity as it were problematically, without assessing whether it is suitable for the production of the representation; or we determine the representation insofar as we have assessed the ground of its faculty for the production of the representation. The first is an inactive desire or a wish. But there are still two kinds of activities: one of these is mechanical, and is produced by an external power; the other is animal or practical. Here the power is determined from an inner principle. The faculty for acting according to satisfaction or dissatisfaction is the practical, active faculty of desire. The faculty of desire should thus be active and consist in acting. But our faculty of desire goes still further; we also desire without being active, without acting; that is an inactive desire or yearning, where one desires something without being able to obtain it. But active desire, or the faculty for doing and for refraining according to satisfaction or dissatisfaction with the object, so far as it is a cause of the active power for producing it, is the *power of free choice* (<*arbitrium liberum*; G: *freie Willkühr*>). This desire is active and forceful, and has the might to achieve what is desired. With each choice <*arbitrio*> there are impelling causes <*causae impulsivae*>. – Impelling causes <*causae impulsivae*> are representations of the object according to satisfaction and dissatisfaction, so far as they are the cause of the determination of our power. Every act of choice <*actus arbitrii*> has an impelling cause <*causam impulsivam*>. – The impelling causes <*causae impulsivae*> are either sensitive or intellectual. The sensitive are stimuli <*stimuli*> or motive causes, impulses. The intellectual are *motives* or *motive grounds*. The first are for the senses, the others for the understanding. If the impelling causes <*causae impulsivae*> are representations of satisfaction or dissatisfaction which depend on the manner in which we are affected by objects, then they are stimuli <*stimuli*>. But if the impelling causes <*causa impulsivae*> are representations of satisfaction or dissatisfaction which here depend on the manner in which we cognize the objects through concepts, through the understanding, then they are motives. Stimuli <*stimuli*> are causes which impel the 28:255 power of choice so far as the object affects our senses. This driving power of the power of choice can either necessitate, or by itself it can also only impel. Stimuli <*stimuli*> thus have either necessitating power <*vim*

---

[c] We follow Lehmann in changing *Hinderniss* (in Pölitz) to *Behinderung* (253_{35}).

necessitantem> or impelling power *<vim impellentem>*. With all non-rational animals the stimuli *<stimuli>* have necessitating power *<vim necessitantem>*, but with human beings the stimuli *<stimuli>* do not have necessitating power *<vim necessitantem>*, but rather only impelling *<impellentem>*. Accordingly, the human power of choice *<arbitrium humanum>* is not brute *<brutum>*, but rather free *<liberum>*. This is the power of free choice *<arbitrium liberum>*, so far as it is defined psychologically or practically. However, that power of choice *<arbitrium>* which is not necessitated or impelled at all by any stimuli *<stimulos>*, but rather is determined by motives, by motive grounds of the understanding, is the intellectual or transcendental power of free choice *<liberum arbitrium>*. The sensitive power of choice *<arbitrium sensitivum>* can indeed be free *<liberum>*, but not the brute one *<brutum>*. The sensitive power of [free]ᴸ choice *<arbitrium sensitivum [liberum]ᴸ>* is only affected or impelled by the stimuli *<stimulis>*, but the brute one *<brutum>* is necessitated. A human being thus has a power of free choice; and everything that arises from his power of choice arises from a power of *free* choice. All kinds of torment cannot compel his power of free choice; he can endure them all and still rest on his will. Only in some cases does he have no power of free choice, e.g., in the most tender childhood, or when he is insane, and in deep sadness, which is however also a kind of insanity. A human being thus feels a faculty in himself for not allowing himself to be compelled to do something by anything in the world. Often because of other grounds this is indeed difficult; but it is still possible, he still has the power for it. But the impelling causes *<causae impulsivae>* are either subjective or objective *<vel subjectivae vel objectivae>*; according to the laws of sensibility and according to the laws of the understanding. The subjective impelling causes *<causae impulsivae subjectivae>* are stimuli *<stimuli>*, and the objective ones *<objectivae>* are motives. – The necessitation by motives *<necessitatio per motivas>* is not opposed to freedom, but the necessitation by stimuli *<necessitatio per stimulos>* is wholly repugnant to it. The power of free choice, so far as it acts according to motives of the understanding, is freedom, which is good in all regards. This is the absolute freedom *<libertas absoluta>*, which is moral freedom.

The human power of choice *<arbitrium humanum>* is free *<liberum>*, be it sensitive *<sensitivum>* or intellectual *<intellectuale>*. Now what occurs on the side of sensibility is that the stimuli *<stimuli>*, so far as they are in conformity with the obscure representations, are called *instincts*, e.g., one has an instinct to eat. The instincts are either of appetition or of aversion. E.g., little chicks already have from nature an instinct of aversion to the hawk, of which they are afraid as soon as they merely see something fly in the air.

As regards the degree of sensible impulses, we call them *affections* and *passions*. The affections concern feeling, the passions concern desires. We are affected by the affections, but we are carried away by the passions. It all depends here on the degree of freedom. The degree of the stimuli <*stimuli*> which is a hindrance to freedom is affection. To the extent the stimuli <*stimuli*> not only hinder freedom, but also predominate, to that extent they are called passions.

Now we want to consider the stimuli <*stimuli*> in collision with freedom, or sensuality with intellectuality, the sensible impulses with the motives.

Understanding submits motives for omitting some action; sensibility, on the contrary, stimuli <*stimuli*> for committing it. But this dispute ends either when the stimuli <*stimuli*> no longer drive [us] (then the higher faculty <*facultas superior*> triumphs, and the motives are predominant); or if the understanding submits no motives at all, then sensibility becomes predominant. Now whoever has sensibility and the understanding in his control, so that sensibility does not become predominant, he has self-mastery <*imperium in semetipsum*>.

The greatest freedom in a human being is assessed according to the degree of the outweighing of the hindrances. Our standard for determining the magnitude of freedom thus rests on the degree of the outweighing of the sensible impulses. But there are beings who have no sensible impulses at all; their freedom we cannot assess because we have no standard here, for our standard for assessing freedom is derived from the sensible impulses. The highest freedom of all would thus be where the freedom is utterly independent of all stimuli <*stimulis*>.

Animals can be necessitated strictly through stimuli <*stricte per stimulos*>, but human beings only comparatively. This compulsion <*coactio*> can be either external <*externa*> or internal <*interna*>. External compulsion <*coactio externa*> is compulsion of the intellectual power of free choice <*coactio arbitrii liberi intellectualis*>. One can be forced by sensuality to act contrary to the intellect, but one can also be forced by the intellect to act contrary to sensuality. The more a human being has power, by means of the higher power of choice, to suppress the lower power of choice, the freer he is. But the less he can compel sensuality by the intellect, the less freedom he 28:257 has. If one compels oneself according to rules of morality, and the lower power of choice is suppressed by the higher power of choice, then that is *virtue. – Practical freedom*, or the freedom of the person, must be distinguished from physical freedom, or from the freedom of one's state.*[d]* Personal freedom can remain, even when physical freedom is missing, as e.g., with *Epictetus*. This practical freedom rests on independence of choice from necessitation by stimuli <*independentia arbitrii a necessitatione per stimulos*>. That freedom, however, which is wholly independent of all stimuli <*stimulis*>, is transcendental freedom, which will be spoken of in the Rational

---

[d] G: *Zustand*, i.e., the state or condition of the individual person.

Psychology <*psychologia rationali*>. Everything that happens in nature, happens either according to physical-mechanical laws, or according to laws of the power of free choice. In inanimate nature everything happens according to mechanical laws, but in animate according to laws of the power of free choice. What happens according to the laws of the power of choice, happens either *pathologically* or *practically*. Accordingly, something is pathologically necessary or possible according to laws of the sensible power of choice. – Something is practically necessary or possible according to laws of the power of free choice. Accordingly the necessitation <*necessitatio*> is either pathological or practical.

Practical necessitation <*necessitatio practica*> can be various:

1. problematic necessation <*necessitatio problematica*>, where the understanding cognizes the necessity of the use of the means under the condition of the given end, e.g., in geometry.

2. pragmatic necessitation <*necessitatio pragmatica*>, where the understanding cognizes the necessity of the use of the means with respect to the universal end of every thinking being.

3. moral necessitation <*necessitatio moralis*>. This is the necessity of the use of the power of free choice, not as means to an end, but rather because it is in itself necessary. –

All propositions of practical necessitation are expressed by imperatives <*imperativos*> that the action *should* happen, i.e., it is good that the action happen. Here there is thus no stimulus <*stimulus*>, and this practical necessitation is objective. An objective necessitation can also be subjective (the pathological is always subjective), namely if the mere cognition of the action *that* it is good moves my subject to perform it; then it is an incentive. If the cognition of the understanding has a power to move the subject to the action *merely because* the action *in itself* is good, then this motive power is an incentive which we also call *moral feeling*. Thus there should be moral feeling, whereby a motive power arises through the motives of the understanding. This incentive of the mind, however, is not pathologically necessitating,[18] and indeed it does not necessitate pathologically, because we comprehend the good through the understanding, and not so far as it affects our senses. We should thus think of a feeling, but one which does not necessitate pathologically, and this is to be the moral feeling. One is to cognize the good through the understanding, and yet have a feeling of it. This is obviously something that cannot be properly understood, but over which there is also dispute still. I am supposed to have a feeling of that which is not an object of feeling, but rather which I cognize objectively through the understanding. Thus there is always a contradiction hidden in here. For if we are supposed to do the good through a feeling, then we do it because it is agreeable. But this cannot be, for the good cannot at all affect our senses. But we call the pleasure in the good a feeling because we cannot otherwise express the subjective driving power of objective practical necessitation. That is a misfortune for the human race, that moral laws, which are here objectively necessitating are not also at the same time subjectively necessitating. Were we also at the same time subjectively necessitated, then we would still be just as free, because this subjective necessitation arises from the objective one. We are subjectively necessitated by a condition, because the action is objectively good. Moral compulsion is always practical, but not every practical compulsion is moral. If the motives enunciate the absolute good <*bonum absolutum*>, then they are moral motives <*motiva moralia*>. But to the extent the motives <*motiva*> enunciate the comparative good <*bonum comparativum*>, to that extent they say only what is good in a conditional way; to that extent they are only pragmatic motives <*motiva pragmatica*>. Thus the moral motives <*motiva moralia*> must not be confused with the pragmatic ones.

The proportion of the principles and sources of our desires is called character <*indoles*> or *disposition*. Upright character <*indoles erecta*> is the noble disposition where the higher faculty of desire rules; low character <*indoles abjecta*>, on the other hand, the ignoble disposition where the lower faculty of desire, sensibility, rules.

Noble and liberal arts <*artes ingenuae . . . liberales*> are what bring us from the desires of enjoyment to the desires of intuition, which make human beings free from the servitude of the senses; for whoever finds, e.g., gratification in poetic matters is already freed from crude sensibility. 28:259 The proportion among the sensible impulses is *temperament*.

ON THE INTERACTION <*COMMERCIO*> OF THE SOUL WITH THE BODY

When we consider the soul of a human being, we regard it not merely as intelligence, but rather when it *stands in connection with the body* as soul of a human being. But it is not merely in connection, but rather also in *community*, for we can also stand in connection with other bodies, e.g., with our children, but that is no community. A *community is a connection where the soul constitutes a unity with the body, where alterations of the body are at the same time alterations of the soul, and alterations of the soul at the same time alterations of the body.* No alterations happen in the mind that do not correspond with the alterations of the body. Further, not only does the alteration correspond, but also the *constitution* of the mind with the constitution of the body. As for the correspondence of the alterations, nothing can take place in the soul where the body is not to come into play.

This happens:

1. through *thinking*. The soul thinks nothing where the body is not also affected by the thinking. The body suffers many shocks by reflection, and

is quite strained by it. The more active the soul is, the more worn out is the body. The ideas of the soul correspond to something bodily. These conditions of the body, under which alone the thoughts can take place, are called material ideas <*ideas materiales*> or material correlates of the ideas. Just as we cannot calculate a large problem right away in the head (which indeed can be done with smaller ones), but rather must use numbers that correspond to our thoughts, so must there also be impressions in the body that correspond with the thoughts and accompany the idea, for otherwise we would not be able to think. Thus there must be impressions in the brain of that which one has thought; there must be something bodily with thinking. Thus the soul affects the brain quite a bit by thinking. The brain, of course, does not work out the thoughts, but rather it is only the slate upon which the soul draws its thoughts. Thus the brain is the condition of thinking; for all of our thinking concerns objects. But the objects are that which affect me. Accordingly thinking concerns things that affect my body; thus my thinking is directed toward the impressions of the brain which my body receives. These bodily impressions are the material ideas <*ideae materiales*>. From this it thus follows that the body is also affected by thinking. We can go no further here in the investigation.

28:260

2. *Willing* affects our body even more than thinking. The power of free choice moves the body at one's discretion; the voluntary influence of the desires on our body is wholly clear, as is deliberate influence as well; but when contrary to our intention our desires produce motions in the body, which nevertheless have their natural origin (e.g., when someone is frightened and wants to run away from something, and from fear cannot or falls down), then there was still the intention to run, but the falling down must here have followed naturally from the fear. The body is also quite affected when a human being is delivered over to affections and passions; e.g., anger can often make one sick. This feeling also affects the body considerably, so, e.g., one can blanch over a letter in which one receives distressing news.

3. *Outer objects* affect my senses as well. The nerves are thereby affected, and through this affection of the nerves the play of sensation occurs in the soul, according to the faculty of pleasure and displeasure, whereby the whole body is then set into motion.

On the other hand, the body again affects the mind through its corporeal constitution. This corporeal constitution is the cause of the character <*indoles*> and the temperament of the mind. The sort of temperament a human being has depends heavily on the body; the head as well, even the powers of the mind, appear to depend considerably on the body. So the liveliness of one's understanding and wit is seen already in the eyes, and from another stupidity beams from^ the forehead. Accordingly with re-

---

^ We follow Lehmann in changing *vor der* (in Pölitz) to *von der* (260₃₃).

spect to our desires and the faculty of pleasure and displeasure, much also rests on the body.

On the other hand, the constitution and also the state of the mind rests on the constitution and the state of the body. E.g., one can enliven the mind by bodily motion, and vice versa (e.g., in society) enliven the body 28:261 again by mental motions. We can thus get at the body through the mind, and at the mind through the body.

The question is: from which side is the *most* to be derived, from the body or from the soul? Further: would the soul, if it were to come into another body, have the same or another constitution and another state? We can say *nothing* about this, for here we consider the soul in community with its body, and thus cannot know what the soul would be *without* this body, and the body *without* this soul. Many maintain that all souls are the same, and the difference in the variety stems merely from the body. This amounts to *materialism*. If on the other hand we put all might in the soul, then we arrive at *Stahlianism*. *Stahl* was a physician who maintained this.[19] One cannot wholly contradict this opinion, for all properties of the soul are already to be read in the countenance and lineaments of the body; thus the soul must have placed its properties in the body. Some opined that it also even *makes* it body.

In concluding the empirical psychology, the question is still to be raised: whether all powers of the soul are unified, and *can be derived from one basic power*, or whether various basic powers are to be assumed, in order to explain from them all the actions of the soul? *Wolff* assumes one basic power and says: the soul itself is a basic power which represents the universe. It is already false when one says: the soul is a basic power. This arises because the soul is falsely defined, as the Ontology teaches. Power is not what contains in itself the ground of the actual representation, but rather the relation <*respectus*> of the substance to the accident, insofar as the ground of the actual representations is contained in it. *Power is thus not a separate principle, but rather a relation* <*respectus*>. Whoever thus says: the soul is power <*anima est vis*>, maintains that the soul is no separate substance, but rather only a power, thus a phenomenon and accident. Now in order to answer and to treat the question, whether all powers of the soul can be derived from one basic power, or whether several of them are to be assumed, we must of course say: because the soul is indeed a unity, which will be demonstrated later, and which the I already proves, then it is obvious that there is only one basic power in the soul, out of which all alterations and determinations arise. But *this is a wholly other* 28:262 *question: whether we are capable of deriving all actions of the soul, and its various powers and faculties, from one basic power.* This we are in no way in the position [to do], for we certainly cannot derive effects which are actually different from one another from one basic power; e.g., the motive power and the power of cognition cannot possibly be derived from one power, for the cause of the one power is different from that of the other. Now since in the human soul we meet real determinations or accidents of essentially different kinds, the philosopher strives in vain to derive these from one basic power. It is indeed this which is the main rule of the philosopher: that he strive to bring everything to one principle, so far as it is possible, so that the principles of cognition^f are not increased too much; but whether we also have cause to reduce various powers in the human mind to one power does not follow from that. E.g., memory is only a reproductive imagination of past things, thus no separate basic power. But we cannot derive the reproductive imagination itself any further. Accordingly, the formative faculty is already a basic power. Likewise is reason and understanding *a priori*. We find accordingly that we must assume various basic powers, and are not able to explain all phenomena of the soul from one; for who would want to try to derive the understanding from the senses? *Accordingly, the faculty of cognition, the faculty of pleasure and displeasure, and the faculty of desire are basic powers.* In vain does one strive to derive all powers of the soul from one; even much less, that the power which represents the universe <*vis repraesentativa universi*> could be assumed as the basic power. But the proposition that all diverse actions of a human being must be derived from diverse powers of the soul serves in order to treat empirical psychology all the more systematically.

Rational psychology

OVERVIEW OF THIS.

28:263 In rational psychology the human soul is cognized not from experience, as in empirical psychology, but *a priori from concepts.* Here we are to investigate *how much of the human soul we can cognize through reason.* The greatest yearning of a human being is not to know the actions of the soul, which one cognizes through experience, but rather its future state. The individual propositions of rational psychology are not so important here as *the general consideration of its origin, of its future state, and of survival.* Here we must try to see how much we can cognize of that through reason.

The concept of the soul in itself is a concept of experience. But in rational psychology we take nothing more from experience than the mere concept of the soul, *that* we have a soul. The rest must be cognized from pure reason. That cognition where we abandon the guiding thread of experience is the *metaphysical cognition* of the soul.

Accordingly the soul is considered from a threefold point of view:[20]

---

^{f} We follow Lehmann in changing *Erkenntnissquellen* (sources of cognition) in Pölitz to *Erkenntniss* (262$_{14}$).

1. absolutely; *in and for itself*, according to its subject, merely from pure concepts of reason alone. The first part thus includes in itself the absolute consideration of the soul. This is the *transcendental* part of rational psychology.

2. *In comparison with other things in general*, either with bodies, or with other thinking natures outside it, to what extent it differs from bodily natures, and agrees with thinking natures. In the first case we investigate whether the soul is material or immaterial; and in the second, how far it agrees with animal souls, or other higher spirits.

3. With respect to *the connection of the soul with other things*, and this indeed because it belongs to the concept of the soul that it is connected with a body; thus with respect to^g the connection of the soul with the body, or the interaction <*commercio*> between both. Here will be treated:

   a. the *possibility* of this interaction <*commercii*>;

   b. the *beginning* of the connection of the soul with the body, or of our birth;

   c. the *end* of this connection of the soul with the body, or of the state of the soul with our death. With the beginning of the connection, the state of the soul *before* the connection is investigated; does it occur? And finally at the occasion of death, or at the end of the connection, the state of the soul *after* the connection is investigated, whether it will also survive. Thus this hangs together in a certain way quite well.

28:264

But since we consider the soul according to these three parts, various other sorts of matters must be brought in as well. Namely, when we consider the soul *absolutely* in the first section, thus from transcendental concepts of ontology, then we will examine, e.g., whether the soul is a substance or an accident, whether it is simple or composite, whether a single or many souls are in a human being (oneness is not the same as simplicity), whether it is a spontaneous substance <*substantia spontanea*>, or whether it is necessitated from outside. Thus *transcendental freedom* is treated here: whether the soul is a being which is independent and is necessitated by nothing. This is all treated and proved in the first section. – When in the second section we treat the *comparison* of the soul with other things, then immateriality will be proved there: that the soul is not only a simple substance, but also distinguished from all simple parts of bodies. Further, in *comparison with thinking natures*, the degree of its perfection will be shown; how far it goes beyond the animal soul, and how far it stands below the perfection of higher spirits. But this part can be treated only hypothetically <*hypothetice*>, i.e., it is shown what likely can be

---

^g We follow Lehmann in changing *von der* (from the) in Pölitz to *in Ansehung der* (263₃₁).

thought and cognized about this through reason. – In the third section, where the *connection* is treated, and indeed of its beginning, the state of the soul *before* the connection is considered and seen: whether we can cognize something of that from concepts through reason. But from this it will be clear that our transcendental concepts go no further than experience leads us, and that it directs only cognition *a posteriori*. Indeed we can come *up to the boundaries* of[h] experience, as much from before as after <*a parte ante . . . post*>, but *not beyond the boundaries* of experience. But here we will philosophize with advantage because we thereby hold within limits the false sophistry that only undermines true cognition. We will *not* speak 28:265 *dogmatically* here of the state of the soul before birth and after death, *although one can speak far more of that of which one knows nothing than of that of which one knows something.* Accordingly we will determine the limits of human reason here, so that under the semblance of rational cognition false sophistry[i] cannot undermine our true principles with respect to the practical.

FIRST SECTION OF RATIONAL PSYCHOLOGY

If we consider the soul *absolutely* in the transcendental part of rational psychology, then we apply the transcendental concepts of ontology to it. These are:

1. that the soul is a substance;
2. that it is simple;
3. that it is a single substance; and
4. that it is a spontaneous agent, simply speaking <*simpliciter spontanea agens*>. These are the transcendental concepts according to which we consider the soul.

When I speak of the soul, then I speak of the I in the strict sense <*in sensu stricto*>. We receive the concept of the soul only through *the I*, thus through the inner intuition of inner sense, in that I am conscious of all my thoughts, accordingly that I can speak of myself as a state of inner sense. This object of inner sense, *this subject, consciousness* in the strict sense <*in sensu stricto*>, is the soul. I take the self in the strict sense <*in sensu stricto*> insofar as I omit everything that belongs to my self in the broader sense <*in sensu latiori*>. But the I in the broader sense <*in sensu latiori*> expresses me as the whole human being with soul and body. But the body is an object of outer sense. I can perceive every single part of the body through outer sense, just like all other objects. But the soul is an object of

---

[h] The emphasis of *der*, added by Lehmann, has been removed (264₃₅).
[i] G: *Vernünftelei* (false sophistry); this term indicates a misuse of reason (*Vernunft*). Cf. also 264₃₈, above.

inner sense. Now so far as I feel myself as an object and am conscious of this, this means the I in the strict sense <*in sensu stricto*> or only selfhood alone, the soul. We would not have this concept of the soul if we could not abstract everything outer from the object of inner sense: therefore the I in the strict sense <*in sensu stricto*> expresses not the whole human being, but rather the soul alone.

Now when we speak of the soul *a priori*, then we will talk of it only to the extent we can derive all from the concept of the I and to the extent we can apply the transcendental concepts to this I. And this is the *true philosophy, to indicate the source of cognition*, for otherwise one could not know how I can cognize something *a priori* of the soul, and why transcendental concepts can no longer be applied to it. –

28:266

We will thus cognize *a priori* no more of the soul than the I allows us to cognize. But I cognize of the soul:

1. that it is a substance, or: I am a substance. The *I* means the subject, so far as it is no predicate of another thing. What is no predicate of another thing is a substance. The I is *the general subject* of all predicates, of all thinking, of all actions, of all possible judgments that we can pass of ourselves as a thinking being. I can only say: I am, I think, I act. Thus it is not at all feasible that the I would be a predicate of something else. I cannot be a predicate of another being; predicates do belong to me; but I cannot predicate the I of another, I cannot say: another being is the I. Consequently the I, or the soul through which the I is expressed, is a substance.

2. The soul is *simple, i.e., the I means a simple concept*. Many beings taken together cannot constitute an I. If I say: I think, then I do not express representations which are divided among many beings, rather I express a representation that takes place in one subject. For all thoughts can be only simple or composite. One and precisely the same simple thought can take place only in one simple subject. For if the parts of the representations should be divided among many subjects, then each subject would have only one part of the representation, therefore no single subject would have the whole representation. But for the whole representation to be wholly in a subject, all parts of the representation must also be in the one subject. For if they are not connected together in the one subject, then the representation is not whole. E.g., if the saying: whatever you do <*quidquid agis*>, etc., were distributed among many subjects so that each had a part; that is, if whatever <*quidquid*> were spoken into the ear of one, you do <*agis*> into that of another, so that no one heard the whole saying, then one could not say: the whole thought is together in the many minds, so that each had a part of the thought; but rather the thought is not at all, because each has only the thought of one word, but not a part of the whole representation. Accordingly many beings can indeed have one and the same thought at the same time, but each has the whole thought. But many

28:267

beings together cannot have one whole representation. Accordingly that subject which has a whole representation must be *simple*. The soul is thus either a simple substance or a composite <*compositum*> of substances. If it is the latter, then it cannot think at all. For even if a part thinks, all parts together still cannot have one thought, thus a composite <*compositum*> of substances which is a plurality of substances cannot think at all; accordingly the soul must be a simple substance.

3. The soul is a *single soul* (the oneness, the unity of the soul), *i.e.*, *my consciousness is the consciousness of a single substance*. I am not conscious of myself as several substances. For if there were several thinking beings in a human being, then one would also have to be conscious oneself of several thinking beings. But the I expresses oneness: I am conscious of myself as one subject.

4. The soul is a being which acts spontaneously, simply speaking <*simpliciter spontan*>; i.e., the human soul is free in the transcendental sense <*in sensu transcendentali*>. Practical or psychological freedom was the independence of the power of choice from the necessitation of stimuli <*stimulorum*>. This is treated in empirical psychology, and this concept of freedom was also sufficient enough for morality. But now the transcendental concept of freedom follows; this means absolute spontaneity, and is self-activity from an *inner principle* according to the power of free choice. Spontaneity <*spontaneitas*> is either absolute or without qualification <*absoluta vel simpliciter talis*>, or qualified in some respect <*secundum quid talis*>. – Spontaneity in some respect <*spontaneitas secundum quid*> is when something acts spontaneously *under a condition*. So, e.g., a body which is shot off moves spontaneously, but in some respect <*secundum quid*>. This spontaneity <*spontaneitas*> is also called automatic spontaneity <*spontaneitas automatica*>, namely when a machine moves itself according to an inner principle, e.g., a watch, a turnspit. But the spontaneity is not without qualification <*simpliciter talis*> because here the inner principle <*principium*> was determined by an external principle <*principium externum*>. The internal principle <*principium internum*> with the watch is the spring, with the turnspit the weight, but the external principle <*principium externum*> is the artist who determines the internal principle <*principium internum*>. The spontaneity which is without qualification <*spontaneitas simpliciter talis*> is an absolute spontaneity. –

28:268

But it is asked: do the actions of the soul, its thoughts, come from the inner principle which is determined by no causes, or are its actions determined by an external principle <*principium externum*>? If the latter were [the case], then it would have only spontaneity in some respect <*spontaneitatem secundum quid*>, but not without qualification <*simpliciter talem*>, and thus no freedom in the transcendental sense. If it is assumed (but this will be settled only in the Rational Theology <*theologia rationali*>) that the soul has a cause, that it is a dependent being <*ens dependens*>, is an effect of another <*causatum alterius*>, then the question here is: whether absolute spontaneity <*spontaneitas absoluta*> can be attributed to the soul, as a being which has a cause. This is a difficulty which detains us here. Were it an independent being <*ens independens*>, then we could in any event think in it absolute spontaneity <*spontaneitatem absolutam*>. But if I assume: it is a being derived from another <*ens ab alio*>, then it appears to be quite probable that it is also determined by this cause in all its thoughts and actions, thus has only spontaneity in some respect <*spontaneitatem secundum quid*>; that it indeed acts freely according to the inner principle, but is determined by a cause. Now the question is: whether I can think [of myself]ᴸ as soul? Do I have transcendental spontaneity <*spontaneitatem transscendentalem*> or absolute freedom <*libertatem absolutam*>?

Here the I must again help out. It is true, the absolute spontaneity <*spontaneitas absoluta*> cannot be conceived through reason in a dependent being <*ente dependente*>; the pure self-activity of a being that is an effect <*causatum*> cannot be comprehended. *But although absolute spontaneity <spontaneitas absoluta> cannot be conceived, it also still cannot be refuted.* Therefore we only have to look to this, whether self-activity can be claimed for the I, whether I can act freely by myself without any determination of a cause? When I do something, do I do it myself, or does another effect it in me? If the latter happens, then I am not free but rather determined by a cause outside me. But if I do it from an inner principle which is determined by nothing outer, then absolute spontaneity <*spontaneitas absoluta*> in the transcendental sense is in me. But the I proves that I myself act; *I* am a principle and no thing which has a principle <*principiatum*>, *I* am conscious of determinations and actions, and such a subject that is conscious of its determinations and actions has absolute freedom <*libertatem absolutam*>. That the subject has absolute freedom <*libertatem absolutam*> because it is conscious of itself, that proves that it is not a subject being acted upon <*subjectum patiens*>, but rather [one] acting <*agens*>. To the extent I am conscious to myself of an active action, to that extent I act from an inner principle of activity according to the power of free choice, without an outer determination; only then do I have absolute spontaneity <*spontaneitatem absolutam*>. When I say: I think, I act, etc., then either the word I is applied falsely, or I am free. Were I not free, then I could not say: *I* do it, but rather I would have to say: I feel in me a desire to do, which someone has aroused in me. But when I say: I do it, that means spontaneity in the transcendental sense <*in sensu transcendentali*>. But now I am conscious to myself that I can say: I do; therefore I am conscious of no determination in me, and thus I act *absolutely freely*. Were I not free, but rather only a means by which the other does something immediately <*immediate*> in me, that I do, then I could not say: I do. I do, as action <*actio*>, cannot be used otherwise than as absolutely free. All practical objective propositions would have no sense if human beings were not free. All practi-

28:269

cal prescriptions would be useless; one then could not say: you should do this or that. But now there are such imperatives <*imperativos*> according to which I should do something; therefore all practical propositions, problematic as well as pragmatic and moral, must presuppose a freedom in me; consequently I must be the *first cause* of all actions. But since we have proven practical freedom in the Empirical Psychology, according to which we are free of necessitation by stimuli <*necessitatione a stimulis*>, then practical propositions can take place simply on that account; *therefore in that respect morality, which is also our most noble end, is certain.* But we must always think: we are in the Rational Psychology <*psychologia rationali*>, here we must not call upon any experience, but rather demonstrate absolute spontaneity <*spontaneitatem absolutam*> from principles of pure reason; *thus here I go out beyond the practical* and ask: how is such practical freedom possible according to which I act from an inner principle <*principio*>, determined by no outer cause? Thus the discussion is not of the will; later it surely can be applied to the free will; but here I rather am positing the I or the substrate <*substratum*> as a basis of all experience, and am affirming sheer transcendental predicates of it. In that case I am in rational psychology <*psychologia rationali*>. I or the soul has absolute spontaneity of actions <*spontaneitatem absolutam actionum*>. These are sheer transcendental concepts. But examining this proposition any further must still be postponed until later when *divine freedom* is discussed in the Natural Theology <*theologia naturali*>. It will still be hard to comprehend by speculative understanding how a derivative being <*ens derivativum*> can perform original acts <*actus originarios*>; but the reason that we cannot comprehend it lies in our understanding, *for we can never conceive the beginning*, but rather only what happens in the series of causes and effects. But the beginning is the boundary of the series, yet freedom makes wholly new divisions for a new beginning; it is on that account difficult to comprehend. But because the possibility of such freedom cannot be comprehended, it does not yet follow from this that, because we cannot comprehend it, there also could not be any freedom. *But freedom is a necessary condition of all our practical actions.* So just as there are other propositions that we do not comprehend but which presuppose a necessary condition, so are we also independent by the concept of transcendental freedom.

28:270

But it is asked whether there can be a stoic fate <*fatum stoicum*>, according to which our actions, which we call free, are^j necessary through the relation of the highest cause, to the extent each member in the order is already determined. If this were so, then no imputation would be valid. E.g., a Stoic said: by fate he had to steal from his master; but his master also had him hanged by fate. But this is sophistry, and although we cannot refute fatalism, another still cannot prove it. There is here, in any event,

---

^j We follow Lehmann in changing *sey* (in Pölitz) to *seyen* (270₂₀).

no way out, and we do well *if we remain standing where we cannot proceed further*. But with respect to the practical we cannot admit fatalism, because we find with ourselves that we are not determined to our actions by any cause.

Religion and morality accordingly remain secure. – The concept of freedom is practically adequate, but not speculatively. If we could explain free original actions from reason, then the concept would be speculatively adequate. But this we cannot do, because free actions are those which arise from the inner principle of all actions without any determination of an external cause. Now we cannot comprehend how the soul can perform such actions. This difficulty is no objection, but rather a subjective difficulty of our reason. An objection is an objective difficulty, but here reason has hindrances in comprehending the matter. But the matter in itself 28:271 suffers nothing here *if the difficulty lies in us.* Here the conditions are lacking under which reason can comprehend something; these are the determining grounds. But our free actions have no determining grounds, thus we also cannot comprehend them. This is a ground for comprehending the limits of the understanding, but not for denying the matter. But with respect to us the subjective difficulty is just as if it were an objective difficulty; *although the subjective hindrances of inconceivability are essentially different from the objective hindrances of impossibility.* –

SECOND SECTION OF RATIONAL PSYCHOLOGY

In the second section of rational psychology the human soul is considered in *comparison with other things*.

But here we consider the soul in comparison

1. with bodily natures, and
2. with other thinking natures.

If we compare the soul as an object of inner sense with the objects of outer sense, is it material or immaterial? Is it an object of outer or inner sense? The I shows that I have no concept of the soul other than of an object of inner sense. All objects of outer sense are material, and when they are present in space through impenetrability I thereby become aware of the objects of outer sense. But I am conscious of the soul through inner, and not through outer, sense; thus I comprehend that the soul is given to me as an object of inner sense. Further, we see that all actions of the soul, thinking, willing, etc., are not objects of outer sense. A thinking being, as such, cannot at all be an object of outer sense; we can perceive through outer sense neither thinking nor willing nor the faculty of pleasure and displeasure; and we cannot imagine how the soul as a thinking being should be an object of outer sense; but since it is not that, then it is also not material. Were the soul an object of outer sense, then it would have to

28:272 be such by virtue of impenetrability in space; for only thereby do we become aware of objects through outer sense. But because we are acquainted with the actions of the soul from the side that is no object of outer sense, the soul as well must not be an object of outer sense, but rather must be immaterial. But this we also cannot maintain so firmly and certainly, rather only so far as we are acquainted with it.

But we have already demonstrated that the soul is a substance, and then that it is a simple substance. From that *Wolff* believed already to have proved immateriality; but that is false; immateriality does not yet follow from simplicity, for the smallest part of a body is still actually something material and an object of outer sense. Although it is not immediately an actual object of outer sense, it can still become an actual object of outer sense through the putting together of many such small particles. Thus even if the soul were simple, it could still be material, and if it were put together out of other such simple parts, then it could become an actual object of outer sense. E.g., if we imagine a cubic inch filled with matter, and one asked: if the soul is merely simple, would it take up space there so that precisely such a simple part would have to be taken away, in whose position it would enter? Or would it have a place therein, without that happening? If the first is maintained, then it would have to follow that if I continue this with the second, third, fourth, and following souls, I ultimately remove all matter from the cubic inch and have the whole cubic inch full of souls, which would be present in space through impenetrability, without taking up a space. The soul can thus always be simple and yet material. But what is no object of outer sense, that must not in the least degree be something bodily; and no matter how many such simple parts are put together, it still need not become a noticeable object of outer sense, for it is immaterial. –

Now what is the source of this cognition? (The philosopher must always go back to the source of this cognition; this is better than if he knows all proofs by heart.) *From what* can a philosopher prove the immateriality of the soul, and *how far* can he go? He can take the thoughts from nothing more than the expression: *I*, which expresses the object of inner 28:273 sense. Immateriality thus lies in the concept of the *I*. – We *cannot prove a priori* the immateriality of the soul, but rather *only so much: that all properties and actions of the soul cannot be cognized from materiality.* But these properties do not yet prove that our soul should have nothing outer; rather only so much, that I cannot assume materiality as a ground of explanation of actions. I thus exclude only materiality. For if I wanted[k] to assume it, then I would not cognize anything more of the soul. Thus one may not arbitrarily assume materiality; *but for immateriality I have a ground.* Here one could even deceive someone, and prove from that immateriality, al-

---

[k] We follow Lehmann in changing *sollte* (in Pölitz) to *wollte* (273₉).

though it does not follow from it. But one still has a ground for immateriality, and that is this: everything that constitutes a part in the whole of space is between two boundaries. The boundaries of space are points; whatever is between two points is in space, whatever is in space is divisible, accordingly there is no simple part of matter, but rather each matter is in space, and thus is divisible to infinity. Now if the soul were material, then it would at least have to be a simple part of matter (because it is already proved that the soul is simple). But now no part of matter is simple, for that is a contradiction; thus the soul is also not material, but rather immaterial.

Now we consider the soul *in comparison with thinking natures*, and indeed its agreement with animal souls and with other spirits. From the concept of the immateriality of the soul one came to the concept of spirits. An immaterial being that is considered separately from all matter, and can think for itself, is a *spirit*. The concept and doctrine of spirits in psychology came about in such a manner. The path which we have taken in considering the soul is this: that we showed the soul to be a substance; a simple and freely-acting substance; an immaterial substance. Now the question is: *is the soul also a spirit?* Of a spirit it is required not only that it be an immaterial being but also that it be a thinking being itself separated from all matter. – If I confer the name soul on my immaterial being, then it follows from the meaning of the word that it is a being which stands not only in connection but rather also in interaction *<commercio>* with a body. *Now if this being is separated from the body, then the name soul also ceases.* Now 28:274 it is asked: Is the soul merely an immaterial being that one can think only in interaction *<commercio>* with the body, *or is it a spirit*, [i.e., something] that can also think separated from the body? Here it is not being investigated whether the soul is actually that now, but rather whether it has a faculty (disregarding that it stands in interaction *<commercio>* with the body now) for thinking even without community with the body; that is, whether it can also survive and live as a spirit separated from the body. We will thus compare the human soul, which is connected with the body, with beings that stand in no community at all with bodies, *and these are spirits*; or with such beings which stand in the same community with the body as the human soul, which are beings that have mere sensibility and power of representation, and these are *animal souls*. We will thus speak:

a. on the soul of the brute *<de anima bruti>*, whose community depends on bodies;

b. on spirit *<de spiritu>*, which is in no community at all with the body, and

c. on the human soul *<de anima humana>*, of which we have mainly spoken so far, which does stand in community with the body, but is independent in that it can also live and think without body as a spirit.

But when we compare the soul of human beings with animals souls and with other spirits, then one must not hope to hear many secrets and discoveries here which no one else knows, and which the philosopher has obtained from a secret source; but one will still await a discovery here which has cost much trouble and which only a few know: namely *to cognize the limits of reason and of philosophy and to comprehend* how far reason can go here. We will thus become acquainted here with *our ignorance*, and comprehend *its ground*; why it is impossible that any philosopher can go farther in this, and also will not go, and *if we know that, then we already know a great deal.*

Animals are not mere machines or matter, rather they have souls;²¹ for everything in the whole of nature is either inanimate or animate. All matter as matter (matter as such <*materia, qua talis*>) is inanimate. From what do we know that? The concept which we have of matter is this: matter is an extended, impenetrable, inert thing <*materia est extensum impenetrabile iners*>. When, e.g., we perceive a mote on a paper, then we look to see whether it moves. If it does not move of itself, then we hold it to be inanimate matter, which is inert <*iners*>, and which would remain lying for all eternity if it were not moved by something else. But as soon as a matter moves, then we look to see whether it moved itself voluntarily. If we perceive that in the mote, then we say that it is *animate*, it is *an animal*. An animal is thus an animated matter, for life¹ is the faculty for determining oneself from an inner principle according to the power of choice. But matter, as matter, has no inner principle of self-activity, no spontaneity to move itself, rather all matter that is animate has an inner principle which is separated from the object of outer sense, and is an object of inner sense; there is in it a separate principle of inner sense. An inner principle of self-activity is just thinking and willing, only thereby can something be moved by inner sense; this is simply a principle for acting according to will and the power of choice. Thus if a matter moves, then it follows that there is in it such a separate principle of self-activity. But only a being that has cognition is capable of this principle of thinking and willing. Matter can move only by means of such a principle. But such a principle of matter is the soul of matter. Thus: all matter which lives is alive not as matter but rather has a principle of life and is animated. But to the extent matter is animated, to that extent it is *ensouled*. A principle of life thus underlies animals, and that is the soul. –

We are to undertake a comparison of these souls of animals and of our souls, *a priori* without any experience, and see wherein the difference consists; but if we are to cognize beings that have a power of representation, and indeed *a priori*, where do we get the differences from when they are not at all given to us? Are we to cognize souls that are outside of us,

28:275

---

¹ G: *belebt* (animated), *Leben* (life).

and for which we have no data <*data*> at all? But this difference and the data <*data*> for it we take again from ourselves and from the concept of the I. We are acquainted with our soul merely through inner sense; but we also have an outer sense; accordingly all difference will rest merely on our outer and inner sense. When we imagine beings *a priori*, then we will notice the difference not by degree, but rather by species; the difference and the comparison must thus rest on our outer and inner sense. Accordingly we can imagine beings that have a faculty of outer sense but forgo the faculty of inner sense, and these are animals. 28:276

Accordingly, animals will have all representations of the outer senses; they will forgo only those representations which rest on inner sense, on the consciousness of oneself, in short, on the concept of the I. Accordingly they will have no understanding and no reason, for all actions of the understanding and of reason are possible only insofar as one is conscious of oneself. They will have no general cognition through reflection, no identity of the representations, also no connections of the representations according to subject and predicate, according to ground and consequence, according to the whole and according to the parts; for those are all consequences of the consciousness which animals lack.

We can attribute to animals an analogue of reason <*analogon rationis*>, which involves connection of representations according to the laws of sensibility, from which the same effects follow as from a connection according to concepts. Animals are accordingly different from human souls not in degree but rather in species; for however much animal souls increase in their sensible faculties, consciousness of their self, inner sense, still cannot be attained thereby. Even though they have better phenomena in sensibility than we do, they still lack inner sense.

Since we have inferred from the nature of spirit that everything that is a principle of life must also live, we must also concede such to the souls of animals. Accordingly, just as our intellectuality will increase in the other world, sensibility in animals can also increase, but they will never become equal to us. Now we can think problematically that such beings exist which have no inner sense, for it is no contradiction to suppose such. How many phenomena can be explained, without assuming an inner sense, from the faculty of outer sensibility in such beings that have no inner sense? The consciousness of one's self, the concept of the I, does not occur with such beings that have no inner sense; accordingly no non-rational animal can think: I am; from this follows the difference that beings that have such a concept of the I possess *personality*. 28:277

This is psychological*[m]* personality, to the extent they can say: I am. It further follows that such beings have *freedom*, and everything can be imputed to them; and this is *practical personality*, which has consequences

---

[m] We follow Lehmann in changing *physikalische* (in Pölitz) to *psychologische* (277₃).

in morality. But if one wanted to introduce phenomena which can be explained merely from outer sensibility, then one could explain the whole empirical psychology of animals quite well. But because this is interwoven with physics, we would stray thereby too far from rational psychology <*psychologia rationali*>. But we see from the actions of animals undertakings which we would not be able to bring about other than through understanding and reason. Accordingly sensibility is with us such a state as with animals, except theirs is far advanced over ours. But for this privation we have received compensation through the consciousness of ourselves and through the understanding that follows from it. We are also not at all required to assume reflection in animals, rather we can derive all of this from the formative power. Accordingly we ascribe to these beings a faculty of sensation, reproductive imagination, etc., but all only sensible as a lower faculty, and not connected with consciousness. We can explain all phenomena of animals from this outer sensibility and from mechanical grounds of their bodies, without assuming consciousness or inner sense. The philosopher must not increase the principles of cognitions without cause.

Since we have now compared our soul with beings that are *below* it, we want now to compare it as well with beings that are *above* it. Since we have an outer and inner sense, and we can think of beings that have merely an outer sense, we can on the other hand also think of beings which have no outer sense at all, which do not at all meddle with the senses, and thus are immaterial. Accordingly we can imagine immaterial beings that are gifted with consciousness of themselves. An immaterial thinking being that is gifted with consciousness of itself (from which it already follows that it is also a rational being) is a spirit. From spirit must be distinguished that which is *spiritual*. *Spiritual beings* are those which are indeed connected with a body, but whose representations, whose thinking and willing, can continue even when they are separated from the body. Now it is asked: is

28:278 the human soul a spiritual being? – If it can continue to live even without a body, then it is spiritual; and if the souls of animals can also do that, then they are of spiritual nature as well. But a spirit is that which is actually separated from the body, which can nevertheless think and will without being an object of outer sense. Now what can we cognize *a priori* of spirits? *We can think of spirits only problematically, i.e., no a priori ground can be introduced to repudiate them.* Experience teaches us that when we think, our body comes into play; but we do not comprehend that it is necessary. We can quite easily imagine beings that have no body at all, and nevertheless can think and will. Accordingly we can problematically assume thinking rational beings with consciousness of themselves which are immaterial. Something can be assumed problematically when it is absolutely clear that it is *possible*. We cannot prove it apodictically, but neither can anyone refute us, [saying] that such spirits do not exist. Likewise we cannot demonstrate the existence of God apodictically; but there is also no one in the position to prove to me the opposite, for from where will he derive it? – Now we can say nothing more of these spirits than what a spirit, which is separated from the body, can do. They are no object of outer sense, thus they are not in space. *We can say no more here; otherwise we degenerate into phantoms of the brain.* The concept of animal souls and of higher spirits is only a game of our concepts. The result is: we experience in ourselves that we are an object of outer and inner sense. Now we can imagine beings that have merely outer sense, and these are animal souls; but we can also imagine beings that have merely an inner sense, and these are spirits. When we imagine beings that have an inner as well as an outer sense, then these are *human souls.*

We can prove nothing of this, but rather can only assume it problematically, in that the impossibility of it cannot be demonstrated. Fortunately experience still teaches us that there actually are such beings of which we say in rational psychology <*psychologia rationali*> that they have only an outer sense; but that there are beings which have merely an inner sense, *of that experience cannot possibly teach us.*

THIRD SECTION OF RATIONAL PSYCHOLOGY 28:279

In the *third* section of rational psychology the *connection of the soul with other things* is treated.

We treat first of the *connection of the soul with the body*, or of the interaction <*commercio*> between the two.

An interaction <*commercium*> is a reciprocal determination. The dependence of a determination which is not reciprocal is no interaction <*commercium*>, but rather a *connection.*" God stands in such a one-sided connection with the world. But the interaction <*commercium*> between soul and body is a reciprocal dependence of determination. Accordingly we ask first: how is such an interaction <*commercium*> possible between a thinking being and a body? (I cannot say between the *soul* and the body, for the concept of soul already presupposes an interaction <*commercium*>.) The ground of the difficulty in comprehending this interaction <*commercii*> rests on this: the soul is an object of inner sense, and the body is an object of outer sense. I am aware of nothing internal with the body, and nothing external with the soul. Now it cannot be conceived through reason how that which is an object of inner sense is supposed to be a ground of that which is an object of outer sense. Thinking and willing are mere objects of inner sense. Were thinking and willing a motive power,

---

" The "connection" in the previous two paragraphs was *Verknüpfung*; here it is *Verbindung* (279₈). Although generally used synonymously, here we find *Verbindung* used in the weaker sense of a one-sided, or non-reciprocal, connection.

then they*o* would be an object of outer sense itself. But now because thinking and willing are merely objects of inner sense (thus a ground of inner determination), then this is difficult to comprehend, how these can be a ground of outer determination. And since on the other hand motion, as an object of outer sense, is a ground of outer determination, it is hard to determine how this can then be a ground of inner determinations and representations. We cannot have insight through reason into the reciprocal determination between thinking and willing and between*p* moving. *The impossibility of comprehending this through reason, however, does not at all prove the inner impossibility of the matter itself.* But through experience we can comprehend it; and indeed this applies not here alone, but rather all basic powers are given to us through experience, and none can be comprehended through reason. We are thus acquainted only with those powers in the body whose effects are phenomena of outer sense; and in the soul we are acquainted with no other powers than those whose effects are phenomena of inner sense. Now how the powers of outer sense of the body can be grounds of the phenomena of the soul, and the powers of the soul can be*q* grounds of the phenomena of the body, cannot at all be comprehended. But not only is the interaction <*commercium*> between the soul and body difficult to comprehend, but rather also the interaction <*commercium*> between bodies among themselves. We can indeed comprehend it, but only if we already assume powers of interaction <*commercii*> beforehand. E.g., if I assume impenetrability, then this is already a basic power of the interaction <*commercii*>. No being whose reason is not intuitive, but rather discursive, can comprehend this basic power of the interaction <*commercii*> among bodies. Accordingly all systems of explaining the soul's interaction with the body <*systemata explicandi commercium animae cum corpore*> are fruitless and in vain; for no system can explain how motion arises from thinking, and the reverse, thinking from motion, because one cannot comprehend any basic power. One has already philosophized enough if one only comes *up to the basic power.*[22] All systems of explaining interaction <*systemata explicandi commercium*> amount to that because they see the unlikeness between thinking and moving. Therefore they fabricate in every way because they fancy that natural influence is impossible. But with respect to the soul, the phenomena show that the will has an influence on the body and the reverse, that the soul has a power to move the body. But we can give no ground of that, for it is a basic power, a basic faculty. Accordingly the interaction <*commercium*>, because it happens according to determinate laws, is a natural influence, and the commu-

28:280

---

o We follow Lehmann in changing *Wäre . . . wäre es* (in Pölitz) to *Wären . . . wären sie* (279₂₁₋₂₂).

p This extra "between" (G: *zwischen*) seems to have been inserted unnecessarily.

q A *seyn können* omitted by Lehmann (following *Körper*) has been replaced (280₄).

nity is natural. Because one believed that the interaction <*commercium*> could not possibly be natural, one put a third being into play and said, like Leibniz: either God has already arranged the actions of the soul and the body in the beginning, so that they agree, or like *Descartes*, that at each occasion God so arranged the actions of each that they agree. But of the interaction <*commercium*> between bodies among themselves as well as that between the soul and the body, we can comprehend nothing other than that it is possible, insofar as all substances are here through one [being]; on that account they stand in community. But *how* this happens between the soul and the body is not to be comprehended.

Now since the soul stands in interaction <*commercio*> with the body, we ask: where does the soul have its *seat* in the body? The location of the soul in the world is determined by the location of the body; *my soul is there where my body is*. But where in the body does the soul have its seat? The location of the body in the world is determined only by *outer* sense; now since the soul is an object of *inner* sense, but no location can be determined by inner sense: *the location of the soul in the body also cannot be determined*, for no outer relation can be determined by inner actions. But the soul intuits itself only through inner sense: thus it cannot intuit itself in a location and be conscious of a location. I cannot feel the place in the body where the soul resides, for otherwise I would have to intuit myself through an outer sense; but I intuit myself through inner sense. As little as an eye can intuit itself, just as little can the soul intuit itself externally. But it can be conscious of outer parts of the body, especially of those which contain most of the causes of its sensations. But the cause of all sensations is the nervous system. Without nerves we cannot sense anything outer. But the root of all nerves is the brain; the brain is accordingly aroused with each sensation because all nerves concentrate themselves in the brain; accordingly, all sensations concentrate themselves in the brain. Thus the soul must put the *seat of its sensations* in the brain, as the *location of all conditions* of the sensations. *But that is not the location of the soul itself*, but rather the location from which all nerves, consequently all sensations as well, arise. We find that the brain harmonizes with all actions of the power of choice of the soul. I feel each part in particular. When, e.g., I hold a finger to the fire, then I experience pain in it; but in the end all sensations from every particular part of the body are concentrated in the brain, the stem of all nerves; for if the nerves from one part of the body are cut, then of course we feel nothing from that part. Accordingly the principle of all sensations must be in the brain. Now one imagines that the soul has its seat there in the brain so that it can move all nerves, and can itself be affected by the nerves. But we do not feel the seat of the soul in the brain, but rather only that the brain harmonizes with all the alterations of its soul. E.g., the head aches from pondering. We do not intuit the location, but rather only infer that the brain is the seat of the soul, because the

28:281

91

28:282 soul works there the most. When we imagine a position in the brain which is the first principle of the stem of the nerves where all nerves run together and end in one point, which is called the seat of the senses <*sensorium commune*>, but which no physician <*medicus*> has seen, then the question arises, does the soul reside in this seat of the senses <*sensorio communi*>? Has it taken up a little spot there from which it directs the whole body, somewhat like an organist can direct the whole organ from one location; or does it have no location at all in the body, so that the body itself is its location? Granted, if the soul took up a little spot in the brain where it plays on our nerves as on an organ, then we could believe that if we had gone through all the parts of the body we ultimately would have to come upon this little spot where the soul resides. Now if one took away this little spot, the whole human being might still be there, but the location would be lacking where the organist is supposed to play, as though on an organ: but this is thought very materialistically. But if the soul is no object of the outer senses, then the conditions of outer intuitions also do not belong to it. The condition of outer intuition, however, is space. Now since it is no object of outer intuition, it is also *not in space*, but rather works only in space; – and although we say by analogy <*analogice*>, it is in space, we must still not take this in a bodily way. Likewise one says that God is in a church. Accordingly we maintain the second, namely: the soul has no particular location in the body; but its location in the world is determined by the body, and it is immediately connected with the body. We do not comprehend the possibility of this interaction <*commercii*>; but we must not posit the conditions of this interaction <*commercii*> simply as they are among bodies among themselves, namely through impenetrability, for otherwise it becomes material. To indicate a location and place in the body for it is nonsensical and materialistic.

Now we consider *the soul* in interaction <*commercio*> *with the body* according to time; and in particular the state of the soul in the *beginning* of the interaction <*commercii*>, or at *birth*; in interaction <*commercio*> itself, or in *life*; and at the *end* of the interaction <*commercii*>, or at *death*.

Life consists in the interaction <*commercio*> of the soul with the body; the beginning of life is the beginning of the interaction <*commercii*>, the end of life is the end of the interaction <*commercii*>. The beginning of the interaction <*commercii*> is birth, the end of the interaction <*com-*

28:283 *mercii*> is death. The *duration* of the interaction <*commercii*> is life. The beginning of life is birth; but this is the beginning not of the life of the soul, but rather of the human being. The end of life is death, but this is the end not of the life of the soul, but rather of the human being. Birth, life, and death are thus only *states* of the soul, for the soul is a simple substance, thus it also cannot be produced when the body is produced, and also not decomposed when the body is decomposed; *for the body is only the form of the soul.* The beginning or the birth of the human being is thus only the beginning of the interaction <*commercii*>, or the altered state of the soul; and the end or the death of the human being is only the end of the interaction <*commercii*>, or the altered state of the soul. But the beginning of the interaction <*commercii*> or the birth of the human being is not the beginning of the principle of life, and the end of the interaction <*commercii*> or the death of the human being is not the end of the principle of life; for the principle of life does not arise through birth and also does not stop through death. The principle of life is a simple substance. But from substantiality or simplicity it does not at all follow that the birth of the human being is the beginning of the substance, and the death of the human being the end of the substance; for a simple substance does not arise and pass away according to natural laws. Therefore the substance remains, even if the body passes away, and thus the substance must also have been there when the body arose. – The substance always remains unaltered; accordingly birth, life, and death are only different states of the soul. But a state *already presupposes an existence*, for the beginning is no state, but birth is a state of the soul, thus no beginning of the soul.

Since we have considered the state of the soul at the beginning of the interaction <*commercii*>, now we must discuss the soul *before* the beginning of the connections, or its state before birth, and *after* the end of the connection, or its state after death. Between the state of the soul before birth and after death there is a great agreement. For if the soul had not lived before the union with the body, then we could not infer that it would also live after the union with it. For if it had arisen with the body, then it could also cease with it. For that which it is supposed to be after the union it can also have been *from just the same grounds* before the union. But we can also infer from the state after death, which we will prove, to the state 28:284 of the soul before birth; for from the proofs that we will give for the survival of the soul after death it *appears to follow* that *before* birth we were in a pure, spiritual life; and that through birth the soul, so to speak, came into a dungeon, into a cave, which hinders it in its spiritual life. But here the question is whether the soul in its spiritual life before birth had a full use of its powers and faculties; whether it possessed all the cognitions, the experiences of the world, or whether it acquired them for the first time through the body? We answer: from the fact that the soul was in a pure, spiritual life before birth, it still does not at all follow that it had in it such a full use of its powers and faculties, and just the same cognitions of the world (which it acquired only after birth); but rather it follows that the soul was in a spiritual life, had a spiritual power of life, already possessed all abilities and faculties; but such that these abilities developed only through the body, and that it acquired all the cognitions that it has of the world only through the body, and thus had to prepare itself through the body for future survival. *The state of the soul before birth was thus without consciousness of the world and of itself.*

ABOUT THE STATE OF THE SOUL AFTER DEATH

Now we want to consider the state of the soul *after* death.

Here we have two questions to pose:[23]

1. whether the soul *will* live and survive[r] after death, and
2. whether by its nature it *must* live and survive, i.e., whether it is *immortal*.

If the soul lives, it does not yet follow that by its nature it necessarily must live; for after all it could be kept alive by God, out of certain intentions of reward or improvement. But then, if it lived only *contingently*, then the time could come where it could cease to live. But if it is immortal *by its nature*, then in a *necessary way* it must always survive. Accordingly we will have to prove here not the *contingent* life of the soul (that it will merely live follows already from its substantiality, in that every substance survives, the substance of bodies as well; for when wood is burned, the parts are merely decomposed, but the substance always remains), but rather that it is *immortal. Immortality is the natural necessity of living.* To prove this involves much more than a merely contingent life, which can be demonstrated with many proofs taken from the justice, wisdom, goodness, etc., of God. But that proof which is taken from the nature and the concept of the matter itself is always the only possible proof, and this is *transcendental.*[24] Many proofs of a matter cannot be given *a priori.* The other proofs for the immortality of the soul that one otherwise has are not proofs for its immortality, but rather prove only the *hope* for a future life. The proof for the immortality of the soul, which is taken from the nature and from the concept, rests on this: life is nothing more than a faculty for acting from an *inner* principle, from spontaneity. Now it lies already in the general concept of the soul that it is a subject that[s] contains spontaneity in itself for determining itself from the inner principle. It is the source of life which animates the body. Now because all matter is lifeless[25] (for that is the concept of matter that we have of it, because we do not know it otherwise), everything that belongs to life cannot come from matter. The act <*actus*> of spontaneity cannot proceed from an outer principle, i.e., there cannot be outer causes of life, for otherwise spontaneity would not be in life. That lies already in the concept of life, since it is a faculty for determining actions from an *inner* principle. Thus no body can be a cause of life. For because body is matter, and all matter is lifeless, the body is not a ground of life, but rather a hindrance to life that opposes the principle of life. The ground of life must rather lie in another substance, namely, in the soul; a

28:285

---

[r] The German *fortdauern*, which in this context is translated as "to survive," is elsewhere translated as "to continue" or "to endure."
[s] We follow Lehmann in changing *Subject sey. Die* (in Pölitz) to *Subject sey, das* (285₂₁₋₂₂).

ground which, however, rests not on the connection with the body, but rather on the inner principle of its spontaneity. Accordingly neither the beginning of the life of the soul, nor the survival of its life will proceed from the body. Thus even if the body ceases, the principle of life still 28:286 remains, which the act <*actus*> of life has exercised independently of the body, and thus the same act <*actus*> of life must also exercise [it] unhindered now, after the separation from the body.

Life in a human being is *twofold*: animal and spiritual life. The animal is the life of the human being as human, and here the body is necessary for the human being to live. The other life is the spiritual life, where the soul, independently of the body, must continue to exercise this same act <*actus*> of life. The body is necessary for the animal life; the soul is in connection with the body then; it works in the body and animates it. Now if the machine of the body is destroyed so that the soul can no longer work in it, then the animal life does cease, but not the spiritual. But one could say: all actions of the soul, e.g., thinking, willing, etc., happen by means of the body, which experience shows; thus the body is the condition of the life of the soul. Of course, as long as the spirit represents a soul, as long as the spirit stands in interaction <*commercio*> with the body, so long also are the actions of the soul dependent <*dependent*> on the body; for otherwise there would be no interaction <*commercium*>. As long as the animal lives, the soul is the principle of life; but the body is the instrument <*organon; G: Instrument*> through which the living acts <*actus*> of the soul are exercised in the world. If we thus consider two substances in interaction <*commercio*>, then of course it cannot be otherwise than that the one substance is a condition of the other. Therefore, e.g., the soul cannot think when the body is sick. All sensible cognitions rest on the body, for it is the instrument <*organon*> of the senses. As long as the human being lives, the soul must[1] be able to bring forth its sensible representations through the brain, as though drawn on a slate.

With a soul that is attached to a body, it is as with a human being who is fastened to a cart.[26] If this human being moves, then the cart must move with him. But no one will maintain that the motion proceeds from the cart; likewise the actions proceed not from the body but rather from the soul. As long as the human being is attached to the cart, this is the condition of his motion. If he is freed of it, then he will be able to move more easily, thus this was a hindrance to his motion. But as long as he is still bound to it, so long will the movement also be easier for him the better the condition of the instrument. Now if the soul is once bound to 28:287 the body, then the alteration of the hindrances is a promotion of life; just as motion is easier when the wheels on the cart are greased, although it would be even easier upon liberation from the cart. Thus a good constitu-

---

[1] We follow Lehmann in omitting a *so* (in Pölitz) preceding *muss* (286_{28}).

tion of the body is also a promotion of life, as long as the soul is bound to the body, although the promotion of life would be greater still upon liberation from the body. For since the body is lifeless matter, it is a hindrance to life. But as long as the soul is bound with the body, it must put up with this hindrance and attempt to lighten it in every way. But now if the body wholly ceases, then the soul is freed from its hindrance, and only from now on does it properly begin to live. Thus death is not the absolute suspension of life, but rather a liberation from the hindrances to a complete life. This lies already in every understanding and in the nature of the matter. The consciousness of the mere I proves that life lies not in the body, but rather in a separate principle which is different from the body; consequently that this principle <*principium*> can survive without the body as well, and its life is not diminished thereby but rather increased. This is the only proof that can be given a priori, which is derived from the cognition and the nature of the soul, which we have comprehended *a priori*.

Now we can introduce yet another *a priori* proof, but from the cognition of another being.

But which being do we cognize *a priori*? We do cognize the existence of our soul from experience, but its nature we comprehend *a priori*. That being which we can cognize *a priori* must be absolutely necessary. I can cognize contingent beings only through experience; I would know nothing of them if they were not given; but what is necessary, of that I comprehend *a priori* that it must be absolutely necessary. This absolutely necessary being is the divine being. Now if we want to infer the immortality of the soul from the necessity of this divine being, then we cannot cognize this *a priori* from the divine nature, for then the soul would have to be a part of the divine nature. Thus if I cannot cognize it from the nature of the essence of the soul, then what is left? Answer: *freedom*; for nature and freedom are all that can be cognized in a being. Accordingly from the cognition of the divine will we will infer to the necessary survival of the soul. This is the moral or (because the cognition of God is involved) the theological-moral proof. It rests on this: all our actions stand under practical rules of obligation. This practical rule is the holy moral law. This law we comprehend *a priori*; it lies in the nature of actions that they should be so and not otherwise, which we comprehend *a priori*. But what matters here are primarily dispositions, that they are adequate to the holy law, where the *motive* is also moral. But all morality consists in the summation of *rules* according to which we *become worthy to be happy* when we act according to them. It is a guide not of actions through which we *become* happy, but rather only of those through which we become *worthy* of happiness. It teaches only the *conditions* under which it is possible to attain happiness. Through reason I comprehend these conditions, this law. But now there is no way in this world to attain happiness through these actions. We see that the actions through which we make ourselves worthy of happiness cannot procure happiness for us here. How often must honesty languish? At court one does not prosper through uprightness. But now since I do comprehend the law, but on the other hand have no promise at all, and cannot at all hope that my actions will be rewarded some day if they are adequate to this law; since I comprehend that I made myself worthy of happiness by having followed this law, but on the other hand cannot at all hope ever to share in this happiness; then all moral rules have no power; they are deficient because they cannot procure what they promise. It appears to be better that one make no effort at all to live adequately to this law, but rather attempt to promote one's happiness in the world as much as possible. In this manner the cleverest rogue is the happiest, if only he knows how to be clever enough not to get caught; and he who endeavored to live according to the moral law would be a proper fool if he set aside the advantages in the world and hankered after such things as the moral law promises him, but cannot deliver.

Here theology, or the cognition of God, comes to our aid. I compre- 28:289 hend an absolutely necessary being which is in the position to apportion to me that happiness which I have made myself worthy of through observation of the moral law. But since I see that in this world I cannot at all share in the happiness of which I have made myself worthy, but rather quite often must sacrifice much of my temporal happiness through my moral conduct and through my integrity, then there must be *another world*, or a *state where the well-being of a creature is adequate to its proper conduct.*" Now if a human being assumes another world, then he must also arrange his actions according to it; otherwise he acts like a knave. But if he does *not* assume the other world, then he would act like a fool if he wanted to arrange his actions in conformity with the law which he comprehends through reason; for then the most evil knave would be the best and smartest, because here he is attempting merely to promote his happiness, because after all he cannot hope for any future happiness.

This moral proof is practically adequate enough for believing in a future state. The human being on whom it is supposed to have its effect must have *already* embraced moral convictions beforehand; then he does not need such a proof any more; he never hears the objections that are made; for him it is fully adequate. This is the incentive to virtue, and whoever wanted to introduce the opposite suspends all moral laws and all incentives to virtue; then moral principles are only chimeras. But according to speculation, according to logical correctness and according to its standard this proof is *not adequate* enough. For because we do not see that vice is punished in this life and virtue is rewarded, *it does not at all follow from this that there is another world;*[27] for we indeed cannot know

---

" *Wohlbefinden* (well-being) and *Wohlverhalten* (proper conduct) (289₁₀₋₁₁).

whether the vices and virtues are not already rewarded and punished here. It can well be that each already feels his punishment here; and even if his vices and crimes appear to us to be greater than their punishment, then it can well be that the crimes which we hold as being so punishable are just as human and just as small according to his temperament as with another who commits lesser crimes, but has a better constitution of temperament, and can more readily refrain from vice. If on the other hand we see the virtuous as not as happy as he has deserved, then perhaps his virtue was yet quite tainted, and thus perhaps he also did not deserve so great a happiness. Further one could object: even if we assume that for this reason there is a future, so that each will be rewarded or punished:* one need not for that reason live eternally in order to be rewarded or punished. When each has received his reward or punishment, then that is the end of him and his life is over; for the relation of the crime to the eternity of punishments is obviously too large, and the same is also true of the rewards; thus life can always stop once everything is rewarded and punished. Further, quite a few persons would not need to appear before the divine seat of judgment at all merely for rewards or punishments because they cannot have exercised either good or evil actions, e.g., small children who died early, savages who have no use of reason and know nothing of a moral law. Thus according to this proof all persons of that sort could not assume any reckoning on a future life, and even if the others were transferred into the future state, they still would remain in it only as long as their rewards and punishments last.

28:290

Accordingly it is not enough that one prove that the soul will live after death; rather, it must also be proven that it must by its nature live *necessarily*; for otherwise, if I am supposed to die sometime, even if it should happen after several thousand centuries, then I will rather die soon than spend yet*ᵛ* a long time with worries and view the comedy. –

Thus from this proof also no necessary survival can be demonstrated. But the previous proof, which is given from the nature of the soul and from the concept of spirit, proves that the soul, according to its spiritual nature, should necessarily survive eternally. Now if the soul is already *immortal* by its nature, then this is true for all, small children as well as savages, for the nature of all souls is the same. But the moral proof is an *adequate ground of belief.* But what can this belief bring about? The cognition of a being who will reward and punish all actions in accordance with this pure and holy moral law. Whoever believes that, lives morally. But the

28:291

---

* [Author's note] One could just as well ask here: Why do we not already appear here before the divine judge? Why must we first die? But if one wanted to venture so deeply into questions, one could also ask: Why does a horse not have six feet and two horns?

ᵛ A *noch* (following *dass ich*) omitted by Lehmann has been replaced (290₂₆).

mere concept cannot move him to it; accordingly, this moral proof is adequate practically for an honorable man; but a rogue denies not only the law but also its author.

The third proof is the empirical one which is derived from psychology. It is taken from the nature of the soul *so far as it is borrowed from experience*. We essay, namely, whether we can derive a proof from the experience that we have of the nature of the soul. – We note in experience that the powers of the soul increase just like the powers of the body, and decrease just like the powers of the body. Just as the body decreases, so the soul decreases as well. But from that it still does not at all follow that: if the body decreases, and entirely ceases,^w the soul also would entirely cease with it. The body is indeed the condition of animal life; accordingly the animal life does indeed cease, but not yet the entire life. But this empirical proof still cannot at all demonstrate the *immortality* of the soul. The general reason why we cannot demonstrate the future survival of the soul without the body from the observations and experiences of the human mind, is: because all of these experiences and observations happen *in connection with the body*. We cannot set up any experiences in life other than in connection with the body. Accordingly these experiences cannot prove what we could be *without* the body, for of course they have happened *with* the body. If a human being could disembody himself, then the experience that he might set up then could prove what he would be *without* a body. But since such experience is not possible, one cannot demonstrate without this experience what the soul will be without the body. But this empirical proof has a *negative* use, namely in that we cannot derive from experience any certain inference *against* the life of the soul; for from that, that the body ceases, it still does not at all follow that the soul will also cease. – Thus no opponent can find an argument *from experience* which would demonstrate the mortality of the soul. The immortality of the soul is thus at least secured against all objections that are derived from experience.

The fourth proof is empirical-psychological, but from cosmological grounds, and this is the analogical proof. Here the immortality of the soul is inferred from analogy with the entirety of nature. – Analogy is a proportion of concepts, where from the relation between two members that I know I bring out the relation of a third member, that I know, to a fourth member,^x that I do *not* know. The proof in itself is the following: in the entirety of nature we find that no powers, no faculty, no instruments belong to either inanimate or animate beings which are not aimed toward a certain *use* or *end*. But we find in the soul such powers and faculties

28:292

---

^w We follow Lehmann in omitting a *dass* (preceding *auch* in Pölitz) (291₁₅).
^x We follow Lehmann in changing *zum Verhältnis des dritten Gliedes, das ich kenne, das Verhältnis des vierten Gliede* (in Pölitz) to *das Verhältniss des dritten Gliedes, das ich kenne, zum vierten Gliede* (292₅₋₆).

which have no determinate end in this life; thus these faculties (since nothing in nature is without use or end), if they here have no use and determinate end here, still must have a use *somewhere*; there must thus be a state where the powers can be used. Thus it can be supposed of the soul that a future world must be in store for it where it can employ and use all of its powers. If we go through this proposition piece by piece, then we find through experience in the whole of nature that all animals have no organs, no powers and faculties in vain, but rather that they all have their use and determinate end. Now it is asked: Are the powers of the human soul so constituted that their use stretches only over this world; or are there also abilities and faculties in it that have no use and determinate end at all in this life? If we investigate this, then we will find the latter confirmed. We need assume only the faculty of cognition of the soul to see that this stretches much further than the needs of this life and the determinations in this world require. Several sciences prove this. Mathematics shows that our faculty of cognition stretches far beyond the boundaries of our present determination.*ʸ* We possess a desire to know what is the case with the whole structure of creation; we contrive observations with great effort; our desire to know stretches over every bright point of the heavens, as astronomy proves. Now it is asked, do all these efforts which consist in the satisfaction of our desire to know have the slightest use for our present life? It is quite well known that all the sciences through which we satisfy 28:293 our desire to know do not have the slightest use for*ᶻ* our life in this world, in that many nations exist which know nothing at all of it, who are quite indifferent to the Copernican system, and who seem quite content with the lack of this insight. One can always live without such sciences; indeed, the most important point of astronomy is precisely the least interesting. The calendar and navigation would easily be the most prominent use that we have of it in this world; but one could live without that as well if one should do no more here than *just* live. These are also the consequences of the luxury of the understanding, which do not aim at this life. For all that we can live without the luxury that navigation brings our way. The worth of our person does not consist in that, that we adorn ourselves with wares and clothes from foreign regions of the world; thus it also has no determinate end in this life. But our desire to know stretches even further. A human being investigates and asks: what was he before birth? What will he be after death? He goes even further and asks: where does the world come from? Is it infinite or contingent, or from eternity, and does it have a cause? How is this cause constituted? All these cognitions do not at all interest me in this life. If I were for this world alone, what need did I have

---

ʸ The term *Bestimmung* (determination) can also be translated as "vocation," but it is related to *bestimmt* (determinate, definite).
ᶻ We follow Lehmann in changing *auf* (in Pölitz) to *für* (293,₁).

to know where I or the world come from, and who the cause of the world is, and how it is constituted; if I am and can live only here. Now since all these faculties cannot be in vain, they must have their use in some other state. Even those ends which in this life can be the most interesting, e.g., how a good beer, etc., can be made, appear in our consciousness as quite inferior; on the other hand, investigations which have no determinate use here seem to be the determinate and higher end. Thus it would be not only useless, but also nonsensical to raise one's powers beyond one's determination, end, and use. Accordingly another life must be in store for us where one has one's end and use. Further, the sciences and speculation require such: that one part of humanity works more so that another part retains more time and leisure for speculating, and need not care for the means of livelihood and nourishment. But now if there were no other determination, then this inequality among human beings in this life would be quite improper. Indeed, the human being who devotes himself to sciences and speculations puts aside many advantages of this life; he   28:294 shortens his life and weakens his health. Thus since sciences of this sort are not at all fitting for our present determination, then there must be another determination to be awaited where they will have more worth <*valeur*>. Further, the shortness of human life is inadequate for making *use* of all the sciences and cognitions which one has acquired. Life is too short to cultivate one's talent fully. When one has done the utmost in the sciences, and now could make the best use of it, then one dies. If, e.g., a Newton had lived longer, he alone would have discovered more than all human beings together would have discovered in a thousand years. But when he had done the utmost in the sciences, then he dies. After him comes again one who must begin from the A, B, C, and when he has brought it just as far, then he dies as well; and it goes similarly with the following. Accordingly the shortness of life has no proportion at all to the talent of human understanding. Now since nothing in nature is in vain, then this as well must be reserved for another life. *The sciences are the luxury of the understanding which give us a foretaste of what we will be in the future life.*

If, on the other hand, we consider the powers of the will, then we find an incentive to morality and integrity in us. Should this be made for us merely in this life, then nature is making fools of us. Everything would be useless if the determination of the soul had no further extent. Suppose another being, a spirit, were to come to our earth, and he were to see a pregnant woman opened up in whose body was another being. Were he to see further that this being had organs but ones that it could not at all use in the state in which it finds itself, then this spirit would necessarily have to infer that another state was in store for this being, in which it will be able to use all its organs. And we ourselves infer just the same; when we see, e.g., a caterpillar, and become aware that it already has all the organs that it will use later as a butterfly: that it will avail itself of them after its development. Likewise the soul of a human being is armed with powers of cognition and desire, with drives and moral feeling which have no adequate determination at all in this life. Now since nothing is in vain, but rather everything has its end, these abilities of the soul must also have their determinate end. Now because this is not fulfilled in the present life, it must be kept in store for a future life.

28:295

The difficulty that accompanies this proof rests on the following objection: the begetting of human beings is contingent, it always rests on human beings, whether they want to put themselves in the state to beget children or not, it rests merely on their inclination, on their whim. Often children are even produced in an illicit manner, when persons get on with one another out of great passion. Thus persons can also be bred just as well as other animals. Now no creature which is set into the world through birth by means of the contingent decision of its parents can be determined for a higher end and a future life. This is indeed true, if human beings would otherwise not at all have come into life, but for the end of animal birth, which is quite contingent; then this would be not only a perfect objection, but even a proof. But we see, on the other hand, that the life of the soul does not rest on the contingency of the begetting of animal life, but rather that it has already lasted *before* the animal life, and thus its existence depends on a higher determination. *Consequently the animal life is contingent, but not the spiritual.* The spiritual life could still survive and be exercised, even if it had also been contingently united to the body. Even if the beings which were not born, or could not have been born, have not taken part in human life, still this spirit, which then would have been developed through the sheath of a body, can be developed in another manner. Even if this answer to the objection does not yet fully prove the matter, it is still useful to this extent that the objection which opposes it is not valid, and thus we are secured in our belief in assuming a future life.

We will not be able to say anything with reliability here as to what concerns the constitution of the state of the soul beyond the boundary of life because the limits of our reason stretch up to the boundary, but do not go beyond it. – Accordingly only concepts will occur which can be opposed to the objections to be made. It is first asked whether the soul will be conscious of itself in its future state or not. – If it were not conscious of itself, then this would be *spiritual* death, which we have already refuted by the previous concepts. But if it is not conscious of itself, although its life-power is still there, then this is *spiritual slumber*, in which the soul does not know where it is, and cannot yet rightly adapt itself in the other world. But this kind of deficiency of life-power and of consciousness cannot at all be proven, for because the soul itself is the life-power, it then can have no lack of it.

28:296

However, *personality*, the main matter with the soul after death, and the identity of the personality of the soul, consists in this: that it is conscious to itself that it is a person, and that it is also conscious of the identity; for otherwise the previous state would not at all be connected with the future one. Personality can be taken *practically* and *psychologically; practically,* if free actions are ascribed to it; *psychologically,* if it is conscious of itself and of the identity. The consciousness of itself and the identity of the person rests on inner sense. But because the body is not a principle of life, inner sense still remains even without the body, thus likewise the personality.

But now if the soul is conscious of itself, the question is: is it conscious of itself *as a pure spirit, or connected with an organic body?* Of this we can say nothing reliable. There are two opinions on this:

1. one can think either a restitution of the animal life, which can be either of a worldly or otherworldly kind. According to the worldly kind my soul would have to assume this or another body; according to the otherworldly kind, which would be a transition from this into another animal life, the soul would have to assume a transfigured body. Or one can also

2. think an entirely pure spiritual life, where the soul will not have any body at all.

This last opinion is the most suitable for philosophy. For if a body is a hindrance to life, but the future [life] is supposed to be perfect, then it must be *fully spiritual.* But if we now assume a full spiritual life, then here one can ask again: where is heaven? Where is hell? And which is our future determined location? The separation of the soul from the body is not to be posited in a change of location. The presence of the spirit cannot be explained locally <*localiter*>. For if it is explained locally <*localiter*>, then when a human being is dead I can ask: does the soul still reside for a while in the body? Or does it leave immediately? Is it accordingly in the room or in the house? And how long might it spend on its trip, be it to heaven or to hell? Or where else is it? But all these questions fall away if one does not assume and explain the presence of the soul locally <*localiter*>. Locations are relations only of bodily but not of spiritual things. Accordingly the soul, because it occupies no location, is not to be seen in the whole bodily world; it has no determinate location in the bodily world, rather it is in the spiritual world; it stands in connection and in relation with other spirits. Now if these spirits are well-thinking and holy beings, and the soul is in their community, then it is *in heaven.* But if the community of spirits in which it finds itself is evil, then the soul is *in hell. Heaven is thus everywhere where there is such a community of holy, spiritual beings,* but it is nowhere, because it occupies no location in the world, in that the community is not set up in the bodily world. Accordingly heaven will not be the immeasurable space which the heavenly bodies occupy and which shows itself in blue color, to which one would have to travel through the air if one wanted to get there; rather the spiritual world

28:297

is heaven; and to stand in relation and community with the spiritual world means: *to be in heaven.* Accordingly the soul will not arrive in hell if it has been evil; rather it will merely see itself in the society of evil spirits, and that means: *to be in hell.* –

We have a cognition of the bodily world through sensible intuition insofar it appears to us; our consciousness is bound to animal intuition; the present world is the interaction <*commercium*> of all objects, insofar as they are intuited through present sensible intuition. But when the soul separates itself from the body, then it will not have the same sensible intuition of this world; it will not intuit the world as it appears, but rather as it is. Accordingly the separation of the soul from the body consists in the *alteration of sensible intuition into spiritual intuition; and that is the other world.*

28:298 The other world is accordingly not another location, but rather only another intuition. The other world remains the same with respect to its objects; it is not different with respect to the substances, but it is *intuited spiritually.* Those who imagine the other world as if it were a *new location* which is separated from this one, and into which one must first be transferred if one wants to arrive there; they must then also take the separation of the soul locally <*localiter*> and explain its presence locally <*localiter*>. Then its presence would rest on bodily conditions, as on contact, extension in space, etc.; but then many questions would also occur, and one would degenerate into materialism. But since the presence of the soul is spiritual, the separation must likewise consist not in a going away of the soul from the body and a going into the other world; rather, since the soul has a sensible intuition of the bodily world through the body, it will then, when it is liberated from the sensible intuition of the body, have a spiritual intuition, and that is the other world. – If one comes into the other world, then one does not come into the community of other things, say, to other planets; for I am already in connection with them now, although only in a distant way; rather one remains in this world, but has a spiritual intuition of everything. Thus the other world is not to be distinguished from this one with respect to location; the concept of location cannot be used at all here. Accordingly the state of blessedness, or heaven, and the state of misery, or hell, which all comprise the other world, must also not at all be sought in this sensible world; rather if I have been righteous here, and after death receive a spiritual intuition of everything, and enter into the community of just such righteous beings, then I am in heaven. But if according to my conduct I receive a spiritual intuition of such beings whose will opposes every rule of morality, and if I fall into such a community, then I am in hell. To be sure, this opinion of the other world cannot be demonstrated, but rather it is a necessary hypothesis of reason which can be set against opponents.[a]

---

[a] The phrase "which can be set against opponents" is not in Pölitz. We follow Lehmann in adding this clause on the basis of Heinze (*Vorlesungen Kants*, p. 556).

The thought of *Swedenborg* is in this quite sublime.[28] He says the spiritual world constitutes a special real universe; this is the intelligible world <*mundus intelligibilis*> which must be distinguished from this sensible world <*mundo sensibili*>. He says all spiritual natures stand in connection with one another, only the community and connection of the spirits is not bound to the condition of bodies; there one spirit will not be far or near to the other, but rather there is a spiritual connection. Now as spirits our souls stand in this connection and community with one another, and indeed already here in this world, only we do not see ourselves in this community because we still have a sensible intuition; but although we do not see ourselves in it, we still stand within it. Now when the hindrance of sensible intuition is once removed, then we see ourselves in this spiritual community, and this is the other world; now these are not other things, but rather the same ones, but which we intuit differently. Now if a human being, whose will is a well-meaning will which devotes itself to exercising the rule of morality, was righteous in the world, he is already in this world in community with all righteous and well-meaning souls, be they in India or in Arabia, only he does not yet see himself in this community until he is liberated from sensible intuition. Likewise an evil being is also already here in the community of all knaves who abhor one another, only he does not yet see himself in it. But when he is liberated from sensible intuition, then he will become aware of this. Accordingly every good action of the virtuous is a step towards the community of the blessed, just as every evil action is a step towards the community of the vicious. Accordingly the virtuous does not go to heaven, but rather he is already there; yet only after death will he see himself in this community. Likewise the evil cannot see themselves in hell, although they are already actually there. But when they are liberated from the body, only then will they see where they are. What a horrible thought for the knave! Must he not fear every moment that his spiritual eyes will be opened? And as soon as these open he is already in hell.

28:299

I do not at all comprehend how the body should be necessary for this spiritual intuition. Why should the soul still be surrounded with this dust if it is once liberated from it? This is all that we can say here in order to purify the concept of the spiritual nature of the soul, of its separation from the body, of the future world which consists in heaven and hell. –

To conclude the Psychology, *spirits in general* should still be treated; but of that we can comprehend no more through reason *than that such spirits are possible*.

28:300

But one question still remains: whether the soul, which already sees itself spiritually in the other world, will and can appear in the visible world through visible effects? This is *not possible*, for matter can be intuited only sensibly and fall only in the outer senses, but not a spirit. Or could I not to some extent already *intuit here* the community of departed souls with my soul, which is not yet departed, but which stands in their community as a spirit? E.g. as *Swedenborg* contends? This is contradictory, for then spiritual intuition would have[b] to begin already in this world. But since I still have a sensible intuition in this world, *I cannot at the same time have a spiritual intuition.* I cannot be at the same time in this and also in that world, for if I have a sensible intuition, then I am in this world, and if I have a spiritual intuition, then I am in the other, but this cannot take place at the same time. But granted that it would be possible that the soul could still appear in this world, or that such a spiritual intuition were already possible here, because we still cannot prove the impossibility of that, then still the maxim of healthy reason must be being opposed here. But the maxim of healthy reason is this: *not to allow, but rather to reject all such experiences and appearances that are so constituted that, if I assume them, then they make the use of my reason impossible and suspend the conditions under which alone I can use my reason.* Were this to be assumed, then the use of my reason in this world would wholly cease, *for then many actions could happen on account of spirits.* This requires no closer consideration, however, since one already sees from experience that if a wrongdoer shoves the guilt of his actions onto an evil spirit, who supposedly lured him to it, the judge cannot allow this as an excuse. For otherwise he of course could not punish such a human being.

28:301　In general we still allege *that it is not at all suitable here to our vocation to worry much over the future world; rather we must complete the circle to which we are here determined, and wait for how it will be with respect to the future world.* The main point is that we conduct ourselves well at this post, righteously and morally, and attempt to make ourselves worthy of future happiness. Likewise it would be absurd if one occupied the lowest post in the military, and concerned oneself about the state of the colonel or the general. For there is time for that only when one has arrived at it.

Providence has locked up the future world from us, and has left over to us only a small hope, which is adequate enough to move us *to make ourselves worthy of it*; which we would not do so eagerly if we were already precisely acquainted in advance with the future world.

The main point is always morality: this is the holy and unassailable, what we must protect, and this is also the ground and the purpose of all our speculations and investigations. All metaphysical speculations aim *at it. God* and *the other world* is the single goal of all our philosophical investigations, and if the concepts of God and of the other world did not hang together with morality, then they would be useless.

---

[b] We follow Lehmann in omitting *sich* (in Pölitz), following *müsste* (300₁₂).

PART III
Metaphysik Mrongovius

1782–1783 (AK. 29: 747–940)

Introduction to metaphysics
\<Prolegomena metaphysices\>[1]

Our cognitions are connected in a twofold way: *first* as an aggregate, when one is added to another [in order to]^L constitute a whole, e.g., a sand hill is not in itself a connection of things, but rather they are arbitrarily put together (there is nothing determinate here),[b] *second*, as a series of ground and consequences, the parts of the series being called members because we can cognize one part only through the others, e.g., in a human body each part is there through the others. We easily comprehend that a connection of cognitions as an aggregate provides no determinate concept of a whole, and it is as if I add one small piece to another until a hill arises, etc., until a planet or terrestrial body comes into being; at least we can so think of it. In a series there is something that makes the connection according to a rule, namely, grounds and consequences. With grounds and consequences we must think of *a priori*[c] boundaries, i.e., a ground that is not also a consequence, and *a posteriori* boundaries, i.e., a consequence that is not a ground, e.g., with human generations: human beings are members in a series, yet here we must think of a human being who does conceive but is not born, thus an *a priori* limit \<*terminus*\>, and of one

---

[a] We have altered the sequence of these lecture notes as they appear in the Academy edition in two sorts of instances. The first sort is where the editor (Gerhard Lehmann) apparently misplaced some of his photocopied pages of the manuscript while preparing his transcription for publication; here a simple inspection of the original manuscript (or, in our case, a microfilm) makes evident the error and the need for repagination. The second sort is where Mrongovius, in copying his notes, accidentally omitted some sections and later inserted them with a sign indicating this. We offer footnotes explaining each change. With all of this repagination, especially with that of the second sort, we are indebted to the work of Werner Stark at the Kant Archive in Marburg (Germany); see Zelazny and Stark, "Zu Krzysztof Celestyn Mrongovius und seinen Kollegheften nach Kants Vorlesungen," in *Kant-Forschungen*, 1: 283–4.

All repagination is noted in the text. A list of the sequence of pages (as we offer them here in translation) follows: Introduction (747_1–750_{27}, 751_5–752_{38}, 750_{27}–751_4, 752_{38}–753_{14}, 755_6–756_{17}, 753_{14}–755_5, 756_{18}–765_{39}, 767_8–768_{39}, 766_1–766_{26}, 773_{10}–784_6), Ontology (784_7–822_{33}, 766_{27}–767_7, 769_1–773_9, 822_{34}–848_7), Cosmology (848_8–864_{24}, 921_2–937_{15}, 864_{25}–875_3), Psychology (875_6–920_9), unassimilated text (937_{17}–940_{10}).

[b] Parentheses added by Lehmann (747_6).

[c] Only *priori* is underlined in the ms, as if to emphasize that it is not *a posteriori* (747_{16}).

who is born but conceives no one, thus an *a posteriori* limit <*terminus*>. We consider here (in metaphysics) not things as they are connected as grounds and consequences, but rather cognitions, which also have a descent like human beings or other things. I can imagine a cognition that is not a consequence, thus the highest ground, and [one] that is not a ground, thus the last consequence. {The last consequence is an immediate experience, e.g., something-body-stone-limestone-marble-marble column.}[d] We thus have an idea of a connection of cognitions as grounds and consequences. Cognitions which are the grounds of grounds that follow a certain rule are called principles <*principia*>.[e] Thus insofar as cognitions are in a series, there must also be principles <*principia*> – – . *It is remarkable that I can make a consequence into a ground, but one out of which the other does not [follow]*[L], but rather through which I always arrive at [only][L] the cognition of the other. Thus they are not principles of being <*principia essendi*>, but of cognition <*cognoscendi*>, e.g., I cognize God's existence from the world. The world is nevertheless not the ground of God, but rather the reverse, but through the world I am able to arrive at the concept of God, and to this extent I can move from the principled <*principiatis*> to the principles <*principiis*> – the consequences that are used as grounds, for going back in reverse to their own grounds, are called *a posteriori* principles <*principia*>. If I begin from the consequences, then I cognize something *a posteriori;* if I begin from the grounds, then I cognize *a priori*. If something is given to me then I can test whether I could indeed have cognized it *a priori* from grounds, e.g., experience teaches that sunlight melts ice, but we would have hardly cognized this *a priori*. Cognition that is taken from experience [is] eminently <*per kat'exochen*>[f] *a posteriori*, and from now on when we call cognitions *a posteriori*, then we are always understanding these to be from experience, because experience contains the last consequence of our cognition, for which we seek grounds by means of reason. If we take experience as the principle <*principium*>, then the principle is empirical: e.g., experience teaches all bodies are heavy (insofar as we are acquainted with them), we can accept it as a principle and say: since all bodies are heavy, it follows that. . . . [g] *a priori* principles are those which are not borrowed from any experience.[h] Whether there are such must be investigated shortly.

29:748

---

[d] Marginalia (747_{28-9}) alongside text printed at 747_{30-1}, and is inserted with a sign ('*F*') before this text. We follow Lehmann in the insertion. The period is added by Lehmann. Paragraph breaks added by Lehmann have been removed.

[e] Lehmann misreads, *und Folgen. Erkenntnisse, die Gründe* as *und Folgen Erkenntniss Die Gründe* (747_{31}).

[f] Lehmann misreads *per* as *ist* (748_{15}). Latin: *per* (by), Greek: *kat'exochen* (eminently), written in Greek letters in the ms.

[g] Ellipses added by Lehmann (748_{22}); there is only a period in the ms.

[h] We follow Lehmann in adding a period here (748_{23}).

There can arise from the conglomeration of our cognition a unity, i.e., science, or a connection can be met with that is systematic. (A)*i* We can think of a connection of our cognitions as science, from the first grounds up to the last consequences, and this would comprise in it the entirety of all inferred cognitions; but this goes beyond our powers. {The first ground is simple – namely of something – but to have the last consequences we have to go through the whole field of experience, which cannot be done.}*j* Since this is thus not feasible, we can (B) draw off the essence of it. I want to have only a piece of the system of the whole of human cognition, namely the science of the highest principles of human cognition, and such a project is modest. For a long time people have had it in mind to work out such a science and called it metaphysics. (C)*k* Meta-physics is thus the science of the first principles of the entirety of human cognition,*l* which thus contains the first members of the series. But this concept is*m* not determinate enough as to how much or how little belongs to it. For if I give a concept of science, then it must be determined what belongs to it and what not, and also human beings cannot know through the given concept*n* how far down into experience these principles reach and where we stop. – Every series can be divided into two parts: that which precedes the other is comparatively the first, for example, a church history of the first centuries. Nothing is determined here; the 3rd, 7th, 8th, can be the first century.*o* The *a priori* boundary of metaphysics is determined, namely, that there be no principles from which it could be derived. One speaks of the possible, the impossible, something and noth-ing, a human being can rise no higher.[2] World, accident, fate, natural, supernatural – cause of the world, existence, God so far have been spoken of through mere concepts. Only of the human soul, there it was presumed that something could be said, if it did not attend to itself. Thus the body can also fit in here, and now, for all I know, the whole doctrine of nature.

29:749

---

i We are adding round brackets to this and the following letters: A–F. All of these letters are in darker ink and appear to have been inserted later into the ms ($748_{27, 35}$; $749_{2, 33}$; 750_3; 751_{12}).

j Marginalia (748_{32-4}) alongside text printed at 748_{30-6}, inserted after the first sentence of this text with a sign. We follow Lehmann in the insertion, but paragraph breaks added by Lehmann have been removed.

k Lehmann omits a *C* here without note (749_2), and mistakes part of the sign for *nicht* at 749_5 as a *C* (see below).

l We follow Lehmann in changing *des gesamten Menschen* to *der gesamten Menschlichen* (749_3). Lehmann does not note changing *des* to *der*.

m A *C* added by Lehmann without note has been removed (749_5).

n Parentheses added by Lehmann have been removed (749_8).

o We do not follow Lehmann in his interpreting a *J* in the ms as *Jahresrechnung* (reckoning of the years), interpreting it instead as *Jahrhundert* (century) (749_{13}). We read the entire passage as *es kann der 3, 7, 8, ?se ersteren J seyn* and not, as Lehmann reads it, *es kann das 3, 7, 8 folgende unserer J seyn*.

111

Here it becomes evident that I cannot set the boundaries for metaphysics in the series of consequences and grounds according to degree, as when I consider it homogeneous and related to other sciences, but rather I must think of it as heterogeneous and entirely different from the others.[p] {*a priori* [principles][L] always carry necessity with them, *a posteriori* principles do not, e.g., everything that happens must have a ground – is an *a priori* proposition, for experience teaches only that such is the case – but it cannot deny that there might sometime occur something without a ground.}[q]

There are two[r] kinds of cognitions, *a priori* and *a posteriori*, which are wholly distinct from each other. E.g., God can be cognized merely *a priori*. (D) Now we say that metaphysics is the science of the *a priori* principles of human cognition <*est scientia principiorum cognitionis humanae a priori*>.[3] Does mathematics not belong in metaphysics, although it is also pure cognition <*cognitio pura*>? No, but clearly the principles of the possibility of mathematics – – for it contains the principles of the possibility of all *a priori* cognitions. Now the concept is determined and settled. All cognitions that require an experience in order to be attained are outside the field of metaphysics; {(E) *a priori* cognitions are twofold: (a) mathematical (b) philosophical with the difference: logic – here we are taking only the latter – –, therefore mathematics does not belong in metaphysics, although it is also pure cognition <*cognitio pura*>, but clearly the principles of the possibility of mathematics do, for it contains the principles of the possibility of all *a priori* cognition. – – But we can philosophize about mathematics.}[s] In order to determine the concept I must (F)[t] add a special species of principles. {Something is *a priori* (a) simply speaking <*simpliciter*> and *a priori* (b) in some respect <*secundum quid*>[4] – *a priori* in some respect <*secundum quid*> when I cognize something through reason, but from empirical principles, e.g., if I throw a stone horizontally – so that it does not fall straight down – one can determine the curve *a priori*, but

29:750

---

[p] The following text, which followed . . . *verschieden denken* (749₂₆), is crossed out in the ms: *die doch die ersten princ / enthält. [¶] Welches sind den diese princ. prima?* (which yet contain the first principles. [¶] Which then are these first principles <*principia prima*>?). Marginalia were added here (see below) without an insertion sign, and were possibly meant to replace the deleted text.

[q] Marginalia (749₂₇₋₃₀) alongside text printed at 749₃₁₋₂. This is without an insertion sign, although it may have been meant to replace deleted text (as noted above). A nonsense word, *ozi* (749₂₈), added by Lehmann without note, has been removed, as have various blank lines and paragraph breaks.

[r] Lehmann misreads *2* as *5* (749₃₁).

[s] Marginalia (751₁₂₋₁₈) alongside text printed at 750₁₋₃ (at the bottom of the ms page), and is inserted into the text with a sign after *Metaphysik* (750₃); Lehmann ignores this insertion sign. We omit a second *E* inserted into the text after this insertion sign, and add the capitalization following the marginalia. Much of this marginalia is verbatim from 749₃₄₋₇.

[t] Lehmann misreads the inserted *F* as *E* (750₃).

according to laws of gravity, which we cognize *a posteriori*.}[u] A cognition that is not burdened with any experience is pure, {pure philosophical cognitions are metaphysical. What is philosophy? The system of the cognitions of reason through concepts. Metaphysics is thus the system of pure cognitions of reason through concepts.

The system must be based on an idea, through which the parts, the connection of the parts, and the completeness of the parts is determined,}[v] or metaphysics is the science of the principles of pure cognition <*scientia principiorum cognitionis purae*> or only pure philosophy <*philosophia pura*>, that is a proper touchstone, e.g., the soul does not belong in metaphysics either; psychology is merely tacked on. The use of reason must be pure <*pura*> – thus isolated, i.e., freed from all experience and independent of the same. – Natural science is also philosophy, but applied philosophy <*philosophia applicata*>, it is an application of reason to objects of experience, where we start from empirical principles <*principia*>.[5] We have two fields of the use of reason. It can proceed when it has *a priori* principles <*principia*>, or when it has *a posteriori* principles <*principia*>, wherein it draws upon the advice of experience. The first part of this use is called metaphysics. Here there must be two main parts:

1. We must consider reason itself – – or the first part is the science which has reason for its object. It would deal with the sources, extent, and boundaries of our pure reason[6] – or with nature, i.e., with the possibility of judging *a priori*. (a)[w] First we will examine: can our rational cognition cognize something *a priori* – the possibility of *a priori* cognition must first be demonstrated. (b) Further: the extension, how far it can come, which objects it can come to without experience. – (c) Finally, when it wants to judge without experience the boundaries over which it dare not step[x] without falling into confusion and errors. This first part could be called transcendental philosophy, or critique of pure reason. Pure reason is that which judges independently of all experience. One could also call this part pure metaphysics <*metaphysicam puram*>; and second, the application of *a priori* principles <*principia*> to objects of experience, would be applied metaphysics <*metaphysica applicata*>. We will indicate later what these are.

29:751

---

[u] Marginalia (751_{19-23}) alongside text printed at 750_{3-7}, and is inserted with a sign after the first sentence of this text. Lehmann ignores this sign, inserting the marginalia much later in the text; also, an *F* added to the beginning of the marginalia without note by Lehmann has been removed.

[v] Marginalia (751_{24-9}) alongside text printed at 750_{8-9}, and is inserted with a sign after *rein* (750_5). Lehmann ignores this sign, inserting the marginalia much later in the text.

[w] Lehmann misreads *a* and *b* as *1* and *2*, respectively ($750_{22, 24}$).

[x] Lehmann misplaces a page of ms text here, inserting ms 6 between 4 and 4'. We continue here with ms 4'–5' (751_5–752_{38}), removing a period added by Lehmann without note (750_{27}).

Mathematics[y] teaches that[z] pure cognitions of reason are possible, for it is such a pure cognition of reason: since its propositions always carry their own evidence with them, and furthermore each of them can be confirmed through experience, it would not be necessary to go so far to fetch its possibility; but our pure reason, however, has a special discipline of cognitions, with which it is not the same as with mathematics: they are not so fortunate as to have evidence and are also not confirmed by experience – furthermore they are also of the kind that, although a person easily takes himself to be convinced of one and then the other, yet not one is such that it has not been disputed; since general human reason, i.e., the summation of the reason of all human beings in the philosophy of pure reason, that is, in metaphysics, is in dispute with itself, it is necessary to investigate the possibility of pure cognitions of reason, and so we will also investigate the possibility of pure metaphysics, not in order to favor it, but so that we might at the same time learn through this the possibility of pure philosophy.

29:752

Applied metaphysics <*metaphysica applicata*>, which contains the *a priori* cognition of objects, constitutes a system of pure reason, and that system of pure cognition of reason is called metaphysics in the strict sense. Transcendental philosophy is the propaedeutic of metaphysics proper. Reason determines nothing here, but rather speaks always of only its own faculty, and in metaphysics proper it makes use of this faculty, and metaphysics is always taken in this sense. No one has had a true transcendental philosophy. The word has been used and understood as ontology;[7] but (as it is easy to make out) this is not how we are taking it. In ontology one speaks of things in general, and thus actually of no thing – one is occupied with the nature of the understanding for thinking of things – here we have the concepts through which we think things, namely, the pure concepts of reason[a] – hence it is the science of the principles of pure understanding and of pure reason.[b] But that was also transcendental philosophy, thus ontology belongs to it – one has never treated it properly – one treated things in general directly – without investigating whether such cognitions of pure understanding or pure reason or pure science were even possible. There I speak already of things, substances and accidents, which are properties of things that I cognize *a priori*. But I cannot speak this way in the *Critique*. Here I will say substance and accident are also found among the concepts that are *a priori*. How do I arrive at that? What

---

[y] This entire paragraph (751_{30}–752_{10}) has a line drawn along its margin in the ms, as though for emphasis, and there is an X drawn at the beginning and end of the paragraph.

[z] Lehmann misreads *Dass* as *Wie* (how)(751_{30}).

[a] The ms reads: *reine Vern und reine Vern Begriffe.* We follow Lehmann in omitting *und reine Vernunft* (752_{24-5}). Lehmann does not note the *und*.

[b] This and the following sentence (751_{21-30}) are bracketed together with X's in the ms, presumably for emphasis.

can I accomplish with that? What is possibly cognized *a priori* of objects, insofar as they are substances? I examine thus the source of the concept, how far it would be able to go.*ᶜ* I am not saying: that is substance, that accident; for here I would be examining not reason itself, but rather would be dealing with the objects. Transcendental philosophy is thus to be sharply distinguished from metaphysics proper, i.e., the system of cognition through reason. We naturally ask how we arrive at such *a priori* cognitions where certainly the principles are entirely *a priori*, e.g., no experience can teach whether the world has a beginning or not, nevertheless reason asks about this and*ᵈ* it lays considerable weight on deciding this. It is thus a question for pure reason, not for that which is supported from empirical principles, for this cannot give us an answer here. – Here the question naturally arises, how does reason mean to cognize this independently of experience? The answering of this question belongs to transcendental philosophy, where we see that there are *a priori* principles. Now again I do not know, how far will they bring me? I must thus attempt to acquaint myself with its whole faculty,*ᵉ* and its source, and become acquainted with how far they reach, and their boundaries. That is the business of the critique of pure reason. Granted, if we paid no attention to the establishment of the principles and immediately*ᶠ* made a system in which we assume principles*ᵍ* whose validity has arisen through their use, then we would have a metaphysics proper, but with what assurance could we avail ourselves of it? Eventually we would arrive at such difficulties that we would no longer be able to find our way out, and reason would destroy even its own products – critique is therefore highly necessary. If reason errs, no experience can set it aright. If we consider the critique of pure reason independently of all experience then this is the genuine pure philosophy, i.e., the consideration of the faculty of reason itself is pure philosophy. *ʰ*In all cognitions where principles of reason arise, and indeed from concepts, there is only science*ⁱ* of science, that is, what is a product of reason and separated from all experience. Because they arise from different sources of cognition, we must separate as much as possible in all the sciences the pieces that are heterogeneous, how many rest on mere philosophy and [how many on] mere experience, e.g., in the doctrine of nature much is *a priori*, e.g., nothing happens without sufficient reason, substance does not pass away but rather only form, etc. If I take this (apart and separated from that which experience teaches) with all consequences

29:750

29:751

29:752

29:753

29:755

ᶜ Lehmann jumps here (752_{38}) from ms 5' to ms 6'. We continue with ms 6 (750_{27}–751_4).
ᵈ An *und* omitted by Lehmann without note has been replaced (750_{35}).
ᵉ Lehmann jumps here (751_4) from ms 6 to ms 4'. We continue with ms 6' (752_{38}–753_{14}).
ᶠ Lehmann misreads *gleich ein System* as *gleichsam [ein]ᴸ system* (752_{2-3}).
ᵍ Lehmann misreads *principien* as *principien a priori* (753_3), i.e., *prin/cip:* as *prin/ap:*.
ʰ An *X* is placed in the ms before this sentence, perhaps for emphasis (753_{13}).
ⁱ Lehmann jumps here (753_{14}) from ms 6' to ms 8'. We continue with ms 7–8 (755_6–756_{17}).

that can be drawn from it, this is the metaphysics of the doctrine of nature; there is thus a metaphysics of politics, legislation, etc., yet it can take place only where there are principles of reason; metaphysics of history is nothing. Such a metaphysics is very good, for if I lack [something] in a science then I can see right away whether it is due to reason or experience and the illusion of the senses. The object of philosophy must lie in the system of metaphysics, it is the extent of all that which only pure reason can think – it contains everything together that, as said above, is distributed in the various sciences. Metaphysics is the greatest culture of human reason. We come to be acquainted with all illusions, to comprehend their cause and avoid them, it presents the elementary concepts, e.g., substance, necessity, and principles which reason avails itself of everywhere. ^{j} Thus a metaphysics must be possible in every science where reason rules, e.g., in the doctrine of nature, namely, that which reason has for principles without experience. Even mathematics institutes a metaphysics:[8] it refers to objects only insofar as they have a magnitude – and the general use of reason's principles on all objects underlies mathematics and is its metaphysics. – Mathematics, one can say, is the philosophy of all philosophy – Transcendental philosophy is in respect to metaphysics what logic [is]^L in respect to the whole of philosophy. – Logic contains the general rules of the use of the understanding and is to this extent an introduction to all philosophy. Transcendental

29:756 philosophy is an introduction to pure philosophy <*philosophiam puram*>, which is a part of the whole of philosophy. In transcendental philosophy we consider not objects, but rather reason itself, just as in general logic^k we regard only the understanding and its rules. Thus transcendental philosophy could also be called transcendental logic. It occupies itself with the sources, the extent, and the boundaries of pure reason, without busying itself with objects. For that reason it is wrong to call it ontology <*ontologiam*>. There we consider things already according to their general properties. Transcendental logic abstracts from all that;^{l} it is a kind of self-cognition. Reason tests whether it cannot set itself beyond experience on the wings of ideas. It speaks, e.g., of spiritual being. – Now what does it have for sources, in order to establish a system of such things? If it has explained this [system], then the question arises: upon which things can this be applied? It thus concerns not the object, but the subject – not things, but

29:753 rather the source, extent, and boundaries of reason^m in its pure use, i.e., free of experience. One can then regard it more as critique [than]^L as doctrine in

---

^{j} An X is placed in the ms before the sentence, perhaps for emphasis (755$_{28}$).
^{k} Lehmann misreads *Logik* as *Metaphysik* (756$_3$), i.e. *L* as *M*.
^{l} A period added by Lehmann without note has been removed (756$_{10}$).
^{m} Lehmann jumps here (756$_{18}$) from ms 8 to ms 10'. We continue with ms 8'–10' (753$_{14}$–755$_5$). The period following *Vernunft* (756$_{17}$) belongs to an abbreviation (*Vern.*), and is not the close of a sentence.

which we are dogmatic. A cognition is dogmatic which is presented in its connection with grounds. In the critique we do not present a cognitive connection, but rather we first explore the sources of the possibility of such a cognition without experience. Now the second part of metaphysics is the system of pure reason. Philosophy means a system of rational cognition from concepts. – Here pure philosophy is to be presented in a system. Our reason should have objects, which are of two kinds: they belong either to nature or freedom. Both are subject to rules and laws. Our reason cognizes them in that it brings them under rules. Reason considers necessary laws, and everything that can be cognized through reason is necessary. We should cognize objects through reason, thus according to that which is necessary to them and belongs to them; our cognitions of reason should thus have the character of necessity in them. We can cognize either (1) what there is, or (2) what there should be. The former belongs to nature, the latter to freedom. Nature is the summation of what there is, and the summation of what there should be is morals. We thus have two parts of philosophy. The philosophy of nature considers things that are there. Philosophy of morals concerns free actions that ought to happen. Since we said above that there was a metaphysics in every science, we can also think of a metaphysics of nature, which contains the principles of things insofar as they are – and a metaphysics of morals, which contains the principles of the possibility of things insofar as they ought to happen*, but the ought applies only to free actions. {All our cognitions are theoretical which consider things as they are; or practical, which say how something ought to be and carry necessity with them, etc. We treat the metaphysics of nature here, and of the metaphysics of morals (which sets aside the rules of life that we abstract° from the nature of the soul out of experience) we will draw upon only something from natural theology <*theologia naturalis*>, where we think of God as lawgiver.}ᵖ Metaphysics of nature has various parts: it is philosophy of (a) bodily, (b) thinking, (c) entire nature, (d) the highest ground of all nature. The objects of metaphysics are (a) nature or world, (b) the world creator, thus general cosmology <*cosmologia generalis*> and rational theology <*theologia rationalis*>. We cognize objects either through outer sense, i.e., general physics <*physica generalis*>, or through inner sense, i.e., rational psychology <*psychologia rationalis*> according to Wolff's classification; although this is incorrect, one reckons only general physics <*physica generalis*> to cosmology and rational psychology <*psychologia rationalis*> separately.

29:754

ⁿ We do not follow Lehmann in changing *geschehen* to *seyen* (754₂).

° We follow Lehmann in changing *abstrahirt* to *abstrahiren* (754₁₈).

ᵖ Marginalia (754₁₃₋₂₀) alongside text printed at 754₂₋₄. It comes without an insertion sign, *pace* Lehmann; we insert it after the first sentence of this text, while Lehmann inserts it after the paragraph. There is a *7* after the *etc*, but its meaning is unclear, and there is no corresponding sign in the text.

Metaphysics of morals[9] is pure morality, which we are setting wholly aside.[q] Metaphysics of nature contains the principles of the speculative use of reason, and metaphysics of morals the principles of the practical use of reason; everything that is there can be classified (A) into that which is given to the senses, and (B) that which does go beyond the use of the senses but is connected with the objects of the senses. – Regarding <*ad*> (A) the objects of the senses are either objects of the outer sense of the five bodily [senses],[L] or of the inner sense, which is the soul. We thus have a doctrine of the body and a doctrine of the soul; regarding <*ad*> (B) we consider the summation of all objects of the senses, i.e., [the][L] entirety of nature. We can also think of the whole series of things and then we must assume a highest creator of nature, i.e., God; that is the last part of metaphysics. The metaphysics of bodily nature is rational physics <*physica rationalis*>, that of thinking rational psychology <*psychologia rationalis*>, that of the entirety of nature or of the world rational cosmology <*cosmologia rationalis*>, that of the highest creator of nature and of all beings natural theology <*theologia naturalis*>. The concept of a being

29:755 insofar as it contains the ground of the possibility of the entirety of nature is the concept of God. The last part of metaphysics is thus rational theology <*theologia rationalis*>. Now we clearly comprehend that everything empirical must fall away. For otherwise it would not be pure philosophy <*philosophia pura*>. But the concept of the body is still an empirical

29:756 concept and likewise the[r] concept of the soul. We call soul namely that of which I am conscious when I think. So how can rational physics and psychology <*physica . . . psychologia rationalis*> be brought in here? We note that an object can be given through experience only when we regard it according to principles which are *a priori*. E.g., the concept of a thinking and bodily being is given through experience. But if I do not take the principles <*principia*> of the properties from experience, then the object is given but not the principles <*principia*>, and thus can belong within metaphysics. Thus rational physics and psychology <*physica . . . psychologia rationalis*> lie in the field of metaphysics. The empirical doctrine of bodies is called the doctrine of nature proper, physics does not belong here. There is also empirical psychology <*psychologia empirica*>, where I must presuppose observations in order to say something about the soul. – It also does not belong here; but psychology, as it will be treated here, still has a rational and an empirical part. The latter considers the soul from experience, the former from concepts.

Now how does the empirical part get into metaphysics? They do not

---

[q] We follow Lehmann in omitting a doubled *bey* (754₂₁).

[r] Lehmann jumps here (755₅) from ms 10 to ms 7. We continue with ms 10'–20' (756₁₈–766₂₆). A *der* (following *und so auch*), omitted by Lehmann without note, has been replaced (755₅).

gather it from the bad definition of empirical physics <*physicae empiricae*> introduced above, but what they do not comprehend is that empirical psychology <*psychologia empirica*> did not belong in there either: joy, contentment, and all motions of the mind are but mere observations. {Special physics <*physica specialis*> and empirical psychology <*psychologia empirica*> belong with equal right in metaphysics, each as little as the other – – .}⁵ A psychology of observations could be called anthropology.¹⁰ – But we will expound it here because the sciences are classified not only as to how reason sorts them, but rather as academic instruction demands. It has not yet matured enough that a special course of lectures <*collegium*> can be made from it. One pushed it therefore into metaphysics. Here there is a passing over into another genus <*metabasis eis allo genos*>.ᵗ One can still distinguish anthropology from it, if one understands by this a cognition of human beings insofar as it is pragmatic.

29:757

HISTORY OF METAPHYSICS

As old as reason is, metaphysical investigations are just as old. It is remarkable that human beings began to judge about that which goes beyond the senses earlier than about that which is given to them. The doctrine of nature was worked out only poorly. The cause is probably this: philosophizing about nature requires persistent diligence, observation, and collection of all manner of laws of experience. But everyone can find in himself the ideas of the understanding and of reason and one, as it were, *spins*ᵘ them from oneself. Without any doubt human understanding is also impelled by natural needs to know where all of its ends lead. It is not satisfied with what the sensible world delivers to it; rather it must know what the future has in store for it – whoever believes that everything ends with death must have a low concept of his life. These needs, to be acquainted with God and the other world, which are so closely connected with the interest of human reason, went beyondᵛ nature, which forʷ human beings has much less interest. Although all of this was quite difficult, nevertheless they were compelled by the importance of the objects to further investigations, even though some miscarried. No peoples had metaphysics prior to the Greeks, just as they had no philosophy. If we begin to reckon correctly, we find a time in which the Greek language was so limited and unsuited for expressing philosophical considerations that

---

ˢ Marginalia (Ak. 29: 1150) which we insert at 757₁. It comes without an insertion sign, and is written alongside the beginning of this paragraph in the ms.

ᵗ This is written with Greek letters in the ms (757₇).

ᵘ Lehmann misreads *spint* as *spürt* (traces), and adds a *man* without note (757₁₀). A second *spint*, which we omit, is written above the line. See Kant's parallel claim at 787₁₂, below.

ᵛ We follow Lehmann in changing *sie der* to *an der* (757₂₇).

ʷ We follow Lehmann in changing *auf* to *für* (757₂₈).

everything had to be expressed poetically. Orpheus, Hesiod, and others had many sparks of philosophy in their poetry. At that time the manner of expressing ideas was to clothe them in images so that as a rule one finds philosophy carried out poetically, which also happened in part in order to impress religion all the better into memory. But poetry is for us always a play of sensibility. Pherecydes is said to have been the first philosopher to express himself in prose.[11] But we have nothing from him and Heraclitus, whose writings were exceedingly obscure, so that even Socrates, who knew them, for later they were lost, said: that which he understood was excellent, thus he believed that that which he did not understand would be likewise. {Heraclitus was so difficult for him that he said: one needs a Delian swimmer <*delio natatore opus est*>.}[x][12] That comes about because there were not enough words, and thus the ones that were newly invented were for the most part unfamiliar. Impossible <*impossibile*> is not a Latin word.[13] Cicero says: it cannot happen <*fieri nequit*>, or one used [the Greek term] impossible <*adunaton*>.[y] It is not as easy to invent new words as one thinks, because they are contrary to taste and in this way taste is a hindrance to philosophy. Pythagoras clothed philosophy even more in the language of pure reason.[14] But for a long time the mistake still stuck to Greek philosophy of clothing ideas and concepts in images in order to give them a proper meaning, through which a concept loses much of its purity. Aristotle went the farthest in this; he invented words for the most abstract ideas, for which the Greek language was very pliant. German is similar to Greek in this respect. It has many apt expressions. If one word does not fit, then another does, and one always expresses more than the other. One does not find this at all with French. Professor Kant attributes this to the spread of religion in Germany: the missionaries had no proper words to express their thoughts and concepts, thus they invented new ones which are closely related to Latin, because they knew that. E.g., simple <G: *einfaltig*> means literally that which has one fold, in Latin simple <*simplex*>, which comes from single <*simplus*> and fold <*plica; G: Falte*>; in this way our language is much enriched. At the time of Pythagoras and the Eleatic sect there reigned [a][L] philosophical system where objects of the senses and of the understanding were distinguished. The first were called sensibles <*sensibilia*> and phenomena, the other intelligibles <*intelligibilia*> and noumena. The Eleatic sect said: there is no truth in the senses <*in sensibus nihil inesse veri*>.[15] They provide appearances, not as matters are, but rather

---

[x] Marginalia (758_{10-11}) alongside text printed at 758_6 has an insertion sign before *Heraclitus* (758_6). We follow Lehmann by inserting it at the end of the sentence. Parentheses added by Lehmann have been removed. See the endnote regarding the Latin phrase.

[y] This is printed in Greek letters in the ms. The ms appears to read *adunaton* rather than the *adunatos* printed in Lehmann (758_{14}).

as they affect us.[z] {One should not have divided things into intelligibles   29:759
<*intelligibilia*> and sensibles <*sensibilia*> or noumena and phenomena,
but rather said that our cognition is twofold (first intellectual and second
sensitive), which would have prevented the coming about of a mystical
concept of the intellectual which distances itself from the logical [and]
through which metaphysics deteriorated into wild fantasy.[a] They should
not have divided philosophy in terms of objects.}[b16] Shortly before or
during the time of Alexander there arose two parties here, of which
there are two quite famous leaders with whom we are acquainted.
Namely, Epicurus, philosopher of sensibility, and Plato, philosopher of
ideas. The latter said there was no reality in the senses, the sensible
appearances could be otherwise if we had other senses, without the
object itself being altered thereby.

Note. Sense and appearance have been confused. Illusion[c] lies in the
understanding, but in the senses there is no false illusion. They give
appearances, and the understanding judges about these; now the understanding can judge falsely in connecting appearance, which produces
illusion, for which the senses are not really guilty, but rather the understanding, because it has not investigated closely enough what it is judging
about before it judges – those on the side of the intellectualists said: truth
is only in the understanding, and some added yet to that: false illusion is in
the senses. This was the method in the old days, which still derived from
the Eleusinian mysteries. Some doctrines are to be expounded as exoteric,
i.e., for everyone's need and grasp <*captus*>, and others as esoteric for
confidants and the trusted under the seal of secrecy, so to speak within
veils <*intra vela*>. E.g., of the one invisible divinity, of the correctness of
their theogonies and mythologies. At certain times this can be good, e.g.,
at the origin of such doctrines; but later it can cease and indeed must,
because they are not justified in holding alone a monopoly for promoting
wisdom. In Plato's time there were several esoteric doctrines, but the
exoteric ones were always held back. At his time there also arose the
question: how do our intellectual cognitions arise? Sensitive cognitions
need not be explained, they come from the senses. – We note that either
our understanding has an intuitive faculty of another kind than the sensible, this latter delivering only appearances of things, but the former things   29:760

---

[z] A paragraph break added by Lehmann has been removed (759₈).

[a] *Schwärmerei;* this term was often used by Kant with connotations of reveries, enthusiasm, or
zealotry in religious contexts.

[b] Marginalia (759₁₋₇) alongside text printed at 758₃₆₋₉. We follow Lehmann in inserting it
immediately after this text. Parentheses are added by Lehmann. Blank lines and paragraph
breaks added by Lehmann have been removed. Lehmann does not note that this text is
marginalia.

[c] The German terms are closely related here: *Erscheinung* (appearance), *Schein* (illusion,
seeming), *scheinen* (to seem), *erscheinen* (appear).

as they are. Then there would be intellectual things through intuitions <*intellectualia per intuitus*>; or it has a conceptual faculty for making concepts through reflection on the intuitions of things; these would be intellectual things through concepts <*intellectualia per conceptus*>. Intellectual things through intuitions <*intellectualia per intuitus*>[17] are objects which only the understanding alone can intuit, and through concepts <*per conceptus*> would be concepts which the understanding makes. The first is a mere phantom of the brain; the understanding cannot intuit, but rather the senses [alone can], thus there are only intellectual things through concepts <*intellectualia per conceptus*>. [d]Professor Kant calls the first mystical, the other logical intellectual things <*intellectualia*>.

The philosophers were classified accordingly. Plato maintained mystical intellectual things <*intellectualia*>, Aristotle logical ones. {Aristotle accepted noumena not as object[s] of the intuition of the understanding, but rather as intellectual concepts.}[e] Plato says we have concepts that are not borrowed from the senses, e.g., of a primordial being, etc., which we obtained through a higher intuition that our understanding had previously, in which there was intuition of things, thus something which goes beyond the senses intuitively. We have had, he says, an intuition of God from which we derived all remaining ideas, [and] of which we now have only weak memories, that occur to us on the occasion of sensible appearances. Now we no longer have this because our soul is locked up in our body as though in a prison. All concepts of divinity are only copies of the intuition which the soul had before it was united with the body. Logical intellectual things <*intellectualia*> arise through the reflection of the understanding. It reflects upon the objects of the senses; if it leaves the object, then the concept is a logical intellectual thing <*intellectuale*>: e.g., we see from experience that water flows downhill if there is no obstacle. The understanding cognizes this as necessary. If it now lets the water run away, then it has the concept of the necessary, which is a logical intellectual thing <*intellectuale*>. Aristotle took everything to be logical intellectual things <*intellectualia*>. From this schism arose a philosophical dispute whether the concepts of the intellect <*conceptus intellecti*> were innate <*conati*> or acquired <*acquisiti*>. According to Plato they were innate <*conati*>, for at least we have not acquired them now, but rather everyone brings them along as renovated ideas (note: the ideas of Plato 29:761 refer to mystical intuition and are different from the concepts <*conceptus*> of Aristotle). We note that our understanding can think but not intuit. If one accepts the latter, then they are all innate <*conati*>. Aristotle

[d] An *X* is placed in the ms before this sentence (760$_8$).
[e] Marginalia (760$_{13-14}$) alongside text printed at 760$_{11-12}$. We follow Lehmann in inserting it immediately after this text. There is no insertion sign, unless it is the *X* noted above at 760$_8$. Paragraph breaks and blank lines added by Lehmann have been removed.

says: the concepts of the understanding are not innate <*conati*> but rather acquired <*acquisiti*>, we obtained them on the occasion of experience, when we reflect upon the objects of the senses. Now one says: our concepts are innate but not, as Plato says, that they are renovated ideas which we originally acquired, but rather God has placed certain fundamental concepts in everyone, to direct the understanding later. To these belong the concept of cause and effect. Whether we take the intellectual things <*intellectualia*> as logical or mystical, we can still ask whether they are innate, since we neither can nor may come to them through reflection, or nothing is innate in us other than the ability of the understanding. In modern times Locke was the follower of Aristotle. He said: nothing is in the intellect which was not first in the senses <*nihil est in intellectu quod non antea fuit in sensu*>. {Locke maintained: a practiced understanding can even comprehend the manner in which something can come from nothing, and yet he wanted to cull all cognition from experience. He proceeded quite inconsistently.}[f] Leibniz was the follower of Plato, believed in innate ideas <*ideas connatas*>, but left the mystical aside. Crusius also maintained this, although he does not express himself quite so obscurely regarding this. – One can say that the school of Plato has still retained something of the mystical intellect <*intellectus*>. But this opinion is fanatical; everyone can imagine much here – c.g., standing in community with spirits, etc.[18] If we take the logical intellectual things <*intellectualia*> as a basis, there arises the question, how do we arrive at them? E.g., the concept of the necessary, the contingent, etc., are sheer concepts of the understanding. Now one can take two ways: either they arose from the understanding, then one follows Plato, though not his mysticism, but rather in what he maintains of their origin; and Aristotle said: nothing is in the intellect which was not first in the senses <*nihil est in intellectu quod non antea fuit in sensu*>. But there is a misunderstanding here: our concepts never arise other than upon the occasion of objects of the senses, upon which the understanding reflects. In this Aristotle is right. For if nothing is given to us, then we cannot reflect on anything. Plato says, on the contrary, they are not borrowed from the senses, and in that he was also right, for could our senses ever bring about the concept of the necessary or the possible? In which would it lie, in smell, in taste, etc.? The concepts of the understanding are nothing other than actions of reflection. But since it is impossible to reflect if I have no object, which the senses deliver it to us, the understanding would not reflect if the senses provided no stuff. Pure understanding produces concepts, but they would not occur if there was no stuff. So Plato was also right. Aristotle meant to

29:762

---

[f] Marginalia (761_{16-19}) alongside text printed at 761_{14-20}. We follow Lehmann in inserting it before the last sentence of this text; paragraph breaks and blank lines added by Lehmann have been removed.

maintain that matter, but not form, came from the senses; had he so expressed himself, and Plato in turn: the form for reflecting is what the understanding has independently of the senses, then no dispute would have arisen and both kinds of systems could easily have been united. Here the one cannot dispense with the other. All concepts of the understanding would mean nothing if the senses delivered no objects and examples. If, e.g., I explained however well what a substance was and yet did not know to give an example, then it would be all for nothing; and again, without understanding we would have no concepts, and we would gape at everything. We think of form through concepts of the understanding, as the understanding makes concepts of the appearances; now I can leave aside the appearances, but then the concept would still have no meaning without them. But it is entirely correct that the concepts of the understanding are not derived from the senses, for they arise out of reflection, but the senses do not reflect. Now one can err in saying all concepts of the understanding are derived from the senses, and of this Aristotle is guilty; he had not expressed his opinion precisely enough, and Plato again goes too far and says we have representations of the understanding independently of the senses; without any of the senses the understanding would cognize things, indeed even much better, for the senses, instead of being helpful to us, even hinder us. But now he already deteriorates into fantasy: he says we see only the shadows of things; the understanding [sees] the things in themselves. If only he had said that we have concepts that we draw not from the senses but which rather occur in the understanding independently of the senses, and if only he had admitted that they alone do not provide objects as long as the senses do not deliver them. With his symbolic nothing <*nihil*>, etc., etc., Aristotle still leapt to things which go entirely beyond the senses, e.g., the cosmos, the primordial being. Of

29:763 these the senses can teach us nothing. {Aristotle was right that there were no innate concepts <*conceptus connatos*>, but that did not justify his proposition: nothing is in the intellect which was not first in the senses <*nihil est in intellectu quod non antea fuerit in sensu*>. All of metaphysics builds on that, and of all the ancient metaphysicians with whom we are acquainted, Aristotle is the greatest.}[g]

We will show that all concepts are acquired <*acquisiti*>, only not all from the senses; we also have many through the pure use of reason. A scholar proceeds inconsistently if he behaves contrary to his accepted principles, and Professor Kant calls empiricists those who take all concepts of the understanding from experience, and now we say almost all empiricists, Aristotle, Locke, etc., act inconsistently. For if all concepts are

---

[g] Marginalia (763$_{1-4}$) alongside text printed at 762$_{38}$–763$_5$. We follow Lehmann in inserting it after this paragraph. A paragraph break and blank lines added by Lehmann have been removed.

borrowed from experience, then they can assume nothing other than what [rests]^L on experience. But God is not in any experience. Thus we cannot say anything of him. Epicurus belongs to those who proceed very consistently. Epicurus seems to have feigned worship of the gods,[19] and this in order to avoid the priests' censure. Plato is the philosopher of the intellect and Epicurus of sensibility. Although his propositions were strange, one still must forgive him because perhaps he was not rightly understood. In his philosophy he sought to restrict the proofs of things, but not the things themselves. That is always a great difference. He said: no concept has a meaning if a corresponding object in experience cannot be given for it. We have no text from him, but we have his opinions from the poet Lucretius. In philosophy one should not attach very much credence to a poet. He said: we can reflect only on the objects of the senses. He also made up gods, but they were entirely sensible, namely, composed from the finest atoms <*atomis*> of the world. Leibniz was a follower of Plato; he began to go further than the senses reached, but he did not say how it comes about that concepts of the understanding, which we have without the senses, have validity with respect to the objects of the senses. Plato and Aristotle had a metaphysics. But Epicurus none. With him everything was physics, natural science. He said there could be no principles other than those experience confirms. In this he might have been wrong or not, but in any event he was the anti-metaphysician of the ancients. We note the following on the differentiation of philosophical investigations. We can distinguish physiology, critique of pure reason, and system of science. Physiology of pure reason[20] is the inquiry into the origin of concepts. It is an investigation of a matter of fact <*re facti*>, it is, as lawyers say, question of fact <*quaestio facti*>. How has it come to that?^{h} This investigation can be quite subtle, but it does not belong in metaphysics; but since we do have such concepts, we must also ask by what right we avail ourselves of them. This latter question has a far more important influence in metaphysics, for that is critique, thus question of right <*quaestio iuris*>. The former question has been the business of two philosophers,^{i} of Locke and Leibniz, the former wrote a book on human understanding <*de intellectu humano*> and the latter published a book with this title in French.[21] Locke adheres to Aristotle and maintains that concepts arose from experience through acts of reflection. Leibniz adheres to Plato, but not to his mysticism, and says that the concepts of the understanding are prior to acquaintance with any sensible objects. – And^j physiology is the consideration of the nature of reason: how reason generates concepts of the understanding

29:764

---

^{h} A paragraph break added by Lehmann has been removed (764$_5$).
^{i} Lehmann misreads *2 Phil:* as *der Philosophie* (764$_{10}$).
^{j} An *und* (before *die Physiologie*), omitted by Lehmann without note, has been replaced (764$_{16}$).

in us; it is really a part of psychology. No one has thought of a critique of pure reason until now. Systems without physiology were expounded by authors such as, e.g., Wolff,[22] who also expounds a system without indicating[k] how all this came about. He investigates only the content, but how far the use of the pure cognition of reason goes, with what right we avail ourselves of it, that is critique, thus question of right <*quaestio iuris*>. Critique is thus to be distinguished sharply from physiology and system. E.g., one proves that a spirit thinks; on these grounds one can institute various investigations (1) when these grounds produce conviction in us, and Wolff also allows such an investigation. (2)[l] But how it is possible that reason can know properties of things that are not given in any experience, this[m] belongs to critique. In many cases it appears to be unnecessary, for with cognitions that we have, it appears superfluous to see whether they are possible. But when we see to which illusions reason is subject, then we will comprehend the necessity [of critique]. We thus have before us now a business of such a kind as has never before been pursued. When we see the result of all the cognitions attained through metaphysics, then we see that it can no longer endure like this. Enough systems have been composed which, even where they are in agreement, cannot withstand the onslaught of a mischievous skeptic.[n] If we except the principle of contradiction <*principium contradictionis*>, they contain nothing of use that is so constituted that it[o] can withstand and oppose the attacks of an opponent who is no system maker. Men who have not wanted to exercise their pure reason in vain have either given it up or have continued so far until they found the philosopher's stone.

29:765

[p]Now which way shall we take, the first? That is impossible since we cannot disabuse the understanding of these questions. They are so woven into the nature of reason that we cannot be rid of them. All the despisers of metaphysics, who wanted thereby to give themselves the appearance of having clearer heads, also had their own metaphysics, even Voltaire.[23] For everyone will still think something about their own soul. This resolution[q] consequently cannot be maintained. Reason would *want to* give up all other sciences rather than this. These questions concern its highest inter-

---

[k] We follow Lehmann in changing *vorzugeben* to *anzugeben* (764₂₁).
[l] A 2 (following *Wolff*), omitted by Lehmann without note, has been replaced (764₂₉).
[m] We follow Lehmann in changing *sind. Die* to *sind, diese* (764₃₀).
[n] Lehmann misreads *Scepticers* as *Scepticismus* (765₁).
[o] We follow Lehmann in changing *die . . . sind . . . sie* to *das . . . ist es* (765₂₋₃).
[p] There is a hatch mark in the ms at the beginning of this paragraph (765₇). It may be an insertion sign for the long marginalia (767₈–768₃₀), i.e., where the "two ways" in the following text are the immanent and transcendent uses of reason as discussed in the marginalia (768₇).
[q] Presumably, to abandon metaphysics.

est, and to say reason should no longer occupy us with these matters is to say it should stop being reason. We are thus left with the critique of reason. It criticizes how far reason can go in its pure use, from which reason creates principles independent of experience, and the critique can be wholly satisfying. Up to now in metaphysics we still have not had anything satisfactory, for all systems can be shaken. The teacher of metaphysics can proceed in such a way that he conceals the weaknesses of the proofs from his students and merely shows off with this illusory wisdom. In the future, if they read and think more on this, they will see how little had been sound, through which many minds have gone to waste. Our reason can make mighty strides without critique; it convinces itself of the correctness of its use through its basic advances. E.g., with mathematics we can safely avail ourselves of reason without criticizing it beforehand; the cause of this is that it can exhibit its concepts in intuition, but it also must not go any farther. Intuition convinces it of the correctness of its use. In philosophy I dare not bring forth cognitions which have a presumed self-evidence, for in that way many illusions can occur. In mathematics, as already said, illusion is prevented by intuition, but in metaphysics by critique. We thus comprehend the necessity of this [critique]. Thus the difficulties which come up in discovering a critique must be overcome.

{'and this transcendent use of pure understanding' has the difficulty   29:767
that one can confirm nothing about it through experience – but it has the advantage – that no one can refute it through experience. Metaphysics is concentrated in the transcendent use of reason, because the most interesting objects are there, and it finds no satisfaction in experience. We would not take the trouble to prove and dissect principles – and to produce a science – for the sake of the immanent use of reason unless this seemed to prepare us to climb up to the ideas. We have many *a priori* cognitions that we cannot do without in experience. E.g., when something happens, there must be a cause. This proposition is *a priori* because of [its] "must" – and necessary with experience because otherwise we would have no connection in the series of experiences. We do not need metaphysics for the principles that are necessary in experience, although it is a good thing – and culture of the understanding, to separate in experience what belongs to reason and to the senses. We must thus first examine the use of pure reason with respect to experience – for this is its simplest use, and it

---

' The following passage (767_8–768_{39}) comes from the margin of ms 19'–20' (alongside the text printed at 765_{21}–766_{21}). It begins with: *X und dieser trscdent trscdtlte Gebrauch*, and ends with: *vide supra X*. (The *tl* of *trscdtlte* is possibly crossed out, so we are omitting it as an unwanted repetition of "transcendent"; Lehmann omits the *und* and *trscdtlte* without note.) Lehmann claims that there is an insertion sign for this marginalia, but he does not indicate *what* sign or where, and we cannot find one. We insert the marginalia here before the discussion headed "The Use of Metaphysics" (766_1).
' Lehmann misreads *des reinen Verstand* as *der reinen Vernunft* (767_8).

occurs in the transcendental analytic (transcendental philosophy is that which investigates the possibility^t of metaphysics), where we dissect the *a priori* concepts that are necessary for the purposes of experience – but this still is of no benefit, e.g., we already make use of everything that happens [has a cause],^{u} as a proposition which is true only through induction <*per inductionem*>. – But reason does not find its satisfaction in experience, it asks about the "why," and can find a "because" for a while, but not always. Therefore it ventures a^v step out of the field of experience and comes to ideas, and here one cannot satisfy reason – except by cognitions of its own nature and by answers that can be given through cognition of its sources –

29:768 extent – and boundaries. This part, [to which]^L we ascribe the *a priori* concepts that go beyond experience, is called transcendental dialectic, and here metaphysics is necessary because the most interesting objects lie beyond the boundaries of experience, and metaphysics will receive its value from the necessary relation of our reason to objects beyond experience. –

There is a twofold use of pure understanding: the immanent is namely where the *a priori* cognitions have their objects in experience. Likewise there are also *a priori* basic propositions which apply to objects of experience, that is pure reason, but in its immanent use – and if we separate it from experience, then it is analytic – and the transcendent [use] namely where the *a priori* cognitions do not have their objects in experience. Metaphysics which expounds the transcendent use of reason occupies itself not with the correctness of propositions,^{w} definitions, and proofs, but with ideas, and this is the realm of necessities^x – although there are also some of these in the immanent use. E.g., a proof of the principle of sufficient reason has been sought to this day – but one still uses it – and no one doubts the principle – but with the transcendent [use of reason] there is no proposition whose truth has not been doubted. Until now no metaphysician has thought of distinguishing these uses of reason. – That is invalid, for in cosmology and also in ontology there are propositions which have objects in experience,^{y} and also those which do not – hence the critique of reason must assume quite different basic propositions with respect to its immanent as opposed to its transcendent use.

---

^{t} Lehmann reads *Mögl* as *Möglichkeiten*. We read it as *Möglichkeit* (767_{28}).

^{u} "Has a cause" is our interpolation. The text has only "everything that happens (etc.)," (762_{31}) but we conjecture the proposition is related to the one about happenings and causes mentioned earlier at 767_{18-19}.

^{v} Lehmann misreads *einen Schritt* as *keinen Schritt* (767_{35}).

^{w} We follow Lehmann in omitting a *deren* following *Sätze* (768_{17}).

^{x} Lehmann's reading of *Notwendigkeiten* (768_{15}) makes sense but is questionable; the text looks more like *S – r – – gkeiten* (perhaps *Streitigkeiten* (disputes)).

^{y} We follow Lehmann in omitting a dash (following *Erfahrung haben;* 768_{24}). Lehmann does not note the omission.

128

We have classified metaphysics into the part which contains the immanent use of reason and that which contains the transcendent. Transcendent and transcendental are definitely to be distinguished. Transcendental pertains not to concepts but rather to science, i.e., to the use of the understanding. Transcendental philosophy is that which considers the pure use of the understanding – and to that belong all the concepts and principles of pure understanding and of pure reason. But some concepts are of immanent use, others of transcendent. Transcendental philosophy considers the entire faculty of pure understanding and of pure reason for cognizing something *a priori*. The concept of ground and cause and [that] of God belong to transcendental philosophy, but the former is immanent. See above *<vide supra>*[z]}

THE USE OF METAPHYSICS 29:766

Now we ask, as with every science: what is its end? The end of each science can be speculative or practical. We have either an intention to widen our cognitions or one that concerns our interest. If we consider the first case then we see that the objects of speculation are twofold, either of experience, or they go beyond experience. In order to become acquainted with the first, we do not need metaphysics. Now we ask: would it really be worth the trouble to sketch out metaphysics for that purpose? – As for physics,[24] we note that it allows no other principles *<principia>* than those which are (1) derived from experience, (2) mathematical, (3) or philosophical, which conform to common sense *<sensu communi>*, and experience – or, more briefly, its principles must be borrowed from experience or be confirmed by experience. This takes place in mathematics, whose [principles] are *a priori* but find their confirmation in experience. Physics concedes that every thing has a cause, for experience confirms it; but it does not investigate the grounds further. Physics wants to have no metaphysical principles. Metaphysics serves just as little to give a deeper experiential acquaintance with the soul. We can discover various things with it, draw out consequences, but without any metaphysical principles – rather they must be confirmed in experience. Metaphysics can thus add little of significance to the cognition of nature. For[a] to explain the appearances of the soul and body[b] it is best to take principles from experience, since otherwise they are unreliable[c] and we can also get on well here without any 29:773

---

[z] This *vide supra*, omitted by Lehmann, has been replaced (768₃₉). It is followed by an X in the ms. See the note at 767₈, above.

[a] An *um* added by Lehmann without note has been removed (766₂₄).

[b] A *des* added by Lehmann has been removed (766₂₅).

[c] Added here above *unzuverlässig sind* (766₂₆) are several illegible words preceded by the words *vide arcum trans*. We follow Stark here, who suggests that this is a reference to 773₁₀ᵇ i.e., the top of ms 25, which begins with these same words *unzuverlässig sind* (and which does

metaphysical principles, yet it can be said that a metaphysic or critique of pure reason serves a use here, for if the first sources of judgment are not checked then one runs the danger of false metaphysical judgments. The use here is therefore negative, to warn against false metaphysics, and not positive, to expand science. Since the object of metaphysics does not lie in bodily and thinking nature, what is it then to which metaphysics applies? It must be an object beyond the senses. Metaphysics means beyond natural science, beyond the natural things <*meta ta physica*>,[d] it means beyond physics <*trans physicam*>. Some have held this name to be unsuitable and believed Aristotle named it such because it followed the physics in his convolutes: *meta* means not "after," but "beyond," and this designation is most fitting and appears to have been carefully thought out by Aristotle. It is the science of things which go out beyond all appearances, what lies beyond nature. Here we take nature not in the broad sense <*sensu toto*>, but rather the strict one <*proprio*>. For it is called the summation of all objects of the senses. Here I can think of nothing other than God and an other world. A being which is distinguished from all other things, and a life that follows upon this and is distinguished from it, these two propositions rule the whole of metaphysics: if we are indifferent here, then we can be indifferent in all parts. Given these two propositions, which are the hinges <*cardines*> upon which the entirety of metaphysics turns, then the question is: for what do we need to answer these two questions? – If we name that part of metaphysics which deals with the primordial being rational theology <*theologia rationalis*>, and the part that deals with future life, because it presupposes the immortality of the soul, rational psychol-

29:774 ogy <*psychologia rationalis*>, then metaphysics has only these two parts: rational psychology <*psychologia rationalis*> and rational theology <*theologia rationalis*>. Regardless of the uses these have, they must still interest us in a certain way. – This is all the same to us with respect to speculative being, for I will explain natural appearances as though they came from the constitution of nature; I cannot call on God. For that would mean putting aside all philosophizing. It is likewise with the immortality of the soul, for here I can say: let us wait until we arrive there, where we can make experiments. – Through speculation we can accomplish and settle noth- ing. There must thus be a practical intent. What will I do if there is a God and another world? Now it is clear that this interests us very much. I must now comport myself entirely differently than when I see that only the sensible world exists. – Now I avail myself of things as suits my intentions, as I can promote my gratification, still my desires. (All human beings want

not seem to follow the text on ms 24′). Apparently Mrongovius (or the copyist) had inadver- tently begun copying material from the Ontology section (viz. 766$_{27}$–767$_7$, 769$_1$–773$_9$), and then finished copying here the Introduction section (viz. 773$_{10}$–784$_6$).
[d] This is written with Greek letters in the ms, as is *meta*, later (773$_{22}$).

to be happy – reason prescribes laws and conditions under which alone one is worthy of happiness. – Morality, which contains these conditions, does not teach us the path to happiness, but rather *only* the conditions under which we are worthy of such, and that is the practical interest of reason in the principles of life's way. – But religion is also joined <*connexa*> with a speculative interest – I ask, can I also hope to share in happiness if I am not unworthy of it? Here we must presuppose a wise world ruler. – Were nothing resting on this for us, that the rules of morality would have influence over us and a motive power, then we could be spared all speculation about this. As soon as we have no practical interest, i.e., as soon as we do not worry about our worthiness to be happy, that all falls away.) If I have a ground to suspect there is another world and a world author, then an entirely other interest opens up. What must I thus do? In the practical respect these two propositions are thus of the highest importance and more important than all other ends. – They concern our ultimate ends. If there is yet another world, a world author upon whom my destiny in that world depends, what am I to do in order to partake in a lasting happiness? Granted now that all speculation about the two questions can give us no sufficient and satisfying instruction, what use would metaphysics then yield? We must see whether there might not be another way to arrive at it. Let us think what I should do if there is God and another world, then we see that morality teaches what I must do if I am not to be despicable in my own eyes and if I want a share of happiness. (We do not find that happiness is always distributed in the right proportion. The vicious triumph and the virtuous must show no concern. Thus if our present life completes our existence, then we cannot say that we would be happy to the same extent as we are worthy. – We must thus accept yet another world. – From these two needs, God (for we can expect nothing from blind necessity, that it should make us happy insofar as we are worthy of that, rather we must assume for that a wise world ruler) and another world, metaphysics arises; everything in [the]^L immanent [world]$^{L e}$ refers to this, and [among]^L all the questions which speculative philosophy can ever cast up, none are so urgent and interesting that they should move us to entwine ourselves in such difficult speculations. Both of these objects are entirely beyond the field of experience (God and another world, which is just what lies beyond the circle of all my presently possible experience); empirical principles can thus be of no use to me now; rather, here pure reason alone must decide. Theology and psychology are thus the proper parts of metaphysics. In the latter we seek to get to know this much of the nature of the soul, that it can still survive when its animal life ceases, and indeed [as] a spiritual life.) (Pure philosophy has yet another use: it enlightens the understanding, we explicate our con-

29:775

---

^{e} Lehmann does not note his addition of *Welt* and *unter* (775_{16}).

cepts here. The use is logical, but much too small for the trouble which we must expend on it. Its primary use is to liberate us from errors with respect to these objects. It does not serve to obtain them for us, for it is quite easy to comprehend that cognitions which are such great needs will not lie so high that the highest speculation is necessary for them, but rather that common sense can be convinced of them as well, and so it is also in fact. It finds so many traces of wisdom in the world, from which it concludes that there must be a wise world author; if along with this it unites the command which reason or rather this wise world author gives to

29:776 it, then it must hope for another world, because it finds that virtue and vice do not receive their rightful desert.

It is indeed true that speculative reason is not necessary [to]$^{L.f}$ produce these concepts – but for many it will nevertheless turn out [to be necessary], for speculating and this speculative reason can lead our beliefs into such error and make it so inconstant, even bringing us into errors (which common reason can as well), that we must of necessity have similar weapons against it, and that is metaphysics.)^g

Everyone readily comprehends that it is unfair to demand happiness without conducting oneself worthy of such. Morality teaches this. It thus rests not on metaphysics, since I can ground a morality that does not presuppose metaphysics; thus I have a law of conduct for becoming worthy of happiness, which it teaches apodictically. But that, we see, still always lacks something. Can I then also hope to partake of happiness if I am worthy of it? If my disposition and conduct are directed by and based upon morality, then it is necessary to bind myself with the basic moral proposition: to carry out no actions but those in accord with the law of duties, a belief in a gracious world ruler who wants to have us partake in happiness, and in another world in which we will be able to partake in it. But can metaphysics expand this belief? No, but this belief is [not only]$^{L.h}$ supported by the consideration of the entirety of nature, but this [also]^L makes it secure against all objections of speculative reason, to which it sets boundaries. – Metaphysics is thus not the foundation of religion – how could it look otherwise with the non-metaphysical minds – but rather the bulwark against the attacks of speculative reason. For this is quite dangerous and its attacks are unavoidable. Its use is thus negative: to hinder errors, but it is immense, because these are so ruinous.

Morality is the cognition of that which I must irremissably do according to the basic propositions of reason, which concern my entire end.[25] This is already given to us and requires no metaphysical principles and

---

^{f} This *zu* is not apparent, but may be hidden in the fold of the ms (776$_4$).
^{g} A closing parenthesis omitted by Lehmann without note has been replaced (776$_8$), as well as the following paragraph break, likewise omitted by Lehmann without note.
^{h} Lehmann adds *nicht nur* (776$_{23}$), support for which is found at 778$_{20-2}$, below.

does not need to presuppose God and another world. But the motives of morality will be strengthened more if I see that there is a God and another world. The moral laws must also precede the theological ones, they exhibit to us the most perfect will of God. But first we must recognize the perfection of our wills and then set up the divine as our model. Morality is a canon. Every lawgiving is a canon insofar as it is absolutely commanded; it must presuppose no condition. Not even that of God and another world. It must be recognized from the nature of action what is to be done and what omitted. Morality teaches what I should do. But it gives no ready incentives to do that which reason prescribes as duty. The summation of the incentives to actions is happiness, and these no mortal can dispense with – and these are lacking with morality; I cannot hope, or I cannot comprehend whether I can hope, to partake in happiness. Morality teaches not this, but how to become worthy of happiness. The same can be comprehended *a priori*, without cognition of propositions about God and another world. – Laws are not complete which do not carry with them a threat and a promise apart from their fulfillment. – Moral laws have no threat or promise that we should partake in happiness or be deprived. Nor can it be so in this world, for here well-being and acting well are not bound together. – But for morality there still remains one belief, that there perhaps might be a wise world ruler and another world. If this were not so, moral laws would have no success. Now we can imagine a practical dilemma, i.e., a proposition that shows that one[i] is delivered into pure absurdities, turn where one may, if one does not concede something. A practical dilemma is one where if I do not presuppose something then I will always plunge myself into a practical absurdity <*absurdum practicum*>. That is twofold: (1) a principle according to which I give up all claim to honor, honesty, and conscience. (2) A principle according to which I give up all claim to happiness. – If we assume moral principles without presupposing God and another world, then we trap ourselves in a practical dilemma. Namely, if there is no God and no other world, then I must either constantly follow the rules of virtue, [and] then I am a virtuous dreamer, because I expect no consequences which are worthy of my conduct – or I will throw away and despise the law of virtue, tread over all morality because it can bring me no happiness, I will[j] give way to my vices, enjoy these enjoyments of life while I have them, and then I form a principle through which I become a knave. We must thus decide to be either fools or knaves. – This dilemma indicates that the moral law that is written in our reason is inextricably bound with a belief in God and another world. – With the ancients such pure virtue was not taught as

29:777

29:778

---

[i] We follow Lehmann in moving a *man* from after *einraümt* to after *dass* (777_{24}). Lehmann does not note the change.
[j] Lehmann misreads *werde* as *würde* (777_{38}).

with us, but they could also exercise virtue without believing in God and another world. They exercised only a political virtue, which is mere cleverness that brought respect, happiness, and advantages of life their way. Here is the question: whether someone can adhere to the purest virtue, by which many gratifications of this life must be sacrificed, without belief in God and another world. Such is wholly impossible. In his eyes he would always be worthy of honor, but for all that a dreamer. Belief in God and another world is inextricably bound with the cognition of our duty, which reason prescribes, and of the moral maxims for living according to it. The mere beauty of an action cannot incite us to it;[26] that is a great motive, but we still sacrifice it to advantage. If we thus should attain no knowledge through metaphysics according to logical conditions, then there remains only a moral belief, which will be not only not contested by the consideration of the entirety of nature, but rather will be strengthened. If we do not satisfy reason in its speculative use, still we do in the practical, and this moral belief is as unshakable as the greatest speculative certainty, indeed even firmer, because that which is grounded on the principles of resolution is way above the principles of speculation – and here we receive freedom to examine impartially with the greatest scrutiny all proofs of God and of the immortality of the soul, so as to remove illusion from them when they promise to do more than they really do and can do, to throw away everything sophistical; and if none remained, these great truths will nonetheless lose nothing, because if we are not convinced enough in a speculative respect, then we still are in a practical respect. Here we have the true freedom to philosophize[k] without any compulsion or partiality. With most of our philosophizing we shall not find anything other than others have already found, approving what others held to be true, but not making the slightest change. With these things we want now to concern

29:779 ourselves more extensively. [l]The whole of metaphysics is nothing other than a chain of built-up and overthrown systems. No book has yet appeared where there is something permanent. It is not a science which has the fate to be permanent. The more the understanding begins to become enlightened, the more value it yet receives, because no one can cast off metaphysical questions, because they are too closely tied to the interest of human reason. It will be objected that Wolff and Crusius have published metaphysics. Without checking the matter itself, look only at the success. They have all collapsed already. A few propositions were true, but not the whole. With respect to such metaphysical propositions one can adopt the dogmatic path, i.e., to become acquainted with one's pure reason as far as possible. A treatment of science is dogmatic when one does not trouble to investigate from which powers of the mind a cognition arises, but rather lays

[k] We are reading *philosohiren* as *philosophieren* (778₃₅).
[l] A paragraph break added by Lehmann has been removed (779₁).

down as a basis certain general and accepted propositions and infers the rest from them; a treatment is critical when one attempts to discover the sources from which it arises. In mathematics the latter is not needed since everything that it says can be confirmed by experience, but in philosophy this is not so, and here in the use of many cognitions we often find great difficulties and contradictions then, although they seem to be immediately certain, just like basic propositions of mathematics, e.g., everything that exists is in time. We must therefore investigate the powers of the mind out of which the cognitions arise, in order to see whether we can trust them, regardless of whether they seem to be obviously true – – and then, to cognize something *a priori*, which is what the faculty in general is based on. The critical method examines the proposition not objectively or according to its content, but rather subjectively. – Accordingly, the method of metaphysics is critical and*m* dogmatic in order to find a criterion for distinguishing between the cognitions which legitimately arise from understanding and from reason, and those which come about through*n* an illusion or through one's deceiving oneself. In metaphysics we will not ask whether the propositions: there is a God and [there is] another world are true, but rather whether the understanding can get that far through mere speculation. One can become so convinced of something practically, according to all rules of rational belief, that no reason will deny it,*o* but not in a speculative respect. – With the first question, whether the propositions are true in general, we will show that no one can deny them without abandoning all rational basic propositions, for which however we will merely need common sense, to enlighten it just a little. With the second question,*p* whether we can proceed so far through mere speculation, without a practical intention, we will show that such is not feasible. – We want to call that logical truth, thus we cannot become logically certain of the propositions – with critical investigations we will find weaknesses of the understanding which are large, and that it pretends to much cognition that it does not have. Here metaphysics has no positive use, but many negative ones: until now one has always criticized propositions, but no one [has criticized] reason itself, and therefore nothing permanent has been achieved here. (In no science is the negative use so great as in metaphysics, for in no other are the errors so great and dangerous. Critique is thus needed here more than in any other science, for here everything has negative use. We can show that the principles with which an opponent argues against me and wants to shake belief in God and another world are

29:780

---

m An *und* omitted by Lehmann without note (following *critisch*) has been replaced (779₃₀).
n Lehmann misreads *durch* as *ohne* (779₃₃).
o A period added by Lehmann without note has been removed (779₃₉).
p *Absicht* (780₄) is here translated as "question" so as to avoid confusion; it is the same term that is translated as "respect" and "intention" elsewhere in the paragraph.

not at all grounded in reason – thus the incapacity of reason to hold something against religion.) The first way was to discover propositions and to bring them into a system; then [as]^L one saw that this caused discord, one began to examine reason itself, not in order to debate the matters but rather to investigate what sort of sources they have, how far it can go without experience. These were investigations of the subject, and this decision was very reasonable. For when we cannot advance with the object, then it is good to direct our attention itself^q to the subject itself, and this had to come about sometime, for if I cannot be certain of things speculatively, I still must be certain of the sources, boundaries, and principles of reason. With many things we cannot provide a solution, as e.g., in natural science, and we cannot judge here whether they somehow are possible, because all of our insights in natural science depend on experience, and we cannot know how far we will get with it. Here one cannot possibly determine the boundaries of human reason. Nor with respect to mathematics, because everything is grounded in intuitions there, from

29:781 which consequences flow; since the intuitions can be infinite here, the consequences can also be infinite. One can thus not determine whether or not many more properties of the circle still will be discovered. In metaphysics we use pure reason, without grounding ourselves in intuitions. It is pure philosophy which cognizes objects through pure concepts. It is a special science of the use of reason through concepts. If we have still not come very far here, which is how it actually is, we still can determine with certainty something with respect to reason. The boundaries of pure reason must allow^r themselves to be determined with certainty because the objects are reflected from intuitions, for if we are not given objects through experience then we do not have any objects of reflection. We will thus be able to reckon all the concepts of pure reason, [and] also to enumerate the basic propositions and to show how far the use of pure reason reaches and within which limits it must be held, and now we can show whence illusion arises and which questions are either answered or proposed, and which prevailed in so many systems. We will be able to secure morality and religion against the illusory objections of speculative reason, and in this human reason attains its complete satisfaction, and such a work is possible. (In the previous century <*saeculo*>, when all sciences underwent a great revolution, when experimental physics came into fashion, one also began to examine reason, but physiologically, not critically. This was actually an explanation and investigation of the origin of concepts. Locke and Leibniz had not thought of a critique of concepts of reason; they investigated merely how we arrive at the concepts. Locke

---

^{q} A *selbst* (following *Aufmerksamkeit*) removed by Lehmann has been replaced (780$_{28}$).
^{r} Lehmann misreads *muss* as *lassen*. A *lassen* (following *bestimmen*) omitted by Lehmann has been replaced (781$_9$).

said all concepts are borrowed from experience. Leibniz no. We also have some through pure reason. That is easy to distinguish, e.g., can experience really provide the concept of cause and effect, of God, etc.? But Leibniz did not ask how reason comes to a concept independently of all experience – upon what is the faculty grounded for cognizing something *a priori* at all? How far does it reach? Something similar to a critique of pure reason was found with David Hume, but he sank into the wildest and most inconsolable speculation[s] over this,[27] and that happened easily because he did not study reason completely, but rather only this or that concept.) 'An investigation of practices <*facti*>, how we arrive at cognition, whether from experience or through pure reason." Locke accomplished much here, and this can 29:782 also have uses, but it is not especially needed and also scarcely possible – it would be better to ask how many concepts are of pure reason, what is their meaning, i.e., to which objects can they apply, how can they be used, and within which boundaries must they be held? That is a critique of pure reason. We see here with what right we avail ourselves of concepts apart from experience, whether we do this not illegitimately. Through critique I do not arrive at a certainty regarding questions, insofar as they are to be answered dogmatically, but rather of what reason can execute with respect to all metaphysical questions. Such a critique is yet[v] to be published, save from Professor Kant Riga 1781."[28]

(Note. Metaphysics can be classified into metaphysics as natural predisposition and metaphysics as science. The summation of all our cognitions of reason through concepts, which are inherent in every human being and of which he avails himself in experience, is natural metaphysics <*metaphysica naturalis*>. Every cognition of reason, insofar as it is concrete <*in concreto*>, or not speculative, is natural, and of these there is a considerable number; thus the common use of the understanding also has a metaphysics, and this metaphysics surely deserves to be raised to a science. Not every natural use of reason may be changed into a scientific one, because of the ends to be attained, e.g., in morals one is not to represent the rules abstractly <*in abstracto*> but rather merely concretely <*in concreto*>. It is difficult, e.g., to *prove a priori* the illegitimacy of lying or to demonstrate this abstractly <*in abstracto*>,[x] to be sure, it can be done concretely <*in concreto*>; but with[y] metaphysics it is necessary. We have various *a priori* cognitions which do find their confirmation in experi-

---

[s] Lehmann misreads *Speculation* as *Scepticism* (781₃₆), although he notes at Ak. 29: 1155: *Text wie: Speculationen.*
[t] A paragraph break added by Lehmann has been removed (781₃₈).
[u] A dash added by Lehmann without note has been removed (781₃₉).
[v] We follow Lehmann in omitting a *nicht* between *noch* and *nie* (782₁₁).
[w] A blank line added by Lehmann (as noted Ak. 29: 1109) has been removed (782₁₃).
[x] We follow Lehmann in reading *zeigen oder in abstracto* as *oder in abstracto zeigen* (782₂₇).
[y] Lehmann misreads *mit* as *in* (782₂₇).

ence – but also transcendent concepts, and here natural^z metaphysics cannot help, since the confirmation of general principles is lacking in experience; so I flutter about as in empty space, and if^a science does not confirm itself through itself *a priori*, then I run the danger of lapsing into phantoms of the brain.^b The natural use of reason occurs when we remain in experience, but is inadequate as soon as we go beyond that, and since this is necessary here, metaphysics as science is necessarily unavoidable for reason – it searches whether it can find solutions there to the entangled

29:783 questions which even true reason proposes; even practical reason looks about for one, treating metaphysics as a science, or testing it by itself, and no cognition has such a need to be a science as metaphysics. It is ridiculed as a useless and easily dispensable affair, but the same could also easily be said of the topic of the circulation of the blood[29] – one cannot excuse oneself with that: it concerns reason and our cognitions; in nature there are mysteries, but the things are outside of me and I should study them, here covers are drawn over; but I think something, I think things *a priori* which are only creations of my understanding, so information must be able [to be]^L given with respect to them, as to whether my claims have a ground or not. It is not research into a thing, but rather into an understanding, whose basic propositions and concepts must be open to study, for it all lies within me.) ^c However, we do want to see that we do not incur the loss of the dogmatic method, hence we will present it just like our author. We will accordingly not establish metaphysics as a teaching, as a doctrine, because in the following one will still find that it is all a delusion; rather, we will append the critique of pure reason, through which all dogmatic pretensions will fall to the side. Critique shall thus produce a system of the self-cognition of our reason. In the system of metaphysics we will first go through concepts analytically and merely explain what our reason understands, when it avails itself of this or that concept. That is of great use even if we leave undecided for the moment whether the questions of metaphysics will be answered or not. This elucidation (not extension) of our cognitions is very useful, for wherever there is reason there are metaphysical concepts. Metaphysics is the summation of all pure cognitions of reason, which is greatly clarified through analysis. The answering of all questions of reason is the synthetic part of metaphysics, where we extend our cognition through pure reason and seek to acquire pure cognition. This is of another kind than analysis, for here concepts of the understanding are dissected, but no questions are an-

---

^z Lehmann misreads *naturl.* as *materiale* (782_{30}).

^a We follow Lehmann in omitting a *sie* (following *wenn*) and a *sich* (following *a priori*) (782_{32-3}).

^b Lehmann misreads *Hirn Gespenst* as *Hirn Geschäfte* (782_{34}).

^c A paragraph break added by Lehmann has been removed (783_{15}).

swered, thus our cognition is not extended, but only elucidated. But in the synthetic [part]^L it is extended and there we need critique because there we make attempts to go beyond experience without reason. Although as   29:784 yet not all philosophers adopt the way of the critique of pure reason, they will still need^d to come to it sometime. Need will teach them this, because only critique offers complete satisfaction, and without it our reason will remain constantly in discord with itself.

ENDOFTHEINTRODUCTION <*FINIS PROLEGOMENORUM*>.

^{d} We follow Lehmann in omitting a *zu* (preceding *seyn*)(784$_3$).

Ontology <Ontologia>

We now begin the science of the properties of all things in general, which is called ontology. (Ontology is supposed to be the science that deals with the general predicates of all things, which are such predicates as are common to the most things – should the predicates not be universals <*universalia*>, i.e., which are common to all things, then who knows what ontology is. They must belong to all things, if not copulatively, i.e., that they each belong to them, then at least disjunctively, one of the two, e.g., composite and not composite. – These predicates belong to all higher [things], but not copulatively, i.e., [such] that both predicates should belong to them, but rather disjunctively, one of the two. If I say general predicate, an exception still always occurs, and how far does it extend?) One easily comprehends that it will contain nothing but all basic concepts and basic propositions of our *a priori* cognition in general: for if it is to consider the properties of all things, then it has as an object nothing but a thing in general, i.e., every object of thought, thus no determinate object. Thus nothing remains for me other than the cognizing, which I consider. (The science that deals with objects in general, will deal with nothing but those concepts through which the understanding thinks, thus of the nature of the understanding and of reason, insofar as it cognizes something *a priori*. – That is transcendental philosophy, which does not say something *a priori* of objects, but rather investigates the faculty of the understanding or of reason for cognizing something *a priori*; thus with regard to content it is a self-cognition of the understanding or of reason, just as logic is a self-cognition of the understanding and of reason with regard to form; the critique of pure reason belongs necessarily to transcendental philosophy. But since one used to treat ontology without a critique – what was ontology then? An ontology that was not a transcendental philosophy. Thus one philosophized back and forth without asking: can one do that? Transcendental philosophy is the result of critique, for if I can represent the extent and the sources in a connection then the connected representation of the *a priori* principles is transcendental philosophy, and if I take all the consequences that flow from that, then that is metaphysics; without critique I do not know whether the concepts of pure reason and pure understanding are all there or whether some are still missing – because I have no principles. One set no boundaries to reason, and thereby went as far as one was able. They indeed comprehend that in matters of experience they cannot mix everything together, but *a priori* they can comprehend everything, and that because no one can refute them.)*e*

(Metaphysics is special in that one can wholly complete it, one can measure out the faculty of reason according to its sources, extent, and boundaries. Metaphysics cannot hope to make discoveries into the nature of things, rather reason must teach everything; I can thus settle which concepts lie in reason independently of experience – it is here as with a grammar, which can be complete, but not a lexicon, because during the time the author is writing it, new words will be made again.)

(Something can also be completed in moral philosophy, namely, as Mr. Kant calls it, metaphysics of morals,[30] i.e. the first principles of morality, which are from pure, but practical, reason.)

(The author's ontology is a hodgepodge <*farrago*>, gathered up knowledge which is not a system, but instead rhapsodic[31] – although otherwise he was one of the most acute philosophers. The cause is that one still knew nothing of critique.) A science which is supposed to treat the properties of all things in general must be an *a priori* science. Thus it is a cognition from mere reason, [and] cannot be created from experience, for experience does not reach so far that it can be applied to all things; it does not teach what must belong to things in general, but rather what our senses show us; while ontology has no determinate object,[32] it can contain nothing but the principles of *a priori* cognizing in general: thus the science of all basic concepts and basic propositions upon which all of our pure cognitions of reason rest is ontology. But this science will not be properly called ontology. For to have a thing in general as an object is as much as to have no object and to treat*f* only of a cognition, as in logic. The name, however, sounds as if it had a determinate object. But this science has no object that would be distinguishable from the essence of reason, but rather it considers understanding and reason itself, namely their basic concepts and basic propositions in their pure use (or of pure reason and pure understanding); the most fitting name would be transcendental philosophy. A cognition is called a pure cognition of understanding or reason insofar as it is *a priori* possible, and is to be distinguished from the empirical. A pure cognition of reason is, however, not transcendental. But the consideration by pure reason of the nature and possibility of such a pure cognition of reason*g* is transcendental, e.g., the concept of cause and effect is pure but not transcendental, but the consideration of the possibility of such a concept is transcendental. – Between two points only one

29:786

---

e Several blank lines added by Lehmann after the following paragraphs have been omitted ($785_{14, 23, 26}$).
f We follow Lehmann in changing *handeln* to *behandlen* (786_7).
g A comma added by Lehmann without note has been removed (786_{18}).

straight line is possible, is an *a priori* proposition, but not a transcendental proposition, for it deals with an object. But if I consider how it is possible to arrive at such an *a priori* cognition, then that is transcendental. Transcendental philosophy contains the principles of the possibility of *a priori* cognition. It contains all basic concepts of our pure reason and pure understanding, in general all the basic propositions of the possibility of *a priori* cognition, the extent and boundaries of all reason *a priori*. It determines how far pure reason can go without experience; but before that, we must know the content of pure reason, the basic propositions, basic concepts, principles, and conditions of the use of the concepts of pure reason. With the extension of our cognition it is quite necessary to be acquainted with the boundaries beyond which we cannot go, for otherwise we run the danger of working at a loss. We venture to extend our cognition and do not know whether we are in the field of truth or of phantoms of the brain, and even our true cognitions become dubious. *The boundaries of empirical*

29:787 *cognition, as said above, do not allow themselves to be determined.* Physics, i.e., *philosophy concerning the appearances of nature*, thus also has no determinate boundaries, and likewise mathematics, because it can multiply its intuitions without end. The objects of pure reason are such as can [not]*ʰ* be given in experience, e.g., God, world, whole, etc. Now what are the boundaries of pure reason? It must be possible to determine them, for with pure reason the object is not given to me at all; I am thus permitted to study only reason itself, for it is given to me. But with natural science one receives the cognition from elsewhere, namely from experience. With pure cognitions of reason I presumably spin everything out of my self, here experience and intuition cannot help me; since the whole can thus be drawn from my cognition in advance, I have reason in me, thus the boundaries of pure reason must admit of determination – and transcendental philosophy is the determination of the boundaries of the use of pure reason. – Now we proceed to actual cognition, and before we consider it and its elements, i.e., boundaries, sources, and extent, we must note something beforehand, namely, the difference between analytic and synthetic judgments. We can judge in two ways, in that either in judging we attribute to a subject a predicate which already lies in the concept of the subject – *or* in judging we go beyond the concept of the subject and attribute to it a predicate which does not lie in its concept. The former is analytic, the latter synthetic, e.g.: every body is extended, is an analytic judgment. If I think a body, then at the same time I think something extended. – Here I can find the predicate through analysis of the subject. They are called dissecting judgments. Mr. Kant says: elucidating judgments, because they elucidate our cognition. – Every body is heavy is a synthetic judgment, heaviness does not at all lie in the concept of body.

ʰ We presume that this was an inadvertent omission (787₉).

Everything that happens has a cause. In the concept: it happens, the concept of cause is not contained. To happen means that something becomes which earlier was not, here the concept of cause does not lie within this at all; this judgment is *ampliative*. Everything that happens exists in time, is analytic. It happens means: there was a time wherein it arose, which another time preceded, in which it was not. In order to bring out the judgment, I am permitted only to dissect the concept: everything happens. The possibility of analytic judgments is easy, for I cognize only that which I had already in 29:788 the concept of the subject, I am permitted only to dissect the concept. Whether synthetic judgments are possible is a question: synthetic *a posteriori* judgments are easily possible. E.g., every body is heavy, experience teaches this. Now there still remains to be shown the possibility of synthetic *a priori* judgments, and that is difficult to answer, but it constitutes the spirit of the entire transcendental philosophy. Had the philosophers already investigated this instead, then they would have already advanced in many areas. *Mathematics* has a great many synthetic *a priori* judgments. Thus they must be possible. Now we must see how they are possible, since reason makes a great multitude of such synthetic judgments about experience. I have a concept of which I am to say not at all what lies inside it, but rather outside it, and this indeed *a priori* without assistance from experience. How is that possible? E.g., everything that happens has a cause, i.e.: something must precede what happens, from which the latter follows according to a rule, and that which happens is considered as effect. How can I extend for myself a cognition *a priori* in this way? This question <*quaestio*> was never posed so generally, yet it is so exceedingly necessary. Indeed, one can say that the entire transcendental philosophy is an investigation into the possibility of synthetic *a priori* judgments. Before we speak in detail of the answer to this question, let us return again to analytic judgments.

All judgments must have a principle which is the criterion of truth. For without that there is absolutely no difference between true and false judgments. (Metaphysicians no doubt saw that synthetic judgments must have another principle – Leibniz made it the principle of sufficient reason <*principium rationis sufficientis*>: everyone believes this proposition, but how do we arrive at it? Wolff ventured to add *to this* a proof from the principle of contradiction,[33] – but he surely comprehended that it was not adequate, thus said in the note to it that, although this proof was not strict, one could appeal here to common sense. – That is quite true, but if it is supposed to be an *a priori* proposition, it must also be proven *a priori* – and fully, [for] this proposition cannot also be the principle, i.e., principle of judgment,[i] because it itself requires a proof.)[j] What is the principle of

---

[i] Lehmann interprets *Ur* in ms as *Urteilsprincip* (788$_{37}$). Perhaps *Urprincip* (ultimate principle) is meant.

[j] A closing parenthesis omitted by Lehmann without note has been replaced (788$_{38}$).

analytic judgments? For everyone easily comprehends that the synthetic ones must have an entirely different one. – For saying something that lies in the concept, is quite different from going beyond the concept. The principle of analytic judgments is the principle of contradiction: to no subject does there belong a predicate opposed to it <*cuilibet subjecto non competit praedicatum ipsi oppositum*>.[k] All analysis is nothing more than the consciousness that a certain feature is contained in the concept of the thing. The feature that is contained in the concept of the thing is in part one and the same with the thing. Every analytic feature is identical with the concept, not with the entire concept,[l] but rather with a part of it, e.g., every body is extended, is really judged by identity. All analytic affirmative judgments rest on the principle of identity: to any subject there belongs a predicate identical to it <*cuilibet subjecto competit praedicatum ipsi identicum*>[m] (the predicate can be identical in part <*ex parte identicum*>,[34] e.g., every body is composite – or totally identical, in which case it is an empty proposition). Man is an animal, here I say nothing other than what I already think in the concept of man. The principle of identity indicates nothing more than the analysis of the concept (all analytic judgments are easy – and *a priori* propositions – for we need only go through our concepts and see what lies therein, they are falsely presented as propositions of experience). There are also analytic negative judgments. An analytic negative judgment is one where I find through dissection that a certain feature conflicts with the thing, e.g., no body is simple. The simple conflicts with the composite. The principle <*principium*> is: everything must be denied of the thing that contradicts the concept of the thing – the principle of contradiction <*principium contradictionis*> expresses the negation by which I am not permitted to go outside the concept of the thing. Are these the principles of all analytic judgments? Yes, all analytic judgments, affirmative as well as negative, stand under the principle of contradiction. For when a predicate is identical with the subject, then its opposite contradicts the subject, and I will cognize the falsity at once by the principle of contradiction <*principium contradictionis*> when I cognize the truth through the principle of identity <*principium identitatis*>; and vice versa, I will cognize the truth *at once* through the principle of identity <*principium identitatis*>, just as I cognized falsity through the principle of contradiction <*principium contradictionis*>; as long as I can infer here from one to the other, I will accept the principle of contradiction <*principium contradictionis*> as the general principle of all analytic judgments, e.g., a body is simple, i.e., the concept of body is contradicted by the simple, not the composite. The composite thus belongs to it. It is the

29:789

29:790

---

[k] Lehmann misinterprets *subj* as *subjecti* and *praed* as *praedicato* (789_{3-4}).

[l] For clarity, we have removed the parentheses enclosing this clause (789_8).

[m] Lehmann misinterprets *subj* as *subjecti* and *praed* as *praedicato* (789_{11-12}).

same whether I say: a concept contradicts the thing, or its opposite is identical with it – and: a concept is identical with the thing or its opposite contradicts it. The principle of contradiction *<principium contradictionis>* is thus the principle of all analytic judgments. – Can we not also say: the principle of all human cognition? Response *<responsio>*: yes, but then it is not a principle from which all judgments can be derived, but rather a criterion of truth, to which no true cognition can be contrary, because then the thought itself would be contradictory, but that which is not contrary to the principle of contradiction *<principium contradictionis>* is not on that account true, thus it is a negative criterion of truth. The thought of something can be possible, but the matter is not possible on that account: e.g., we can think of a power of the mind by which we think others' thoughts, here nothing is contradictory, but the matter is not yet on that account possible. Here the principle of contradiction *<principium contradictionis>* cannot be a criterion of truth. But it is false, according to the principle of contradiction *<principium contradictionis>*, that at the same time I think and do not think – or stand in immediate connection with a distant object. The principle of contradiction *<principium contradictionis>* is a general principle of all human cognition, but only falsehood is derivable from it. It is indeed general, but not sufficient. There can be no contradiction, and the matter can still be false. The principle of contradiction *<principium contradictionis>* is the general negative criterion of all truth, what is contrary to it is false (the impossible *<impossibile>* in the principle of the author can be nothing other than modality – it should indicate merely the apodicticity of the proposition – which of course, as also here, is not always necessary to express, because it is self-evident). Our author expresses it:[35] it is impossible for something to be and not be at the same time *<impossibile est aliquid simul esse et non esse>*. How can we use this, since we have not yet spoken of time, and thus have many acute authors gone wrong (we first must, or rather can, ask, to what extent is time possible?). The author believes this is at the same time the definition of the impossible.[36] The impossible is what is and is not *<impossibile quod est et non est>* or what contradicts itself. (As we expressed it: to no subject does there belong a predicate opposed to it *<nulli subjecto competit praedicatum ipsi oppositum>*, the at the same time *<simul>* falls away and [the proposition] is still generally valid – for a subject can never take a predicate that opposes it – but clearly a subject can take a predicate which is opposed to another predicate of the same subject, only not at the same time, e.g., a moved body which is at rest[n] is a contradiction, but a body which is at rest and in motion is no contradiction, namely in succession when a subject can take a predicate that is opposite *<oppositum>* another predicate of the same subject; [this] one must and can cognize only

29:791

---

[n] Lehmann misreads *in Ruhe* as *einfach* (simple)(791,).

through experience, or experience teaches the possibility that a thing can be altered.)

(The principle of contradiction <*principium contradictionis*> is the criterion[o] of possibility, and one can also say of truth, only not a sufficient one, but rather a necessary condition <*conditio sine qua non*>.) If that is so, can I reverse: what does not contradict itself, is not impossible (if a definition belongs to something, then the thing defined belongs to the thing <*cui competit definitio competit definitum*>)? That is false, for otherwise all fantasies that do not contradict themselves would be possibilities. – The principle of contradiction <*principium contradictionis*> should precede all cognition, thus cannot depend on the concept of time. Some have expressed it thus: that something be and not be <*ut aliquid sit et non sit*>, that is also false, for it is possible that a thing be and not be, but in succession. All things, as we know, can be altered and alteration is just the succession of predicates opposed after the manner of contradiction <*successio praedicatorum contradictorie oppositorum*>. He expressed the principle of identity thus:[37] whatever is, is that <*quicquid est illud est*>.[p] (The principle of identity enunciates positively what the principle of contradiction enunciates negatively; for if the subject takes identical predicates, then were it to take the opposite, that would be an opposed predicate <*praedicatum oppositum*>, but that is contrary to the principle of contradiction <*principium contradictionis*>.[q] – This principle of contradiction is the highest logical negative principle, and identity is the highest logical positive principle.) (From the two principles combined springs a third, namely, the principle of the excluded middle between two contradictories <*principium exclusi medii inter duo contradictoria*>,[r][38] i.e., of two opposing[s] predicates a subject must always take one, for if I attribute both to it at the same time, one cancels[t] the other, and I think nothing; if I negate both, then I also think nothing (logical), that is, where one is A, the other is non-A. With the principle of the excluded middle <*principium exclusi medii*> we do not compare two contradictorily opposed judgments, but rather a thing with all possible predicates of things in general. Understanding aims to furnish a given concept with predicates from all possibilities.) That is an empty proposition; all empty propositions are not means for arriving at clarity, because the same <*idem*> is explained through the same <*per idem*>; thus no clearer concept arises, e.g., a body is, is a true proposition but empty, and likewise the proposition whatever is, is that <*quicquid est illud*

---

[o] We are assuming that *Critic* (in the ms) was a miswrite of *Criterium* (791_7).
[p] We are adding a period and capitalization here and in the next parenthetical passage ($791_{19, 26}$).
[q] We are reading "p. contr." (in the ms) as *principium contradictionis* rather than Lehmann's *praedicatum contradictum* (contradictory predicate)(791_{23}).
[r] A period added by Lehmann without note (after *medii*) has been removed (791_{27}).
[s] A sign (similar to our uppercase *F*) precedes *opponirt*, as well as the *logisch*, below ($791_{28, 30}$).
[t] We follow Lehmann in adding *auf*, thus reading *aufhebt* instead of *hebt* (lifts)(791_{29}).

est>.[u] When I explain a concept through itself, then I have thought noth- 29:792
ing else. We have not said with our explanation: a predicate identical with
its subject as such *<praedicatum subjecto per tale identicum>*. That would
also be empty, e.g., body is body, but rather identical in part *<ex parte
identicum>*. The predicate is a criterion of falsity *<criterium falsitatis>* of
all human cognition, but [it is] a positive actual predicate of all analytic
judgments which are derivable and provable from it. (An analytic judgment is one where the subject and predicate are identical; now if I attribute an identical predicate to the subject, then if I am attributing an
opposite *<oppositum>* to it, I thereby am also contradicting myself – but
not with a synthetic one, because there the subject and predicate are not
identical.) Now the only way the truth of analytic judgments can be
cognized is that either the predicate is identical with the subject, or its
opposite contradicts the subject. With synthetic judgments, however,
there is no contradiction, therefore I cannot judge them with the principle
of contradiction *<principium contradictionis>*, e.g., that something happens without anything having preceded it, is not self-contradictory, nevertheless it is still false. Hence a contradiction arises only when what is
cancelled is the same as what is posited in the concept of the subject. The
truth of synthetic judgments does not rest on the principle of identity. For
the synthetic judgment consists in this, that I posit something other than
what is identical to the thing, e.g., everything that happens has its cause.
Cause is not identical with what happens, but rather is something completely different.

The author says[39] the *negative* nothing *<nihil negativum>*[v] is as much as
impossible *<impossibile>*; that is as usual and quite right. It is to be
distinguished from the privative nothing *<nihil privativum>*, which
means a lack, e.g., light is something *positive*, darkness something *negative*.
Bright darkness is a negative nothing *<nihil negativum>*. Negative nothing *<nihil negativum>* is that of which no thought at all is possible. I can
think something affirmative and negative, but I think nothing at all when I
think the affirmative and negative at the same time, e.g., bright darkness.
Here I cannot think darkness, because I think brightness, and not brightness, because I think darkness – thus nothing at all. If I think of two[w]
opposed things, then I have two thoughts; if I set them together, then I
think nothing at all. In the advance of cognition one must guard against
pairing together actual thoughts in such a way that in the end nothing at
all is thought.

Contradiction is classified into real and apparent *<in veram et appar-*

---

[u] Lehmann misreads *illud* (that) as *aliud* (other)(791₃₉).

[v] *Negativum* is underlined with a pale ink, presumably the pale red ink found elsewhere in the
ms.

[w] Lehmann inadvertently omits a 2 after *ich* in the ms (792₃₄).

entem>, e.g., no one seems to be a pious fraud <*pia fraus*>⁴⁰ and this is

29:793   indeed an actual [contradiction]ᴸˣ, because whoever is pious cannot deceive, and vice versa. That the earth immediately attracts the moon without touching it is an apparent contradiction. Further, they are *hidden* <*latentes*>,ʸ where the contradiction can be cognized only through analysis, e.g., a permitted lie in emergency is a hidden contradiction; one needs only to show the concept, for emergency cannot give permission to lie. – Evident <*patentes*>, where no dissection is necessary. One must not immediately accuse someone of an obvious contradiction, *for* were it known to him, he wouldᶻ not contradict himself. The evident ones <*patentes*> are thus only relatively evident <*patentes*>. If one wants to accuse another of absurdity, i.e., of evident <*patentis*> contradiction, then he must change the hidden <*latentem*> into the evident <*patentem*>, and if the opponent still persists in it, then he accepts an absurdity.

    Hereby we can introduce the principle of the excluded middle between two contradictories <*principium exclusi medii inter duo contradictoria*>. Two opposed predicates, A and not A <*opposita praedicata, A et non A*>, cannot be posited at the same time; that is a contradiction. To cancel two opposed predicates at the same time also will not do, rather the principle of the excluded middle <*principium exclusi medii*>, etc., says that one must belong to the thing, e.g., round or not round; according to the principle of contradiction <*principium contradictionis*> both cannot belong to the subject, but according to the principle of the excluded middle <*principium exclusi medii*>, etc., both cannot also be denied of the subject. This cannot be derived from the principle of contradiction <*principium contradictionis*>: for if two opposed predicates cannot belong to one thing, but rather one must be rejected, then the other must at the same time be posited in its place. Consequently the principle of contradiction <*principium contradictionis*> is still the *first*. We can make many analytic *a priori* judgments according to this principle, we may dissect the concept and see what is contained within, and affirm the one or deny its opposite, e.g., body, there I think of an extended thing. Thus I say, a body is extended, or no body is not extended. – That is an analytic *a priori* judgment. One can pass analytic *a priori* judgments on all concepts which allow of dissection; if they are simple, then they cannot be dissected, e.g., being, something. – We come now to the synthetic judgments. – Experience is something other than a chain of synthetic *a posteriori* judgments. But we do not want to ask: how are synthetic *a posteriori* judgments possible, that is clear; e.g., I have gold, I want to know more of it than lies in my concept of gold, so I

29:794   make use of experience, place it in various circumstances through which I

ˣ Lehmann does not note his addition of *Widerspruch* (792₃₉).
ʸ Lehmann misreads *latentes* as *latenter* (793₃).
ᶻ Emphasis added by Lehmann to *würde* has been removed (793₉).

become aware of more and more of it and notice, e.g., malleable, fire-resistant etc., then I have a synthetic *a posteriori* judgment. The whole of experience is nothing other than the synthesis of perceptions. Perception is consciousness of sensation. From pure sensations one cannot make any concepts or communicate them to others, for it is the manner in which one finds oneself with something. Someone else finds himself quite otherwise. But one can make concepts from the synthesis of perceptions. Because we are not passive there, we can thus be conscious of all that we must do – .[a]

Experience yields synthetic *a posteriori* judgments. Can we not have synthetic *a priori* judgments? Upon the answering of this question rests the possibility of the whole of metaphysics. (Many reject synthetic *a priori* judgments and thereby the whole of metaphysics – if metaphysics is possible, then such synthetic *a priori* judgments are also possible, and whether they are is the first cardinal question *in* metaphysics.[b] Here we immediately find great difficulties. – We attribute to a subject a predicate which was not in its concept, e.g., all substances are perdurable, all accidents alterable; that is a synthetic proposition. There is nothing in the concept of substance other than that it is *not a property of another thing, but rather is itself a thing.*[c] – Is it *a priori* or *a posteriori*? In order to decide this one must see whether the proposition contains a necessity or not. For experience teaches merely that things are, not that they should be. – Necessity is here with this proposition, thus *a priori*. If something arises that earlier was not, *then we say that it must have a cause.* – That is a synthetic proposition, for to happen is not the same thing as to have a cause. – It is thus a synthetic proposition and indeed *a priori*.) At first we ask: are not certain synthetic *a priori* judgments necessary for the possibility of experience or synthetic *a posteriori* cognitions? Must there not be certain synthetic *a priori* judgments through which the synthetic *a posteriori* judgments are possible? And they would certainly be true, because they are the basis of experience, and it is true. – Thus we see first whether an experience is possible which is not based on synthetic *a priori* judgments.

Experience has matter, i.e., data <*data*>, and form, i.e., the connection of the data <*datorum*>. Perceptions constitute the matter. The unity of multiple perceptions is experience. The unity is the form of the percep-

29:795

---

[a] A dash at the end of the sentence omitted by Lehmann without note has been replaced (794₁₀). Lehmann changes the text, believing the ms to be corrupt here, but it appears corrupt only given his mistaken reading. Lehmann reads the ms (at Ak. 29: 1157) as: *können wir uns also alles dessen bewusst seyn? was wir thun möchten.* (can we thus be conscious of all that we would like to do?). The ms actually reads *können uns also alles dessen bewusst seyn was wir thun müssen – ,*
[b] Emphasis added by Lehmann has been removed (794₁₇).
[c] The underlining in the ms is very light here (794₁₉₋₂₄); this is probably in the pale red ink found elsewhere in the ms.

tions. Yet here there must be a rule of the connection of the perceptions through which all experience is possible. Now this rule cannot again be *a posteriori* for it must precede all experience, thus *a priori*. There will thus have to be an *a priori* rule of the unity of perceptions which makes experience possible. There will be synthetic *a priori* propositions which contain the principles of the possibility of experience, given that experience is [not]^{Ld} an aggregate of perceptions but rather a unity of perceptions ordered according to certain rules, which we will be illustrating in the following. We have now come far enough to see, as though far off in the twilight, that synthetic *a priori* judgments must in some way be possible; because some must even be the basis of experience. Now we must investigate which synthetic propositions may indeed *a priori* precede all experience. – I notice in my experience a duality: intuition, which rests on the senses and is called empirical intuition; and concept, which does not rest on the senses but rather comes about through categories, thus rests on the *understanding*. I thus have *intuition*, which belongs to the *senses*, and *concepts*, which belong to the *understanding*. Now it is asked whether there might be *a priori* intuitions and concepts, or if all is *a posteriori*. Empirical intuitions are representations of an object, how our senses are affected by it. Empirical intuition has two parts: matter and form, and empirical concepts likewise. – The matter of everything empirical – of empirical intuition, is sensation; the form is the shape. The concept has matter, i.e., content, representations, data <*data*>, which are given – the form is the reflection of the understanding, by which it brings the sensations together in such a way that it thinks something general through it. The concept is a sum of sensations processed by the understanding. The empirical constitutes the matter in the perceptions and intuitions and concepts. – The empirical rests on sensations which are *a posteriori*. The matter of all representations is sensation and is given to us *a posteriori*. – If I omit everything from intuition, I still retain the form, i.e., the shape. There is something empirical for all empirical intuition, i.e.,

29:796 sensation, and something that can be represented *a priori*. There is matter in every empirical concept, i.e., sensation, and form, which belongs to the understanding, for it is logical. Now I can retain the intellectual, the form, when I omit everything empirical, e.g., if with chalk I omit the intuition, only the form remains, size, shape, that is *a priori*. *A priori* cognitions of the form of intuition and of the form of concepts are the basis of synthetic *a priori* judgments. We thus must have concepts which are possible before all experience, which are its basis and are synthetic. Sensation constitutes the matter of all experience. If we omit all of that, the shape still remains. I can invent a thousand different shapes in empty space. In geometry real shapes are thought *a priori*, e.g., cones, etc.: thus I will call the form of intuition that which remains of extended beings when I omit all the matter

---

^{d} This *nicht* is probably hidden in the fold of the ms (795_9); see the parallel passage at 934_{17}.

of perception. With a body I think of nothing more than space and shape, i.e., the form of intuition. Everyone has the representation of space *a priori*, that it is extended in length, breadth, and height, that between two points a straight line is possible – therefore they are absolutely necessary. We thus have an intuition of space. – If we omit everything empirical, like weight, density, and color, I still retain the form and shape. Now I ask, can I also omit that? Yes, but then for me no body is left. Through body I think of a substance, so the concept still remains for me. Through substance I think of a subject that is not a predicate of another. In that case I am already arriving at concepts. It is a concept which remains when I omit everything else from the object. Every body has a power in it, i.e., a ground of action, that is again a concept. It has form, a multitude of parts – or it is a whole, here I am also not permitted to think of space. Finally, there still remains the concept of a thing, which is substance, has power, parts, is a whole, which presupposes no shape or figure. Thus pure intuition ultimately remains, and if it is left out, then the pure concept: it is pure because it contains nothing empirical and also has no intuition, is thus transcendental. All pure concepts belong to the understanding. Intuitions are their basis, they provide the object – our understanding reflects, but does not intuit. What are intuitions? They are nothing other than the ways in which our senses are affected by an object. We have no archetypal intellect <*intellectum archetypum*> which would be the productive cause of $\quad$ 29:797 things so that the object arises concurrently with the representation. Thus, because this is not – how can we represent objects to ourselves which the understanding does not produce? Each representation must agree with the object, otherwise there is no cognition. The agreement is possible in two ways, either when my representation produces the object, or when the object produces my representation. Now since our cognition is not of the sort that it produces objects itself, there remains only this, that the things themselves produce cognition, these are thus cognitions which rest on the way we are affected by objects. On this rests all our cognition. Granted, were we not affected by any thing, then we could not have a concept of any thing. Sensibility is the property of the power of representation that shows us how we are affected by things. Sensibility is thus a receptivity,ᵉ according to which we are affected by things. Accordingly all intuitions are sensible. For if nothing affects us, then we also have no representation, for if we are supposed to cognize objects that are given to us, then we can never have the slightest representation of them if they do not affect us. Empirical intuitions thus belong to sensibility and even pure intuitions will belong to it, e.g., the empirical intuition of body contains warm, cold, but even when we take only space, and the extension

---

ᵉ The text includes here two synonyms: *Receptivitaet, Empfänglichkeit* (797₁₆).

of the body, then as pure intuition that will [be]$^{L f}$ nothing other than the form of our sensibility for being affected by things through outer circumstances. Space is thus nothing other than the form of outer intuition. It is likewise with time. We find in our soul alterations and inclinations of the will, if we take everything together then there is still always a connection, since either something is concurrent or one succeeds the other. Time is thus being concurrent and successive, it is thus nothing other than the form of inner intuition, or of inner sense. Thus the pure form of sensibility precedes all experience, we can know nothing *a priori* of sensations, e.g., who can see in aloe that it is bitter? But we can know *a priori* how we will be affected by things that are mere shapes, e.g., if I omit everything empirical from a die, then I still retain the shape; if I see it from the corner then I catch sight of three quadrilaterals, I can know that *a priori*, for that is pure intuition. Thus there are *a priori* cognitions which are possible with respect to pure intuition. We thus find in our sensibility a rule through which we are capable of *a priori* intuitions, but no more, of course, than the form of intuitions. On the other hand we also have pure concepts of reason. Each object of experience must be a subject of a substance. We thus can think of various *a priori* concepts through mere understanding, for mere thinking can be considered separately from all pure intuition, separately from all intuition and sensible sensation. So far as they are objects of pure thought, I can know *a priori* the properties of things, just as well as the objects of pure intuition. Here it is clear that we are capable of pure^g *a priori* cognition of things of experience, for everything rests on the form of sensible intuition which I can know *a priori*, for I can say something *a priori* about space without an object being there. I can say much *a priori* without experience, so long as the objects of experience are thought by me, and if I were not to think that which I intuit, then I would not at all be able to say that I had experience. Thus I do have *a priori* intuition. The intuitions are forms of sensibility which I can know in advance; for before I am affected, the mind must still represent to itself a form of how it will be affected. But we would also not get any concept of things which are intuited here if we could not think any intuitions. We can make concepts of things in general only through the understanding, even if no object is given, because we are representing to ourselves only the manner in which we can think an object. We thus see that all experience is based *a priori* on a pure intuition^h

29:798

---

^{f} We follow Lehmann in adding a *sein;* Lehmann reads a *sind* in the text and claims to be changing it to *sein,* but we find no *sind* (797$_{25}$). Also, Lehmann omits an *uns* (after *wenn wir*) without note (797$_{24}$).

^{g} The ms is ambiguous between an *r:* (*reiner;* pure) and *k:* (*keiner;* none). Lehmann is possibly correct in reading the latter (798$_{14}$), but we are reading the former because it makes more sense.

^{h} The ms reads *eine V Anschauung,* where – in this particular handwriting – the *V* could also be construed as an *R* (*Reine,* pure), which is our reading. Lehmann interprets the text as *eine*

which is nothing other than the form of our sensibility, through which it is possible that we can perceive something; and that all empirical intuitions are finite, secondly [there are] pure *a priori* concepts, for since experience is not possible through perception alone, but rather concepts must be added to it, so there must be underlying *a priori* concepts through which I can bring perceptions under concepts: they underlie experience as substance, and if we did not have *a priori* concepts then we also would not obtain any [concepts]. – Sensations make no concept. This *a priori* cognition will thus have two parts, the first contains the form of *a priori* sensibility, the other the form of the understanding or *a priori* thinking. Thus if we want to consider the first source of experience, then we have two; the one is aesthetic, which shows what belongs to the senses and how we are affected by objects; the other is logical and considers the form of thinking. We thus have [a] transcendental aesthetic, which considers *a priori* intuition and the *a priori* conditions of sensibility, and through which we cognize the possibility of aesthetic judgments; and when we have gone through this synthetic *a priori* cognition according to its entire extent, then we can say that we have *a priori* principles on which [rests]^L the possibility of experience, which concerns all objects; we will show that they are certain because experience is certain and it rests on them. We will be able to determine *a priori* the boundaries of cognition, because as long as^i all *a priori* cognitions have no other meaning than that they are the conditions of the possibility of experience, they also cannot be valid any further than for the field of experience. The endeavor of transcendental philosophy will thus be to show that all our *a priori* cognitions can go no further than the objects of experience, and thus [to] hinder our reason from climbing beyond the boundaries of experience and risking ventures which aim away from possible objects of experience. –

29:799

The manner in which we are affected by things makes sensible representation possible. – All sensible intuition has a certain form which is proper to human nature. Outer sensible intuition has the form that all outer things appear to us in space. That is a particular manner in which we intuit things. The relations of space are not something in itself, but rather a form of sensibility that arises from the relations of representations. Time is also the form of pure intuition; yet it is not something that we cognize immediately, and all representations are possible according to this double form of sensibility. We must cognize it first, before we have impressions. We will thus have *a priori* intuitions without objects being given to us. We may have nothing but the form of intuition, which rests

---

^{L} *Verstandes Anschauung* (an intuition of the understanding), which, however, is a highly unusual expression, especially for Kant (798$_{30}$).
^{i} We do not follow Lehmann in his changing *können, die dieweilen* to *konnen. Dieweil* (799$_{15}$).

not on things but rather on us. According to the diversity of the subjects one will be affected by the same things in diverse manners, e.g., the raven is agreeably affected by spoiled carrion, and we run from it. Every subject has its own manner of being affected. Its representation thus rests not on the object, but rather on the particular manner of intuition. Our human nature is of the manner that, when we are affected by external things, they are represented to us in space; this form of intuition can be considered only *a priori* because it is the basis of every representation, thus precedes them. Likewise time can be considered *a priori*, i.e., the form which we cognize of our inner state through the inner sense.[j] – That is all possible because our intuition is sensible. – It rests on the receptivity[k] of being affected by things. We can think of a being that intuits spontaneously from its own power, by itself without being affected by objects, so one imagines God; we cannot comprehend how this is possible, other than perhaps through this, that the power of cognition produces things, for he affected them, not they him; but we also have no concepts of this: our intuition is receptivity. By intuition we understand sensible intuition through all organs, not merely through sight. With every manner in which we are affected there are two parts: matter, i.e., the impression of sensation, and form, i.e., [the][L] manner in which the impressions are unified in my mind. Otherwise I would have millions of impressions but no intuition of a whole object. – [l] Intuition rests on nature just like sensation, which presumably differs for everyone although we have the same words for it. – All objects of our intuition are appearances. We never see things as they are, but rather as they are presented to our senses – if a being had intellectual intuition, as we think of God, it would intuit beings as they are, not as they appear. Our intuitive representations are only representations *about* the appearances of things. We are thus acquainted only with the appearances of things. – Thus, to our experience belongs, first, intuition, second, thinking, which does not belong to the senses. To intuit does not mean to have experience. Experience is a cognition that we have of an object of intuition. Thus that requires thinking, which can be considered separately. Thinking constitutes one part of experience, [i.e.,] insofar as the understanding plays a part in it. Intuiting [is][L] a part of experience insofar as sensibility participates in it. We can omit everything empirical, then pure intuition remains, i.e., space and time remain.[m] If we omit that, then pure

29:800

29:801

---

[j] Lehmann claims the ms is corrupt here and thus changes it to read: "i.e., the form through which we cognize our inner state." He reads the ms itself as follows (Ak. 29: 1158): *d.i. die Form die wir durch den innern Sinn unsern Zustand erkennen.* Lehmann omits here (without note) an *innern* after *Sinn unsern*. We have ignored Lehmann's change (800₈₋₉).

[k] The text includes here two synonyms: *Receptivitaet, Empfänglichkeit* (800₁₀₋₁₁).

[l] This and the next dash, omitted by Lehmann without note, have been replaced (800₂₃,₂₅).

[m] An *übrig* (following *Zeit*) omitted by Lehmann has been replaced (801₁).

thinking remains – if we think of objects in general and the conditions under which they are, then we call these pure concepts of the understanding or categories. They come down from Aristotle, but since he had no principle with which to number them with certainty and could not deduce where we have them from, they finally passed into decay, because one had no certainty here. He also named them predicaments <praedicamenta>. We want to sketch beforehand a system of the categories which exhaust all concepts of which the understanding avails itself in experience. (The investigation as to how synthetic *a priori* cognitions are possible is called critique of reason.) Every system of cognition is dogmatic if it is not preceded by a critique. We can thus think a dogmatic metaphysics. And this is how all metaphysics was until now. – All dogmatic procedure without critique – which could also be called anticritical procedure – is but a gamble of reason. – This question falls into two. First: how are speculative concepts possible *a priori*; second, [how are] judgments [possible *a priori*]? The concept of ground is a synthetic concept, for I think under it something upon which something else follows according to a rule. Before we are able to answer this question (namely, how can our reason connect a manifold without the rule of identity) we must exhibit the table of *a priori* concepts which are the basis everywhere. First [the table] of judgments, with which every classification of concepts is connected

(1)	(2)[41]	(3)
Quantity	Quality	Relation
universality	affirmative	categorical
particularity	negative	hypothetical
singularity	infinite	disjunctive
	(4)	
	Modality	
	problematic	
	assertoric	
	apodictic	

Thus there are as many categories as moments of the understanding in judging. We have the advantage through this table that we comprehend their origin. – Logic deals with the connections of concepts, metaphysics with their origin. We see from this that understanding performs the same action when it makes concepts for itself as when it connects them.

29:802

All actions of the understanding reduce to judgments. There must be as many moments with respect to the thinking of objects in general as there are moments of each judgment, i.e., we must have as many categories as there are moments of judgments.

(1)[42]	(2)	(3)
Quantity	Quality	Relation
unity *<unitas>*	reality	substance to the accident
multitude *<multitudo>*	negation	cause *<causa>* to the effect *<causato>*[n]
totality *<omnitudo>*	limitation	reciprocal action *<actio mutua>* or interaction *<commercium>*

(4)
Modality
possibility *<possibilitas>*
existence *<existentia>*
necessity *<necessitas>*

These categories can be called predicaments *<praedicamenta>*. Under these basic concepts stand derivatives which are called predicables *<praedicabilia>*: under totality *<omnitudo>* lies wholeness, perfection, under multitude *<multitudo>*: number *<numerus>*, infinitude *<infinitudo>*, under order *<ordo>*, etc., and so we get a full system of pure thinking which can be thought without recourse to intuition. – Space, time, and sensation belong to sensibility, thus not to the categories.[o] – We therefore divide transcendental philosophy into two parts: into the transcendental aesthetic, i.e., science of the senses *<scientia sensuum>*, the science of sensibility and its *a priori* representations. – The science of *a priori* sensible cognitions thus deals with nothing other than space and time, for there are no other sensible cognitions – It is thus an entirely separate part – and transcendental logic, which contains pure *a priori* thinking or the pure form of the understanding. – This transcendental logic is distinguished from common logic by the following: the latter concerns cognition without troubling over whether the objects are *a priori* or *a posteriori*; the former considers the cognitions of the understanding insofar as they cannot be *a posteriori* or the possibility of pure *a priori* cognition of the understanding, the categories belong here. Aristotle had ten (many are ours) (1) substance and accident, (2) quality *<qualitas>*, (3) quantity *<quantitas>*, (4) relation, (5) action *<actio>* passivity *<passio>*,[43] (6) when *<quando>* (belongs to time), (7) where *<ubi>*, (8) position *<situs>* (both belong to space), (9) disposition *<habitus>* (that is, suitability of a thing for receiving a form, ability *<habilitaet>*).

29:803

He found by experiment that something was still missing, so he supposed yet four postpredicaments *<postpraedicamenta>*: opposition *<oppositum>*, before and after *<prius et posterius>*, at the same time *<simul>*, motion *<motus>* (is entirely empirical), having *<habere>* (that also cannot be a category).[44] Through this table we have the advantage that we do

[n] Lehmann misreads *zum* as *cum* ($802_{9,10}$).
[o] We are adding a period (802_{23}).

156

not gather together concepts randomly, but rather we can number the elements of our pure understanding here so that no gap remains. (We also have the requisite order and would prefer to begin from quantity, since they are the clearest, rather than, as the author does, with modality,[45] which are considerably harder, yet we must follow him here.) The predicables <*praedicabilien*> are also pure concepts of the understanding, but are derived from the categories; the concept of the whole is a predicable <*praedicabile*> that stands under the category of totality <*omnitudo*>, and so we can[p] have many predicables <*praedicabilia*>[q] under this category. When one speaks now of categories, predicaments <*praedicamenten*> and predicables <*praedicabilibus*>,[r] one appears to be warming-up the old scholastic philosophy. – But in fact there remains nothing more than the names from Aristotle, whose notion of enumerating the pure concepts of reason here and bringing them under an index was quite good and worthy of a philosopher, but did not succeed. – In every system the slightest deficiency reveals a gap, because an idea of the whole underlies it here. With a sand hill we do not see if some grains are missing, but with a pyramid [we do] at once. This is just what also occurs when we sketch a system of categories. – We can then know which are the concepts that constitute the whole extent of pure reason. – What are categories? They are pure concepts of reason, i.e., those that are fully *a priori*. Now the place in the understanding of a concept of experience is set by the category, e.g., the concept of body, where, however, there is much which is empirical, i.e., which contains nothing more than sensation – and also pure intuition as space which, as said, can be represented *a priori*. If we omit all that, then substance, power, etc., remain. The pure concept of reason lies in experience, where I must leave everything else that belongs to sensibility. That is first sensation, second intuition, through which the object appears. Thus nothing is left over here except the pure thinking of appearance, which the categories are. They are thus the pure thinking of objects insofar as they are given through intuition. Our experience consists in intuiting and thinking. Empirical intuition is the manner in which we are affected by things. Nothing is given thereby other than appearance. It can be considered with respect to matter and form. Space and time belong in the aesthetic. Thinking also belongs to experience; a category is an *a priori* concept through which alone thinking in experience is possible. Here we abstract from the differences of all objects of experience, as much with respect to sensation as to intuition. The categories are preconditions of appearances, through which concepts of experience arise, although they

29:804

---

[p] We follow Lehmann in changing *kennen* (to know) to *können* (803₁₅); Lehmann does not note the change.

[q] Lehmann misreads *praedicabilia* as *Predicate* (predicates)(803₁₅).

[r] Lehmann misreads *praedicabilibus* as *praedicabilien* (803₁₇).

are not concepts of experience. – Our common language already contains everything that transcendental philosophy draws out with effort. – These categories are already all contained in us, for without them no experience would be possible, e.g., snow has fallen. Herein lies that snow is, substance; fallen means an accident, upon the earth means an influence, that is, action <*actio*> thus belongs to cause <*causa*>. Today refers to time, fallen to space. If we omit all sensations, as well as space and time, substance remains, which acts in a certain way, thus they must be connected so that the concept of experience arises. If we posit that we had no such pure[s] concepts of the understanding, then we could not think or speak at all. – Experience is the ordering of appearances and of concepts; the concepts are categories, they are thus the conditions of the possibility of experience insofar as that requires thinking – just as space and time are the conditions of the possibility of experience insofar as that requires intuition. Categories are pure concepts of the understanding without which there would be no concepts of experience, therefore no experience. Through them intuitions are brought into a concept of experience – and then impressions of sensibility must still be added to it. The transcendental aesthetic contains the elements of our cognitions that lie in sensibility. The transcendental logic [contains] the elements of our cognition that lie in the understanding. It is divided into the transcendental analytic, transcendental dialectic, as with general logic. The former contains all pure cognitions of the understanding, insofar as they are valid only for objects of experience – and is called the logic of truth of the pure concepts of the understanding; it has to do with pure cognitions of reason, which concern only objects of some possible experience. Transcendental dialectic contains pure concepts of reason insofar as they are to go beyond objects of all possible experience, thus beyond the boundaries of experience, and that is logic of illusion; for they cannot go beyond experience because they have no other meaning than that experiences arise through them out of given appearances. They have truth insofar as they apply to objects of possible experience, for they are nothing other than thinking, which must be added to appearance so that experience arises. – They are nothing other than concepts through which given appearances are expounded, i.e., make a concept which is a concept of experience. Insofar as a part of transcendental philosophy contains nothing other than the principles of possible experience, it is then a logic of truth. An *a priori* proposition that precedes all experience is certain, for what is more certain than experience, and it is certain only to that extent. Here there is something quite peculiar with the understanding: it attempts to fly beyond experience with the concepts of which it avails itself to make experience possible. What comes of this? They must lose all meaning as long as the categories have no object beyond the boundaries of experi-

29:805

---

[s] Two synonyms are used here: *pure Reine* (804$_{21}$).

ence, thus all cognition through categories is illusion when it goes beyond experience, and the dialectic is logic of illusion. We will not show, as is easy to comprehend, how to contrive an illusion, but rather how an illusion can be discovered – and the dialectic is the greatest end of transcendental philosophy. But the analytic must come first. We will analyze the concepts and proceed dogmatically here. When we come to the synthetic propositions we will show that that which is supposed to be proven only from pure concepts, can be proven only with recourse to possible experience. – We want to leave aside the dialectic here and postpone that which belongs to it to where it can be best inserted, and here we will become practiced in critique.

We want now to return to our author. But we cannot possibly proceed according to a system without laying a foundation under it. Our author had the intention, like everyone else, of sketching a system, but freedom was entirely lacking, or the principle for ordering the manifold. The idea of metaphysics was lacking altogether: it was no system, but rather an aggregate. Therefore the author as well cannot give an accounting as to whether that would be all the pure concepts. – when we thus have no system, we will then analyze all concepts that he presents, even though they do not have the 29:806 order of the categories. In the meantime we will call upon the categories and note under which category this or that concept belongs. In the *Critique of Pure Reason*, which Professor Kant published, the extent of pure reason is dissected, the idea established from which all concepts of the understanding can be classified. The concepts themselves are not all analyzed, because it was not necessary, our concern there was only to establish the extent and boundaries of pure reason, thus the parts could be left out. They are dissected as far as was necessary to fit them into the system of pure reason. Now we must undertake this work of dissection, though not according to the order of the categories. But we want to refer to them. That' which we have before us is analytic, here we are at once missing something essential, namely a principle of all synthetic *a priori* propositions. One can say the sum of metaphysics amounts to showing the possibility and the criterion of truth of all synthetic *a priori* propositions. A principle of all synthetic *a posteriori* judgments is experience; but we do not yet have one for all synthetic *a priori* judgments. All concepts which we have contain a synthesis, and if we have comprehended how it is possible, then we will soon also have a criterion of truth. We want to criticize our author, who presents synthetic *a priori* propositions, but actually not him, for that would serve little use, but rather the whole human reason, e.g., the principle of sufficient reason. We will show that it is impossible to prove such synthetic *a priori* propositions

---

' We follow Lehmann in omitting an *ist* after *Das* (806₁₂). Lehmann does not note his omission. As Lehmann notes, there is a sign following this omitted *ist*, which resembles our lower-case *b*, and which is preceded by what could be a comma.

through pure concepts, and to indicate for each of them a place in the system according to the categories, which is easy.*" We first take the concept.*v* The author has here aligned himself with Wolff, for he clearly comprehended that a principle of contradiction <*principium contradictionis*> is not sufficient <*sufficient*>,[46] so he took in addition the principle of sufficient reason <*principium rationis sufficientis*>. Therefore the author here immediately treats of ground. We first take the concept [of ground and consequence.]

SECOND CHAPTER *w*

On ground and consequence

Ground <*ratio*>, relation <*respectus*>, is a manifold [of elements][47] insofar as one is posited or canceled by another. Thus all relation is relation either of connection or of opposition <*relatio vel nexus, vel oppositionis*>, e.g., the

29:807   citizens of a republic are in the relation of connection <*in relatione nexus*> whereby one is of use to the other, or in the relation of opposition <*in relatione oppositionis*> insofar as the interests of one conflict with those of another. (The relation of ground and consequence and vice versa is connection <*nexus*>. – Were a thing not a ground of another, and this its consequence, then the things would be wholly separate. The thing as ground relates *a posteriori* to its consequence, i.e., connection <*nexus*>, and the reverse is *a priori* connection <*nexus*>. – Something that would not be in such a connection <*nexu*>, therefore not ground and consequence, would be isolated, which is an Italian word and means an island <*isola; G: Insel*>; then we would not at all know how we had come to it – . We would thus*x* also have no sign as to whether it would belong to our cognition, therefore all of our cognitions are in connection <*in nexu*>.) – (Connection <*nexus*> as well as opposition <*oppositio*>*y* are either analytic, if the connection is according to the principle of identity, or synthetic if it is not according to

---

u Lehmann changes this sentence (806$_{25-7}$), reading the ms (Ak. 29: 1158) as: *dass es unmöglich sey ohne solche Sätze a priori zu beweisen durch pure Begriffe und jedem derselben eine Stelle im System anweisen nach den Categories welches nicht ist.* We read the ms as follows: *dass unmöglich sey ohne solche synth Sätze a priori zu beweisen durch pure Begriffe und jedem derselben eine Stelle im System anweisen nach den Categorien welches leicht ist.* That is, Lehmann adds an *es* (after *dass*), omits *synthetisch*, and misreads *leicht* (easy) as *nicht* (not). We are ignoring Lehmann's reading.

v *Wir nehmen zuerst den Begriff* (806$_{27-8}$) is apparently a miswrite in the ms; the same phrase closes the section a sentence later at 806$_{31-2}$.

w *2tes Capitel* (806$_{33}$) was apparently added later; it is scarcely visible on microfilm, and in the ms it is written in a pale red ink. The underlining is in this same red ink.

x An *also* (thus) omitted by Lehmann without note, and a dash (after which we have added a period) have been replaced (807$_{10}$).

y A dash omitted by Lehmann has been replaced (807$_{12}$).

this principle – opposition <*oppositio*> is analytic – according to the principle of contradiction <*principium contradictionis*>; [it] is synthetic when it
is not according to the principle of contradiction <*principium contradictionis*> – one can[z] call that real connection and opposition <*nexus . . .
oppositio realis*> – one can call the analytic connection <*nexus*> logical;
connection and contradiction rest on grounds, are logical or real. – They
can be grounds of positing <*rationis ponendi*>, where something is posited
according to [the] rules of identity, or not according to [the][L] rules of
identity, – and of denying <*tollendi*>, where something is canceled according to the principle of contradiction[a] or not, e.g., extension is a ground of
divisibility, the latter is posited through the former[b] according to rules of
identity, – but: every body has attractive power, here the latter is posited
through the former (body), but not according to the rules of identity, and
this connection <*nexus*> is real, the former logical. It is possible to cognize
a real connection <*nexus*> only *a posteriori*.[c] A conflict is logical when it
takes place by the principle of contradiction <*principium contradictionis*> –
and without that [it is] real – logical opposites taken up at the same time
give the negative nothing <*opposita, simul sumta dant nihil negativum*>,
i.e., the impossible; real opposites taken up at the same time give the
privative nothing <*realiter opposita simul sumta dant nihil privativum*>, i.e.,
lack, and that is by all means conceivable; if two opposing grounds are in
the same subject, the result is zero, therefore if there are two logically
opposing grounds, the result is the impossible. Logically opposed[48] is that
through which, when posited, the other is denied <*quo posito tollitur
aliud*> – really <*realiter*> opposed is that through which, when posited,
the real ground is denied <*quo posito tollitur ratio realem*>, not the other
<*aliud*>.) We can regard opposition as a connection with an opposite,
e.g., something is opposed to motion, thus it is connected with the bodies'
rest. – By conjunction <*connexum*>[49] we are to understand all relation,
connection <*nexus*> as well as opposite <*oppositum*>, and say: those
things are joined of which it is the case that when one has been posited,
the other is posited <*connexa sunt, quorum uno posito ponitur aliud*>, e.g.,   29:808
when horses move, then the wagon is also moved; in another connection
there is a relation <*respectus*> of two, namely one which is posited, and
another which is posited when the first one has been posited <*unum, quod
ponitur, et aliud, quod uno posito ponitur*>. A is posited, another thing B
which is posited because A has been posited <*A ponitur, B aliud quod*

---

[z] We follow Lehmann in changing *sind synthetisch* to *ist synthetisch* (807₁₅) and *das sind kann* to
das kann (807₁₆). A period added by Lehmann (after *real*) has been removed (807₁₉). Lehmann notes neither of these changes.

[a] Lehmann misreads *des W[iderspruchs]* as *der Identitaet* (identity)(807₂₂).

[b] Lehmann misreads *dieses . . . jenes* as *diese . . . jene* (807₂₃).

[c] We are reading *Mogl:* in the ms as *möglich* instead of Lehmann's *Möglichkeit* (807₂₇).

posito A ponitur>, therefore two correlates *<correlata>* are in every connection *<nexu>*; the one through which, when posited, another is posited *<unum quo posito ponitur aliud>* we call ground, the other *<aliud>*, consequence. A is the ground *<est ratio>*, B the consequence *<rationatum>*. In the relation of ground and consequence we distinguish the ground. It is[d] namely that through which I posit something – and consequence, which is that which is posited. I cannot distinguish ground and consequence by definition. For I can just as well say: when B has been posited, A is posited *<posito B, ponitur A>* (namely with hypothetical judgments, where we say: when the antecedent has been posited, the consequence is posited *<posito antecedens, ponitur consequens>*, but not vice versa, rather: the consequence is posited because of the antecedent *<posito consequens ponitur quod . . . antecedens>*). We must now turn back to logic, which contains the forms of our understanding without distinguishing objects. With this we see that from the ground we can infer the consequence, but not the reverse, from the consequence to a determinate ground. The connection *<nexus>* of the consequence with a ground is certain, but not with a said ground. Now our definition is brought right into order: the ground is that which, having been posited, another thing is posited determinately, the consequence is that which is not posited unless something else is posited *<ratio est id, quo posito aliud determinate ponitur, rationatum quod non ponitur nisi posito alia>*. – (['One can also say: the consequence is that which, having been posited, another is posited – but indeterminately *<rationatum est quo posito ponitur aliud – sed indeterminate>*; for if there is a consequence, there must likewise always be a ground, and if something is a ground, there must likewise always be a consequence, but in the first case it is indeterminate *<indeterminate>*, in the other determinate *<determinate>*.) With many things one can see that there is a consequence, but we cannot know the ground. Now we have a criterion of the ground, namely: that which, having been posited determinately, another is posited *<quo posito determinate, ponitur aliud>*. Determinately *<determinate>* means according to a general rule *<secundum regulam generalem>*. Every ground gives a rule, therefore the connection *<nexus>* of the ground and the consequence is necessary. (Logical ground is a cognition from which another follows according to a rule. E.g., necessity is the ground of unalterability. The one is not the cause of the existence of the other. Real ground is a thing upon which another follows.) If something is posited, then something else is posited by that according to

---

[d] An *er ist* (following *Grund*) omitted by Lehmann (and replaced by him with a dash) has been replaced (808_{7-8}).

['] We are adding an opening parenthesis here (808_{21}), although the fold of the ms obscures (on our microfilm) whether there actually is one in the ms. Without an addition, the closing parenthesis at 808_{25} is without a mate.

a general rule. The expression consequence[f] is indeterminate, one often uses it of time, we will therefore often make use of the expression consequence <*rationatum*>. Here it means the connection with the former which contains its ground and upon which it follows according to a general rule,[g] e.g., he has always had fever, but since he used quinine, it disappeared, thus quinine is the ground of the disappearance of the fever. The criterion of a ground is not that something follows upon it but rather that something follows according to general rules. – Where does the concept belong? In the category of relation. – But for the[h] concept of cause to presuppose the concept of ground, ground would[i] be the predicament <*praedicamentum*> of the former, and we have not brought it into the table of the categories. Response <*responsio*>: the two concepts of ground and consequence are logical, but not transcendental. Cause and effect are things. Cause is that out of which the existence of another follows. Existence is not at all discussed in logic – rather, [what is discussed is] not how a thing is the ground of other things, but how a concept is the ground of other concepts.

29:809

We have spoken here of such a relation of concepts, where one can be determinately inferred from the other;[j] but that there might be such things, of which I can infer one from the other, belongs to metaphysics. We now want to consider the possibility of a real ground, where if one thing is posited, the other can be determined by it – not a logical [ground], where I can infer from one to another. – When the thing which is to be inferred is really <*realiter*> distinguished from the other, then no human reason can comprehend the possibility that one thing could be the ground of another thing, experience teaches it, but reason cannot make it conceivable to us. (All grounds are either grounds of cognizing <*rationes cognoscendi*>, where a cognition is a ground of others, e.g., composite is a cognitive ground of divisible – or if one sees a human footstep, then one says there were human beings there, the former is thus a cognitive ground, not a ground of becoming <*ratio fiendi*>, otherwise the footsteps

---

[f] *Folge* (i.e., that which follows)(808₃₅).

[g] Lehmann misreads *H[ier] bedeutet es den Zusammenhang mit dem vorigen we[lches] s[einen] Grund enthält und worauf es nach einer allg[emeinen] Regel folgt*, as *So bedeutet er den Zusammenhang mit dem vorigen. (Grund enthält das, worauf es nach einer allgemeinen Regel folgt,)* (So it means the connection with the former. Ground contains that upon which it follows according to a general rule.)(808₃₇₋₈).

[h] Lehmann misreads *der* as *dem* (809₅).

[i] An illegible word follows *wäre* (809₆).

[j] We follow Lehmann in changing *Wir haben hier eine solches Verhältniss von Begriffen da man von einem auf den andern bestimmt schliessen kann* (We have here such a relation of concepts, since one can be determinately inferred from the other) to *Wir haben hier von einem solchen Verhältniss von Begriffen geredet, wo man von einem auf dem andern bestimmt schliessen kann* (809₁₄₋₁₅).

would have to be the ground of the existence of the human being.[k]
Ground of being <*ratio essendi*> is the ground of that which belongs to a
thing considered according to its possibility, e.g., the three sides in the
triangle are the ground of the three corners. Here I speak merely of a
possible triangle; considered in actuality = of becoming <*fiendi*>,[l] e.g.,
ink and quill are the ground of becoming <*ratio fiendi*> of the triangle,
and the ground of becoming <*ratio fiendi*> is cause.) But they must be
different really, not in a hidden way, otherwise they are still one, e.g., if I
posit A, by which B is posited,[m] [this] is not at all to be comprehended. –
But still I can so infer, otherwise logic would not be right. But I cannot
with really <*realiter*> different things. Things are logically different when
they are really one, but in a hidden way, and the connection <*nexus*> of
the ground and consequence is analytic according to the rule of identity:
(what exists as consequence <*rationatum*> is dependent <*dependens*>),
e.g., because something is a body, it is divisible. The inference which one
has in general logic from ground to consequence, which is a logical
connection <*nexus logicus*>, is comprehended easily, but a real connection
<*real nexus*>, which is synthetic, is not at all, where the consequence is
really distinguished from the ground, e.g., snow with salt causes frost.
There is here no connection <*nexus*> according to the rule of identity.
The ground receives a consequence which did not at all lie in the concept
of the ground, and this synthetic connection <*nexus*> no human reason
can comprehend. There is a remarkable property of the understanding: it
infers from the ground to the consequence, and the possibility of this it
cannot comprehend – and then there is even more to it. – All relation is,
as said, a connection of opposites <*nexus oppositorum*>. If we think of a
logical opposition <*oppositio*>, it is analytic. Real opposition is synthetic.
Logical opposition is of contradictories <*contradictoria*>. An angular circle is a contradiction. Two logical opposites <*opposita*> completely cancel
themselves and nothing remains (the negative nothing <*nihil negativum*>). Two real opposites <*opposita*> do not cancel themselves, rather
the consequences cancel themselves, and what arises through their connection is zero, null, the privative nothing <*nihil privativum*>, e.g., I get
an inheritance, that causes pleasure, I must repay just as many debts,
[that][L] causes displeasure. The opposites <*opposita*> can indeed be together, only the consequences cancel themselves, and I remain in a condition of parity. Two real opposites <*opposita*> can thus be in a thing at the
same time, for only the consequences will be canceled, but logical opposites <*opposita*> cannot be [in][L] a thing at the same time (logical opposites

29:810

---

[k] Lehmann misreads a period as a comma (809_{13}).
[l] Ms reads: *mögl Δ = fiendi ie Wirklk be/trachtet*. Lehmann misreads *fiendi ie* as *in* (809_{33-4}).
[m] Lehmann misreads *dass durch B gesetzt wird, ist da* as *und doch B gesetzt wird, ist es* (809_{37}). In
any case, the sense of the sentence is unclear.

<*opposita*> are either contradictory opposites <*contradictorie opposita*>, like e.g., A and not A <*A et non A*>, or disparates <*disparata*>, e.g., every body is either red or green. Disparates <*disparata*> contain besides the opposite contradiction <*contradictio opposita*> still something which is added, e.g., if something [is]^L either red – the contradictory opposite <*contradictorie oppositum*> would be not red. With [the]^L opposition of disparates <*disparaten*> something is still left over, namely green. The principle of the excluded middle <*principium exclusi medii*> does not say that a thing takes one of two disparate predicates <*disparaten praedicaten*>, but rather [of] contradictory opposites <*contradictorie opposita*>"). One can say that the entire play of alteration of the universe <*universi*> comes from real oppositions. – Because only consequences are canceled by this, the thing that is the same will not be canceled, but rather something else, namely, the consequence. Real oppositions can thus be together. We come to the concept

29:811

Of possibility and impossibility^o

The author speaks first of impossibility, then of something and of the possible.^50

(^pNote: if two concepts are opposed, for example here: possible and impossible, then they always stand under a higher concept – for opposition always presents a disjunctive proposition. Now there must be a divided concept that has the opposing^q concepts as members of the division, and it is a higher concept. What is possible or impossible? Object (for object can also be thought with impossible predicates) is thus surely the highest concept in ontology. The possible we call thing, something, and opposed to it is the impossible, nothing. But nothing is opposed to object, therefore it would surely be a still higher concept than something. E.g., under thing is understood (1) object in general, (2) the possible, (3) the positive or reality, (4) that which is actual.) Possibility is falsely defined when one says that the possible is that which contains no contradiction; what contradicts itself is impossible, but not vice versa, the thought of it is possible, but whether the matter is objectively possible is not yet certain. That the thought of which is not self-contradictory is not possible, also not impossible. It is difficult to define it so that it applies to matters as well as to thoughts. Whatever would agree with all possible rules of thought

---

^n We are reading *contra opp.* (in the ms) as *contradictorie opposita* rather than Lehmann's *contra opposition* (810_{35}).

^o A *Der* omitted by Lehmann (as noted at Ak. 29: 1111, note to 811_1) has been replaced (811_1), but we agree with him in taking out a period after *Begriff* (810_{39}).

^p We are adding an opening parenthesis here, as a mate to the closing parenthesis at 811_{16}.

^q Ms has *oppost.* written in Latin; Lehmann interprets this as *opponirten* (811_8).

would be possible, but then one would have to know all possible rules. Logically possible is that of which the thought of a possible metaphysics is possible; that of which the thought is possible, and the matter in and for itself without recourse to experience is not impossible,[r] e.g., [a][L] four-cornered circle, is logically impossible. For the thought is impossible. Logical possibility is possibility of the concept, and the principle of contradiction <*principium contradictionis*> is its adequate criterion. Real possibility is different from this, here the principle of contradiction <*principium contradictionis*> does not suffice. What[s] is logically impossible is also really impossible, but [it is] not [the case that] what is logically possible is also really possible. (The impossible is twofold: (I) when either the concept itself is nothing, e.g., four-cornered circle, (II) or where no possible object corresponds, e.g., fairy tales.) Logical possibility is that wherein there is no contradiction. Metaphysical possibility is where the matter in and for itself is possible without relation to my thoughts. No human being can comprehend this. How am I to judge a matter, what it is in and for itself, without reference to experience? The possibility of the thought does not constitute the possibility of the matter. We cognize the matter itself purely through concepts, and then no feature of possibility remains for us. We can comprehend logic, but that[t] does not settle anything with the matter. Physical possibility is that which does not conflict with the laws of experience; this one can easily comprehend, e.g., that a large palace could be built in four weeks is physically impossible. Morally possible is that which is possible according to the rules of morals, and does not conflict with the general law of freedom. It is necessary to notice these differences. Many philosophers have confused logical with metaphysical possibility, e.g., the possibility or impossibility of ghosts cannot be demonstrated by logical philosophy, but no rational person must[u] believe in them because he has no concept of their possibility or impossibility. – Here one must not build on experience, for it is commonly weak people who experience them, and they experience much that is not true. –

When a synthesis is thought in a concept not through the principle of contradiction or identity, then it cannot at all be cognized by the principle of contradiction, for it is [not][L] logical, but rather real, and here we have no logical mark of possibility, e.g., every body is extended, can be cognized through the principle of contradiction. An unextended body is a non-thing or impossible. Here we cognize the possibility *a priori*, but analyti-

29:812

---

[r] We do not follow Lehmann in his changing *L. Mögl.* to *K[ein] Mögliches* and *unmögl* as *möglich* (811₂₅, ₂₈); he makes these changes, and also adds *ein*, without note (811₂₈). In either case, the sense of the sentence is unclear.

[s] An *aber* added by Lehmann has been removed (811₃₂).

[t] We follow Lehmann in changing *aber* to *das* (812₇).

[u] We follow Lehmann in omitting a *kann* preceding *muss* (812₁₆), but it is difficult to say which auxiliary is intended.

cally, and the possibility of an analytic ground can be easily comprehended *a priori*, e.g., [that] every body has alterability, [has an] analytic ground: there is a multitude of parts that can be separated, thus the concept of body contains the analytic ground of alteration. The possibility of an analytic ground and its consequence flows from the principle of contradiction. But if I think a ground whose consequence is really <*realiter*> different, then that cannot be cognized from the principle of contradiction. – It does not at all contradict itself, that because A is posited, for that reason B is as well, but it cannot for that reason be accepted as possible, because it is a synthetic judgment and we do not have the slightest concept of how that happens. – Real possibility cannot be comprehended *a priori* without pure concepts. In the following we will see that the criterion of the possibility of things is this: that synthesis is possible which contains the possibility of the conditions of experience, but this applies only to the objects of experience. (If something is considered outside the connection <*nexu*>, one says: it is observed through itself or internally <*spectatur per se . . . interne*>; inside the connection <*in nexu*> one says: internally observed[v] <*interne spectatur*>.)[51] – Something is possible internally or in and for itself, and relatively in reference and connection with other things. (The internally impossible <*interne impossibile*> is the negative nothing <*nihil negativum*>; nothing through a mere lack is named nothing. – Much is possible internally <*interne*>, that in connection is not possible externally <*externe*>, i.e., conditionally possible as well; the condition is here as much as a ground, e.g., it is possible in itself that a human being can become rich, but also conditionally, for his parents are rich, so there is yet another ground for that. – To take condition in this way is not in accord with linguistic usage – it actually means a restriction, e.g., many a commander can give orders if the people agree to it.) The inner criterion of things is the principle of contradiction, but [it is] not close to being sufficient, and the possibility of a thing is relative with respect to its grounds or consequences. E.g., it is possible that a human being should arrive at vast riches, but due to laziness, unsuitability, and a lack of wealthy relatives it is impossible. – What contradicts the conditions under which something is possible, is hypothetically impossible; what contradicts itself, is absolutely impossible. Something can be possible in itself, while hypothetically, under either its logical or real hypothesis, it is impossible. Hypothetical impossibility presupposes absolute possibility tacitly <*tacite*>, for what is nothing at all in itself can be considered in logical relation. We come now to the famous principle of

29:813

---

[v] In §15, Baumgarten links considering a thing internally and it not being in a connection; in §16 he links considering a thing externally and it being in connection; consequently, the passage would make more sense if we assumed that the auditor or copyist inadvertently wrote *interne* instead of *externe* (externally) (813₆₋₇).

sufficient reason (which is the first synthetic *a priori* proposition).*ʷ* The author speaks here not of existing, but rather of possible things.⁵² Expressed in its entire generality it says: nothing is without a ground <*nihil est sine ratione*>. Here we want to substitute other words: that which is without some ground is a consequence <*id quod habet sine rationem aliquam est rationatum*>, thus: everything possible is a consequence <*omne possibile est rationatum*>, is entirely the same thing. (So the author expresses it, but he still maintains afterwards a being which is a ground but not a consequence – and helps himself out by saying that it has a ground in itself, which is absurd; a ground must always be some-

29:814 thing else, and if it is not, there is no ground. It is as if I say, I want something. Why? Because I want it. I.e., there*ˣ* is still really no ground, and the wanting <*velle*> must be named original <*originarium*>,*ʸ* likewise the highest being the original being <*ens originarium*>.) Now the proposition in view looks very contradictory; we see sheer consequences and no sufficient ground which would be merely a ground. The summation of all things would be something which would not be posited unless nothing were posited <*quod non poneretur nisi posito nihil*>. The ground of the possibility of all things would thus be a non-thing. We will therefore have to use a restriction. Namely: everything contingent has a ground, contingent is that whose opposite is possible, which we cannot cognize from pure concepts. The logically possible, indeed [we can], but not the real. Logical contingency allows itself to be cognized from pure concepts, but the real possibility of the opposite can in no way be comprehended. Since the contingency of things cannot be cognized *a priori* through pure concepts, we must say everything empirically contingent has its ground, i.e., the contingent in appearance; empirically contingent is that whose opposite is empirically possible, as when experience shows that something is which previously was not. That something happens always means empirical contingency. Thus the proposition also reads: everything that happens has a ground. The happening contains in itself a coming about or passing away, the latter are the species, the former the genus. This principle of sufficient reason should be proven, but not from pure concepts. For it is a synthetic proposition, where I go out beyond my concept in order to add another which was not contained in the one given me. But we still find a certain partiality in us for this principle as presented by the author. For every claim which is ungrounded is false. Right here is the delusion. If we must provide a ground for

---

ʷ There is no punctuation sign here in the ms. We are replacing Lehmann's comma with a period (813₃₁).

ˣ We do not follow Lehmann in changing *es* to *noch;* Lehmann does not note his change (814₂). The preceding short sentences have been broken up from one long sentence beginning "It is as if . . . ."

ʸ An opening parenthesis added by Lehmann without note has been removed (814₃).

everything that happens, it still does not follow that things in themselves must have a ground, and one gets confused in this, e.g., the highest being has no ground, and nevertheless we must introduce grounds that it is there. The proposition can also be expressed thus: everything which follows in sensibility or sensible intuition, follows in the concepts of the understanding. Or, what can be represented as a consequence of sensibility can be represented as a consequence through the understanding. This proposition recommends itself through this – since, as just said, it cannot be proved from pure concepts, it will have to have another proof. – We will see in the following that synthetic *a priori* cognitions have a validity insofar as they are principles of the possibility of experience.[z] (All our judgments have a ground as to why the predicate belongs to the subject; with analytic judgments the ground is analysis, with synthetic ones synthesis. – We also have *a posteriori* judgments; these are either judgments of perception or of experience, the latter always presuppose the former, – the first have only subjective validity; I say, e.g., I am cold. The latter [have] objective or general validity. Thus that [example] has merely subjective validity, should it have objective validity or be a judgment of experience then the sequence[a] of perceptions must be determined according to rules, i.e., be necessary – then, one says, there is also a sequence in the object; that one follows the other according to a rule, is a ground, thus the principle of sufficient reason <*principium rationis sufficientis*> is the ground of the possibility of experience, without which there would be no experience.) How is experience possible, or how does the understanding make cognitions of things from perceptions? It must have principles which are synthetic propositions and to these now belongs the principle also.[b] (Perceptions can follow one another without the things thereby following. I can, e.g., first perceive the roof of a house, then the foundation, then the windows, etc., without the things following thusly, for they are concurrent.) It (the principle) is valid for all objects of experience and we will see that it cannot be proved other than as a proposition which is valid for all objects of experience, but not beyond them, and so it is with all synthetic *a priori* propositions; and all mistakes of metaphysics consist[c] in this, that propositions that apply only to experience are used beyond this, for they are nevertheless valid only for all possible objects of experience, not for things in themselves. They are rules of the synthesis of appearances, by which mere experience is distinguished from a dream, and thus also the principle of sufficient reason <*principium rationis sufficientis*>. The author

29:815

---

[z] We insert a period and capital here (815_2).

[a] For the following it is important that the term *Folge* can mean either "sequence" or "consequence," and that "to follow" (*folgen*) can have a temporal, logical, or causal meaning.

[b] We insert a period and capital here (815_{18}). The "principle" is presumably the principle of sufficient reason.

[c] We are changing *besteht* to *bestehen* (815_{26}).

has proven it, but rather remarkably,[53] namely: if a thing were to have no ground, then its ground would be nothing. Then nothing would be the ground of something, but that is a contradiction. He has here confused the logical and metaphysical nothing, which is hardly pardonable. One can easily refute this proof if one parodies it, that is, proves something absurd from it, e.g., you have money in the chest – for if you did not have that, then there would be nothing of money in the chest, then nothing would be money, thus you must have money. The mistake is that nothing *<nihil>* is meant one time as negation, another time as a concept. It is not the same whether I say: nothing is without a ground *<nihil est sine ratione>*, or nothing is a ground *<nihil est ratio>*. (That does not admit being proved from the pure concept; we would have to take yet a third, with which the concepts agree, namely the concept of a possible experience. Empirical cognition, insofar as it is considered valid in general, i.e., necessary, is called experience; empirical cognition insofar as it is subjectively valid, perception, and it is indisputable, but only for me, e.g., should the proposition: upon sunshine follows warmth, be a proposition of experience, – then it must read: upon sunshine follows warmth for everyone or necessarily. But what is that upon which something follows in a necessary way? Ground. Thus should the above perception become an experience, then I must represent to myself that the ground of warmth lies in the sunshine, for it is valid for everyone. Now these principles of the necessary connection of perceptions are synthetic *a priori* principles, and to this also belongs our proposition – no experience can take place without it. Should the above proposition become a proposition of experience, it must stand under the principle of the necessary connection of perceptions. The chief connection is that of ground and consequence. – Should connections of things be general, there must be a constant rule, otherwise I cannot say that the sequence of things should be generally valid and then again it is not an experience.

But we have said above that empirical cognitions or experiences contain no necessity. It does not teach that something is necessary, abstracted from all perceptions. – They presuppose principles which are necessary and under which alone it is possible. It[d] does not teach the necessity of the things. – All principles of synthesis which I think *a priori* are principles of the possibility of experience and apply merely to things of experience, but yet are *a priori* because they precede all experience, which is possible only through them. They are also synthetic, just like experience, for it is nothing but synthesis of perceptions, which is necessarily valid, which I can

---

[d] The references of these pronouns and the person of the verbs are not entirely consistent with each other in the first sentences of the paragraph – sometimes meaning "experiences," sometimes seeming to make an implicit reference to "experience" – but they have been left as in the ms.

cognize through *a priori* concepts. A synthesis which is not given in any experience is here plainly impossible. But I can comprehend these synthetic *a priori* principles, and actually do comprehend them, because otherwise there would be no experience. I can comprehend them, for they are mere cognitions which lie in my understanding. The author says,[54] if everything has its ground and its consequence, then everything is conjoined <*connexa*> *a priori* and *a posteriori*; that is right, but does not apply to all things, for otherwise there would not be any highest ground.)

29:817

On sufficient and insufficient

A ground is sufficient in a twofold manner: (1) we can represent the ground to ourselves as a whole like an aggregate, (2) like a series. The completeness of a ground as aggregate is sufficient, as series it is also sufficient. The ground, by which everything in the consequent is determined, is sufficient as aggregate, therefore everything must have a sufficient ground. An insufficient ground is also true; it is a part of the sufficient. The ground in the series of grounds subordinated to one another is only sufficient when we trace everything back to the first ground. It is commonly named sufficient when the consequences are capable of being immediately understood from it.

The author proves the proposition that everything has its consequences, as well as that everything has its ground; but it does not admit of proof from pure concepts.[55] We consider grounds in a series when one is the consequence <*rationatum*> of the other. In a series there is always an immediate ground, and each is in part a ground of the consequence. – We can thus represent grounds as complete, coordinate, and subordinate. All of our grounds are connections, are coordination, i.e., the connection of parts in an aggregate – and subordination, i.e., the connection of parts in a series. A ground is sufficient simply speaking <*simpliciter*> or in some respect <*secundum quid*>. Something is a ground of something else mediately when it is a ground by means of another, – immediately, when it is a ground not mediated by another, a remote positing or inference <*remota posita . . . ratiocinium*> of something through many intermediate grounds <*rationes intermedias*>. With the coordination of grounds one is the complement <*complementum*> of the other for a sufficient ground, with subordination one ground is the consequence of the other. In a series grounds <*rationes*> are immediate, mediate, or without qualification <*immediatae, mediatae et simpliciter talis*>. The coordination of the grounds is the connection of them in an immediate <*immediaten*> sufficient ground; the subordination of grounds is the connection of them in a mediate sufficient ground.)[e] (A ground can be sufficient in view of its consequences, and in view of itself; in

---

[e] Neither this parenthesis nor the one following has a mate.

29:818   view of its consequences, when it determines everything that is contained in these, in view of itself, when it presupposes no other ground. If I take the summation of all mundane causes, they contain the complete ground of the world's present state, but it is not sufficient for itself, i.e., without qualification <*simpliciter talis*>, but rather only in view of its consequences, i.e., in some respect <*secundum quid*> – we do not find grounds without qualification <*rationes simpliciter talis*> in the world. The relation of ground and consequence contains only the logical sequence, i.e., if one is posited, so is the other as well and indeed necessarily, and to that extent it contains the ground of the possibility of the connected perceptions, i.e., experience. In the series of subordinated concepts, that which is sufficient in a certain respect is sufficient in some respect <*sufficient secundum quid*>, [that which is sufficient] in every respect [is sufficient] simply speaking <*simpliciter*>; we must introduce the following canons <*canones*>:[56]

when the ground has been posited, the consequence is posited <*posita ratione, ponitur rationatum*>, is already clarified from the definition of the ground, further

when a consequence has been posited, a specific ground is not posited <*posito rationato, ponitur ratio quaedam non certa*>. E.g., if one is strangled, he is dead, but if he is dead, he need not specifically have been strangled.

To determine means to attribute to a thing one of two contradictorily opposed[f] predicates. I can compare everything with any one possible opposite of a predicate and with the predicate itself. If I attribute the predicate to the thing, the opposite will be excluded. Of two opposed predicates <*praedicatis oppositis*> one must belong to the thing, thus every thing must be determinable. (The inferences of the author belong in logic, they are also all presented there, but there ground <G: *Grund*> is called antecedent <*antecedens*> and consequence <G: *Folge*> [is called] consequence <*consequens*>. When the consequence has been denied, the ground is denied <*sublato rationato tollitur ratio*>, for if the ground were to remain, the consequence would also remain, but [it is] not [true that] when the ground has been denied, the consequence is denied <*sublata ratione tollitur rationatum*>, for the consequence can have another ground.)[57] (Since every consequence takes one of two contradictorily opposed predicates, each is thoroughly determinate – but one still says, a thing is undetermined in view of certain opposed predicates <*praedicata opposita*>, if by the concept which we have of it neither of the two belongs to it, e.g., every human being that is here is either learned or unlearned, but whether he is learned or unlearned is undetermined by the concept that I have of a human being. There is only one being which is thoroughly determined by its concept, namely since all reality belongs to it, otherwise things are undetermined in

---

[f] In the ms, the phrase *contrad. opp.* is written above *entgegengesetzten*, presumably as a synonym (818₂₀).

many aspects in view of or by their concept.) In itself, a general concept is   29:819
not determined, e.g., a human being is either learned or unlearned, is
undetermined. But a learned human being is determined. One can determine only through synthesis, not through analysis, for in view of that which
lies within it, it was not undetermined. For I can determine the concept only
when I add something. Every ground of determination is called the determining ground <*ratio determinans*>. Our cognition, if it is to be determined, must have a ground, so also with things. When two things are
undetermined in view of two predicates, they can be determined by a
determining ground. Determination is distinguished from logical predicates. (The logical predicate can be analytic, but determination is always
synthetic, e.g., one says, the concept of body is determined by extension – I
determine the concept by a predicate when it would be undetermined
without it, – but the concept of body is not undetermined without extension, for that already lies in its concept, but weight is a determination.)
(Can every ground be determined or not, or is it only the sufficient? Most
still always make a distinction here, but that is wrong – ground consists just
in this, that which, having been posited, another is posited determinately
<*quo posito, determinate ponitur aliud*> – the insufficient ground deter-
mines something in the consequence – the sufficient everything.) Determination is a predicate of a thing by which the opposite is excluded. That is the
customary manner for thinking of determination, namely, one views it as a
predicate which is attributed to the thing, by which the opposite is excluded.
That is not enough. Determination is a synthetic predicate.[g] E.g., a body is
extended. It is not yet determined by this. A learned human being is determined, for learnedness does not lie in the concept of human being. – A
predicate belongs to the thing internally if it lies already in its concept,
externally if it belongs to it in relation to another. ([h]Internal predicates are
ones that belong to things in themselves. – Further, they are also divided
into absolute and relative.[58] The latter are relative (to internal or external
matters <*ad interna . . . externa*>.) The relation to the external <*respectus
ad externa*> is relation; e.g., that a human being is master over his passions,
is relative, but to the internal <*ad interna*>; I consider here the relation of a
power to what is subjected under it. Thus there is here a relation <*respectus*>; it is relative to the external <*ad externa*> if I consider it as master   29:820
and servant. The author explains what same <*idem*> and different <*diversum*> is:[59] A and B are the same <*sunt eadem*> insofar as the representation of B is nothing but a repetition of the representation of A – if through
the representation of A I can also represent B. But we see that two things

---

[g] We are adding a period in place of a comma to prevent the misunderstanding that Kant is
suggesting that extension is synthetically related to body (819_{28}).
[h] This parenthesis has no mate (819_{33}). This is also true of the parenthesis later at 820_3 and
the first parenthesis at 821_7.

that we call the same can be the same <*eadem*> only in some respect, because otherwise one would not be able to say: the other. Of this more will be said below. The author speaks[60] of attributes, modes, and affections <*de attributis, modis et affectionibus*>, all of that belongs in logic. We note the following: we find in most philosophies an unsteady distinction between nature and essence. What is the difference? One does not customarily attribute nature to a thing that does not exist for itself, e.g., one says of a triangle it has [no][i] nature; with things that exist for themselves, one makes no distinction. We have distinguished above the analytic relation between ground and consequence; here the ground is logical, – and the synthetic relation between ground and consequence; here the ground is a real ground. The relation of the ground and the consequence is analytic if the predicate can be cognized analytically, synthetic if it cannot be so cognized. What is first analytically would be ground of all predicates of a thing and is called the logical essence – what is first synthetically would be ground of all predicates of a thing, is called the real essence or nature[61] (essence is the first inner ground of all that belongs to the possibility of a thing – and that which belongs to the actuality of a thing is nature, e.g., one will not assign a nature to the triangle in geometry; in the concept of each thing there is always something separable and [something] inseparable from it, the second[j] is called what pertains to the possibility of a thing or to the essence <*ad possibilitatem rei seu ad essentiam pertinens*>, the first [what is] apart from the essential <*extra essentiale*>, what does not go together necessarily with the concept or possibility of the matter. The first can again be as of a ground <*ut rationis*>, that is, essence <*essentia*>, or as consequences <*ut rationata*>, that is, attributes <*attributa*> – an essential complex <*complexus essentialiam*>, i.e., nature is the first true higher ground of all that which belongs to the existence of a thing) or the first logical inner ground of all determinations of a thing is essence, the first inner real ground of determinations of a thing is nature. It is impossible to find the complete inner real ground of all determinations. The logical is easy, here I need only to analyze my concept until I come upon such concepts that can no longer be derived from others. (When we complain that we are not acquainted with the essences of things, that concerns merely the nature; with the essences we can surely be acquainted – for if something is not actual,[k] then it lies merely in my concept. – Thus if I treat of that which belongs to the possibility of the thing, then I treat of that which lies in my concept of the thing – and that I can indeed know. If, like Professor Kant,

29:821

---

[i] We are reading *eine* (a) as *keine* (no)(820₁₃) since the former conflicts with what is said below at 820₂₅₋₆, which states Kant's doctrine that a triangle has an essence but not a nature.

[j] We have reversed *1te* and *2te* in the text (820₂₈₋₉).

[k] Lehmann misreads *denn ist* as *denn so*, and then adds an *ist*, which we remove (821₂).

174

one classifies essence into logical and real essence, then the latter is nature.) (The attribute which can flow only from the entire essence of the thing is its own <*proprium*> – for another thing would have another essence. That which is always logically consequent <*consectarium*> on a part of the essence is common <*commune*>, for the part can also take place with other things, e.g., man is a rational animal. – On account of the former he has reason, by which he is not to be distinguished from spirit; on account of the latter he has senses, here again he is indistinguishable from animals.) But what human being wants to undertake to show the whole real essence of things which are given through experience? We can call something the real essence comparatively, or we can stop with the investigation of the real essence in a certain respect, and with that be content. We often hear the complaint [that] the essences of things are unknown, [that] we are acquainted with only the surface. That is entirely right, but is valid only for the real essence. We can cognize much that belongs therein, but not everything. This real essence is nature.

We now come to the concept of

Existence

Under the fourth heading, namely under modality, we have introduced the categories: possibility, actuality, and necessity,[62] and then we deemed that they are not at all determinations of a thing, or synthetic predicates; they are namely concepts by which a thing is posited with all predicates. Possibility is nothing other than the agreement of a thing with conditions of thought. The conditions are analytic or synthetic; should it not agree with the former, then it is impossible on account of the principle of contradiction. But it must also agree with synthesis. The principle which contains the synthetic conditions of thought is provisionally this: all synthesis must contain the conditions under which the manifold is brought into a unity – or: to no thing can a synthetic predicate be attributed unless it is a possible experience. All synthetic *a priori* judgments express nothing more than the conditions of a possible experience. E.g., everything that exists in the sensible world is in space, i.e., insofar as it is in experience. If I say a thing is possible, then I think nothing more in addition. It is not a predicate that belongs to the thing, but rather to the positing of the thing insofar as it agrees with the laws of thinking. Actuality is absolute positing <*positio absoluta*>,[63] necessity [is] when absolute positing <*positio absoluta*> is so constituted that its cancellation contradicts the laws of thinking. Possibility, actuality, necessity are not concepts of things in themselves; rather possibility already presupposes the thing with all its predicates, and is the comparison of the thing with the laws of thinking, whether it can be thought or not. (Actuality is that to which an object in experience corresponds; necessity is

29:822

175

actuality that follows from possibility.) (With actuality, the object is added to a concept, but nothing is added to the object.) Likewise actuality; they are differentiated only in the manner that a thing is posited. Although we [have]^L indeed said that they are not predicates of the things in themselves, but rather modes <*modi*>, how it is posited, we must nevertheless concede that all concepts, modal concepts as well, can be made into predicates, but not into real predicates or determinations, but rather logical ones, e.g., God is possible. Possibility, actuality, and necessity presuppose a thing, but its determinations are not themselves determinations. Possibility is a positing relative to our thinking, actuality is absolute positing <*positio absoluta*>. More is contained in actuality than in possibility, i.e., not that more is represented of the thing by actuality than by possibility, but more is added to our thinking. First I posit a thing relative to my thinking, then I posit it absolutely by which I obviously think more. For illustration we want to note the following: – .^{l}

29:766 ^{m}The connection between friends is more certain than that between citizens of a state. The basis of the connection is a matter of degree. Order is a quality, nevertheless it can be as great with a few things as with many; it rests on the truth of the rules of the connection of the manifold. Transcendental perfection is the same.[64] Its degree rests on this, the more a manifold is in agreement, the more there is perfection,^{n} one to which a manifold agrees is an associate <*unum ad quod varium consentitur est socius*>; thus the more that are associates <*socii*>, the greater is the perfection; if I do not take it metaphysically, it is only relative. Metaphysical perfection is the degree of reality, and we cannot appraise that because

29:767 we have no concept of the highest degree of reality. The author speaks further of the magnitude of alteration. Sameness can also be large or small![65] Alteration is the existence of opposite determinations <*existentia determinationum oppositorum*>. The opposites <*oppositi*> cannot occur at the same time, but only successively. That is thus successive existence <*existentia successiva*>. Something alterable is that in which the determina-

---

^{l} The remainder of this ms page (bottom third) is blank, and the following page (reverse of this one) is blank, with written at the top: *hier fehlt sehr viel-*. (much is missing here-.), and in smaller writing below the dash: *indess dadurch* (because thereby). With respect to the Baumgarten text that Kant is following, discussion of the second half of Ch. 1, sect. 3 ("being") through Ch. 2, sect. 5 ("mathematics of intensive magnitude"), i.e., §§61–190, is missing here. The paragraph prior to the discussion of substance and accident (below) may come from §190. It also parallels *Metaphysik Dohna* (28:633$_{1-6}$).

^{m} Following Stark, we are inserting here (after 822$_{33}$) a passage that was originally included in the Introduction section (viz. 766$_{27}$–767$_7$, 769$_1$–773$_9$). On this, see the corresponding break in the Introduction section (above) between 760 and 773. We retain a paragraph break added here by Lehmann (766$_{27}$).

^{n} Lehmann misreads *Der Grad derselben beruht darauf, in ie mehreres* as *Der Grund derselben beruht darauf, wie in mehreren* (Its ground rests on this, as in several). Also, there is a series of dashes and periods in the right margin of the ms here (766$_{32-3}$).

tion of opposites <*determinatio oppositorum*> is*[o]* possible; the greater the determination <*determinatio*>, the greater is the alteration.*[p]* We come 29:769 now to the concepts of

Substance and accident

With the category we have spoken of the relation of substance to accident – of the cause <*causa*> to the effect <*causato*> and of the active to the passive. We want to call*[q]* the second the category of principle <*principii*>, the first the category of subject <*subjecti*>, the third [the]*[L.r]* category of interaction <*commercii*>. The three are possible only in real relations. In all judgments there is a relation of predicate to subject; if that is all, then it is categorical, if thé relation is of ground to consequent, then it is hypothetical, if various judgments are considered as in one whole of cognition, then it is disjunctive.*[s]* We know that the table of categories is [an analogue]*[L.r]* of the table of the functions of the understanding in judging – in the latter we find categorical judgments which form the basis of all the others – they contain the relations of the subject to the predicate. That which cannot exist otherwise than as subject is substance, what cannot exist otherwise than as predicate is accident. Thus everything here is so: as the categorical judgments are the most preeminent, so also is the category of substance the most preeminent, while the concepts of accident are as it were only secondary concepts <*conceptus secundarii*>. Substance is therefore also called the substrate <*substratum*> of appearances, and is the first, for I can think of substance or subject without accident or predicate, but not the reverse. Therefore substance is also called the substrate of accidents.[66] – Accidents are mere modes <*modi*> of the existence of substance and these cannot be apart from that substance; for they exist as predicates and these cannot be apart from the subject. The ancients therefore said: accidents do not move from a substance into a substance <*accidentia non migrant e substantia in substantiam*>, that would indicate that they had their own existence. If we go back then we find that

---

[o] We follow Lehmann in changing *seyn sind* to *ist* (767₆). The ms is barely legible here, and the presumed underlining may have been meant as a deletion of *seyn*.

[p] A long marginalium (767₈–768₃₉) belonging to the Introduction section was inserted into the text here by Lehmann, and we have removed it to that section (just prior to the subsection on "The Use of Metaphysics," 766ff). The text before and after this note is continuous in the ms, without a paragraph break, although "Substance and Accident" is on a new line by itself. A *40* added by Lehmann without note (before *Wir*, 769₁) has been removed, and the text has been restructured in accordance with the appearance of the ms. Lehmann apparently read a page number as part of the text in adding the *40*.

[q] *wollen wir nennen* is written twice in the ms (769₅); this is not noted by Lehmann.

[r] Lehmann does not note his addition of *die* (769₆).

[s] An *X* precedes this sentence (769₁₁).

[t] In the ms, there is only the sign # (769₁₂).

substance and accident lie at the basis of reality. (Note: a predicable accident <*accidens praedicabile*>[67] is a contingent accident, opposed to the necessary – predicamental accidents <*accidens praedicamentale*> are contradistinguished to substance.) Accident is also an existence, but only as inherence, and something really positive must be there. Therefore negative predicates are also not accidents, nor are logical predicates, which apply merely to the actuality of a thing, e.g., triangle is not a substance and three corners not an accident. With the expression inherence one imagines the substance carrying the accidents, as if they were separate existences, but requiring a basis; however that is simply a sheer misuse of speech; they are simply manners in which things exist. – Insofar as a thing is determined positively, accidents <*accidentia*> inhere in it; insofar as it is negatively determined, they do not inhere in it. They do not exist for themselves and are not merely supported by the substance like a book in a bookcase.

29:770

That which exists without being the determination of another is substance; that which exists only as determination is accident. We consider first the category substance: that which cannot be represented other than as subject is substance, and what cannot be represented other than as predicate is accident; they are taken from the logical concepts of subject and predicate. A logical predicate can be anything. E.g., human being, considered as real, cannot be the predicate of a thing.

Learnedness cannot exist for itself alone. – The categorical judgments are the basis of hypothetical and disjunctive ones. Since we cannot cognize anything without judgments, and even each concept is a judgment, the categorical judgments constitute an essential condition of experience. In every experience the real is the relation of substance to accident. The category of substance is thus the basis of all other cognition. All determinations <*determinationes*> are either positive <*positivae*> or negative <*negativae*>.[68] These are not accidents <*accidentia*>, because accidents <*accidentia*> involve an existence <*existens*>: every existence is subsistence – that whose existence is inherence is an accident <*omnis existentia est subsistentia – cujus existentia est inhaerentia, est accidens*>. With a substance we can have two relations <*respectus*>: in relation to accidents <*respectu accidentium*> it has power insofar as it is the ground of their inherence; and in relation to the first subject without any accidents, that is the substantial. Power is thus not a new accident, but rather the accidents <*accidentia*> are effects produced by the power. Sometimes the accidents <*accidentia*> do not differ really, then the powers also differ only logically, e.g., to illuminate and to warm. All powers are called derivative <*derivationes*> which differ logically from others, or where the difference can be canceled through analysis. Thus we have primitive and derivative powers in every substance: one assumes, and indeed with high probability, that there must be a primitive power from which all others come. But we cannot reduce all powers to one, because the accidents are so different that we cannot take them as the same. If we leave aside all accidents then substance remains, this is the pure subject in which everything inheres or 29:771 the substantial, e.g., I. All powers are set aside here. The other relation <*respectus*> is [that]ᴸ of the substance with its accidents to the substantial, i.e., to the subject, which is distinguished from all *other* accidents. Concerning power, it is to be noted: the author defines it as that which contains the ground of the inherence of the accidents;⁶⁹ since accidents inhere in each substance, he concludes that every substance is a power.ᵘ That is contrary to all rules of usage: I do not say that substance is a power, but rather that it has power, power is the relation <*respectus*> of the substance to the accidents, insofar as it contains the ground of their actuality, e.g.: I cannot say that the faculty of thinking within us is the substance itself – the faculty belongs to it – nor even [that] an accident of the thoughts is the accident. We thus have something that is not substance, yet also not accident. What then is the faculty of thinking? The relation of the soul to thought insofar as it contains the ground of its actuality. We have absolutely no acquaintance with the substantial, i.e., the subject, in which no accidents inhere, which must be necessarily distinguished from the accident, for if I cancel all positive predicates then I have no predicates and cannot think anything at all. Substances are occasionally taken for predicates by mistake, that is, predicated substance <*substantia praedicata*>; but this is only seldom – more often predicates are transformed into substances, e.g., some theologians [on] original sin.

Categories are indeed pure concepts of the understanding, but they can also be applied to objects of experience, then they retain their names, with the additional phenomenon, here as well: there is phenomenal substance <*substantia phaenomenon*>. E.g., body, which is indeed an appearance, but by means of this the substratum of other appearances. That which is nothing butᵛ a summation of accidents, but is presented only as substance, is a substantiated phenomenon <*phaenomenon substantiatum*>, e.g., a rainbow.⁷⁰ Only through reason does substance prove its existence.ʷ A remarkable consequence, it arises from the false activity of power. It is not a thing, but a relation <*respectus*>, therefore an accident. If I take subject and accident, then substance is; if I leave aside the accidents, the substantial remains.⁷¹ Of that we cannot make the least concept, i.e., we cognize nothing but accidents. For our understanding cognizes everything through predicates; we never cognize that which underlies the predicate. E.g., all human beings are mortal means that all that I cognize under the predicate human being I also cognize under the predicate of mortality. 29:772

ᵘ There is an *X* in the ms between *Kraft* and *das* (771₈).
ᵛ We follow Lehmann in omitting a second *als* (771₂₉).
ʷ There is an *X* following *Daseyn* (771₃₁).

Human being is the essence, the bodily, the animal, eating, thinking, wanting, etc., these are sheer accidents <*accidentia*>. The concept of human being is thus composed of sheer predicates, that of substance is something in space, to which accidents belong, but with which we are not acquainted. If I speak of myself, I want, I do, these are accidents, I is substantial. Can we [then]$^{L.x}$ be acquainted with anything other than through accidents? Elsewhere we have not the least concept of such. When we speak specifically of appearances, we will see that we are acquainted with mere powers. The thing in which the powers inhere remains unknown to us. Negations are not accidents and actual [accidents] can be cognized only according to their actuality, i.e., according to the real which is within.^{y} Powers are derivative whose accidents are one with the accident of another power. A primitive power is one whose accidents are not one with the accident of another power, or which cannot be reduced to a higher one. All natural philosophy occupies itself with the reduction of powers to a single basic power which we cannot further explain,[72] namely that because something is, something else thereby follows. All basic powers must be given through experience.^{z} The coexistence of alterable things with fixed things is state <*coexistentia mutabilium cum fixis est status*>.[73] Something is perdurable in every thing, that is, fixed <*fixum*>. The alterable, insofar as it coexists with existence, is state – it is thus nothing but the determination of a substance in time. In time only alterations are possible; if the determinations in different times are different, then the state is altered; if they are the same, then the state is not altered. The unchanging accordingly has two states, hence the real thing <*ens reale*> does not. An inner state is a coexistence of the inner alterable determinations with the existent, an outer state is coexistence of the relations with the existent, modification is alteration of the inner state – if someone receives more evil, he is not modified. The outer state can be altered without the inner, and the latter without the former. Now we come to weightier concepts. Action can be derived from power,[74] and other things from both; corresponding to it is suffering <*passio; G: Leiden*>. The possibility of acting is faculty <*facultas*>, the possibility of suffering is receptivity <*receptivitas*>. A substance, insofar is it contains the ground of that which belongs to the being of *one thing*, acts <*agirt; G: handelt*>; insofar as the ground of that which belongs to its own being is contained in another substance, it suffers passively. Every substance acts, because the subject subsists. The predicates inhere in each substance, the accidents (which we call merely that) cannot exist other than in the substance,

29:773

---

^{x} We follow Lehmann in changing *das* to *denn* (772₇).
^{y} We follow Lehmann in changing *kennen wir* to *können nur* (772₁₂).
^{z} There is an *X* in the ms following the period; a dash added by Lehmann has been removed (772₂₀).

thus it contains the ground of something which belongs to existence, thus it acts.[a] In natural science one has good reason to regard the attracting and repelling powers <*vim attrahentem . . . pellentem*> as primitive powers. Can there be in one substance many or only one basic power? For[b] our reason there must be several[c] because we cannot reduce everything to one, but the unity of each substance requires that there be only one basic power. Substance acts, insofar as it contains not merely the ground of the accidents, but rather also determines the existence of the accidents; or substance, insofar as its accidents inhere, is in action, and it acts insofar as it is the ground of the actuality of the accidents; that substance suffers (passive) whose accidents inhere through another power. How is this passion possible, since it was said earlier that it is active insofar as its accidents inhere? Every substance is active insofar as its accidents inhere, but also passive, insofar as they inhere through an external[d] power, this is not self-contradictory. E.g., a representation of a trumpet sound inheres in me through an external power, but not alone, for had I no power of representation <*vim repraesentativam*>, then it could be sounded forever and I could not have a representation. From the union of one substance with another an effect comes about, namely, the representation of the trumpet sound. We can never be merely passive, but rather every passion is at the same time action. The possibility of acting is [a][L[e] faculty <*facultas*>, and of suffering receptivity <*receptivitas*>. The latter always presupposes the former. Every substance is self-active, otherwise it could not be substance; it can be suffering in one relation <*respectu*>, but can also be active in the same. A merely suffering substance is a contradiction <*contradictio*>; otherwise it could not have any accidents. The inner actions <*actiones immanentes*> [are those] which a substance produces[f] in itself, [the] transeunt <*transientes*> [are those which] act upon another substance or [have] influence <*influxus*>.[g] The substance being acted upon <*substantia patiens*> is acting in itself <*eo ipso agens*>, for the accident would not inhere if the substance had no power through which it inhered in it, hence it also acts; influence <*influxus*>[75] is therefore an unfitting expression, it

29:822

29:823

[a] There is an *X* here (773[5]) at the right margin, possibly corresponding with a similar sign at 772[20].
[b] The ms appears to read *Auf*; Lehmann changes this to *Auch* and says the text is illegible (773[8]).
[c] This ends the inserted section (766[27]–767[7], 769[1]–773[9]). The text begins again at 822[34], which in the ms is a page following and facing a blank page with the words "Much is missing here – ." Text begins in the top left corner of the page, with no indication that it should be inserted somewhere.
[d] Lehmann misreads *fremde* as *trennende* (823[6]).
[e] Lehmann does not note his addition of *eine* (823[14]).
[f] Reading *hervorbringt* for *hervorbringen* (823[20]).
[g] There may be an *X* in the ms following *influxus* (823[21]).

implies that the accident migrated out of a substance. What then is genuine passivity <*passio*>?[76] The acting substance <*substantia agens*> determines the power of the substance being acted upon <*substantiae patientis*> in order to produce this accident, therefore all passivity <*passio*> is nothing more than the determination of the power of the suffering substance by an outer power.

Transeunt action <*actio transiens*>, when I make something actually outside me, is twofold: the action <*actio*> (*actuare* means to make actual) of a substance or accident outside itself <*substantiae vel accidentia extra se*> – the first, when I make actual a substance actually outside of me, is called creation <*creatio*> – if I make actual accidents outside of me, then if it is determined,[h] it is called influence <*influxus*>. An action that consists of many actions is composite <*composita*>, that which is not put together from smaller actions is simple <*simplex*>.

Power is a faculty insofar as it suffices for the actuality of an accident. The difference between power and faculty is difficult to determine. Faculty, insofar as it is determined with respect to an effect, is power, and insofar as it is undetermined, *becomes* faculty. Power contains the ground of the actuality of an action, faculty the ground of the possibility of an action.

29:824

That power which contains the internal and external sufficient ground of an action, is living power – insofar as it contains merely the internal sufficient ground of an action, it is dead power; in comparison to the living, there are infinitely many dead powers in the world. The connection of two powers which resist each other is confluence <*confluens*> – as such each power is living – for if it exists, then the effect must also exist.

Reaction is not counteraction, but rather reciprocal action.[i] Counteraction is that reciprocal action which is opposed to the action of the other, or the opposed action on the agent of the one acted upon <*actio opposita patientis in agentem*>, which is also called impediment <*impediment*>;[77] that is twofold: (1) negative, where there are no efficient causes, or [there is] a lack of them in the cause, which would constitute the completion <*complement*> of the same; (2) positive, there are efficient causes of what is being acted upon <*patientis*>, which are opposed to the actions of the agent.

The author now speaks of presence, distance, absence, and contact.[78] The first could still belong here, but not the last – that concerns extended beings that have a surface and are impenetrable, for that is contact <*contactus*>, as when two bodies conflict with each other in space through

---

[h] *wäre es bestimmt* (823_{33}) is written above the line and inserted. It is difficult to read, and it may well not be *bestimmt*.

[i] The terms are *Reaction* (reaction), *Gegenwirkung* (counteraction), *Wechselwirkung* (reciprocal action), and *Handlung* (action) (824_{10-11}).

their impenetrability. A substance, one can say, is present to another if it influences it. That can happen mediately <*mediate*>, also immediately <*immediate*>. Presence <*praesentia*> is either bilateral <*bilateralis*>, if two substances reciprocally influence each other, or unilateral <*vel unilateralis*> as when God has an influence on all things, but they do not on him – all things in the world are in presence.[j] It[k] is unilateral <*unilateralis*> when in respect of one substance another is merely being acted upon <*mere patiens*>, bilateral <*bilateralis*> if they can be viewed as acting reciprocally <*reciproce agentes*>. With influence <*influxu*>, the substance must be present. The internal sufficient ground of an[l] action of a substance is power. It is distinguished from being acted upon <*patientia*>, to which something more must be added if it is to become power. Power that suffices internally but not externally is dead power; that which suffices internally and externally is living power. Dead power is a ground whereby an effect can exist but does not exist due to outer circumstances. If the ground is internally sufficient and the effect is still missing, then there must be a real power whose effect is an even stronger object, or a hindrance, i.e., something which opposes the effect of a given power. If the ground of the opposite of an effect is a power, then it is called resistance <*resistenz; G: Widerstand*>;[79] dead powers <*vires mortuae*> are those which have no actuality because another power resists them. If they are increased internally, or the hindrances are taken away, then they can clearly become externally sufficient. The difference between dead and living powers is not in them but due to hindrances. If we take away the hindrances, then many effects will happen in the world without an augmentation of active powers. 29:825

The author speaks now of contact <*contactu*>.[80] Two bodies are in contact if they have a common boundary. He believes that this is the same as immediate presence <*praesentia immediata*>. A substance is present to another if it has an influence on it. If this is immediate, then according to the author it is contact <*contactus*>. But that is valid only of space and the extended, and is a physical concept which presupposes impenetrability. Presence <*praesentia*> is either unilateral or bilateral or reciprocal <*vel unilateralis vel bilateralis vel mutua*>. With every contact <*contactu*> there is a reciprocal influence <*influxus mutuus*>, but contrariwise, where there [is][L] reciprocal influence <*influxus mutuus*>, there is not always contact <*contactus*>. With sensible beings to be sure, but not with spiritual ones. We now speak on

[j] The term transcribed by Lehmann as *praesenz* is unclear in the ms, although it is probably not *praesenz;* the text appears to read: *auf ihn – in p??/bil: sind alle Dinge* (824₂₇). Also, an *X* is at the end of this sentence in the ms.

[k] An *Einfluss*, added by Lehmann without note, has been removed (824₂₈).

[l] We do not follow Lehmann in his changing *Grund einer* to *Grund der* (824₃₁).

The simple and composite

Quantum <*quanto*> and composite <*composito*> have already been spoken of above.[81] With a quantum <*quanto*> one must be taken several times, not with a composite <*composito*>. We suppose that many constitute a one; but nothing can be considered as quantum without the identity of many <*identitas plurium*>. A composite <*compositum*> is classified into real, i.e., composite from substances <*compositum ex substantiis*>, and into ideal,[82] i.e., into composite <*compositum*> that is composed from something that is not substance, or from accidents; the real is also called: [composite] strictly speaking <*strictus dictum*>. {Insofar as there is [something] contained in one, much has been represented by substance, but not parts, e.g., the soul does not consist of thoughts; they inhere in it. It is thus a connection <*nexus*> that is a connection <*nexus*> not of composition but rather of inherence. We take now the first: the composite <*compositum*>, insofar as it is not viewed as part of something else, is whole <*totum*>. A whole <*totum*> and composite <*compositum*> both refer to parts. – The many, insofar as it becomes a one in an aggregate – that one is called composite <*compositum*> and, when the many is homogeneous, quantum. We speak now only of the composite insofar as it has been composed <*compositum quatenus est compositum*>.

A real composite <*compositum reale*> is that whose parts can also exist for themselves apart from a connection <*nexu*> with others – that whose parts can never exist apart from the connection with others is ideal <*ideale*>, e.g., inference is an ideal composite <*compositum ideale*>, whose parts can exist only in the soul. Body is a real composite <*compositum reale*>.}[m] When the parts exist for themselves, then the composition is an action through which the parts are connected; when the parts can exist before the composition, then it is a real composite <*compositum reale*>; when the concept of the composite <*compositum*> precedes the concept of the parts, then it is an ideal composite <*compositum ideale*>, e.g., space, which I cannot think as composed out of small spaces, rather I must think of the small space as being in the large space. The composition is thought of later than the composite <*compositum*>. We consider here the substantial composite <*compositum substantiale*>, whereby we note:

29:826   1. matter, or the parts, out of which the composite <*compositum*> consists,

2. the manner and way in which the parts are composed, i.e., the form.

---

[m] Marginalia (826_{8-22}) alongside 825_{21-30}. It begins at the top of the page (ms, p. 63′) alongside the section heading, and ends roughly where we have inserted it (825_{20}), viz., after the last full sentence of this text. We thus do not follow Lehmann, who inserts it at the end of the paragraph; likewise, paragraph breaks and blank lines added by Lehmann have been removed.

The essence of each composite <*compositi*> consists in the form, i.e., in the manner of composition <*in modo compositionis*>. The ancients said: form gives being to a thing <*forma dat esse rei*>.[83] By that they understood the matter in each thing is something real, but the form constitutes the difference of things; and we must think of it before the stuff.

The author speaks further of coming about and passing away and says the alteration from non-existence into existence is origin <*ortus*>, and the reverse is death <*interitus*>.[84] Origin from nothing <*ortus ex nihilo*> is the origin of substance, of accidents one cannot say that they have come about from nothing – originated from nothing is <*ex nihilo ortum est*> that whose parts would have had preexistence. Annihilation <*annihilatio*> also concerns only the substance, the accidents are merely modes of existence <*modi existentiae*> of the substance. But that[n] is not alteration of a thing itself, for alteration can take place only with existing things. Origin <*ortus*> means the being that a non-being precedes. And death <*interitus*> that which a non-being follows. In appearance, substance is what remains there while the determinations change. That is the condition under which we call something the first substantial, namely that it perdures. For were there nothing perdurable, that would not have come about and passed away, then we could not have any experience of alteration. There must be a substantial, of which we can perceive only the alteration. In that which perdures there was the state A, and now the state B, thus it is altered through something, and this perdurable <*perdurabile*> we call substance. When one says everything in the world is alterable, then that means: there comes to be and passes away nothing except accidents and connections of bodies.

29:827

The parts of a real composite <*compositi realis*> are in interaction <*commercio*>, and all substances, insofar as they stand in interaction <*commercio*>, constitute a real composite <*compositum reale*>. Interaction <*commercium*> is reciprocal influence <*influxus mutuus*>, for how else is the interaction <*commercium*> of different substances possible than by one determining something in the other, for the substances have an effect in each other, e.g., with a body all parts are in interaction <*commercio*>; what is not in interaction <*commercio*> does not belong to it. The connection of the highest cause with its effects <*causatis*> connects nothing, is no interaction <*commercium*>. The cause accordingly does not belong to the effects <*causatis*>.

Every whole of substances consists of simple substances. We also note that the author maintains against Leibniz that a composite <*compositum*> should not be named a substance, although the parts are substances, for composition is only an accident. That is surely true, but mere subtlety. Leibniz says bodies are substantial phenomena, they appear to be sub-

---

[n] Presumably "that" refers to annihilation (826[29]).

stances, but only the parts are. He presumably had another sense here than that which Wolff and the author impute to him, otherwise he could well have kept this to himself, that can be easily comprehended by anyone. *(Monad <*monas*> means the same as unity of an indivisible substance, i.e., what cannot be thought further as aggregate of many substances. Now the question arises: can one say of every substantial composite <*compositum substantiale*> that it consists of simple substances, i.e., is it a whole consisting of monads <*monadatum*>? Yes, insofar as it is noumenon, for all connection is nothing other than relation. Since the substances by definition <*ex definitione*> are privy to outer existence for themselves, one can remove all relation and the substances remain and are simple. For were they not simple, then the composition would not be removed. But how is it with a real composite <*composito reali*> phenomenon? Where something is represented only through the senses as a substantial composite <*compositum substantiale*> – and the substances are substances only for the senses – that falls aside here, for the proof falls aside. The appearance of a substance is not the substance itself, and what is valid for it is not valid for the latter. Suppose a body were to consist of simple parts, then its shadow may not

29:828   consist of simple parts. If we take away all composition then nothing remains.) If in a composite <*composito*> of substances nothing is substance except the parts from which we abstract all composition, which is only an accident of their reciprocal relation, then the substances remain; these are without composition, accordingly the substances are the simple parts in every substantial composite <*composito substantiale*>. If I set aside all relation, the simple remains. That is entirely correct if I speak of composites insofar as they are <*compositis quatenus sunt*> noumena, for through the understanding I cannot think any composite <*compositum*> without previously thinking of simple substances. The simple is the substrate <*substratum*> of everything composite in the noumena <*noumenis*>. Composition <*compositio*> is the relation of substances insofar as they are in community; but this does not take place with a phenomenal composition <*compositio*>. A real composite <*compositum reale*>, insofar as it is appearance, is considered in space. Space does not consist of simple parts, thus neither does the composite <*compositum*>. I cannot say of a perduring appearance that which is valid of substances, insofar as they are thought through the understanding. Bodies are appearances and in space, thus do not consist of simple substances. If we would cognize the unknown that is the basis of bodies and produces the bodily appearances, then we would cognize something sheerly simple that would be in interaction <*commercio*>. We make the phenomena in appearance into substances, but we must then remain with the concept of substance, for the perduring appearance suffers. To

---

* We follow Lehmann in adding parentheses here and below in place of *X*'s in the ms (827₂₅, 828₂).

speak of simple beings we must go beyond the world of the senses, but then we have no proof for the objective reality of our concept, for we can give no example; but that applies for all appearances. Composites <*composita*> of which I can give examples are substantiated phenomena <*phaenomena substantiata*>. But what is valid for the noumena <*noumenis*> is not valid for them.

Have we comprehended anything new through this doctrine? No, for through the category of substance we are acquainted with no things. Experience must give us examples – and these are appearances. Just as little can we comprehend how substances are supposed to constitute a whole – [we can,] to be sure, of appearances that are in space – but not how substances in themselves do, for here we have to leave space aside, because it is the form of sensible intuition. We speak now on

Space and time[85] 29:829

Space and time are not determinations of things insofar as they are thought through the understanding, but rather insofar as they occur to sense, thus they are forms of intuitions. (We come now to the important concepts that are of the kind that, once we have been able to unfold their nature, they alter the entire plan of metaphysics, and banish all contradictions that [have][L,p] discredited metaphysics.)[q] Space, of outer sense, and time, of inner. The matter of all appearances is sensation, and what corresponds to it is real. Philosophy: we cognize the real only *a posteriori*, but the formal *a priori*. *The representation of the impression of the object on us is sensation*, thus is something subjective that we all must cognize *a posteriori*. In our sense cognition there is something of which we have a representation *a priori*; that is the form of appearance, of the outer, space, of the inner, time. They are the form, how objects will appear to us when they affect us, therefore we can imagine much that we have never seen, e.g., cones and pyramids as in geometry; accordingly one can cognize space and time *a priori*. Something else besides appearance belongs to experience, for it is not merely perception, but rather the unity of perceptions connected with one another according to general rules. The matter must be given, the form consists in the concepts of the understanding. These are the categories, which constitute the form of all human experience – and the unity of the appearances is *a priori*, these are also the categories, e.g., substance, they are namely the connection of the manifold of appearance according to rules. – We can thus cognize *a priori*:

1. the form of intuition, that is space and time and
2. the form of understanding, insofar as it is applied to sensibility; or

---

p Lehmann does not note his addition of *haben* (829₈).

q An *X* follows the parenthesis in the ms (829₈).

the form of the thinking of objects which appear to us; that is a concept of the understanding and constitutes the form of experience. Space and time, belonging to sensibility, and the categories, belonging to the understanding, constitute the concepts that we can have *a priori* and of which we can give corresponding objects in experience. We also have yet other transcendent concepts, but of these no objects in experience can be given; they must be distinguished from transcendental ones. Those are ones through which I represent merely the possibility of synthetic *a priori* cognition. Transcendent can be expressed in German as beyond bounds <G: *überschwenglich*>. Concepts are immanent if their example can be given from experience or according to the analogy of an experience. – These concepts are the ground of the possibility of an *a priori* cognition – and of synthetic *a priori* cognition. They have always been a stumbling block. Of space one says [that if it]^L were something in itself, then without things it would be nothing at all, for in space there are locations; the location, or the manner in which things are next to each other, is not there if no things exist. Nonetheless, our understanding supposes: it precedes all things, it is viewed as an all-encompassing receptacle <*receptaculum*> containing nothing except places of things. Nor could it be relations, for one cannot imagine that they should exist without things. Space is not a thing, nonetheless something wherein I can represent to myself all relations. What then is space? It is just the same with time. Time is that in which alterations subsist, it is not a thing, but rather things are in it; it does not presuppose the existence of things, but rather I must have a time in which I posit the thing. If I take all things away, then there is a time in which nothing is, but wherein something can be. So what is it? A flow of moments. And again what are these? Since they^r were required to regard space and time as something but not as a thing, they did not know what they were to do with them. (The author says the order of successive things is time – posited connected things succeed each other one after the other <*ordo successivorum est tempus*[86] – *post se invicem posita coniuncta succedunt*>. Time is thus the connection of things insofar as they follow upon one another – but he leaves out being concurrent, and that is an important relation. When are things concurrent? When they are in the same time; and successively, when they are things in different times. And no human being has grasped sequence without presupposing time, hence the definition is false – space is the order of simultaneous things posited outside each other <*ordo simultaneorum extra se positorum*> – that things can be outside another, space is needed for that. One says things can be represented outside one another without being in space, e.g., I say one substance is other than another – yes, but the positing outside <*extra*> also presupposes a space, the author says that as well:[87] of simultaneous things

^{r} I.e., previous philosophers.

posited outside and within each other <*simultaneorum extra et intra se posita*>, otherwise I cannot see what sort of relations the different things have to each other.)

The author explains space through the order of things posited outside 29:831 each other <*ordo extra se positorum*>. Things in different locations are posited outside each other <*extra se positorum*>. The concept of location presupposes the concept of space, and the concept is accepted as already familiar: the order of many things, insofar as they exist after each other, is time <*ordo plurium, quatenus post se existunt est tempus*>; to be successive is to be at different times, thus the same <*idem*> is explained through the same <*per idem*>.

The main question is whether they[s] are things existing in and for themselves, for they are different from all possible things that are in them. For the most part all of the ancient philosophers rejected that. Now a few believed space to be a determination of things. Because space and time contain and consist of sheer relations one believed that this relation of things insofar as they are connected constitutes space and, insofar as one determines the other in a series, time, thus they would be true relations which, without things, would fall away, which can be thought of by the understanding as possible. For others, there was nothing but a general concept of relations in general. We want to see whether such is the case. – Were they relations, we could not have any *a priori* concept of them, yet this occurs in geometry, or we would have to be able to cognize the properties of space from the relations of the things, and synthetic *a priori* propositions would be impossible in the whole of geometry; we can cognize the properties *a posteriori*, but there are then no apodictic propositions. Space is no concept, but rather an intuition. The concept presupposes intuition. We cannot prove any properties of a triangle without drawing them. We have only one space, and by many spaces we mean parts of the one united infinite space. But that is not so with a concept, e.g., virtue is not a part of general virtue, but it is otherwise with all-encompassing space. To intuit a thing *a priori* means to intuit a thing that is not at all given, and so I can intuit nothing other than the form of sensibility, how I intuit things, which is in me. Space must also be something like that, namely the form of outer appearance. It is something which lies not in things but rather in us ourselves. Now I can explain it: it is the formal aspect of outer appearances, and thus properties of space can be cognized *a priori*. This condition under which appearances are possible is pure outer intuition. Now it is comprehensible how they can precede things or, rather, appearances. They concern merely the nature of sensibil- 29:832 ity, according to which it can be only affected. (Space and time give us *a priori* cognitions prior to all experience, therefore they cannot be bor-

---

[s] I.e., space and time.

rowed from experience. – We recognize *a priori* propositions by their necessity, we have such necessary propositions in geometry, e.g., between two points only one straight line is possible – time also provides such necessary propositions, e.g., two times cannot be concurrent, thus they cannot be properties of things in themselves. To comprehend things in themselves *a priori* is *here* plainly impossible. Since they are thus not determinations of the objects, they must be determinations of the subject – thus the forms of our sensibility. – Space is the form of how we intuit outer things, time, of how we intuit ourselves. What we cognize through outer and inner sense is mere appearance, not things in themselves. – Could one say: Surely we can cognize ourselves? Yes, where we are self-active, one can say that does not belong to sensibility, but if we observe ourselves that is nothing but a series of inner appearances. We can still observe everything only as we are inwardly affected.) (We can now also see how we cognize time and space *a priori*. We cannot view things in themselves *a priori* – but how can we view appearances *a priori*? Because I can know how they will affect me – for they are not things in themselves, e.g., I will not see a body except when light rays from a point of the body strike on a point on my retina – that I can comprehend *a priori*.) (Space and time will thus also not be valid for things in themselves – but things as phenomena are in space and time, that is the foundation of the transcendental aesthetic. Aesthetic is the doctrine of sensibility. The ancients classified everything into sensibles <*aistheta*> and intelligibles <*noeta*>,[']now one uses it for sensible satisfaction and calls it doctrine of taste. – Since this does not actually admit of being raised to a science, it is better to remain with the meaning of the ancients. Transcendental aesthetic is the consideration of things as objects of the senses; insofar as we can cognize them *a priori*, it indicates the grounds of the possibility of *a priori* sensible intuitions, which rests on space and time.) (If I say that something is extended, then it is appearance – for extended is a determination of space. If we speak of coming about and passing away, alteration, etc., then we speak merely of phenomena. This has no meaning when we speak merely of the noumenon.) We cannot have the concept of time *a posteriori*, for how should we begin to create it *a posteriori*; we would not have any experience at all that one follows upon another if the concept did not underlie it. It is not a concept of relations of things, otherwise we could not have any properties *a priori* or apodictic propositions of time, e.g., between two moments there is only one time – two times are not concurrent – time has only one dimension, but were the properties concepts of relation, then we could not have any of the propositions – time is also intuition. All things are in the same time. – All times are parts of the same time. Intuition contains not the constitution of the thing, but rather

29:833

['] These terms are written with Greek letters in the ms (832_{30}).

the subjective form of sensibility, how I am affected. The form of inner sense is time. I can comprehend *a priori* how my inner sense intuits itself, and can say much about it *a priori*. Do the concepts also have objective reality, or are they beings of reason <*entia rationis*>? Most certainly they do have objective reality, but they are limited to mere objects of the senses, they apply to all appearances. Crusius says: all things are somewhere or sometime,[88] that must be limited to appearances. The summation of all possible objects of the senses is the sensible world, the concepts thus apply only to the sensible world – [the] world is the aggregate of appearances. To be sure, just as we represent a sensual world,*u* I can think of an intelligible world that can be cognized through the understanding alone, but the understanding does not have the faculty to intuit, but rather to reflect on appearances; thus it cannot know what things in themselves are. It can have experiences, but thereby it has cognized only the connection of appearances, not the things in themselves. Appearance and illusion must be distinguished.[89] Appearance can be true as appearance. Illusion is a perception through which I want to make a concept without taking into account all other perceptions. Appearance does not judge. If we want to judge about appearances, we judge truly when this occurs with all perceptions; if I want to judge from only one perception, then this is illusion. God cognizes things in themselves, for his cognitive power produces the things. We cognize only the appearances, i.e., the manner in which we are affected, and things must affect us, otherwise we know nothing at all of them. – Space and time are nothing but representations of things, and now we have a key to many problems. If appearances are nothing but representations, and*v* all sensible things are appearances, then all sensible things are nothing but representations. Appearances thus exist only in the representation itself. We can accordingly say: only so much exists in the sensible world as lies in our representation, e.g., supposing that human beings were to lose their hearing in the midst of music, then there also would exist no music for them, just like for those who are tone deaf. The objects in themselves do not exist. Through this we are spared many mistakes, e.g., is the world finite or infinite? The question, which has made so many difficulties, now falls away and means: in the series of my perceptions, will I go on without end or not? And to that the answer is determined: without end.

29:834

---

u We are following Lehmann's changes to the text (833_{23-4}). Unchanged, the ms reads (in translation): "I can easily imagine an intelligible w[orld] intellectual for that is valid only of representations just like a sensual world" (see Ak. 29: 1163). Contrary to Lehmann, we read a *W* in the ms instead of a *Z* (*Zeit*).

v Lehmann misreads *und* as *wie* (how)(834_3).

On the finite and infinite

Magnitude which cannot be immediately intuited as magnitude is appraised by way of sequence. I represent it to myself as quality. That the quantity of quality <*quantitas qualitatis*> is degree, see* definition of the author,[90] is wholly correct, i.e., it is not immediately represented as quantity, but mediately, namely through a sequence. Likewise one can also say: quantity of the ground <*quantitas rationis; G: Grunds*> is degree. Degrees are opposed to extensive magnitudes, which are space and time and everything that is within them. For inner magnitude one uses the expression degree, not magnitude, which holds only of extensive magnitudes. All reality has degree. There are degrees from sensation to thought, i.e., up to apperception, where I think myself with respect to the understanding. Something can have so little degree that I can scarcely notice it, but nonetheless I am still always conscious of it. There is, properly speaking, no largest and smallest in experience. We have three concepts: of the greatest <*maximi*>, the unlimited <*illimitati*>, and the infinite <*infiniti*>, which are quite closely related and yet distinct from each other. The greatest <*maximum*> is that beyond which nothing larger is possible. The unlimited <*illimitatum*> is the negative representation of the largest. With the greatest <*maximo*>, the concept is of a totality that lacks nothing which is requisite for a certain kind of thing. (What contains all of a certain kind is unlimited <*illimitatum*>; what does not have everything, etc., etc., is limited, the limited <*limitatum*> is thus opposed to the totality <*omnitudo*>.) Unlimited <*illimitatum*> can thus mean the greatest <*maximum*>, insofar as it is represented through a negative concept. Something can be unlimited <*illimitatum*> comparatively, but not absolutely; greatest <*maximum*> is a positive, and unlimited <*illimitatum*> a negative concept of totality. With infinite <*infinito*> I represent the relation of the magnitude of a thing to the essence. The relation of the magnitude to the possibility of measuring it determines either the magnitude or the infinity; I do not say how large the thing is – larger than all concepts that I have so far used for measuring. It has been confused with unlimited <*illimitatum*>: we appraise magnitudes by successively adding one of a thing <*successive unum rei addendo*>. All counting is a progression <*progressus*> in the construction of a magnitude. The magnitude whose construction is possible through finite progression <*progressus finitum*> is a finite quantity <*quantitas finita*>, and infinite <*infinita*> if its progression <*progressus*> is infinite <*infinitus*>. I cannot call a thing in itself infinite <*infinitum*>. Language usage is such that one often calls the unlimited <*illimitatum*> the infinite. In itself, they are not the same. With the phenomena <*phaenomenis*>, one can say that is unlimited <*illimi-*

29:835

---

* Lehmann misinterprets *s.* (*sehe*) as *ist* (is)(834_{19}).

tatum> and infinite *<infinitum>*. We imagine the highest being *<ens summum>* as unlimited *<illimitatum>*, but can we call it infinite *<infinitum>*? That is not fitting, for I do not say as much with that [term] as with highest being *<ens summum>*, i.e., that which contains everything that a being can contain, or with all-sufficient,[x] i.e., that which lacks nothing; but with infinite *<infinitum>* I do not say what the being is itself, but rather only that its magnitude cannot be determined in relation to a measure; by this I do not know how large it is itself, whether it is large or not, but rather only that it is too large for any of my concepts, but on that account it need not be the largest among all things. (Infinite *<infinitum>* means not how large a thing is in itself, but rather relative to a measure it is larger than every number. All appraisal of what is larger in space and time is relative, e.g., the sun is far from the earth, relative to the fixed stars it is close to the earth, and the smaller the measure the larger the number. – Absolute magnitude is totality, so if we take something in relation to the totality, it is limited. The absolute metaphysical magnitude is that of the most real being *<ens realissimi>*, through totality we also cognize things in themselves through limitation of the totality *<omnitudo>*.) (The concept of the infinite *<infiniten>* concerns only phenomena, thus only space and time, and everything that is possible within them, and we must apply it only to these as well. If I say God is an infinite being *<ens infinitum>*, that means unlimited *<illimitatum>*.) (There is with the noumena *<noumenis>* a greatest *<maximum>*, but with the phenomena *<phaenomenis>* there occurs neither a greatest *<maximum>* nor a smallest *<minimum>*.) Infinite *<infinitum>* means the continuation to infinity in measuring magnitude. The infinite *<infinitum>*, in distinction to the unlimited *<illimitatum>*, is called the mathematical infinite *<infinitum mathematicum>* and insofar as it is the same as the unlimited *<illimitatum>*, it is called the real infinite *<infinitum reale>*. The quantum relative to any givable unity greater than every number *<quantum relative ad unitatem aliquam dabilem omni numero maius>* is infinite; when it is larger than any number, then it goes beyond my concept, for I can make a determinate concept of magnitude for myself only through number. A being that has a determinate concept of magnitude without number can also grasp the infinite *<infinitum>*. With the highest being we cannot avail ourselves of this word, for it presupposes that we have a measure. Homogeneity is needed for that, but the highest being has no homogeneity *<homogeneum>*. I compare the unlimited *<illimitatum>* with no measure, and the concept of the infinite can be applied only to phenomena; for it presupposes that the progression *<progressus>* from one to another is larger than any number. The progression *<progressus>* happens in

29:836

---

[x] Lehmann misreads (at Ak. 29: 1163) *durch allgenugsam d.h.* as *d.h. allgemein d.h.* (i.e., general, i.e.)(835₂₁).

time. With appearances, is the object infinite <*infinitum*> or the progression <*progressus*>? I cannot call the phenomenon infinite, for it is nothing outside of me. Were the sensible world a thing in itself then one could ask whether it was infinite <*infinitum*> or not. So I cannot ask: is the world infinite with regard to space; but rather: in the world must I continue to infinity? Yes, the pro- and regression to infinity <*pro- ... regressus in infinitum*> is possible, but on the other hand one cannot represent to oneself that a quantum is infinite. A future eternity is infinite, it is not an infinite given <*infinitum datum*>, but rather an infinite possible continuation of alterations that can follow upon one another, it is an infinite possibility, not actuality. (Infinity is progressive when concerning potential <*potentiale*> magnitude, or collective <*collective*> when concerning actual <*actuale*> magnitude. Actual infinity <*infinitum actuale*> cannot be thought, but potential <*potentiale*> clearly can be, e.g., future eternity is not something actual, but rather the composition of several times, and this can be infinite. – If we wanted to think of a fulfilled collection of this sort <*collective tale*>, we would have to represent [it] as though all the parts were actual – we would have to run through and take them together, but that is contrary to the definition of the infinite <*infiniten*>, on that account the infinite collection of this sort <*infinitum collective tale*> is not impossible in itself, for we say nothing further than that without number the magnitude cannot be determinately cognized – for because we go into infinity, we cannot express it through any number – but with an understanding which may not posit magnitude through numbers, it would be otherwise.) (The concept of the infinite <*infinitum*> was meant at the same time to be the concept of the greatest <*maximi*> beyond which nothing greater is possible – but that is the unlimited <*illimitatum*>; whether the infinite <*infinite*> thing contains everything, is not yet clarified by that. One has attempted to prove various things from that. An infinite number <*numerus infinitus*>, one says, is impossible <*impossibile*>. That is apodictically true. – That would be a number that would be larger than all numbers, but an infinite multitude <*multitudo infinita*>, e.g., an infinite space, is not impossible on that account, as was further inferred. We say it is a number of miles – here there is no number at all, which was proved thusly: the infinite multitude <*multitudo infinita*> would be the largest according to its definition; but to each magnitude yet another unit can be thought, therefore a largest, hence infinite, magnitude is impossible – when one carves such definitions, one can prove whatever one wants.) Some authors say: because there is no infinite number, there is also no infinite. The highest infinity is a contradiction <*summus infinitus est contradictio*>, but not an infinite multitude. One must distinguish an actual and a potential infinite <*infinitum actuale ... potentiale*>. Potential <*potentiale*>, in which infinite progression <*progressus in infinitum*> is possible, is that which is not given, actual <*actuale*>, that which

29:837

is given. The unlimited belongs to the noumena <*noumenis*>; I represent to myself that it lacks no reality, [that it] bounds a concept that applies to phenomena. We think of boundaries in space and time, limits with noumena <*noumenis*>; whatever contains a ground of limit in itself either in time or in space <*quod rationem in se continet limitis vel in tempore vel in spatio*> is boundary, which can thus be only with phenomena. The mathematical infinity is not givable <*infinitum mathematicum non est dabile*>, i.e., it cannot be represented to me as entirely existent; e.g., future eternity cannot be entirely given, otherwise it would not be eternity. Through what do we represent to ourselves magnitudes as entirely existent? Only through the progression <*progressus*> of the addition of one to one. An infinite magnitude can therefore not be given, because the infinite progression <*progressus in infinitum*> would also have had to be entirely given, or the progression <*progressus*> would have had to be complete, and that is impossible to represent. One can no sooner represent to oneself an infinite <*infiniten*> space, but the progression <*progressus*> in space can be represented as infinite <*infinit*>. If we wanted to represent to ourselves that it exists even prior to the progression <*progressus*>, then we have made for ourselves a concept with a property with which we cannot at all think it, for we cannot think a magnitude other than through a progression <*progressus*>. (Measure is a magnitude that we can cognize intuitively.) Infinite progress <*progressus in infinitum*> occurs, for I can continue a magnitude to infinity <*in infinitum*> and always proceed further in the addition; it can also be thought in the coming eternity. Indefinite progression <*progressus in indefinitum*> is less than infinite <*in infinitum*>. Here there is merely no determinate boundary posited for me. We speak now   29:838

On agreement and diversity

The author now speaks on the relative predicates of beings <*de praedicatis entium relativis*>.[91] He calls them predicates of connection (relation); that is not good. Predicates serve for cognizing identity and diversity, but then no relation is permitted, e.g., two human beings can be quite similar or agree in many features without having the slightest relation to one another. We note the following:[92] the definition of quality is similarity <*similitudo*>, of quantity equality <*aequalitas*> – they are either partially or wholly similar <*vel partialiter vel totaliter similia*>; total equality <*aequalitas totalis*> is equality with respect to all predicates. If we imagine that two total equalities <*aequalitates*> are also similar <*similia*>, then they should be totally equal, hence totally the same as well. The equal <*aequale*> is identical quantity. Homogeneous things <*homogenea*> can be compared, however, only by magnitude. E.g., I cannot compare a year and a mile; if they are fully equal, then they must also be fully homogeneous, for if they are supposed to be equal with respect to all determinations, then they must also be^y homogeneous. Identity is threefold: (a) qualitative, (b) quantitative, both together constituting inner identity, (c) relational <*relationum*>, i.e., outer identity, e.g., that one thing is in different times – one should think wholly congruent things <*totaliter congruentia*> could be diverse by reason of relation <*ratione relationis*> – one also should think wholly similar things <*totaliter similia*> could be different. Therefore the author also says:[93] quantity is an internal difference of fully similar things completely the same as pertaining to inner and outer determinations <*quantitas est discrimen internum, mere similium totaliter eadem tanquam ad internos et externos determinationes*>; says the author, they are numerically the same <*sunt numerice eadem*> – or not many <*plure*>;^{z} many things totally the same are impossible <*plura totaliter eadem sunt impossibilia*>, otherwise there would be no inner difference of the things. An outer difference does not make a difference of things, but rather of outer relation – thus they are not different in kind – for I have no ground to say that that is something other. – ^{a} Further: perfectly equal things are impossible <*perfecte aequalia sunt impossibilia*>, for according to the preceding they would have to be fully similar – therefore wholly congruent things <*totaliter congruentia*>, which are impossible. Further:^{b} fully similar things are impossible <*mere similia sunt impossibilia*>, for were they fully similar, they would differ according to magnitude – one is larger than the other. – The one is thus fully equal and similar to the part of the other, thus wholly congruent <*totaliter congruentia*>, therefore impossible. Wolff, Baumgarten, and before them, Leibniz, have maintained these propositions; he had the principle of indiscernibles <*principium indiscernibilium*>.)^c[94] (This principle of indiscernibles <*principium indiscernibilium*> falls aside with the sensible world; it is also absurd to think that God should have created as diverse every tiniest particle that was supposed to have one and the same effect as others, etc.)

29:839

Wholly the same <*totaliter eadem*> are those where there is no diversity, partially the same <*partialiter eadem*> those diverse with respect to single relations. Internally the same <*eadem*> are those that agree in inner determinations, externally the same <*eadem*> that agree in relations. Things that are entirely one and the same are called numerically the same <*numero eadem*>, for it is one and the same thing <*unum idemque; G: ein und eben dasselbe Ding*>. Where is numerical unity or total identity, and numerical plurality <*pluralitas numerica*> or numerical diversity?

^{y} We follow Lehmann in omitting an *als* (after *auch*) (838$_{20}$).
^{z} We are adding the semicolon after *plure* (838$_{29}$).
^{a} We are replacing three dashes omitted by Lehmann without note. They precede *Weiter, mithin,* and *eines,* respectively (838$_{33, 34,}$ 839$_1$).
^{b} Lehmann misreads *Weiter* as *Weder* (838$_{35}$). We add a colon here to parallel the colon added above by Lehmann after an earlier *Weiter* (cf. 838$_{33}$).
^{c} This closing parenthesis has no mate (839$_5$).

Leibniz wanted to bring a proposition into metaphysics,[95] namely, that things that agree with respect to quantity and quality and also in inner determinations, are thus the same <eadem>, but if they are only in different locations then they are already diverse. It is to be noted here: if objects are considered as noumena then this is true, because here we consider the two things merely through the understanding, and it does not differentiate them at all, even when they are placed in different relations, A with B and C with D, it is all the same whether A is compared with D or C with B; two noumenal beings <entia noumena>, which differ in nothing themselves, are the same. But if I consider things as phenomena, then it is otherwise, they are not the same <eadem>, however much they are equal according to quantity and quality, and are in diverse locations. For if they are already many <plura> and diverse <diversa>, then that does not mean our representation of the space of the things [which][L] are outside each other and thus are diverse. Leibniz calls this the principle of indiscernibles <principium indiscernibilium> and wanted to use it to prove that in the world there were not and could not be two things equal and similar. The first is contingent and may well be true, but not absolutely, e.g., that God could not make a thing found at one location similar to one at another location. That is absurd. Accordingly we call things that are in diverse locations diverse in number <numero diversa>. But diversity of time gives no numerical diversity, e.g., I live at diverse times and am still the same; we speak of things that are next to each other.

Simultaneity <simultaneum> is a mathematical concept.[96] Location is determinate position <determinatus positus>, i.e., relation to other things in space <in spatio>; there is also a position <positum> in time, i.e., age <aetas>, position <positus> is nothing but the determinate relation of one thing with others, it is related to space and time. The position <positus> in time is determined (1) by that which is concurrent, (2) precedes, (3) follows upon something. Location is no space, rather locations are in space, and one location cannot have many locations. That in space which is not a space is a point, therefore each location is a point. Since a location must always be the simple in space, no space can consist of points. (Location is always something simple, e.g., if I want to determine the location of Paris, it is not irrelevant in which way I go – rather it happens in observation <observatorio>, there is once again a space. But[d] formally <formaliter> one takes it for a point because relatively it is quite small.) For if space consisted of locations, then the locations would have to be able to be thought previously, which cannot be done. (A thing cannot be concurrently in diverse locations, for were that so it would be as far away from itself as the one location from the other, which is absurd.) Likewise, time does not consist of moments, for these are positions of

29:840

---

[d] We are adding *aber*, which Lehmann says is not clear in the ms (840,13).

determination in time <*positus determinationis in tempore*>. (Motion is continuous alteration of location, where I successively go through all intermediate spaces – were I to go from one location into the other without going through intermediate locations, but rather being nowhere in the intermediate time, then that would be interrupted alteration <*mutatio interrupta*>. Rest is the perduring presence of a thing at a location, i.e., which is over a time.) In a boundary there is something positive, in limits negative, for here a reality is lacking. The boundary of the line is a point, the boundary of a surface is a line, of a body a surface (limits are the negations of some being insofar as it is not the greatest <*limites sunt negationis entis alicuius quatenus non est maximum*>; a boundary is a space and time, and something positive, which contains the ground of the limits and that by which they are determined). A space which is not the boundary of another space, is called a solid or complete space; it can touch on the boundary of another, but is not it. One can think of a planar space which can be only the boundary of another (the solid). – A line is the boundary of a planar space, and a point the boundary of the line. From this one also sees that space cannot consist of points, because points are boundaries. (The following actually does not belong here. In the actuality of every accident one must think of power. Motive power is the opposite <*oppositum*> of inertial power, which is a contradiction in the predicate <*contradictio in adjecto*>; a power that is the ground for nothing being done is not a power; one can say resisting power <*vis resistens*>, but that is not inertial power <*vis inertiae*>: what resists, is also material. Space, which is nothing other than the form, is distinguished from matter. Matter is that which can be intuited in space. One distinguishes matter and body. By matter one always understood something passive that lies at the basis of all appearances. – Body would be the active principle. That is false. No substance is merely <*mere*> passive – if matter is substance, and that lies in its concept, then it is active, otherwise no motion could inhere in it; one must characterize it thus: matter determined with respect to figure and quantity is a body <*materia quoad figuram et quantitatem determinata est corpus*>.)

29:841

A complete space is a solid space. Motion is the continuous alteration of the location of things. Things which are outside each other cannot be in the same location, and a thing cannot be concurrently at different locations, for then one would also see it in other locations and would have to call it [an]ᴸ other thing. Measuring is the action by which I make a distinct concept of magnitude merely through the successive addition of unity. Power which begins, continues, and resists a motion is motive power. The power of resistance is called inertial power <*vis inertiae*>. But the name is ill-suited.

On the relations of time.⁹⁷ They concern only appearances, because time is not the representation of the constitution of a thing in itself. The concept of time is not a concept of things in themselves, but rather order in appearances. The present, past, and future is to be distinguished in time. Actually we can imagine two relations of things in time, namely insofar as they are concurrent, and insofar as they are successive. Present is that which is together with the representation of time; past, what precedes the present; future, what follows upon the present. In themselves things are neither present nor past nor future, but rather these are relations of how the things have become in time. To the concept of time also belongs the concept of existence, namely, in the present, past, and future. Temporal existence can be considered as magnitude, and the magnitude of existence is duration; by this I do not understand the magnitude of the thing in itself. Of the existence of the thing in itself (potential beings <entia in potentia> are such as can become in the future and whose ground of existence is already met with now). (Ground of existence is duration. – The existence of God cannot be measured in time, also cannot be compared with it.)

29:842

How can we make for ourselves the concept of the magnitude of existence? If existence is considered with phenomena, then it is posited in time; if it is a long time, then it is large duration, if a short time, then a short duration. We cannot imagine duration without time, there is indeed no contradiction <contradictio> of concepts, but it has no objective reality, is thus problematic. – (The perdurable <perdurabile> is that whose existence endures – or whose existence is the same as a time – existence that is not perdurable is instantaneous <existentia non perdurabilis est instantanea>[98] – the moment is that in time which itself is no time, thus that which the point is in space. What is a point? [It] is always the boundary of a line, where one line begins and the other ends, thus no part; likewise the moment. The moment that concludes one year begins the next at the same time.) Duration in the time of a thing is the measure of the magnitude of the existence of the thing insofar as it is a phenomenon. That whose existence has no duration is properly instantaneous <instantaneum> – thus one must not say: something endures, but rather a moment exists. Instantaneous <instantaneum> and enduring <durabile> are thus different. We can imagine a moment as a boundary of time, but not as a part of time, for they presuppose time – just as little as points are parts of space. On beginning and end.[99] An existence upon which an entire duration follows, is a beginning, and the existence which an entire duration precedes is an end.)[e] (Eternity can be represented as time as potential <in potentia> – if I imagine it as elapsed, then that is nothing. – Eternity, one says, is duration without limits. Of that we have no concept. – Duration of a thing in time, insofar as time is without limits, is existence at all times. That is phenomenal eternity <aeternitas phaenomenon> or

[e] The closing and opening parentheses have no mates (842₂₇).

199

sempiternity <*sempiternitas*> and is to be distinguished from noumenal eternity <*aeternitas noumenon*>;[100] this I think of as not in time and can attribute it to God. Sempiternity <*sempiternitas*> is the boundlessness of an existence in time. It can be thought from the earlier part <*a parte priori*> and from the later part <*a parte posteriori*>. (['f']Both have no magnitude. The beginning is the boundary from the earlier part <*a parte priori*> of duration, and end the boundary from the later part <*a parte posteriori*> of duration, thus itself no duration. Duration without beginning or end is the negative concept of eternity, but also problematic, for I cannot describe it concretely <*in concreto*>. Eternity from the earlier part <*aeternitas a parte ante*> does not allow itself to be conceived in time because the procession can be infinite and absolute <*processus infinitus ut absolutus*>. By eternity <*aeternitas*>, as duration without beginning and end, we gain nothing, because the concept does not at all apply to noumena <*noumenis*>. Sempiternity <*sempiternitas*> is existence at all times. We speak now

29:843

On cause and caused[g]

That which contains the ground of the existence of something is cause. (The principle <*principium*>, says the author, is the ground[101] – actually it expresses a cognition, insofar as it is the general ground of other cognitions according to a general rule – but also occasionally the ground of a matter, for example the Manichaeans affirmed a principle of good and evil <*principium boni et mali*>.[102] – The effect <*causatum*> corresponds to the cause. – What can exist only as effect <*causatum*> is a thing derived from another or dependent <*ens ab alio sive dependens*> – better a thing derived from another <*ens ab alio*>, for occasionally a thing of reason <*rationis*> can be dependent <*dependens*> in its state, but not in itself, e.g., the domestic animals of human beings – opposed to this is the thing by means of itself <*ens a se*>. – But we cannot comprehend how a thing is for itself, that is a merely negative concept.) Essential properties <*essentialia*> contain the ground of the attributes <*attributa*> and are logical grounds <*rationes logicae*>, but are not causes, because I ask only about the possibility. A thing derived from another is an effect <*ens ab alio est causatum*>; a thing by means of itself <*ens a se*> [is] self-sufficient, because it does not exist as an effect <*quod non existit ut causatum*>. The concept of a self-sufficient being is not the concept of a necessary being, for I say, it exists by means of itself <*a se*>, without making the distinction between self-sufficient and necessary. But the author says: thing by means of itself

---

[f] This opening parenthesis has no mate (842₃₆).

[g] Paragraph breaks and the separation of the words *Von Ursach und Verursachtem* are introduced by Lehmann (843₆₋₈).

<*ens a se*> is alone necessary and a contingent thing <*ens contingens*> is an effect of another <*causatum alterius*>.[103] Necessary is a concept of the understanding, I cannot cognize existence through reason, except when it must be necessary simply or through something else. From the author's proposition it follows that everything that we cognize as contingent must have had its existence from something else. In what do we cognize the contingency? A contingent thing <*ens contingens*> is that whose non-being is possible. But in what do I cognize the possibility of non-being? Were the lack of contradiction enough, then everything is contingent. We have no concept of impossibility other than through the principle of contradiction, a non-being is a contradiction, thus nothing is necessary, and [there is] no highest cause and everything [is] an effect <*causatum*>. We 29:844 have no concept of absolute necessity, nor of absolute contingency. For we say: contingent is everything that is not necessary in itself, or whose non-being is possible in itself – that whose non-being can be thought without contradiction, is thus contingent; everything is thus contingent. The proposition of the author, taken generally, would have a meaning if I could cognize something as contingent in itself. We can have a concept of the contingent and necessary, but only in appearance. That which happens in time is contingent; what does not pass away nor come about is necessary in appearance. We have no concept of the necessity and contingency of things. Do substances come about or pass away? No, that was above a main principle.[h] We will say: all alterations are effects of another <*causata alterius*>, but not substances, for in them I do not at all cognize contingency; they are perdurable. That every state is an effect of another <*causatum alterius*> can easily be grasped. While the proposition of the author is correct, we cannot believe that it can be immediately applied to things, but rather only to states, for we have no concept of the contingent in itself. – Every cause is a principle insofar as other effects <*causata*> flow out from it. – The principle of becoming <*principium fiendi*> is cause (principle of becoming <*principium fiendi*> is that which contains the ground of actuality), [principle] of cognizing <*cognoscendi*> [contains the ground of] judgment, [principle] of being <*essendi*> the ground of possibility, and concerns the essence of things. Many causes, insofar as they belong to one effect <*causato*>, are called co-causes <*concausae*>, they are either subordinate to each other <*sibi subordinatae*>, when one is the cause of an effect <*causa causati*> by means of the other – or coordinate <*coordinatae*>, when none are remote causes <*causa remota*>, but rather all are viewed as immediate ones <*immediatae*>. The co-causes <*concausae*> are subordinated, either essentially <*essentialiter*>, when they are subordinated with respect to causality <*quoad causalitatem*> or according to the determination whereby they are the cause of the effect

---

[h] Cf. Ak. 29: 832–3, above.

<causati>, – or accidentally *<accidentaliter>*, when they are subordinated not with respect to causality *<quoad causalitatem>*, but rather with respect to other determinations *<quoad ceteras determinatibus>*. (Correlates *<correlata>* signify the limit *<terminus>* and the subject of the relation – in the relation something is a principle *<princip>* of the relation, i.e., limit *<terminus>*; what depends on that is subject and both are correlates *<correlata>*, e.g., apprenticeship is limit *<terminus>* and apprentice subject. Every relation is one-sided – when one ground follows another and is not consequence as well as ground – or two-sided, when the consequence is ground and vice versa. The first can be called heteronymous correlates *<correlata heteronyma>*, the other homonymous *<homonyma>*. When a cause is the supplement for the sufficiency of another, they concur – and their connection *<nexus>* is called a concurrence *<concursus>*.[104] The less principal *<minus principialis>* is called the concurring one – the cause of the cause *<causa causae>* is the cause of the effect *<causa causatae>* insofar as it contains the cause of the causality of the subordinate causes *<causae subordinatae>*, e.g., a father is cause *<causa>* of the evil of his son, or when he does evil, not insofar as he brought him into the world, but rather if he spurred him on to evil, that is used in natural theology *<theologia naturali>*.) Causes are either efficient *<efficientes>* or final *<finales>*, efficient *<efficiens>* is cause through action *<per actionem>*. Cause is what is the ground of the existence of another, be it positive or negative, material or formal. All efficient causes *<causae efficientes>* are thus determinations of powers; so far as they are coordinated, [i.e.,] or efficient coordinate *<efficientes coordinatae>* [causes], [they] are called associate *<sociae>*. The less principal one *<minus principalis>* is called auxiliary *<auxiliaris>* (the efficient *<efficienz>* is the opposite of formal cause *<opposita causa formalis>*, e.g., by its form a wedge is the cause of the[i] split wood – or it contains the formal conditions of that – the mallet, with which it is struck, and the firm matter of the wedge are efficient causes *<causae efficientes>*). The causality of an auxiliary cause *<causalitas causa auxiliaris>* is assistance *<auxilium>*.[105] Event *<eventus>* is a single action with its issue, event considered in its connection is called the connection or relation with other things in the same time (the outer connection in which the event *<eventus>* happens is circumstance – local circumstances *<circumstantiae loci>*, insofar as they concur with the event, are called temporal opportunities *<opportunitates temporis>* – timeliness[j]). Circumstance *<G: Circumstanz>* or the relation of an event with respect to simultaneous things is circumstance *<relatio eventus respectu simultaneorum est circumstantia>*.[106] The coordinate co-causes *<concausae coordinatae>* hide in the circumstances *<circumstantiis>*. Concurrence is the action (causality) of

29:845

---

[i] Lehmann misprints *des* as *dse* (854_{14}).
[j] *Tempestivität*, presumably a Germanized form of the Latin *tempestivitas* (845_{29}).

coordinate co-causes <*concursus est actio . . . concausarum coordinatarum*>, not subordinate ones <*subordinatarum*>; all circumstances insofar as they concur with an event are called opportunity; which is either opportunity of time or of location, and much depends on both. The concurrence of the circumstances of time is timeliness <*tempestivitas*>,[107] of location opportunity <*opportunitas*>. One says: the smallest circumstances alter a matter <*minima circumstantia variant rem*>. For, if I want to have all co-causes <*concausas*>, then it depends on the slightest circumstance, even that can be a co-cause <*concausa*> (further place and time do not alter the matter <*locus et tempus non variant rem*> – for they are mere positions wherein events happen). Univocal effect <*effectus univocus*> is that which is of one kind with the cause, equivocal <*aequivocus*>[108] that which is not of one kind with it. In physics, equivocal effect <*effectus aequivocus*> is denied, but that will not do in general, otherwise God would have to be homogeneous with the world.[k] (E.g., equivocal effect <*effectus aequivocus*> would be if insects were to arise out of carrion.[109] Here cause and effect would be specifically distinguished. Equivocal effect <*effectus aequivocus*> has until now not been fully refuted. But the author makes this general and says: equivocal effect <*effectus aequivocus*> is general,[110] that will not do. What is God and world, clockmaker and clock?) The effect testifies to the cause <*effectus testaur de causa*>. The effect indicates the ground of the causality, i.e., the determination of the cause to act, through which the effect <*causatum*> exists, for the effect <*effectus*> shows only living powers <*vires vivas*>, applied powers, not dead [powers] <*mortuas*>, which have no effect. (An effect can be mediate <*mediatus*>, also immediate <*immediatus*>, full <*plenus*> and less full <*minus plenus*>. By full <*plenus*> is understood the whole aggregate of coordinated effects, i.e., the whole series of subordinated effects; properly it is the former, but the latter is also named full effect <*effectus plenus*>. – With the former is meant merely all immediate effects <*effectus immediatos*> – with the latter also all mediate ones <*mediatos*> and thus one can say: a cannonball can produce an infinite series of alterations and we receive a full effect <*effectus plenus*>. Full effect <*effectus plenus*> (or the whole aggregate of coordinated effects) is equal to the efficient powers <*est aequalis viribus efficientibus*>. The author says: *the living* <*vivis*>, that is the applied [powers],[111] that is, the effects prove the degree of the power, but not of the faculty, in the effects there can be no more worth than in the cause, i.e., no more reality. Here we consider merely the metaphysical worth, which rests on the degree of reality. For both the effect testifies to the cause <*effectus testatur de causa*>, i.e., the effect reveals the existence of the cause – also its quantity and quality. The connection <*nexus*> between an efficient cause <*causa efficiens*> and the effect <*effectus*> is an effective connection <*nexus effectivus*>.)

29:846

[k] We are adding a period and capital here (845$_{37}$).

On the useful, that does not belong here at all.[112] Use presupposes, namely, an object of willing. Willing in turn the concept of pleasure and displeasure. None of that belongs in ontology. What is a means to the good is useful. The degree of usefulness is worth or price <*pretium*>; the outer worth is price, the inner dignity <*dignitas; G: Würde*>, and only a human being, insofar as he is morally good, has dignity. Misuse is a use which is contrary to utility. (Good is that which serves as the ground to something else. Things are good absolutely or respectively, absolute good <*bonum absolutum*> is dignity <*dignitas*> – relative good <*bonum respective*> [is] usefulness <*utilitas*>. The price of something is other than the worth – it means something else that can be put in place of this as equivalent – thus presupposes a standard. – A human being is called valuable, also invaluable – valuable, whose worth can be valued, that is, what[l] has little or high worth, and then it comes close to the invaluable.) We must speak yet

On matter and form.[m][113] The Scholastics differentiated matter in all things, i.e., genus and form, that is specific difference <*differentia specifica*>. In every judgment, subject and predicate constitute matter, and the relation of both the form. In inference <*ratiocinio*>, the premises [constitute] the matter, and the consequence the form. The form always constitutes the essence of the matter. Matter out of which <*materia ex qua*> is, for example, the wood when a cabinet is made from it, around which <*circa quam*>, what one is occupied with, in which <*in qua*>, the data <*data*> in which the determinations already inhere.

Besides the concepts of the understanding we have still other *a priori* concepts that are called concepts of reason or ideas, i.e., those necessary concepts of reason for which no corresponding object in experience can be given. The meaning of a concept is determined by naming an example, and without that it has no meaning at all. Are ideas like these in us? Yes, e.g., the wise Stoic in morality is a mere idea. Wisdom is perfect morality without lack or exception, such I cannot find, for every human being has at least a propensity to vices; but that already does not agree with wisdom. One cannot say such a concept is contradictory, but rather that it is quite possible, even necessary. Above all ideas are the transcendental ones, with which we have to deal. These are ideas of pure reason, and that with which we are now occupied is the idea of the world. (Besides the effective connection <*nexu effectivo*> there is yet a connection of usefulness <*nexum utilitatis*>, and everything is in a connection of usefulness <*in*

29:847

---

[l] We follow Lehmann in omitting a second *kann* (following *Werth*), but we replace a *was* omitted by Lehmann after *oder* (847₁).

[m] We are removing the paragraph breaks added by Lehmann (847₃₋₅) and have changed the wording back to the form of the ms. *Materie und Form* are *not* set off as a separate line, nor are they underlined. *Von* precedes *Materie und Form* and begins a new line.

nexu utilitatis>. The connection of uses <*nexus usuum*> depends on human beings – always;[n] i.e., the possibility of producing the useful, that is [a matter] of providence.[o] End, means, intention belong to psychology. The end is that which I represent to myself as good, and for whose sake something else is viewed as a means for the good; impelling cause <*causa impulsiva*> is in every end, i.e., the good in the end, for which something else pleases as a means. End and final end can be distinguished. End can be coordinated, here are then co-ends <*cofines*> – or subordinated, and that to which all ends are subordinated is called final end.) (Matter and form go through all parts of philosophy. Matter is the determinable <*determinabile*> – form the determination. – Matter from which <*ex* 29:848
qua>, e.g., three sides, – that is the determinable, around which something is occupied <*determinabile, circa quam quidam occupatus est*>, e.g., of what the preacher treats.[p] If the determination already happened, then there is matter in which <*materia in qua*>, e.g., the wooden clock.) That one whose likeness is intended <*id cuius simile intenditus est*>, [is][L] an exemplar, the copy is exemplifying <*exemplatum*>. An exemplar not exemplifying <*exemplar non exemplatum*> is original – on the sign and thing signified <*de signo et de signato*>[114] does not at all belong here.)[q]

[n] This last word could be either *immer* (always) or, as Lehmann believes, *meiner* (mine) (847_{28}).

[o] We are not following Lehmann in his changing *d.h. Möglichkeit Nutzen hervorzubringen das ist von der Vorhersehung* to *Die Möglichkeit, Nutzen hervorzubringen ist von der Vorhersehung* (847_{28}).

[p] We are replacing the question mark added by Lehmann with a period (848_3).

[q] This closing parenthesis is without a mate (848_7).

On cosmology <De cosmologia>[r]

INTRODUCTION TO COSMOLOGY

The concept of a world in general is one of the limitations of the sensible world by reason. But we have now two sorts of concepts in our soul: concepts of understanding and of reason. Concepts of reason come about when one enlarges a concept of the understanding to infinity. Thus we have sensible *a priori* concepts, *a priori* concepts of the understanding, and *a priori concepts of reason*. Concepts of reason are called *ideas* and are those *representations* whose object *cannot be given adequately in any possible experience*, but are extremely necessary to reason and do not at all contradict themselves. These transcendental ideas also have the use that, in leading us beyond all possible experience, they make us believe that [there][L] can also be things outside the field of experience. All these ideas relate to and consist in the absolute totality of the conditions in the world. The absolute totality of the series of the conditions which occur with the objects of experience is the cosmological idea. This divides into four specific ones according to the categories:

1. Into the cosmological idea of the quantity of the world. We cannot at all be acquainted with this through experience. For were the world infinite, then this would be out of the question. But were it finite, then I could not experience the boundary; for I cannot experience anything negative.

2. [Into the cosmological idea][L] of quality or of decomposition, that the world consists of simple [parts],[L] which I also cannot cognize from experience; since experience happens through the senses and these forms of sensibility, space and time, do not consist of simple parts.

3. [Into the cosmological idea][L] of relation or the absolute totality of the natural order. Since in the world the cause of the conditioned is always itself a condition, I search for the unconditioned in order to attain absolute totality, which experience cannot give me since it is not to be met with in the world, but rather is beyond it.

4. The cosmological idea of the necessary, that the highest being is necessary for the sake of absolute totality. – These ideas have the use that

29:849

---

[r] In the ms, this title occurs two-thirds down the left-hand page (ms, p. 83′), after which the page is blank; the facing page is also blank (ms, p. 84), as well as the next (ms, p. 84′). The "Introduction" heading begins ms, p. 85.

they propel us, with the events of the world, [1.] to infer always from one cause to the other in order to arrive at the absolute totality. 2. To teach us that there must yet be something present beyond the sensible world. To this extent they have immanent use. But since they have no examples in experience, they are empty concepts and can teach us nothing of their objects.

First section
On the concept of a world

FIRST CHAPTER
ON THE POSITIVE CONCEPT OF THE WORLD

The world is a substantial whole which is not a part of another, i.e., the absolute and non-relative which in no respect is part of another <*totum substantiale quod non est pars alterius, i.e., absolutum et non respectivum quod nullo respectu est pars alterius*>.[115] Only the connection of the coordination of things in interaction <*commercio*> is connection of the parts into a whole; but connection, subordination as effect and cause is not that. Therefore with the connection of the world with God, the world is not a part of God. This explanation of the world is an explanation of the intelligible world <*mundi intelligibilis*>, where we understand by substances things as they are in themselves, and is certainly to be distinguished from sensible world <*mundus sensibilis*>, which is a complex, given <*complexus, datum*> of all appearances, where we understand by substances the perduring in appearances. All antinomies in cosmology arise accordingly through the confusion of these two concepts. If I say: the sensible world is a whole <*totum*> of substances, then this is contradictory, since space and time are infinite. I can maintain of the sensible world that it is finite, also that it is infinite; that comes about because and when I hold it to be one and the same with the world of the understanding. I thus err with the second cosmological idea as well, if I assume the sensible world as consisting of simple parts. I can indeed say that of the noumenal world <*mundus noumenon*>, because, if I remove the composition here, the composed substances remain for me which, if they are no longer composite, must necessarily be simple. But if I remove composition in the sensible world, then nothing remains for me. The sensible world is nothing other than the synthesis or the placing of one after the other in a series of my representations of objects according to the forms of space and time. Thus if I remove the latter, I remove at the same time the sensible world. Space and time do not consist of simple parts. These and other antinomies are the main object and content of cosmology. Little is presented of the intelligible world <*mundo intelligibili*> since we can cognize little more of it through the understanding than what follows from the definition. See <*vide*> Kant's *Concerning the Form and Principles of the Sensible and Intelligible World*. Königsberg. <*De mundi intelligibilis atque sensibilis Forma et Principiis. Regiom.*> 1770.[116] A foreigner called it wild

29:850

fantasy to speak of the intelligible world <*mundo intelligibili*>. But this is just the opposite, for one understands by it not another world, but rather this world as I think it through the understanding. –

Each word is significant in the definition given of the world. Therefore we want to develop it more. There are sheer ontological concepts here. Therefore it belongs to transcendental philosophy. The world is thus a substantial whole <*totum substantiale*>, hence not merely ideal. We can think of diverse ideal wholes <*tota idealia*>, but they do not constitute a world, e.g., I can represent to myself a syllogistic whole <*totum syllogismorum*>, an accidental whole <*totum accidentale*>, or a whole in space, etc.; but these are mere ideal wholes <*tota idealia*>, which consist of concepts. But the world is a real whole <*totum reale*>, which consists of substances. The author conflates these two kinds of wholes <*totis*>.[117] For he explains series <*series*> through multitude <*multitudo*> and whole <*totum*>, because he holds them to be synonyms <*synonyma*>.

Matter and form are met with in every whole. Matter as the data <*data*> and form as the manner of connecting them.

In a composite <*composito*>, the matter consists of parts, and in metaphysics these are the substances, which can also be spirits. For here we do not take matter bodily, but transcendentally <*transcendentaliter*> as what is in any way determinable <*quacumque ratione determinabile*>. If substances are accordingly the matter of the world, then the accidents are not that, but rather belong merely to its states.

29:851   Now the form of the world is the connection <*nexus*> of the substances.

If the world is a connection <*nexus*> of substances, then I cannot think of the world egoistically,[118] i.e., I cannot say: I am the world. Everything outside of me are not things, but rather mere illusion. For since a world requires many substances and yet in addition a connection <*nexum*> of them, then I as a single substance cannot constitute a world. –

The connection <*nexus*> is *ideal* if I merely *think* the substances together, and *real* if the substances actually stand in interaction <*commercio*>.

The form of the world is a real connection <*nexus realis*> because it is a real whole <*totum reale*>. For if we have a multitude of substances, then these must also stand together in connection, otherwise they would be isolated. Isolated substances, however, never constitute a whole <*totum*>. If the substances are together, thus a whole <*totum*>, then they must also be a real whole <*totum reale*>. For were they ideal, then surely they could be represented in thought as a whole <*totum*>, or the representations of them would constitute a whole <*totum*>; but things in themselves would still not constitute a whole on this account.

Accordingly the author's definition of the world through a series is false[119] because it brings with it the concept of the ideal whole <*toti idealis*>. Finally, totality <*omnitudo*> belongs to the definition of the world, which is not part of another <*quae non est pars alterius*>.

208

A composite <*compositum*> can be either a relative <*respective*> or an absolute whole <*absolute totum*>. It is a relative whole <*totum respective*> insofar as it is not a part of a whole of the same kind, but an absolute whole <*absolute totum*> insofar as it is a part neither of the same nor of another kind, e.g., a house is a relative whole <*respective totum*> insofar as it is a whole of its kind; but it is not an absolute whole <*absolute totum*>, for it is a part of another kind, namely of a street.

The world is no relative whole <*respective totum*>, but rather an absolute whole <*absolute totum*> in the metaphysical sense. In the physical sense the world is the earth considered relatively <*relative spectatum*>.

The concept of the cosmos is a mere problem, a concept of reason, which I can think easily abstractly <*in abstracto*>, but can never give concretely <*in concreto*>. For should we give it concretely <*in concreto*>, we would have to represent it in the space which it occupies. Now if this space were unbounded, we would not be able to finish counting it, but rather something would always be left over. Therefore we cannot experience the totality of the world. But even if space were bounded, we still could not experience its boundary. For how can we experience that nothing more is there? We cannot perceive something more, but it still does not follow from this that there also is actually nothing more. $\quad$ 29:852

But then are these transcendental or dialectical ideas (also specious concepts) not mere phantoms of the brain (beings of the reasoning reason <*entia rationis ratiocinantis;* G: *Hirngespenste*>)?

No. It is necessary for reason to bring all of its concepts to completion and therefore also to make complete the absolute composite <*compositum absolute*>, for nature brings with it the projecting of general rules, therefore it can stand nothing incomplete.

The unity of the manifold is threefold: composite <*compositum*>, quantum, and whole <*totum*>. Composite <*compositum*> is unity insofar as it is composite, whole <*totum*>, when this composition is complete, and quantum means this unity in relation to still other unities.

The world is composite <*compositum*> because it has a multitude of substances, and whole <*totum*> because all of these stand in interaction <*commercio*>. Finally, also a quantum, when we see whether it is finite or infinite. This comprises the whole of cosmology.

In ontology we have the concept of a monad <*monas*>, a part that is not also a whole, and in cosmology the concept of a world: a whole that is not also a part.

These are the two extremes in composition and decomposition. For in the decomposition[s] I come no further than to the monad and in the composition no further than to the world.

The author says in his definition that the world is a series of finite

---

[s] *Auflösung (Decomposition):* two synonyms are used here (852₂₅).

substances. But this is unnecessary, that he adds of finite things <*fini-torum*> (or, like others, of contingent things <*contingentium*>), for it follows already from the definition itself. For if the world is a whole <*totum*> of substances, but each of these requires the other as its complement for the whole <*complementi ad totum*>, then of course each cannot be infinite. Therefore the world consists of finite substances. Further, because the substances in the world stand in interaction <*commercio*> and find themselves in action and reaction <*in actione et reactione*>, then each, or rather its state, is dependent on the acting of another. Consequently [each is] alterable and contingent.

Now the author comes to the proposition: nothing is isolated in the world <*in mundo non datur insula*>, i.e., everything in the world is in thoroughgoing connection <*nexu*>.[120] This already lies in the concept of the whole. For one substance separated from all the rest, thus isolated, would not at all belong to the world, because it would then not be connected with the whole. Indeed, a great multitude of isolated substances would not constitute a world (isolated substances are only the stuff for a world), because they would not constitute a whole, but rather each of them would be entirely alone and without any community with the others. Now we come to the important question: is there only one world, or are still other worlds possible? But this question is ambiguous, for there is possible a disjunctive plurality of the world, such that in the place of one another could be; or a plurality of the world collectively or jointly <*collective vel copulative*>, [such] that one could be next to the other.

Accordingly, is (1) a disjunctive plurality of the world possible? Yes, for the world is not necessary, therefore another could also have been in its place. That the world is contingent follows from the interaction <*commercio*> of the substances in it.

But is a collective diversity of the world possible? The author says a plurality of the world is impossible[121] and, admittedly, if in following his definition one takes the world for a complex of all things, then as collective <*collective*> it can be only one. For two universes <*universa*> cannot exist. But that is the concept of a world which constitutes an ideal whole, but not a real whole of substances. For not all things are allowed to belong in a real whole of the world, rather only those substances which stand in interaction <*commercio*> with one another. Those substances not standing in interaction <*commercio*> are isolated and can again constitute a separate whole <*totum*> if they are connected with each other. This whole <*totum*> can be another world that may stand in no connection at all with this one, could in any event also have a separate creator.

We can consider the world in general as noumenon and phenomenon. The definition is a cognition of the noumenal world <*mundi nou-meni*>. For I abstract here from the manner in which such a whole

29:853

<*totum*> of substances supposedly can be intuited, and find no contradiction in this idea of reason. I also find no contradiction in this absolute whole not occurring in appearances or in the sensible world. But it is nevertheless impossible for me to experience it, because the connection of substances consists in the sensible world and space and time, but these are continuous quanta <*quanta continua*>, whose totality one can never 29:854 find out, for an infinite progression <*progressus in infinitum*> is here, and yet totality is possible only through a completed progression <*progressus*>. Therefore the concept of totality in metaphysics is called only noumenal and phenomenal world <*mundus noumenon . . . phenomenon*>.

Only one sensible world is possible, and two times cannot take place together, for there is only one space and one time, but both make up the ground of the interaction <*commercii*> of all substances in the sensible world, so again only one sensible world is possible.

CHAPTER TWO
ON THE NEGATIVE CONCEPT OF A WORLD

Here we consider the world as a quantum and indeed according to the absolute totality of its composition and decomposition. With composition we consider the world as a quantum and move from the parts to the whole. With decomposition we consider the world as a composite <*compositum*> and move from the whole to the parts.

With respect to composition the question arises: is the world finite or infinite, and with respect to decomposition: is the world bounded or not? Does it have simple parts or not? The first question: is the world finite or infinite? There is a double infinite <*infinitum*>: a real infinite <*infinitum reale*> or the so-called unlimited <*illimitatum*>, and the mathematical infinite <*infinitum mathematicum*>, which applies only to the appearance of things in space and time and is thus valid only with phenomena. (The mathematical infinite <*infinitum mathematicum*> is taken here not as potential <*potentiale*>, but rather as actual <*actuale*>. For we can always think a potential <*potentiale*> or future infinity.) Since we are speaking here of the sensible world, we thus understand by the infinite here the real infinite <*infinitum reale*>, and ask accordingly whether the sensible world is infinite or not in space or in time. Neither are true. That both contradictory judgments here are concurrently false comes about because the underlying concept is false. If I say, e.g.: a four-cornered circle must either have corners or be round, then both predicates apply – because the subject is false. It is likewise here as well. For the question whether the world is infinite or not presupposes that the sensible world is something in itself. But now the sensible world is merely the sum of appearances and no whole of things. Thus if we consider it in itself, there is a contradiction in the predicate <*contradictio in adjecto*>. Hence occur these contradictions

29:855 of reason with itself, which in the *Critique*[^t] are called antinomies of pure reason, for if one assumes that the world is finite or infinite, then one finds oneself in both cases entangled in contradictions and absurdities.

If one assumes the world to be infinite in time, then an eternity has already elapsed and it is absurd to keep this in mind. But should the world have taken a temporal beginning, then there still would have to have been a previous time, for the beginning is an existence that follows upon non-being. Thus if a previous time has been, then it must also not have been an empty time, for in that one cannot imagine a time. Thus there must again have been a world in that time. Consequently a world has always been, and yet also had a beginning. What a contradiction! A beginning is always something which happens. Everything that happens has a cause. Thus something must have preceded the beginning. Nothing can have taken place in God, thus what took place must belong to the world, thus there would be no beginning of the world after all. – Wolff of course wants to extricate himself when he says: before the beginning there was no time at all.[122] But then there was also no beginning, for this always presupposes a time. One can also say that in the empty time preceding the beginning, the necessary highest being would have existed. But then it would have effected nothing in this empty time, and effected something at the time of creation,[^u] consequently an alteration must have taken place with it. And why had this author not created the world earlier? Sheer unavoidable difficulties. If I assume further that the world is infinite with respect to space, then I maintain thereby that the world is a whole that, through all possible composition, nevertheless could not be thought of as a whole, and therefore with it the composition will never be completed. But to think totality and infinite composition concurrently is a contradiction. Finally, if I maintain that the world is finite with respect to space, then I also assume yet an empty space outside the space that the world occupies.[^v] (Through experience I cannot at all make out that the world is finite. For were I to come to the boundary of the world, experience would still teach me nothing more than that I notice nothing more, but not that there is nothing more there at all. –)

But why is it not also in empty space? Is it in motion or at rest? It can move and alter itself to infinity <*in infinitum*>, without something being
29:856 altered either in the world or outside it in empty space. Hence there would occur an alteration whereby nothing would be altered. How absurd. From these antinomies we clearly see that the world can be neither finite <*finitum*> nor infinite <*infinitum*> with respect to time and space. We

---

[^t]: *Kritik* is not designated as a title in the ms, but it seems clearly to refer to Kant's *Critique of Pure Reason* (854_{37}).
[^u]: Lehmann misprints *Schöpfung* as *Sèhöpfung* (855_{22}).
[^v]: We are adding a period here (855_{33}).

can indeed think that, in the noumenal world <*mundo noumeno*>, the world is finite and consists of simple parts, but not with the sensible world. What is it then? The sensible world is no whole of things, but rather merely a sum of appearances.^{*w*} (The sensible world is nothing other than the serial connection of my representations of things, which I receive through sense according to the concepts^{*x*} of space and time, consequently it lies merely in my head and is given not in itself, but rather in the progress of my experience of things. E.g., a rose is not red before I view it. For its redness rests on the constitution of the eyes. Indeed the cause of the redness is in it, but^{*y*} that it is actually red rests on my eye. In fact, there are human beings who see no color at all, but rather view everything as light and shadow, as in a copper engraving. – Now this progress can proceed with us into infinity. Things underlie the appearances, but these constitute the noumenal world <*mundum noumenon*>, and according to its concept as a whole <*totum*> it is obviously finite. The progression to infinity <*progressus in infinitum*> is a potential infinity <*infinitum potentiale*>, but not an actual one <*actuale*>, for the latter is absurd. Therefore it still does not follow from this that the world is infinite.)

Now I can experience the sum of appearances, and this experience can proceed into infinity, or have a progression to infinity <*progressus in infinitum*>, without my determining thereby that the world itself is infinite. For the expressions: it is something infinite, and it continues into infinity, are distinguished from one another. If I say the world or the progression <*progressus*> continues into infinity, the infinity here does not belong to the object, but rather to my concept of it. For I cognize all assessment of magnitude through counting. This shows us, however, not the magnitude of the things themselves, but rather the relation of them to my faculty of assessment. It is merely a condition of our understanding.

Therefore I cannot immediately say: the world is accordingly infinite in itself, but rather only my progression <*progressus*> in its appearances is infinite, and it is this merely for our nature, since for a higher being the world would still be finite. But are not these sums of appearances things themselves?

No. For the sensible world lies merely in my senses. These, however, 29:857 show us only the manner in which they are affected by the things, but not the latter themselves. They show us merely the appearances of the things. But these are not the things themselves. They indeed underlie the appearances, and I can therefore surely infer the^{*z*} actuality of the things from the appearances, but not the properties of the things themselves from the

^{*w*} We are adding a period here (856₈).
^{*x*} Lehmann misreads *Begr* (i.e., *Begriffe*) as *Beziehungen* (relations)(856₁₀).
^{*y*} We follow Lehmann in omitting a *da* (preceding *aber*)(856₁₅).
^{*z*} We follow Lehmann in omitting a second *wol* (preceding *auf*)(857₆).

213

properties of the appearances, e.g., the colors of the rainbow are the mere appearance of it, mere refractions of light, but not actual things. We do not see the water drops, however, which are the cause of these refractions and consequently are the things in themselves, but rather merely their appearance; and this is surely something wholly other, and from this we also cannot in the least infer the water drops. The present sensible world thus rests merely on our senses. Had we other senses, then the world would appear quite otherwise to us; we would see a new world. And even if the whole sensible world passes away sometime, the things in themselves can still remain, only the appearances would then be altered. Perhaps this can be the case with a future world, that we will intuit things there as they are in themselves; that would be an intellectual world. Because God is the cause of the noumenal world <*mundi noumeni*> and of the possibility of the interaction <*commercii*> in it, if we could intuitively cognize its source then we would also cognize things in themselves thereby. But we cannot comprehend the possibility of that. Malebranche and others built on this,[123] but here tried to have intuitions of God already, which is a wild fantasy since God is not an object of possible experience.

There is also an intelligible world that exists merely in my understanding apart from all possible experience; but in this, space and time are out of the question. –

The sensible world exists only in the senses and in their composition of appearances. But this is a progression <*progressus*>. Now the question is whether the progression <*progressus*> of the composition of the appearances is finite or infinite. This is infinite, i.e., it continues so that I cannot determine its end. –

In the appearances there is no first because space and time have no first parts. Granted, if the progression <*progressus*> were finite, then it would also have to be bound. The sensible world lies merely in experience; accordingly I would also have to experience the boundary of the appearances. But I cannot experience the end, because it is nothing. Accordingly the progression <*progressus*> is infinite.

Likewise the regression <*regressus*> in time is infinite. For if we wanted to know the beginning of time, then we would have to have been before the world was, and yet would still belong to the world. The beginning of time is the existence of that, before which a time preceded where it was not. A contradiction, for here time is presupposed. And so all the contradictions are then lifted away if we assume that there occurs in the sensible world a progression to infinity <*progressus in infinitum*> with respect to space, and a regression to infinity <*regressus in infinitum*> with respect to time, but that the world in itself is neither finite nor infinite because we know nothing of things in themselves, and also cannot infer to them from their appearances. The mistake in the representation that the world in itself is finite or infinite lies in this, that reason took a regulative principle <*principium*> for a constitutive one. The world is therefore not an infinite composite <*compositum*>, but rather my composition of it is infinite.

It is likewise with decomposition or with the question whether or not the world consists[a] of infinite parts. Both concepts are false. For if I assume, e.g., that a line consists of finite parts, then it consists of simple parts. Now these are points, points are locations, and thus the line would consist of locations. Accordingly the locations would be thinkable prior to space; but that is contradictory. ([b]The simple parts in space are points. But these do not make space possible, which would have to be if space consisted of points, but rather space makes them possible. If I think of two points, then I cannot think of them otherwise than there being a space in between. Thus space does not consist of points and of any simple parts. For if I remove the composition, then nothing remains for me. So it is with space and so with appearances.

If on the contrary I assume again that a line consists of infinite [parts],[L] then its composition must be infinite. But since I can actually compose a line, my composition is complete, but finite. Accordingly the composition here is finite and infinite, which is a contradiction.

Here the noumenon is thus confused again with the phenomenon. For the world, considered as noumenon, must consist of simple parts, because otherwise it cannot be composed. But as phenomenon it is different. The things in themselves have neither finite nor infinite parts (at least we cannot know this), but the regression <*regressus*> of my decomposition is infinite.

29:859

For in space and time there is no last [item]. They are continuous quanta <*quanta continua*>. Consequently my decomposition of them is infinite, thus also of the remaining ones that are found in these. These questions of com- and decomposition in the world concern the totality of the synthesis of appearances insofar as they constitute a composite <*compositum*>, and this is mathematical synthesis.

Now we come to the dynamic synthesis in appearances, insofar as the things are connected with one another as causes and consequences. This is a deduction of causality, and the relation between effects and cause is thus its object. But the mathematical synthesis is merely synthesis of the aggregation.

We speak now of mere series in the connection of our multiple representations, and[c] a series is whenever one representation is the condition of another. The continuation in space and time is also a series, but a series of appearances.

---

[a] We follow Lehmann in changing *nicht beschaffen* to *nicht bestehen* (858₂₁).
[b] This opening parenthesis has no mate (858₂₆).
[c] An *und* omitted by Lehmann without note has been replaced (859₂₀).

*d*If in the series of causes I go from the conditions to the conditioned, that is progression <*progressus*>, from the conditioned to the conditions is regression <*regressus*>. The progression to infinity <*progressus in infinitum*> is a potential infinity <*infinitum potentiale*> and therefore does not allow being thought of as totality. But with space we represent the things all at once, and that must be totality. The whole cosmology has to do with the regression <*regressu*> of time. For reason demands the totality of the conditions, not of the conditioned. Pro- and regression <*pro-* . . . *regressus*> are the same in space, for there every part is at the same time condition and conditioned. The constitutive principle <*principium*> of reason is: the world is infinite <*infinit*> with respect to causes. That is, in the series of subordinated causes in the world, there is no first. But if one maintains that there is a first, then one maintains a regression to the definite <*regressum in definitum*>. In the world one can think neither regression to infinity <*regressus in infinitum*> nor to the finite <*in finitum*>, neither a first cause nor a causality leading into infinity. These are again antinomies of reason whereby noumena and phenomena are again confused.

29:860 Things in themselves are possible only in a series, i.e., in the connection between cause and effect. But the series cannot be infinite, but rather must have a first cause which is no longer an effect of another. Here is accordingly regression to the finite <*regressus in finitum*>, that is with the noumenal world <*mundo noumenon*>. Here no infinite regression <*regressus*> is possible, for since beyond this infinite series of conditions no further condition would take place, then one of the conditions of this series must not be conditioned again, but rather a first condition: because were it not unconditioned it would be at once conditioned and yet without condition, which is a contradiction. The regression <*regressus*> is straight <*rectilineus*>, if I always so continue, or circular <*curvilineus*> if the last effect is, at first, cause of the first cause, and it goes around as in a circle. But still there is always a first cause. This is valid just as little as is a circle in a proof. A commandant during a siege in a Flemish fortress had food supplies but no money. He thus sold the first to the merchants, these gave him money which he paid to the soldiers; these [gave it] to the merchants, who again to him, etc. So a quantity of money ran around and around in a circle as long as the food supplies lasted; yet these were the highest cause.

But in appearance there is no regression to the finite <*regressus in finitum*>. For here there is no first in time, i.e., something before which nothing else precedes. But if time is infinite in the regression <*regressu*>, then the series of events in time must also be infinite. Nature is the connection of appearances according to general laws. Now this connec-

---

d A paragraph break omitted by Lehmann without note has been replaced (859$_{23}$).

tion is diverse, and the series also belongs to it, e.g., inherence in a subject is also a connection,ᵉ but not a series; for the subject itself does not inhere.

In all appearances of an event the causality of the cause of the event is itself an event. Now if all causes themselves have causes, then there is nothing in the world except nature. Now since there is nothing in the sensible world except events, we can go to infinity; everything that we will experience will still be either event or effect. For were it not an event, it would not be an object of experience at all. Experience consists just in this, that my perceptions are connected with each other by the connection of cause <*causa*> and effect <*causato*>. If this does not exist, then my perception is not much more than a dream that has merely private validity for me – but never can be called experience. We thus come to experience no event in the world which would be the first, for our regression <*regressus*> goes to infinity <*in infinitum*>. But there is no actual infinite <*infinite*> series of causes, but rather merely a regression <*regressus*> [that] is infinite <*infinit*>.

29:861

If we thus never come upon the first cause in the sensible world, there must yet nevertheless be one, for to think of no first cause would contradict our reason. Thus, since the sensible world, i.e., all objects of possible experience, are and can be nothing but events, and therefore always have a cause underlying them; then the first cause cannot be in the world, but rather is an extramundane being <*ens extramundanum*>. It is thus merely a regulative, not a constitutive principle of reason, to say: the appearances and therefore also the connection of them according to cause and effect go on to infinity. For they are not things in themselves, and also not actual before we have arrived that far in regression <*in regressu*>.

If an event ensues from [a]ᴸ·ᶠ cause which is no event, then it is said to occur spontaneously <*sponte accidit*> from it. It happens first, for no event precedes it. Freedom is the faculty for beginning a series of states oneself.[124] If something is an effect of nature, then it is already a continuation of the series of states; if it is an effect of freedom, then it is a new state: that is the transcendental concept of freedom. E.g., if due to hypochondria I always stay at home, then that arises from my nature. But if I do it merely because I want to, then this arises from my freedom. Now the question is: is everything in the world nature or freedom? When we look upon the appearances, they all fit together according to the laws of nature. But still all appearances also have a transcendental cause which we do not know, e.g., body is composite, i.e., an appearance. But there must still be a transcendental cause that contains the ground from which this appearance arises. This cause is unknown to us; but because it does not belong to the sensible world, it also cannot be determined by other causes in it, conse-

---

ᵉ *Verknüpfung;* elsewhere in the paragraph *Zusammenhang* is used for "connection" (860₂₈).
ᶠ Lehmann does not note his addition of *eine* (861₁₈).

quently it likewise does not stand under the laws of nature or of the sensible world and is thus transcendentally <*transcendentaliter*>[g] free.

29:862　　There is thus in the world, on the one hand, nature and on the other freedom. What happens can also be viewed as an effect that does not have its ground in the series of appearances, which are connected according to the general laws of nature, but rather occurs spontaneously <*sponte*> according to laws of freedom; e.g., if I do something according to the guidance of my understanding then this is freedom, insofar as it springs from the understanding; but it is nature insofar as it happens according to the laws of nature (namely that I can also accomplish that which I want). For it also happens in the world, and what happens in the sensible world is nature. –

If I want to explain an event in the world, and I derive this from the general laws of nature, then that is a natural event. In the world as a series of appearances, we cannot and must not explain any event from spontaneity <*ex spontaneitate*>, only the reason of human beings is exempted from this. It does not belong to the series of appearances. It is independent of the laws of nature, and just in that consists freedom. With respect to the powers of the mind, a human being belongs[h] to the noumenal world <*mundo noumeno*>, for through the understanding he can cognize things as they are, as e.g., his moral relations, truth, etc., and in this regard his actions are free, as well as the phenomenal world <*mundo phaenomeno*>, insofar as through his actions he belongs to the chain of appearances.[i]

We now come to the negative principles with respect to the world.[125] They are the general principles <*principia*> of formed nature. These negative principles are four, according to the number of the four types of categories: (1) concerns quality, (2) quantity, (3) concerns relation, the (4th) concerns modality; thus: (1) there is no leap in the world <*in mundo non datur saltus*>, (2) there is no gap <*non datur hiatus*>, (3) [there is no][L] chance <[*non datur*][L] *casus*>, (4) [there is no][L] fate <[*non datur*][L] *fatum*>. These all refer to the connection <*nexum*> in the world.

(A)[j] There is no leap in the world <*in mundo non datur saltus*>. Leap <*saltus*> is in general an event <*eventus*>. (Thus with an advance in arguing <*avancement in argumentando*>; but where one can understand the intermediate grounds, there it is a legitimate leap <*saltus legitimus*>. Here leap <*saltus*> is the immediate transition from a quantum <*quanto*> to that which is not quantum. Space and time are continuous quanta <*quanta*

---

[g] Lehmann misreads the abbreviation *trscdtaliter* as *totaliter* (totally)(861₃₇).

[h] A *so* (preceding *wohl*) omitted by Lehmann has been replaced (862₁₇). The *so* was added to *wohl* above the line in the ms.

[i] A blank line inserted by Lehmann has been removed (862₂₂).

[j] The author's confusing numbering system is retained, viz. (A) *saltus*, (II) *hiatus*, (III) *casus*, (IV) *fatum*.

continua>, the real in these is also quantum. For internally the real is the sensations, externally that which corresponds to them. But sensation has a degree and an infinite multitude of degrees. With respect to quanta *<quanti>*, the simple is zero. From that to the quantum are infinitely many parts. A thing thus consists not of finite degrees, also not of finite parts, for that would be an infinite given *<infinitum datum>*, but rather the regression *<regressus>* in division is infinite.) The leap *<saltus>* is an immediate sequence of two states wholly unconnected with each other, without passing through the states which are between them. Each body has extensive magnitude insofar it is in space and in time, and also intensive magnitude or a degree of reality.[k] No bodies are so closely related to one another that the difference between them could not be still smaller. There is no step over from one appearance, quality, to another, without a transition through infinitely many intermediate degrees;[l] between the slightest bit of reality that we may ever assume and nothing, are infinitely many intermediate degrees. In the world there is no smallest appearance, because there is no thing [that is] smallest in space and time, but rather everything proceeds in an infinite continuity. This proposition could also be expressed so: everything is connected according to the law of continuity *<lege continui>*, e.g., the transition from an appearance is possible only if I pass through all infinite intermediate degrees. Thus no appearance can consist of the simple, because from the simple to matter there would be a sudden transition to something which is distinguished from it generically *<in genere>*. Strictly speaking, one especially needs this proposition in the alterations of the states of things, for every alteration has its degree as well.[m] No body can transfer from one state into another without passing through all the intermediate states, or intermediate degrees, e.g., if a body which is at rest moves all at once, then it must pass through all the intermediate degrees from total rest up to the degree of motion that it now has. This shall now be proven:

Suppose a thing is in the state A and wants to transfer into the state B. Now[n] these are two different states, therefore they cannot also exist at the same time, but rather each in a specific time. The thing would thus be in A in one moment and in B in the other. Between two moments there is a time (it may be as small as it wants), for the moments themselves are only positions in time. In this time the thing will thus be in neither of the two states, also in no other state, because these are the immediately following ones. There thus remains nothing left of it other than that it finds itself in transition from one state to the other. But between two states there is a

29:863

29:864

---

[k] We follow Lehmann in changing *Realitaeten* to *Realitaet* (863₈); Lehmann does not note the change.
[l] We are adding a semicolon (863₁₂).
[m] An *auch* omitted by Lehmann has been replaced (863₂₄).
[n] Lehmann misreads *nun* as *nur* (only)(863₃₁).

degree and the transition to this degree will thus happen without a series of intermediate degrees. Accordingly the thing will pass in its transition from one state to the other through the intermediate degrees. Because the opposite of this would be a leap <*saltus*>, the proposition is demonstrated now: nothing happens in the world through a leap <*nihil fit in mundo per saltum*>.

Thus everything in the world alters by degree, for the causes always work little by little. There could be no empty time between the two moments, rather the cause had to work, otherwise no effect would have arisen. And the cause must have worked ever stronger there until the effect attained the degree that it was to reach. E.g., if there are obscure representations in my soul, then it must seek to make the representations ever clearer until they finally obtain an adequate degree of clarity.

Thus because all alterations proceed without a leap, but rather continuously <*in continuo*>, this is also called law of continuity <*lex continui*>.

I cannot describe a triangle or other straight figure by continuous motion <*motum continuum*>. For at each corner I rest for some time; with the motion of a body from A to B I rest a moment at B, and from B until C I rest a moment at B. Between two moments there is a time in which the body ceases in its motion, thus this is interrupted motion <*motus interruptus*> and not continuous <*continuus*>. Curved lines have, on the other hand, a continuous motion <*motum continuum*>.[*o*]

29:921 Kaestner proposed this and said: whoever wants to prove the law of continuity <*lex continui*> must prove this proposition.[*p*126] Otherwise it would be a leap if one were to come from one direction immediately to the other. It can continuously alter its direction only in a curved line. Therefore Newton also says that light rays fall upon a mirror in a curved line, and are likewise reflected back by it, although the angles x=y are equal.)[*q*127]

This law of nature can also be applied to the kinds and species of things (however this application of the proposition, how far it can go, is unknown), namely if one says: no kind or species is so closely related to another that another intermediate kind or intermediate species might not be able to occur between them. (The law of continuity <*lex continui*> serves for refuting the monadology; the world cannot consist of monads, for with respect to quanta <*quanti*> the simple is a null. But the transition from null to a quantum <*quanto*> is a leap. I can put together as

---

[*o*] We follow Stark here (at 864_{24}), who inserts 921_2–927_{15}. This is text found toward the end of the ms, a section that Lehmann separates as being *aus einer anderen Fassung* (from another version), and was apparently inadvertently omitted from its proper place during the process of copying the notes. Its content strongly suggests this present insertion. Introductory ellipses added by Lehmann have been removed (921_2).
[*p*] We follow Lehmann in omitting an extra *will* (following *beweisen*)(921_3).
[*q*] This closing parenthesis has no mate (921_8).

220

many simples as I want, but they will never become a quantum. The simple is certainly something positive with respect to quality, but not with respect to quantity. A complete concept of the law of continuity <*lege continui*> cannot be obtained if one does not take the first state in which a thing is for the infinitely smallest part of the state in which a thing is yet to come. Thus zero must be taken as the infinitely smallest part of the following state. Rest, e.g., as the infinitely smallest part of motion. The first state must not be taken merely as zero with respect to the consequent, for zero is wholly different from every state. We must arrive at this law <*lex*>; for two states are never next to each other, rather there is a moment still in between them. Everything in the world is according to the law of continuity <*lege continui*>, therefore also all motion according to curved lines.) The latter is also called the law of nature and indeed the mechanical [law of nature],ᴸ since the former is called the cosmological. We find it, of course, becauseʳ it is so constituted; but we cannot prove through reason that it must be so. Therefore it does not at all belong in metaphysics. This is also called the chain of things, to which God is then also counted, that he would thus have merely an infinitely higher degree of perfection than creatures. Voltaire ridicules this when he represents it as a great procession in which were God, the Pope, the angels, the cardinals, etc.[128] It is also in vain to include God in this chain, of course, for he is quite specifically distinguished from creatures. He is cause <*causa*> of everything, the creature is effect <*causatum*>, that would be as if, in order to describe a plane, I continued a straight line without stopping. It would not become a plane even in eternity.

29:922

(II) There is no gap in the world <*in mundo non datur hiatus*>.[129] There is in the world no empty space and no empty time. This proposition belongs under the category of magnitude. There are two kinds of empty space possible.

1. An empty space outside the world or extramundane vacuum <*vacuum extra mundanum*>, which encloses it. And that is nothing. For the sensible world has no boundaries, at least we cannot determine them by any possible experience. Therefore we also cannot at all comprehend an empty space outside the world, because it is not an object of our experience at all and is nothing real. But here the question is also not of this empty space, but rather

2. of the empty space in the world or the interrupted or concrete vacuum <*vacuo intermisso vel concreto*>. Experience concerning this is also impossible for us. Further, by a gap <*hiatus*> two things in the world would also be separated from their connection <*nexu*>, and that will not do since the world stands in a thoroughgoing connection <*nexu*>. Moreover a gap <*hiatus*> would at the same time also be a leap <*saltus*>; and

---

ʳ We follow Lehmann in omitting a *da* (following *weil*)(921₃₃).

that this latter does not take place has already been proved earlier. An empty time in which nothing passed away would be a leap <*saltus*>. An empty space is also a leap <*saltus*>. For if a body merely moved in an empty space, then nothing would be altered, neither in it itself nor outside it. There would thus have happened no alteration at all. Consequently on the previous alteration another would immediately succeed at once, without this attaining a degree in the meantime through a gradual increase. But that would be a leap <*saltus*>, e.g., if a body falls through a hollow ball, and this has an empty space, then the time which it took in falling through would be an empty time. For neither would it be altered in itself, nor something outside it, because there would then be nothing outside it. But through its motion it would not be altered at all. But the empty time between two states is a leap <*saltus*>.

29:923

(III) There is no chance in the world <*in mundo non datur casus*>. Chance is an event in the world not determined according to natural laws <*casus est eventus in mundo non determinatus secundum leges naturales*>. Chance is the coming about of an event without cause and sufficient ground. This runs contrary to the principle of sufficient reason <*principium rationis sufficientis*>, without which, however, no experience is possible. The world is a sum of appearances. In the world everything happens according to natural laws. The actions of human beings also happen according to natural laws although their will does not stand under natural laws. Between natural necessity and chance is something intermediate, namely: freedom. This can certainly be contrary to the causes of that which happens, but chance not at all. For I cannot explain the slightest from chance. The proposition: [in the world there is no]^L chance <[*in mundo non datur*]^L *casus*> is true only of events – thus merely of the sensible world.

Chance is also called a blind accident and for this reason: something through which one cannot see is sometimes called blind, e.g., opaque glass.^{s} Now if we assume chance as the cause of the events, we cannot at all comprehend why and for what the event happened, because we lack a sufficient ground.^{t} In the world everything happens according to general standing rules. That holds only for the sensible world. For happening presupposes a time, consequently nothing happens in the noumenal world <*mundo noumeno*>, therefore the principle of sufficient reason <*principium rationis sufficientis*> holds only for phenomena <*phenomenis*>. – For the sensible world is objectively the sum of all possible experiences, and only through sufficient reason <*ratione sufficienti*> is experience possible. Cause is that upon which an event follows according to a necessary rule.

---

^{s} *blindes Glas* (923$_{18}$), literally *blind glass*.
^{t} We are adding a period here, and omit, at the beginning of the next sentence, an opening parenthesis that has no mate (923$_{21}$).

In the sensible world the causality of an event is itself an event, for in the sensible world everything happens. Therefore no totality is in the series of conditions here. The causality of an event is also itself an event. For had it been causality at all times, then the event would have been at all times. But that contradicts the concept of event, which signifies the coming about of a thing, thus presupposes a time at which the thing was not. The causality thus also came about, therefore [is] also an event. An entire series of such events must also contain an unconditioned: for if the series is whole, then it must be unconditioned. Thus there must be an unconditioned first cause. But if I say: God gave the world a beginning, then he was the 29:924 causality of it, and since I connect him thus with time, his causality was itself an event. In order to get out of this difficulty I must recall that God is being considered as a thing in itself. With such, causality is not an event. The arrangement that everything happens in the world according to stand-ing rules can be called the mechanism of nature. The mechanism of a thing is otherwise called the arrangement of a thing according to laws of motion, but more generally it can mean an arrangement according to any manner of laws. Thus in the sensible world, everything goes according to the mechanism of nature, according to natural necessity. Contrary to this is accident, chance <*casus*>. Between the two is the intermediate – freedom. Now one should think that there is no freedom in the sensible world; but there is still. – Namely, when I think of a thing in itself, then this is clearly a substrate <*substratum*> of appearances and to this extent, as appearance, it belongs under the mechanism of nature, but not as thing in itself. Thus such a noumenon indeed acts as appearance according to the mechanism of nature, [but] its actions do not happen thus, but rather according to its will and not by the mechanism of nature. Its causality of an event is not itself an event, for he[u] is no appearance. My reason is a faculty for cognizing things as they are, therefore I must indeed also be a thing in itself. All my actions happen according to the mechanism of nature, etc., insofar as they have their ground in another, but not by the mechanism of nature; rather I have the faculty for determining myself by reason according to objective grounds, independent of all outer circum-stances, stimuli <*stimulis*>, etc. To this extent I have freedom. Thus the difficulty with freedom lies merely in this, that one takes appearances for things in themselves. For they cannot help us out, because with appear-ances everything happens according to the mechanism of nature. Since the soul is also a thing in itself, it is free. For there its causality is not again an event, rather it acts there according to its own motive grounds, which it takes from itself. As thing in itself it does not at all produce its actions in a time sequence, rather they only appear to us that way. And thus the

---

[u] *er* (924₂₂); this masculine first-person pronoun presumably refers to the person who is free, although there is no explicit masculine antecedent.

antinomy that there is freedom and necessity in the world is removed,
29:925 because it is shown that they are not actual opposites <*opposita*>, because
they apply to different objects, namely the first to the noumenal world
<*mundus noumenon*> and the other to the phenomenal world <*mundus
phaenomenon*>, and therefore both can take place at once. It is likewise
with the following antinomy: whether everything in the world, conditioned
as well as unconditioned, is contingent, or whether something is necessary
in it. The first is true of the phenomenal world <*mundo phaenomenon*>.
For nothing is necessary in space and time, because everything that has a
cause is an event. But in the noumenal world <*mundo noumenon*> the
cause can be necessary, and thus the latter holds for it. – If a world is,
then something necessary must exist, neither as cause nor as part. Both
propositions are true, however contradictory they also appear to be. If we
consider the world as the content of appearance, then nothing is necessary, because in the sensible world there is no totality. But if we view the
world as the summation of things themselves, then something must be
necessary. With appearances nothing is necessary. For were there a being
that had produced the appearance, then it would also have had to produce
this in time. Accordingly there would have to be a time where God would
not yet have produced any appearance. He would accordingly be himself
an event, himself an appearance, and accordingly would have his ground
in another event. We elude this contradiction if we consider God as thing
in itself whose effects in the sensible world happen indeed according to
mechanism, but not by it, rather by freedom. In the world there is no
chance <*in mundo non datur casus*>, this proposition thus means positively
this much, that everything in the world happens necessarily according to
certain rules. In the world there is thus no chance in itself, but we can call
something chance comparatively that indeed has its ground, but one we
cannot comprehend, and there is plenty of such chance. Such comparative chance is called fortune or misfortune. The cause of our well-being
rests then not on our actions but on other circumstances.

If I assume a blind accident, then I take no trouble in scouting for the
grounds of the events, and this proposition is, like the following, a crutch
for lazy reason.

(IV) There is no fate in the world <*in mundo non datur fatum*>.[130]
Destinies are deviations from maxims. The latter are basic propositions
which are taken from the subject, and principles are basic propositions[v]
that are taken from the object. They are speculative or practical. The
former require that which promotes the interest of my reason. Destinies
29:926 conflict with the interest of reason. For if I accept them, then I must
renounce the use of reason; destiny also opposes the practical maxims

---

[v] Here *Grundsätze* (usually translated as "principles") is translated as "basic propositions"
and *principien* as "principles" (925_{36-7}).

which are in connection with the will, e.g., Mohammedanism, that life depends upon blind destiny, that for each human being it was determined even before birth how long it is to live.

Fate <*fatum*> means something once pronounced. Destiny is a blind necessity without law. Natural necessity is still according to laws; the events in the world occur according to this necessity. Blind necessity is the contrary <*contrarium*> of chance. But of that, that something should be without any grounds and causes, and yet be necessary, we have not the slightest concept. For we find nothing at all contradictory in this, that something would also not have happened. To want to explain something by destiny is nonsensical, for calling upon destiny just means that I cannot explain something. When we do something, insofar as it proceeds from physical causes, we must explain it from the laws of nature and not from spontaneity, otherwise we would come to intelligible grounds which belong to the noumenal world <*mundo noumenon*>; and that would be passing over into another genus <*metabasis eis allo genos*>,[v] that takes place only in moral relations. The intelligences <*intelligentia*> (beings of understanding and free beings, and thus also human beings) belong to the noumenal world <*mundo noumeno*>. Here the author begins to speak of the extramundane being <*ente extramundano*>.[131] If this world is a contingent being, then it is the effect of another <*causatum alterius*>. But that it is contingent comes from this: [the] noumenal world <*mundus noumenon*> is a whole <*totum*> of substances that stand in interaction <*in commercio*> with one another. By means of this interaction <*commercii*> the substances depend reciprocally on each other. The substances thus have no necessary existence. For absolutely necessary being presupposes an independent being. But the world does not have that. Accordingly it is dependent upon another being. This being does not belong to the world, for otherwise it would be at the same time cause, in that it would have produced the world, but at the same time also effect, in that it would belong at the same time to the world; but that just cannot be. For cause and effect must be different. Accordingly the world as effect must also be different from its cause. Thus the cause of the world <*causa mundi*> is an extramundane being <*ens extra mundanum*>.

The cause of the world is a being above the world <*causa mundi est ens super mundanum*>, since a cause is more noble <*causa nobilior*> than the effect <*effectus*>, because in it lies the causality of yet more and other effects <*effectuum*>.

What is necessary can subsist for itself or is isolated; the extramundane being <*ens extra mundanum*> is therefore also isolated. It can indeed have an effect in other substances, but other substances cannot reciprocate. The sensible world is certainly contingent, for the appearances are indeed nothing in themselves. The proximate cause of the sensible world is the

29:927

---

[v] This is written with Greek letters in the ms (926$_{19}$).

noumenal world <*mundus noumenon*>, with which we are not now acquainted, but into which we can come after our death as into a wholly other world. –

Second section
On general parts or monadology

FIRST CHAPTER
ON GENERAL SIMPLE PARTS

Egoism is when someone maintains that there is nothing present outside him, but rather everything that we see is mere illusion; and whoever maintains this is an egoist. Egoism can be dogmatic or skeptical. Many have maintained skepticism in earnest, and that is feasible if one maintains namely that all grounds to the contrary are not yet adequate. The egoist says: in dreaming I also imagine a world,[132] and am in it, and nevertheless it is not so. Can it not also be the same with me when awake? But against this is that dreams do not connect with each other, rather I now dream this, now that, but when awake appearances are connected according to general rules. Egoism is a mere problem which has no ground for itself at all – but nonetheless is also very difficult to prove and to refute. I cannot refute the egoist by experience, for this instructs us immediately <*immediate*> only of our own existence. We do experience mediately <*mediate*> that other things are there through the senses; but the egoist says that in these senses there lies only the ground by which we would become aware of appearances. But they would be nothing in themselves. Since nothing can be settled this way, one uses moral proofs, and indeed the following: the human being is limited, thus contingent. Accordingly he must have a cause. This highest cause must be unlimited, because it depends on nothing, and thus it also cannot be limited by anything. Thus it cannot be assumed that one is here all alone.

29:928

Dualism (pluralism)[x] is opposed to egoism.[133] The dualist believes in thinking beings and bodies outside him. In general it is so absurd that it may well never occur to anyone to affirm this error seriously, even if it were irrefutable as well.

Idealism is when one imagines that outside oneself thinking beings are indeed present, but not bodies.[134] This error is likewise refutable neither from experience nor *a priori*. For it is not necessary that there are bodies. But here one also has a moral ground. One says, namely, God is the most perfect being and author of me. Therefore he would have also made my senses through which I am constantly seeing bodies. The illusion would

---

[x] We follow Lehmann in adding parentheses (928₃). *Pluralism.* is written above *Dualismus* in the ms.

also have to come from God by which we are persuaded to hold something which is mere delusion of our senses. But that He will delude us is not to be presumed. This ground, however, is quite lame, for one can rightly object against it: that we deceive ourselves when we believe what our senses teach us. Truly, it remains rather in our power to believe this or not.

Idealism also has actual grounds for itself and is therefore also more probable than egoism. In particular, Bishop Cloyd[135] in Ireland said: if spiritual beings were in interaction <*commercio*> in such a way that their bodies were mere effects of their imagination, then the world would lose nothing in its worth. For this properly rests on thinking beings. Therefore, according to the principle: beings must not be multiplied without necessity <*entia non sunt sine necessitate multiplicanda*>, it is thus useless to assume a bodily world. Bishop Berkeley in Ireland went even further, for he maintained that bodies are even impossible, because one would always contradict oneself if one assumes them. This is dogmatic or crude idealism, that no bodies exist outside of us, but rather that appearances are nothing and lie merely in our senses and our power of imagination. But there is also a critical or transcendental idealism, when one assumes that appearances are indeed nothing in themselves, but that actually something unknown still underlies them. That is correct.

Materialism is when one assumes that everything is material.[136] This hypothesis is assumed in full seriousness by many. There is a difference between matter and material. Material is that which is or can be a constituent part <*pars constitutiva*> of some matter, and matter is the extended thing <*extensum*> that consists of such parts <*partibus*>, or an impenetrable whole. Thus whoever maintains: matter consists of simple parts or monads, also maintains that these parts are indeed not matter, but material things <*materialia*>. Thus if I say: the soul is simple, then I still cannot prove from this that it is immaterial, and distinguish material from immaterial monads. No, if the soul is simple, then it can also be material, but on that account it need not yet be matter. If the monads of bodies are also actual, then they must have a representation as much as the soul, which Leibniz also maintains.[137] The soul would then also be such a monad, thus material. Should bodies thus consist of simple parts, then the materialist would not be wrong. The grounds from which Leibniz wanted to derive the existence of monads and their power of representation are: world, he says, is a whole consisting of simple parts or of monads <*monadatum*>, for what is composed presupposes something simple from which it is composed. There are thus monads. But what do these have in the way of powers? All powers with which we are acquainted in things concern merely outer relations, e.g., motive power is merely alteration of location, impenetrability indicates perdurability in a location. These inner realities still must be, although we are not acquainted with them. They

29:929

must be the causes of the outer ones. But we cannot become aware of these inner powers in any thing except our soul. For we cannot perceive them through outer, but rather only through inner sense. And here we find that their inner power is thinking, from which arise willing, pleasure, and displeasure. Now since the monads are also simple like the soul, they can also have powers of representation <*vires repraesentativae*> and their influence can be merely the modification of powers of representation <*modificatio virium repraesentativarum*>. (They can also have faculty of desire <*facultatem appetitivam*>, which is in conformity with the representations <*repraesentativae*>.) Accordingly the monads have power of representation of all parts of the world through which they are affected. But because they are not alone, but rather are always connected with other monads, they are hindered by this in their power of representation, and therefore have obscure representations, are slumbering <*sopitae;* G: *schlummernde*> monads.[138] Thereby they are distinguished from the soul. Here Leibniz also actually understood merely the noumenal world <*mundum noumenon*>, only he did not express himself very clearly.

29:930

Now that is the famous doctrine of monads of Leibniz. But it is a mere phantom of the brain. For Leibniz committed the error here of confusing the noumenal and phenomenal world <*mundum noumenon . . . phaenomenon*> with each other,[139] for it is true only of the noumenal world <*mundo noumenon*> that bodies consist of monads. But of these we know nothing other than the mere names. But we are unacquainted with their nature. (With respect to the noumenal world <*mundi noumenon*>, bodies consist of simple parts. For if I remove the composition of the substantial composite <*compositum substantiale*>, then the parts still remain. Now as these are then not composite, they must be simple. But it is otherwise with the phenomenal world <*mundus phaenomenon*>. If I remove the composition here, then nothing remains for me. For space and time are here the essentials of composition; without these no thing can appear to me.)

But with respect to the phenomenal world <*mundi phaenomenon*> it is obviously false. For all these inferences, those of Leibniz as well as those of the materialists from this proposition of Leibniz, come tumbling down due to the following proposition: matter, or rather its appearances in the sensible world, do not consist of simple parts, for first, no part of space is simple, second,[y] a body must consist of as many parts as the space consists of which the body occupies. Therefore body is infinitely divisible, because space is infinitely divisible. The bodies themselves can perhaps consist of simple parts, but not the appearances, for they are not the bodies themselves. Now I can say: thinking beings are simple. But matter is not simple, nor is the material. Accordingly souls are immaterial. Impenetrability belongs to physics.

[y] Lehmann misreads *2 aus soviel* as *2tens soviel,* and then adds an *aus* after *2tens* (930_{23}).

Leibniz and the author distinguish mathematical and physical points.[140] The latter are monads, the former locations in space. They say: all monads are simple, therefore not in space, otherwise they would be divisible. Therefore they are points, which are indivisible. But now space does not consist of points. Therefore that which is in space also does not consist of points.

SECOND CHAPTER
29:931
ON THE FIRST ORIGIN OF BODIES

The author now speaks of the first possibility of the production of bodies[141] and proves *a priori* various propositions here. (Here possibility is understood not physically, but rather metaphysically. The author explains the possibility of a body as that of a monad <*monadati*>[142] – the alteration of space is always reciprocal <*reciproque*>. Of a ship that goes to Pillau, I say: it moves there. But I can also say:^{z} Pillau moves ever closer to the ship just as much as the ship [to]^L it.[143] That can be strictly proved. And from that I can also prove *a priori* the possibility of interaction <*commercii*>. The author attempts to explain the possibility of motion from the power of representation <*vi repraesentativa*>.[144] But it is simply impossible to prove that what is an object of inner sense can be a cause of that which is an object of outer sense.) (No concept can be given *a priori* of motion, because it is inevitably based on something empirical. Material is either that which is matter, or what is at least a constituent part of matter <*pars constitutiva materiae*>. Those who make the human soul into a monad cannot have the difficulty that follows from many souls constituting a body; our elements are the basic parts of the body. Qualitative elements <*elementa qualitativa*> are those basic parts which are no longer decomposable into elements of different kinds. Quantitative elements <*elementa quantitativa*> are those basic parts which cannot at all be further divided; they are called atoms <*atomi*>.)

The proposition that substances reciprocally influence each other by action <*actio*> and reaction <*reactio*> is certainly correct. But this can be proved only in physics from experience, and in no way *a priori* in metaphysics. The expressions war of all against all <*bellum omnium contra omnia*>, etc.,[145] are improper. It signifies only harmony, e.g., the coachman effects the horses, and the horses effect the wagon and pull him forth. But reaction <*reactio*> is an opposed effect, a resistance. The author wants to prove this *a priori* here from the connection <*nexu*> of substances, but from that flows only the interaction <*commercium*>. But the author errs

---

^{z} A *so gut* (following *zum Schiff*) omitted by Lehmann without note has been replaced, and a *gut* (after *eben so*) added by Lehmann has been removed (931$_{8-9}$).

because he holds reaction <*reactio*> and impediment <*impediment*> for receptivity.

Now he also wants to prove *a priori* that the monads are connected. But how can I comprehend *a priori* that a substance has a power? Contact is only one kind of immediate action and counteraction in virtue of impenetrability. But this is a physical concept.

Moreover attraction is wholly different; there one body affects another in such a way that the other wants to penetrate the space where the effective one is. The [power] in contact does not belong here, rather it applies to matter and is due to impenetrability. This we can prove only *a posteriori*. Immediate <*immediate*> effect is a concept of the understanding. The author has therefore proved it quite poorly.

That which does not consist of any more parts, but rather is simple, is atomic (indivisible) <*atomus (indivisibile)*>, either absolutely or mathematically <*mathematice talis*>;[146] or physically <*physice talis*>, when it cannot be divided through any further chemistry, even if it still does consist of parts.

Something absolutely atomic <*atomus absolute talis*> would be a monad, and that is not to be assumed – the physically atomic <*atomus physicus*> is assumed, however, by all physicists. Figure, they say, constitutes the specific difference <*differentiam specificam*> and can never be decomposed. For were they to be decomposed to monads, then their figure would also have to cease; therefore there would no longer be any difference between them, and all manifold in the things in the world would cease. But we see now that gold remains gold, even if it is decomposed into the subtlest parts.

The [set of] principles that assumes physical atoms <*atomos physicos*> as the first basic parts, is philosophy of the lazy <*philosophia pigrorum*>.

That which explains phenomena by corpuscles <*corpusculis*> (invisible parts) is corpuscular philosophy <*philosophia corpuscularis*>. (Corpuscles <*corpuscula*> are physical atoms <*atomi physici*>.[147] According to Descartes's hypothesis they are indivisible and constitute the differences in matter.) (For him the atoms <*atomi*> are also the basic stuff of body. Body is that whose spatial limits are determined by matter.) Gassendi, Descartes, etc., etc., accept these.[148] The atomism <*atomistica*> of Epicurus is the same as that, only he accepted with it a vacuum or empty space <*inane*>.

That which explains appearances by monads is metaphysical atomism <*atomista metaphysicus*>, and that which [explains][L] it by corpuscles <*corpusculis*> or physical atoms <*atomis physicis*> is physical atomism <*atomista physicus*>.

The ancients called that lazy reason <*ignava ratio*> when one goes at once from the proximate ground <*ratione proxima*> to the most remote <*ad remotissimam*> without touching the intermediate grounds <*rationes intermedias*>. When one refers the explanation of all events immediately to God, without investigating the proximate natural causes.

THIRD CHAPTER
ON THE NATURE OF BODIES

The objective principles are the general grounds of reason, why things should happen.[a] (Nature is the existence of a thing insofar as it is internally determined according to general laws.[b] We cannot comprehend how a single created being can cognize things in themselves. We would not cognize things if we did not cognize them through action. These are the dynamic principles of nature. The ground of the determinability of appearance must lie in the understanding, [and so] also [must] the ground of the determinability of essence. These are determined in space and time according to their essence. The understanding is the faculty of rules; without this there is no experience. Prior to experience, we must thus premise natural laws that the understanding provides. Space and time make appearance possible, and so also the natural laws of experience. – Our understanding therefore prescribes laws to nature. But one says: but how will things arrange themselves according to my understanding? Appearances cannot become experiences if they do not fit the understanding. That means merely this. Thus they are called the highest dynamic principles.[149] – The understanding does not prescribe all laws of nature, or comprehend them, but rather only those that belong to the possibility of experience. (1) Only substance perdures, and states change. (2) What happens has a cause. (3) In all appearances there is no action without a counteraction.) Now nature is the first general inner objective principle of all that which belongs to the existence of the causality of a thing. It is thereby distinguished from essence, which is the inner principle of the possibility of a thing.[150] Nature is the first principle, and thus subalternate to no other, e.g., the ground of discoveries is reflection. This comes again from the understanding; this again from consciousness, and this is nature.

Nature is further a general principle from which I can explain all things. Finally it is also an inner principle which is met in things themselves. It is thereby to be distinguished from a miracle. This is also a principle, although outer; e.g., if someone ill becomes well by his nature, then that comes from himself, from the construction of his body. But if he is cured by a miracle, that comes from another cause outside of him.

Finally, nature is the principle of the existence of things. It is thereby to be strictly distinguished from possibility. Even perceptive men have failed

---

[a] We are adding a period and capital here (933_3).
[b] A closing parenthesis added here by Lehmann without note has been removed (933_4). The actual closing parenthesis is found at 933_{24}.

to heed this difference, as e.g., Reimarus explains nature through essential power, which is false.[151] For powers belong to nature because actuality belongs to nature. If a substance is actual, then it has power insofar as it can be the ground of something else.

But formal conditions of outer powers also belong to nature. E.g., a wedge must be pointed because it is supposed to split wood. This is what is formal in the power and belongs to the nature of the wedge. What is merely possible has no nature, e.g., a triangle. The explanation of nature by Reimarus is thus (1) incomplete, for to nature belong not merely powers, but also the connection of these with one another. Further it is (2) confused with essence.

All objects of experience have their nature, for without this no experience is possible. Experience is not an aggregate of perceptions, but rather a whole of perceptions connected according to a principle. Consequently there must be a principle in every thing, according to which the perceptions are connected and this is – nature.

Nature can be taken in a twofold meaning. First substantively or materially <*materialiter*>. This is called simply the nature of all things. It is the whole of all natures, the unity of all connected nature, in short, the general nature of all things, or that which all things have in common with one another.

Second, nature is also used as the specific nature of each thing, or adjectivally or formally <*vel formaliter*>. Each thing has its own nature, according to which it is different from others, e.g., the nature of body is extension and motive power. The nature of the soul is thinking and willing, etc.

Finally nature is also called, and indeed most often, the order of things according to certain general laws.

It is rational to explain everything that happens in the world according to these laws; but one must also not do this everywhere, where it does not at all belong. It is just as great a mistake as when we accept unknown powers as grounds of cognition. For there I have actually explained nothing. One often uses nature as a person or as a form, which is not a

29:935 substance and yet is held for one. Aristotle called this*c* substantial form <*forma substantialis*>, and for him too that was the soul.

Nature is opposed to (1) accident. But because all things have a nature, nothing is by accident. Everything is according to laws. Fate <*fatum*> [is] a necessity without (2)*d* laws, without ground.

Freedom is also a nature, insofar as it is not determined by others but by itself. Human beings have this. Animals do determine their instinct, but still

c Lehmann misreads *das* as *des* (935₁).
d A *2* (before *Gesetzte* in the ms) omitted here by Lehmann without note has been replaced (935₅).

the latter is already determined beforehand for that by God. To call the beginning of nature life (as the author wants),[152] and the end death, fits only living, but not lifeless creatures. That would be too symbolic. A machine <*machina*> is not a body movable according to the universal laws of motion <*corpus secundum leges universales motus mobile*>, as the author explains it,[153] but rather according to particular laws <*secundum leges particulares*>. Otherwise every body would be a machine. Mechanism is the mode of composition <*modus compositionis*> of a machine. It is the formal aspect, just as the motive power [is] the[e] material law in nature.

Explaining something from the nature of bodies is called physical, and explaining from the nature of thinking beings [is called] pneumatic. If I explain something not from nature but rather from a cause which goes beyond nature, then this is explained hyperphysically. But if this happens from hidden qualities <*qualitatibus occultis*>, then it is hypophysical. A body which can be explained from motive powers is in a mechanical connection <*in nexu mechanico*>. There are further two physical modes of explanation: (1) mechanical philosophy <*philosophia mechanica*>, which explains all phenomena from the shape and the general motive power of bodies. This is also explained mechanically <*mechanice*> or by mechanical physics <*physico mechanice*>. Here I explain not the origin, but rather the alteration of motion from motions already present. E.g., one explains how vinegar dissolves chalk mechanically this way: vinegar has in its atoms <*atomis*> sheer pointed particles, which look like spears. Now these drill through the chalk and thus it is dissolved. This power which drives the vinegar spears into the chalk comes from the warm outer air. But where does that come from? There we are stuck. Thus the phenomena cannot be explained mechanically after all.

(2) The dynamical mode of explanation, when certain basic powers are assumed from which the phenomena are derived. This was first discovered by Newton and is more satisfactory and complete than the former. Thus to explain something mechanically means to explain something according to the laws of motion, dynamically, from the powers of bodies. With either explanation one never comes to an end. The correct mode of explanation is dynamical physics <*physico*>, which includes both in itself. That is the mode of explanation of the present time. The first is the mode of explanation of Descartes, the second that of the chemists.[154] So, e.g., Descartes explains the attractive power of bodies thus, that he assumed a material which flowed around bodies and held them together. But if one asks whence this matter comes, then it cannot be derived from anywhere except God. Newton explained this appearance dynamically,[155] so that God had put a power in the substance to attract the bodies together. 29:936

[e] Reading *des* as *das* (935₁,₇).

Third section
On the representation of the whole

FIRST CHAPTER
ON THE BEST WORLD

(^{f}All things are heterogeneous in the transcendental sense and consequently one cannot say in this sense that one thing is more perfect than another. One must therefore look for a certain similarity of things, and then the distinction can be made between the good, best, and the most perfect. Good is that which [is]^L the objective ground of our choice, for the subjective ground of our choice [is]^L what is agreeable. The greatest objective ground of our choice is the best. Perfection is the ground of the greatest objective unity of cognition. So, the good is for the will, the perfect for the understanding. To the greatest perfection of the world belongs: (1) the greatest multitude of substances according to their extensive, intensive, and protensive magnitude. (2) A complete connection of these according to the rules of the greatest unity. This last above all belongs to it and is the most noble.) One can think of the highest original and derivative good <$summum\ bonum\ originarium \ldots derivativum$>. The world is the latter. For a whole <$totum$> is always contingent and therefore an effect <$causatum$>. The topic here is actually the perfection of the world.[156] The author has confused that with the best <$optimum$>, yet it is quite different from that. Perfection, insofar as it means a completeness of the whole and mutual harmony and connection of the whole, is transcendental perfection. Thus here the perfection of the world also means the perfection of the whole, which lacks no part that could yet be added to it, and that stands in the best order and connection.

29:937

Thus with the perfection of the world we have two matters to note: (1) perfection with respect to parts, or extensive magnitude (2) perfection in connection, or intensive magnitude. No world is absolutely complete with respect to its parts. More substances can still always be added; just as something more can be added to any multitude. But the multitude of parts does not constitute perfection, but rather only its manifold. A largest is nevertheless still possible, e.g., from the multitude of the subjects in a country I cannot at once infer to the perfection of the state.^{g}

---

^{f} We follow Lehmann in adding an opening parenthesis (936_{16}).

^{g} This paragraph ends here (937_{15}) at the bottom of ms, p. 124' with the following paragraph beginning at the top of the facing page (ms, p. 125); there is no blank line or empty space separating them, and the only indication that the text "breaks off" (as noted by Lehmann) is the very different subject matter of the two paragraphs. They nevertheless appear to be written by the same person and at the same time (judging from the similarity of ink). We follow Stark in viewing Ak. 29: 927–37 as a portion of text that was inadvertently copied into the wrong section of the ms, and so we return now to the remainder of the Cosmology section at 864_{25} (ms, p. 93).

I can represent the world to myself as infinite with respect to possible 29:864
completeness and manifold. But since this material does not yet constitute
the perfection of the world, the connection of substances with one another
is needed for this. Ultimately substances in this world become a complete
whole which lacks nothing in its perfection. It cannot be complete according to this connection and arrangement, although it could well be according to another. This is the complete nature of the world: its formal perfection and certainly the most noble [perfection], namely that all is in the
most beautiful harmony and order. This natural order is so holy and
inviolable to us that we would certainly despise and rank far behind our
world a world that was by reason of its matter <*ratione materiae*> much
better than this world but by reason of its form <*ratione formae*> much
worse. One can also think of the perfection of the world in the teleological
sense (i.e., according to ends, or practically). If all possible ends can be 29:865
united into a main end, then it is called the highest good <*summum
bonum*>. – The perfect <*perfectum*> and the best <*optimum*> are thus to
be distinguished from one another. The entirety of nature is thought of as
a kingdom. A kingdom is the relation of many to a one as the highest
commander <*summum imperantem*> or law[giver],L and so it is in nature
as well. What happens once under certain circumstances will happen
under the same circumstances on into eternity. The highest good <*summum bonum*> is accordingly the most perfect kingdom of nature as the
most complete system of all ends.157

SECOND CHAPTER
ON THE RECIPROCAL INFLUENCE OF
SUBSTANCES IN THE WORLD

The possibility of the connection <*nexus*> of substances is the possibility
of formal perfection in the world. I can comprehend this just as little as I
can the possibility of the first basic power of things. For by its concept
each substance exists for itself, therefore appears to be isolated, and has
nothing at all to do with an other substance. One even says that it could
not be otherwise, for if a body moves, then it moves with it the body that is
in its way, and thus acts upon it. But here connection <*nexus*> in space
and time is already taken as a basis, and then one would have to ask how is
space and time possible? This question no sooner came into philosophy
than the question was raised as to how soul as a spiritual, and body as an
extended being, could stand in interaction <*in commercio*> with one another. One generalized this now and asked:h how are substances in interaction <*in commercio*> with one another possible at all?158 Leibniz was the

---

h Lehmann misreads *Dieses machte man nun allgemeiner und frug* as *Dieses müsste man in
allgemeiner [Hinsicht] fragen* (865₂₆₋₇).

first to put this the right way. After him this investigation was brought to its height by Wolff (in whose philosophy the proposition first stands) and Baumgarten. But now since one seeks mere popularity, and with that gladly abandons thoroughness, this proposition has also been left lying, although it is one of the most important in the whole of philosophy. (Real influence <*influxus realis*> presupposes a passion which however is at the same time action <*actio*> as well. I cannot at all derive from the concept of substance how this is possible. It is possible in the phenomenal world <*mundo phaenomenon*> from the mere existence of substance in space. –

29:866   For space connects them all. In the noumenal world <*mundo noumenon*> it is possible only if one assumes a common cause, i.e., God, which has already put that in the nature of substance. That is Leibniz's pre-established harmony <*harmonia praestabilita*>. Physical influence <*influxus physicus*>[159] is a hidden quality <*qualitas occulta*>, for nothing is cognized through the term. The concept of space accomplishes in the sensible world <*mundo sensibili*> what the divine omnipresence does in the noumenal world <*mundo noumenon*>, and one can therefore call it as it were a phenomenon of the divine omnipresence. Perhaps God wanted thereby to make his omnipresence sensibly cognizable to us. Newton called it the seat of the senses <*sensorium*> of the divine omnipresence.[160] Perhaps space is also the only sensibility that belongs to all rational beings other than God.) (N.B. Leibniz presumably also understood his system as it is represented here, but because he expresses himself obscurely it was taken in another sense, which is false.) All connection of substances among themselves can be viewed as real connection <*nexus realis*> or substantial interaction <*commercium substantiarum*>, when substances act on each other reciprocally, or as ideal connection <*nexus idealis*>, i.e., harmony of substances without interaction <*harmonia substantiarum absque commercio*>. The ideal connection <*nexus idealis*> is not connection in the things themselves, but rather merely in the idea of the observer who considers them, i.e., if I hear the most agreeable music then I sense in my hearing a harmony of all the instruments. But now this harmony is merely in me and my thoughts; the instruments, however, do not have the slightest harmony with one another. Two systems were invented according to this ideal connection <*nexus idealis*> which are supposed to explain the interaction <*commercium*> of substances among one another. To them belong (1) the Cartesian system of harmony established occasionally <*systema harmoniae occasionaliter stabilitae*> or system of occasionalism or of assistance <*systema occasionalismi vel assistentiae*>.[i]

(2) The Leibnizian system of preestablished harmony <*systema harmoniae praestabilitae*>. Both are externally established systems <*systemata externa stabilita*>. For since the interaction <*commercium*> can never be

---

[i] A paragraph break omitted by Lehmann without note has been replaced (866₂₈).

explained from the nature of substance, they derive it from an extramundane being <*ente extramundo*>.

(1) The system of assistance <*systema assistentiae*> of Descartes consists in this, that with every cause and effect or with every influence <*influxu*> of substances, God would be the intermediate cause <*causa intermedia*> and would have arranged the effects harmoniously with the causes. E.g., with Leibniz[161] the custom is that only one clock strikes by itself, [the others][L] are struck with a clapper by certain people. In such a way all the clocks strike together. Now each of these harmonize in my ear, but this harmony between the first clock as cause and the others as effect does not arise from the first clock, but rather from intermediate causes <*causis intermediis*>, the people who strike the clocks, and these make the harmony among the clocks. So it is as well with the connection <*nexu*> of substances in the world. At first Descartes had invented this system in order to derive from it the interaction <*commercium*> of the soul with the body. For because he could not imagine how the soul could act immediately on the body, he assumed an intermediate cause <*causam intermediam*> besides, which at every occasion ruled the body according to the will of the soul.

29:867

(2) Leibniz's preestablished harmony <*harmonia praestabilita*>. Is nearly the same as the former. Both assume an extramundane intermediate cause <*causam intermediam extramundanum*>. But Descartes assumes it with every alteration of substance. Leibniz, on the other hand, affirmed that the highest being would have already so arranged things from eternity that they harmonized with one another, and thus the alteration of one would appear to be the work of another, e.g., when clocks, all of which are self-driven through one clockwork, strike at the same time, then this harmony arises not from them but rather is preestablished. Their creator arranged them thus. But both of these systems rest on the ideal connection <*nexus idealis*>. If however the substances stood in no other connection <*nexu*>, then there would be no world, but rather only an ideal whole in thoughts. There each substance would indeed be rational and isolated, if it did not itself care to effect anything. The objection has rightly been made that with regard to the soul bodies would be wholly superfluous. For God could also have allowed representations of body to come about in the soul, either as occasioned <*occasionaliter*> or as preestablished <*praestabiliter*>, without actual bodies being necessary. These representations could indeed always harmonize with the soul. All this amounts to idealism, as can be seen. Accordingly one can also say that, because of bodies <*ratione corporum*>, souls[j] would be superfluous. For since the souls effect nothing, without them God could still effect all alterations in bodies. Further, one body, as opposed to or with respect to

---

[j] Lehmann misreads *Seelen* as *Sachen* (affairs, matters)(867₃₀).

another, would also be superfluous. Each could be isolated. One sees from all this that these systems are like siblings.

But there is yet a second connection <*nexum*> in the world, namely real connection <*nexus realis*>, or influence <*influxus*>, where substances reciprocally influence one another by action and reaction <*per actionem et reactionem*>. Now this is possible in a twofold way: either as original <*originarius*> or as defective <*defectivus*>;[k] the former is the influence <*influxus*> of those substances that merely by their existence are already capable of having an effect in another. Now the question is: can original <*originarie*> substances be in interaction <*commercio*>? No, for original substances <*substantiae originariae*> are existent through themselves <*per se existentes*>, thus independent or isolated. But then because they would exist so that no determination of their existence would depend upon something else, they would also not be in interaction <*commercio*> with one another. A whole <*totum*> of original substances <*substantiae originares*>[l] is therefore impossible. Secondly, derivatively <*derivativus*>[m], when substances exist so that the possibility of their interaction <*commercii*> depends upon a third substance. If substances are in interaction <*commercio*>, then they are dependent upon one another, therefore contingent and the effect of another <*causatum alterius*>. But the cause <*causa*> must be an original being <*ens originarium*>. But there cannot be many original beings <*entia originaria*> that are the cause of the world and its interaction <*commercii*>. For since each original being <*ens originarium*> would be isolated, its work would also be fully isolated from the work of the other. But we do not find that in the world, for there everything is in thoroughgoing connection <*nexu*>. Accordingly the world must also have only one cause. The connection <*nexus*> of substances is on that account to be thought possible only as derivative, but with that not as ideal, but rather concurrently as real. This proof holds, however, only for the noumenal world <*mundus noumenon*>. In the phenomenal world <*mundus phaenomenon*> we do not need it, for it is nothing in itself. Here everything is in interaction <*commercio*> in virtue of space. The systems of occasional and predetermined harmony take place only in the sensible world. For here the question is whether God arranged[n] the harmony in the beginning or in the duration, and this presupposes time. Physical influence <*influxus physicus*> is called [influence] in the crude original sense <*crasiori sensu originarie*>, insofar as God in this case effects nothing in it; subtle or derivative sense <*sensu subtiliori* . . .

29:868

---

[k] This is likely a miswrite or miscopy of *derivativus* (derivative) (867₃₈).

[l] We do not follow Lehmann in changing *Ein Totum v Subs. orig* to *Ein Totum originarium von Substanzen* (An original whole of substances)(868₆₋₇).

[m] Lehmann misreads *derivativus* as *Derivationes* (868₇).

[n] We follow Lehmann here in adding a *hat* (868₂₄).

derivatus>, when the possibility of the influence *<influxus>* still arises from God as the prior origin *<ante originario>*. –

Physical influence *<influxus physicus>* happens according to general laws, but the two systems of ideal connection *<nexus idealis>* do not. –

THIRD CHAPTER
ON THE NATURAL

Nature can be taken in a double sense:[162] (1) adjectivally as the particular nature of each thing, (2) substantively of the world according to general principles and laws, which is the entirety of nature or the sensible world with respect to its connection (universal nature *<natura universa>*). In the substantive sense *<in sensu substantivo>* there is only one nature, in the adjectival sense *<in sensu adjectivo>* as many natures as things. Natural is that which can be explained from the nature of a thing, or an event is natural if its cause is met with in the cosmos. Now it can be properly   29:869 natural, when[a] it can be explained from the nature of the thing with which it occurs, or it is also natural relatively if its ground lies in another thing. So art is also natural in that it springs from the nature of some thing. Absolutely natural is that whose cause is met with in the entirety of nature. This is also called simply natural (course of nature is succession of the series of events), or the course of nature is the connection of events insofar as it is connected with experience. I experience what happens according to the course of nature. The order of nature is the ground of this connecting of appearances. – Course of nature points to the regularity of experience, order of nature its necessity.

An event belongs to the course of nature insofar as it is a part of the alterations[b] that arise in the world. The order in nature excites wonder and respect in us at all times. But whence does it come? From the fact that without nature we would not have any objects of the understanding. Without nature nothing is an object of the understanding since the understanding cognizes nothing without rules. But now we would not be able to make any rules if everything in the world happened first as though without the slightest order. We would then have either useless understanding, or none at all. Thus, since this nobility of the soul which raises us to humanity, the worth of our understanding, rests on nature, we thus regard this natural order as if it were something holy, and hesitate injuring it;[c] even when it should also work to our disadvantage, e.g., if due to age a wall collapses and strikes a man dead, then we will certainly not rejoice over it. But because this happens according to the order of nature, we do wish

---

[a] Lehmann misreads *wenn* as *wie* (how)(869₂).
[b] To agree with the verb, we are changing *Veränderung* to *Veränderungen* (869₁₆).
[c] We follow Lehmann in changing *scheuen sie uns* to *scheuen uns, sie* (869₂₆).

that the man had not gone by at that time, but we find it absurd to wish that the wall had stood longer than it could stand given the laws of nature. –

FOURTH CHAPTER
ON THE SUPERNATURAL AND
THE POSSIBILITY OF MIRACLES[163]

Supernatural <*supernaturale;* G: *übernaturlich*>, is that which cannot be explained from the entirety of nature. Contrary to nature <*praeternaturale;* G: *wiedernatürlich*>, is that which is contrary to the particular nature of a thing, but which can still be explained from the nature of other things or from the entirety of nature, e.g., that a human being cannot sleep[r] does not come from his nature, but still from the nature of other things which are the cause of it. Not everything supernatural <*supernaturale*> is a miracle, but rather that which happens contrary to the order of nature in the world. What happens outside the world contrary to the order of nature is not a miracle, e.g., creation is no miracle. Miracles are either strict or comparative miracles <*miracula rigorosa . . . comparativa*>;[164] the former are those which cannot be explained from the entirety of nature and have as author an extramundane cause <*causam extra mundanam*>, and because the natural order is interrupted here, only the author, namely God, can do that. – The strict miracles <*miracula rigorosa*> are again either occasioned <*occasionalia*> or preestablished <*praestabilita*>; the former is that which God effects immediately <*immediate*> at each occasion and thereby interrupts the natural order. This is the proper miracle. (2) Preestablished miracle <*miraculum praestabilitum*> is what God effects mediately <*mediate*> through natural causes, but which is used by God for special purposes, or what God already determined from the beginning and whose execution requires natural causes. This is also called an effect of nature, but it is just as much a miracle as the occasional one. For it does have as a proximate cause a natural cause, but this lies not in the laws of nature, but rather in the prior determination of God who wanted to effect it just at that time and under those circumstances. An occasioned miracle <*miraculum occasionale*> is also called material, and a preestablished <*praestabilitum*>, formal. (A material miracle <*miraculum materiale*> is where cause and causality of the miracles are outside of the world, or where God produces something new by his sheer power. Formal <*Formale*> – where the immediate <*immediate*> cause does lie in nature, but the causality of it is in God. Both are alike miracles, for that depends merely on the form; the form gives being to a thing <*forma dat esse rei*>.) One explains pre-established miracles <*miracula praestabilita*> as

29:870

[r] Lehmann misreads *schlaffen* as *schaffen* (provide)(870₃).

miracles of nature, for one says: God still effects them according to nature, although not according to general laws, but still to special ones. With these one must, however, again assume a special divine direction, and thus this is the emanation of God. It is just as unnatural as the occasioned. So, e.g., Whiston believes to be able to explain the biblical flood naturally when he assumes that a comet had come, had shaken off its watery tail and thereby it happened.[165] After this it then drew the water back to itself. But that is still a miracle. For it is still no law of nature that a comet should have flooded over the earth just then, and for the reason that its inhabitants were godless. (Teichmayer[166] also believed himself to have discovered something great when he showed that if a cloud of ice came before the sun, its shadow would then retreat so far, and thus the miracle with Ahaz's sundial would be easily explained.)[167] The pre-established miracles <*miracula praestabilita*> are yet greater miracles, for they are thought up even more artificially. But one would gladly make all the miracles preestablished ones because this way one pays a compliment to one's own reason for being able to devise it so artfully.)' Meanwhile one still believes to find more of reason in the explanation of a miracle as a preestablished miracle <*miraculum praestabilitum*>. It is not that we do not believe in the possibility of a miracle in general, but rather that with the supposition of a miracle which is occasioned, all of our understanding in explaining it must cease. And if one thinks that God has previously determined these miracles, that they should have happened through usual natural causes, then one judges of God in terms of human senses <*anthropopathisch*>,' for just as it costs human beings more trouble to do something little by little than all at once, so one believes that it costs God more trouble to do miracles with each occasion than if he had already arranged it thus at creation.

29:871

However it is still always good when one attempts to explain miracles naturally – at least better than when one attempts to make something a miracle. Now it is asked: how are miracles at all possible? Indeed, the effect testifies to the cause <*effectus testatur de causa*>. Now since an extramundane cause <*causa extramundana*> is the cause of the order of nature, it can also suspend the order. No world can be thought without deficiencies, without certain negations and limitations, and thus to make up the defect of nature, miracles are possible in the best world also, and even probable according to the concept of God's goodness and truth. But [it]ᴸ is still asked: how often" is reason authorized to assume miracles? For in general we must admit that miracles are possible, but with particular

---

' This closing parenthesis is without a mate (871₁₁).
' We follow Lehmann in reading *anthropoapatios* (written with Greek letters in the ms) as *anthropopathisch* (871₁₉). Lehmann does not note that it is written in Greek.
" Lehmann misreads *oft* as a second *ist* (is) and then omits it (871₃₂).

cases we must always resist assuming them since they oppose the subjective maxims of our reason, which command assuming only that which takes place with a use of reason.)^v (1) Every miracle presupposes the order of nature. For if this were not, there would not be any miracle. Everything

29:872 would be a miracle. But since this is not so, we see that miracles are merely an exception from the order of nature. But exceptions cannot be frequent, otherwise all rules and their certainty cease. Thus miracles also cannot be frequent. Even the concept of the word distinguishes it from the everyday. (2) If we view nature as a cause of things existing for itself, and thus God not as creator but rather as their architect and ruler, then we could assume more frequent miracles. For since matter then would not have arisen from God, it could also have many deficiencies, which could be improved only little by little. But since God is creator of the world, he will likely have created it as unimprovable. Thus in such a world miracles can occur exceedingly seldom. It is thus also false if one says that whoever disavows miracles recognizes nature as a cause existing for itself. Quite the opposite occurs here. For he does this simply because he represents God as the creator of the world, and not merely as its architect. But since he represents God as the cause of the order of nature, then he also believes on this account that all events in the world arise from God. He thus assumes God only as mediate cause <*causa mediata*> of all events; on the other hand, whoever affirms miracles views God thereby as immediate cause <*causa immediata*>. Whoever views nature as a cause independent from God can just for this reason^w rather believe in miracles, because he imagines and can imagine nature and God as from time to time coming into collision, and God, because he is more powerful than it, making exceptions to its rules. – Indeed, he can then wish for miracles because he cannot expect from a blindly running nature that it would properly attain perfection. Again, he who assumes miracles everywhere, because he believes thereby to glorify God's^x power, does exactly the opposite. For he maintains with that the incompleteness and inadequacy of the natural order, whose deficiencies will be corrected by miracles. But since^y the natural order is God's work, he says thereby that God made an imperfect work, and with this God's wisdom and omnipotence suffer considerably. From all that has been cited we see that miracles, if they are at all in the world, must come to pass only exceedingly seldom. Now we also want to see by which grounds our reason can then be moved to assume miracles.

29:873 (If the cause of an event is not met in nature, then there is a gap <*hiatus*>.

---

^{v} This closing parenthesis is without a mate (871$_{37}$).

^{w} Lehmann misreads *deswegen* as *destoweniger* (872$_{24}$).

^{x} Lehmann misreads *Gottes* as *Gotter* (872$_{30}$).

^{y} We follow Lehmann in changing *das* to *da* (872$_{33}$). Lehmann misreads *das* as *dass* at Ak. 29: 1168.

The consequences of what arises from that have no connection with what preceded; but in order to know this, I must be acquainted with all causes in the world in order to know that this is not in the world. Each object which is connected with others is experience. Miracles are spoken of as objects of experience. The cognition of miracles does not rest on mere perception. Miracles presuppose nature and are mere exceptions to it, thus must not be frequent, otherwise they suspend the order of nature and would not be miracles.) Historical testimonies cannot prove them, rather moral ones must be added as well. Thus in order to demonstrate the believability of a miracle one must presuppose a natural order of the human will, that it is impossible to lie. But this comes to nothing. For here I must believe that something is contrary to the order of nature on account of a testimonial that follows the order of nature. But cannot the moral order of nature be just as easily suspended? Can a human being not lie, and is pious fraud <*pia fraus*> so unheard of? Further, it is also no miracle to deceive oneself. For it requires nearly another miracle to distinguish events of nature from miracles and to know in each case what a miracle is. Historical and moral testimonies can thus still not convince us of the existence of miracles. This must thus yet be added, that reason comprehends there to be an event which is indispensable to the perfection of the world and yet is impossible according to the order of nature. But this event cannot add anything to the perfection of nature for this was made unimprovable by God; rather, it can contribute merely to the promotion of our moral world. This does not at all depend upon the order of nature. Thus, when miracles happen confirming a doctrine which contributes toward our moral perfection, then they are believable. For we comprehend at once that God could not put them in nature at the beginning of the world and yet necessarily had to do them.

Now that is the only case where we can assume miracles and which is not contrary to our reason and the wisdom of God. For the small loss which is brought about by the interruption of the natural order is seen here to be richly compensated by the great advantage that humanity has from it. Miracles would then also be possible if the hypothesis were true   29:874
that the highest perfection would be attained if human beings were destined to a certain community with the highest being. –

(2) Comparative miracles <*miracula comparativa*>. These are events which supposedly happened from higher beings or unknown powers of nature. But there is no such thing. For if I do not recognize the cause then I also can conclude nothing from it. But the unfamiliarity of not merely the cause, but rather also of its causal law belongs to a comparative miracle <*miraculo comparativo*>. Natural causes whose causal law is indeed known, if not also the causes, are not comparative miracles <*miracula comparativa*>, and that is the case with hidden qualities <*qualitatibus occultis*>. They are indeed unknown, but not their causal laws; thus their

effects are also not comparative miracles <*miracula comparativa*>. With higher beings, on the other hand, to whom we ascribe comparative miracles <*miracula comparativa*>, e.g., with devils, we are acquainted neither with them nor with their causal laws. But then it is entirely contrary to reason to assume them as cause of many events. For since we do not know how to offer any rules of their effects, we of course cannot determine what arises from them or not. Thus we assume them merely arbitrarily. To believe in comparative miracles <*miracula comparativa*> would be all right in word but not in heart. Many human beings believe everything that they do not comprehend; they acknowledge the supernatural at once because they do not want to use their reason. But whoever believes in the natural can sooner expect the supernatural from God than can the opponent. But human beings who love the supernatural so much also have a special reason. They do it namely from pride. For there are two paths to arrogance: either to raise oneself over others, or to pull others down to oneself. The latter is the easiest. Now since these people do not want to employ reason so much, or do not even have it to comprehend the natural causes of such events, they thus envy those others and want to make them into the blockheads that they themselves are. Therefore they attempt to offer them in a hidden pious language belief in the supernatural. Yet how is it that everywhere only ancient miracles are mentioned rather than current ones? Not because now no more miracles are necessary anymore, for one can never prove that, but rather because: the ancient miracles and their consequences have already been brought under certain rules. With new miracles, however, we do not know the consequences that can arise from them. They could enter into our rational morality and overturn everything, and for that reason we do not accept them at once.

29:875

On psychology[z]

INTRODUCTION

All cognition of things is twofold. Either they can be given through experience or not. Both kinds of cognition belong to pure metaphysics or transcendental[a] philosophy. Transcendental philosophy should be simply ontology, but the cognitions in this are twofold, as we have already indicated. The objects of ontology can be given in experience and are cognitions of the understanding. But there are also cognitions of reason, which cannot be given in experience. These arise from the cognitions of the understanding, but reason extends them so that they never can be given in experience. It does this by giving them absolute totality. There are two such ideas of reason: (1) the absolute totality of many things, i.e., the absolute cosmos, (2) the [absolute totality][L] of one thing, i.e., the most real being <*ens realissimum*>. Now these are treated in cosmology and theology, therefore these actually should belong to ontology, and these three: ontology, cosmology, and theology, constitute pure metaphysics <*metaphysicam puram*>. In pure metaphysics <*metaphysica pura*> there occur the intuitions of sensibility as space and time, the categories of the understanding, and the ideas of reason. The second part of metaphysics is applied metaphysics <*metaphysica applicata*>, whose objects are in experience, but which still rest on *a priori* principles. That is the metaphysics of nature, and indeed (1) of bodily nature or objects of outer sense, that is general physics <*physica generalis*>, and (2) thinking nature, or of the objects of inner[b] sense, i.e., rational psychology <*psychologia rationalis*>. Both constitute applied metaphysics <*metaphysicam applicatam*>. General physics <*physica generalis*> occurs in cosmology, but rational psychology <*psychologia rationalis*> will follow.

Both of these sciences are opposed to empirical physics and psychology, which obtain their principles merely from experience, and not *a priori*. But on that account these do not at all belong in metaphysics. Empirical physics also constitutes a separate science; empirical psychol-

28:876

---

[z] We have deleted, for the sake of uniformity, the words "Third Part."

[a] Ms reads: *trscdt* (875₉). This is Mrongovius's normal abbreviation for *transcendent*. *Transcendental* is normally abbreviated *trscdtal*.

[b] We follow Lehmann in changing *äussern* (outer) to *innern* (875₃₁).

ogy is not yet so complete that it could furnish a separate science, since work on it has begun only recently. Because one knew of no other science with which it could be paired, that is why it is joined to rational psychology <*psychologia rationalis*> as a stranger and guest, since it is still most closely related to this. We are guided by the author, and thus want to consider empirical psychology first.

First section
On empirical psychology

FIRST CHAPTER
ON THE EXISTENCE OF THE SOUL[168]

The soul is the object of inner sense. – Thus whoever rejects it, also rejects inner sense. (Soul is called soul <*pneuma*>,[*c*] but that means a wholly free and pure spirit, actually it is more commonly called mind <*psyche*>, which means butterfly <*papillon; G: Schmetterling*>, and is quite fitting since it furnishes an excellent symbol of its unloading of the burden of the body, which perishes in dying, and the transition into a better life. [*d*]The word soul actually means the interior of a thing, e.g., with a feather, cannon).[169] My thoughts are not an object of the outer senses for they of course have no figure. Of myself I have the body as an object of the outer senses. But this is to be distinguished from the soul. Its determinations are different, for the form of its intuition is different. The form of intuition with bodies is space, with the soul time, for thoughts are not in space.

Here we consider the soul merely as the object of inner sense, and that rests on our own experience which no one can deny. Furthermore, we are not worrying here about the question whether the soul [is][L] material or not, because we cannot prove this from experience, and thus it belongs in rational psychology <*psychologia rationalis*>. The soul is merely our I, not the body, but body and soul together, as human consciousness, are also
29:877 called I. In empirical psychology we consider our I as soul and as human being. But we consider the body, on the one hand, as an organ of the soul which depends on the soul, but on the other hand as a lodging, since the soul also often depends on it. A short anthropology is thus presented in empirical psychology. We suppose it an indubitable experience that the soul exists. But Descartes, and in a similar way the author, attempt to bring this out only through an inference. The former says: I think therefore I am <*cogito ergo sum*>. But that is unnecessary, for I think <*cogito*>

[*c*] *pneuma* (876₁₆) and *psyche* (876₁₈, below) are written with Greek letters in the ms.
[*d*] An opening parenthesis added by Lehmann has been removed (876₂₁); he claims that one is missing, but in fact the opening parenthesis is printed at 876₁₆.

or I am a thinking [being] <*sum cogitans*> is the same.[170] Descartes even said that I am immediately <*immediate*> conscious of myself as an actuality as an object of inner sense.[171] But of the actuality of the objects of the outer senses, e.g., of my body, I can become conscious only mediately <*mediate*> through an inference, and yet here he infers the existence of the soul and thus sins against his own rule. That I exist as a human being is already an inference, and indeed an inference that provides no mathematical certainty, for the idealist denies the existence of bodies. Empirical psychology divides into two main parts:[172] namely, (1) into the consideration of the soul in itself – (2) [into the consideration]ᴸ of the community of the soul with the body. The powers of the human soul divide into three major classes: (1) the cognitive faculty, (2) pleasure or displeasure, (3) the faculty of desire. Pleasure precedes the faculty of desire, and the cognitive faculty precedes pleasure. Just as the cognitive faculty is diverse, both of the following are likewise diverse.[e] There is a higher and a lower cognitive faculty. The former is understanding, the latter sensibility. So there is also a rational and sensible feeling of pleasure or displeasure (and so is it also with the faculty of desire).[f] The subject itself is passive through the sensible cognitive faculty, and therefore it is said to have receptivity; it is self-active through the higher [faculty], and therefore it has spontaneity. These two faculties are thus differentiated by the manner in which the subject is thereby conditioned.

We have pleasure or displeasure without desiring or abhorring, e.g., if we see a beautiful area, then it enchants us, but we will not on that account wish at once to possess it. Pleasure or displeasure is thus something entirely different from the faculty of desire.[173] But on the other hand we can desire or abhor nothing which is not based on pleasure or displeasure. For that which gives me no pleasure, I also do not want. Thus pleasure or displeasure precedes desire or abhorrence. But still I must first cognize what I desire, likewise with what gives me pleasure or displeasure; accordingly, both are based on the cognitive faculty. There are also many representations which are connected with neither pleasure nor displeasure, and thus the cognitive faculty is wholly distinct from the feeling of pleasure or displeasure. Taken together, these three major powers of the soul constitute its life.

29:878

(Consciousness is the principle of the possibility of the understanding, but not of sensibility. Consciousness with the power of choice is attentiveness – the repetition of that is abstraction. The self underlies consciousness and is what is peculiar to spirit. But we can consider this self in three ways: I think as intelligence, i.e., the subject of thinking is intelligence. I think as subject which has sensibility, and am soul. I think as intelligence

---

[e] A misprinted repeat at 877_{25-6} has been removed.
[f] We follow Lehmann in adding a closing parenthesis here (877_{20}).

and soul, and am a human being. A body which is animated only by a soul, and not by intelligence, is an animal. The faculty for grasping the thought: I am, belongs solely to the intelligence. This I remains [even] when everything has changed, when bodies and principles have changed. Now what the identity of its self consists in is difficult to know; everything is related to this, everything can change, only consciousness and apperception, or the faculty for referring representations to one's self, remain. This apperception provides representations in certain degrees distinct, in lesser degrees obscure. These thus differ by degree, not kind. But clarity in intuition is quite different from clarity in the concept. The former is aesthetic clarity, the latter logical. Abstraction is the actualization of attention, whereby only a single representation is made clear and all the remaining are obscured. Attention does not stop with abstraction, but rather it is only directed from one or several objects to one, and all the remaining representations obscured[g] and the one clear.)

The first and major representation is that of the I or the consciousness of my self, apperception (as Prof. Kant calls it in his *Critique*).

29:879 Now this belongs to the human soul alone, and distinguishes it from all animals. An animal has no apperception, and therefore it is also incapable of any moral principles, of the use of understanding and reason, as will be shown further after this. The body of mine is my body because its alterations are mine. For only through it can I receive representations of outer things and through them my body is affected.[174] A being that is merely an object of inner sense cannot know its relation to things that are objects of outer sense. Wherever my body is, there is my thinking I as well, for only through it can I know the position of my self. But I myself do not occupy any particular space in the body since I cannot be intuited according to the form of space. The body determines only my relation of place with respect to other things (namely that I am in it), but not with respect to myself and where I am in it. Our representations are either obscure or clear, etc. Obscure representations are those of which I am not immediately conscious, but nevertheless can become conscious through inferences.

On the other hand, Locke makes the objection: I am not conscious of obscure representations. Whence does one know then that I have obscure representations? Not to be conscious of something and yet to know it, is a contradiction in the predicate <*contradictio in adjecto*> – but that is mere chicanery.[175]

Obviously we do not know it immediately <*immediate*>, but we do through inferences, e.g., when we observe it with the naked eye, we are not conscious to ourselves that the Milky Way consists of sheer small stars, but through a telescope we see that. Now we infer that since we have seen the entire Milky Way, we must also have seen all the individual stars.

[g] A period added by Lehmann has been removed (878₃₅).

For were that not so, we would have seen nothing. But what we have seen we must also have represented to ourselves. Since we know nothing of these representations, they must have been obscure. Thus we have obscure representations, and these indeed in such a great multitude that their number far exceeds that of our clear representations. It is as if our soul were a map on which just a few places were illuminated. Should all of our obscure representations become clear at once we would be stunned by the multitude. We would see ourselves as though transferred into another world. The obscure representations constitute the depth of the soul and their multitude is the field of the obscure representations. This designa- 29:880 tion is drawn from analogy (with a map).

SECOND CHAPTER
ON THE LOWER COGNITIVE FACULTY

All of our cognitions, pleasure, etc., and desires are either sensuous or intellectual. So there are also sensible and intellectual representations.

According to the author they are distinguished merely by logical form,[176] but this is false. In this the author, along with Wolff and Leibniz, differ from all philosophers and cause great confusion. They distinguish them merely with respect to distinctness and indistinctness. But that is not an essential difference. For intellectual cognitions can also be obscure or indistinct, and sensible cognitions can again be just as distinct; the former, on that account, still remain intellectual and the latter sensuous, e.g., the concept of justice and injustice is obscure and yet intellectual, while the concept of tones is quite distinct and yet sensible. (Distinct cognition is not a cognition different in kind <in specie>, but rather it rests simply on the relation of consciousness to cognition.) Therefore the cause of its difference must lie in its different origin. Sensible representations are representations according to the manner in which I am affected by things; intellectual representations are ones that are independent of that. Cognition that rests on receptivity is sensible, that which [rests]L on spontaneity is intellectual. Through sensibility I cognize things as they are for *us*; but through understanding, as they are in themselves. For all objects of our senses are mere appearances. Sensibility is the material in all of our cognitions. (It is the faculty of intuition, and the science of that is aesthetics.)[177] Everything that we represent to ourselves comes from the senses. For only through them can we intuit things. If we had intellectual intuitions, then our understanding would have to be creative and produce the things themselves. Since that is not so, the things must produce the representations in us, and this through sensible intuition. Understanding thus adds nothing but the form to experience. In cognition sensibility provides the sensation. In pleasure or displea- 29:881 sure, the gratification. In the faculty of desire, the incentives.

The power to produce sensible representations is the sensible faculty of cognition, and the power to produce intellectual ones is the intellectual faculty of cognition. The former is called the lower, the latter the higher faculty of cognition.

The sensible faculty of cognition can be classified (A)[h] with respect to time, since it is (α) the faculty of intuition of the present or the senses, sensation <*sensatio*>, (B) of the past or reproduction, and (C) of the future or anticipation <*praevision*>[178] (reproduction, or reproductive power of imagination connected with consciousness, is memory <*memoria*>).[i][179]

Time and space are conditions of sensible representations, all of which rest on the faculty of intuition. The faculty of intuition, insofar as it begins from the presence of the object, is sense; insofar as it is without object, but yet is in respect to time, is power of imagination; and without any relation of the object to time, the fictive faculty. These three faculties constitute the intuition of objects.

(B) With respect to the production of representations, the cognitive faculty is (a) the faculty of comparing <*facultas comparandi*>.[180] To this belongs wit as the faculty whereby we find similarity, and the power of judgment[181] [as the faculty][L] whereby we find difference in things. (b) The fictive faculty <*facultas fingendi*>[182] or the faculty of generating new representations, i.e., productive power of imagination. (c) The faculty of signifying <*facultas signandi*>, the faculty of connecting representations with a subject, or [the faculty][L] of characterization <*vel* [*facultas*][L] *characteristica*>,[183] or the faculty of generating representations by certain others as means, or the faculty of producing vicarious or subsidiary representations <*repraesentationes vicarias . . . subsidiarias*>, which have no validity in themselves, but which yet serve to produce in us other representations. E.g., the word Rome produces the representation of a city in Italy. Language also rests on this. The sensible cognitive faculty rests on the manner that we [are][L] affected by things – therefore receptivity, or a passive property for being determined by other things – ; the intellectual cognitive faculty rests on spontaneity, or the faculty for determining oneself, for it is independent of sensation. Understanding belongs to spontaneity, thus to the higher cognitive faculty. But the feeling of pleasure or displeasure is part spontaneity, part receptivity.

29:882

THIRD CHAPTER
ON SENSE

A. Sense (sensation <*sensatio*>)[184] is twofold: (1) inner and (2) outer sense. The faculty of inner intuition is inner sense. Inner sense is the

---

[h] The confusing section markings here (A, α, B, C) and in the next paragraph (B, a, b, c) are left as in the ms (881$_{7-24}$).
[i] A paragraph break omitted by Lehmann without note has been replaced (881$_{12}$).

consciousness of our representations themselves. (Apperception is the ground of inner sense.) It has the soul as its object. If the soul is conscious of itself to itself, without being conscious of its state, that is apperception. If it is also conscious of its state, then it is sensation or perception. Outer sense is classified (1) into organ senses, which limit themselves to certain parts, of which, as is known, there are five, and (2) into the vital sense, or the sense for sensing something without a special organ. This is wherever there is life, and since life is in the nervous system, this is particularly in the outer ends of the nerves. This is found in a certain mild well-being, in shuddering, loathing, etc. It is the sixth sense of the French, namely the sensation of lust in sexual relations. The vital sense can also be called vague sense <*sensus vagus*> and the others fixed <*fixus*>. – All organ senses have something subjective and objective, but some are more subjective than objective, and vice versa. That is: with some we represent more alterations of the subject than of the object, and vice versa.[j] (Other creatures can have more or fewer organ senses and [this][L] is known of some animals. So, e.g., the turtles that swim at a certain season from the Yucatan island three hundred miles to Cayman Island must have a special sense for that;[185] we may also possess still more senses, but these we count as feeling.) Smell and taste are more subjective. For if one merely smells or tastes, one can not yet distinguish one thing from another. I cannot know color, shape, etc. Therefore these also affect us most. We can fall into a swoon from strong odors, and from foul taste nausea can be aroused and thereby set the entire body into convulsions. Feeling, seeing, and hearing are more objective than subjective. One cannot doubt with feeling, but then one connects it with inner sensation, and that is the vital sense, which certainly refers more to the subjective than the objective. But here the discussion is of outer feeling, or of the sensation of things through touching. This consists predominantly in the fingers. Through this I can determine the figure, hardness, and softness of a thing. It is the basis of all other senses. The congenitally blind can distinguish even colors through feeling,[186] and when they become sighted, at first this sight still is of no use to them: sight has even more objectivity in itself. If I look about myself, I do not feel what is transpiring in my eyes, for it is so weak that one does not always notice it. Hearing is more objective than subjective. For if I hear speech, I feel no striking and pushing of the air on my eardrum. Unless someone really shrieks; yes, that hurts one's ears. Now the question is whether there can be still more senses. O yes,[k] for how many fine matters might there be which we do not perceive for want of an organ, e.g., magnetic matter. It is believed that animals have certain senses of which we have no concept, and that is entirely possible, e.g., when the

29:883

---

[j] We are adding a period and capital here (882_{21}).
[k] Lehmann misreads *O ja* as (*Ja* (883_{10}).

wild geese travel in summer to cold lands, they move in the darkest night and yet in the straightest line to the north. Some senses have a large sphere in which they can perceive things. Feeling and taste have the narrowest sphere, but smell one still wider, e.g., the eagle smells carrion from up to a mile away. Hearing has a still wider and sight the widest. – It is worthy of wonder that we can even see stars, the closest of which are up to 200,000 times more distant than the sun. That is also in part because air is only a fine matter through which light, as one still finer, can easily pass. Now we come to the fourth chapter on the[l]

B. reproductive power of the soul, or imagination.[187] This is the faculty for representing past states to oneself. We become conscious of our past representations, and that indeed according to the laws of association <*association; G: Vergesellschaftung*> as associated ideas reproduce each other <*ideae sociae sese invicem reproducunt*>.

The faculty of imagination <*facultas imaginationis*> is reproductive <*reproductiva*> with respect to past time, anticipating <*praevidendi*> with respect to future, and productive <*productiva*> with respect to no time. The first has the law of the association of related ideas <*lex associationis idearum sociarum*>, through which ideas which were connected with one another follow each other again as well, the second the law of expectation of similar outcomes <*lex expectationis casuum similium*>,[188] the third the law of compatibles <*lex sociabilium*>, that one must make sense of what fits together.

The faculty of imagining <*facultas imaginandi*> can be classified (a) into the faculty of anticipating <*facultas praevidendi*> or the fictive [faculty] <*fingendi*>, when my soul produces new representations through the power of imagination and (b) into the faculty of reproducing <*facultas reproducendi*>, when it merely renews those it had. The reproductive power of imagination refers either to inner or outer sense. Connected with it is:

C. The faculty of anticipation <*facultas praevisionis*>, when I infer to my future state (*[m]*The faculty of anticipation <*facultas praevisionis*> or anticipatory power of imagination rests on the reproductive. E.g., if a bell sounds, then it occurs to me that it is time to eat; that is the reproductive power of imagination. But at the same time I infer from this that when the bell is sounded, a dinner follows. Anticipatory power of imagination with consciousness is prediction <*praesagition*>, without this it is presentiment <*praesensio*>.), and I infer the future when there has already been a similar case upon which something followed, and believe thereby that this case will also have a similar consequence. It is thus merely an application to future time of the law of the reproductive power of imagination. All three of these

29:884

---

[l] A blank line added by Lehmann has been removed (883_{25}).
[m] We are adding a capital here and a period at the closing parenthesis ($884_{6, 12}$).

cognitive faculties can be accompanied by apperception or not. When they are, then they belong only to human beings, when not – then animals also have them. We ought, therefore, to have two different names for these, but for this [faculty] there is only one, namely, the reproductive power of imagination; for this is called memory when accompanied by apperception. Now we come to the second difference of the sensible cognitive powers, namely,[n] (II) with respect to their production, and indeed (A) to the faculty of comparing <*facultas comparandi*>. This is entirely different from the faculty of conjoining or composing <*facultas coniungendi seu componendi*>.[189] For in comparison I do not set concepts together, but rather hold them only against one another in order to produce new representations. Here we look to sameness <*identitatem*> and diversity <*diversitatem*>. The faculty for recognizing sameness <*facultas ad cognoscendum identitatem*> is wit <*ingenium*>; but acumen <*acumen*> [is] for recognizing diversity <*ad cognoscendum diversitatem*>.[190] The use of wit <*ingenium*> is positive, but that of acumen <*acumens*> negative. The latter protects us from errors, for it shows us not to accept things as the same which are not. But it does not have the pleasant and entertaining quality of the wit <*ingenii*>.

CHAPTER SEVEN
ON THE FICTIVE FACULTY

The fictive faculty <*facultas fingendi*> is the faculty for producing representations of things that we have never seen. This is either <*aut*> imagination or fantasy. Imagination is when *we* play with the power of imagination, and fabricate something for certain purposes and ends. Fantasy is when the power of imagination plays with *us*. The former is voluntary, for we can cancel and direct it as we please, but the latter is involuntary. Each fabrication must occur according to the analogy of experience, otherwise it is unbridled <*effrenis*>, unruly fantasy. We can therefore fabricate nothing materially <*materialiter*>, but rather only formally <*formaliter*>. If the fabrication is according to the analogy of experience, then it is disciplined fantasy <*phantasia subacta*>.[191] If it is involuntary, then it is specifically called unbridled fantasy <*phantasia effrenis*>.[o] Hypochondriacal people commonly have this; whoever has it is called a fantasizer. (The feeble imagination is just like the donkey in England, with which one still makes fun at the end of the race. Namely, when the rider is almost to the finish line he spurs the donkey and, since it cannot tolerate this, it comes to a sudden standstill. Likewise with the over-spurred power of

29:885

---

[n] A paragraph break added by Lehmann has been removed (884_{23}).
[o] In his *Metaphysica*, §571, Baumgarten translates *phantasia subacta* as *wohlgeordnete Einbildungskraft* (well-ordered power of imagination) and *phantasia effrenis* as *ausschweifende Einbildungskraft* (unbridled power of imagination).

imagination. If unruliness and unbridledness are united with the power of imagination, there arises what is called *frenzy*. This is occasionally attributed to studying too much, but from that nothing will come if one did not already have it, or at least was disposed toward it when one came to study. Insanity consists in this, when we take as actual the images of the power of imagination, and madness when one passes wholly perverse judgments.[p][192] The criterion of being disturbed is when one is incapable of comparing one's judgment with that of others and never even asks about this. Another phenomenon of the power of imagination is the dream. It arises quite naturally. For since the power of imagination is constantly active, and in sleep the effects of the understanding stop, this remains and thereby receives a free rein, and makes for us representations of things in place of the understanding – thus it also occurs that these appear necessary to us. It is so as with the moon.)[193] This productive power of imagination expresses itself predominantly in dreaming.[194] It is a series of fabrications, but these are involuntary. In waking we live in a communal world, but when dreaming in our own. – It is quite similar to the fictive power when awake, except with the difference that in dreaming the productive power of imagination is involuntary, without order and purpose. But when awake I can generally give any manner of direction and order to my

29:886   fantasy, and always be able to call myself back if I so prefer. When awake fantasy is indeed on occasion also involuntary, but the ideas are still not as clear as in a dream, because the impressions of the senses hinder us here, while there all senses rest, and the productive power of imagination alone rules the field. For a dream suspends all consciousness of our state. Therefore the peculiarity also arises that we represent past time to ourselves without knowing that it is past. Here we have, so to speak, merely opened a drawer of the reproductive power of imagination, in which we rove about without being conscious of our present state.

Dreaming nevertheless has its uses, like everything in the world. For if the mind is not always in consciousness, then it appears that the body is not agitated enough. It would be quite harmful to our body should it be affected neither internally nor, because it is asleep, externally. In dreaming the mind is moved, and by it likewise the body, especially by the affections. The soul thereby works on the sources of life, and that is quite healthy and necessary for us, for we cannot replace the sources of life in consciousness and activity by any bodily consciousness, but rather can merely promote the circulation of the blood. The soul works especially on the respiratory system, and without this we certainly cannot endure. E.g., if someone has exercised well and thereupon goes to sleep, he generally sleeps quite soundly. Since he then also dreams nothing, he loses his breath, and then he normally receives frightening dreams from

[p] *Wahnsinn* (illusory sense, insanity); *Wahnwitz* (illusory wit, madness) (885_{21-2}).

which he again awakes. One is also much more awake in the morning after dreaming than otherwise, because this way life*q* is as it were strengthened. What, then, is sleep?[195] It is a phenomenon which belongs to the physiology or to the science of the human body, and as a consequence does not admit of being determined metaphysically. – Whoever is healthy, also sleeps well.

If one compares the productive power of imagination with the signifying power <*vi signatrici*>, there arises the art of interpreting dreams. Dreams are taken as signs of future events,[196] and this partly because they so often have little in common with experience, and because they represent the events as so lively that one believes these have really happened. These prognostic signs <*signa prognostica*> can be (1) natural and (2) voluntary. Natural signs <*signa naturalia*> are representations of their effects. These by all means take place, and in this light dreams can always be prognostic signs <*signa prognostica*>, e.g., if gall   29:887 flows in a human being at night, he receives frightful and vexatious dreams; these are the cause that he arises in the morning with melancholy, and because of his ill-humored and morose state of mind finds everywhere ill-humor, annoyance, and quarrels. Thus gall is the actual, but dreams only the mediate, cause of the ill-humor of the following day.

(2) Arbitrary signs <*signa arbitraria*>. That is mere superstition, for I find here not the slightest connection. Indeed, I cannot at all know what they mean. The use of the lower cognitive powers depends on the higher, and indeed the higher govern over the lower by means of the imagination. It is worthy of wonder when the lower cognitive powers do not*r* allow themselves to be ruled by the higher ones. This is the state of the person who cannot abstract or attend to anything. The imagination must rest entirely on our power of choice, and it is constituted like the function of the lungs in breathing, which we have in our control, yet not so that we could entirely dispense with them. We must therefore at times give our imagination a free rein, yet so that we can always govern it and always restrain it. But when it does [not]*s* respect the guidance of the understanding, then it is unbridled <*effrenis*>.

ON THE SIGNIFYING FACULTY

The faculty of characterization <*facultas characteristica*>[197] is the faculty for laying down certain signs in the understanding, or associating represen-

---

q We follow Lehmann in changing an *ist* (before *Leben*) to *das* (886$_{28}$).
r A *nicht* omitted by Lehmann without note has been replaced (887$_{14}$).
s A *nicht* probably follows *respectirt* in the ms, but is obscured in our microfilm (*respectirt* falls at the end of the line in the ms, next to the fold) (887$_{22}$).

tations so that the one is the means of reproducing the others, and is also called the faculty of signifying <*facultas signandi*>. It is mechanical, i.e., without any exertion of power, and also involuntary, e.g., if I say Rome, then the representation of this city immediately springs forth. I may want it or not. This comes from habit. I fabricate signs in order to express thereby that which I think. These are words and are either (a) demonstrative <*demonstrativa*> or representative <*repraesentativa*>, which concern what is at the same time, e.g., the pulse is a sign of health or illness; (b) reminiscent <*rememorativa*>, which relate to the past, e.g., Cicero; (c) prognostic <*prognostica*>, which relate to the future, as e.g., the low flight of swallows is a sign of impending rain.

ON UNDERSTANDING, THE POWER OF JUDGMENT, AND REASON

The higher [faculty]^L has spontaneity in its representations. Consequently, we view ourselves as the compelling cause for it. Thus the will also belongs to the higher cognitive faculty, thus it is its own master, and the inclination to receptivity of the higher [cognitive faculty]^L is in general called understanding. The intellectual cognitive faculty is the faculty for thinking or for making concepts for ourselves. It represents only the object in general, without looking to the manner of its appearance. The latter is discursive, the former intuitive.^{t} Intuition <*intuitus*> is an immediate representation, concept <*conceptus;* G: *Begriff*>, [is representation] mediated by a feature.^{u} (The faculty of the consciousness of the manifold through concepts is, however, an imperfect faculty, and the larger and more perfect the faculty the closer it approaches to intuition. The most perfect understanding would therefore be that which cognizes merely through intuition, but of course not through sensible intuition. This is how we represent to ourselves the divine understanding. Here the question arises whether we can arrive at general representations only through comparison.^{v} But [concerning the claim] that for us general concepts arise in comparison, it is rather the opposite that is correct.^{w} Thus we arrive at, e.g., the concept of a triangle not through comparison; rather, when we see one for the first time we are immediately aware that its magnitude does not restrict us at all from conferring the name triangle on all three-cornered figures which we see in the future.) A concept is the consciousness that the [same] is contained in one representation as in another, or

---

^{t} The text has a more natural sense if "latter" and "former" are reversed here (888_{9-10}).
^{u} We are adding a period and a capital (888_{11}).
^{v} A question mark added by Lehmann has been removed (888_{19}).
^{w} A comma added by Lehmann here has been replaced by a period, and we have inserted a phrase that seems needed to make the passage consistent (888_{20}).

that in multiple representations one and the same features are contained. This thus presupposes consciousness or apperception. Animals indeed compare representations with one another, but they are not conscious of where the harmony or disharmony between them lies. Therefore they also have no concepts, and also no higher cognitive faculty, because the higher cognitive faculty consists of these. This [faculty] is thus differentiated by apperception from the lower cognitive faculty. As animals, we have the latter in common with them, but the former raises us as thinking beings over animals. Whoever can make concepts for himself, thinks. All thinking is threefold:[198] (1) through concepts, and the faculty for this is called understanding. (2) Through composition of two concepts, i.e., through judgments, i.e., the power of judgment. (3) Through derivation of a concept from another by inferences, i.e., reason. Understanding is the faculty for bringing various representations under a rule. It rests on apperception. (It is the faculty for determining the particular by the general. With the higher cognitive power the cognitive faculty is considered not in relation to intuition, but rather to the unity of consciousness. This is the representation of one's representations and therefore is also called apperception. Without the consciousness of the sameness of a representation in many representations, no general rule would be possible.[199] For a rule is a necessary unity of the consciousness of a manifold of representations, relation of the manifold of representations to one consciousness.) But how are concepts possible through apperception? In that I represent to myself the identity of my apperception in many representations. The concept is a common perception <*perceptio communis*>, e.g., the concept of body. This applies to metal, gold, stone, etc. In this I represent to myself a one in a manifold. The logical function of this consists in generality. This is the analytic unity of apperception, and many in one is its synthetic unity. The analytic unity of apperception represents nothing new to us, but rather is merely conscious of the manifold in one representation. The synthetic deals with many, insofar as it is contained in one. As long as the understanding judges according to this it is a pure understanding. The understanding makes rules. From the multiple representations it draws out the general, that which is met in all. It is consequently also called the faculty of rules. Experience presupposes understanding because it is a connection of perceptions according to rules. It has *a posteriori* and *a priori* rules.

29:889

(Without the power of judgment we would not cognize the specific difference <*differentia specifica*>, and without perception the genera.) (Each profession needs the power of judgment, but some more than others, e.g., the physician more than the lawyer. In the latter are many instances where if one does not decide correctly the other still will, but in the former it is not so.) The power of judgment brings objects under rules. Reason applies rules to them, thus is the faculty of acting according to principles. Reason determines the particular from a general rule.[200]

29:890 Principles are the determinations of the particular from the general. The power of judgment sees under which rule each thing stands, and whether this thing is contained under this rule or not. There are persons who [think]^L much abstractly $<in\ abstracto>$ and little concretely $<in\ concreto>$, i.e., they have understanding and no power of judgment, for it must be innate and cannot be learned. For then one would have to give new rules as to how the rules of the understanding should be applied, but one would have to learn again how to apply these new rules, consequently there would have to be new rules again, and it would continue like that without end. Cleverness consists in power of judgment. Therefore many are well educated and yet not clever. Reason infers that^x that which the rule says in general is true also for this or that thing in particular. Understanding draws the general from the particular, namely, from the various things in experience.^{y} Reason draws the particular from the general. One finds these three cognitive powers in the syllogism. The understanding gives the general rule, major premise $<propositio\ major>$. The power of judgment is the subsumption of one concept under others. Reason finally makes the conclusion, for it infers that that which is valid in general is valid also for the subsumed thing. What a cognition of reason cognizes is necessary, but it is very restricted, because it takes nothing from experience. One must attempt to cultivate through practice the power of judgment, and to improve it. Now we come to the second main section of this psychology, namely, to the feeling of pleasure and displeasure.

ON PLEASURE OR DISPLEASURE^z

One cannot define pleasure or displeasure if one does not presuppose the faculty of desire. The cognitive faculty is connected with the faculty of desire by the feeling of pleasure or displeasure. The author calls it pleasure $<voluptas>$ and displeasure $<taedium>$.[201] That is false, for this is true only of sensible satisfaction. – For the understanding can frequently find dissatisfaction with that which best satisfies the senses. This should be named the faculty of satisfaction and dissatisfaction $<facultas\ complacentia \ldots disputlicentia>$.[202] This could be properly called internal sense $<sensum\ internum>$, because it applies to our own state, although no one has yet properly developed the concept of it. The feeling of pleasure is the ability of my power of representation to become determined by a given representation to its maintenance or promotion or avoidance. With dis-

---

^{x} We follow Lehmann in changing *das* to *dass* (890$_{10}$).
^{y} Lehmann misreads *dem besondere nehmlich* as *dem besonderen. Besonderen, nehmlich* (890$_{12}$), and he adds a comma (after *Erfahrung*) that we have replaced with a period (890$_{13}$).
^{z} A *Von* (before *Lust oder Unlust*) omitted by Lehmann without note has been replaced (890$_{24}$); the *Von* was apparently added later, being in a much paler (red?) ink.

pleasure we summon up our entire faculty to prevent a representation   29:891
from penetrating further into the mind. Whatever excites the feeling of
the promotion of life, arouses pleasure. (The faculty of a subject is called
the faculty of desire insofar as through pleasure in an object it is determined to produce this object.) It is striking that our representations can
become the cause of the actuality of objects, e.g., the musician is the cause
of the notes which he produces by his instrument. Pleasure is thus the
consciousness of the agreement of an object with the productive power of
imagination of our soul. This definition will be made still clearer in
knowing the will.[a]

– Our satisfaction or dissatisfaction is either mediate or immediate; the
former is intellectual, the latter sensible. Something pleases me mediately
when it pleases not in itself, but rather only as a means to an immediate
satisfaction. It is no special object of pleasure but rather an object of
reason, which recognizes that I will partake in a pleasure through this,
e.g., I have a mediate satisfaction in money. For it does not please me in
itself,[203] but rather merely because I can procure thousands of gratifications by means of it. This is also an object of reason since I need reason in
order to recognize whether something is good as a means to its end.
Therefore we must have satisfaction from a means simply because of the
end, and if not then we behave foolishly, e.g., whoever finds satisfaction in
money itself without viewing it as a means to an end, and so always keeps
it locked in his chest, is a miser. That in which I have merely mediate
satisfaction is also called useful or beneficial. This is not general, but
rather according to the purpose of each person. To one a thing is useful,
to another that same thing is harmful. But of that nothing can be discussed. The other kind of satisfaction is immediate satisfaction, which
pleases us in itself. Now this is twofold: either subjective or objective.
Subjective, if it rests on the alteration of our state, and thus lies merely in
the subject. This is called the agreeable; it is also called private satisfaction, because it takes place only in relation to the senses of this or that
subject and thus is not general, e.g., warmth, for one person can find quite
agreeable a certain degree of warmth that is insufferable to another, which
arises from the constitution of his life and from his state in general. That   29:892
satisfaction is objective which rests not at all on the subject, but rather
merely on the object, therefore it is a general satisfaction because it must
please all who sense the object. Now this pleases in general either according to laws of sensibility, and then it is beautiful. The beautiful pleases in
the imagination; or according to laws of the understanding and reason,
and then it is good. The good is immediate and mediate. Mediate good is
the useful, e.g., the punishment of evil pleases not in itself, but rather as a
means to the attainment of a good end. Therefore it is useful and good for

---

[a] A paragraph break omitted by Lehmann has been replaced (891_{11}).

us. Much is good mediately, but only morality is immediately good. A human being is not immediately good when acting like a cannibal or slave trader; [but he is good] immediately, when he is moral. For he is himself an end.[b]

The beautiful pleases generally,[204] thus it has general rules, e.g., a person who pleases everyone is beautiful. But if she has a charm merely for this or that subject, then she is merely agreeable. Therefore it happens that we dispute only about the beautiful, but not about the agreeable, because the former rests on general rules, and thus one could rather say: matters of taste leave room for disagreement *<de gusto est disputandum>*. The faculty for judging the beautiful is taste. The faculty for judging the agreeable has no name, and also needs none. Taste judges according to general rules; the agreeable is judged according to its source, sensation. The power of judgment is thus an objective faculty. The general rules of taste hold only for the sensibility of human beings and for beings that have a sensibility the same as theirs. The general rules of the good stretch over all rational beings, even God, for they apply to cognition. With taste, sensibility and understanding are connected in judging. For since it rests on general rules, the understanding must provide these; but it must sense the object through the senses. Whatever pleases in sensation or in the agreeable gratifies; whatever pleases by the sensible power of judging, namely, the beautiful, pleases in the stricter sense. Something pleases me if I am indifferent to its existence, e.g., a beautiful plan can please me even if the thing itself does not yet exist, but I am not indifferent to the existence of the agreeable. If a beautiful area pleases me, it pleases me because I would enjoy it even were it not there, but rather I imagined it only in thoughts. – What gratifies me I either possess, or its existence is not a matter of indifference for me. Every mediate gratification presupposes an immediate one. The beautiful is the generality of the sensible satisfaction or the evaluation of the object according to general satisfaction. Feeling has to do with matter, but taste with the form of the composition of the manifold in sensation. Talent belongs to taste, but not to sensation. The agreeable has more degrees or intensive magnitudes than the beautiful, and the latter again more extensive magnitude than the former. The good has even more extensive magnitude. Because with taste some exceptions still always occur, some fall into the extremity of denying its generality. Beauty is the object of satisfaction in sensible intuition or also, according to the author, phenomenal perfection *<perfectio phaenomenon>*,[205] if one understands by perfection *<perfectio>* the object of sensible satisfaction. The goodness or good constitution of a thing is the object of the satisfaction according to concepts of the understanding. The agreeable gratifies, the disagreeable hurts, [the][L] beautiful satisfies, the bad dissatis-

29:893

---

[b] *selbst Zweck;* translated here as "himself an end," when written as one word is commonly translated as "end in itself." See also 907₇, below.

fies; the good is approved, the evil is disapproved. Sensation belongs to the agreeable (the agreeable pleases on account of the matter); taste [belongs]ᴸ to the beautiful – (the beautiful [pleases]ᴸ on account of the form) and a manner of thinking (sentiment) [belongs] to the good. Virtue is a true inner good, but nothing agreeable. There are intellectual and not sensible judgments with it. But it still has something that comes close to the beautiful. For if one represents an entire realm of the virtuous in thoughts,[206] then the order and regularity of their conduct, which necessarily would have to spring from it, awakens in us a sensible satisfaction.

ON THE FACULTY OF DESIRE

Causality <*causalitas*> is the determination of a cause by which it becomes a cause, or the determination of the relation of a thing as cause to a determined effect. Thus the cause is always to be distinguished from the causality, e.g., a human being is the cause of letters but not by means of his head or feet, etc., but rather by means of his fingers. – The faculty for producing objects by one's representations is the faculty of desire. The faculty of desire rests on the principle: I desire nothing but what pleases, and avoid nothing but what displeases <*nihil appeto nisi quod placet, nihil averto nisi quod displicet*>.[207] But representations cannot be the cause of an object where we have no pleasure or displeasure in it. This is therefore the subjective condition by which alone a representation can become the cause of an object. Therefore desire is also a complex <*complexus*> of the actuality of the object and of the faculty of desire. The faculty for determining one's behavior to conform to the object of the satisfaction. The objective [condition] of desires is the physical faculty for them. But this belongs to the mechanism of nature. But we presuppose it, otherwise our desires would be empty. But here we consider desires in general.ᶜ (Besides the things which are moved by outer causes, there are living things which are moved by inner ones. A being is living if its power of representation can be the ground of the actuality of its objects. Life is thus the causality of a representation with respect to the actuality of its objects. Now this causality of representations with respect to the subject is the feeling of pleasure or displeasure. But with respect to the object [it is] the faculty of desire.)

29:894

Pleasure is the representation of the agreement of an object with the productive power of the soul, and displeasure the opposite. The faculty of desire is the causality of the object which is produced. Accordingly, pleasure is the agreement and displeasure the conflict with our faculty of desire. But now pleasure is also the feeling of the promotion of life, and whence this? – From the following. A thing lives if it has a faculty to move

ᶜ We are adding a period and capital (894₁₃).

itself by choice. Life is thus the faculty for acting according to choice or one's desires. But now this is, practically speaking, the faculty of desire. Since pleasure is thus agreement with the faculty of desire, it is also agreement with life, and displeasure [is] conflict with life. But pleasure and displeasure presuppose sensation. Accordingly I can also say: pleasure and displeasure is a feeling of agreement and conflict or, what is the same, of the promotion or obstruction of life. All desires are always directed to something in the future. All desires are, like pleasure and displeasure, intellectual or sensitive. –

29:895   That which is the cause of the desires is the impelling cause <*causa impulsiva*> or incentive of the soul <*elater animi*>. Now, if they arose from sensibility then they are called stimuli <*stimuli*> and their effect desire aroused by stimuli <*appetitio per stimulos*> or sensible desires. But if they originate from the understanding, then they are called motives <*motiva*>, their effect [is called] desire aroused by motives <*appetitio per motiva*> or intellectual desires.

Stimuli <*stimuli*> originate from the agreeable because this is for the senses and is merely a private judgment. The beautiful and good is intellectual because their judgment is logical, therefore also the source of the motives or motive grounds. Furthermore desires are idle (<*otiosae;* G: *müssige*>) if the objects do not stand within our control. They are also called fantastic and contemplative desires, e.g., if we wish to see a comet this year then we have idle desires, likewise with the readers of novels.[d] (In affection one feeling is stronger than all the others, and likewise in passion one inclination. Consciousness of the agreement of all our inclinations is contentment. Affections destroy the comfort. Passions the ends.) We often desire something before we see whether it is possible for us to obtain it. But why has nature given us this? In order to incite us all the more to activity. For we are thereby impelled to investigate properly whether they stand within our control; but if we find that they do not stand within our control, and we nevertheless harbor the desires, then we behave unnaturally and absurdly. We also have a contemplative satisfaction, for many things happen with which we gratify ourselves without their standing within our control. This is always taking place – but not idle desires. Animals have no idle desires, for even when they apply their powers in vain they still do not know that the thing is not within their control. Idle desires are opposed to practical ones. The latter are desires for such things as stand within our control. If the stimuli <*stimuli*> have become habitual, then they are inclinations and their source is instinct or habit – habitual sensible desires are passions. As desires and affections they concern sensation. There the subject is not capable of comparing the inclination for an object with the sum of all inclinations; here of comparing a

---

[d] We are adding a period and a capital (895_{14}).

sensation with the sum of all. The author explains affection indeterminately by higher degrees of pleasure or displeasure.[208] The harmony of the lower and higher faculty of desire must be negative, namely so that the lower does not lay any obstacle in the way of the higher. Therefore the impelling causes <*causae impulsivae*> to virtue must not be derived from sensible advantages.

29:896

ON THE POWER OF CHOICE

The faculty for desiring practically or faculty of practical desires <*facultas appetitionum practicarum*> is the power of choice <*arbitrium*>.[209] The power of choice <*arbitrium; G: Willkür*> is either sensitive <*sensitivum*>, which represents things to us that are agreeable to the senses, [or][L] intellectual <*intellectuale*> – things of which the understanding approves. But the power of choice <*arbitrium*> is better classified into brute <*brutum*> and free <*liberum*>. Brute <*brutum*> is that which is determined or necessitated by stimuli <*stimulis*>, and free <*liberum*> that which [is][L] determined by motives <*motiva*>; animals have the former, human beings the latter, therefore it is also called human <*humanum*>. A human being can of course be affected by stimuli <*stimulis*>, but not necessitated, for he is independent of the stimuli <*stimulis*>.[210]

ON FREEDOM

The power of free choice <*arbitrium liberum*> is determined by motives <*per motiva*>. Since these originate only in the understanding, they are intellectual impelling causes <*causae impulsivae intellectuales*>. These are the concepts of the good. The power of free choice <*arbitrium liberum*> is will <*voluntas*>. Freedom is thus a faculty for acting according to the concepts of good and evil.[e] (With a pure intelligence, objective necessity is at the same time subjective. So it is with God.) That is its positive concept in the practical sense. Negatively, it is the faculty for choosing at the level of the understanding independently of sensible stimulations; thus are we indeed free from stimuli <*stimulis*>, but not from motives <*motivis*>. This can be called the higher faculty of desire because its rules (the concepts of the good) are general. (What is determined by motives is an end, what precedes decision [is] deliberation. I desire nothing unless under the aspect of the good – and [avoid] nothing unless under the aspect of evil <*nihil appeto nisi sub ratione boni – et nihil nisi sub ratione mali*> is indeed valid as a principle, but is false as a proposition of experience, for under the representation of the agreeable I often signify evil, and under the representation of the disagreeable I disavow the good.)

[e] We are adding a period and a capital (896_{21}).

263

From what do we know that the will is free? – Freedom is not a property that we learn from experience; for we cannot experience anything negative. Indeed we do many actions by which we appear to act contrary to all stimuli <*stimulos*>, but we can not yet infer it from that – for a secret stimulus <*stimulus*> can still have induced us, e.g., when despite torture and all affliction a criminal does not confess, then he acts indeed against all stimuli <*stimulos*>, but still in favor of a stimulus <*stimulus*>, namely the fear of death. Thus the inference that there are no stimuli <*stimulos*> because I notice none can accordingly be very uncertain.

We ourselves are also not immediately conscious of freedom.[211] We are conscious only of the incentives or stimuli <*stimulorum*> which are clear representations. But we can also have obscure representations and stimuli <*stimuli*> for something of which we thus are not conscious.[f] (All of our actions are voluntary actions <*actiones voluntariae*>, but again these are either willing <*libentes*> (actions that happen gladly) if we are conscious of no desire to the contrary, or unwilling <*invitae*> insofar as we are conscious here of one or several grounds to the contrary. The latter are composed out of desire <*appetitio*> and aversion <*aversatio*>, only that the first is stronger. Compulsion <*coactio;* G: *Zwang*> is necessitation of an unwilling action <*necessitatio actionis invitae*>.[212] It [necessitation] is either from oneself <*in se ipsum*> or from another <*ab alio*>. It can be physical or moral. It is physical either through enticements <*illecebras*> or threats <*minas*>. Through enticements <*illecebras*> there is in fact no compulsion, but rather necessitation, e.g., hunger is enticement <*illecebra*> of the thief to steal. Physical compulsion without enticement <*illecebras*>, and threat <*minas*> is extortion <*extorsio*>. Compulsion is not necessitation of the sensitive power of choice <*necessitatio arbitrii sensitivi*>, but rather of the intellectual <*intellectualis*>; for were it necessitation by stimuli <*necessitatio per stimulos*>, then a human being would be an animal. But even with the strongest physical necessitation a human being can outweigh sensitive representations through reason. That is: the will cannot be coerced physically, but it can power itself by willing <*voluntas non potest cogi physice, sed semet ipsam cogere potest volendo*>.[213][g] Thus we can compel others if we represent motives <*motiva*> to them that move them to compel themselves. Obligation is the necessitation of an unwilling but morally good action <*necessitatio actionis invitae moraliter bonae est obligatio*>,[h] that is practical compulsion. Were the practical, or also objective, compulsion in a human being at the same time always subjective, then he would be perfectly free. Moral obligation can be thought only in relation to a sensible power of choice which is affected by

---

[f] We are adding a period and a capital (897_{13}).

[g] *volendo* here (897_{29}), and *invitae* below (897_{31-2}) are very unclear in the ms.

[h] Lehmann misreads *invitae* as *invicem* (897_{31-2}).

stimuli <*stimulos*>. There is therefore no moral obligation with animals, but much necessity. Every created being, however perfect it may be, has moral obligation. For they all have needs which certain stimuli <*stimuli*>   29:898 provide, with which they have to struggle. A human being therefore has not holiness, but virtue. We can, of course, have satisfaction in an object when we lack an incentive of the soul <*elater animi*>; these [stimuli] are thus not the causes of pleasure or displeasure. If satisfaction is connected with my state, then I will not be indifferent to the existence of the object, i.e., I will have interest in it. With virtue, then, we must also have an interest. But the moralists are not in accord with respect to its incentives.

Freedom is a mere idea and to act in conformity with this idea is to be free in the practical sense. Practical necessity is objective and not subjective. Here I must do something; but the natural necessity of stimuli <*stimulos*> says only: it will happen. Practically necessary is that without which our actions do not take place, namely without laws of the understanding and of reason. Freedom is thus practically necessary – thus a human being must act according to an idea of freedom, and he cannot otherwise. But that does not yet prove freedom in the theoretical sense. All the difficulties and contradictions that the concept of freedom has caused thereby fall away. One may prove or also refute freedom in the theoretical sense, as one wants, nevertheless one will still always act according to ideas of freedom. There are many people who do not concede certain propositions in speculation, but still act according to them.

Freedom is merely the capacity for acting according to the intellectual power of choice <*arbitrio intellectuali*>, and not the power of choice <*arbitrium*> itself. The intellectual impelling causes <*causae impulsivae intellectuales*> are either in some respect <*secundum quid*> or without qualification <*simpliciter talis*>. A cause that is impelling in some respect <*causa impulsiva secundum quid*> is when I merely choose a good means for attaining my end which proceeds from a stimulus <*stimulo*>, e.g., when someone writes a book, he commonly claims to be doing it out of love of truth, although he is just as often doing it to earn money. The means that he uses, namely, writing a good book, is good. He must overcome considerable stimuli <*stimulos*>, such as the love of laziness, he can also serve the world, but his intention is still not intellectual, but rather sensible. A future life of comfort was his end; this was thus a cause which is impelling in some respect <*causa impulsiva secundum quid*>. But if someone writes a book simply from a love of truth and allows it to be made public only upon his death, when he cannot hope for any more profit from the world, then his end is good and the intellectual impelling   29:899 cause <*causa impulsiva intellectualis*>. This depends on no other stimuli <*stimulo*>. Morality has such simply intellectual <*simpliciter intellectuale*> laws, and yet freedom must be presupposed with morality. All human beings choose good means, whatever the intention may be. They proceed cleverly because their desires are always going toward something good, but merely as a means to a sensible end, whatever the intention may be. He views the end as agreeable, the means through understanding and reason as good. Here he always acts in some respect <*secundum quid*>.*[i]* The power of choice <*arbitrium*> is purely intellectual if it is without qualification <*simpliciter tale*>. Not the means but rather the ends determine the desires. If reason is what discerns what is really good, or specifies the ends, then it looks after its interest and is the mistress <*domina*>. If it merely devises a good means for the sake of the end that arises from inclination, then it merely looks after the interest of inclination and is the maidservant <*serua*>. Then it is not the incentive but rather inclination. The power of choice which is simply intellectual <*arbitrium simpliciter intellectuale*>*[j]* is also pure <*purum*>, for there only reason takes place. But where reason and sensibility reign, and the latter is the ruler, there is sensitive or impure power of choice <*arbitrium sensitivum . . . impurum*>, for the impelling cause <*causa impulsiva*> lies now in sensibility. And since the end is more than the means, denomination from the more important <*a potiori denominatio*> occurs. Happiness has two meanings: (1) the sum of all agreeable sensations. But this we cannot determine. (2) The gratification of all present inclinations. When the intention of our actions is merely happiness and the satisfaction of all our sensible inclinations, then our power of choice <*arbitrium*> is merely sensitive <*sensitivum*>. It is thus not virtue when we practice good actions on account of certain advantages, e.g., when a citizen does his duty because he fears punishment, but rather when we do the good because we comprehend that it is good and our duty. Here we act intellectually, but there sensibly. Intellectual power of choice <*arbitrium intellectuale*> or [choice] in the narrower sense <*strictius sic dictum*> or pure power of choice <*arbitrium purum*>. So freedom is the faculty for choosing that which is good in itself and not merely good as a means. Thus we are free when we arrange our actions entirely according to the laws of the understanding and of reason, and the more we do this, the freer we are. For even if the will is free from stimuli <*stimulis*>, it can still be not entirely free. For since we desire merely that which pleases us, pleasure is the cause of our desiring. But the cause of the pleasure is either sensibility or understanding. No third thing is possible. Thus if I do not desire something from sensibility, then I must desire it because it pleases my understanding. But should I desire neither according to understanding nor to sensibility, then I would want that which displeases me, I would act without incentive and cause, and that is impossible. Understanding and reason give laws to the will according to which it must conform if it is to be free. But we cannot be determined by

29:900

---

[i] We are changing a comma to a period here (899₉).
[j] Lehmann misreads *simpl* as *simul* (simultaneously) rather than *simpliciter* (simply) (899₁₇).

266

mere representations of reason; it must also give us incentives, and these it also gives us, because our conscience approves or disapproves. For when we follow it, then we can attain a calm conscience and every spiritual happiness. Here it exerts not only legislative power <*vim legislatoriam*>, but also executive <*executivam*>. What follows it is thus not only objectively necessary, but rather subjectively possible as well. A human being is on this account still free, for he can choose between sensibility and understanding, but were he to act according to sensibility, then he would become the same as the animals. But reason raises him above the animals, and the more he acts according to it, the more moral and at the same time freer he becomes.[214] For morality is the science of that which is good, otherwise the concept of freedom would be superfluous, if there were no morality; and then reason would also be superfluous. For it is there only for the sake of the morality of the laws. The field of morality is either affected by inclinations or not. In either case there is a power of free choice <*arbitrium liberum*>. For here we also still have the freedom to act according to the understanding. The intellectual power of choice <*arbitrium intellectuale*> is when we act independently of inclinations, though we still have them. And now we can consider whether we should follow them or not. We are free only in order to follow the laws of morality. For otherwise we would not need reason. So far we have spoken of freedom in the practical sense. But freedom in the transcendental sense is a faculty for determining oneself independently of all remote or natural causes. Here again is an antinomy[k] of reason. For whether I suppose this or the opposite, I lose myself in contradictions. Sensibility is determined by objects; these by laws of nature, and these by God. Therefore God determines our sensibility and we are not transcendentally <*transcendentaliter*> free. But if we suppose that everything happens merely according to necessity, we never arrive at the first, and then we can also ask by what God is determined. But all these speculative considerations of contradictions do not damage the practical concept of freedom. For this concerns not how something happens, but rather that it should happen, and should presupposes freedom. If with the use of our will we have regard only for empirical happiness, then reason determines not by the concept of the highest good, but rather by the concept of the highest comfort. There inclination reigns, determines the end, and reason is the slave which must provide here for the means. But morality says the senses are not supposed to rationalize; reason alone must be lord. For I cannot entirely fulfill my desires, new ones always arise. – But I can reach the highest good.[215] Therefore the concept of an intellectual power of choice <*arbitrii intellectualis*> must necessarily underlie it, and it must itself be important [for][L] every human being.

29:901

---

[k] Lehmann misreads *Antinomie* as *Autonomie* (900_{33}).

ON INDIFFERENCE AND EQUILIBRIUM ^{l}

We are indifferent regarding that for which we have neither agreeable nor disagreeable sensations, thus the same as insensitivity. We are also indifferent when we neither desire nor abhor something. But equal is that which we equally desire and abhor, or for whose realization we have equal grounds and counter-grounds.

One wants to prove, through the faculty for choosing between indifferent things, that freedom is a lawlessness from all incentives. But the freedom of indifference <*libertas indifferentiae*> is a non-thing.[216] For what does not please me I also cannot want, thus I remain in the same state. Equilibrium <*aequilibrium*> or equality is when we equally desire and abhor something: but with human beings this occurs only seldom. We do not find a total equilibrium <*aequilibrium*> even with scales. Equilibrium <*aequilibrium*> can be either (1) equilibrium of stimuli <*aequilibrium stimulorum*>: when the incentives of sensibility are equal on both sides. Here, one says, a human being will still do one of the two and can choose, and thus can act freely. But no, he will rather do neither of them, and refrain from acting. This refraining is also equilibrium, or it still always remains for him to change and to determine himself by reason, e.g., if to do something determinate someone is allowed the power of choice to take either five Reichsthaler [or]^{L} one Friedrichsd'or, he is in a state of equilibrium <*statu aequilibri*> with respect to what he ought to take. But he is not allowed to take either of them if he wants to act uprightly.

29:902

(2) Equilibrium of motives <*aequilibrium motivorum*>. But here complete equality can never take place. Were there complete equality then one could not choose; for when there is no ground, there is also no choice, or one can also refrain from the action. There is no complete equality for even when the objective grounds of both sides are equally strong, special subjective grounds can still be added to one side which give them more weight, e.g., when freedom is given to me to choose one of two wholly equal ducats, then the objective incentives for the two sides would be of equal strength. I would thus reflect a moment as to which I should take until finally a subjective incentive, greed or also impatience from delaying so long, would so stimulate me that I would take as best the first^{m} that caught my eye then, or out of comfort^{n} I would take that which was closest to me. Thus we see that an object must be given priority by a subjective

---

^{l} There is a play on the German in the following paragraphs. The components of *Gleichgültigkeit* (indifference) mean "equal validity," while the components of *Gleichgewicht* (equilibrium) mean "equal weight."
^{m} We follow Lehmann in omitting a *den* (preceding *besten*)(902$_{16}$).
^{n} We follow Lehmann in changing *Unbequemlichkeit* to *Bequemlichkeit* (902$_{17-18}$).

cause, of which there could be countless many, according to the then-current constitution of our mind, and which often remain obscure to us and tend to work secretly. Otherwise a human being in a complete equilibrium <*aequilibrium*> will not be able to choose anything. The freedom of equilibrium <*libertas aequilibrium*> is thus nonexistent. For we do always act here according to the larger multitude of incentives and thus not according to mere whim. Finally, some have posited the concept of true freedom[217] in this, that one commonly can choose that to which impelling causes <*causae impulsivae*>[218] drive us. This is called the freedom of contrariety <*libertas contrarietatis*>.[o] But that comes about because the concept of freedom was conceived as merely negative. But we still must have a positive concept of it, otherwise we have no concept at all. The positive concept is the faculty for acting according to concepts of good and evil. – Because freedom is not subject to physical laws or the laws of sensibility, one believes that it is subject to no law. But this is to conclude too much. Our prerogative is that we are free from the laws of sensibility. Animals are not, and are therefore merely passive.[219] But we are not passive when we act according to laws of the understanding, because these do originate from ourselves. We are thus [determined][L] by no one, but rather determine ourselves and thus we have spontaneity. Since here our own reason is the incentive of the laws, we are indeed free, since we govern ourselves. Freedom is thus not at all a faculty for choosing evil, but rather the good, because our reason commands only the good. When we are free from stimuli <*stimulis*> we still must have a motive ground according to which we can conform ourselves. For to act without a motive ground would not at all be a prerogative for us but rather a disgrace. For what would one hold of a human being who, in order to demonstrate his freedom, danced in the gutter in fine clothes? The freedom of contrariety <*libertas contrarietatis*> is merely a fabricated dream, for we will still find with all our actions that they happen from causes, and it would also be contradictory not to want that which satisfies me in the highest degree, but instead its opposite. The good is always that which each human being wants, and he would also always do it if only it were not hard for him to carry it out; and if our nature were so constituted that we always acted according to the concept of the good, then we would be truly free. But because reason always arises from other causes, man is merely free in some respect <*secundum quid*>. Still one raises an objection when one says: a being so created that according to its nature it can do only good, is not free. For then it could not lie and would have to speak the truth, and would accordingly be compelled and not free. To this one can answer: it would stand in his power, or be physically possible, that it could lie, but it would never want to lie. Yet a spirit so created is restricted by the highest

29:903

---

[o] Lehmann misreads *contrarietatis* as *contrarietalis* (902₂₈); cf. 903₁₀.

cause and acts like a clock. All of these disputes about the transcendental concept of freedom have no influence on the practical. For I here look not to the highest cause, but rather to the ultimate end.

Second section
Rational psychology

INTRODUCTION[p]

This should be derived solely *a priori*, wholly independent of empirical principles. Here we have to observe three things: (1) the transcendental predicates of the soul, whether it be substance and perduring, finite or infinite, etc., (2) the soul in comparison with other beings, and indeed (a) in comparison with matter, (b) [in comparison with][L] other thinking beings, (3) the connection of the soul with other beings, (a) with the body, (b) with the world by means of the body. This connection is called interaction of the soul and body <*commercium animae et corporis*> and constitutes life. Thus (a) possibility of life, (b) its beginning, (c) the end or death, (d) then the state after death, immortality.

29:904

ON THE NATURE OF THE HUMAN SOUL

Here we treat of the transcendental predicates of the human soul. Here it is asked (1) is it material or immaterial? The I is already a sign of the immateriality of the human soul. The I is throughout an object of inner sense, and everything of myself of which I am myself[q] conscious is merely an object of inner sense. All efforts are therefore in vain that want to make the faculties of the soul distinct through bodily intuition. We find not the slightest analogy between thinking and matter.

(2) The soul is substance,[220] and not only that, but rather I am also conscious of the substantial of the soul. For of matter only the accidents are known to me, but not the substantial. I am the ultimate subject and cognize myself without accidents. But of the substantial, in body as well as in me, I have no proper concept; I know nothing of it but that it is a something. Now it all comes down to deriving the properties of the soul from this sterile concept of a something. The entire rational theology[r] is supposedly built upon this; we easily comprehend that this is impossible, for nothing can be conceived from the concept of a something. We cannot

---

[p] This heading, as written in the ms, could be read either as *Einleitung* (Introduction) or *Einteilung* (Classification). Lehmann takes the latter reading, but the absence of an "h" following the "t/l" (*Einteilung* was commonly spelled with a "th") suggests that this letter is probably meant as an "l" (903₃₁).

[q] Lehmann misprints *selbst* as *selbet* (904₁₂).

[r] *Theologie; Psychologie* (psychology) was likely intended here (904₂₅).

prove that the soul is a substance from its perdurability. For from where do we know this? Substance is that which still remains through all alterations. We have experience of the soul, experience up until death. Whether it will still remain after death, I do not know. Thus if we call the soul a substance, then we can say nothing more than that substance is here a logical function – namely the subject and not the predicate. If I consider this subject alone without any predicates, then I consider the substantial or the something. To pick all properties out of that is not possible. But if we cannot discover any new properties, we can at least 29:905 avoid false inferences and errors. Thus I can determine, e.g., from the narrow concept of the subject, from the I, that the soul is not a composite <compositum>. – The I is the ultimate subject. But the ultimate subject is never composite. Further, we cognize the soul through such sheer predicates, none of which can be cognized through sensible intuition. They are merely objects of inner intuition. But we cognize matter, as object of outer intuition, in its extension and in its figure. Thinking takes no extension, no figure. – Therefore the soul must also be something other than matter. If this investigation has no positive use, it still has a negative one, which consists in this, that we do not fall into the mistakes of the materialists and explain the actions of the soul physico-mechanically. Here the materialist really commits [the fallacy of] passing over into another genus <metabasin eis allo genos>.⁵ That the soul is not matter can be distinctly discerned; but it can still be that the substrate <substratum> of matter is the same as the substrate <substrato> of the soul. Still the phenomena are different. – One proves the simplicity of the soul, and thus its immateriality, in the following manner. Should the soul be composite, then its representations would have to be so divided that in every part of the soul there would be a representation which, taken together, would constitute the entire representation.' (With every single thought there is a unity of consciousness, always the same I, which therefore also presupposes a unity of the subject.) That would be as if in a society of my thoughts each member of the society would say one word. But it is impossible that the entire thought could arise in this way and I be conscious of it, rather there then must again be a subject that puts together all the parts of the thought and thus constructs the entire thought. But now cannot the perdurability of the human soul be inferred from its simplicity, as Mendelssohn believes? If we could think of no other perishing than through division, then this proof for the perdurability and immortality of the soul would be irrefutable. But there is possible yet another perishing of the soul, namely though evanescence. – Its reality can become ever smaller until it disappears. The soul is not matter, but it can still be material, i.e., the substrate <substratum> of the

---

⁵ This is written with Greek letters in the ms (905₁₅).
' We have added a period here (905₂₃).

29:906 soul: the I, the ultimate subject, can be of the same content as the substrate <*substratum*> of matter, and could have become the substrate <*substratum*> of matter. So thought Leibniz, and the monadology brought him to this thought. Namely, because he believed that all monads had powers of representation <*vires repraesentativas*> and the soul also had a power of representation <*vim repraesentativam*> and was a monad, he held the two to be the same. But we have not the slightest cause to assume that the soul is material since thinking is entirely different from all accidents of matter, and do not comprehend why we should assume something for which we have no ground. Therefore we say that the soul is immaterial or pneumatic, although we cannot prove this. But it does not follow from this what was a necessary consequence of the Leibnizian monadology, namely, that through the composition of many souls a composite <*compositum*>, an appearance, would arise in the end. The author explains soul <*animam*> through the power of representation <*vim repraesentativam*>.[221] But that is false; for from this it follows that the soul could be only one basic power. Several basic powers would then constitute several souls. Accordingly it is better [to say]: the soul is the power of representation <*anima est vis repraesentationis*>. For soul <*anima*> is not the same as power <*vis*>, for power <*vis*> is the effect <*effectus*> of the soul upon a causality. –

ON THE SOULS OF ANIMALS[222]

We come now to the second part of rational psychology, namely, the comparison of the soul with other beings. – We can think of beings who have only the lower cognitive faculty, and who lack entirely the higher faculty. We call these brute substances <*substantias brutas*>. Do animals not have the higher cognitive faculty, or is it simply buried in them? We cannot demonstrate that they do not have it. But why should we assume more than is necessary for the explanation of certain appearances?[223] Therefore we assume that animals can endure to eternity and that their powers can steadily grow, and yet not attain to understanding, because first an essential piece must then be added to their sensibility, through which alone understanding becomes possible, namely, apperception. Perhaps animal souls persist for eternity and also stand in service to human beings in the next life as in this one. But they will still never become human souls, because they differ from human beings not merely by degree, as Meier believes, but by kind.[224] But it is easy to think that since
29:907 animals are at present a part of human needs, likewise in that life when man will be perfect, there will be more perfect animals who will serve him. Meanwhile these always remain mere fantasies. Just as are the different opinions and wild fantasies about beings higher than human beings. Even

if there are such beings, human beings are not less than they, for a rational being is itself an end*u* and capable of happiness, if it makes itself worthy.

PSYCHOLOGICAL SYSTEMS OF THE INTERACTION <*COMMERCIUMS*> OF THE SOUL WITH THE BODY[225]

We come now to the third part of rational psychology, namely, the connection of the soul with other beings, and in particular, with (a) matter. This connection is (α) immediate with its body, (β) mediate with other matter by means of the body. I say: that is my body, its alterations are my alterations. Why that? The soul can never indicate its position in the world by the mere consciousness of itself – rather, the body determines its position. The soul is not an object of outer sense, and for that reason one also cannot determine where it has its seat; hence it is also not possible to say properly where it is in the body. For this purpose soul and body are in interaction <*commercio*>, and this interaction <*commercium*> is so strong that even mere thinking already has an influence on the body. The soul works immediately on the nervous system, and the remaining parts of the body are mere instruments through which it works by means of the nervous system. It is the business of anthropology to determine this interaction <*commercium*> more closely. We consider now (a) the possibility of the interaction <*commercii*>. We already have difficulties in explaining the mere interaction <*commercium*> of bodies amongst themselves; how much harder will it therefore be to comprehend the possibility of the interaction <*commercii*> of the soul with the body. This interaction <*commercium*> manifests itself in the fact that, merely by willing, the soul can cause motions in the body. Now on this the following is of use: motions are not effects, but rather phenomena of effects. Motion is the successive alteration of the location that a body occupies, but not an effect, rather a phenomenon of an effect which is unknown to us. Whether that which has influence and effects is a Leibnizian monad we do not know. But we do know that a homogeneity between cause and effect is not necessary, but rather mere heterogeneity can occur. (The primary difficulty that one runs up against in the explanation of the interaction <*commercii*> with the body is that motion and thinking are so different that one cannot comprehend how the one is supposed to have an effect on the other; but the body is a phenomenon and consequently its properties are as well. We are not acquainted with its substrate. Now how this could be in interaction <*commercio*> with the soul amounts to how substances in general can be in interaction <*commercio*>, and the diffi-

29:908

---

u *selbst Zweck;* translated here as "itself an end," when written as one word is commonly translated as "end in itself." See also 892$_{13}$, above.

culty due to heterogeneity now falls away. That bodies are mere appearances follows quite clearly from this because all their properties and powers issue from the motive power. Likewise with impenetrability. Motion is successive presence in different locations. But what causes this, that a thing can be at a particular location, and successively at different locations, we do not know.) Therefore the power to think can be completely different from the body, and the heterogeneity causes no difficulty at all. We are thus not at all required for that reason to think of a preestablished harmony <*harmoniam praestabilitam*>; here only the system of efficient causes <*systema causarum efficientium*> is to be assumed. The connection by preestablished harmony <*per harmoniam praestabilitam*> is merely ideal. According to it, the body must be capable of the same performances even if it lacked a soul, even if the soul were already separated from it. Thus the soul is superfluous here. The best system is that of efficient cause <*causarum efficientium*> or determinate physical influence <*influxus physici*> – it is because the soul is connected with the body that it is called soul. The soul avails itself of the nerves as instruments and through these immediately influences the remaining parts of the body; on the other hand the nerves are also the instruments through which the body influences the soul. If a nerve is constricted, I see nothing. Descartes said: there are material ideas <*ideas materiales*>, impressions in the brain that the soul produces as upon a tablet. When we think, we impress this upon the brain, and this leaves traces behind which are struck again and refreshed by several related brain-nerves. Thus is memory to be explained. Bonnet is also of the same opinion.[226] But materialism, as we have already seen, is nothing. It could leave its thought impressions behind, but it is still a pointless artifice, e.g., if one wants to remember something his head might ache, but these are not ideas, rather they serve merely to awaken ideas. Likewise when it portrays[v] intuitions through the power of imagination.

29:909

Where does the soul have its seat? In general it has it in the body; but where specifically? That is a great dispute. The ancients said: in the diaphragm, because this is moved by certain affections. Descartes said it was in the pineal gland.[227] But this is often found calcified and human beings have still survived (the physicians call it seat of the senses <*commune sensorium*>, whence the soul first begins its effects; they have now sought to ascertain that in every manner possible). The ancients also said: the soul is whole in the body, but yet wholly in a part of it <*anima est tota in corpore, sed totum tamen in parte ejus*>. This is nothing. Many have assumed that there is in every part of the body some proper degree of motion, and that consequently there would also be many souls bound with a single body. Bonnet put it in the corpus callosum <*corpus callosum; G:*

---

[v] Lehmann misreads *mahlt* as *macht* (makes)(909₃).

Hirnschwiele>, but had no other ground for this than the suspicion that it must be in that part of the body where there are not two of everything. But are all these opinions really rational? The soul is an object of inner sense and therefore occupies no space. But if I attribute spatiality to it, then I make it into an object of outer sense and into matter. Therefore its presence in the body cannot be determined locally *<localiter>* but only virtually *<virtualiter>* by the influence that it has on the body. This influence is immediate only on the nerves (i.e., the soul is immediately present to each nerve) and is strongest in the brain, because there the nerves come together. With matter, presence at a location does precede influence, but not with a soul. – Thus God's omnipresence is also to be explained not otherwise than as virtual *<virtualiter>*. – Since the soul cannot be conscious of its location in the body, because it cannot be intuited with any outer sense, it is also incapable of leaving the body at its own discretion. – Does the soul leave the body immediately after the death of the body? If it is an atom, then presumably it must still remain within until the body is destroyed.

CHAPTER THREE
ORIGIN OF THE HUMAN SOUL

As for the birth of a human being, it arises through begetting. Were the soul material it would also arise in the same manner as the other matter of the body. All the parts of this matter were already present, and through the generation they receive only a new form. A composite *<compositum>* can arise without creation because the substances are already present. But a simple must arise through creation, thus also the soul, since it is simple. Creation is actuation of substance *<actuatio substantiae>*. The author's explanation: actuation out of nothing *<actuatio ex nihilo>*, is not right.[228] For it already follows from the concept of a substance that it would have to arise out of nothing. For were the parts already present, then only its form would have sprung forth, which is an accident but not substance. But now the question is: did God or the parents create the soul? Substances that are in the world cannot possibly create others. For all substances stand in interaction *<commercio>*. But if one produces the others, then it creates something with which thereafter it is itself passive. It is thus passive for itself, which is not at all thinkable. – Those who assume that the parents have created the souls of children are called Traducians.[229] The propagation through transference *<propagatio per traducem>*, by one soul which produced the others, is a crude concept. It rests on materialism. Parents cannot, by dividing, convey the soul to children, otherwise theirs would be composite. Thus God created the soul. But when? At birth, or at the beginning of the world? The first is maintained by Inducians (Concreation-

29:910

ists), the latter by Preexistencers.*w* The latter are correct. For all substances must be created at the creation of the world. Were souls still being
created, that would always be a miracle, since every creation is a miracle.
But if they become common, they are contradictory.

IMMORTALITY OF THE HUMAN SOUL

Here we have the following questions to answer: will the soul continue to
live (1) as a human being or as an intelligence? (2) Does this survival flow
from the constitution of its nature (i.e., it is properly immortal) or from a
special divine decree? (3) Will this survival be general or particular? With
respect to the first question the materialist needs only trouble with
whether a human being will also survive, but the pneumatist with whether
he will survive as intelligence as well. We can set aside the first question
for it can be of indifference to us, and the human body appears, even from
its first determination on, to incline toward the earth.*x* (Priestley is a
29:911 materialist[230] and assumes that the body will be reawakened after death,
but then that is no immortality. For there is no surviving life and it is also
not I, the I who would be awakened, but rather a similar being. For it is
the same whether God composes such a body from the parts of my body
or from other matter, for as matter or substance they are entirely the
same.)*y* Priestley says the doctrine that a human being has a soul is a
senseless doctrine and entirely contrary to holy scripture. For soul
<*pneuma*>*z* is a breath and indicates something external. But whether a
human being will survive as intelligence is more important for us to know,
and there we must again ask whether one's survival after one's death is
necessary as a general law of nature, or is based on an extraordinary divine
decree. The first is more important to us, for with the latter the survival
could be particular. Here it is not a question of future life in general, for
we can prove that teleologically;[231] rather, we want to be convinced of the
immortality of the soul, or the impossibility of its dying. For then we are
certain of the survival of all souls after death. (For immortality it is needed
to prove: (1) the natural impossibility of dying, (2) the survival of the soul
with all its powers and as the same, for otherwise life would be nothing,
(3) the survival of its personality, that it remains conscious of its previous
life. For otherwise I do not survive, but rather another spiritual being.) A
natural and a moral proof will be possible of the immortality of the soul.
For all philosophy concerns either nature or morals. Morality is the deter-

---

w We follow Lehmann in changing *Concreatianer. Die das letzte* to *(Concreatianer), das letzte*
(910_{22-3}).
x We are adding a period here (911_2).
y A closing parenthesis omitted by Lehmann (without note) has been replaced (911_9).
z This is written with Greek letters in the ms (911_{11}).

mination of action according to laws of freedom. Philosophy, as much of morality as of nature, is based upon *a priori* principles. The natural proofs are of three kinds: (1) from experience or the experientially known nature of human beings, (2) from rational psychology, (3) from the analogy of the nature of the soul with the entire natural order. As regards the empirical proof, it has very uncertain arguments. Since we have not the slightest experience of immortality, all conclusions from the experiences of this life are mere speculations. Experiences happen only during animal life, thus I can know the powers of the soul only when it is in interaction <*commer-* 29:912 *cio*> with the body. Therefore they cannot shed for us the slightest light on how the soul will be constituted after the interaction <*commercio*> with the body.

[(1)] (In order to adduce a proof from experience, we would have to be able to place ourselves outside of the interaction <*commercio*> with our body, or else be able to interrogate other souls so placed, neither of which, however, is feasible. One also compares the soul with a caterpillar which, after its apparent death, becomes a beautiful butterfly <*papillon*>, and wants to find in this an analogy in nature.[232] But it is entirely false, for if the caterpillar is killed it will never become a butterfly <*papillon*>. There is in general nothing similar to it in nature and experience.) One says: with old age the body grows ever weaker, but the mind ever stronger. People who fantasize during a feverish illness become rational shortly before death, and from that it is inferred that the soul, if it were freed from the body, would be able to think better and more freely than now. But to that one can object in part that these appearances can be so explained that, when a human being dies, the life fluid in the brain becomes more lively the more the lower part of the body dies; in part one also has experiences which attest the opposite: namely that the body has much influence on the soul, that e.g., a blow to the head can produce madness and stupidity, that the soul changes with the body. (ᵃIn old age memory, wit, and an easy overview of the whole dwindle, but there arises through long experience a practiced power of judgment. Therefore the elderly are the best advisers, and for ages one has chosen them for that.)ᵇ In rational psychology we have three items to prove: (1) the perdurability of the soul as substance, (2) the survival of this after death, as intelligence, (3) its survival as a person. One believes oneself to be done with the first since substance is perdurable. But since the soul is cognized as substance only through the I, we do not at all know whether it is substance in the sense that as such it could not perish. Mendelssohn attempted to prove the immortality of the soul as substance first, but he did not succeed.[233] He says: it is simple, therefore cannot be decomposed through division. But it can expire and

---

ᵃ Lehmann misreads an opening parenthesis as *etc* (912₂₄).
ᵇ A paragraph break added by Lehmann (without note) has been removed (912₂₇).

its reality gradually diminish. He says that would be a leap: but it could still happen by the law of continuity <*lege continui*>. But even if its

29:913 survival as substance is certain, that does not yet prove its survival as intelligence. The previous proof proves the incorruptibility of the soul. But on that account it can fall into an eternal dream or everlasting sleep after death, which is called the sleep of the soul. But if it survives as intelligence, then that is not at all to be feared. Finally, the survival of its personality must be proven. Immortality is the impossibility of dying. Dying is the end of life. Life is animal in interaction <*commercium*> with the body, and spiritual without interaction <*commercium*>. The animal life can clearly end, therefore, but not the spiritual. The life of the thinking being consists in personality, that it is conscious of itself. Immortality will be the necessary survival of this personality, not brute life <*vita bruta*>. If the soul loses its personality or becomes another person, then it would no longer be the same and one could not say that it continued its life. So, e.g., migration of the soul <*metempsychosis*> is such an interruption where personality is altered.[234] Immortality will thus be continuous life. It must connect the following state with the previous and know that it is the same as it previously was. If the soul in the next world were to be conscious of nothing that had happened with it here, then its substance would surely survive, but not its person.

(2) The rational proof. All matter is lifeless, has no faculty for determining itself, and the principle of life is something other than matter. For every matter remains in motion or at rest until it is altered by something else. Matter thus has mere receptivity or passivity. The principle of life, however, is spontaneity or the faculty for determining oneself from inner principles.[*] (The body is a hindrance to life because it contributes nothing to the promotion of life and yet very strongly influences the soul. It is just like one who is welded to a cart and must always pull it along. If the cart is well oiled until death then he can pull it more easily and more quickly, when not, he must go more slowly. Now should one think that he could not go at all if he were free from the cart? No, he would go much more easily, better.) Matter has no principle of life in itself, therefore also does not contribute to the promotion of life. Because it is entirely lifeless, it also

29:914 furnishes no condition of life. Thus the principle of life with human beings is not the body, but rather the soul, and the body also does not serve the promotion of life. On this account the separation of the body from the soul also need not be an alteration of life. It must just mean, e.g., the separation of a horse from the wagon it had been pulling. But when for all that we still see that the body influences the soul, then it must be a hindrance to life. For other kinds of influences are not thinkable. Death is thus a promotion of the life of the soul, and its future life will be its first

---

[*] We have added a period and capital here (913_{29}).

true life. The animal side is nearly half lifelessness. This proof is also not very rigorous. For the lifelessness of matter is merely a property of appearance, namely of the body. But whether the substance underlying the body also has life we do not know, yet the proof is good against the materialists.[d] But here again the difficulty is that the body, even if it contributes nothing to life, can still be the sole condition on which life depends. If the soul had no senses and sensations, then it would also not have stuff for thinking. Thus were the soul separated from the body, its life power may indeed not stop, but its life would. One can lose one's memory through illness. Therefore the soul might perhaps require the body for memory. Perhaps in the future it will be able to be self-conscious without body, for I must be conscious of myself through clear representations. But these rest on the body, since they are sensations. For all that, this proof still has much in its favor and shows that it is not necessary that the soul would have to stop with the body. Moreover it also serves to renew the difficulties which oppose the acceptance of immortality. This was thus a proof from the particular nature of the soul. From this we will clearly never be able to prove it with certainty, but perhaps we can prove it by analogy from the entirety of the nature of all things. That is what we now want to do, and thus

(3) carry out the proof from the analogy of the entirety of nature with the nature of our soul.[235]

We cannot at all dispense with analogy. Most of our inferences are analogical; we infer, namely: because two things have these properties in common that we know, they will also agree in those properties that we do not know. Of course here deception is also possible, and in many cases actual. Here we prove from the nature of ends, and therefore this proof is teleological. For physically nature is a realm of efficient causes, and teleologically a realm of ends. The principle in the realm of ends is: that everything has an end and nothing is in vain. That is a necessary postulate of reason. For otherwise reason can explain nothing. But it is also confirmed by experience. (Even the atheist must assume ends, otherwise he cannot at all explain the structure and organization of bodies; the students of nature are led by that principle to many useful experiences. There have been human beings who can see without a lens,[236] and one did not know what to make of that. The lens is a thicker fluid than the vitreous fluid that lies underneath it. Therefore it occurred to Euler that it would hinder the gradation of the colors in the eye, and that if one would insert a darker glass than the colored glass in telescopes as well, that the same would occur.[237] Dolland disagreed with him but finally tested it and produced the flint glass and the Dolland telescope.)[238] But we find in nature that everything not only has its end, but rather is also determined to develop com-

29:915

---

[d] We omit a closing parenthesis here that seems to have no mate (914_{15}).

pletely and to attain its complete end, because it actually attains it. Animals have instincts which are exactly suited to their desires. All members have their appointed use. Now in human beings there are predispositions of the soul that do not at all attain their vocation*e* in this life. Therefore we infer that a time must come wherein they will attain their vocation. Now everything rests on the proof of the minor premise <*minoris*>, and this is the following: the human soul has three abilities: cognitive faculty, feeling of pleasure-displeasure, and faculty of desire. As for the first, it is not at all satisfied here. Here we especially find that our curiosity extends to things whose cognition can be of no use to us in our life, indeed, that we find a greater gratification in the cognition of things, and the cognition more sublime, the further the things are from us, e.g., stars. We despise a human being who thinks merely of what will serve the maintenance of his life. Of what use to Newton was the discovery of the laws of attraction and other philosophical investigations? None of this is the least necessary for this life. It would thus be superfluous if there were

29:916 no future life, and further, we also do not satisfy*f* our curiosity in this life. The striving after cognition, carried to a certain degree, appears to be even against our vocation on earth. One weakens his mind through this, is less able to care for his physical happiness, cannot fulfill his animal vocation. That is the way it is likewise with the feeling of pleasure or displeasure. Of what help is it to us that moral beauty pleases us, and with respect to the faculty of desire a human being feels laws in himself that drive him to the good and that he values more than his life; and here we cannot ever properly carry them out, for in order to carry them out we would often have to risk and forfeit even our life, for which a human being can expect no reward here. Even when he knows that no human being recognizes his good deeds and he is only inwardly convinced of them, this still provides him the most precious gratification. But that would be fantasy and chimera if he were determined for only this life. Thus all talents are disproportionate in this life. Newton, a man of such great talents,[239] becomes barely sixty years old, has scarcely begun to discover something new; then he dies. Had the man lived only twice as long he would have been able to build even further on his experiences and with time discover as much as the entire human race will not discover in a thousand years. A human being only rightly comprehends how things are, when he rightly comes to his reason, but then he also dies right away. Add to this that it is never advisable to develop all one's predispositions because this often runs contrary to our physical determination. Thus one can lead oneself to an early death by heavy studying. One harms oneself in domestic concerns. Many are thereby prevented from ever marrying. This proof was discov-

---

e *Bestimmung* (915₂₅); this is usually translated in other contexts as "determination."
f We follow Lehmann in omitting an *uns* (following *wir*)(916₂).

ered by Fordyce, who made use of a parable:[240] if a higher being should perceive in the uterus <*utero*> of a mother a creature that had eyes, ears, and other members, it would infer thus: this creature is determined to a life where these members could be used. – This proof is therefore especially admirable, because we infer here from a general law of nature. For according to this all human beings are immortal. The previous proof went still further, for it also proved the immortality of animal souls. This one, however, does not prove that. But these also are of not so much interest to us. I still do not know from this proof whether the human soul will live eternally. Who knows if I do not die once all these predispositions have developed? Granted, that I will live even that long, if I do finally stop then, I would rather wish to have stopped earlier. Now comes the moral proof. All moral arguments abstract from the nature of the soul, but they do not deny immateriality. But because of this, that they do not build the proofs on immateriality, they are more understandable to the common man than the others. This proof is either moral-theological or *theological-moral*, the ground of the *latter* are the moral properties of the highest being. It rests on God's goodness and justice, but it is quite weak. One says: virtue is so little rewarded here in the world, and vice so little punished. If God is just, then a future life is to be hoped for where this disproportion will be removed. But if only we could precisely judge the virtuous then his vices certainly will amount to more than his virtues. (Who is acquainted with the innermost of each human being so as to know whether his vicious actions have not already been punished here and the virtuous rewarded? And then it is audacious to want to judge God's justice and goodness.)[g] But if we allow a future compensation it does not at all follow that this will be eternal. Now can we actually demand an eternal reward for our few virtues? And if we then also wanted to have a myriad of years which then would pass,[h] how would that help us? Finally, this proof also shows only that the future life will be particular. For children, idiots, and the wholly stupid, people whose lives were neither morally worthy nor unworthy, are excluded according to this proof, or at least are not included in it. One has yet a proof from the wisdom of God, namely, that this wisdom would suffer a great offense if rational beings should not survive after the alteration of the world, so that they regard the proof of the divine goodness as an entire source. Otherwise there would be sheer fragments; the universe would be in vain if rational beings should not intuit the whole. But it does not follow in the least from any of this, for there could well be other rational beings that God determined for that. Now the moral-theological proof still remains left for us. This is grounded in the moral laws, which are as it were geometrically necessary. Morality would be without incen-

29:917

29:918

---

[g] We are adding a period here (917_{22}).

[h] Dashes added here and below by Lehmann have been removed ($917_{26, 29}$).

tives if there were no immortality of the soul. Without belief in immortality, morality would have power only in the idea, but not in reality. Since morality thus lacks reality, the hope of immortality cannot be separated from it. Accordingly, without it human beings cannot embrace any resolution for good actions, and the hope and belief in immortality is a practical postulate of reason. (One objection is made against the survival of the soul, that there is something so contingent about birth. How many millions of embryos are nipped in the bud or die at the earliest age? A regent can multiply his underlings as a farmer his chickens when he promotes all the branches of nourishment. How should so contingent an affair as the coming about of a human being be determined to immortality? Answer: the soul must already have previously existed, although birth is the first beginning of its life in the sensible world. The migration of the soul *<metempsychosis>* of the Indians is, however, an unusual idea, namely, that the soul was previously a pure spirit (deva *<Dewa>*)²⁴¹ which is connected to a human body as a test, afterwards traveling into other animals, until it once again becomes a human being, where it is then completely holy, which is the rebirth of the lama, and then it is thrown into the abyss of all spirits, i.e., God.) Morality rests on the concept of freedom and is a necessary hypothesis. Although we may not be able to grasp it immediately, nevertheless we must necessarily assume it. If human actions appear to flow only from the mechanism of nature, then that is true only of their appearances. What underlies the actions, namely the purer manner of thinking of human beings, is unknown to us. We cannot grasp freedom in the speculative sense. It is a practical postulate. This is to be distinguished from hypotheses.²⁴² A hypothesis is a proposition that one assumes for explaining certain phenomena, but which yet could well be explained through another hypothesis. But a practical postulate is the only possible thing that can explain certain appearances. That human beings are bound to act honestly and to be good is an apodictic proposition. Only immortality can provide incentives for this. Therefore it is a practical

29:919   postulate that the soul is immortal. The analytic and moral proofs[i] for immortality are quite strong, especially the latter. Although this cannot be counted among the scientific proofs, for all that it has strength. For with it I bring the opponent to a practical absurdity *<ad absurdum practicum>*.[j]

How can we think of our state after death?²⁴³ Either that the soul will be entirely free from my body, or that a new body is given over to the soul. If the latter, then a rebirth *<palingenesie>* takes place. Priestley and other materialists have had to assume that the present body of the soul would surround it in my new life as well. It is an audacious thought to compare resurrection with the transformation of a butterfly. For when a caterpillar

---

[i] We are reading *der . . . Beweis* as *die . . . Beweise* (918₃₉).
[j] Lehmann misprints *practicum* as *praticum* (919₄).

282

is burned, no pupae arises from it. Entire nations have differed with respect to the manner in which they thought of the immortality of the soul – the Romans, e.g., viewed the body as a prison of the soul and burned it in the end. The Egyptians believed, on the other hand, that it was a necessary vehicle <*vehiculum*> of the soul, and sought to preserve it and to protect it from decay. – We have nothing to say either for or against whether the soul is dispatched into a period of sleep immediately after death. Also granted that it is so, no human being need be unsettled by this for in contrast to eternity the shortness of the sleep disappears. But what do we have to imagine of the separation of the soul from the body? Nothing more than the beginning of the intellectual and the end of the sensible [life].ᴸ It is a materialistic representation if one thinks that the soul would, as it were, leave the room when the human being dies; for it has no local presence. The soul begins from then on to intuit things differently than it had been accustomed to while it was connected to the body. Now we find ourselves already in the intelligible world, and each human being can count himself as belonging, according to the constitution of his manner of thinking, either to the society of the blessed or of the damned. He is now only not conscious of it, and after death he will become conscious of this society. Thus the human being does not come for the first time into heaven or hell, rather he merely sees himself as being there. This is a grand representation. Where is heaven and hell? If we ask after the location, then that is sensible and turns the soul into a body. Heaven is the realm of the rewarding and hell [the realm]ᴸ of the punishing judge. We are now already conscious through reason of finding ourselves in an intelligible realm; after death we will intuit and cognize it and then we are in an entirely different world that, however, is altered only in form, namely, where we cognize things as they are in themselves. The opinion of Leibniz, that the soul has here already and also will have in the future a vehicle <*vehiculum*> of matter which is indestructible, is sensible and explains nothing.[244] –

29:920

END OF THE PSYCHOLOGY

[Unassimilated text]

^kWere there no hope for a future life then the vicious, who by any means and intrigue attempted to put himself in possession of earthly happiness, would be the happiest.

29:937

Therefore one sees that metaphysics first arose from this practical interest of our reason.

The use of metaphysics is

(2) Logical, in which it amplifies our understanding, for in dissecting the concepts of our understanding we clarify it thereby. But this use is too insignificant to have been able to give occasion to the discovery of metaphysics, and were it alone then the whole of metaphysics would be dispensable.[l]

One does not need metaphysics for the sake of physics or mathematics. For from experience itself one sees daily the principles of the possibility of experience in experience itself, and I can quickly discover an error in experience, if I repeat it. Besides that, metaphysics does not concern natural science, but rather goes beyond it. Viewed generally, the use of metaphysics is either positive or negative. The positive use of a matter always consists, namely, in how we can attain some more perfection through it; the *positive* use of metaphysics is thus the attainment of a knowledge of God and of the hope of a future life. The *negative* [use]^{L m} to guard us from errors.

29:938

The negative [use]^L of metaphysics is the greater because it consists in the prevention of imperfection. But then it is certainly more important to alleviate pain than to provide pleasure. The negative use of [metaphysics]^L is also nearly the only one, for the existence of God and the hope of a future life can be cognized by any human being by common sense by considering nature and one's state, and thus one has no need of speculative inquiry, which in any event can occur with only very few human

---

^k This text begins at the top of ms, p. 125. Its facing page (124′) has text from the misplaced Cosmology section, and ends at the bottom of the page as a paragraph end. There is no blank line and no indication that the text "breaks off" (as Lehmann reports) other than the difference in content between ms, p. 124′ and p. 125. The handwriting appears the same on ms, p. 124′ as on the following pages, although the ink is darker beginning with p. 124′. The content clearly indicates that it is material from a general Introduction section, concerning the uses of metaphysics.

^l We follow Lehmann in changing *unentbehrlich* (indispensable) to *entbehrlich* (937_{26}).

^m Lehmann does not note his addition of *Nutzen* here or below (937_{37}, 938_1).

284

beings. But this is merely a practical faith, with which a human being can be puzzled by every speculative doubt. In order to dissolve these speculative doubts and investigations, which cannot be refuted by practical faith and yet [are]^{Ln} indispensable to our reason, speculative principles must also be opposed, and metaphysics does this. Its main use is thus to purify our cognition from errors and to guard it from them. The main ends of all metaphysics are the cognition of God and the hope of a future life. If metaphysics wanted to discuss merely this question: is it true that there is a God and a future life? then it would not at all be necessary, rather one can comprehend this with the greatest probability according to the rules of a rational practical faith. But it rather investigates whether we can arrive at a cognition of God and a future life by mere speculation, and how far we are in a position to do that. There are two ways to treat a science, dogmatically and critically. (1) The dogmatic method is when I take some cognitions as unprovable propositions as a basis and build the others upon that. (2) The critical [method],^{L} when I investigate the principles themselves according to the way they came about, from which power of the mind they arose, and according to their possibility, how they could have arisen *a priori*. One proceeds dogmatically in geometry, as well as in other sciences, e.g., the proposition: there can be only one straight line between two points. It is not at all necessary to investigate this, for one can confirm it at once from experience. Therefore indemonstrable propositions also hold good in mathematics; but in philosophy, especially metaphysics, one cannot proceed dogmatically. E.g., if I assume the principle: everything that comes about is in time, then I can *infer many propositions* and derive many inferences from this that are false and incomprehensible.^{o} I can say, if all things are in time then the first cause of them must also be in time. It must thus also have first begun to be effective only^p in time. But then why could it not have become effective sooner? This is unsolvable for the understanding, and if it inquires further into the matter, then it eventually falls into errors. Therefore it is impermissible to proceed in philosophy according to principles, because they are not certain and adequate for explaining all the consequences drawn from them. The critical method applies not to cognition itself or to the object, but rather to the understanding. Therefore it is not objective, but rather subjective. Thus if I have assumed a principle in philosophy, I must first have proved it. But if I cannot prove it, then it is suspect and not to be used. For if the cognitions inferred from it contain a contradiction, I cannot remove it, for metaphysics passes beyond experience and I thus cannot test the principles against experience. Critique is most indispensable in metaphysics because one

29:939

---

^{n} We follow Lehmann in changing *ist* to *sind* (938_{14}). Lehmann does not note the change.
^{o} Lehmann misreads *unbegreifliche* as *unbeweisbare* (938_{39}).
^{p} An *erst* (following *Zeit* in the ms) omitted by Lehmann has been replaced (939_3).

can otherwise err very easily, since it has no guiding thread, because it climbs over the boundary of experience; therefore the use of *metaphysics* is *also* negative and indeed this use is thus the greatest, because the critique of metaphysics is the most necessary. Because it is thus built upon critique and guards us from errors, it is a bulwark of religion against all speculative doubt. We will connect both methods in our presentation, at first dogmatically and then afterwards criticize it step by step. For if critique does not accompany dogmatism, then we have no touchstone of truth. If I speak, e.g., of the beginning of the world, then it is indeed impossible that I have this from experience, I likewise can never confirm it through experience, rather this passes beyond all experience and is thus a mere idea in my reason. – But I must then ask, how does my understanding arrive at it and how far does it reach? It is remarkable that these questions still have almost never been investigated. The questions have indeed been posed[q] and investigated as to where our concepts come from; but that does not belong here.

In each science that contains concepts of reason, one represents to oneself a metaphysics of science which certainly must be distinguished from this metaphysics. If in a science of the understanding I separate the pure cognition of reason from the empirical, then this collection is – a metaphysics of that same science. It is thus the pure product of reason in the sciences. This is quite useful in a science, to separate the cognition of reason from empirical cognition, in order to comprehend the errors all the more distinctly. Metaphysics is the spirit of philosophy. It is related to philosophy as the spirit of wine <*spiritus vini*> is to wine. It purifies our elementary concepts and thereby makes us capable of comprehending all sciences. In short, it is the greatest culture of the human understanding.

29:940

HISTORY OF METAPHYSICS[r]

[q] We follow Lehmann in changing *angestellt* to *gestellt* (939_{34}).
[r] The remainder of the page (ms, p. 126'), about one-half of a page, is blank, as is the facing page, other than the pagination in the upper right corner (namely, ms. p. 127).

PART IV

Metaphysik Volckmann

1784–1785 (AK. 28: 440–450)

Metaphysics lectures
of Prof. Kant
written in the years
1784 and 85
by
I. W. Volckmann

[Rational psychology]

wanted to annihilate.[a] However, both presuppose this: that we have a soul, therefore one could insert another idea here, namely: that we have no soul at all, and yet will live after death, this idea considers life only as property of the body, and so even the materialist can hope for a future life. In England, Priestley maintained this.[1] One cannot demonstrate, however, the complete impossibility of the transitoriness of the soul, but rather only the impossibility of its passing away like a body. With this there is to prove (1) its perdurability, i.e., the survival of the substance, (2) its survival as intelligence, i.e., of a being whose faculty of reason and its acts <*actus*> also survive, (3) the actual survival of the personality of the human soul, that after death it be conscious of itself that it was the same soul, for otherwise I could not say that *it itself* exists in the future world, but rather that there would be another rational being there. – One can infer the immortality of the soul either from empirical or pure rational psychology, from the empirical one would have to do it in this manner: that from the experiences which we have of the soul, its survival followed; but this is not feasible, for from all perceptions of it in interaction <*commercio*> with the body we cannot infer how it would be constituted outside the interaction <*commercio*> with the body, we would then have to have a faculty for positing our soul outside the interaction <*commercio*> with the body, or we would have to observe other souls (e.g., if there were ghosts), neither of which is feasible. Yet another empirical proof is the usual one by an analogy <*analogon*> with animals, namely, from those which at first appear to die, mature in another husk, then gradually break the outer shell in two, and come out as butterflies <*papillon*>; however this is merely a schema for making immortality more

---

[a] This passage begins abruptly with the last two words of a sentence: *vernichten wollte* (440_{28}).

conceivable. Thus from empirical psychology the least proof of the survival of the soul cannot be furnished. – Now in rational psychology we can infer to it either from the concept of life in general, and primarily from the life of a being with intellect <*intelligens*>, that it cannot be canceled by death, or *secondly*, from the analogy of the entirety of nature. The first proof is furnished in the following manner: *all matter is lifeless* (this is a principle of physics: matter is inert <*materia iners*>, and inertia <*inertia*> is as much as lifelessness) *if that is so, then it also cannot contain in it any proper principle of life, but rather it can be only an organ of life, for what itself is lifeless cannot be a ground of life, thus also not with human beings, therefore life lies in the soul, what is not a ground of life also cannot be a ground of the promotion of life, consequently the separation of the soul is also no ground of the diminishing of life, from which it follows that the body was rather a hindrance of life.* But here matter means only the appearance of outer things, these we indeed find lifeless, but we do not cognize whether the substances that underlie them perhaps contain life. However, this argument is still very nice against the materialists. Further, it also seems to follow from this that the soul led a more perfect life before its connection with the body, and that this connection with the body is as it were a death for it. – The second proof is taken from the analogy of nature with other living beings in general,* and this appears to be the best among them all, although it is also in part empirical, in that it advances a principle without which we cannot at all judge the nature of a connection according to ends. We find in nature a certain connection of causality that is efficient connection <*nexus effectivus*>, and a connection of ends that is a connection of finality <*nexus finalis*> and this rests on the highest principle: that no organ is ever met with in any living being that would be superfluous, which principle serves for making perfect our cognitions of the ends of the organic things; and these we now also apply to human beings, in that we find so many furnishings of the mind which cannot be used in this life, thus we have, e.g., a faculty of reason and strong impulse to use it; it can make a very disproportionate use of these talents of the mind, which conflicts with the teleological principle of nature, therefore we infer it must possess them in order to use them sometime in the future. Further proof is served by the principles of the will and of morality; the moral principles in the reason of a human being intend that he should not attend even to the advantages of life and even life itself. Now it is obvious that no proportionate use can be made of such principles in life, therefore such

28:442

---

* The proof from the analogy of the entirety of nature is thus twofold with respect to cognition and with respect to the will, the first goes this way, that we attempt to cognize things for which we have not the slightest use in our life, but which are still magnificent to know, e.g., all astronomy. The objection that not all human beings seek to extend their cognitions is removed when one considers that, with many, bodily circumstances or their situation hinders the development of their powers, so there can be, e.g., many Newtons walking behind a plow.

moral ideas obviously go further than the world. Now this still must have a use sometime, therefore there must be another world, otherwise we also would not act according to our determination in this world, for we must work for the station at which we are, otherwise we act contrary to duty, but it still appears that a human being wants to anticipate cognitions in another world. Now can organs really be given to us by whose use we would become confused? – Thus it is wholly impossible to prove the immortality of the soul from the *a posteriori* or *a priori* known nature of a thinking being, for granted I know *a priori* the soul is a substance, that it is immaterial as well as simple, still I am also at an end here, I will never get perdurability from it, this can be proved only in relation to the possibility of experience; it thus holds only for objects of experience, we must thus presuppose the proposition with respect to the possibility of experience. The proof that the human soul will live after death would indeed be very good, yet working it out is not feasible, for it is unsuitable to build it upon the divine will; for we do not know what he will do in accordance with his goodness and justice; it is also audacity to want to determine according to our wisdom what God will do. The grounds of it are taken from morality: that God brings an execution of his holy laws into effect: hereby we presuppose that the bad-minded are not yet punished enough here in life, which we still cannot know, or that our virtue, which also did not deserve such a great reward, is not yet rewarded enough; and if we are punished or rewarded all at once, then it would indeed also be feasible that we could take leave again after a determinate series of years, therefore eternity cannot be brought forth from this proposition; it also could not be inferred from it that all human beings should live, e.g., why [are there] the inhabitants of Tierra del Fuego,[2] or New Holland,[3] or further, the children who are born? These have still not done anything good yet. Meanwhile it still remains that God would have had no end with the creation of his creatures, if the rational beings should not have survived, for these just are the end of creation, and if these always take leave, then no connection comes about, then all are only fragments. A being must go through the entire series of alterations of nature, therefore we could infer: souls would also have to be after death in order to connect the course of things: but from this it again follows, it would hold not for all human beings, but rather only for those who can reason about ends. But children have not yet had any influence at all. But the proof according to the analogy of nature is one that is *general*, therefore the ground of hope also lies in this. – *The objections against the immortality of the soul* are the following, which are also taken from empirical observations that we can make of our soul in life; namely there appear on the other hand great phenomena for proving the dependence of the human soul [on the body], this rests namely on: our thought directs itself according to the state of the body, and there is also a certain use of it that appears to have principles separately, e.g., rage often

28:443

28:444

rests on nothing but the constitution of the body; as a human body grows, its powers of mind grow as well, until it finally receives the power of judgment, after many years again wit loses its liveliness and other powers of mind, and then there remains only a mere power of judgment acquired through much experience, which is rather melancholy, and whereby after countless attempts of judgment one then grasps the decision which is appropriate. If finally a human being becomes so weak that he lapses back into his childhood, then the powers of the soul also finally disappear completely, thus it appears that the soul cannot think without body; however this holds merely *as long as* the soul is in interaction <*commercio*>, although the existence of the interaction <*commercii*> is not necessary. Thus it does not at all prove that the soul cannot at all think without body. It would be just as if someone were welded to a cart; if its wheel is well greased then it goes quickly, if not, then it goes slowly, could one then say that this human being could *not* go *at all* without a cart? – The second objection is something more important, and is also taken in part from the analogy of nature: if we consider the coming to be of thinking beings in the world, among which we also want to reckon animals, then we are astonished over the wastefulness of the generative powers which are not all used, a being that is so contingent, should that be for eternity? – One also says: life here in the world must be viewed as only an interlude of our life; while this could have also been without existence in the sensible world, it still goes according to a course of nature unknown to us, it is as it were only the first act <*act*> of our life, the spiritual life would be the beginning, a special act <*actus*>, schema of existence, whereby however something dubious again emerges, for from it would follow that, if we can no longer remember our previous state, then the next one could perhaps

28:445   also be such that we appear again in it as another being, which is true migration of the soul <*metempsychosis*>. Being born is the beginning of consciousness in the sensible world. But it is not reckoned as though it were the beginning of all life; it constitutes for the thinking being no main ground, but rather it is only one of the many means in nature by which it takes its steps to greater perfection. – *The consideration of the state of the soul after death*. The first question with this is: if the soul lives after death then *where* is it? If the bodily world is only appearance, then we cannot at all posit the soul in it, but rather in another world, heaven, which means the whole of intellectual beings; if the souls will cognize the same things *as they are*, then this is another world. Now we can say: the virtuous is already here in heaven only he is not conscious of it, for he cognizes things in themselves, and the rational kingdom is considered under moral laws: the kingdom of God and the kingdom of ends, and he is a true member in the kingdom of ends, the transition into the other world would be merely the intuition, that is called coming into another world; the latter is another only with respect to form, but with respect to content it is always the same world, we cannot go any further in this. That the soul, according to Leibniz, will have a corpuscle <*corpusculum*>, vehicle <*vehiculum*> that already lies in human beings, is a far too coarse representation.[4] Leibniz also said: the soul would still be buried with the body because it could not so easily work itself loose, until the parts of the body have passed over into decay, where it can then more easily come away, but then the soul would still have to be dug up sometime; death is also merely the end of sensibility; if this has an end, then we are separated from the body. – The last question is: can one think of a sleeping soul? I.e. whether the acts <*actus*> of its thinking will also be suspended a while, about which however one can say nothing at all. (The migration of the soul <*metempsychosis*> was a pleasing idea of the Oriental peoples, although somewhat coarse. It was their purgatory <*purgatorium*>, which they named *devas*,[5] if the soul migrated into an animal there, then this was called the lamaistic rebirth, and if the soul came again into a human being as a reward, then that was called *burham*,[6] from there, they believed, the soul would be flung back into the abyss of all souls, namely God, out of which it had gone.) Cutting off all further pondering on this is the best remedy, that we can say: another world means only another intuition of the 28:446 same things, the sensible world thus entirely ceases for us, therefore we also cannot hope to be transferred to any place in it. Now it is asked: will the soul exist as pure intelligence? But it is indeed that when it is not sensible; will there not be yet another sensible intuition? No human being can discern this, or also whether after death souls will intuit things according to the same form, only more finely and more perfectly[.] We also cannot know that, but then the soul would still always remain in the same world, and there would be no other world, but rather it would perhaps be only at another location in this world, but should there really be another world, then I must separate it from this manner of sensibility. But one also cannot think how a being that is created should cognize things in themselves. We will thus presumably come only by degrees to a greater perfection of cognitions and have another kind of intuition in the same or in another world. Here no philosophy goes any further. – The author now speaks also of blessedness and damnation, etc., etc.[7] Here on earth happiness[b] is nothing but a progress, each sensation of our state drives us to go from one to another, accordingly we cannot at all think a *perduring* state after this which would be happy in a constant way, for we think of happiness only in progress, but if it is always in progress then it also can never be completed, were this to happen, then happiness would cease. We think of an entirely complete happiness only in the other world, which state, without any added pain, is called *blessed*. *Blessedness* is contentment insofar as it springs from the power of the rational subject, or so far as the subject is itself

---

[b] The German counterparts of "blessedness" and "happiness" are closely related, namely, *Seligkeit* and *Glückseligkeit*, respectively.

sufficient. If the moral good that someone does is adequate for contentment, then he has a foretaste of blessedness, but this degree is only a small mixture of heavenly sparks, accordingly a human being is not blessed in this life, but in the strictest sense it also could not become [this], for it depends on other things whose possession is required for its contentment. But we almost cannot think that a creature can be damned or robbed of all happiness, for then we would have to imagine it as almost dead, it would

28:447 proceed from no other state and so all activity would cease. In the future world we can thus think only a progress to blessedness or to misery, we cannot at all imagine that all will be in one pile. The morally good and evil is therefore also never perfect with a human being, but rather consists only in progress. We will thus also be able to think of the other world with respect to moral and physical perfection only in a progression <*progressus*>, both of which ultimately must be connected with well-being. If the moral worth of a human being can never be attained all at once, then it is still peculiar that human beings so imagine it, since, if a human being stands in a progression of getting worse, more evil in this life, it is not to be expected that after his death it will take another path, therefore there is an indiscernible future of a fall into a worse state <*in deterius*>, and thus my state as well will fall ever more into misery and unhappiness. Therefore improvement in the last moment of life is also very dubious according to this. – The progression to the good also goes into infinity, for we see no reason why it should cease. The state in the progression of the moral and physical *good* is called blessedness, and the progression of the moral and physical evil is called *damnation*, but one cannot discern whether this will last for eternity. But in the practical sense we can also say the concern with evil is eternal, for I have no reason to believe why the human being should be different there (*practically indiscernible* is thus that where I have no reason to posit bounds), similarly we are also not in a position to establish positively that it will last eternally. – *On the possibility of community with departed souls.* The imagination of this came about because one could not represent to oneself of a human being that it was dead, and therefore often represented him again to oneself in fantasy, whereby one finally lapsed into this: although a human being is not visible, yet he must be there invisibly, which representation increased the aversion to annihilation even more. Those who assume this say: it would indeed be possible, which possibility can be twofold, either the soul assumes a body, and then souls would come before us as bodily appearing beings, or *secondly* they would be *internally* present, which Swedenborg maintained. To engage here in disputing the possibility of this would be vain work, I can neither

28:448 prove it nor thoroughly refute it, for experience gives us no instruction of it. The maxims of reason or the maxims of self-preservation, meanwhile, require us not to assume any of this; I cannot say that reason has no further use if I admit this; however, with respect to the effect of such beings, there is no use of reason at all possible, for because they are spirits, they therefore cannot be grasped and observed by us, then neither can there be any use of reason on them at all. All spirits and ghosts, appearances, interpretations of dreams, prophecies of the future, sympathy of temperaments are altogether a thoroughly reprehensible delusion, for it cannot be explained by any rule or by compared observations. A human being who reckons on that, takes away all those means by which alone a use of reason is to be made, namely: that the things of the world stand under natural laws, and even if there actually were ghosts, a rational person still must not believe in them, because it corrupts all use of reason. There also lies a certain mischief in this, for the ignorant would gladly like to cancel the difference between him and the rational scholar, and in this the cleverest is just as stupid as the ignorant. – But now it is asked whether it could hold of spirits other than the human,ᶜ which however have a merely *spiritual* existence, and can they influence us? The entire delusion of the Neo-Platonic philosophers (who were also called eclectics <*ecclectices*>)[8] is thereby broached, out of which arose theurgy, which was the entire art of entering into community with such beings, to which belonged penance, sacrifice, and all manner of superstitious formulas, etc. There are quite a lot of phantoms of the brain here, which one also finds in modern times, but it is foolish to assume that a created being should be the governor <*gubernator*> of others. – Rational beings which are at the same time bodily are called *living beings* <*animalia*>. *Each body or matter perdures in its rest and motion, except when it is compelled by an external cause to alter its state.* An internally active power in a being is called life, our own state is a state of representation <*status repraesentativus*>, accordingly in a living being we can always imagine a power of representation <*vim repraesentativam*>; motive powers cannot work otherwise than by outer causes, they are therefore also determined only externally, internally I cognize nothing, but should it be living then it has a faculty for acting from an *inner* principle, and this principle is a subject that has powers of representation <*vires repraesentativas*>. *To live*, properly speaking, means to have a faculty for performing actions in conformity with one's representations. We call an animal *alive* because it has a faculty to alter its own state as a consequence of its own representations. Someone who maintained that in animals the principle of life has no power of representation <*vim repraesentativam*>, but rather that they act only according to general laws of matter, was Descartes, and afterwards also Malebranche, but to think of animals as machines is impossible, because then one would deviate from all analogy with nature, and the proposition: that a human being is itself a machine, is utter foolishness, for we are conscious of our own representations, and all natural science rests on the proposition: that

28:449

ᶜ We are moving a question-mark and changing the capitalization (448₂₀₋₂).

matter can have *no representations*. Everything mechanical is external and consists in a relation in space, our thinking *refers* indeed to *things in space* but itself is still not in space; but thoughts would have to be objects of outer intuition if they are supposed to be machines. That thinking is thus a mechanism is absurd, this would mean to make thinking in one's own consciousness into an object of the outer senses. Matter can indeed be a necessary requirement for the support of our thoughts, but thinking itself is not mechanical. – Now how can we conceive animals as beings below human beings? We think higher beings without having need of the hindrance or support of matter, on the other hand we can think of things which are *below* us, whose representations are different in species and not merely in degree. We perceive in ourselves a specific feature of the understanding and of reason, namely consciousness, if I take this away there still remains something left yet, namely, sensation <*sensus*>, imagination <*imaginatio*>, the former is intuition with presence, the latter without presence of the object, we can also think a reproduction <*reproduction*>, anticipation <*praevision*>, without the least self-consciousness, but such a being could not prescribe rules to itself, for the possibility of a rule requires making consciousness of oneself the object of one's intuition, one must be conscious of what different beings agree in; if many beings exhibit a large degree of the effects which can arise in human beings through reason, it still does not at all follow from that that they also would have reason, for, if they are lacking consciousness, then they are also 28:450 missing understanding and reason, and sensibility alone reigns. With animals one calls this an analogue of reason <*analogon rationis*> and there is an instinct of sensibility whereby they need no reason, but rather which an external being placed in them for acting, or for working according to instinct; the analogue of reason <*analogon rationis*> is the summation of all lower powers. To imagine that these beings will receive reason in the future world is to base oneself much too much on speculation; also one has no reason at all to assume it, because they can also always grow within their species through greater instincts. –

PART V
Metaphysik L$_2$

1790–1791? (AK. 28: 531–594)

(1) ON PHILOSOPHY IN GENERAL

All human cognitions are, according to form, of a twofold kind: (1) *histori-cal*, which are from things given <*ex datis*>, taken merely from experi-ence; and (2) *rational cognitions*, which are from principles <*ex principiis*>, taken from certain principles. The rational cognitions are again: (1) *philo-sophical*, cognitions from concepts, and (2) *mathematical*, from the construc-tion of concepts. One can distinguish cognitions according to their *objec-tive* origin, i.e., according to the sources from which alone a cognition is possible; and according to the *subjective* origin, i.e., according to the man-ner in which cognition can be acquired by a human being. With respect to the former, cognitions are either rational or empirical, with respect to the latter, rational or historical; in itself the cognition may have come about however it will. – The system of rational cognition through concepts would thus be philosophy. But first we must consider the cognitions themselves, and then the system of them. – Because mathematics and philosophy agree in that they are rational cognitions, we must first define rational cognitions. The rational cognitions are opposed to the historical ones. The historical ones are derived from things given <*ex datis*>, and the rational cognitions from principles <*ex principiis*>, as we have already indicated above. The first, namely, the historical, are cognitions which are possible only insofar as they are given. The latter arise from this, that one cognizes their grounds and obtains them *a priori*. This must be elucidated. A cognition can have arisen out of reason and still be only historical, and indeed subjective; but objectively it is a philosophical cognition. One can thus *learn* philosophy, without being able to philosophize. Thus whoever properly wants to become a philosopher: he must make a free use of his reason, and not merely an imitative, so to speak, mechanical use.

We have said of rational cognitions that they are cognitions from princi-ples <*ex principiis*>, they must thus be *a priori*. There are two cognitions that are *a priori* but which nevertheless have many noteworthy differences: 28:532 namely *mathematics* and *philosophy*. One tends to say that they differ ac-cording to the object, but that is false. The first, it is said, deals with quantity, the latter with quality. But the difference of these sciences does not rest on the object, for philosophy applies to everything cognizable, and mathematics in part as well, because everything has a magnitude. Magnitude is also an object of philosophy, but the kind of treatment, however, is different than in mathematics. Now what makes the difference in the kind of cognizing through reason in mathematics and philosophy? The specific difference rests on this: all philosophy is rational cognition from mere concepts, but mathematics [is] rational cognition from the construction of concepts. I construct concepts when I exhibit them in intuition *a priori* without experience, or when I exhibit an object in intuition that corresponds to my concept. – *A priori* intuition is that which does not depend on experience, but rather that which everyone can give to himself. – The mathematician can never avail himself of his reason with mere concepts, just as the philosopher can never avail himself of his reason with the construction of concepts. – In mathematics one avails oneself of reason concretely <*in concreto*>, but the intuition is not empirical, rather here one makes something *a priori* the object of the intuitions. We thus see that mathematics has an advantage here over philosophy, because the former cognitions are *intuitive*, the latter *discursive*. – The cause of our considering magnitudes more in mathematics is that magnitudes can be constructed *a priori* in intuition; but qualities cannot be exhibited in intuition. Philosophy *in the scholastic sense* <*in sensu scholastico*> is thus the system of the philosophical rational cognitions from concepts; but *in the cosmopolitan sense* <*in sensu cosmopolitico*> it is the science of the ultimate ends of human reason. That gives philosophy *dignity*, i.e., absolute worth; and it is that which alone has *inner* worth, and gives worth to all other sciences. – Philosophy in the scholastic sense <*in sensu scholastico*> concerns only skill, but in the cosmopolitan sense <*in sensu cosmopolitico*> usefulness. Philosophy in the first sense is thus the *doctrine of skill*, but in the other *of wisdom*. Thus it is the lawgiver of reason. But the *philosopher* must be distinguished from the *artist of reason*. The latter points out rules for the use of our reason for discretionary ends; he aims at *merely* speculative knowledge, without seeing how much it contributes to the ultimate end of human reason. The *practical* philosopher is the *genuine* philosopher. – Philosophy is the idea of a perfect wisdom, which shows me the ultimate ends of human reason.

28:533

Two parts belong to philosophy in the scholastic sense <*in sensu scholastico*>: (1) a sufficient supply of rational cognitions; (2) a systematic connection of them. Not every science allows of a systematic connection. Systematic connection is the connection of various cognitions *in one idea*. Now philosophy is the only science that has a systematic connection, and it is that which makes all the other sciences systematic. – Our historical cognitions are useful for this, that our reason can make a use of them which serves its ends. But the ends are again subordinated, so that one end is the means to another; thus there must be a *higher* end in which the others have unity. Since means have a worth only in regard to ends, our use of reason also can have worth with respect to this science only insofar as it is determined how far these cognitions concern the ultimate final ends of human reason. – If we call the inner principle of the choice among the various ends *maxims*, then we can say: *philosophy is a science of the highest maxims of the use of our reason.* Then the philosopher is designated more according to his conduct than according to his science. – Philosophy in the scholastic concept is merely an instrument *<organon>* of skill. The philosopher in the cosmopolitan sense *<in sensu cosmopolitico>* is he who has maxims of the use of our reason for certain ends.

The philosopher must be able to determine:

1. the sources of human knowledge;
2. the scope of its possible and advantageous use;
3. the boundaries of reason. –

The field of philosophy in the cosmopolitan sense *<in sensu cosmopolitico>* can be brought down to the following questions:

1. What can I *know*? *Metaphysics* shows that.
2. What should I *do*? *Moral philosophy* shows that.
3. What may I hope? *Religion* teaches that.   28:534
4. What is man? *Anthropology* teaches that.

One could call everything anthropology, because the three former questions refer to the latter. – Philosophy in the scholastic concept is skill; but philosophy in the eminent sense *<in sensu eminenti>* teaches what this is to serve. – Philosopher is an elevated name, and means *knower of wisdom*, which no one can properly presume. But one usually calls everyone a philosopher who broods over concepts only, without bothering oneself as to what they are useful for. –

How can one learn philosophy? One either derives philosophical cognitions from the first sources of their production, i.e., from the principles of reason; or one learns them from those who have philosophized. The *easiest* way is the latter. But that is not properly philosophy. Suppose there were a true philosophy, [if] one learned it, then one would still have only a historical cognition. A philosopher must be able to *philosophize*, and for that one must not *learn* philosophy; otherwise one can judge nothing. One believes, e.g., that everything that Plato says is true; for one cannot reproach what is learned. But even if I learned a true philosophy, I still must not think that I can philosophize. *But there is also no such true philosophy. We learn to philosophize; so we are permitted to view all systems of philosophy only as [the] history of the use of our reason, and as objects for the practice of our critical abilities.* From this it becomes apparent that some use their understanding dialectically, i.e., give their cognitions an illusion of wisdom. But this is the office of a sophist. A philosopher must have two things:

301

1. the cultivation of his skill; this is necessary, because we need it for all ends;
2. an aptitude in the use of all means for discretionary ends.

Both must be *together*. One can never become a philosopher without cognition; but *cognitions alone never* constitute a philosopher; there must be a purposeful unity of this skill here, and an insight into the agreement of this skill with the highest ends. – One wants to say of Epicurus that he neglected science, and only so much the more looked to wisdom. Whether this procedure is grounded or not we do not want to investigate here. But 28:535 so much is certain, that this claim is false; for wisdom *without science* is a mere silhouette of a perfection to which we will never attain. Whoever hates science and all the more loves wisdom is called a *misologist*. Occasionally some will also degenerate into misology who were at first immersed in science with diligence and fortune; *this* misology arises then because their knowledge could not do enough for them. Philosophy is the only thing that knows how to procure this inner satisfaction for us; it closes as it were the circle, and then the sciences receive order and connection. We will thus have to look *more* to the method of our use of reason than to the propositions which we have arrived at thereby.

(2) HISTORY OF PHILOSOPHY[2]

No people had properly begun to philosophize before the Greeks; everything previously had been represented by images, and nothing by concepts. The Greeks were the first to find that rational cognition is not to be cultivated by the guiding thread of images, but rather abstractly <*in abstracto*>. No people had investigated what virtue is, although one prescribed rules for it. The Egyptian wisdom cannot at all be compared with the Greek. The Greeks were also the first in mathematics who demonstrated every proposition from the elements <*ex elementis*>; but that is not very old even with them, and one cannot really know when and where the philosophical spirit arose. The *Thracians* appear to have been an old, clever people; we find Orpheus among them. One can begin to calculate just after the building of the city of Rome, at which time the seven sages in Greece flourished through their epigrams, which the Orientals already had long ago. Aphorisms are what one calls many thoughts compressed into a few words. The one among the seven sages from whom one dates science is called Thales, with the nickname of the Physicist. He is supposed to be the originator of the Ionian school, to which Anaximander, Anaximenes, and Anaxagoras belong. There are also some peoples, like the Chinese and some Indians, who treat of matters taken from reason alone, e.g., of the immortality of the soul. But they do not distinguish the concrete <*in concreto*> from the abstract <*in abstracto*> use of reason. –

Persians and Arabs have also borrowed something from Aristotle, thus from the Greeks. With Zoroaster there is, judging by the Zend-Avesta,   28:536 not the slightest trace of philosophy.[3]

Especially to be considered are the steps human reason takes to elevate itself to a speculative use. – Among the Greeks there was a difference between the physicists <*physicis*> and theologians <*theologis*>. There were many theologians <*theologi*> from the Eleatic school. The Epicureans were the greatest physicists, but hardly theologians, so that one almost held them to be atheists.[4] The first stimulus to philosophy was clearly the progression that human beings made through common reason from the visible world to its invisible author. This step is also quite natural, for the order of the world already betrays an author, and in addition to this comes also the incomplete series of causes in nature. The interest of reason is so great with this that it interwove mathematics into the speculations, whose object seemed worthwhile despite all the trouble that they had with it and all the miscarried attempts; – and so the first philosophers were likely theologians. – That some became physicists already presupposes much culture, for we do not have the same stimulus to that, because experience always remains the same. –

Poetry is older than prose, for the first philosophers clothed everything in images. The first poet was Orpheus, then Hesiod. Pherecydes[5] was supposedly the first to have written in prose. One says of him as well as of Heraclitus that their writings were quite obscure. This came about because philosophical language was still new then. – As regards poets, the manifold of images and expressions is remarkable. – The *Eleatic* school, whose founder was *Xenophanes*, followed after the Ionian. Its principle was: in the senses is deception and illusion, but in the understanding alone is truth. This school began at once to revolt against the poets, for these clothed everything sensuously. Otherwise this school served no great use. – *Zeno* of Elea was among them a man of great understanding and acumen. – Dialectic now indicated the pure use of understanding, or it denoted the faculty of availing oneself of one's understanding according to concepts separated from all sensibility. – Therefore we find so many encomia of it among the ancients; and in this sense it is also praiseworthy. The philosophers who now wholly rejected the senses had to deteriorate   28:537 necessarily into subtleties, and there arose dialectic in the sense that we take it; it became an art for maintaining and disputing every proposition; it was merely an exercise of the sophists, lawyers, and orators. *Sophist* was previously a good name; one gave this name to those who could speak rationally and with insight on all matters. But when they wanted to rationalize about everything and devoted themselves to it, then this name became hated and the name philosopher came about. On top of this, *Socrates* drove the sophists into a corner with his irony and made them laughable. *Carneades*, a Stoic, came to Rome and gave speeches, and *Cicero* said of him:[6] he would attack no proposition which he did not dispute and over-turn, and maintained none that he did not strengthen and make certain. Yet *Cato*, the censor, supposedly said:[7] he could not find the truth among his grounds. – – About the time of the Ionian school a man of unusual genius arose in Magna Graecia (Naples), namely *Pythagoras* of Samos, who set up a school and made a project the equal of which had never been. He founded, namely, a society of philosophers who were bound by silence. He had doctrines that were exoteric, i.e., which he delivered to the entire people. He made certain ones novices <*novitii*>, who had to make a vow, and to whom he revealed more; and he took some into his special circle of friends, who were entirely separate. The former he named auditors <*acusmatici*>, who were allowed only to listen, but the latter disciples <*acroamatici*>, who could also ask questions. The vehicle <*vehiculum*> of his secret doctrine was physics and theology: doctrine of the visible and the invisible. His project appears to have been to purify religion from the folly of the people, to moderate tyranny, and to introduce more lawfulness into the realms. This entire sect was extirpated shortly before his death. Of his doctrines one can say nothing because one does not properly know them. Those of his pupils who were still remaining were novices <*novitii*>, who did not know much. Later many proposi-tions were ascribed to Pythagoras which were certainly only fabricated. He was besides that a mathematical mind.

Later a man arose among the Greeks who took a new step among the speculative minds, and led human beings to the true good; that was *Socrates*. Among almost all of them, it was he whose behavior came closest to the idea of a sage. His most distinguished pupil was called *Plato*, who occupied himself more with the practical doctrines of Socrates. His pupil was *Aristotle*, who elevated speculative philosophy. – Then came the *Epicu-reans*, who placed all good in a cheerful heart, which they called delight; and the *Stoics*, who placed all happiness in the elevation of the soul, according to which one can do without all the diversions of life. One can also say of the former that they were still the best natural philosophers of all the schools of Greece. –

The most prominent Greek schools had special names. – The school of *Plato* was called *Academia*; of *Aristotle Lyceum*; of *Zeno* of Cittium *Porticus*; of *Epicurus Hortus*. *Lyceum* was a place where the youths exercised in physical training. The members of this school were also called Peripa-tetics <*peripatetici*>. The walkway (<*porticus*: G: *Spaziergang*>) was a covered way; in Greek, *stoa*[a]; from this the Stoics also have their name. The school of Epicurus was called a garden <*hortus*> because he taught in gardens. There was, with the first Epicureans, the greatest moderation in the enjoyment of all pleasures. – After Plato's Academy there followed

28:538

---

[a] This is printed with Greek letters in Lehmann (538₁₃).

yet others which were founded by his pupils. *Speusippus* founded the first, *Arcesilaus* the second, *Carneades* the third. Plato delivered many of his doctrines in dialogue, i.e., grounds pro and contra were introduced, whereby he decided nothing, although he was otherwise very dogmatic. The *method* for investigating truth must be doubting. The first pupil of Plato, Speusippus, was doubting; Arcesilaus also concurred with this, and Carneades carried it still further. Therefore the doubters were also called Academics <*Academici*>; otherwise they are called *Skeptics*, and the Skeptics were subtle and dialectical philosophers. *Pyrrho*,[8] among others, was a great Skeptic. From the school of Aristotle, one finds no great successors other than *Theophrastus* and *Demetrius Phaleraeus*;[9] but there are no writings from them, and one also does not see from the ancients that they enlarged the philosophy of Aristotle. – The *Stoics* were dialectical in speculative philosophy; practical in moral philosophy, and showed much dignity in their principles. This school begins with *Zeno* of Cittium. Thereupon followed two famous men: *Cleanthes* and *Chrysippus*. – The *Epicurean* sect was never able to attain the reputation that the Stoic did, and they were sworn enemies to one another. One can cite no report of the Garden <*hortis*> other than that of the poet *Lucretius* in Rome, to whom however the strictest belief is not to be accorded.

The Academy fell into Skepticism; and if one begins to count from   28:539 Pyrrho on, then one finds an entire school of doubters, who differed from the Dogmatists. The Dogmatists said: that one could become certain merely through the understanding without assistance of experience. The Skeptics, on the other hand, believed: if the understanding spins something from out of itself then it is nothing more than sheer illusion. But later they went further, and said not only that in the general judgment of the understanding separated from experience there is nothing but mere illusion, but rather also in all experience. Nothing is left us of these Skeptics except the work of *Sextus Empiricus*, who brought all doubts together.

When philosophy went from the Greeks to the Romans, it did not expand; for the Romans always remained only pupils. *Cicero* was a pupil of Plato in speculative philosophy, a Stoic in moral philosophy. Among the Romans we find no natural scholars other than *Pliny* the Younger, who left behind a description of nature. Among the Romans *Epictetus* and *Antoninus Philosophus* belonged to the Stoics.

Finally culture disappeared with the Romans, and barbarism arose, until the *Arabs* flooded parts of the Roman empire, began to apply themselves in the seventh century to science and brought Aristotle again into the forefront. When the sciences prospered again in the Occident, one followed Aristotle in a slavish manner. The *Scholastics*, who illustrated Aristotle and drove his subtleties into infinity, came into prominence in the eleventh and twelfth century <*seculo*>. This muck was swept away by the Reformation, and here there were *Eclectics*, i.e., those who subscribed to no school, but rather searched for truth wherever they found it.[10]

The improvement of philosophy *in our* time came about because a greater study of nature came into prominence, and because mathematics and natural science had been connected. The order in the thinking which arose thereby also spread over the other parts of philosophy. The greatest investigator of nature was *Bacon of Verulam*, who made human beings attentive to observations and experiments. Descartes also contributed much to giving distinctness to thinking. It is difficult to determine where the improvement of *speculative* philosophy comes from. Among the improvers of this belong *Leibniz* and *Locke*. The dogmatic philosophizing characteristic of *Leibniz* and *Wolff* is quite defective; and there is so much deceptive in it that it is necessary to suspend this procedure. But the other procedure that one could adopt was *critique, or the procedure of investigating and judging reason. Locke* had dissected the human understanding, and showed which powers belong to this or that cognition; but he did not complete the work. His procedure was dogmatic, and it served the use that one began to study the soul better. At the present time, *natural philosophy (which proceeds along the guiding thread of nature)* is in the most flourishing state. In moral philosophy we have come no further than the ancients. As for metaphysics: it appears as though we have become perplexed in the investigation of truth; and one finds a kind of indifferentism, where one makes it into an honor to speak deprecatingly of metaphysical ponderings, although metaphysics is *philosophy proper*. Our age is the *age of critique, and one must see what will become of these critical attempts*. Of a newer philosophy one cannot properly speak, since everything goes as in a flux; what the one builds, the other tears down.

28:540

Introduction <Prolegomena>*ᵇ*

Philosophy, like mathematics as well, can be divided into two parts, namely into the *pure* and into the *applied*. – *Metaphysics* is the system of pure philosophy. The word metaphysics means a science which goes beyond the boundaries of nature. (Nature is the summation of all objects of experience.)

A principle <*principium*> is a general rule, which again contains other rules under it. If we take together all pure concepts which can be entirely separated from the empirical ones, then we attain thereby a science. Philosophical cognition consists of mere concepts *a priori*.

Physics is the philosophy of nature insofar as it depends on principles from experience; but *metaphysics* is the philosophy of nature insofar as it depends on *a priori* principles. *Moral philosophy* teaches us the practical principles of reason. The concepts *toward which everything seems to be aimed* is the concept of a *highest being and of another world*.

28:541

Metaphysics is *necessary*. Its ground is reason, which is never to be satisfied by empirical concepts. Reason finds satisfaction neither in the consideration of things, nor in the field of experience, i.e., in the sensible world. The concepts of God and of the immortality of the soul, these are the two great incentives on whose account reason went out beyond the field of experience.

A major question is: *how are* a priori *cognitions possible?* The whole pure mathematics is a science which contains only *a priori* concepts, without its supporting their ground on empirical concepts. That there are thus actual *a priori* cognitions is already proved; indeed, there is a whole science of sheer pure concepts of the understanding. But the question arises: how are the *a priori* cognitions possible? The science that answers this question is called *critique of pure reason*. Transcendental philosophy is the system of all our pure *a priori* cognitions; customarily it is called *ontology*. Ontology thus deals with things in general, it abstracts from everything particular. It embraces all pure concepts of the understanding and all principles of the understanding or of reason.

The main sciences that belong in metaphysics are: *ontology, cosmology,* and *theology*. – All science that has nature as an object is called *physiology*.

ᵇ The word *Metaphysik* preceding *Prolegomena* has been omitted as redundant. See note 1 to Ak 28:531.

The doctrine of bodily things is called *physics*, and the metaphysical doctrine of the soul is called *psychology*. Both are physiology. Physics is either empirical <*empirica*> or rational <*rationalis*>. One can also call the latter general <*generalis*>. Psychology is likewise either empirical <*empirica*> or rational <*rationalis*>. Empirical physics <*physica empirica*> and empirical psychology <*psychologia empirica*> *do not at all belong properly to metaphysics*. But one has constantly brought empirical psychology <*psychologia empirica*> into metaphysics, because one did not know what metaphysics actually was. We must also bring it in because it cannot be properly presented by itself.

Ontology is a pure doctrine of elements of all our *a priori* cognitions, or: it contains the summation of all our pure concepts that we can have *a priori* of things. *Cosmology* is the consideration of the world through pure reason. The world is either the bodily [-world] or the soul-world. Thus cosmology contains two parts. The first could be called the science of *bodily nature* and the other part the science of *thinking nature*. There is therefore a doctrine of body and a doctrine of soul. Rational physics <*physica rationalis*> and rational psychology <*psychologia rationalis*> are the two main sections that belong to general metaphysical cosmology. – The last main metaphysical science is rational *theology*.

28:542

(1)
Ontology

Ontology is the first part that actually belongs to metaphysics. The word itself comes from the Greek, and just means the *science of beings*, or properly according to the sense of the words, the *general doctrine of being.*ᶜ Ontology is the doctrine of elements of all my concepts that my understanding can have only *a priori*.

ON THE POSSIBLE AND THE IMPOSSIBLE

The first and most important question in ontology is: *how are a priori cognitions possible?* This question must be solved first, for the whole of ontology is based on the solution of this question. *Aristotle* decided the proposition in that he rejected all *a priori* cognitions, and said that all cognitions were empirical, or that they were based on the first principles of experience. For his main proposition was: nothing is in the intellect that was not first in the senses <*nihil est in intellectu, quod non antea fuerit in sensu*>. Through this he overturned all *a priori* cognitions. But *Plato* said that all our *a priori* cognitions arose from an original intuition.

We have no innate concepts (<*notiones connatae*; G: *angebornen Begriffe*>) at all, but rather we attain them all, or we receive acquired concepts <*notiones acquisitae*>. The understanding acquires concepts by its paying attention to its own use. All that can be said of that is this: that there are certain *a priori* cognitions, even when it seems that they are taken from experience, or that they are used beyond the boundaries of experience. There is in our reason a certain dialectic, that is: a certain art of illusion, which shows me either something true or false. A good dialectician must maintain at the same time and with the same facility thesis <*thesin*> and antithesis <*antithesin*> of a matter, or he must at the same time prove the truth and falsity of a matter, or be able to say yes or no. Dialectic contains a conflict which indicates that it is impossible to proceed dogmatically here in metaphysics. It is impossible to be and not to be at the same

28:543

ᶜ G: *Wesen* (542₁₄); translated here as "beings" and "being," it is also translated in other contexts as "essence."

309

time <*impossibile est, simul esse et non esse*>.[d] *Simul* means at the same time; but time is not yet explained. One can thus better say: to no subject does there belong a predicate opposed to it <*nulli subjecto competit praedicatum ipsi oppositum*>. The negative nothing <*nihil negativum*> is that which cannot even be thought.

The highest concept of the whole human cognition is the concept of an object in general, not of a thing and non-thing, or of something possible and impossible, for these are opposites <*opposita*>. Each concept that has an opposite <*oppositum*> always requires a yet higher concept that contains this division. Two opposites <*opposita*> are divisions of a higher object. Thus the concept *of the possible and impossible*, or of a *thing and non-thing* cannot at all be the highest concept of human cognition.

The principle of *contradiction* is not the definition of the impossible. Impossible is that which contradicts itself. *Apodictically certain* is that of which the opposite cannot at all be thought. Impossibility is a necessary *apodictic* negative judgment, the impossible is that which contradicts itself <*impossibile est illud, quod sibi ipsi contradicit*>. Each definition can be reversed. Each definition can be exchanged with the defined <*definito*>, and when this does not allow of substitution, then it is a sure indication that it is no definition. What contradicts itself is *impossible*. It thus follows from this: what contains no contradiction is *not impossible*. What is not impossible, is possible. Now if my thoughts contain no contradiction, then they are possible. That of which the thought contradicts itself is absolutely impossible, that is the negative nothing <*nihil negativum*>. *Reality* is something; *negation* is nothing, namely a concept of the lack of an object. Imaginary being <*ens imaginarium*> is a non-thing, of which the thought, however, is possible. Such a non-thing is nothing, it is no object that can be intuited. We must indeed not take the possibility of thoughts for the possibility of objects; one must guard oneself very much against this. The principle of contradiction <*principium contradictionis*> is a criterion of truth, with which no cognition can conflict. The sign for distinguishing truth is a criterion of truth <*criterium veritatis*>. The principle of contradiction <*principium contradictionis*> is the highest negative criterion of truth. It is a necessary condition <*conditio sine qua non*> of all cognitions; but not the sufficient criterion of all truth.

28:544

ON SYNTHETIC AND ANALYTIC JUDGMENTS

A judgment is *false* if it contradicts itself; but it does not at all follow from this that a judgment that does not contradict itself is true. All *analytic* judgments must be derived from the principle of contradiction <*principio contradictionis*>. Nothing <*nihil*> is that which contradicts itself and of

---

[d] We have changed *ac* (in Lehmann) to *et* (543₇).

which even the concept is impossible; this is also called the negative nothing <*nihil negativum*>. An imaginary being <*ens imaginarium*> is a mere phantom of the brain, but of which the thought is still possible. What does not contradict itself is logically possible; that is, the concept is indeed possible, but there is no reality there. One thus says of the concept: it has no *objective reality*. *Something* means any object of thinking; this is the *logical* something. The concept of an object in general is the highest concept of all cognitions. One also calls an object a something, but not a metaphysical, rather a logical something. The principle of contradiction <*principium contradictionis*> is: to no subject does there belong a predicate opposed to it <*nulli subjecto competit praedicatum ipsi oppositum*>. The principle of identity <*principium identitatis*> is subordinate or coordinate to this principle <*principio*>. This is: to every subject there belongs a predicate identical to itself <*omni subjecto competit praedicatum ipsi identicum*>. – The contradiction <*contradictio*> is either evident <*patens*> or hidden <*latens*>; identity is also either evident <*patens*> or hidden <*latens*>, either *obvious* or *hidden*. The evident identity <*identitas patens*> must be avoided. No one will commit an evident contradiction <*contradictio patens*> because it quite obviously contradicts itself. The proposition or the principle <*principium*> of identity is just as valid for the affirmative propositions as the principle of contradiction is valid for the negative propositions. Fundamentally these two principles <*principia*> can be considered as one; for if I posit the one, the other also follows from this already. The principle of identity <*principium identitatis*> is already conceived in the principle of contradiction <*principio contradictionis*>. The principle of the excluded middle between two contradictories <*principium exclusi medii inter duo contradictoria*> is also contained in the principle of contradiction <*principio contradictionis*>. This thus reads: to any subject there belongs one or the other of contradictorily opposed predicates <*cuilibet subjecto competit praedicatorum contradictorie oppositorum alterutrum*>. The contradiction <*contradictio*> is either apparent <*apparens*> or actual <*vera*>. Our concept often appears to contain a contradiction, although in fact there is none; e.g., when one says: to hurry slowly. There appears to be a contradiction here, but there is none, for it just means: to hurry in a way that it is not immoderate and does not overstep the prescribed end. 28:545

All judgments are of two kinds: namely *analytic* and *synthetic*. An *analytic* judgment is one in which I say nothing of a subject other than what was contained in its concept, and what I can draw out through analysis <*per analysin*>. A *synthetic judgment* is one in which I attribute a predicate to the subject, which I add to the concept, and do not draw out through analysis <*per analysin*>, e.g., if I say: gold is a yellow metal, then that is an analytic judgment. But if I say: gold does not rust, then that is a synthetic judgment. Analytic judgments are mere *elucidatory* judgments, but the synthetic *amplificatory* judgments. The use of analytic judgments is that they elucidate the matter. They are of great importance; the whole of philosophy is loaded with them. Almost the whole of morality consists of sheer analytic judgments.

How are analytic judgments a priori *possible?* All analytic judgments are *a priori* judgments because the predicate is drawn out from the concept of the subject. All analytic judgments follow from the principle of contradiction <*principio contradictionis*>. But a synthetic judgment is not at all based on the principle of contradiction <*principium contradictionis*>. Synthetic judgments can be classified: (1) into *a posteriori* judgments or judgments of experience, and (2) into *a priori* judgments. All our experiences consists of sheer synthetic judgments. Our judgments of experience are thus all synthetic. But now it is asked, how are synthetic *a posteriori* judgments possible? They arise by the connection of empirical intuitions, or whenever one adds empirical perceptions to perceptions. But that there really are synthetic *a priori* judgments one can see from a multitude of examples. The whole of mathematics proves this; arithmetic and the whole of geometry contain almost only synthetic *a priori* judgments. It is asked, whether there are also *synthetic a priori judgments* in philosophy. Here there are synthetic *a priori* judgments through concepts: but in mathematics through the construction of concepts. The whole of philosophy is full of analytic judgments, for everything must be analyzed here. Now how do we recognize the judgments, whether they are *a posteriori* or 28:546 *a priori?* Everything that happens has a sufficient ground, or cause. A cause is something else, which something must follow according to a standing rule. Every substance perdures; only the form alters. Before one has nonanalytic cognitions, it is not at all worthwhile to think of synthetic cognitions. There is only a single way open in which I can cognize something synthetically *without analysis* <*analysin*>, or how *synthesis* is possible without *analysis*, namely, merely through experience. But if I can find something through *analysis*, then I do not need any experience at all. All experiences are nothing other than synthetic judgments. *A priori* judgments are not at all possible through experience, but rather the reverse: only through *a priori* cognitions is experience possible. If there were no *a priori* cognitions, then no experience would ever take place, for this is based merely on *a priori* cognitions. In all my cognitions, there are two sorts of things: namely (1) concepts and (2) intuitions. All our cognitions presuppose concepts, and the concepts themselves absolutely require intuitions. One can use concepts concretely <*in concreto*> and abstractly <*in abstracto*>. If I want to have concepts, then I must also have intuitions. Intuition is the immediate representation of a single object. But the concept is the mediate representation of a single object. If we have *a priori* cognitions, then we must first have *a priori* concepts and then also *a priori* intuitions, upon which the concepts can be applied. Intuition is thus the single representation of an object. *Space and time are* a priori *intuitions.*

312

An *a priori* concept is the unification in One consciousness of the manifold of pure concepts of the understanding. *Logic* speaks merely of the *formal* laws of the concepts of the understanding. Space and time are *a priori* intuitions; prior to experience, we can say much of space and of time. There are also *a priori* concepts; for if there were not, then *metaphysics would not at all be possible*. We can determine all these concepts, of which the understanding is capable only *a priori*, according to a single principle <*principio*>: that is (1) *the ground from which they arise* and (2) *how many there are*. By virtue of the *a priori* concepts we can expound metaphysics as a system. We must see what the concepts are based on *a priori*, and out of what they arise. Everything *formal* in the understanding will be treated in detail in logic. Following Aristotle, we want to call the   28:547
pure concepts of the understanding *categories*. All *a priori* concepts arise from the formal aspect of the use of the understanding.

All judgments can be classified

1. according to *quantity*;
2. according to *quality*;
3. according to *relation*, and
4. according to *modality*.

1. The judgments are, according to quantity, *universal, particular*, and *singular*;

2. according to quality, *affirmative, negative*, and *infinite*. The last are the same as the negative ones with respect to content, but are different with respect to logical form.

3. According to relation they are *categorical, hypothetical*, and *disjunctive* judgments.

4. According to modality they are *problematic, assertoric*, and *apodictic*.

The concepts of the understanding *correspond* to these judgments.

1. To the judgments according to quantity, the concepts: unity, plurality, totality (unity, multitude, and totality <*unitas, multitudo et totalitas*>).

2. To the judgments according to quality: reality, negation, and limitation <*realitas, negatio, . . . limitatio*>. This is a lack of reality, which is limited.

3. To the judgments according to relation: substance and accident to the categorical, – cause <*causa*> and effect <*causatum*> to the hypothetical, and composite <*compositum*> and parts <*partes*> to the disjunctive judgments. With one name they can be called: inherence, causality, and interaction <*commercium*>.

4. To the judgments according to modality correspond the concepts: *possibility, actuality*, and *necessity*.

There are absolutely no pure concepts of the understanding that would not be included under these.

Modality is something quite special; I look merely at the manner in which I posit something, either as *problematic* or *possible*; *assertoric* or *actual*; and as *apodictic* or *necessary*.

A representation that is referred not to the object, but rather merely to the subject, is called *sensation*.

28:548 Through sensations alone we cannot cognize anything at all. Intuitions without concepts, and the reverse, concepts without intuitions, give no cognitions at all. We must have intuitions and *a priori* concepts at the same time, for without them no cognitions are possible. Sensation makes intuition empirical. We can call *a priori* intuitions pure intuitions, and these are ones in which no sensation takes place. *A posteriori* intuitions, or empirical intuitions, are those which are connected with sensations. The explanation of the possibility of pure concepts of the understanding we call *deduction*. The deduction is actually the answer to the question, what is right <*quid juris*>? The deduction of the pure concepts of the understanding is a proof of the validity of the pure concepts of the understanding.

ON GROUND

The concept of ground and consequence belongs in logic, and thus not in metaphysics, but rather it is taken as presupposed; but we can include it here. The *logical ground* is the relation of cognition, how one is inferred from the other. In metaphysics ground belongs under the concept of causality. The word category is drawn from *Aristotle*. *Aristotle* introduced ten categories, namely: (1) substance <*substantia*> and accident <*accidens*> (was one category), (2) quality <*qualitas*>, (3) quantity <*quantitas*>, (4) relation <*relatio*>, (5) action <*actio*>, (6) passivity <*passio*>, (7) when <*quando*>, (8) where <*ubi*>, (9) position <*situs*>, and (10) disposition <*habitus*>. Action <*actio*> and passivity <*passio*> are actually not categories, but rather predicables; they belong to relation. The concepts when <*quando*>, where <*ubi*>, and position <*situs*> belong to the concepts of space and time. But space and time must not come among the categories. Disposition <*habitus*> belongs to possibility; but one does not find possibility, actuality, and necessity in the categories of Aristotle. Thus one easily sees that the categories of Aristotle are in part not sufficient, in part not distinct.

We want to try out giving a correct definition of ground piece by piece, because it is wholly indispensable. *Ground* is that by which something else is posited. The concept of ground is a concept of relation. Consequence <*rationatum*> is that which is not posited unless another thing has been posited <*quod non ponitur nisi posito alio*>. Ground is that upon which something follows in a wholly necessary way; or ground is that upon which something follows according to universal rules; basically it amounts to the same thing. When the consequence is posited, a ground must also follow;

but the ground is not determined through this. But if I posit the ground, then a consequence must follow necessarily. A ground is that whereby, when it is posited, another thing is determinately posited <*ratio est id, quo posito determinate ponitur aliud*>. But there are cases where something is posited, and another thing is posited after, yet where the one is not a ground of the other. E.g., when the stork comes, good weather follows. But to posit <*ponere*> does not mean something follows the other accidentally; for the stork could also be brought on the mail coach.

28:549

That which is regarded as consequence is called a dependent thing <*dependens*>. A dependent thing <*dependens*> is that which contains in itself consequences from others; e.g., a human being can be a thing dependent <*dependens*> on another. An independent thing <*independens*> is that which contains in itself nothing which is a consequence <*rationatum*> of other things. Only God alone can be an independent thing <*independens*>. The connection <*nexus*; G: *Verknüpfung*> between ground and consequence is twofold: the connection <*nexus*> of subordination and coordination. Every connection <*nexus*> is in relation <*respectus*>. But relation (<*respectus*; G: *Beziehung*>) is twofold: connection <*nexus*> or opposition <*oppositio*>. To both belong a ground, thus the ground of positing and denying <*ratio ponendi . . . tollendi*>; the positing and denying relation <*respectus ponens . . . tollens*>; a ground can be required of both. Every ground is twofold;[11] either a *logical* or a *real ground*. A logical ground is that by which something is posited or canceled according to the principle of identity. But a real ground is that by which something is posited or canceled according to the principle of causality. The first is analytic, and the other synthetic. Agreement (<*consensus*; G: *Übereinstimmung*>) is only a negative connection <*nexus*>. Logical connection <*nexus logicus*> can indeed also be comprehended according to the principle of contradiction <*principio contradictionis*; G: *Satz des Widerspruchs*>, but much more distinctly and easily according to the principle of identity <*principio identitatis*>. The logical ground (<*ratio logica*; G: *logische Grund*>) is: that which, having been posited, another is posited according to the principle of identity <*quo posito ponitur aliud secundum principium identitatis*>. I derive the concept from the other, according to the derivation which happens through analysis. Thus the consequence lies in the ground, and is implicitly <*implicite*> in and for itself the same with it, but not explicitly <*explicite*>. Therefore the diversity is not real, but rather only according to the form. A real ground is that whose consequence is a real consequence; e.g., my will is a real ground of the motion of my foot.

Between two logical opposites <*logice oppositis*> there is no third (<*tertium non datur*; G: *giebt's kein Drittes*>); but between two real opposites <*realiter oppositis*> there is a third (<*tertium datur*; G: *giebt es ein*

Drittes>). The concept of the real ground is a synthetic concept. That which the real ground contains of something is called *cause*. I can *not* comprehend the concept of the real ground from experience; for it contains a necessity.

Here the question about the *possibility of synthetic* a priori *judgments*
28:550 can best be answered. Every cognition consists of judgments; i.e., I must refer a representation as predicate to a subject. With respect to the concepts that are derived from the senses, it is all the same in which form I judge. But should the representations refer to an object, then it is no longer all the same in which form I judge, because they are determined by the object as [it is] in itself. Representations, insofar as they are not referred to an object, are only predicates for possible judgments; but if they refer to an object, then I must ascertain a form of judgments in which I refer them to an object. Now, cognition is empirical cognition, or the relation of the representations to an object; it is thus possible only through judgments, and to be sure, their form must be determined. Now the concepts that with respect to each object determine the form of the judgments about that object are the pure concepts of the understanding, or categories, and *these* are thus the *grounds of the possibility of all experience*. They are that which the form of the judgments determines *a priori* for all objects. All representations of the senses have a relation to an object. The connection of the ground with the consequence is the representation of the connection of two appearances, insofar as they are thought according to universal rules. Every motion must have a cause. Experience is nothing other than a cognition of an object through sensible representations. The form of judgments indicates how many representations can be connected in a consciousness. Through senses we can cognize only the properties or predicates of the object. The*ᶜ* object itself lies in the understanding. –

Something can be considered *as internally* and *as externally possible*. The internally possible is called the absolutely [possible], and the externally possible the hypothetically possible. This expression is very equivocal. Every condition limits, and is not valid universally; but here possibility is considered not as limited, but rather as amplified. What is possible not merely in a thesis <*thesi*>, but in a hypothesis <*hypothesis*>, is that which is possible not only internally, but rather also externally. Conditioned possibility is thus a narrower degree of possibility; but it should be extensive. Absolutely possible is that which is possible in every regard; hypothetically possible [is] when something is possible under certain conditions (<*sub conditione restrictiva*; G: *unter gewissen Bedingungen*>). What is impossible in itself is also possible under no conditions (<*sub nulla hypothesi*; G: *unter gar keinen Bedingungen*>) at all.

ᶜ We do not follow Lehmann in his changing *erkennen. Das* (in Pölitz) to *erkennen, das* (550₂₆).

ON THE PRINCIPLE OF SUFFICIENT REASON <PRINCIPIO RATIONIS SUFFICIENTIS>

In the metaphysics textbooks the principle of sufficient reason <*principium rationis sufficientis*; G: *Satz des zureichenden Grundes*>, or the principle of sufficient reason, reads: nothing is without reason <*nihil est sine ratione*>. *Leibniz* thought that if this principle were placed in a better light, one could make better use of it. But *Wolff* used this principle without any restriction.[12] (Everything that is has a ground; thus everything that is must be a consequence.) In order to comprehend the falsity of this universal principle, one need only put it into other words: whatever is, is a consequence <*quidquid est, est rationatum*>. Here one sees at once that it will not do. So all things are consequences? From what then do they follow? The impossibility of this principle thus strikes the eye at once. If one wants to demonstrate it distinctly, so that one says: if something is, and it has no ground, then it is nothing; – then one confuses the logical with the transcendental nothing. Thus I cannot say of all things: they are consequences; but rather I will use the principle according to a certain restriction. The relation of consequence to ground is a relation of subordination; and things which stand in such a relation, constitute a *series*. Thus this relation of ground to consequence is *a principle of the series*, and it is valid merely of the *contingent*. Everything contingent has a ground; contingent is that for which the opposite is possible. The principle of sufficient reason <*principium rationis sufficientis*> is thus: everything that happens has a ground. The principle of sufficient reason <*principium rationis sufficientis*> does not apply to concepts in general, but rather to the senses. There has not yet been a philosopher who has proven the principle of sufficient reason. The proof of this principle is, so to speak: the cross of the philosophers <*crux philosophorum*>.[13] It is not possible to prove it analytically, for the principle "if something happens, there must be a ground *why* something happens" is a synthetic principle. It cannot be brought forth from mere concepts; it is possible *a priori* through the relation of concepts in relation to a possible experience. The principle of sufficient reason is a principle upon which possible experience rests. A ground is that upon which, when something is posited, something else follows according to universal rules. Experience is possible only through *a priori* concepts of the understanding. All synthetic judgments are never valid for things in themselves, but rather only through experience. All experience is synthesis, or synthetic cognition of things, which is objectively valid. The principle of the empirical necessity of the connection of all representations of experience is a synthetic cognition *a priori*.

The difference between the sufficient and insufficient ground is this: the ground which contains *everything* that is to be met with in the consequence is called the *sufficient* ground; but the ground which contains *only some* of what is to be met with in the consequence, is the *insufficient* ground. Grounds are classified into *mediate* and *immediate*. The mediate ground is the ground of a ground, but the immediate [is] the ground without an intermediate ground *<absque ratione intermedia>*. Something can be called the *highest* ground (first ground *<ratio prima>*), and this is either in some respect *<secundum quid>* or simply speaking *<simpliciter>*. Independent ground *<ratio independens>* is *the* ground which depends upon no other. Grounds can also be considered as coordinated. – If the ground is posited, then the consequence is also posited; but not the reverse, if the consequence is posited, then the ground is also posited.

The object of thinking is something in the logical sense *<aliquid in logico sensu>*, and this is the highest concept. Two opposites *<opposita>* cannot be in one concept. *To determine* is nothing other than to posit one of two opposites *<oppositis>*. Objects which we have through concepts are not determined. Every concept is determinable insofar as it is universal. To determine each thing in every way *<omni modo>* is impossible; for one would have to know all predicates of all things, and no one can do that, except one who is all-knowing. The determining thing *<determinans>* is the ground. We call determinations not analytic predicates *<praedicata analytica>* but rather synthetic predicates *<praedicata synthetica>*. The difference between determinations is: they are either affirmative or negative. This belongs to the quality of the judgments. Whether I use the predicate affirmatively or negatively is the same in logic; it considers merely the form of the judgment. Reality and negation are categories, that is: pure concepts of the understanding. The difference between reality and negation is: reality is that whose concept contains in itself a being; negation, whose concept contains in itself a non-being. This is easy to distinguish; but occasionally it causes difficulties and then it concerns intellectual things. Error is not negation. There is yet a third, that is not between these, but rather is connected with them, and that is: *limitation*. All determinations are either inner determination, or relation, a reference to others.

THE CONCEPT OF ESSENCE

28:553   The concept of essence belongs properly in logic.[14] Essence is either a logical essence, or a real essence. A *logical essence* is the first ground of all logical *predicates* of a thing; a *real essence* is the first ground of all *determinations* of an essence. For an essence is either logical or real *<essentia est vel logica vel realis>*. We posit a logical essence through the analysis of the concept. The first ground of all predicates thus lies in a concept; but that is not yet a real essence. E.g., that bodies attract belongs to the essence of things, although it does not lie in the concept of the body. Accordingly, the *logical essence* is the first inner ground of all that which is contained in the concept. But a *real essence* is the first inner ground of all that which belongs to the matter itself. – If I have the logical essence, I still do not yet have the real essence. In metaphysics, essence should never be understood as logical essence, for this belongs in logic. Logical essence is found through principles of analysis: but real essence through principles of synthesis. Predicates belonging to the essence, but only as a consequence, are called attributes *<attributa>*; what on the other hand belongs to essence as a ground is called an essential property *<essentiale>*. Attributes *<attributa>* and essential properties *<essentialia>* belong to essence. Modes *<modi>* and relations are properties apart from the essence *<extraessentialia>*, which do not belong to essence. Modes *<modi>* are internal properties apart from the essence *<extraessentialia interna>*. Some predicates belong to the concept of the thing as an inner ground, others only as consequences of a given concept. The former are essential properties *<essentialia>*, the latter attributes *<attributa>*. The complex *<complexus>* of the essential properties *<essentialium>* is essence *<essentia; G: Wesen>*. The real essence is not the essence of the concept, but rather of the matter. E.g., the predicate of impenetrability belongs to the existence of body. Now I observe through experience much that belongs to its existence; e.g., extension in space, resistance against other bodies, etc. Now the inner ground of all this is the nature of the thing. We can infer the inner principle only from the properties known to us; *therefore the real essence of things is inscrutable to us*, although we cognize many essential aspects. We become acquainted with the powers of things bit by bit in experience. The attributes *<attributa>* of a thing belong either to this thing alone, and then they are proper *<propria>*; or common *<communia>*, when they are common to several. A proper attribute *<attributum proprium>* must flow from all essential properties *<essentialibus>* together; a common one *<commune>* follows only from some, or from one, essential property *<essentiali>*.

ON EXISTENCE

This concept, although it is simple, is still quite difficult, because we apply it to concepts which are sublime beyond all experience and example. E.g., to the concept of God. It belongs to the class of modality, i.e., according to the possibility for judging in general. The difference between problematic and assertoric judgment is this: that in the first case, namely problematic, I think something of the object, or I attribute to the subject a predicate in my thoughts; in the other case, namely assertoric, I attribute to the object a predicate outside of me, and not in thoughts. Likewise the categories of possibility and actuality are different. Through actuality no more is given to the subject than through possibility; but now the possibility, with all its predicates, is posited absolutely; in possibility these predicates were pos-

319

ited only in thoughts, relatively. The first is absolute positing <*positio absoluta*>, the latter relative <*respectiva*>. I cognize logical possibility through the principle of contradiction. Everything that exists is, to be sure, thoroughly determined; but with existence the thing is posited with all its predicates, and thus thoroughly determined. Existence, however, is not a concept of thoroughgoing determination; for I cannot cognize this, and omniscience is required for it. Existence must thus depend not on the concept of thoroughgoing determination, but rather the reverse. If something is only thought, then it is *possible*. If something is thought because it is already given, then it is actual. And if it is given because it is thought, then it is *necessary*. Through existence I think nothing more of the thing than through possibility, but only the manner of positing it is different, namely the relation to me. Existence thus gives no further predicate to the thing. One says in the schools: existence is the complement <*complementum*> of possibility. But it is added only in my thoughts and not to the thing. The true explanation of existence is: existence is absolute positing <*existentia est positio absoluta*>. It thus can be no complement <*complementum*>, no predicate of a thing, but rather *the positing of the thing with all predicates*. Existence is not a separate reality, although everything that exists must have reality. Existence, possibility, actuality, and necessity are special kinds of categories which do not at all contain predicates of things, but rather only modes <*modos*>, for positing the predicates of things. Possibility can be inferred from existence <*ab esse ad posse valet consequentia*>, but not: existence can be inferred from possibility <*a posse ad esse valet consequentia*>. One can infer to possibility from existence, but not the reverse, to existence from possibility. Nonexistence can be inferred from impossibility <*a non posse ad non esse valet consequentia*>; but impossibility cannot be inferred from nonexistence <*a non esse ad non posse non valet consequentia*>. One infers to non-being from impossibility, but not to impossibility from non-being. According to our limited concepts, according to which we cannot comprehend *a priori* the possibility of things, we *must* infer from existence to possibility <*ab esse ad posse*>. –

Being <*ens*> and non-being <*non ens*>. Something <*aliquid*> in the logical sense means an object in general; in the metaphysical sense (in the real sense <*in sensu reali*>) [it means] the possible (imaginary being <*ens imaginarum*>); it is usually also called: being of reason <*ens rationis*>; whose concept is indeed possible, but of which we cannot say that the matter is possible; it is not self-contradictory. Entire books of pneumatology are like that – e.g., *Lavater's* views of eternity,[15] where much is said of the community of spirits – are nothing other than beings of the reasoning reason <*entia rationis ratiocinantis*>. E.g., that after death our spirit will go from one heavenly body to another, can be thought through reason and is no contradiction. A being of the reasoning reason <*ens rationis ratiocinantis*> is an *ideal*. Reason is constrained to assume such an ideal of perfection *as a greatest* <*maximum*> in a matter, according to which the other is judged, e.g., a model of the most perfect friendship. Such an ideal is the greatest, and for that reason only one; for the greatest is only a single one. – Imaginary beings <*entia ficta imaginaria*> are things which we can think; but these are not ideals. For *ideals are a matter of reason and without intuition.* They are necessary substrates <*substrata*> of reason. Chimeras and ideals are different from each other. An *ideal* arises by a necessary use of reason; a *chimera* on the other hand is an arbitrary predicate of straying reason.

ON UNITY, TRUTH, AND PERFECTION

There is an old scholastic doctrine: everything is one, true, good or perfect <*quodlibet ens est unum, verum, bonum seu perfectum*>. (1) Each thing is one; (2) each thing is true. To attribute truth to a thing is contrary to common usage; one surely says: cognition is true. The ground of truth must be in the thing. (3) Each thing is perfect, i.e., each thing contains all that is required for it.

The representation of each object contains: 28:556

1. the unity of the determinable;
2. the plurality and harmony of the multiple determinations among each other;
3. the totality of the determinations, insofar as it consists in the many determinations being taken together in one object.

Transcendental truth, unlike the logical, consists in the agreement of the predicates that belong to the essence of a thing, with the essence itself; for since they are the predicates of the thing, then they must also agree with its essence. Each thing is true in the transcendental sense. Perfection, transcendentally considered, is the totality or the completeness of many determinations. Each thing is transcendentally perfect.

The criteria of thing and non-thing are:

1. the *unity* of the object, which is thought in my concept;
2. the transcendental *truth* in the connection of the multiple determinations;
3. the *completeness* or totality.

Things can be considered:

1. *physically*, insofar as they are represented through experience;
2. *metaphysically*, insofar as they are represented through pure reason;
3. *transcendentally*, insofar as they are represented through pure reason so that something *necessary* belongs to their essence.

321

Physical perfection consists in the adequacy of the empirical representations. Metaphysical perfection consists in the degrees of reality. Transcendental perfection in this, that it contains all that the thing requires. One thing is metaphysically more perfect than the other. One has more reality than the other. But each thing is transcendentally perfect.

ON THE NECESSARY AND THE CONTINGENT

The agreement of an object with the conditions of thinking is the possibility of it; actuality is absolute positing <*absoluta positio*>, i.e., the object is posited in itself, and not in relation to thinking. Actuality, insofar as it can be cognized *a priori*, is necessity. Now this necessity can be *hypothetical*, when the existence of a thing is cognized *a priori* in some respect <*secundum quid*>, or absolute, when the existence of a thing is cognized *a priori* simply speaking <*simpliciter*>. To cognize something *a priori* in some respect <*secundum quid*> is: when I cognize something from concepts without experience, but cognize the ground from experience. I can never cognize the existence of things fully *a priori*, from mere concepts, for it cannot be derived from mere concepts, but rather from the very beginning through experience. A ground must be given that still can be cognized through experience. For were this merely thought through concepts, then there would be more in the consequence than in the ground, because a concept indicates only the relation of the thing to my thinking in general. But actuality is an absolute positing, so that the object is posited in itself, and not relative to my understanding. Therefore I can never infer to actuality from possibility, but clearly to possibility from actuality. Thus I cannot cognize the existence of a thing fully *a priori*; absolute necessity is that which is to be cognized *a priori* simply speaking <*simpliciter*>. Something outside of thought must still be added, and this is the intuition of something actual, or perception. Perception is the representation of the actual. Thus the cognition of the existence of a thing is never possible without experience; either I cognize things wholly from experience, or I cognize the grounds of experience. It is thus wholly impossible to cognize absolute necessity, although we do not comprehend its impossibility. The cognition of necessity is therefore a hypothetical cognition. All things have derived necessity <*necessitatem derivativam*>; I can cognize them *a priori* in some respect <*secundum quid*> from grounds of experience. Necessary is that of which the opposite is impossible; possible <*possibile*> is that which is in agreement with the rules of thinking; contingent <*contingens*> is that of which the opposite is possible. These are nominal definitions, mere verbal explanations. *Logical* possibility, actuality, and necessity are cognized according to the principle of contradiction. Logical necessity does not prove the existence of a thing. But logical possibility is, as shown, not real possibility. Real possibility is the agreement with the conditions of a possible experience. The connection of a thing with experience is actuality. This connection, insofar as it can be cognized *a priori*, is necessity. This is, as shown, always hypothetical. We have a logical concept of absolute necessity. Necessity can be classified into real and into logical necessity. The logical absolute necessity of judgments is always a hypothetical necessity of the predicates of judgments, or a necessity under prior conditions. Absolute real necessity cannot be elucidated by any example. Only hypothetical necessity can be comprehended.

28:558

ON THE ALTERABLE AND THE UNALTERABLE

It is asked in which categories the concept of the alterable and the unalterable <*mutabilien . . . immutabilien*; G: *Veränderlichen . . . Unveränderlichen*> belong. We must first explain what *alteration* is; it is namely: the succession of opposite determinations of the same thing <*successio determinationum oppositarum in eodem ente*>. E.g., a body is altered externally if it is set out of rest into motion. Thus the concept of the alterable and unalterable belongs in the categories of existence. To exist *at the same time* means: to be in one and the very same time. Things succeed or follow upon one another when they are *different* in time. We regard as phenomena all things that we set in time and in space. The existence of opposite determinations in the same thing <*existentia determinationum oppositarum in eodem ente*> is a concept of the understanding. Existence, determination, opposition, thing, are all sheer concepts of the understanding. The possibility of alteration presupposes time. The opposite determinations <*determinationes oppositae*> that *follow upon one another* are contrarily opposed <*contrarie oppositae*>. The contrarily opposed determinations <*contrarie oppositae determinationes*> do not contradict themselves. A thing is contingent in whose place the opposite <*oppositum*; G: *das Gegenteil*>, can be thought. Contingency cannot yet be inferred from the existence of the opposites <*oppositorum*> that follow upon one another. To infer contingency from alteration appears, however, to be quite natural; for the opposite of that is indeed not possible. Nevertheless one cannot so infer, because alteration does not prove the contradictory opposite. Logical opposition is a negation which cancels the previous opposition. What matters most here is, how is alteration possible? I.e., how can opposed determinations be in one thing? One must *not* at all times believe that one comprehends what one understands; for comprehending is: cognizing something *a priori* through reason. With respect to experience we always need alteration. There is a general metaphysical canon: the essences of things are unalterable <*essentiae rerum sunt immutabiles*>; underlying this is the proposition: the essences of things are necessary <*essentiae rerum sunt necessariae*>, but from necessity follows unalterability, thus: the essences of things are

28:559

unalterable <*essentiae rerum sunt immutabiles*>. In the same sense that a thing is alterable, it is also contingent; and in the same sense that a thing is unalterable, it is also necessary. But the *logical* essence of things is necessary; and we are speaking here *not of the real*, but rather *of the logical essence*. For: the essences of things are unalterable <*essentiae rerum sunt immutabiles*>, one should say: to each thing belongs the essence of things in a necessary way. We cannot alter the essence of things without canceling it; when the essence of a thing is preserved <*salva rei essentia*>, nothing can be altered that belongs necessarily to the essence. Thus if we say: the essences of things are unalterable <*essentiae rerum sunt immutabiles*>, then this is understood of logical alteration, and not of real. One believed to be hearing much that was new when one attempted metaphysics; but one always received back only identical propositions for hypothetical ones. But an identical proposition has the illusion of containing something special. The cause of that is because the word *essence* is taken in a twofold sense. In the first sense it means *substance*; *Aristotle* took it that way already when he said: substances are unalterable. But in ontology one is not speaking of essence in this sense, but rather only of the first concept that I make of a thing.

ON THE REAL AND THE NEGATIVE

In all that of which one is conscious, one distinguishes something real and something negative. Negation is opposed to reality. An opposite is either logical or real. When someone denies something, then this is a logical opposite <*oppositum*>. Reality and negation cannot be posited in one and the very same thing. *Real* opposition consists in the connection of two real grounds, of which one ground cancels the consequence of the other. Among realities there can be an opposition. A reality is opposed not only to negation, but rather also to another reality that cancels the consequence of the other. The opposition of real grounds makes all alteration possible. If one finds negation in the world, then there are two grounds there, namely a real ground and an opposing ground. All realities are in harmony. A reality <*realitas*> is either phenomenon or noumenon. Everything that is exhibited positively to our senses is called: phenomenal reality <*realitas phaenomenon*>; and everything that is exhibited positively to our pure understanding is noumenal reality <*realitas noumenon*>. Phenomenal reality <*realitas phaenomenon*> or reality in appearance (or apparent reality) is that which lies only in our senses. Realities in appearance constitute the greatest part of all.

28:560

We can think in one thing: *reality*, *negation*, and the third determination that is to be added is *limitation;*[f] this is that negation which contains

---

[f] Two equivalents are given here: *Limitation oder Einschränkung* (560_{11-12}).

reality. The limitation of limitation refers especially to quantity. Reality is that whose concept already in itself means a being; negation is that whose concept is in itself a non-being. Each thing is reality. Thingness, so to speak, rests merely on reality. The perfection of a thing in general is nothing other than the magnitude of the reality. But [the] simply perfect is without any negation, and that is the greatest reality. A being that is real in every respect <*ens omnimode reale*> is thus, in the metaphysical sense, the most perfect.

THE SINGULAR <*SINGULARE*> AND THE UNIVERSAL <*UNIVERSALE*>

A universal thing <*ens universale*> cannot be thought and is only a concept of a thing <*conceptus entis*>; a completely determinate thing is a singular thing <*ens omnimode determinatum est ens singulare*>. The *scholastic* dispute between the realists and the nominalists was over the question, whether the universals <*universalia*> were actual things or only names. An individual, or singular thing <*ens singulare*>, is that insofar as it is thoroughly determined in itself. All difference is either numerical <*numerica*> (these either with the same or a different number <*eodem numero . . . diverso*>), or according to genus <*generica*>, or according to species <*specifica*>.

ON THE WHOLE <*TOTALI*> AND THE PART <*PARTIALI*>

The concept of the whole lies in quantity. Many, insofar as it is one, is totality. That thing, in which there is the totality of many things, is a whole <*id, in quo est omnitudo plurium, est totum*>. Quantum as well as composite <*compositum*> contains the concept of plurality. But the concept of composite <*compositi*> is universal; for the parts can be heterogeneous here. But with the concept of quantum <*quanti*> it is always presupposed that the parts are homogeneous. Thus each quantum is a composite <*compositum*>, but not every composite <*compositum*> is a quantum. Of quantum <*quanto*> as well as composite <*composito*> I ask: does it exist as a whole, or only as part? All parts that belong to a composite <*composito*> are called component parts <*compartes*>. A thing that can be thought only as part of a whole is an incomplete thing <*ens incompletum*>. Each quantum is a multitude <*multitudo*>; each quantum must thus also consist of homogeneous parts. But an infinite multitude is greater than all numbers, and we cannot have a distinct concept of it. Each quantum is either continuous <*continuum*> or discrete <*discretum*>. A quantum through whose magnitude the multitude of parts is undetermined is called continuous <*continuum*>; it consists

28:561

325

of as many parts as I want to give it, but it does not consist of individual parts. Each quantum, on the other hand, through whose magnitude I want to represent the multitude of its parts, is discrete <*discretum*>. A discrete quantum <*quantum discretum*> must be distinguished from a continuous quantum <*quanto continuo*> which is represented as discrete <*discretum*>. A quantum in which I determine the parts is discrete <*discretum*>, but not in itself <*per se*; G: *an sich selbst*>. A quantum continuous in itself <*quantum continuum per se*> is one in which the number of parts is indeterminate; a quantum discrete in itself <*quantum discretum per se*> is one in which the number of parts is arbitrarily determined by us. Discrete quantum <*quantum discretum*> is therefore called number <*numerus*>. Through number we represent each quantum as discrete <*discretum*>. If I make a concept of the discrete quantum <*quanto discreto*>, then I think of a number. Assignable parts <*partes assignabiles*> are the parts that, connected with each other, make a number concept. A multitude <*multitudo*> that can be thought in a continuous quantum <*quanto continuo*> is always greater than every assignable part <*omni assignabili major*>. Something is larger than the other if the latter is only equal to a part of the former. For something to alter into a larger is to increase, and for something to alter into a smaller is to decrease. Each quantum can be increased or decreased. A quantum that cannot be decreased at all is the smallest <*minimum*>. With a continuous quantum <*quanto continuo*> no smallest <*minimum*> can be thought, for each part is again a quantum, therefore there is no smallest. There is also no smallest time; for each small part is again a continuous quantum <*quantum continuum*> that consists of parts. Leibniz calls such concepts misleading ideas <*conceptus deceptores*>. Space and time are continuous quanta <*quanta continua*>. A largest and a smallest in space and in time cannot be thought. *The* space in which all assignable <*assignabile*> parts are contained is called *infinite* or absolute space. *The* time in which all assignable <*assignable*> parts are contained, is *eternity*. But these are *ideas* that we cannot grasp.

28:562

ON MAGNITUDES

All magnitudes (quantities <*quantitates*>) can be considered two ways: either extensively or intensively. There are objects in which we distinguish no multitude of homogeneous parts; this is *intensive* magnitude. This magnitude is the degree. The objects in which we distinguish a multitude of homogeneous parts have *extensive* magnitude. The intensive magnitude is the magnitude of the degree, and the extensive magnitude is the magnitude of the aggregate. Everything that is represented in space and in time has extensive magnitude. All reality in space and in time has a degree. –

Something simple can be thought of as a magnitude, although no multitude can occur there; thus as intensive magnitude.

ON THE DEGREE OF POSSIBILITY

Inner possibility has no degree, for we can cognize it only according to the principle of contradiction <*principio contradictionis*>. But the *hypothetical* has a degree, because every hypothesis is a ground, and every ground has a magnitude. Every ground has a degree, but the consequences can again be considered extensively and intensively. A ground that has many consequences is a *fruitful* ground. A ground that has great consequences is an *important* ground.

Hypothetical possibility can be viewed as diminishing, because it can be decreased into infinity. One speaks in the philosophical schools of the magnitude of unity, truth, and perfection. Transcendental unity, truth, and perfection have no magnitude at all, and cannot at all be compared according to magnitude. Things can be compared according to magnitude only with a third, but not with their own essence, as with transcendental unity, truth, and perfection. But the agreement of a thing with a ground can be larger or smaller. The agreement with the *sufficient* ground is the greatest conformity.

ON SUBSTANCE AND ACCIDENT

Relation is threefold: the relation of judgments of the subject to the predicate, the relation of a ground to the consequence, and the relation of the members of a division to the divided concepts. Judgments are, according to the relation: categorical, hypothetical, and disjunctive. To these correspond the categories of subsistence, of inherence, and of *interaction* <*commercii*>. Substance is that which exists in itself only as subject; accident, what exists only as predicate or determination of a thing, or whose existence is mere inherence. That whose existence is mere subsistence, is substance. If some maintain that substances could also exist as inhering items, but that it is not necessary, then that is incorrect.

Accidents <*accidentia*> are manners of thinking of the existence of a thing, and not different existences; just as *Locke* says, that the substance is a bearer of the accidents, therefore it is also called substrate <*substratum*>.[16] The relation of the accidents to the substance is not the relation of the cause to the effect. Substance can clearly exist as consequence <*rationatum*>, but not as predicate. These are wholly different concepts. We are indeed acquainted with the accidents <*accidentia*>, but not with the substantial. This is the subject which exists *after the separation of all accidents* <*accidentia*>, and that is *unknown* to us, for we know the substances only through the *accidents* <*accidentia*>. This substantial is the

28:563

something in general. I cannot cognize something of a thing other than through judgments, and predicates always underlie these. We can cognize substances only through accidents. Through reason we cannot comprehend *a priori* how something could exist only as subject, or again, something as a predicate of something else. We cannot comprehend *a priori* the possibility of subsisting, the impossibility of subsisting, and the necessity of inhering. But that we cannot comprehend the substantial, but rather merely the *accidents* <*accidentia*>, comes from this: because we are much too short-sighted, and because the understanding can think only through concepts, and concepts are nothing more than predicates. *Descartes* said: substance is that which requires for its existence no existence of another thing, i.e., what exists without being the consequence of another thing. But that is not a substance, rather an independent thing <*independens*>. *Spinoza* also followed this concept, which was the cause of his error. The existence of a substance is subsistence, the existence of an accident <*accidentis*> is inherence. – We also have a principle among the substances and accidents; this is the principle of the perdurability of substances. All philosophers have used the principle of the perdurability of substance. This principle is of the utmost importance, for without it no physics is possible. We want to call *vicissitudo* alteration <G: *Veränderung*>, and *perduratio* or *stabilitas*, perdurability <G: *Beharrlichkeit*>. All alterations presuppose a subject, upon which the predicates follow. The concept of alteration constantly presupposes the perdurability of the substance. But why something would perdure necessarily, we do not comprehend.

28:564

ON POWER

The concept of cause lies in the concept of power. The substance is considered as subject, and the latter as cause. Accident is therefore something real because it exists by inhering <*inhaerendo*> and not for itself. Causality is the determination of something else, by which it is posited according to general rules. The concept of the relation <*respectus*> or of the relation of the substance to the existence of accidents, insofar as it contains their grounds, is *power*. All powers are classified into primitive or basic powers and into derivative or derived powers. We attempt to reduce the derivative powers <*vires derivativae*> to the primitive powers. All physics, of bodies as well as spirits, the latter of which is called psychology, amounts to this: deriving diverse powers, which we know only through observations, as much as possible from basic powers.

Hidden quality <*qualitas occulta*> is a hidden property of things, for there are very many properties of things unknown to us, e.g., the true cause of magnetic power; the cause as to why saltpeter makes water cold, and many others.

ON STATE

State means the thoroughgoing determination of a thing in time. No state can be assigned to a necessary being; for if the outer state is altered, then the thing itself is altered. Thus the word state cannot at all be used of God. God has no state. He indeed stands in relations with outer things, yet these do not affect him, but rather only the world, and on this account he is unalterable.

WHAT IS ACTING?

Acting and effecting can be assigned only to substances. Action is the determination of the power of a substance as a cause of a certain accident   28:565
<*accidentis*>. Causality <*causalitas*> is the property of a substance insofar as it is considered as a cause of an accident <*accidentis*>. We can cognize the powers of things through alterations. Action <*actio*> is either inner or transeunt <*immanens . . . transiens*>. If an *inner* action <*actio immanens*; G: *innere Handlung*> is performed, then one says: the substance activates. Transeunt action <*actio transiens*> is also called influence <*influxus*; G: *Einfluss*>. Suffering obviously corresponds to influence <*influxus*>, but not to inner action. Suffering is the inherence of an accident <*accidentis*> of a substance by a power that is outside it. Interaction is the relation of substances with reciprocal influence <*commercium est relatio substantiarum mutuo influxu*>. *Faculty* and *power* are different. With a faculty we imagine only the possibility of power. Between faculty and power lies the concept of endeavor <*conatus*; G: *Bestrebung*>. When the determining ground for an effect is internally sufficient, then it is a *dead* power. But when it is internally and externally sufficient, then it is a *living* power. Power which is merely internally sufficient, without being able to produce the effect, is always opposed to an opposing power which hinders its effect, an impediment <*impedimentum*>. Thus as soon as the impediment <*impedimentum*> is removed, the dead power becomes living.

A faculty that is sufficient for all sorts of things is an aptitude <*habitus*; G: *Fertigkeit*>. With this one has to distinguish: *effecting, acting,* and *doing. Acting* (<*agere*; G: *handeln*>) can contain everything possible, relative to the consequence <*rationatum*> of the action. Action <*actio*> is when a real consequence arises out of it. Doing (<*facere*; G: *tun*>) means acting *from freedom*; a deed <*factum*> is always attributed only to an acting substance. –

Impediment <*impedimentum*> is either formal or real; formal or negative impediment <*impedimentum formale s. negativum*> is a lack; real or positive impediment <*impedimentum reale s. positivum*> consists in an efficient cause which stands opposed to the other. –

ON THE SIMPLE AND THE COMPOSITE

The concept of a composite <*compositi*> presupposes parts. When the parts of a composite <*compositi*> can be given prior to the composition, then it is a real composite <*compositum reale*>. But when they cannot be given prior to the composition, then it is an ideal composite <*compositum ideale*>. Indeed it appears as if the parts could always be thought prior to the composition, and thus that there would be no ideal composites <*composita idealia*>; but there really are such, as *space* and *time*. In space one cannot think of parts without first thinking the whole.

28:566   A substantial composite <*compositum substantiale*> is that which is composed of substances. Composition is a relation; I must be able to think the correlates <*correlata*> prior to the relation. A substantial composite is the joining of many substances in one connection <*compositum substantiale est complexus plurium substantiarum in uno nexu*>. A complex <*complexus*> is not always already a composite <*compositum*>; I may only think it as a composite <*compositum*>, e.g., the invisible church; those who belong to that are composed in the idea. A formal composite <*compositum formale*> is that whose parts cannot be represented otherwise than in the composition; they cannot be thought as separated. I can easily imagine parts of space; but this is always based upon the idea of the whole. There is only one united space. –

Birth and death <*ortus et interitus*> are not alterations. Creation is no alteration. The succeeding determinations in the thing are alterations; these determinations in a thing come about and pass away; that is change <*mutatio*>. The thing comes about means: being follows upon non-being. It always presupposes a time. The coming about is the existence upon which the whole duration follows. The passing away is the non-being that follows the whole duration.

The main question is: whether a substantial composite <*compositum substantiale*> consists of simple substances? If I want to think of a substantial composite <*compositum substantiale*>, how is this at all possible other than by an interaction <*commercium*> such that the substances have reciprocal influence on each other? For interaction <*commercium*> consists in reciprocal influence <*influxu mutuo*>. Matter and form is in each substantial composite <*composito substantiali*>. The substance is matter; the relation of the substances is form. Thus I can think simple parts in each substantial composite <*compositum substantiale*>.[g] The main principle here is: in all alterations of the world, matter perdures, the form is altered. Substance does not pass away. This law of the perdurability of substance is comparable with the law of causality, that nothing happens without cause, and [it] concerns the same pairs. All alterations are the coming

[g] In Lehmann: *comp. subst.* (566₂₅).

about or passing away of accidents <*accidentium*>. Namely: if we consider things in time and the change of time, then we can say: the state of all things is flowing, all is in the flow of time. But we would never be able to notice this if something were not perduring; time, the succession of various things, could never be perceived if everything changed, nothing were perduring. All change, all alteration requires at the same time something perduring, if our experience of that is to be possible. Substance perdures; only the accidents alter. The changing is always connected with the   28:567
perduring, and the determination of existence either in time or in space is possible only if something is perduring. If something does not perdure there is no possibility of the experience that alterations take place. To compare it merely with something coarse, the sailor on the sea would not be able to observe his movements if the sea moved with him: if there were not something perduring, like an island, with which he could note how he moved away.

ON SPACE AND TIME

If I take away all existence of things, the form of sensibility still remains yet, i.e., *space* and *time*; for these are not properties of things, but rather properties in our senses; they are not objective, but rather subjective properties. I can therefore imagine space and time *a priori*, for they precede all things. Space and time are the conditions of the existence of things; [they] are individual intuitions and not concepts. These intuitions concern no object; [they] are empty, are mere forms of intuitions. Space and time are not things themselves, not properties, not a constitution of things, but rather the form of sensibility. Sensibility is the receptivity[h] for being affected. The forms of intuition have no objective reality, but rather merely subjective [reality]. If I assume space to be a being in itself, then Spinozism is irrefutable, i.e., the parts of the world are parts of the divinity. Space is the divinity; it is united, all-present; nothing can be thought outside of it; everything is in it. – Time is either *protensive* or *extensive* or *intensive*; *protensive* insofar as one follows after the other. *Extensive* concerns the multitude of existing things at the same time; *intensive* concerns reality. Space occurs only with things, as appearances. Appearances teach us nothing as to *how the things are*, but rather how they affect our senses. A simple substance cannot be extended. – Division <*divisio*> is either *logical, metaphysical*, or *physical*. The division of the pure concept is logical. Each concept has a sphere <*sphaeram*>; the sphere <*sphaera*> can be classified. Thus the concept of a human being; the concept of animal includes even more in it. These are   28:568
classifications, not divisions. The metaphysical division consists in the distinguishing of parts; the physical in the separation of parts. *Space* and

---

[h] Two equivalents are used here: *die Receptivität, die Empfänglichkeit* (567₂₁₋₂).

time can be divided metaphysically, but not physically, i.e., they cannot be separated. The distinguishing of parts is not separation. Everything that is extended is divisible. Every part of matter is movable, every motion is separation. Division <*divisio*> is either quantitative or qualitative <*vel quantitativa vel qualitativa*>. The former is the division of substances insofar as they consist of homogeneous parts; the latter is the division of substances insofar as they go into heterogeneous parts; this is called sorting. Such sorting must happen sometimes in thoughts.

ON THE FINITE AND THE INFINITE

The concept of the greatest <*maximi*> belongs to the concept of the how much <*quanti*>, of the quantity; but totality <*omnitudo*> to the concept of the whole <*toti*; G: *Ganzen*>. The greatest <*maximum*> is a relative concept, i.e., it does not give me a determinate concept. So I can say: this human being is the most learned, namely among many learned; but then I still do not yet know *how* learned he is: among others he can in turn be the most unlearned. Totality <*omnitudo*> is an absolute concept. The concept of the infinite <*infiniti*> is quite different from either. The infinite <*infinitum*> is a magnitude for which no determinate measure can be specified. Every magnitude is infinite if it is impossible to measure and evaluate it; but the impossibility lies in the subject, i.e., in us. If we want to measure a magnitude, then it must be given to us, e.g., a rod, a mile. A number always expresses the concept of magnitude. I can indeed look at it; but in order to express the magnitude by a concept I must have a unit which I take several times in order to measure the given magnitude in such a manner, and to attain a determinate concept of it. The cosmos is the greatest quantum, of which I can specify no determinate concept, which cannot be measured.

Infinite can actually be taken in two senses. In the first the concept of the infinite is a pure concept of the understanding, and then it is called: real infinity <*infinitum reale*>, i.e., in which there are no negations, i.e., no limitations. In the second sense the concept of the infinite refers to space and to time, consequently to the objects of the senses; and that is *mathematical infinity*, which arises through the successive addition of one to one. It is said: space is infinite, i.e., the concept of the magnitude of space is never total. With real infinity <*infinito reali*> I think the totality <*omnitudinem*>, and thus I have a determinate concept; but with mathematical infinity <*infinito mathematico*> I can never think the collective totality <*omnitudinem collectivam*>. Mathematical infinity <*infinitum mathematicum*> is a quantum given or givable into infinity <*quantum in infinitum datum s. dabile*>. The given <*datum*> concerns space, and givable <*dabile*> time. Beyond every number I can add a higher one, and I can think it; but a given mathematical infinity <*infinitum mathe-*

28:569

maticum datum> goes beyond all human power of cognition. It is to be the *totality of appearances*. The magnitude of appearances cannot be given, for appearance is no thing in itself, and has no magnitude. There is thus merely the magnitude of my progression *<progressus>* in space and in time. From the concept of the real thing *<entis realis>* and its real infinity its mathematical infinity cannot be inferred. The word infinity is in this case not at all appropriate. But one calls the real thing *<ens reale>* infinite, because this word at the same time indicates our incapacity. But *we cannot conceive* what sort of relation real infinity has with the mathematical or number. Were space and time properties of things in themselves then the infinity of the world would indeed be inconceivable, but not on that account impossible. But if space and time are not properties of things in themselves, then the impossibility of an infinite given world already flows from the inconceivability.

ON SAMENESS AND DIVERSITY

Considered fundamentally these concepts belong in logic; but they occur here because of the principle of *Leibniz*, the principle of the identity of indiscernibles *<principii identitatis indiscernibilium>*. The principle of the identity of indiscernibles *<principium identitatis indiscernibilium>* is: things that agree in all features are the same in number *<sunt numero eadem>*. The things that are wholly the same internally are not different *<interne totaliter eadem non sunt diversa>*. (The inner determinations of a thing are quality *<qualitas>* and quantity *<quantitas>*.) But that is false. If *through the understanding* we think things that are wholly equal, agreeing in all features, then as noumena they are obviously the same in number *<numero eadem>*. But it is different with the objects *of the senses*, for all parts of space are outside one another, are already outer determinations. Objects in space are therefore already plural *<plura>*, *because* they are in space. E.g., if two drops of water or eggs were wholly   28:570
equal according to inner determination, according to quantity and quality, agreeing in everything (although one does not find this in nature), then they would still be different (not same in number *<numero eadem>*), just because they are in different places, one outside the other, not in one and the same place *<in uno eodemque loco>*. –

The *moment* is the boundary of time; it is that which the position *<positum>* determines. It is that which the *point* is in space; therefore one also calls it a point in time. But time does not consist of moments, for I cannot think these before I have a time; nor the boundary of the thing before the thing itself. The determination of the magnitude of a thing by comparison with a unit is called *measurement*. The concept of dimension also does not belong in metaphysics. Space has three dimensions, but time only one. Dimension is properly the representation of the magnitude of a thing, but one which is distinguished from others according to form. The time which is concurrent with the thoughts of time is the present; that which follows the thoughts is the future; that which precedes, the past time. The existence that follows upon nonexistence is the beginning. The nonexistence that follows upon existence is the end.

Everything that exists in time exists either in a moment <*in instanti*> or perduringly <*perdurabile*>. Duration is the magnitude of the existence of a thing. The existence that is smaller than every time is a *moment*; it is the boundary of time. The existence that is larger than every time, or the time without boundary, is *eternity*. Sempiternity <*sempiternitas*> is the future infinite duration, irrespective of the infinite beginning. Eternity, as a concept of the understanding, is only an unlimited duration; but eternity in time is sempiternity <*sempiternitas*>. The concept of limits, which is a pure concept of the understanding, is related to the concept of *boundaries*, which is a mathematical concept; just like the concept of infinity. The measure of a thing in itself is the totality, and this is the absolute magnitude, which is the proper standard of the things, for all things are possible through limitation of this totality. The concept of boundary belongs only to the phenomena <*phenomenis*>, but that of limits to the noumena <*noumenis*>. Solid space has the surface as a boundary, planar space the line, and the line the point. Point is the determined position of space. Point is in space, but is not a part of it. Limit <*limes*> is the negation, so that the thing may not be the greatest <*ut ens non sit maximum*>. But time has only one boundary, namely, the moment.

ON CAUSE AND EFFECT

Cause and ground are to be distinguished. What contains the ground of possibility is ground <*ratio*>, or the principle of being <*principium essendi*>. The ground of actuality is the principle of becoming <*principium fiendi*>, cause <*causa*>. What contains the ground of something is called in general principle <*principium*>. The cause is that which contains the ground of the actuality of the determination or of the substance. The three lines in a triangle are indeed the ground, but not the cause. Cause is also used of negation, e.g., inattention is the cause of errors. Every cause must in itself be something real, for what is the ground of actuality is something positive. The consequence <*rationatum*> of the cause is the effect <*causatum*>. What is an effect <*causatum*> of a cause <*causa*> is a dependent thing <*dependens*>. Cause <*causa*>, as long as it is not an effect of another <*causatum alterius*>, is an independent thing <*independens*>. An independent thing is a thing by means of itself <*ens independens est ens a se*>. It is not called a thing by means of itself <*ens a se*> because it is supposed to be from itself, but rather because it exists without cause. In the series of effects and causes it is the first. A contingent thing <*contingens*> is no thing by means of itself <*ens a se*>, but rather a thing dependent on another <*dependens ab alio*>, thus an effect <*causatum*>. In the series of effects and causes, it is a succeeding member.

A contingent being is also necessary, but only conditionally necessary; but things by means of themselves <*entia a se*> are absolutely necessary. Thus every thing is either absolutely or hypothetically necessary; for were it contingent then it would be valid only for the subject and not for the object. Contingent is that whose non-being is possible. I cannot cognize this non-being by the principle of contradiction. We cannot comprehend the absolute contingency, as well as the absolute necessity of a thing, either from reason or from experience, but rather merely its relative contingency or necessity. One cannot cognize *a priori* from mere concepts whether something is contingent in itself, for I can think away everything; the opposite of all things is possible, thinkable; nothing is contradicted in my concept. I cannot infer to contingency from the successive alteration of a thing, or from the non-being, no more than to the necessity of existence from the existence. For here the question is: whether a thing in the same time, could be or not be in the same moment. But I cannot possibly comprehend this. We indeed assume an absolutely necessary being, but we cannot comprehend how a highest being could exist absolutely necessarily; for the opposite, the non-being, is thinkable, i.e., nothing in my understanding is contradicted. We can cognize the contingency of things only in the coming about and passing away of things, and not from the mere concept; that is contingent which becomes, which previously was not, and vice versa. A contingent thing <*contingens*> is properly that which comes to pass, and such a thing must have a cause. That which happens is either coming about or passing away, or mere alteration of a thing. Alteration belongs merely to the state; and then I can say: its state is contingent, but the thing itself is not thereby contingent; only from the coming about and passing away can I infer the contingency of the thing itself. Thus states must have a cause; but I never ask about the cause of matter. As already mentioned, that which contains the ground of something is called a principle <*principium*>. What contains the ground of actuality is called cause <*causa*> or principle of becoming <*principium fiendi*>; what contains the ground of possibility is called the principle of being <*principium essendi*>. What contains the ground of cognition is called the principle of cognizing <*principium cognoscendi*>. Several causes together can be causes of the actuality of a thing; and then they are called co-causes <*concausae*>. Single cause <*causa solitaria*>, when there is only one cause. The co-causes <*concausae*> are either coordinated or subordinated; subordinated, if one co-cause <*concausa*> is the effect <*causatum*> of the other. But if several co-causes <*concausae*> are causes of an effect <*causati*>, then they are coordinated. Coordinate causes concur <*causae coordinatae concurrunt*>, but subordinated ones do not.

28:572

Each cause *<causa>* is then complemented sufficiently *<complementum ad sufficientiam>*, and to be viewed as a complement of the effect *<causati>*; they are coordinated with each other. God alone is a single cause *<causa solitaria>*; all other causes are subordinated to him, but none coordinated.

Efficient cause *<causa efficiens>*. There is much that does contain the ground of a matter, but is not the actual cause. There are positive as well as negative causes. An efficient cause *<causa efficiens>* is a cause *by efficient power*. A necessary condition *<conditio sine qua non>* is a determination of things that is indeed not negative, but is also not called *efficient* cause, although it is at the same time reckoned a cause. So with cannonballs, the powder is a necessary condition *<conditio sine qua non>*; but the efficient cause *<causa efficiens>* is the soldier who ignites the cannon. Among the coordinate causes, one is the principal one *<principalis>*, the others secondary *<secundaria>*. If one is the principal cause *<causa principalis>*, and the other less principal *<minus principalis>*, then the latter is an auxiliary cause *<causa auxiliaris>*. Instrumental causes *<causae instrumentales>* are subordinate causes *<causae subordinatae>*, as long as they are determined with respect to causality *<quoad causalitatem>* by the principal cause *<causa principalis>*, e.g., the soldiers. What is assigned to the instrumental cause *<causa instrumentalis>* is assigned immediately to the principal cause *<causa principalis>*, that is if it depends completely on the principal cause *<causa principalis>*. If it does not depend completely on the principal cause *<causa principalis>*, then it is not completely assigned to the principal cause *<causa principalis>*, but then it is rather a spontaneous cause *<causa spontanea>*; e.g., what the servant does, so long as he has full authority completely from the master, that will be assigned to the master as principal cause *<causa principalis>*, but not in the aspects where he does not depend on the master.

A single action along with its effects is called *event*. The relation wherein an event occurs is a *circumstance* (*<circumstantia*; G: *Umstand>*). This outer relation is according to either space or time. Circumstances constitute this relation of space and time. The summation of all relations of space and of time, which concur for the event, is called the *occasion*. Thus there is an occasion of location and of time. The occasion of location is called opportunity *<opportunitas>*, and that of time timeliness *<tempestivitas>*. Of the latter one says: it must be seized because time passes away.

One says: *circumstances alter the matter*. The smallest circumstance alters a matter *<minima circumstantia variat rem>*. If the circumstances do not concur, then they do not alter the event. From the above already follows: when the cause has been posited, the effect is posited *<posita causa ponitur effectus>*. But when the cause has been canceled, the effect is canceled *<sublata causa tollitur effectus>* is just as certain; when the effect

28:573

has been canceled, the cause is canceled <*sublato effectu tollitur causa*> is not certain, but rather the causality of the cause is canceled <*tollitur causalitas causae*>. As the cause, so the effect <*qualis causa, talis effectus*> does not mean: the cause is similar to the effect, for cause and effect is not a relation of similarity or a connection in concepts, but rather in the matters. This means that the effects conduct themselves like their causes; or we name the causes only after the effects. Thus if there is another effect, then the cause must also have another name. But cause and effect may not be thought tautologically, for they are wholly different matters. The proposition: "the effect must be *similar* to the cause, and vice versa" is only applicable to the physiology of organized beings. The effect testifies to the cause <*effectus testatur de causa*>. We can already view something as effect before we recognize the cause; e.g., everything contingent. But this proposition must be understood only this way: the effect testifies to the cause as far as the quality of the causality <*effectus testatur de causa quoad qualitatem causalitatis*>; for I cognize the efficient powers of the cause <*vires efficientes causae*> by the whole of all immediate effects, but only according to the causality. Accordingly we cannot cognize God wholly, but rather only as much as he has revealed himself through the world, according to the proportions of the magnitude of the world. The cognition of God is thus equal only to the cognition of the effect of God. Now this depends on how great my cognitions of the effects of God are. Thus the proposition is not to be taken strictly <*stricte*>: the effect testifies to the cause <*effectus testatur de causa*>.

28:574

This connection <*nexus*> is the causal connection <*nexus causalis*>, in particular effective <*effectivus*> [connection]. This effective connection <*nexus effectivus*> is to be distinguished chiefly from the connection of finality <*nexu finali*>, and indeed in the method of philosophizing, so that we do not substitute a connection of finality <*nexum finalem*> for an effective connection <*effectivo*>. E.g., why does a wound heal in the body? If one wanted to answer: providence has already so ordered it, then this would be a connection of finality <*nexus finalis*>, but not an effective connection <*effectivus*>. Here I want to know the cause, how it happens; to comprehend the effective connection <*nexus effectivus*> is true philosophy. If I do not progress in the investigation of the causes, and call upon the principle <*principium*> of the connection of finality <*nexus finalis*>, then this is a begging of the question <*petitio principii*>. Many philosophers assumed the principle of the connection of finality <*principium nexus finalis*>, and also believed to discover much from it. So *Leibniz* assumed, e.g., that a ray of light traverses the shortest way from one location to another, from which he then derived the laws of dioptrics. *Epicurus* wholly rejected the connection of finality <*nexum finalem*>; *Plato*, on the other hand, wholly accepted it. Both are wrong: they must be connected. I must always seek to derive everything from causes, as much as is feasible; and then also assume a being which has arranged everything purposefully. – If I assume the connection of finality <*nexum finalem*> alone, then I still do not know all ends; indeed, I can even think of ends which can rest on chimeras, and I pass by the causes. But this is a great damage to the investigation. To call on only the connection of finality <*nexum finalem*> is a cushion of lazy philosophy. In philosophy one must first seek to derive everything from causes, thus according to the principle of effective connection <*principio nexus effectivi*>. And even if it very often is wrong, it is still no vain effort, for the method and the way of investigating something in *such* a manner is appropriate to philosophy and to human understanding. There are many false presuppositions; but when one proceeds to investigate into them, then one occasionally discovers, contrary to expectation, other truths. E.g., *Rousseau* presupposed: human beings are by nature good, and therefore all evil arises because one does not prevent it; consequently education must be negative, and human beings should be deterred from evil by education. This is quite pleasing, although the

28:575 principle is false. But if I assume that human beings are evil from nature, then no one would make the effort to hinder evil, because it lies already in nature. Then education will rest on the wishes of the highest being, so that it would make an end of evil by a supernatural power.

Thus one must remain with the effective connection <*nexu effectivo*>, even when one sees ahead that one will not advance everywhere in that way.

ON MATTER AND FORM

This difference between matter and form lies already in the nature of our reason.

Matter is the given <*datum*>, what is given, thus the *stuff*. – But *form* is how these givens <*data*> are posited, the manner in which the manifold stands in connection. We see matter and form in all parts. We find matter and form in our judging and effecting. The ancients said: the universal or the genus was the matter, the specific difference <*differentia specifica*> the form. E.g., human being would be the genus, thus the matter; but learned human being [the] specific difference <*differentia specifica*>, thus the form. The ancients placed a great deal on the form; they said it was the essence of matters. That is also quite right, for in no thing can we produce the matter, but rather only the form; e.g., all artists and craftsmen. In our soul the sensations are matter; but all our concepts and judgments are the form.

Matter in the *physical* sense is the substrate <*substratum*> of extended objects, the possibility of bodies. But in the *transcendental* sense every given <*datum*> is matter, but the form [is] the relation of the given <*dati*>. Transcendental matter is the thing that is determinable <*de-*

terminabile>; but transcendental form the determination, or the act of determining <*actus determinandi*>. Transcendental matter is the reality or the given <*datum*> for all things. But the limitation of reality constitutes transcendental form. All realities of things lie as if in infinite matter, where one then separates some realities for a thing, which is the form.

Matter is distinguished into matter out of which <*materia ex qua*>, in which <*in qua*>, and around which <*circa quam*>. – Matter out of which <*materia ex qua*> is the thing itself which is determinable <*determinabile*>, a thing which is already determined. Matter around which <*materia circa quam*> means matter in the act itself of determination <*in ipso determinationis actu*>, e.g., the text of a sermon is not matter out of which <*materia ex qua*>, but rather around which something else moves about <*circa quam aliquis versatur*>. – Matter in which <*materia in qua*> means the subject of inherence. Matter around which <*materia circa quam*> properly means the thoughts by which a matter is given form. E.g., the plan of a building is matter around which <*materia circa quam*>, but the stone, wood, etc., are the matter out of which <*materia ex qua*>. – But the difference is very fine. 28:576

THE TRANSCENDENTAL PHILOSOPHY

The transcendental philosophy is the philosophy of principles, of the elements of human cognition *a priori*. This is at the same time the ground of how an *a priori* geometry is possible. But it is quite necessary to know how a science can be produced from ourselves, and how human understanding can have produced such a thing. To be sure, this investigation would not be so necessary with respect to geometry if we did not have other *a priori* cognitions which are quite important and interesting to us; e.g., of the origin of things, of the necessary and the contingent, and of whether the world is necessary or not. These cognitions do not have such evidence as geometry. We therefore want to know how a cognition of human beings is possible *a priori*; so we must distinguish and investigate all *a priori* cognitions; then we can *determine the boundaries of human understanding*, and all chimeras, which are otherwise possible in metaphysics, will be brought under determinate principles and rules. But now we classify the principles of human *a priori* cognition:

1. into the principles of *a priori* sensibility, and this is the *transcendental aesthetic*, which contains in itself the *a priori* cognitions and concepts of space and time; and
2. into the principles of intellectual human *a priori* cognition, and this is the *transcendental logic*. These principles of human *a priori* cognition are the *categories* of the understanding, which as such have already been indicated above, and these exhaust all of that which the

understanding contains in itself *a priori*, but from which hereafter yet other concepts can be derived.

Were we to so dissect the transcendental concepts, then this would be a *transcendental grammar*,[17] which contains the ground of human language; e.g., how the present *<praesens>*, perfect *<perfectum>*, past perfect *<plusquamperfectum>*, lies in our understanding, what adverbs *<adverbia>* are, etc. If one thought this through, then one would have a transcendental grammar. Logic would contain the formal use of the understanding. Then transcendental philosophy, the doctrine of the universal *a priori* concepts, would be able to follow.

28:577

ON THE IDEA AND THE IDEAL

There are *a priori* cognitions through which objects are possible. That an object is possible merely through a cognition is strange; but all order, all purposeful relations are possible through a cognition. E.g., a truth is not possible without a cognition that precedes. The *a priori* cognition through which an object is possible is the *idea*. *Plato* said: one must study the ideas.[18] He said: with God the ideas are intuitions, with human beings reflections. Ultimately he spoke of them as though they were things. – The idea is unalterable; it is the essential, the ground through which the objects are possible.

An *archetype* is actually an object of intuition, insofar as it is the ground of imitation. *Thus Christ is the archetype of all morality. But in order to regard something as an archetype, we must first have an idea according to which we can cognize the archetype*, in order to hold it for that; for otherwise we indeed would not be able to cognize the archetype, and thus could be deceived. But if we have an idea of something, e.g., of the highest morality, and now an object of intuition is given, someone is represented to us as being congruent with this idea, then we can say: this is the archetype, follow it! – If we have no idea, then we can assume no archetype, even if it were to come from heaven. I must have an idea in order to seek the archetype concretely *<in concreto>*. – The model is a ground of imitation. We can indeed realize actions and objects according to a model, also *without* an idea; but then they agree only *by mere chance* with the model. In morality one must assume no model, but rather follow the archetype which is equal to the idea of holiness.

[Cosmology][i]

of the understanding. The substantial whole which is not part of another $\quad$ 28:581
is the noumenal or intelligible world <*totum substantiarum quod non pars
alterius est, est mundus noumenon . . . intelligibilis*>, the world of the understanding. The difference between intelligible and sensible world <*mundus intelligibilis . . . sensibilis*> must not be taken logically, but rather the
cognition of it is transcendental. The sensible world <*mundus sensibilis*>
is the summation of the appearances that have come about in no other
way than through the senses. The sensory world is also called nature.
The intelligible world <*mundus intelligibilis*> must not be called intellectual <*intellectualis*>. The intelligible world remains unknown to us. Substances are the matter of the world, the formal aspect of the world
consists in their connection <*nexu*> and indeed in a real connection
<*nexu reali*>. The world is thus a *real* whole <*totum reale*>, not ideal
<*ideale*>. – Can one think of only a single world, or of several worlds
outside one another? The author says:[19] one can think of only one. – If I
represent to myself the world merely through the understanding, then
most certainly several can be thought of outside one another. As intelligible world I can represent several to myself, but as sensible world only a
single one. –

The influence of the substances in the world is called interaction
<*commercium*> or reciprocal influence <*influxus mutuus*>. All substances
are isolated for themselves, i.e., they exist as they would exist if there were
no others at all outside of them. Thus they need no other substances for
their existence. All substances must have a ground of their reciprocal
connection. The cause of their existence and also of their reciprocal
connection is God. The interaction <*commercium*> of substances is thus
not at all to be conceived from the existence of substance. Physical influence <*influxus physicus*> is the entirely natural influence which cannot go
beyond nature. In which world do we become conscious of our essence, or
intuit ourselves? Not in the intelligible world, but rather in the sensible
world. This world is an observable world <*mundus adspectabilis*>. –

[i] Text begins at the top of a ms page (ms 83, the front side of a sheet) in the middle of an
unidentifiable word. What follows is the tail-end of the section on cosmology, and then the
section on psychology. The ms of *Metaphysik L₂* is extant from here to the end of the *L₂*
notes. What preceded this was preserved by Pölitz in his edition of that part of the notes.

{Nothing is isolated in the world <*in mundo non datur insula*>, and no thing is independent from the other.}ʲ

Antinomy is the conflict of laws. In the sensible world there is no totality, the sensible world in itself has no boundaries; an absolute world boundary with regard to space cannot be cognized through experience. The sensible world is an object of every possible perception.

28:582   The summation of appearances constitutes nature. What we think with the appearances is experience. There are three rules upon which rests the connection of nature:

1. In all appearances, substance is perduring, this is the principle of subsistence.
2. In all alterations, all that happens [there] is a cause, i.e., everything has its cause, this is the principle of causality.
3. With all alterations there is a connection: this is the principle of interaction <*commercii*>.

Nature is opposed to blind accident and blind destiny. –

The sensible world is a series of phenomena <*phaenomenorum*>, or appearances. –

We distinguish nature from freedom. Freedom is the independence of a causality from appearances, thus freedom does not belong to the sensible world. Causality is the constitution of a thing insofar as it is a cause of something. All events in the world have a cause at the same time in the sensible world. Thus all events are necessary. Mechanism is the natural necessity of motion. If something comes to pass in me without [free]ᴸ cause, then that is the mechanism of nature. We can ask: whether everything in the world is the mechanism of nature, or whether a causality can be thought in the world which would be independent of the mechanism of nature? Mechanism of nature is the connection of appearances according to natural laws. All things in nature, be they inner or outer events, have their determining cause, they all happen according to natural laws and are also determined according to them. An action of a substance in nature that is independent of the mechanism of nature, is called a free action. The faculty of a substance that belongs to nature, for acting independently of the mechanism of nature, is called freedom. If I assume that the appearances in the sensible world are all things in themselves, then freedom would fall aside, therefore we would then also have no morality. For morality presupposes freedom just as necessarily as physics natural necessity. The only way to reconcile freedom and nature is the sensible world; although we are acquainted with it only as appearances, we still say that this is not everything. Natural necessity is nothing other than the causality

---

ʲ Marginalia (581₂₈₋₉) alongside text printed at 581₃₀₋₂. We follow Lehmann in inserting it after the paragraph preceding this text.

of the human soul as phenomenon, the soul is thus to be viewed as a 28:583
cause. How it is possible to be a cause of appearance without itself being
appearance cannot be conceived by any human being, nevertheless, we
can conceive from this cause that the mechanism of nature does not
conflict with freedom, because as appearance a human being is reckoned
to the sensible world, and just the same human being is reckoned as
intelligence to the intelligible world (or as one tends to say, to the intellectual world, which, however, is false). {*Progressive* is the advance from the
condition to the conditioned. *Regressive* [is] when one goes from the conditioned to the condition: from the effect to the cause. E.g., a human being
that is born now exists under the condition that he had parents.}[k] – In
human reason there is an antinomy. We call antinomy the conflict of laws.
But this conflict is at base only an illusion, it is dialectical, an illusory
conflict. Although the illusion can at no time be fully removed, we can still
take care that the illusion does not deceive. This, so to speak, cosmological illusion rests on this, that we view appearances as the matter in itself,
and vice versa, matters in themselves as appearances. – Between freedom
and nature is also an antinomy. The alterations of the world arise either
from freedom or from natural necessity. – At the conclusion of the Cosmology[20] we make yet this general note: the entire dispute rests on this:
whether we should consider the world as phenomenon, appearance, or as
noumenon.

---

[k] Marginalia (582_{21-4}) alongside text printed at 583_{2-9}. Lehmann inserts this at the end of the
Cosmology section; we instead insert it after the first sentence of this text.

Psychology

All experience is twofold, inner or outer. The inner is that which the objects of experience of inner sense move. The outer is the empirical knowledge of the objects of the outer senses. Space is the object of the outer senses. I am myself the object of inner sense. Time applies[1] to all objects of the senses. Time is the form of inner sense. –

To the matter itself. Psychology is the cognition of the object of our inner sense. The object of all inner intuition is the soul. As object of outer and inner sense I am a human being. As object merely of inner sense I am a soul, and as object merely of outer sense I am a body. All determinations of the soul are ordered not according to space but rather merely according to time. The doctrine of body proper is called physics <*physica*>. Psychology is the philosophy of the inner object, which is grounded on principles of experience. Rational psychology <*psychologia rationalis*> would belong to metaphysics. Empirical psychology <*psychologia empirica*> does not belong in metaphysics. But how did it get in? For this reason, because one did not know where one should permit it. It is entirely too small, we have in it too little knowledge, that we could treat it as a separate science. –

28:584

Empirical psychology <*psychologia empirica*>

The powers of the human soul can be reduced to three, namely:

(1) *The faculty of cognition*, (2) *the feeling of pleasure and displeasure*, and (3) *the faculty of desire*. We want to treat of each separately.

One kind of representation can accompany all our representations, this is the representation of our self. The representation of our self is called consciousness, apperception <*apperceptio*>. That representation of which we are conscious through apperception is clear. Clarity, obscurity, distinctness, and indistinctness are distinguished merely according to the connection of consciousness, and not according to their origin, this is a logical difference. All our representations have a twofold origin; they arise (1) from sensibility and (2) from the understanding. The first is called the lower, and the other the higher cognitive faculty. The first belongs to sensuality and the other to intellectuality. Everything that is sensible rests on receptivity;

---

[1] We follow Lehmann in reading *gilt auf* as *geht auf* (583_{30}).

344

but what belongs to spontaneity belongs to the higher powers. We will have sensible cognitions, sensible pleasure and displeasure, and sensible desires. All three of these powers can be sensible. Intellectual pleasure is called moral feeling. Cognitions which are distinct or indistinct are not distinguished other than in the degree to which I am conscious of the representation. Sensible representations can be very distinct, but on that account they still remain sensible, and representations of the understanding can, on the other hand, be indistinct, yet they still*m* remain intellectual. Receptivity*n* is the ability or possibility for being affected.*o*

1. *The faculty of cognition.* The senses give the faculty of intuition. The   28:585 faculty of intuition without presence of the object, but as in the past or future time, is the power of imagination. The faculty of intuition entirely without any time is the fictive faculty. The senses are the faculty of intuition through the presence of the object. There are five senses, in all of our senses is something empirical and something pure. All intuition is either empirical or a pure intuition. Space is a pure intuition. The senses are classified into inner sense and into the outer senses. There are five outer senses and one inner. Some senses are concerned more with sensation without producing cognition, others belong more to cognition than to sensation, the first are called subjective, the other objective senses. The subjective are called crude, but the objective finer senses. Anthropology will treat of this in more detail. Fixed sense <*sensus fixus*> and vague sense <*sensus vagus*>, the latter is feeling. The law of the senses is this: things must be represented in the way they affect us, thus what belongs only to receptivity. The power of imagination is the faculty of intuition, but also without presence of the object. It must be distinguished from the senses as much as from the concepts. The power of imagination is twofold: the reproductive and the anticipatory <*praevidirende*>. The faculty of imagining <*facultas imaginandi*> is the faculty of intuition of the objects of past time, the faculty of anticipation <*facultas praevidendi*> is the faculty of intuition of the objects of future time. The faculty of intuition, insofar as it is not at all bound to time, is called the fictive faculty <*facultas fingendi*; G: *Dichtungsvermögen*>. All three faculties have their laws. The first law is the law of the association of ideas <*lex associationis idearum*>. The law of the power of imagination as a faculty for seeing in advance is the law of expectation of similar cases <*lex exspectationis casuum similium*; G: *Das Gesetz der Erwartung ähnlicher Fälle*>. Of the fictive faculty, the law is the law of the compatibility of ideas <*lex sociabilitatis idearum*>. It (an idea) must be conceived according to the law of compatibility, it must be reproduced according to the law of the association of ideas <*fingendum est*

---

m We follow Lehmann in changing *auch* (also) to *doch* (584₃₆).
n Two equivalents are used here: *Receptivitaet, Empfänglichkeit* (584₃₆₋₇).
o We follow Lehmann in changing *applizirt* (applied) to *affizirt* (584₃₇).

secundum legem sociebilitatis, reproducendum est secundum legem associationis idearum>. There is yet another faculty, the faculty of characterization *<facultas characteristica>*, which does not concern the representation of objects, but rather the representation of representations themselves. Thus the entire sensibility contains nothing but power of imagination, and this is either productive, reproductive, or characterizing. –

28:586 Consciousness underlies the entire higher faculty of cognition. Consciousness is distinguished from the senses. With a rule we think a unity of consciousness. The higher faculty of cognition can be considered as pure, pure cognition *<cognitio pura>*, or as applied *<applicata>*. It is pure when the representation is separated from all sensibility.

2. *The feeling of pleasure and displeasure.* Feeling consists in the relation of a representation not to the object, but rather to the entire subject. Pleasure and displeasure are not cognitions at all. The faculty of the discrimination of representations, insofar as they modify the subject, is the faculty of pleasure and displeasure. It is still entirely peculiar that we also have an intellectual pleasure and displeasure, but we have no other word for it. The discrimination of good and evil belongs to intellectual pleasure or displeasure. With intellectual pleasure or displeasure we must view feeling not as the ground, but rather as the effect of the satisfaction. The feeling of the promotion of life is pleasure, and the feeling of the hindrance of life is displeasure. Pleasure is when a representation contains a ground for becoming determined, for producing again the same representation, or for continuing it when it is there. We can name in a threefold manner the objects of the feeling of pleasure and displeasure, namely: (1) the pleasant, (2) the beautiful, and (3) the good. {This can be pleasant to one, that to another. The pleasant is thus a private judgment; but upon the good we must pass a universally valid judgment. One must well distinguish: the object can please, and the existence of the object can be indifferent to someone, indeed, even displease. So, for example, a depiction of a matter that does not at all exist can please considerably, e.g., if among grain there are many flowers, hedge mustard and others, then that occasionally appears beautiful, and pleases some, while the farmer is vexed.}*ᵖ* The pleasant pleases merely through the senses. We find nothing pleasant other than what we sense; thus only sensation belongs to the pleasant. – The beautiful pleases not merely in sensation, but rather according to universal laws of sensibility, thus that which agrees with our sensibility is beautiful. The good pleases merely according to the laws of the under-

---

ᵖ Marginalia (587₅₋₁₃) alongside text printed at 586₂₁₋₃₄. The example (with the farmer) is written in a different hand than the first part of the marginalia, and is found immediately below this first part. We follow Lehmann in grouping these two marginalia together, but insert them before the text alongside which they are written, whereas Lehmann inserts them after the section on pleasure and displeasure.

standing. But to the discrimination of the beautiful belongs also the understanding, and not merely senses. But all rational beings which also have
senses can discriminate the beautiful, and we human beings are such
beings. Thus the laws of sensibility must hold for all human beings, but
not for merely rational beings. These discriminate merely the good. Usefulness and purposiveness remains without any beauty. – The judgment
of the good must hold for all rational beings. The good is that which
agrees with satisfaction according to the universal laws of reason. What
pleases in sensation, one says: it gratifies. Something can please us which
does not gratify us, indeed, rather hurts. The good must please through
pure reason. {That in whose existence we have a *pleasure* interests [us].}[q]
The good is relatively good (for, one says, it is hypothetically necessary) or
it is utterly good, then it is called absolutely necessary good. All our
pleasure or displeasure is either sensible or intellectual. The pleasant and   28:587
the beautiful is a sensible pleasure, but the good an intellectual pleasure.
The beautiful is indeed a sensible pleasure, but in a finer degree than the
pleasant. {Sensibility and reason are so exactly connected with each other
that they cannot at all be separated when we want to cognize something.}[r]

3. *The faculty of desire.* This is a faculty for making the object actual in
accordance with the satisfaction in the object. Living beings have a faculty
of desire; one can make this into a definition of living beings. To the faculty
of desire <*facultas appetitiva*> is opposed the faculty of aversion <*facultas
aversativa*>, but this is nothing other than the faculty of desiring the opposite <*facultas appetitiva oppositi*>. Each desire <*appetition*> is grounded in
the sense of anticipated pleasure <*sensum voluptatis praevisi*>. Desires
<*appetitiones*> are either sensitive <*sensitivae*> or intellectual <*intellec-
tuales*>. Power of choice <*arbitrium*: G: *Willkür*> is distinguished from
desires. The object of the power of choice is that which we also have a
faculty for accomplishing. An impelling cause <*causa impulsiva*> contains
actually the ground of the desire <*appetition*>, an impelling cause <*causa
impulsiva*> is either a motive <*motivum*; G: *Bewegungsgrund*>, or a stimulus
<*stimulus*;[s] G: *Anreizung*>. Each impelling cause <*causa impulsiva*>, when
it is considered subjectively, is called an incentive of the soul <*elater
animi*>, but when it is taken objectively, is called a stimulus <*stimulus*>.
Virtue gratifies above all else, it is a motive <*motivum*> of reason. Should
the will be moved by stimuli <*stimulos*> or by motives? The stimuli <*stim-*

---

[q] Marginalia (587₁₄) alongside text printed at 586₃₆₋₇. We insert it after the first sentence of
this text, while Lehmann inserts it (with other marginalia) at the end of the section on
pleasure and displeasure.
[r] Marginalia (687₁₅₋₁₇) alongside text printed at 586₃₈–587₄. We follow Lehmann in inserting
it after this text, but we have reinserted other marginalia that Lehmann had also placed here,
and have removed blank lines added by Lehmann.
[s] Lehmann misreads *stimulus* as *stimulans* (587₂₉).

28:588 *uli>* spoil everything. Inclination is the ability to be moved[f] by stimuli *<stimulos>*, i.e., by sensible impulses. Each inclination, desire, has an object, thus the will must also have one. It is impossible that a rational being can wish inclinations for itself, for thereby its contentment becomes very limited. – Affections belong to sensible feeling, passions belong to sensible desiring. Affection is the sensible feeling of pleasure or displeasure, which removes the mind from any position for assessing the worth of all our sensations. If a desire is so great that it puts the mind out of a position for comparing its object with the rest, then it is called passion. Affections and passions, considered in a human being as animal, belong to the perfection of human nature. If reason had total control over a human being, then all of this could also happen without affections and passions. {Low and upright character *<indoles abjecta et erecta>.*}[u] Affections and passions can never be extolled. Noble character *<indoles ingenua>* is opposed to the liberal *<libera>*. Servile and noble arts *<artes serviles . . . ingenuae>*, the latter have a pleasantness about them, but not the servile *<serviles>*. The noble arts *<artes ingenuae>*, to which the humanities *<humaniora>* mainly belong, constantly cultivate taste. The humanities are those arts that make for the promotion of humanity *<humaniora sunt, quae faciunt ad humanitatem promovenda>*. The reading of the ancients, e.g., cultivates taste.

{(Human power of choice *<arbitrium hominis>* is free as far as power *<liberum quoad potentiam>*, and servile as far as actions *<servum quoad actus>*, i.e., acquired aptitudes *<habitus acquisitos>*, therefore one also calls virtue an aptitude. Someone wrote a book *On Free Will <de libero arbitrio>*, Luther then wrote against it *On Bondage of the Will <de arbitrio servo>*,[21] and he was right, if one only distinguishes it exactly.)}[v]

{Power of choice *<arbitrium>* is either free or brutish *<vel liberum vel brutum>*. Power of free choice *<arbitrium liberum>* can occur only with human beings, who have understanding; with animals, on the other hand, brute power of choice *<arbitrium brutum>*. The free *<liberum>* is either sensitive or intellectual *<vel sensitivum vel intellectuale>*. The power of free choice that is determined through the senses is sensitive choice, and that which is determined through the intellect is intellectual *<arbitrium liberum sensitivum quod determinatur per sensus, et intellectuale determinatur per intellectum>*. The intellectual *<intellectuale>* is again either pure or

[f] Lehmann misprints *bewegt zu* as *bewegtzu* (587₃₅).
[u] Marginalia (590₉) alongside text printed at 588₁₁₋₁₂ (somewhat in the manner of a heading). We depart from Lehmann in inserting it after the first sentence of this text.
[v] Marginalia (588₂₀₋₁) alongside text printed at 587₁₈₋₂₁ (viz. the beginning of the section on the faculty of desire). We follow Lehmann in inserting it here at the end of the section (all the text following this is likewise marginalia).

affected <*vel purum vel affectum*>. The pure <*purum*> is that which is determined only by the intellect and is not affected through the senses. The affected is that which, to be sure, is not determined through the senses, but nevertheless is affected by the senses <*quod solum determinatur intellectu, et non afficitur per sensus: affectum quod quidem non determinatur per sensus sed tamen afficitur sensibus*>.}[w]

{The entire field of desires, of the faculty of desire, is (1) a propensity <*propensio*; G: *Hang*>, i.e., the possibility for an inclination. (2) The desire itself, when I actually desire something. (3) Inclination <*inclinatio*; G: *Neigung*> already implies in itself the necessity of desire; if it becomes habitual, disposition <*habitus*> is not merely an aptitude, but rather already necessity. (4) Passion is a ruling inclination which interrupts my freedom.}[x]

28:589

{The intellectual impelling cause <*causa impulsiva intellectualis*> is a motive <*motivum*; G: *Bewegungs-Ursache*>, the sensible impelling cause <*causa impulsiva sensualis*> is a stimulus <*stimulus*>. The intellectual impelling cause <*causa impulsiva intellectualis*> is either purely intellectual without qualification <*simpliciter talis, mere intellectualis*>, or in some respect <*secundum quid*; G: *respective*>. When the impelling cause <*causa impulsiva*> is represented by the pure understanding, it is purely intellectual <*mere intellectualis*>, but if it rests on sensibility, and if merely the means for arriving at the end are represented by the understanding, then it is said to be in some respect <*secundum quid*>. – – }[y]

{Power of choice <G: *Willkür*> comes from election, to elect, *choice, to choose* <G: *Keir, küren, Wahl, wählen*> and is to make something the object of one's desire, which animals can as well, who have a power of choice, but no will; they cannot make a representation of a thing that they desire, much less of an end, why they want or do not want something. –

Actions <*actiones*> are voluntary <*voluntariae*> or involuntary <*involuntariae*>. An action <*actio*> is called unwilling <*invita*>, when there are also impelling causes <*causae impulsivae*> to the opposite <*oppositum*> of that which one does. E.g., a father strikes his unruly child unhappily, if he loves it. So also, e.g., a criminal who waits upon a humiliating death, and who wants to starve himself to death, eats unhappily if he cannot withstand

---

[w] Marginalia (588₂₅₋₃₂) alongside text printed at 587₂₂₋₈ (this is the bottom of the ms page). We follow Lehmann in inserting it here at the end of the section on the faculty of desire.
[x] Marginalia (588₃₃–589₃) alongside text printed at 587₃₁₋₅. We follow Lehmann in inserting it here at the end of the section on the faculty of desire.
[y] Marginalia (584₄₋₁₁) alongside text printed at 587₃₀₋₁ and 588₁₋₅. The first sentence of this marginalia is separate from the remainder, but they are linked together with a sign. We follow Lehmann in combining them, and inserting them at the end of the section.

the strongly enticing food which one then tends to set before him. There are here impelling causes <*causae impulsivae*> to the opposite <*oppositum*>, he is provoked by enticements <*per illecebras*>, thus one can also provoke by threats <*per minas*> to something, by temptations or by threats, by pleasing things or displeasing things <*per placentia et per displacentia*>, by pleasure or pain. The will can also be compelled *morally* by the mere representation of duty or *pathologically* by sensation of the pleasant or unpleasant.

The power of free choice <*arbitrio libero*> is opposed to the servile <*servum*>, when a human being does not have self-mastery <*imperium in semetipsum*>; the brute <*brutum*> [is opposed] to the intellectual <*intellectuale*>, the latter is determined solely by the understanding, and the former is possible without consciousness of oneself. The self-mastery of a human being <*imperium hominis in semetipsum*> is the faculty for freely disposing over the free use of all one's powers but primarily for ruling over sensibility according to one's representations. – Compulsion <*coactio*> is the necessitation to unwilling action <*necessitatio ad actionem invitam*>.[z] The will, the power of free choice, can be compelled in a way <*voluntas arbitrium liberum cogi potest secundum quid*>, i.e., comparatively, if the faculty for the opposite is there. – –

28:590

The community of the soul with the body also belongs in the Empirical Psychology <*psychologia empirica*>. Interaction <*commercium*> is the connection of two substances which have a reciprocal influence <*influxum mutuum*; G: *wechselseitigen Einfluss*> on one another. A human being must be regarded as two substances, as an object of the outer senses and also of the inner.}[a]

Rational psychology <*Psychologia rationalis*>

The first original experience is: I am. Descartes says: I think therefore I am <*cogito ergo sum*>. One can call the proposition, I think, i.e., I exist as a thinking being, I am a thinking [being] <*sum cogitans*>, a proposition of experience. But Descartes still speaks incorrectly when he says: I think therefore I am <*cogito ergo sum*>, just as if it were an inference. In the concept of I lies substance, it expresses the subject in which all accidents <*accidentia*> inhere. Substance is a subject that cannot inhere in other things as accident. The substantial is the proper subject. If I am conscious of myself, do I then have a concept of the substantial? Not at

---

[z] We added a period after *invitam* (590₂).

[a] Marginalia (589₁₂–590₈) alongside text printed at 588₆₋₁₉, 590₁₀₋₂₀ (this marginalia is continuous; the apparent gap is due to the printing of the other marginalia in Lehmann). We follow Lehmann in inserting it here at the end of the section. A blank line added by Lehmann has been removed.

all. The general feature through which we are acquainted with all substances in the world is perdurability. Every substance perdures. The soul is a substance, this is a category. The category is a mere concept of the understanding, of logical form. The pure concepts of the understanding, if they are merely thought, give no stuff for thinking. Consciousness is a quality of thinking and thus has a degree, for every quality always has a degree. My apperception, as we call our consciousness, thus has a quality of thinking. The second proposition that can be inferred from the concept of I is: the soul is simple. Thought consists not just[b] of representations, but rather the representations must also be connected to consciousness. A composite substance is an aggregate of many substances. Unity of consciousness is not an aggregate. Simple is that which is not divisible. Consciousness already allows us to cognize that the soul is simple. The object of inner sense can be represented only in time and not in space. We do not infer from that that the soul is simple, as if we were acquainted with the nature of the soul, but rather because it is an object of inner sense. That the soul in itself is extended is already a contradiction.

28:591

It is asked: whether the perdurability of the soul will continue? So long as we are conscious of it, so long does it perdure, but whether consciousness will continue? The perdurability of the human soul cannot be inferred from the concept of substance. The ancient philosophers inferred that, because the soul cannot perish through division, it will not perish at all. But this is false, for there still remains yet another perishing, namely, when its powers gradually diminish and disappear, until finally they stop altogether and are transformed into zero or into a nothing. – The soul is not material, matter is composite, and not simple, also no part of matter is simple, which is good to note, for the parts of matter must also constantly be material. But the soul is simple, and thus not material. – The soul cannot be thought through any predicates of the outer senses, it is an object of inner sense. We are not acquainted with the substrate <substratum> or the ground of the soul, merely its appearances. How is the soul in interaction <commercio> (in community) with the body? Interaction <commercium> is a reciprocal influence of substances, however bodies are not substances, but rather only appearances. Thus no actual interaction <commercium> takes place here. – No human being can explain basic powers. There is sheer natural necessity in our actions. The human will is the intelligible causality of human actions. –

We can take the proof of the immortality of the soul from empirical and also from rational psychology. We must undertake experiments with either our own soul or with others, but no human being can do that. From

---

[b] A *Sie hat* added by Lehmann has been removed (590₂₉).

empirical psychology it is thus entirely impossible to prove the survival[c] of the soul. In rational psychology we have a double proof: (1) from the concept of the life of an intelligence in general, and (2) from the analogy of nature with other living beings in general. –

The first proof is: all matter is lifeless. No body alters its own condition from itself, it does not bring itself from rest into motion, or from motion into rest, this is the law of inertia <*lex inertiae*>; inertia <*inertia*> is not inactivity, but rather actually lifelessness. Matter is inert <*materia est iners*>. If all matter is lifeless, then it can be only an organ but not a ground of life. Thus the ground of life cannot be in the body. What is not even a ground of life also cannot be a promotion [of life], the body is rather a hindrance to life. Thus the soul of a human being cannot at all lose anything of life by separation from the body. This proof has much that is beautiful about it, but nothing decisive, too much follows from it, one is delivered by it into wild fantasy.

The second proof, from the analogy of nature with other living beings in general, is the best of all that has ever been introduced for the soul. It is based on experience. We find in nature a connection of efficient causes, also connection of ends, this connection is indicated in organized beings, and the connection of finality <*nexus finalis*> with living beings is the highest principle, from which one cannot depart at all: that no organ is met in living beings that would be superfluous, also that no part would be in a living being that would be useless and not have its determinate purpose. Now we find in a human being powers, faculties, and talents which, if they were made merely for this world, are really purposeless and superfluous. The talents and equipment of the soul show that it has powers. The moral principles of the will also go much further than we need here. Thus it is quite obvious that the soul of the human being is not created for this world alone, but rather also for another future world. –

The state of the soul after death. Of this not much can be said, other than what is negative, i.e., what we do not know. We cannot posit the soul after death in the bodily world, also in no other world that would be somehow far away. We say: it goes either to heaven or to hell. By heaven, one must understand the kingdom of rational beings in connection with their superior as the most holy being. The human being who is virtuous is in heaven, only he does not intuit it, but he can infer it through reason. The human being who always finds causes to despise himself and find fault, is already in hell here. Thus the transition from the sensible world into the other is merely the intuition of oneself. According to content it is always the same, but according to form it is different. It is asked: whether the human being after death will assume a new corpuscle <*corpusculum*>

28:592

---

[c] *Fortdauer* (591₃₁); the verb *fortdauern* is translated earlier on this page and elsewhere as "to continue": literally, "to last further."

as the vehicle <*vehiculum*> of the soul? Probably not! – – We could not
form for ourselves any concept of sleep if experience did not teach it to us. 28:593
If we want to compare the state of the soul after death with sleep, i.e.,
since it has suspended its acts <*actus*>, then it is asked: whether the soul
after death will fall into a sleep, or will directly continue its life? Of this
nothing at all can be said. – The migration of the soul <*metempsychosis*; G:
Seelenwanderung> was an agreeable concept of the Orientals which under-
lay the wild fantasies of the Indians; it is their purgatory <*purgatorium*>,
just like purgatory with Catholics. One sees at once how limited is our
knowledge of the state of the soul after death. – This life shows nothing
but appearances, another world means nothing other than another intuition, things in themselves are unknown to us here, but whether we will
become acquainted with them in another world? We do not know. A pure
spirit cannot at all exist merely as soul in the sensible world. As intelligence it does not appear in space, also not in time. The matter of the body
is appearance. – –

Happiness is nowhere complete in this world. Blessedness consists in
contentment so far as it rests on the subject, it is, so to speak, self-
sufficiency. No creature can be blessed in the strictest sense, for as soon
as it is dependent on something, it always has needs and can never be
content. Thus happiness consists in progress. In the future world we will
thus be in progress either toward happiness or toward misery, but whether
this will continue to eternity we cannot at all know. Moral good and evil is
never perfect here, it is always in progress. –

On the possibility of community with departed souls. Human beings
very much abhor annihilation. The possibility of community with the souls
of the deceased is twofold, namely (1) the soul directly assumes a body, or it
already has one, this can be one possibility. (2) By the presence of the spirit,
it does produce thoughts and representations in us, just as if we actually
intuited things. Swedenborg also held this last opinion. The possibility of
refuting appearances of spirits would be a vain task. Possible things of
which we have no experience at all we can judge in no other way than
according to the principle of contradiction. All appearances of spirits are of
the kind that we can neither institute experiments, nor be able to observe
and consider them closely, and thus reason cannot be used here any further. 28:594
All appearances of spirits and ghosts, all interpretations of dreams, prophecies of the future, presentiments and the like are reprehensible in the
extreme, because no rule can be brought out of them. The Neo-Platonic
sect which blossomed especially in the third century, had such visions and
wild fantasies. They called themselves selected <*eclectici*> because they
were, as it were, select.[22] They had special arts. Theurgy is the entire art of
entering into the community of spirits and conversing with them. Theurgy
has as its object the great kingdom of spirits, magic, and cabala, and whatever else there was. It is not worth the trouble here to speak of it any

further. – All matter is lifeless, this is the principle of physics, without this there is no natural science at all. But now what can produce alterations in itself is called living. Living beings <G: *lebende Wesen*> are called animals <*animalia*>. The principle <*principium*> of life must not be represented as material. Each principle <*principium*> of life must have a power of representation <*vim repraesentativam*>. Life means having a faculty for practicing actions in conformity with one's representations. Cartesianism is wholly contrary to the analogy of nature. Animals must have souls, i.e., there must be a principle <*principium*> of life in them. According to quality, we can imagine rational beings as pure intelligences. If animals were different from human beings in degree, then they would have to have less understanding and less reason, but they are different simply in quality. Animals have senses and reproductive imagination <*imaginatio*>. With imagination we can think yet a fictive faculty <*facultatem fingendi*>, of anticipation <*praevision*> and reproduction <*reproduction*>. The faculty of consciousness cannot be attributed to animals. If living beings exhibit effects that with human beings could arise only by reason, we still cannot assign reason to the living beings as long as the effects can be explained merely through their sensibility, without assuming reason. Animals cannot make concepts, there are sheer intuitions with them. Thus we cannot in any manner ascribe reason to animals, but rather only an analogue of reason <*analogon rationis*>. This is mere instinct, where they need no reason, but rather a higher reason has arranged it. However much we extend this instinct, reason will still never arise from it, just as little as, if we infinitely extended a line, a plane could arise from that.

PART VI
Metaphysik Dohna

1792–1793 (AK. 28: 656–690)

Metaphysics   28:613
according to
the lectures of Professor Kant
in the winter semester 1792/93 from 7–8.
by H. L. A. Dohna, begun Monday the 15th
October 1792
(compendium by Baumgarten)

(B) SPECIAL METAPHYSICS [. . .]   28:656

The objects of our *ideas* are *world* and *God* – thus cosmology and theology. The first concerns objects of the senses – (e.g., objects of nature, insofar as they constitute an absolute whole) but now also only insofar as they are not objects of the senses. Objects of the senses are:

1. *of outer sense*, these concern *body*, thus somatology, but only insofar as this cognition is unconditioned does it belong to the transcendental.

2. Of inner sense, this concerns the *soul*. We can think an immanent *doctrine of body* and *of soul*, a *somatology* and *empirical psychology*, [and] in order to indicate the connection of these empirical sciences with the rational ones, we want to mention something of them in the following. We divide metaphysics into:

1. critique of pure reason and ontology {contains immanent and transcendental[a] concepts}[b];

2. into the *transcendent* part of philosophy, now this is the one which contains cosmology and natural theology. – With respect to the transcendent our cognition is dialectical, I can affirm and deny a proposition with equally good grounds, maintain and refute it. This is a peculiar phenomenon of reason, it is called antinomy {conflict in its own subjective laws}[c]. Thus we now go to the *first section* of this second part.

---

[a] Perhaps "transcendent" is meant.
[b] Marginalia (656₂₄₋₅) alongside text printed at 656₂₄. We follow Lehmann in inserting it after this text.
[c] Marginalia (656₃₁₋₂) alongside text printed at 656₃₁₋₃. We follow Lehmann in inserting it after the first sentence of this text, but remove parentheses added by Lehmann.

(I) Cosmology

Contains:

1. Somatology
(Cosmology proper)

36.¹

– Metaphysical doctrine of the world. World in the metaphysical sense is the substantial whole which is not a part of another <*totum substantiarum, quod non est pars alterius*>. The whole of substances, which is no part of another, one can also say: is the absolute whole of substances <*est totum absolutum substantiarum*>ᵈ – is different from the hypothetical whole <*toto hypothetico*>, which is a whole only in one respect, but in another respect a part.

(1) *The material in the world are substances* (egoistic world <*mundum egoisticum*> – egoist: one who assumes here that he is the only existing being) {thus egoistic world <*mundus egoisticus*> is a contradiction in the predicate <*contradictio in adjecto*>}ᵉ *not accidents*. (2) *The formal is the real connection* <*nexus realis*> *of these substances*. Real connection is reciprocal influence (acting and suffering). – {A multitude can consist of isolated parts}ᶠ A *multitude* of substances without connection makes no world. One must thus not define world: the universe of substances, but rather the whole of them. *The third moment* in the concept of the world is *absolute totality*; this makes for us the greatest difficulty, it is a concept which no object of possible experience can display, an idea. We can indeed think an absolute totality, but we cannot give it. A whole of substances is at every time a whole of the finite. Metaphysical infinity <*infinitum metaphysicum*> is what is not limited, has sheer realities and no negations, thus most real being <*ens realissimum*>. The world can never be that, for that which can

---

ᵈ A period has been removed (657₉).

ᵉ Marginalia (657₁₄) alongside text printed here; we follow Lehmann in inserting it after *Wesen*, and replace the closing parenthesis here.

ᶠ Marginalia (657₁₇₋₁₈) alongside text printed here; we remove parentheses added by Lehmann and insert the marginalia before *Eine Menge*.

exist as part can never have all realities. And a whole that consists of such parts, of finite substances (of substances which have negations – limits) in no way forms something infinite. No whole of infinite substances can be thought, or many infinite substances can never form an infinite whole (or they would not themselves be infinite, for one would have to supply what the other lacked). Every whole consists of contingent substances, for they reciprocally influence each other. –

Is there only one world, or can there be several? {The concept is logically   28:658 possible, but not therefore real.}[g] – One can ask: (1) whether *in the place* of the present world yet another one is possible, or (2) whether *beyond* (outside) *it* yet a world is possible. The first is especially difficult and subtle: – we put it off until the Natural Theology <*theologia naturalis*> – it is the matter of the best world. – Now (2) could *next to* a world yet another exist? – Space and time are, as mentioned, not things in themselves but rather mere forms of sensible intuition. Phenomenal world <*mundus phenomenon*> can exist only once, for there is only one space. All things in space stand in a real connection <*nexu reali*>. Because of the unity of space there is thus also only one space possible. There is here only one single universe. If the world depends on a being which is its cause, then it stands with this in a connection <*nexu*> of dependence. An accident can exist only by inhering <*inhaerendo*> in a substance, the latter, [as] thought in reason, can exist in and for itself, even if there were no other [substance] – (as isolated) we can thus represent to ourselves an immeasurable multitude [of substances] in the understanding (not in space), which are independent of one another. – Necessary substances are thoroughly determined, a whole of these thus cannot exist, for connection between them is impossible. Two necessary beings could likewise stand in no connection with one another at all, an evil being could thus have no influence at all on the work of the good, for as necessary they are isolated.

37.[h]

We seek the unconditioned in the phenomena when we hold them as things in themselves. Something unconditioned is met in things in themselves, but not in space and time. This conflict – antinomy can be twofold:

1. *mathematical*, i.e., antinomies which concern *mathematical synthesis* {connection and composition of the homogeneous}[i], e.g., the composition of intuitions.

---

[g] Marginalia (658_{1-2}) alongside text printed at 658_{2-3}. We follow Lehmann in inserting it before this text.

[h] We are omitting an unnecessary *den* (the) (658_{25}).

[i] Marginalia (658_{31-2}) alongside text printed at 658_{30-2} and connected to *mathematische* (synthesis) with a sign. We follow Lehmann in inserting it after this phrase, but remove parentheses added by Lehmann.

2. *dynamic*, which concerns existence, the relation to the effect is always power. {dynamics [=]ᴸ doctrine of powers}.ʲ We find in the mathematical synthesis two propositions, where we find that both can be necessarily false, with the dynamical synthesis – that both propositions are true; a ground can be something wholly different from the consequence. { – namely in the dynamic synthesis}ᵏ Now if we come across an antinomy we will solve it by saying this: both propositions *can* be true, or both *can* be false, – there are only two mathematical antinomies:

28:659

1. the progression <*progressum*> from the parts to the whole, – and
2. the regression <*regressum*> from the whole to the parts, – the magnitude as infinite is given in its absolute totality, an infinite multitude of parts is likewise given. – Now the following propositions: the world has a beginning – if we want to assume it had none, then it would have no first ground, and everything would be conditioned; on the other hand: if I say the world has no beginning, then the former or the latter must still be true – both propositions are false, thus it would be eternal {thus an elapsed eternity}.ˡ Nothing seems clearer than that it has a beginning. We thus think a time before which it did not exist, so what happened previously? We enter here into a whirlwind. We cannot at all assume chance, thus we must think a being as the first cause, but has this been inactive the entire previous time? We cannot think a beginning in time, for all times are only parts of one and the same [time]. – The world cannot be here from eternity, for it is conditioned.ᵐ – Thus both propositions are false – (the unconditioned totality of time leads us astray {nothing is unconditioned in time}ⁿ; we think an absolute totality for phenomena, which they just do not have, etc. –) The second antinomy of mathematical synthesis: the world is infinite in space – (2) the world has its boundaries in space. The latter contradicts itself, for the boundary does make a separation of space. If I think a world that is unbounded, then no contradiction lies in the concept of the understanding. – Yet I can never wholly cognize it in the sensible world, for an infinite given cannot be thought. Only through the progression <*progressus*> can we give space, – if it were a thing in itself, then of course it could be given according to its absolute totality. The mathematical synthesis of the regression <*regressus*> (from the

---

ʲ Marginalia (658₃₄) alongside text printed at 658₃₃. We follow Lehmann in inserting it after this text, but remove parentheses added by Lehmann.

ᵏ Marginalia (659₁₋₂) alongside text printed at 658₃₇–659₁. It appears to be intended for the first sentence of this text, and we insert it immediately after this sentence; Lehmann inserts it within the next sentence after *Antinomie*, and does not note this marginalia.

ˡ Marginalia (659₁₃) alongside text printed at 659₁₂₋₁₃ and inserted with a sign after the first sentence of this text. We follow Lehmann in inserting it here.

ᵐ We are adding this period (659₂₀).

ⁿ Marginalia (659₂₂) alongside text printed at 659₂₁₋₂ and inserted with a sign after *irre*. We follow Lehmann in inserting it here.

whole to the parts) now follows.⁰ (1) Every body consists of simple parts – (2) it does not consist of simple parts, but rather of composites of infinitely many parts. We cannot assume the first, for each body is just as infinitely divisible as the space that it occupies; – a part which has no further part, the indivisible, is the last condition of composition. The parts are given only through the regression <*regressus*> of the parts – in space the progression <*progressus*> is never at an end; likewise the regression <*regressus*>, we will not speak of things in space as things in themselves, but rather merely according to their composition; we can thus divide infinitely and this infinite would be given – but this is not. A regression <*regressus*> to infinity is thus possible, but it never obtains an absolute totality. In the mathematical antinomies both propositions are false, they are opposed as contraries <*contrarie*>, they do not merely negate, but rather assert, they say not merely what it is not, but rather what it *then* is. –

28:660

38. Friday

We come to the antinomies of the totality of the dynamic synthesis (with respect to the *existence* of things). The first says: there is a freedom of actions, the second, everything happens according to natural laws. That is, if one defines freedom: the absolutely unconditioned spontaneity in our actions; we assume no substance can absolutely determine itself. Thus actions would not happen where the subject was determined by no previous ground, thus there can be no freedom – if there would be no first ground, on the other hand, we maintain there is freedom: because unconditionally *some* event still must happen, otherwise we never arrive at totality. The first proposition (there is *none*) is that no action exists which does not have a determining ground outside of it, thus if the determining ground does not lie in the previous time, then everything happens by accident. – Yet something must happen according to absolute spontaneity, but the proposition: every consequence has its ground, contradicts freedom, for as long as it is from the previous time the determining ground does not lie in the control of the one acting. So far we have treated it theoretically, but practically it is otherwise, for through moral laws we must assume absolute spontaneity of actions, for otherwise they could not be imputed to us. With this antinomy we say: both propositions are true, for many actions stand under the law of natural necessity (were this not so they would stand under chance;ᵖ this is the death of all natural science) but other actions stand under absolute spontaneity (if we assume the opposite, then this is the death of all morality).⁹ This conflict is overcome

---

⁰ We are adding this period and the following numeral (659_{34}).
ᵖ We are changing a period to a semicolon (660_{35}).
⁹ We are adding this period (660_{37}).

28:661 this way, that we can consider a human being as phenomenon and noumenon, in the first case he obviously stands under the law of natural necessity, under determining grounds of time, but as noumenon he is independent of them. – But can he consider himself this way? I must yet introduce something where he does not at all stand under the laws of sensibility. Now morality teaches us that we are free, which no experience can; the consciousness of the moral law. Insofar as he is himself the law giver, he also determines himself. All morality falls aside if human beings are not free. A human being stands as phenomenon wholly under the laws of natural necessity. Solely as noumenon is that not so, and solely through morality does he become so acquainted with himself. We express physical necessity: it *will* happen, but moral: it *should* happen. But this makes a very important difference. –

The second antinomy of the dynamic synthesis: there is something absolutely necessary in the world – everything in the world is contingent – for everything is conditioned. But if I assume everything as dependent, then I must still assume something necessary from which it proceeds, an unconditioned ground. If I assume it outside of space (of the world) then it can stand in no connection, for the cause would also have to work in time; – but we think of God as noumenon, and so considered there is an absolutely necessary being.

39.

All antinomies rest on this, that we seek the unconditioned in the phenomenal world <*mundo phenomeno*>, which simply will not do. We want now to treat the synthesis of the things of the world. On that the following cosmological propositions:[2] there is no abyss in the world <*in mundo non datur abyssus*>. (2) There is no leap in the world <*in mundo non datur saltus*>. (3) There is no chance in the world <*in mundo non datur casus*>. – (4) There is no fate in the world <*in mundo non datur fatum*>. The abyss <*abyssus*; G: *Abgrund*>, the given infinite of *composition* as well as *division*; there is no infinite given, but rather with composition merely a progression <*progressus*> and with division a regression <*regressus*>. With time one can indeed think a progression <*progressus*>, but with space? It is given only through the progression – an infinite space, to the extent each possible [space] is only a part, to that extent the whole space is infinite. But we cannot think it, except through the progression <*progressus*>, and because it never comes to an end we can never wholly grasp

28:662 it, because it is *no thing* in itself. With division there is just such an abyss <*abyssus*>, for a drop of water has as many parts as the solar system. There is no leap in the world <*in mundo non datur saltus*>; in space and time there is no immediate step, a continuous quantum <*quantum continuum*> is that of which no part is simple, discrete <*discretum*> what

362

consists of simple parts. *Space* and time are continuous quanta <*quanta continua*>, do not consist of simple parts, but rather are *infinitely* divisible. This proposition is called the law of continuity <*lex continui*>. – Leap <*saltus*> is the immediate connection of a conditioned (of a consequence) with a distant ground without intermediate ground (<*absque ratione intermedia*; G: *Grunde ohne Zwischengrund*>) – a contradiction. No state and no point follows immediately after the other. We can express it: no two points, and no two moments are the *next* ones to each other. Thus in all alterations no state follows another immediately, but rather there is in between still an infinite multitude of intermediate states. No body comes immediately to rest from a motion, but rather it goes only very gradually. No alteration is immediate transition from one state into the other, there are always intermediate states there. But we always make leaps, for we cannot possibly cognize the infinite intermediate states. Two states are always in different times {these are never next to each other}^r, thus, etc.

40.

{The dynamic law of continuous *motion* <*lex continui phoronomica* (G: *Bewegung*) *dynamica*>.}^s Continuous motion <*motus continuus*> (which is perduring) cannot take place in an angle (b c a) for between two moments there is always a time, since it is in the state of transition.

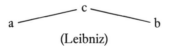

(Leibniz)

There is a *logical* law of continuity <*lex logica continui*>, if something *general* is said of an object, which is in motion, then it also holds of the same body when it is at rest; (one can view it as diminishing – infinitely small – motion).^t The *physical* law of continuity <*lex continui physica*> says [that] the multiple species and kinds in the world are never so diverse that something might not yet be between them that has something in common with each. – {Why an intermediate kind?}^u It is a mere chimera, for if we

---

^r Marginalia (662₂₁) alongside text printed at 662₂₀₋₁ and inserted with a sign after *Zeiten*. We follow Lehmann in inserting it here.
^s Marginalia (662₂₃, ₂₆₋₉) alongside text printed at 662₂₃₋₇. We leave untranslated the German *Bewegung* (motion), which is intended as an equivalent of *phoronomica*. The diagram that follows appears under this text in the margin. We follow Lehmann in inserting the phrase at the beginning of the paragraph.
^t We are adding a period here (662₃₁).
^u Marginalia (662₃₄) alongside text printed at 662₃₅₋₆. We follow Lehmann in inserting it before this text.

are talking about things, then there is no necessary ground of connection for it at all. Law of continuity <*lex continui*> can indeed be thought logically, but it is physically impossible. Continuum of forms <*continuum formarum*> requires an infinite multitude. There is no chance in the world <*in mundo non datur casus*>, no accident, no event without cause. (The word chance <G: *Zufall*> often indicates merely an event which is not according to order or rule – ungoverned. There is no absolute chance <*casus absolutus*>, only relatively such <*respective talis*>.)ᵛ Causality brings necessity with it – the determining ground lies in the previous time, since the previous time does not now lie in the control of the actor – so natural necessity of the action follows, thus no freedom (no faculty to determine one's actions oneself), but we must assume it, as already mentioned, because we have the moral law {(we should, so we can)},ʷ through which a human being represents himself as noumenon. In the sensible world, of course, freedom is not thinkable. Free actions according to moral laws are thus only for noumena, and not according to the laws of the causality of phenomena. The ground for free actions lies in the noumenon itself, in its reason. –

There is no fate in the world <*in mundo non datur fatum*> – no blind destiny. This necessity can be absolute and [it can be] conditioned. The first is Spinozistic. [The second is] not absolute fate <*fatum absolutum*>ˣ – *fate* {not blind destiny}ʸ occurs with human beings in the phenomenal world <*mundo phenomeno*>, but not in the noumenal world <*mundo noumeno*>.

41.

Constituent parts <*partes constitutivae*> – Matter in the transcendental sense, the determinable, what is determined through the form. In the cosmological sense matter indicates: the constituent parts <*partes con­stitutivae*>, constituent pieces of the world. The egoist is he who holds himself, as thinking being, as the only worldly being. The idealist says there are no objects of outer sense, i.e., no matter, he affirms merely thinking beings. The materialist, on the other hand, affirms no thing that is not matter, at least in the world. We call an immaterial thinking being spirit. He who assumes pneumatic (spiritual) as well as material beings is called a realist. Simple substance is called a *monad* <*monas*>. (Matter

---

ᵛ We are adding a period here (663₅).
ʷ Marginalia (663₁₀₋₁₁) alongside text printed at 663₉₋₁₀. We follow Lehmann in inserting it after this text.
ˣ We are adding parentheses here (663₁₉); *nicht absolutum* is written above *Fatum* in the ms.
ʸ Marginalia (663₁₉₋₂₀) alongside text printed here and inserted with a sign after *Verhängniss* (fate). We follow Lehmann in inserting it here.

28:663

insofar as it has a figure [is] body.)^z There is nothing of monads <*monadatum*>, for the world has no simple parts. Would we thus have^a no first elements? Considered as noumenon, the world certainly consists of simples <*simplicibus*>, for composition is just mere relation. But in the world of appearances there are no simple parts. Only the intelligible world, noumenal^b world <*mundus noumenon*> is of monads <*monadatum*>, but we do not at all cognize it. Yet the author wants to enumerate the properties of the monads.[3] –   28:664

Real connection <*nexus realis*> is reciprocal influence <*influxus mutuus*>. But he cannot say generally that everything in the world acts and re-acts.[4] (Discordant harmony, harmonious discord <*concordia discors, discordia concors*> –) Contact is not immediate presence <*praesentia immediata*>, for otherwise the soul would touch the body. The common boundary of extended beings is contact. Monads thus cannot touch one another. Immaterial is not simple, and simple is not on that account immaterial. There is a substance that has simple parts, which also is never part of a material being. But just because matter has no simple parts, we cannot prove that the soul is simple. (The simple according to species – as individual of substance, – composed.) An element [is] a simple part. Is water an element? No, for it can still be decomposed {it consists of vital air and combustible air},^c[5] and we call something that contains no species elementary. (Mechanical division in regard to the magnitude of space; no body is mechanically indivisible.) A monad <*monas*> is called atom <*atomus*>, a part which cannot be further divided; – dynamic chemical division, disintegration, separation, concerns the species – thus we obtain simple matter – but we have no matter that with certainty cannot be divided.

42.

Atom <*atomus*>, the indivisible – The atoms <*atomi*> of Epicurus are corpuscles <*corpuscula*>, small bodies which indeed are mathematically divisible, but cannot be split by any power of nature (primitive molecules <*moleculae primitivae*>).^d The mechanical philosophy explains everything from the figure of the bodies, and the laws of their motion. Corpuscular philosophy arose in order to make the perdurability of the species <*specierum*> conceivable. The method of physics can be divided into the mechanical and dynamic; the first derives all alterations of the world from the

---

^z We are adding a period here (663$_{33}$).
^a We follow Lehmann in reading *hatten* as *hätten* (663$_{34}$).
^b We follow Lehmann in changing *phenomenon* to *noumenon* (663$_{38}$).
^c Marginalia (664$_{15}$) alongside text printed at 664$_{14-16}$ and inserted with a sign after *auflösen*. We follow Lehmann in inserting it here.
^d We are adding a period here (664$_{26}$).

figure of its basic particles; it assumes these as determined, *indivisible* –
atoms <*atomi*>, corpuscles <*corpuscula*>, themselves still matter but un-
splittable.* Descartes gave them certain figures (e.g., hooks in nitric acid).*
All motions are derived from others, which one already assumed. According to Democritus and Epicurus, these atoms <*atome*> have fallen down-
28:665 wards since eternity and bump together by an *accidental* alteration of direction. Descartes assumed the creator first turned the first atoms <*atomi*>
into a ball, and so the world came about.* To philosophize dynamically
means to assign powers to motions, as Newton assigned attraction, a power
which without any motion of its own, even at rest, puts all others into
motion. The dynamic mode of explanation, connected with the mathematical, is called the physico-mechanical mode of explanation, by the drawing
together and connection of powers. –

Nature is the existence of things according to laws of determination
<*natura est existentia rerum secundum leges determinationis*> – Existence,
insofar as it stands under laws, is different from essence,* the possibility of
the existence of a thing according to its principle. *On the best world*
<*mundo optimo*> – Metaphysical perfection – all realities (thingness).* Ev-
ery thing, so far as it contains limits, deficiencies, is metaphysically imperfect. The greatest whole of all realities is the most perfect world, but very
different from the most perfect being. – For it consists of substances
which stand in interaction <*in commercio*>, thus already have deficiencies,
etc. Teleological world <*mundus teleologicus*>, the greatest whole of all
ends – the best world in the teleological sense. These are always two
things – the whole, and the composition, the form, thus the world too –
an infinite multitude, and harmony of substances. – The formal in the
world is the real connection <*nexus realis*> of substances, interaction
<*commercium*>, reciprocal influence <*influxus mutuus*>. How can many
substances stand in such connection? Where no real connection <*nexus
realis*> takes place, a harmony of two substances is possible, a harmony
without interaction <*harmonia absque commercio*> (if one wants, ideal
interaction <*commercium ideale*>) – e.g., two clocks strike at the same
time. Those who affirm an ideal interaction <*commercium ideale*> can be
called harmonists, their opponents influxionists, the latter assume certain
laws. The harmonists are twofold (a harmony without influence <*harmonia absque influxu*> is externally stable <*externe stabilita*>).* Occa-
sionalists {e.g., two clocks strike at the same time because a third party

---

* We are replacing a comma with a period (664₃₄).
* We are adding a period here (664₃₅).
* We are adding a period here (665₂).
* *Wesen*; this can also be translated as "being."
* *Dingheit, Sachheit.*
* We are adding a period here (665₂₉).

directs the movement in the others. – }[k] or Preestablishers {clocks which strike at the same time through their inner arrangement – }.[l] Descartes was of the first class (he *assumes no* real interaction <*commercium*> at all, but rather always a being (God) that connects the two), Leibniz of the second, he assumes an *initial predisposition* in me by which I hear everything, etc., merely developed out of myself, not by influence from outside. – All this is properly a harmony without interaction <*harmonia absque commercio*>. – Physical influence <*influxus physicus*> is *brute* <*brutus*> (original <*originarius*>) or *rational* <*rationalis*> – [if] one assumes the interaction <*commercium*> to be connected with existence, we call it original <*originarius*> (yet a cause must always still be there).

28:666

43. Monday

The way we represent substances in the phenomenal world <*mundo phenomeno*>, all dispute ceases, for space already brings them into an interaction <*commercium*>. But if we think a world merely through the understanding, this is more difficult. The relation of many substances among one another according to general laws is called harmony, this is *without interaction* <*absque commercio*> if no concept of cause and effect between them takes place. Insofar as they actually stand in real interaction <*commercio reali*>, the system of substances can be called a system of *physical influence* <*systema influxus physici*>. The former (the *ideal interaction* <*commercium ideale*>) can be called hyperphysical influence <*influxus hyperphysicus*> – extramundane <*extramundanus*> – presupposes that God is the first cause. The system of *occasional* causes <*systema causarum occasionalium*> [means] at the occasion of an alteration in one substance God produces one in the other [substance], which appears to stand in connection with it. This was Descartes's system. *Preestablished* harmony <*harmonia praestabilita*>, as if God had arranged everything like a clockwork, e.g., as soon as the will is there – the fulfillment follows. Leibniz found a great difficulty here as to how soul and body stand in connection.[6] The author wants to explain it.[7] But ground and consequence can be really <*realiter*> different – so also – thoughts [can differ] from motion. The system of *physical influence* <*systema influxus physici*> is a system <*systema*> of *original or derived* interaction <*commercii originarii vel derivativi*>. Original <*originarius*; G: *ursprünglich*>. If a cause still attaches to the substances – then their community is derivative. (Hidden

---

[k] Marginalia (665[30-1]) alongside text printed at 665[29-33], and attached to *Occasionalisten* with a sign. We follow Lehmann in inserting it after this word but remove parentheses added by him.

[l] Marginalia (665[31-2]) alongside text printed at 665[34-5], and attached to *Praestabilisten* with a sign. We follow Lehmann in inserting it after this word but remove parentheses added by him and are changing a comma to a period (665[32]).

quality <*qualitas occulta*>, when I take a ground of explanation from the matter itself.)*ᵐ* Since hidden quality <*qualitas occulta*> is not adequate for explanation, there thus remains for us but real interaction of *derived* physical influence <*commercium reale influxus physici derivativi*>. That is, there must be a being from which everything proceeds. All substances have their ground in it. If we consider space as real, we assume Spinoza's system. He believed only one substance and all substances in the world he held for – its divinely inhering determinations {he called space the phenomenon of the divine omnipresence}.*ⁿ* A dialectician said – if nothing *is*, then being and not-being are the same. Thus if I say that space remains if I take everything away, then a nothing exists. But space is only ideal, only a relation of things, so if the things are gone, then naturally there is also no relation of them possible, thus also no space.

44.

We arrive at the last portion of the Cosmology – the *contrary to nature*.[8] Nature – the summation of mundane appearances under laws – this is nature (not nature of things) substantively-materially <*materialiter*>.*ᵒ* Something that does not stand under the laws known to us is called *contrary to nature* – (<*praeternaturale*; G: *widernaturlich*>) of which we can make no determinate concept. *Supernatural* <*supernaturale*; G: *übernaturlich*>, what is impossible according to natural laws. Sickness is of the first kind. For the laws of which we can make a determinate concept concern the state of the healthy <*status sani*>. The great diversity with respect to sickness makes impossible a standing rule, thus a determinate concept of the thing. [Something is] *supernatural* as long as the cause of the event <*eventus*> is not met with in the world whole determined according to laws (nature); for we meet it in the *extramundane being* <*ente extramundano*> (i.e., God is, in other words, not part of the world, not somehow the world soul –).*ᵖ* A miracle is a supernatural event in the world <*miraculum est eventus supernaturalis in mundo*>. The creation is thus no miracle, for it was no event in the world, but rather through it the world became. Just as little is conservation a miracle. – It is no event in the world <*eventus in mundo*>. A miracle thus strictly defined is called *strict* <*miraculum stricte sic dictum vocatur rigorosum*>. [How] is such a thing possible? Because there is an *extramundane* cause <*causa extramundana*> that has produced this order of things, thus [it] also can

---

ᵐ We are adding a period (666₂₆).

ⁿ Marginalia (666₃₃₋₄) alongside text printed here. We follow Lehmann in inserting it after the first sentence of this text and replace a colon added by Lehmann with a period.

ᵒ We are adding a period here (667₅).

ᵖ We are adding a period (667₁₆).

produce another. A miracle is thus possible in itself internally <*interne*> (absolutely – on every hypothesis <*in omni hypothesi*> one cannot say).[q] In general, an event in the world whose laws human reason cannot at all cognize is a miracle. Now for us it is the same whether it happens according to – for us unknown – natural laws or by the influence of the highest being. It is enough that the cause is impossible for us to cognize (e.g., of gravity, of attraction).[r] But if a body rises against the laws of gravity, then that is contrary to nature. A miracle is called not something of which we do not cognize the cause, but rather that of which we do not cognize the laws. Thus magnetic power is no miracle, for we cognize its law (but not the cause). Comparative miracle <*miraculum comparativum*>, what is supernatural <*supernaturalis*> in relation to our reason, but otherwise is according to certain laws unknown to us. Rational beings in the world are called demons. One divides them into evil demons <*kakodaimon*> and good demons <*agathodaimon*>.[s] One calls them angels <*angeli*>. So we had theistic (strict <*rigorose*>) and demonic (comparative) miracles. Without being allowed to deny this, we will concede it is possible with respect to the object, but still not affirm it with individual events {i.e., assume it as a basis, a principle}.[t] If one concedes the latter, then it undermines reason (pure reason [is] the faculty of cognition according to principles, practical [reason] concerns actions). For the most part comparative miracles are repugnant to our use of reason, of the theistic ones we can all the more easily make a general concept. – For in the omnisufficiency of the highest being which has no deficiency we find the high properties that we cannot think completely with created beings. No created spirit has the highest holiness of the will or omnipotence. –

28:668

45.

Reason can make no other use of things in the world than insofar as they are considered as events of nature happening according to the order of nature, – according to certain laws that give us a principle of possibility upon which we can reckon with our actions. Thus we suspend all principles when in a given case we get in the business of affirming miracles, assuming them as a foundation, but that does not mean to deny miracles – in general one assumes them as possible. Religion which is built on revelation makes belief in miracles a duty, yet one seeks to dismantle them

[q] We have removed a period after *interne* (667₂₃) and added one here (667₂₄).
[r] We are adding a period here (667₂₉).
[s] *kakodaimon* and *agathodaimon* are written with Greek letters in the ms (667₃₇).
[t] Marginalia (668₃₋₄) alongside text printed at 668₃₋₅ and inserted with a sign after *statuiren*. We follow Lehmann in inserting it here.

as much as possible – {as when it is a small or very rare miracle}.ᵘ – One also clearly affirms miracles in previous times, but not any more now; – the government forbids the doing of miracles. – One assumes ancient miracles, but in no event *new ones*, how come? – Because of the disturbances for the state that would follow; demonic miracles are always more inconceivable to us than theistic ones. It is a hindrance to the use of reason, which is offended – cannot assume it without reluctance – here large or small does not matter, here it is the same whether an atom or a planet is moved from its place *contrary* to natural laws – *everything lies in the formal*; (the difference between the formal miracle *<miraculo formali>* {guiding natural powers against laws of nature is also a miracle}ᵛ and material *<materiali>* is void {for guiding a wind is just as much a miracle as an angel of death, or the like}ʷ). The formal miracles are divided into preestablished *<praestabilita>* and occasioned *<occasionalia>* – those

28:669 which happen at a special occasion, in order to better some remaining error – the preestablished *<praestabilitum>*, what was determined from the beginning; e.g., a wind determined since eternity,⁹ which was to blow exactly at the time, where everything is arranged like a clockwork, but comprehending this is still much less easy than an occasioned miracle *<miraculum occasionale>*.

46.

(Maxims – subjective principles of reason – which the subject makes itself.) With miracles reason looks only to the form, the matter is not the issue. One usually says miracles were only few, and they happen only seldom. The latter is merely tautologous, for seldom means that which does not usually happen. Now every miracle is still something extraordinary, therefore everyone who assumes miracles, also assumes an order of nature from which they are exceptions, exceptions are always seldom { – a tautological proposition}.ˣ Is it possible to cognize a miracle? To cognition belongs perception under the presupposition of certain rules, but with miracles these are unknown to us. In addition there are frequent illusions, even with eyewitnesses, therefore the possibility of the experience that something is a miracle has many difficulties. Ordinary event *<eventus ordinarius>*, an event which happens according to a general rule cognized

---

ᵘ Marginalia (668₂₄₋₅) alongside text printed here. We follow Lehmann in inserting it after this text.
ᵛ Marginalia (668₃₅₋₆) alongside text printed at 668₃₂₋₃ and inserted with a sign after *formali*. We follow Lehmann in inserting it here but remove parentheses added by him.
ʷ Marginalia (668₃₆₋₇) alongside text printed at 668₃₄₋₈ and inserted with a sign after *nichtig*. We follow Lehmann in inserting it here but remove parentheses added by him.
ˣ Marginalia (669₁₄₋₁₅) alongside text printed at 669₁₂₋₁₃. We follow Lehmann in inserting it at the end of the ms page.

by us, extraordinary event <*eventus extraordinarius*> – one we view as an exception to it.*ʸ* One calls the course of nature <*cursus naturae*> the succession – order <*ordo*> – the connection. – The course of nature is also at the same time the order of nature. Thus if the latter is obstructed, then so also is the course of nature. Reason is a law to itself – but if it does not know the laws, then the concept of causality is totally useless to it. Astonishment*ᶻ* is the obstruction of progress in our thought, on account of a hindrance – a kind of fear – that it hits upon something for which it finds no rule – at the same time a hope of finding one in the future, if it is an actual event {e.g., a nebula – ! }.*ᵃ* Therefore all astonishment is quite pleasant. Admiration is an always continuing astonishment which remains even when we know the cause (rule) of it. Actual miracles which allow us no hope – strike down the mind. My cognition is *eo ipso* forbidden to me, all pondering comes to an end. But objects of admiration elevate the mind. { – Can miracles be thought in the best world? Or do they merely make whole the deficiency <*defectum*> of nature? – The moral law gives a   28:670
negative criterion for the possibility of miracles. – }*ᵇ*

47

2. Psychology

Cosmology is called transcendental when {through pure reason}*ᶜ* it considers the world as the summation of substances, empirical when it considers these substances as objects of the senses. Sensibility itself has *a priori* determinations, namely space and time. The world can thus also be [an] object of metaphysics; now when it treats the summation of the objects of the senses, it divides into:

1. metaphysical doctrine of body, somatology, concerning objects of outer sense;

2. metaphysical doctrine of the soul, psychology – concerning objects of inner sense. The doctrine of body can be mathematical – (rational physics <*physica rationalis*>) – and philosophical (somatology) – but from *a priori* principles – from pure concepts. The empirical doctrine of body belongs as little to metaphysics as does the empirical doctrine of soul. One

---

ʸ We are adding a period here (669₂₂) and at 669₂₄.

ᶻ German: *Verwunderung*; this is closely related to *Wunder* (miracle) and seems to mean here the conferring of the status of a miracle onto an event. *Bewunderung* (admiration) is discussed later in the paragraph.

ᵃ Marginalia (669₃₁) alongside text printed here. We follow Lehmann in inserting it here and replace a comma with a period.

ᵇ Marginalia (669₃₇–670₂) alongside text printed at 669₃₃₋₆. We follow Lehmann in inserting this at the end of the ms page.

ᶜ Marginalia (670₆) alongside text printed at 670₅, and inserted with a sign.

can call the latter – anthropology. But rational psychology <*psychologia rationalis*> belongs to special metaphysics, just as much as somatology to cosmology {physiology, which contains doctrine of body and soul}[d] – to the summation of nature, of outer and inner sense. But how can we cognize these *a priori*? Insofar as they can be cognized in many determinations independently of concepts of experience. The conditions according to which they become objects of possible experience are those which our reason cannot go beyond, the cognition becomes transcendent, beyond bounds.

[EMPIRICAL PSYCHOLOGY]

The first is the consciousness of myself, the I, it is the first act <*actus*> of the mind <*psyche*>: the faculty for cognizing oneself as representing subject, and also as object of our own representation. This apperception <*apperceptio*> is (1) empirical <*empirica*>, the consciousness of oneself as a being whose existence is determined in time; insofar as I am self-determining, consciousness is called intellectual <*intellectualis*>, pure apperception <*apperceptio pura*>. It is very hard to grasp. If I say I am, then I take my thinking as an event, by which I immediately imagine something that happens. Pure consciousness is found already in logic. – (All judgments are representations of whose unity we are conscious.)[e] This faculty contains the ground of the difference of sensibility and the understanding (faculty of rules – higher faculty of cognition). I[f] – (1) considered in the thinking subject as human being, is the soul (that which remains when the object of outer sense is taken away), the principle of life in a bodily being.[g] Death – separation of the soul from the body. If I consider myself as object of inner sense as substance, then this substance is my soul. My body is called the body – whose alterations are my alterations (*my* cannot be explained). Soul, insofar as it can also think without body, is called a spirit. – Granted it could not think without connection with a body, then one also cannot call it spirit.[h] §500.[i] The power which represents the universe <*vis repraesentativa universi*>, a representation cognizing oneself as a piece of the world. The author defines the soul: a power to represent oneself[10] – (thus it would not be

28:671

---

[d] Marginalia (670$_{21-2}$) alongside text printed here. Parentheses added by Lehmann have been removed. *Physiologie* is written above *Cosmologie* in the ms, and the rest is inserted after *Physiologie* with a sign.

[e] We are adding a period here (671$_3$) and after the next several sentences (671$_{5, 7, 12, 18}$).

[f] G: *Ich.*

[g] We are replacing a comma with a period (671$_8$).

[h] A paragraph break added by Lehmann (at 671$_{14-15}$) has been removed.

[i] §500 is the last section of the Cosmology in Baumgarten. The number is in the margin alongside *universi*.

substance, but rather merely power of the substance). – Power is not that which contains the true ground of the inherence of the accidents <*accidentium*>, but rather this is precisely *substance*. Power is merely relation of the substance to the accident, no thing in itself. So many errors come from a false definition. – All our natural science concerns seeking out the causes from certain effects. Cause is that which, when it has been posited, something really distinct is posited, according to a universal rule <*quo posito secundum regulam universalem ponitur aliquid realiter diversum*>. We begin by naming causes with the same name as the powers – but that is mere naming, not explanation. One calls this naming a hidden quality <*qualitas occulta*>, e.g., the bell rings because the metal has a ringing effect. To derive – [is] to cognize as power what something has in common with something else. Primitive and derivative power <*vis primitiva . . . derivativa*>, e.g., the sounding, a derivative power <*vis derivativa*> of the elastic power of air. Basic power {homonymous cause <*causa homonyma*>},[j] [is] what cannot be cognized from a yet higher principle. We cognize it only relative to us, e.g., impenetrability of matter – its property that it fills space. As soon as various grounds are assigned to a consequence, reason seeks to derive them all from one ground, in general[k] it always seeks *unity of principle*. Is the power of representation <*vis repraesentativa*> the only basic power of our thinking? We cannot derive it from anything, but everything can be derived from our faculty of representation. We cannot cognize the substantial that contains the first ground of the accidents. If the accidents <*accidentia*> are specifically different, then they cannot be derived from one basic power. E.g., pleasure and displeasure – understanding and sensibility.[l] – The faculty of intuition and [that] of concepts are already two first grounds. – We have in our soul two kinds of determinations, there are either representations themselves (e.g., understanding), or they have reference to representations (e.g., will). The faculty of representations is the *understanding* insofar as concepts underlie it – *sensibility* insofar as intuition underlies it. – Concept is a representation insofar as it is made into a rule. (In logic a common representation <*repraesentatio communis*> – feature common to several.) Understanding [is] thus [the] faculty of rules. We find in us three faculties: the faculty of cognition, the feeling of pleasure and displeasure, and the faculty of desire, unity of principle is impossible here – yet everything is either sensible or intellectual. Sensibility contains senses – faculty of intuition [is] with the presence of the object, and power of imagination [is] faculty of intui-

28:672

---

[j] Marginalia (671_{30-1}) alongside text printed here. We follow Lehmann in the insertion but remove parentheses added by him.
[k] Reading *überhauot* (in Lehmann) as *überhaupt* (671_{35}).
[l] We are adding a period here (672_3).

tion without presence of the object. The senses are either objective – productive of cognition, [or] subjective, providing sensation {feeling – taste – the others are objective}.*m* Further power of imagination – intuitions are in space or time, objects of outer [sense] – objects of inner sense, according to time. Their objects are productive when we provide them, the fictive faculty <*facultas fingendi*>; reproductive as repetition of intuitions had, or signification.

48.

To sensibility thus belong sense and power of imagination. (I) *Sense* is the faculty of empirical intuitions for becoming immediately conscious of existence in space or in time. Sensation is the subjective in the representation of a thing. Insofar as sensation is referred to an object, it can produce cognition. So far as it can become no part of cognition, sensation is called feeling of pleasure and displeasure. That wine is red becomes cognition, that it will be pleasant, not at all. With all sensations we distinguish intuition from sensation. – Pure intuition – and perception (e.g., with taste – we call something beautiful because of the form). Power of imagination – also applies only to the form of the things {without the object being present}.*n* We name only one inner sense – the faculty of the consciousness of one's own existence – in time empirical apperception, in general pure apperception. We name five outer senses, of the inner we can determine merely its relation in time, but this gives no manifold. All things in space are concurrent – my representation[s] of *outer* things, which are objective in space, are subjective in time. To be in time belongs to all things, to be in space only to outer ones. A manifold of feelings does not yet give a multitude of inner senses. Perceptions and their connection do not yet constitute experience; it is only empirical intuition, only a *part* of cognition, therefore we will also have *a priori* concepts, which the possibility of such cognitions contains – which the unity of their consciousness provides. Perceptions are the matter of experience, concepts the form. The fallacy of subreption <*vitium subreptionis*>, when someone takes perception as experience. (Fallacy of subreption.)*o* It can hit the target by accident, but not in general. Subreption <*subreption*> is always a fault <*vitium*> according to form. Whoever takes his inferences from perceptions for experiences, then this is merely his reflection, and can often be badly interpreted perception –

28:673

---

m Marginalia (672$_{18}$) alongside text printed at 672$_{19-20}$, attached to *subjektiv* with a sign. We follow Lehmann in inserting it after the sentence, but omit the parentheses added by him.
n Marginalia (672$_{36}$–673$_{1}$) alongside text printed at 672$_{37}$ and inserted with a sign.
o We are adding this period and the next period (673$_{15, 16}$).

49.

(Deception of the senses <*fallacia sensuum*>) when we falsely take our subjective judgment for objective – the senses do not deceive, for they cannot judge. We can never see that something is *not*. Further – after this therefore because of this <*post hoc ergo propter hoc*> is a very common prejudgment <*praejudicium*> {(fascination, bewitchment)}[p]; we can *perceive* no cause, only judge by the understanding. Dimension of time – many [things] one after another. Two times do not flow next to one another, for there is only one time. The outer senses are five, some are more objective, belong more to the cognition of the object than to the modification of the sensation of the subject. Sensation can also become a part of cognition of something real, which exists outside me. There are representations which contain more sensation than pure intuition. – Of the latter kind is seeing – touching <*tactus*; G: *das anfühlen*> is more subjective, yet also objective in one aspect. We cognize this something only insofar as it affects us, but the object outside us we do not cognize.

(II) *Power of imagination* is the substitute <*vicarius*> of the senses, the faculty of intuitions in the absence of objects. With respect to objects it can be merely reproductive (mere memory); productive (fictive faculty <*facultas fingendi*>) with respect to form, yet it is slow in that and requires much practice. Consciousness is the faculty for grasping representations so that we can reproduce them, the aptitude for that is called faculty of remembering, memory. The law of the fictive faculty is that we fabricate not the matter, but rather the form. – The law of the association of ideas <*lex associationis idearum*>, the law of association, connection, such that when the one is there, the other follows. It is also the law of the expectation of similar cases <*exspectationis casuum similium*; G: *Erwartung ähnlicher Fälle*>. The reproductive power of imagination is so connected with the fictive faculty <*facultas fingendi*> that it is a means to its promotion. Fiction[q] is the faculty of characterization <*facultas characteristica*>. A symbol <*symbolum*> is an object with which I assist the cognition of another through analogy. – Symbolic cognition serves not reproduction, but rather judgment. Intuitive cognition thus stands opposed not to the symbolic, but rather to the discursive. *Understanding and reason* – Understanding is the faculty of rules, only through that is cognition possible. Reason the faculty of principles {unity of the rule}.[r]

28:674

---

[p] Marginalia (673₂₄) alongside text printed at 673₂₄₋₅. We follow Lehmann in inserting this after the clause.

[q] *Das Dichten* (674₁₂); *Dichtungsvermögen* (674₆), above, is translated as "fictive faculty."

[r] Marginalia (674₁₉) alongside text printed here and inserted after *Vermögen* with a sign. We follow Lehmann in inserting it rather at the end of this sentence.

50. Monday the 4th of February

The second part of empirical psychology, the feeling of pleasure and displeasure, is still not at all properly worked-up. Wolff wanted to derive everything from the faculty of cognition, and defined pleasure and displeasure as an act $<actus>$ of the faculty of cognition. He also called the faculty of desire a play of representations, thus likewise modification of the faculty of cognition. Here one believes to have a unity of principle.[s] (This is always a maxim of reason, it makes itself a principle subjectively, {the principle of the unity of the principle is not objective}.)[t] – But this is impossible here. Wolff came to this merely from the cited false definition of substance;[11] thus there were powers which all had to be derived from a basic power, so he assumed the power of representation $<vis\ repraesentativa>$ as basic power – etc. – .[u] But power is nothing but the mere relation of the accidents to the substance. (Perfection is completion, completeness in a certain respect.)[v] Pleasure is matter of perfection – [a] basic property (basic ability, if it is sensible; basic faculty, if it is intellectual) – which cannot be reduced to anything, thus also not to the faculty of cognition. Our representations can themselves become efficient causes (and to that extent are not cognition).[w] The causality of representations is:

first, subjective – they are causes for producing themselves, maintaining themselves.

Second, objective – since they become a cause of the production of objects. The agreement $<consensus>$ in the subjective causality of representations is called the feeling of pleasure – the agreement in the objective causality of representations is called the faculty of desire. Thus a representation which produces the effort $<conatum>$ for maintaining its state of representation $<statum\ repraesentativum>$ is called *pleasure*, one which becomes the cause for the production of an object is called *desire*. The representations which produce determinations are either sensible or intellectual.

28:675

{satisfaction $<complacentia>$
/ \
sensitive $<sensitiva>$ intellectual $<intellectualis>$
/ \
sense-pleasure   sense-displeasure
pleasure $<voluptas>$ displeasure $<taedium>$}[x]

---

[s] We are adding a period here (674_{27}).
[t] Marginalia (674_{28-29}) alongside text printed here, and inserted with a sign.
[u] We are adding a period here (674_{33}).
[v] We are adding a period here (674_{35}).
[w] We are adding a period here (675_3).
[x] Marginalia (675_{14}) alongside text printed at 675_{10-15}. We follow Lehmann in inserting it before the last sentence of this text.

Formal sensible pleasure is called taste, the faculty of a sensitive satisfaction <*complacentia sensitiva*> – pleasure comes about through sensation or through reflection, the faculty of subsumption under rules is power of judgment – if it applies to objects of taste, it is called aesthetic. A sensible pleasure which is not sense-pleasure applies to form, and rests on reflection connected with the faculty of the power of imagination, thus understanding and the power of imagination together give the aesthetic power of judgment, taste. Sensible pleasure, in relation to senses, gives the agreeable, in relation to taste the beautiful. –

51.

Aesthetic power of judgment is the faculty for making oneself conscious through a representation of the agreement of sensibility with the understanding. Everything beautiful rests upon this agreement. Power of judgment in general: subsumption of an intuition under a given concept of the understanding. This is an action of the determining power of judgment <*judicium determinandi*; G: *bestimmenden Urteilskraft*>.[y] If we subsume merely under our faculty of concepts – then this is reflection – an action of the power of imagination, the merely reflecting power of judgment; this pleasure which arises out of the play of the power of the imagination, without immediately connecting a determinate concept with it – is satisfaction. For the power of imagination is still in its freedom, {it would not be this way in a cognition}[z] (e.g., a flower without determinate rule) – schematizing. We call this free play of the power of the imagination, which is still connected with the understanding in general, satisfaction, and so the beautiful is different from the agreeable {which applies merely to the senses}.[a] With the good, a concept must also be presupposed no matter what; the representation of a perfection applies to the good. This is good either in itself {the moral is alone good in itself}[b] – or only in a conditional way, as a means. The beautiful is what pleases in mere reflection (*still without concept*). The beautiful is closer than the agreeable to the good because of the freedom that occurs with it (in reflection – of the power of imagination which has free play); and with the moral good, freedom must be presupposed no matter what. The beautiful also has something similar with the good, that it pleases with-

28:676

---

[y] We are adding a period here (675_{31}).

[z] Marginalia (676_{5-6}) alongside text printed here and connected to *Freiheit* with a sign. We follow Lehmann in inserting it immediately after this word.

[a] Marginalia (676_{9-10}) alongside text printed here and connected to *angenehm* with a sign. We follow Lehmann in inserting it immediately after this word.

[b] Marginalia (676_{12-13}) alongside text printed here and connected to *selbst* with a sign. We follow Lehmann in inserting it immediately after this word but remove parentheses added by him.

out any interest, without looking to the use, but rather, considered solely through reason we give the beautiful like the good our approval. We always find a trichotomy with that which is related to pleasure and displeasure – plus A – minus A, and – o – indifference, which is neither beautiful nor ugly. Pleasure is something positive, displeasure really <*realiter*> opposed. The mind is indifferent when representations produce neither pleasure nor displeasure. But there is nothing like this, for everything arouses either pleasure or displeasure, but if we look at the object itself, we call indifferent <*adiaphoron*>' what is neither good nor evil. Things can be indifferent physically – yet either relatively or absolutely. But the latter we cannot at all determine.

52.

Faculty of desire <*facultas appetitiva*; G: *Begehrungsvermögen*>. Worthless, empty, idle desires <*appetitio inanis, vacua, otiosa*>, empty desires are called wishes (yearnings). The subject can himself be conscious of this emptiness; – effort <*conatus*>, a dead power – consciousness of the causality, but also of the inadequacy. Effective desire <*appetitio efficax*; G: *wirksam*> is not yet efficient <*efficiens*; G: *wirkend*>, one calls it power of

28:677   choice <*arbitrium*; G: *Willkür*> as long as the opposite of my desire is also in my control. Thus, as long as it is elective desire <*appetitio electiva*>, then it is called desiring at one's discretion <*pro lubitu*>. The sensitive power of choice <*arbitrium sensitivum*> – insofar as desire is affected by stimuli <*quatenus appetitio afficitur per stimulos*>. The impelling cause <*causa impulsiva*> is called a motive <*motivum*> if it is intellectual <*intellectualis*>. A power of choice <*arbitrium*> which is determined by stimuli <*per stimulos*> is called brute <*brutum*>. Opposed to this is: free [power of choice], independent from necessitation by stimuli <*liberum, independens a necessitatione per stimulos*>. {We are *affected* by stimuli <*stimulos*>, but *not determined*.}[d] Whoever is determined by motives <*motiva*> is free, for he acts according to the laws of his own reason according to spontaneity and not according to receptivity. Will is the faculty of desire insofar as it is affected by representation of a rule. The will does not have maxims, but rather the power of choice. The power of free choice <*arbitrium liberum*> is: (1) pure <*purum*>, (2) affected <*affectum*>, affected {by matter}.[e] Every object of the power of choice – e.g., reward, punishment – is called matter. Power of free choice is called pure <*pura*> if it is determined merely by the

---

' Written with Greek letters in Lehmann (676₂₈).

[d] Marginalia (677₅₋₆) alongside text printed at 677₇₋₈. We do not follow Lehmann's insertion before the text and instead insert it *after* this text.

' Marginalia (677₁₃) appearing directly after *afficirt*, which is where we (following Lehmann) insert it.

representation of the law, by the form of conformity to the law. Incentives of the soul <*elateres animi*> – incentives of the mind are called impelling causes <*causae impulsivae*> of the power of choice. The faculty of the power of choice, pure power of free choice <*arbitrium liberum purum*>, is the highest degree of freedom, the moral. We would hold it as absurd – if we had no morality. – *Where* we do not at all comprehend the possibility because no experience is given to us, there we can still say we can do it because we *should*. The moral imperative is categorical – unconditioned. –

The mere consciousness of the moral law gives us concept of freedom. That is the great sublimity – independent of the whole of nature as soon as it comes to doing our duty.

53.

The faculty for determining oneself through pure representations of reason is freedom. The impelling causes <*causae impulsivae*> can give mere lawful form. The maxims of action must be taken generally, to agree with a general law { – in that lies the merely formal, free from all matter}.[f] If it cannot be thought in a general system of law then it is unjust. *Will* is the faculty (with power of free choice) for acting with consciousness according to rules – one can also say – it is the faculty of ends. End is in general: concept with which the rule of my action is in agreement: (free will <*voluntas libera*> is tautological, for one understands by it power of free choice <*arbitrium liberum*>). Displeasure is not merely lack, but rather something less <*minus*>. There are also situations that are agreeable and at the same time to be avoided – this state <*status*> is not called indifference <*indifferentiae*> but rather equilibrium <*aequilibrii*>. {(The ass of Buridan)}[g] Buridan said of this state <*statu*> that no one of the two things could be chosen since the motive grounds are fully equal – in empirical psychology, wholly equal incentives cannot be thought (objectively, perhaps, but there again two opposed things cannot be thought).[h] – The faculty of desire <*facultas appetitiva*>, so far as it is determined by merely intellectual motives <*motiva mere intellectualia*> – is called higher <*superior*> – the sensitive power of choice <*arbitrium sensitivum*> stands opposed to it, and is then called lower <*inferior*> – here what matters is not the means, but rather the representation underlying the power of choice. An action happens unwillingly when a desire for the opposite stands opposed to it – [this is] an unwilling action <*actio invita*> – the opposite of which is pleasing <*cujus oppositum placet*>. –

28:678

---

[f] Marginalia (677₃₀₋₁) alongside text printed at 677_{30-2}. We follow Lehmann in inserting it after the first sentence of this text.

[g] Marginalia (678₃) alongside text printed at 678_{2-3}. We follow Lehmann in inserting it before the first full sentence of this text.

[h] We are adding a period here (678_7).

54.

A voluntary action at one's discretion, connected with desire of the opposite <*actio arbitraria pro lubito, cum appetitione oppositi conjuncta*> – this action happens unwillingly, but not involuntarily. The necessitation of an unwilling action is compulsion <*necessitatio actionis invitae est coactio*>. A necessitation of free actions is moral [necessitation]. To be able to compel oneself is the highest degree of freedom – to be able to necessitate oneself through one's own reason. Duty: an action to which I am morally necessitated. Voluntary action <*actio voluntaria*> insofar as it comes about according to maxims (maxims <*maxime*; G: *Maximen*>, principles practically subjective <*principia practice subjectiva*> because they would be the major premise <*propositio major*> in practical syllogisms). Involuntary <*involuntaria*> – not with will, not according to one's maxims. This is a very subtle matter – as a freely acting being, a human being actually cannot do anything without the will – he acts always according to maxims even if not universally <*universaliter*>. The impelling causes conflict with one another <*causae impulsivae colliduntur inter se*> when one determines a carrying out, the other an omitting; a contest of the higher and lower faculty of desire <*lucta facultatis appetitivae superioris atque inferioris*>. Motives <*motiva*> can collide – does this also apply with obligations? No – this is absurd – but two reasons for obliging <*rationes obligandi*> can collide (namely then when they are not yet sufficient <*sufficient*> –) but never obliging reasons <*rationes obligantes*>. The insufficient ground can indeed never contradict the sufficient. Noble or servile character <*indoles ingenua vel servilis*> – the disposition <*habitus*; G: *die Denkungsart*> of the human being with respect to his maxims – in that they are taken either from motives or stimuli <*stimulis*>. The servile character is even mercenary <*indoles serviles est vel mercenaria*> – seeking a reward, or actually slavish – from fear of punishment. (Therefore noble arts are liberal arts <*artes ingenuae liberales*> – where we fully use our freedom.)[i] Affections are motions of the sensitive soul <*motus animi sensitivi*>, which put a human being out of the position to remain in power over himself (master of himself <*sui compos*>) – it belongs to the feeling of pleasure and displeasure, passion – (inclination <*propensio*; G: *Neigung*> is different from that).[j] Passion makes blind – and wholly suspends the faculty for ruling oneself.[k] – This matter belongs to anthropology. – {On the community between soul and body in regard to pathology, D. has written a good work.}[12][l] –

---

[i] We are adding a period here (679$_2$).

[j] We are adding a period here (679$_5$).

[k] We are changing a semicolon to a period (679$_6$).

[l] Marginalia (679$_{7-8}$) alongside text printed at 679$_{9-13}$. We follow Lehmann in inserting it before this text.

The last question in empirical psychology is: is an empirical psychology possible as a science? No – our knowledge of the soul is far too limited. And an empirical cognition becomes science only when we derive it from a principle, we proceed altogether methodically through observing or experimenting; the first is hard, and the latter impossible, for the experiment that we make already alters our state of mind.

55.

Transcendental philosophy is ontology – doctrine of essence, not doctrine of things (discipline,[m] a science which posits limits for our knowledge – doctrine, [one] which extends it). A discipline of pure reason is necessary – we now seek a doctrine of it – metaphysics proper – applied to things which can never be objects of experience, to the supersensible. One can call this doctrine dogmatic in the theoretical respect, it has three parts: first, a metaphysical-dogmatic psychology – pneumatology – doctrine of spirits. Second, a metaphysical-dogmatic cosmology would mean an intelligible world <*mundus intelligibilis*>, noumenon."[n] – Third, metaphysical theology dogmatically considered is called theosophy. All of this is the theoretical – not practical respect – human beings wanting merely to know. Concepts are immanent when corresponding objects can be given to them, transcendent when this is no longer feasible – all concepts of metaphysics are beyond bounds {the human being bounds over the mean}.[o]

RATIONAL PSYCHOLOGY

Doctrine of the soul – soul is the principle of life in an animal. Animal is something bodily insofar as it lives. Life is the faculty for having representations of the faculty of desire. Soul is separate from matter – that which ensouls – a separate substance which connected with the body is called soul. One could call soul <*anima*; G: *Seele*> the subject of feeling, mind <*animus*; G: *Gemüt*>, the subject of thoughts, and spirit <*spiritus*; G: *Geist*> – as the subject of spontaneity – . We will treat first of the existence of the body – we thereby refute the idealists – and second the existence of the soul as a separate substance – against materialists <*contra materialistas*>. We consider the soul first (1) as substance (simple or composite <*compositum*>), (2) according to its personality, as intelligence, in the consciousness of its identity in different states. (3) According to its interaction <*commercio*> with the body – that is animal life <*vita ani-*

28:680

---

[m] Kant gives two synonyms here: *Disciplin, Zucht* (679₁₉).
[n] We are adding a period here (679₂₇).
[o] Marginalia (679₃₃) alongside text printed at 679₃₁₋₂. We follow Lehmann in inserting this after the text.

malis>. With the life of a human being, we will treat first of the beginning, (2) of the survival of the soul in the life of a human being (where it resides – seat of the senses <*sensorium commune*>) {this question is absurd, it cannot be in space. – },[p] (3) the end of life – of this interaction <*commercium*>, death, and (4) the state of the soul after death – ; finally we make comparisons.

56.

Our body is object of outer sense. According to the hypothesis of idealism we have no body, but rather it is mere representation of our thinking principle. This is only a problematic, but not an assertoric proposition. It is likewise with egoism. Both rest on the same grounds, both assume we cannot be certain of the existence of a thing in space. Descartes said in his *Discourse on Method* <*Tractat de methodo*>: I think therefore <*cogito ergo*> – or rather, that is <*id est*> – I am <*sum*>. This he called the sole existential proposition. {Berkeley was an idealist insofar as he said bodies as such do not exist[13] (he looked merely at the form).[q] This is transcendent idealism, opposed to it stands the psychological.}[r] – From an effect we can infer the cause, but we cannot determine it. Idealism is an irrefutable premise (– hypothesis –).[s] Dualism is the hypothesis when a human being assumes a thing outside him. The proof is carried out this way, the determination of my own empirical existence is possible only through the existence of an object outside me, this is sensory representation – if one assumes it without a corresponding object, then it is a representation of the power of imagination. *The idealist* must assume that the intuition of bodily things outside us is representation *of the power of imagination*. The *realist* can refute this hypothesis only this way, if he proves that the intuition of bodily things is a representation *of sense*. Since even the determination of my own existence in time – (the inner sense) would not be possible without something outside me, we must also have an outer sense, because without this we would also have no inner one. Time in itself has only one dimension – it has no breadth – for all things exist in one point of time, thus in my empirical representation nothing is perduring, for it always changes. Idealism is a kind of cancer in metaphysics which until now was deemed untreatable. We can determine our existence in time *by nothing* unless we base it on something perduring. Something must perdure with respect to which everything flows by. The representation of what per-

28:681

---

[p] Marginalia (680_{14}) alongside text printed at 680_{14-16}. We follow Lehmann in the insertion but remove parentheses added by him.
[q] We are adding a period here (680_{28}).
[r] Marginalia (680_{26-9}) alongside text printed at 680_{24-32}. We follow Lehmann in the insertion.
[s] We are adding a period here (680_{31}).

dures – is it only a representation of the power of imagination? It would then belong to our inner sense, *thus be just as little perduring*. Therefore it must be a representation *of outer* sense, corresponding to the object, therefore there are bodies. One cannot say time is everywhere, for things are at one time, but space is for all time, perduring – it does not flow. – What is outside us, – the ground of something outside us, under the form of space, is the intelligible. If idealism cannot be refuted, then this also cannot happen with egoism.

57.

We go now to the *second section*: in our body is a principle of life – a soul. The materialists maintain the opposite. Matter does not think <*materia non cogitat*>. Thus the principle of life – because it thinks, is distinguished from matter. Matter has no faculty of representations at all (it does not represent <*non repraesentat*>) – no power of representation <*vis repraesentativa*> – and so the proposition applies to animals also. All representations are simple or composite. Representations can be made simple only in a subject, but *never* if they are divided singly among several subjects. Since each matter is an aggregate composed of substances outside one another, then it cannot grasp any representations – not think – only the *I* gives the unity of the subject, which cannot possibly be met with in   28:682
matter. ([The] principle of life [is the] faculty of being able to become cause of effects by one's representations.) *In thinking, something simple is required, in matter nothing is simple, therefore matter cannot think.* – The soul is immaterial, no object of outer sense. Can the soul be substrate of matter? (To make into a substance <*substantiare*; G: *zur Substanz machen*>, – a personifying.) A phenomenon is in itself no substance, with respect to our senses we call the appearance of substance itself substance. But this phenomenal substance <*substantia phenomenon*> must have a noumenon as substrate. This can be called transcendental idealism. We can never obtain representations from the motions of matter, thus materialism has no influence on psychology. If we do not assume that only the substrate has representations, then we have no ground for that at all, for with matter we always find nothing but outer relations. Materialism is thus (1) as proven, wholly false, taken in the strict sense <*proprie*> (2) in the extended sense a concept <*conceptus*>. Now we want to refute *fatalism* – the hypothesis according to which one assumes everything is natural necessity, i.e., the necessity of each state of substance, insofar as it is absolutely determined by the previous one. But now a being is free only if in each state it stands in its control to do an action, or to forgo it; therefore fatalism wholly opposes freedom. That a human being has freedom can be proved never psychologically but, to be sure, morally. –

58. Monday

Fate <*fatum*>, blind necessity also concerns bodily things; in other words, human beings have maintained in this way that bodies as well must necessarily change without cause. But this is an obvious absurdity – sheer hidden quality <*qualitas occulta*>. But one also calls fatalism the hypothesis that the human soul has no freedom. We have already treated in the antinomies *of the possibility* of freedom, i.e., of the thought, and proven it; because since everything would be determined in the previous time, then of course a human being also could not act freely, everything would be natural necessity – mere phenomenon – and nothing noumenon. Actions of a human being are natural necessity as events, spontaneity as determination of his will – so both can be united. We can never give supersensible concepts objective reality – [we can] cognize them merely negatively.' – It is beyond bounds, transcendent – for our reason only ideas are possible here. Something supersensible but *not* transcendent are our free actions. – Moral laws, independent of every incentive [and] merely from the pure representation of accordance with the law – from *absolute* spontaneity; that such a thing would be, that something supersensible – *freedom* – lies in us, only the moral law tells us – to live by the immanent use of our practical reason" {the glowing ox of Phalaris[14] – to make oneself never unworthy of life}.' – Absolutely no one can cognize the possibility theoretically (beyond what he is able to do, no man is obliged <*ultra posse nemo obligatus*>). The moral law commands, I *should*, thus *I can*, – we cannot prove this through any experience. We can consider *the personality* of the soul: (1) *morally* – insofar as this being is capable of an ascription (imputation of action), free, – we have just treated of that. (2) *Psychologically*. – Do we indeed maintain identity of person in our whole life? The *I* is intellectual, through that the human being connects his states, thus identity occurs, but that which perdures, empirical consciousness in time, a human being cannot name. Thus identity is not at all to be doubted morally, but (physically) theoretically one cannot assume it, as little as the water in a river always remains the same {(Locke, *Essay*)}.[15]" *The singul(arity)* <G: *Ein(zeln)heit*> (singularity <*unicitas*> – not simplicity <*simplicitas*; G: *Einfachheit*>)ˣ against which some assume three souls (vegetative soul <*animam vegetativam*> – e.g., growth of hair – sensitive

28:683

' We are adding a period here (683₂).

" We are removing a period here (683₉).

ᵛ Marginalia (683₉₋₁₀) alongside text printed at 683₇₋₁₂. We follow Lehmann in inserting this after the first sentence of the text. Parentheses added by Lehmann have been removed but an added period has been retained.

" Marginalia (683₂₃) appearing alongside text printed here. We follow Lehmann in inserting it after this text. *Versuch* is not emphasized, but we are treating it as a reference to Locke's *Essay on Human Understanding* (683₂₃).

ˣ We are removing a period here (683₂₄).

soul <*animam sensitivam*> – cause of actions according to the brute power of choice <*arbitrio bruto*>, and rational soul <*animam rationalem*>, use of reason); but three faculties do not give three souls, and moreover the I brings everything to unity. The question cannot be settled otherwise. A human being constitutes a unity, and we cannot call the principles of life in various parts souls. –

59.

Spirituality, an immaterial being is spirit so far as it can think without body (in connection with a body – [it is] soul).[y] Spirituality belongs to the transcendental concepts – ideas – can never become cognition. Life – [is] existence of the unification of the soul with the body. We can thus contrive no experience through which we could become aware of the faculty of thinking without body. – 28:684

On origin <*De origine*>. In chemistry one distinguishes matter, as *educed* <*tanquam eductum*> {e.g., potash[16] is educt}[z] – what was previously there and only receives a new form; as *produced* <*tanquam productum*>, what was not previously there at all. Either the human soul is *educt* – (natural or supernatural origin <*ortus naturalis aut supernaturalis*>) (Creationists – maintain it is made – hyperphysical <*hyperphysicus*; G: *supernaturalist*>, it arises from the creation) – it is only derived from another substance, – this is the proposition of preexistence. – [Or it arises] as product of the parents, creature of the parents – this system of propagation is:

(1) from *the souls* of the parents <*ex animabus parentum*>, (2) from *the bodies* of the parents <*ex corporibus parentum*>.[a]

(1) Birth of the soul through transference <*ortus animae per traducem*>, (2) materialism underlies this. One can imagine human souls are made from the beginning, and then are developed in preexisting bodies. This is called the system of evolution <*systema evolutionis*>. The systems <*systemata*> of human generation are (1) involution <*involutionis*> (of encasement), (2) epigenesis, that human beings are produced wholly new. In the first case the human being is educt, in the second product; if we have cause to assume the system of epigenesis, then we assume the human being as product – propagation through transference <*propagatio per traducem*> would then occur with the soul. Is it possible that the soul could produce other substances? – This is against the first principles, for sub-

[y] We are adding a period here (683₃₅) and at 684₃.
[z] Marginalia (684₄) alongside text printed here. We follow Lehmann in the insertion but remove parentheses added by him. Two synonyms are given for potash here: *Pottasche Aschensalz*.
[a] We are moving a period here (684₁₃) from after the prior clause.

stances are perdurable – and must in that case be composite – {and the soul is simple substance}.[b] The maintaining of a propagation through transference <*propagatio per traducem*> is absurd, and has not the slightest notion of possibility. (Separation of the simple can hardly be thought – these are games of frivolous reason.) We now go further to the

interaction <*commercio*> *of the soul with the body.* The beginning of the existence of the human being is his birth – the continuation life, the end death. We have just treated of the beginning. Life in the interaction between body and soul <*commercium inter animam et corpus*> is now our object. The harmony is – in real interaction <*commercio reali*>, or without interaction <*absque commercio*>. (Ideal interaction <*commercium ideale*> – without real connection <*nexum realem*>.)[c] The system of *ideal* and [that of] *real* influence. – The heterogeneity between effects and causes gave the ground for assuming ideal influence. { – How can a motion become cause in representations[?]

28:685

$$\text{system} <systema>$$
$$\swarrow \qquad \searrow$$
occasionalist <*occasion.*>   preestablished <*praestabil.*>}[d]

But it is wholly false that the effect must be homogeneous with the cause, for the concept of causality lies just in this, that something is posited by something *really* <*realiter*> *different.* E.g., contact of a string and sound. The interaction <*commercium*> between soul and body thus makes no difficulty.

60.

Bodies as bodies cannot effect the soul because no relation is possible here. The outer relation in which a body stands with another substance can be thought only in space. But the concepts of body and matter themselves contain sheer relations. But with the internal alterations there occur not merely relations, but rather accidents. Substance – something perduring, – bodies [something] possible for us to determine only through relations. Bodies are phenomena, their substrate, – the intelligible noumenon, and it is this which has influence on the soul – one cannot explain this. – *The location of the soul* is there where the location of the human being is. – The soul can never perceive its outer relation in space. A human being is ensouled – effects of a life principle occur in him. Soul in the body means a soul works on the body. Local presence is

---

[b] Marginalia (684_{26}) alongside text printed here. We follow Lehmann in the insertion.
[c] We have added periods at 684_{35}, 684_{36}, and 684_{37}.
[d] Marginalia (685_{1-4}) alongside text printed at 685_1. We follow Lehmann in the insertion.

impossible with it {virtual however [is possible] – },^{e} for in this case it would have to be an object of outer sense – matter. In which location does the soul reside? This question is absurd – we can speak only of the substrate, and we take it immediately as an object of outer sense, thus a seat of the soul <*sedes animi*> is absurd. Although we believe thinking is in the head, this proves nothing. Thinking requires motions of our brain harmonizing with it, etc. When we think, we speak with ourselves. Because the brain is the root of the nerves, thus has uncommonly much influence on our sensations and representations, we feel here the most effects of our thinking, but this does not put the soul in the brain. Descartes put the seat of the soul in the pineal gland <*glandula pinealis*;   28:686 G: *Zirbeldrüse*>^{17} – in the brain, but after it was found filled with sediment, this opinion ceased.^{f} – Later one assumed the pituitary gland – *cortex* – *corpus callosum*. – One found human beings who lost part of their brain, and yet remained living. Thus only virtual presence can be thought – effect on the body. Death – cessation of the community between soul and body. The seat of the soul as phenomenon is in the seat of the senses <*sensorio communi*>, this lies in the brain; all sensations are concentrated here, because all nerves are connected here. At the same time it is the instrument <*organon*> of all motions. The body comes into play with almost all actions of the minds.

61.

The end of the interaction <*commercii*> is death, we know this cessation only through the destruction of the body. Is the end of the life of a human being also the end of all that which belongs to him? Does the soul stop living {[as opposed to] merely not being – }?^{g} – This would be the survival of the personality. – The second task: have we cause *to assume* that the soul will be after death, or can we prove the necessity (future life <*vita futura*> [is] different from immortality <*immortalitas*>)[?]^h It is not enough if we prove that some will live again. If we can prove it only from divine decree, and not from natural necessity, then this is not enough. First, we cannot know this without revelation, and second, it does not follow from this that the future state will be eternal. The arguments on behalf of the future life are the following:

First, *psychological* – from physiology – they can prove nothing. For we

---

^{e} Marginalia (685$_{24}$) alongside text printed at 685$_{22-23}$. We follow Lehmann in the insertion but remove parentheses added by him.
^{f} We are adding this and the next period (686$_{4,5}$).
^{g} Marginalia (686$_{16}$) alongside text printed here and inserted with a sign.
^{h} We are removing periods after *beweisen* and *immortalitas* and adding a period here (686$_{19-20}$).

can never experience the future condition of the soul without body. {For life is interaction <*commercium*>, thus how can we cognize without interaction <*commercium*>?}[i]

Second, *metaphysical a priori* – (what we cognize from *a priori* grounds, we cognize as necessary, thus this proves not merely survival, but immortality) here we prove either from:

a. metaphysical *theoretical* grounds, from the metaphysics of nature

b. metaphysical *practical* grounds, from the metaphysics of morals (morality), these are: (1) from teleological grounds, pure *natural ends*, or (2) *the* 28:687 *ends of God*. The question is: is the [cessation of the] life of this subject the cessation of all life? If someone assumes this, then he maintains that the life of the body depends merely on the body, that it contains the ground of life of the human soul. But all matter is lifeless, therefore the life of human beings cannot depend on it, but rather on another principle, which cannot itself be matter. Hylozoism is the opinion that matter has life – this is the death of all physics.[18] If a being, which is not itself a principle of life, is attached to another principle of life, then the latter will be hindered thereby (restrained), and death is thus rather promotion of activity { – slave chained to the cart – becomes free as soon as he is unchained}.[j] – All of this serves in the refutation of materialism. As for the teleological grounds, we have here:

First, metaphysical cosmological teleological – purely from the ends of nature

Second, theological teleological – from the ends of God. The first are based on the principle of a certain purposiveness which is met with in nature in general. It has placed in no being talents that go further than the ends, so that proportion always remains between the talents and the use. We have astonishing talents of the faculty of cognition – astronomy – yet far more sublime of the faculty of desire – morality . – The command of duty – where there is no proportionate advantage in life at all. Thus the end must be attained in another life. –

62. Monday.

Natural or supernatural teleology <*teleologia naturalis . . . supernaturalis*>. The first gives the proof from the talents of a human being according to the ends of nature, the second gives it from the ends of God; – but the latter we cannot wholly cognize, because he always wants *the best* – but we do not cognize that – and no human being can grasp the wisdom of God – the proof from the analogy of human beings with organized beings of

---

[i] Marginalia (686₁₈₋₁₉) along text printed here and inserted with a sign.

[j] Marginalia (687₁₁₋₁₂) alongside text printed here. We follow Lehmann in the insertion but remove parentheses added by him.

nature is thus for us the most sure. Nothing is in vain – this is the principle – the ends of organization should be fulfilled in this life or in a future one. Since for many talents no proportionate use is possible here at all, then it would be against the general law of nature if they were placed in vain in a human being, if he could not make use of them in a future life. [If] we assume {the Englishman Fordon furnished this proof}[k] an alien being came to the world – and viewed a human being according to his natural talents – life would not be worth the trouble and difficulties – yet we have great incentives: and when a human being has brought it to the highest point in cognitions – then his mental powers sink – thus life is not at all proportionate *in its length* to our cognitions; – the cognition of vast world structures – of the wonderful arrangement of nature – where everything is organized, provides us more gratification than anything else – but in this life such talents attain no advantage – thus a future life – all human beings will survive; – will this survival be eternal? – (Can a human being perish when he has received his reward or punishment? –) Immortality is the necessity of a future life from the natural constitution of the human being (not merely from an extraordinary decree), thus all human beings will live in the future because it lies in their nature – it will last eternally, for, if it must go beyond this life, then I do not have the least ground – why this life should end. This properly teleological proof is noble.[l] – We study more of human nature, get to know our own worth better, – in the intuiting of worlds. – We obtain respect for one's own essence – not for ourselves – , [but] humanity in our person. – The other side also gets a hearing <*audiatur et altera pars*>: of those who are no longer, we know nothing – the contingency of begetting, for it depends quite a lot on the monks (cloisters) – but all of this proves nothing. The best proof would be the one – immediately from the nature *of human beings* (not from nature in general). For the future life is required: (1) the perdurability of the soul as substance, (2) as living being – with representations – (3) the survival of its personality. – Without the last, one cannot say that human beings will exist in the future as rational beings. – Perduring memory <*memoria perdurabilis*>, connection of both states with the consciousness of the identity of the subject, without this the person is dead. Never can psychology become pneumatology with us – showing the life of the spirit without body, [rather] it is only negative – [it] can prove that materialism is not applicable to the human soul (because it contradicts all laws of possible thinking); we can refute all objections to the maintaining of a future life, but can furnish only one proof for it, the moral-teleological. –

28:688

28:689

---

[k] Marginalia (688$_{1-2}$), at top of the ms page, alongside text printed here. We follow Lehmann in the insertion. Lehmann misreads "Fordon" as "Ferguson," but later suggests (in a note) that David Fordyce was probably intended. See the endnote to Ak. 29: 916$_{30f}$ (above).
[l] We are adding periods here (688$_{20}$) and at 688$_{22}$.

63.

On the transition into the future life, this is spiritual, or animal life <*vita animalis*>, the first we call another world, for space makes of all things only one single world; the concept of the spiritual life of the soul is wholly idea. It may be supposed; and if we pass over from the animal life into a purely spiritual life, then this is not all to be sought in space. (Swedenborg – assumed the ideal whole <*totum*> as real, invisible church.)[m][19] Animal life <*vita animalis*>, life in interaction <*commercio*> with the body; a connection, either (1) with the same body, rebirth <*palingenesie*>, (a) through corpuscles <*corpuscula*> which remain indestructible, evolution, (b) through resurrection. { – when *the same* body is resurrected, those who maintained that are materialists},[n] (2) with another body – metamorphosis. The system of rebirth <*palingenesie*>, of evolution, assumes throughout the soul as material – *glorified body* says nothing, it remains thereby always body. The theory of metamorphosis is: (1) formal, where the same matter receives another form, namely from the corpuscle <*corpusculo*>, as from the nucleus, this is the metamorphosis of transformation. (2) The metamorphosis of transmigration, migration of the soul <*metempsychosis*; G: *Seelen-Versetzung*>, soulmigration, a very old opinion with the Indians. Metempsychosists must always assume the cup of forgetfulness <*letheum poculum*; G: *Becher der Vergessenheit*> – but this does not help recovery at all. *The state of the soul after the transition.* The defender of the sleep of the soul <*hypnopsychita*>[20] assumes a sleep of the soul as an intermediate state. The soul is conscious of itself as either in the world of the blessed or of the unblessed – this concerns the moral – blessedness [is] contentment with one's morality, happiness [is] contentment with objects outside oneself. Heaven [is] the greatest <*maximum*> of all good with respect to wellbeing and worthiness – hell the opposite – both are ideals. The greatest <*maximum*> cannot be given with a human being – we think an infinite progression in the good. This is all that rational psychology <*psychologia rationalis*> can judge, – there is a simple principle of life, and materialism can be refuted. We come now to the last chapter of rational psychology: *souls of brutes* <*animae brutorum*>. Can life be a property of matter? – Consciousness is entirely lacking in animals, their actions happen according to laws of the power of imagination, which nature placed in them – by analogy. The principle that guides animals, as analogue of reason <*analogon rationis*>, is called instinct, the faculty for performing

28:690

---

[m] We have added a period and the following capital here (689₁₀).

[n] Marginalia (689₁₃₋₁₄) written in the bottom-right corner of the ms (following *Resurrection*). We follow Lehmann in inserting it after this text, but restore a period (after *Resurrection*) omitted by Lehmann without note.

actions without consciousness, for which human beings require consciousness, a natural desire; they do not learn it, and yet understand it,
the spider works as soon as it has hatched from the egg. Descartes and
Malebranche want to deny the animals souls, the latter from theological
grounds, why should they suffer – since they have perpetrated nothing,
but this is a weak argument; it is clear that in the actions of animals we
do not need to assume understanding, for they perform them without
instruction, nature has placed a drive in them. The subject of representation in each living being is something different from matter, and animals
have souls. The soul of an animal as brute soul <*anima bruti*> can
develop itself to infinity, grow, but always only sensitively, never up to a
rational being. Whoever imagines that animal souls are different from
the human only in degree, not in species, errs, for consciousness effects
total difference and the impossibility that with this lack an animal soul
can ever raise itself to a human one {which would be possible if they
were different merely by degree, and not specifically. – }[o]

[o] Marginalia (690_{20-1}) alongside text printed here, and inserted with a sign.

EARLY 1790S (AK. 28: 753–775)

teaches the nature of the human soul. *Soul is the subject of sensation.* In German it always indicates something inner, as e.g., the soul of a feather, a canon, i.e., the line drawn through the center of the mouth to the center of the ground. Mind *<psyche>*[a] means butterfly *<papillon>*. Thus in this naming of the soul there lies an analogy with a butterfly, which is hidden preformed in the caterpillar, which is nothing more than its husk. This teaches that in this world dying is nothing more than regeneration. *Soul <anima>* is the animating principle in an animal. Matter cannot live for itself. This is a proposition against hylozoism. If one assumes that matter as matter thinks, lives, i.e., acts according to representations, then this is above all contrary to physics; that parts of matter are not moved by others, but rather can move themselves, contradicts the principle of inertia. Pythagoras says something mystical: the soul is a number moving itself *<numerus se ipsum movens>*. *Soul <anima> is the sensible, mind <animus> the intellectual faculty of the soul.* Mind *<mens, nous>* is this in any event. – Soul and spirit are to be sure two distinct relations but only two faculties of one and the same subject.

A living being has only one soul, this is a principle in psychology. The consciousness of the unity of my soul follows already from the consciousness of my subject. Even if we think several principles of life in the body, which are unified, so that much life is united in one, then this is still only one soul. One wants to explain irritability from the mechanical properties of body. This is still dubious. Perhaps an overflowing fluid of the nerves, which looks like slime and clothes the muscles, is the cause of it. With its head, a cut-up wasp grabs its stomach, and the latter defends itself with its stinger. The land crab[1] can leave its claw, and this still continues to pinch the body that it has grabbed. It is therefore not unlikely that multiple lives are concentrated in the body under a single principle. Just because several principles of life are in various parts of the animal, there are not on that account several animals.

There are three important questions: (1) what is the soul in life? (What is its survival in life? N.B. Here the seat of the soul is spoken of immedi-

28:754

---

[a] This is written with Greek letters in Lehmann (753₅).

ately.) (2) What was it before birth? (How is its beginning, the origin of the soul <*ortus animae*>?) (3) What will it be after death or in the future life? (Death is the end of life, i.e., of the interaction of the soul and body <*commercii animae et corporis*>.)

With respect to the first there are again two questions to raise, whether we (1) have a psychology with respect to it, i.e., whether we can cognize it, how it is in the body, how its existence is connected with that of the body. (2) Whether a pneumatology of its nature occurs, i.e., whether we can consider it as not in interaction <*commercio*> with the body, but rather isolated for itself. We do not arrive that far. – A negative property of the soul is: it is an immaterial, non-bodily (simple) being. This is maintained against the materialists. Material is not merely what is matter, but rather also what can be a part of matter. Something simple cannot possibly be a part of matter. All matter is in space, a part of it is thus also in space, but what is in space is always divisible and never simple. The soul is not material. Matter has no faculty of representations, therefore it cannot at the same time be its own principle of life. (The author says: matter cannot think;[2] we say: it has no faculty of representation, and then the proof applies also to animals.) Matter is not the substrate of representations <*materia non est substratum repraesentationum*>. All representations are either simple or composite. Two representations must be united in one subject in order to constitute one representation. All representations refer to one subject, that is a unity in whose representation something multiple is unified. Representations thus cannot be divided among several subjects and then constitute one representation, but rather the unified representation can occur in one subject only as a unity. A being can therefore have no representations without this absolute unity of the subject. If single representations are divided among several subjects, then these, taken together in isolation, cannot constitute a unity; for this consists of the manifold of the representations. – But each matter is an aggregate of substances outside each other, thus matter can have no representations. Matter is no unity of the subject, but rather a plurality of substances. If an aggregate of substances is supposed to think, then a partial part of the representations would have to lie in the single parts, but these together constitute no unity of the representations. A multitude of substances can never have a representation in community. The principle of life is the faculty for being cause of the actuality of objects through one's representations. Something simple is required for thinking, but all matter is composite, consequently it cannot think. N.B. The matter which occupies a space has just as many parts as the space has. – Now *materialism* is the claim according to which one assumes that matter is not lifeless, but rather can ensoul itself, without having necessary a separate substance as a living principle.

28:755

The groundlessness of this is thus now well proved, but not on that account pneumatology. For that this substance recognized as simple could also think without connection with the body cannot be concluded from that. The effects from the faculty of a being can be cognized only from experience. Whether the soul also continues to think outside the body, that cannot be decided *a priori*. One would have to arrange experiences of this. We can arrange experiences only in life, but here we experience only how the soul thinks in interaction <*commercio*> with the body. Therefore it remains undecided whether the soul can continue to think after life, even without interaction <*commercium*>.

Because the soul is not material, one cannot yet on that account maintain its spirituality. Spirit is an immaterial substance that thinks <*spiritus est substantia immaterialis quae cogitat*>, says the author.[3] Spirit is an immaterial substance [about] which one can think also without connection with matter. The spirituality of the human soul belongs to the transcendent concepts, i.e., we can attain no cognition of it, because we can give no objective reality to this concept, i.e., no corresponding object in any possible experience. It is not to be decided whether the body is not an indispensable support <*adminiculum*> of the soul for thinking; for we cannot set ourselves outside the body in order to experience this.

One has sought the seat of the soul <*sedes animae*> in the seat of the senses <*sensorio communi*>, where the soul supposedly receives all impressions of objects. But since, besides the faculty of thinking <*facultas cogitandi*>, it also has a faculty of locomotion <*facultatem locomotivam*>, i.e., for moving the body, then that part by whose motion the soul moves the whole body would be the prime moving power <*primum movens*>. One places both in the brain. Descartes placed it in the pineal gland (<*glandula pinealis;* G: *Zirbeldrüse*>); for since the soul is a unity, one has also sought it in parts which are singular and simple. Yet one has since found that the pineal gland is calcified, indeed Sömmering assumes a calcification with all pineal glands. Bonnet made the corpus callosum (<*corpus callosum;* G: *Hirnschwiele*>) the seat of the soul, although without ground.[4]

28:756

The location of the soul is there where the location of the human being as thinking being is.[5] I cannot perceive myself as soul in relation with other things, therefore not in space. This would have to be perceived through outer sense. The soul would thus have to perceive itself through outer sense, thus perceive itself outside itself, which is a contradiction <*contradictio*>. I see my location in the world as a human being, to be conscious of one's location in the world means to have an outer perception. Should the soul specify its location, then it would have to determine its relation to other things and also specify the point where it finds itself. It can do this only while it sets itself outside, and thus observes. This is absurd. It is absurd to assume a location of the soul in the human body; a human being is an ensouled body, i.e., in connection with a thing that contains the ground of the life-motions. – If we think of an immaterial being, then we can assign it no location, no local relation, but rather only a dynamic one, a relation of virtual, not local, presence. The soul is the ground of the alterations in the body, but the manner and way that it is this is impossible to cognize. The location is not prior to knowing how the soul works. Whatever is an object of inner sense (like the soul) can in no way be cognized as object of the outer. *I can allow the soul no local presence in space*, because I then at once assume it as material. What is supposed to be present in a location, must be object of the outer senses, i.e., matter. I can give the soul not local, but rather virtual presence, i.e., something has an effect. That is a mere thought, through this we merely assume that it is not an absurd representation to assume an effect of the soul on the body. The soul cannot cognize its location. For a thing cannot be in two locations at once, otherwise it would be outside itself and could consider itself as object of outer sense. – *Where is the seat of the soul in the body?* is therefore an absurd question. For it would either have to perceive, grasp, itself, thus be itself object of the outer senses, or we would have to perceive it as object of the outer senses, where it then would have to be body. – The ancients said: the soul is wholly in the whole body, and wholly in each part, i.e., nothing more than: where the human body is, there the soul is as well.

28:757

Against the [claim] that the location of the soul is not to be determined, it is in no way an objection that, e.g., persistent thinking makes [a] sensation in the head, etc. If we believe that we think in the head, then we still do not perceive thereby the seat of the soul in the head; since for thinking we do use bodily organs. Because the brain is the root of all nerves and feelings, the soul works mostly in the head (in the brain)[b] (through the nerves the soul has its faculty of locomotion <*facultatem locomotivam*> through which it moves the other parts, therefore if a nerve is ligated, then its effect ceases), but other internal organs <*viscera*> and nerves will be affected just as much by thinking; for all of our thoughts are accompanied by bodily motions. The presence of the soul is thus virtual <*virtualis*>. Its effects can therefore with full right be assigned a location. This virtual presence can be considered as seat of the soul and be sought in the seat of the senses <*sensorio communi*>. Sensation occurs only to the extent that the nerve reaches the brain. The nerve impels the muscle to voluntary motion, thus the brain is not only the seat of the senses <*sensorium*>, but rather also the common instrument <*organon commune*>.

The interaction <*commercium*> between soul and body is quite intimate in life, i.e., there is no action of the mind without motion of the body. Thus psychology is fully incapable of cognizing an action of the mind without influence of the body.

[b] These brackets are square in Lehmann.

ON THE INTERACTION <*COMMERCIO*> OF
THE SOUL WITH THE BODY

The beginning of the interaction <*commercii*> of the soul with the body is the beginning of the existence of the human being, i.e., its birth. The survival is life, the end is death.

To explain the community of the soul with the body in life is now our goal. This point has occupied philosophers since Descartes.

There is a *harmony* <*harmonia*> between substances *in interaction and without interaction* <*in commercio et absque commercio*>, the latter gives only an ideal connection <*nexum idealem*>. But should there be a harmony in interaction <*harmonia in commercio*> between soul and body, then there is a physical influence <*influxus physicus*>. Thus a system arises here of the ideal and of the real influence between soul and body.

Substances harmonize if the state of one substance corresponds with   28:758
the state of the other.

Since bodily motions produce representations, the heterogeneity of the effects with the causes (in the interaction <*commercio*> between soul and body) has made it that instead of a physical influence (real) <*influxus physici (realis)*>, one assumed an ideal influence <*influxum idealem*>, but that is actually no influence <*influxus*>. For here God would have to assist immediately (i.e., the system of assistance <*systema assistentiae*> or occasionalism), or God would have already determined in the beginning of the world that representations should develop in the soul precisely when certain bodily motions would occur, and this would be the system of preestablished harmony <*systema harmoniae praestabilitae*>. But the heterogeneity of the effect with the cause makes not the least difficulty, but rather how substances in general can act upon one another makes the difficulty, be they homogeneous or heterogeneous.

Once we assume the existence of the soul, then how it acts upon the body makes no further difficulty.

Bodies as bodies cannot act upon the soul and vice versa, because bodies cannot have any relations at all to a thinking being. The outer relation in which a body stands with a substance is only in space, thus this substance must also be in space, therefore a body. Locations are pure relations. Alteration of the locations is alteration of the relations. The filling of space, the figure of the body, i.e., the alteration of the boundaries are sheer relations. With the soul we can name what is altered internally, but these are not relations, but rather only accidents <*accidentia*>, e.g., representations, etc. Since the relation of the body consists only in space, then it cannot be the ground of the inner determinations, e.g., of the representations. The body as phenomenon is not in community with the soul, but rather the substance distinct from the soul, whose appearance is called body. This substrate of the body is an outer determining ground of the soul, but how this interaction <*commercium*> is constituted, we do not know. In body we cognize mere relations, but we do not cognize the inner (the substrate of matter). The extended as an extension <*qua extensum*> does not act upon the soul, otherwise both correlates <*correlata*> would have to be in space, therefore the soul would have to be a body. If we say the intelligible of the body acts upon the soul, then this means this outer body's noumenon determines the soul, but it does not mean: a part of the body (as noumenon) passes over as determining ground into the soul, it does not pour itself as power into the soul, but rather it determines merely the power which is in the soul, thus where the soul is active. This determination the author calls ideal influence <*influxum idealem*>,[6] but this is a real influence <*influxus realis*>; for among bodies as well I can think only such an influence. The body thus contains a ground for determining the power that is in the soul, and thus again the soul contains a ground for determining the power of the unknown something (noumenon of the body), so that an outer motion arises. But without both substances already having powers, no real influence <*influxus realis*> can be between them. Descartes says: God produces representations immediately, e.g., when my eye moves. The third, namely the eye, e.g., is then wholly dispensable, because without an eye God also could produce the representations. Leibniz assumes these representations preestablished by God, that is not much better.

28:759

If the soul is not matter, and cannot think as such, then it is perhaps a substrate <*substratum*> of matter, i.e., the noumenon, of which matter is merely the phenomenon, and then *virtual* <*virtualis*> *materialism* arises. A substantiated phenomenon <*phaenomenon substantiatum*> is an appearance made into a substance that in itself is no substance. Matter is the ultimate subject of the outer senses, it perdures, even if its form is altered, and therefore matter is also called a substance. Because matter is possible only through space, then it is substance not in itself, but rather as appearance. If I take it as substance in itself, then it is a substantiated phenomenon <*phaenomenon substantiatum*>, as Leibniz says. The substrate of the phenomenon of matter is wholly unknown to us, and we do not even know whether it is not a simple being. We cannot know how the substrate might be internally constituted, whether it could have thinking and representations. Thus it can at least be thought that underlying matter is a substrate that could think. This would be *transcendent*[c] *materialism*. – The faculty of life is met with perhaps in all matter, but matter has in itself no faculty of life, but rather this underlies it as a substrate. – Between motions and representations there is not the least connection, thus matter cannot be assumed either positively or negatively. All representations are something

---

[c] *transcendentelle* is used here (759₃₁₋₂); *transcendental* is the ordinary term for "transcendental," and so "transcendent" seems more appropriate.

in us, and we cannot say that they are objects of the outer senses. But all matter is an object of the outer senses, and we can assume nothing of its inner representations. With matter we have nothing other than outer relations and alterations of outer relations. Since bodies are not substances in themselves, then we cannot give representations to them, but rather we cognize in them mere outer relations (representations are but inner determinations). – How matter could have representations is wholly ungraspable and inconceivable to us. Thus it is wholly in vain to assume such a thing. If one maintains that the substrate of matter and the substrate of our own thinking are the same, we can easily grant him that, but he still says nothing thereby; for we can derive nothing from it, because we cognize and comprehend nothing from it.

28:760

Origin of the soul <origo animae>, state of the soul before the birth of the human being. The origin of the soul <origo animae> actually has an analogy with the generation of the human being. Epigenesis is the system where the parents are the productive cause of the children. This has more grounds for it than the system of preformation. The system of little animal seeds <animalculorum spermaticorum> is the system where the seeds are thought as consisting of small animals. This is also the system of free preexistence <praeexistentiae liberae>. If one assumes the system of involution, then one thereby declares great precaution as completely useless. A pig, e.g., that eats an acorn destroys thereby a million trees that were placed in it. Also speaking against that are hybrids and bastard plants which seem to indicate actual production, not mere evolution.

CLASSIFICATION OF THE OPINIONS ABOUT THE ORIGIN OF THE SOUL

(1) A matter is an educt, i.e., what was previously already there in another matter, but now is exhibited as separate. (2) A product, what previously was not there at all, but rather only now is first produced. The human soul can be both in generation, but if in both cases its origin <ortus> is physical <physicus>, whoever assumes this is a physicalist <physicus> with respect to the soul (naturalist). If one assumes the soul is created by God at birth, then its origin <ortus> is hyperphysical <hyperphysicus>, and whoever assumes this is a creationist (hypernaturalist). To assume this is merely a matter of faith, here all investigation is cut off. Whoever assumes the soul as an educt is a preexistentialist, i.e., he assumes the system of the preexistence of the soul. Whoever assumes the soul as product of the parents believes in the system of propagation <systema propagationis>. This system of production is again twofold, either from the *souls* of the parents or from the *bodies* of the parents. The first is called the origin of the soul through transference <ortus animae per traducem>, i.e., parents' souls produce children's souls. If the human souls came from

28:761

401

the body of the parents, then they would themselves have to be material. Materialism would thus underlie this. The systems of human generation are twofold: (1) involution (encasement): all children have lain in their ancestors, (2) epigenesis, according to which human beings, as concerns their bodies, are produced wholly new. According to the first the human being is mere educt (educt was already present before birth, only in connection with other matters, so that it comes forth to appear through separation). If we have causes for assuming the system of epigenesis, then we also have cause for assuming the soul as a product, because otherwise the soul would had to have existed elsewhere and then be connected with this newly created body. Here one would then have to assume a propagation through transference <*propagatio per traducem*> in regard to the soul. But a substance cannot produce any other substance, so likewise with the soul. A soul cannot let other souls proceed out of it; for otherwise it would be a composite <*compositum*>. We know nothing of the substrate of matter (of the noumenon), whether it is of the same kind as the thinking principle in us. To assume the propagation <*propagatio*> of the human soul by transference <*per traducem*> is absurd because we cannot judge anything at all about it. Were the soul a product, then the parent souls would have to have a creative power. Each production of a substance is production from nothing <*productio ex nihilo*>, creation; for before the substance, nothing was there. But a creature itself has not a creative, but rather a formative power, i.e., to separate or compose things which are there. Therefore nothing else remains than to view the soul as preformed, however it may stand with bodies.

N.B. All powers and properties of a substance have a degree, the human soul could perish if the degree of powers gradually waned. One could think of a substance of great power as composite, from which a simple substance could then be separated as a child's soul. Yet this is a game of frivolous reason. The system of epigenesis does not explain the origin of the human body, but rather says that we know nothing of it. –

28:762 Leibniz took all matter to be an aggregate of monads. These monads, he says, have externally the relation that they are a composite <*compositum*> and capable of all bodily properties. Since we have no other concept of the interior of other things than what proceeds in ourselves, which are representations and what follows from them, so he concluded from this that all monads would have these representations (the actuality of something is not also to be assumed when it is possible), and called them powers which represent the universe <*vires repraesentativas universi*> or living mirrors of the universe <*specula viva universi*>. For if all monads were in the world, one would influence the other, but since they have nothing but mere representations, each has representations of all monads in the world. But one had to assume slumbering monads <*monades sopita*>, which, to be sure, have representations but are not conscious of them. According to him these constitute the class of non-rational animals. But there were various degrees of the consciousness of the representations – distinct <*distincte*> – clear <*clare*> – obscure <*obscure*>. The monads went from one state <*status*> to another, from the distinct <*distincto*> to the most distinct <*distinctissimum*>, until God. This is the so-called continuum of forms <*continuum formarum*>, according to the analogy of the physical continuum <*continui physici*>, where the minerals commence the order, through the mosses, lichens, plants, zoophytes through the animal kingdom until human beings. This is nothing more than a dream whose groundlessness Blumenbach has shown.[7] According to Leibniz human souls were already previously present, from the obscure state <*statu obscuro*> they have finally come to the distinct one <*distincto*>. All things press toward divinity and in the end they would disappear into it, which then amounts to an emanative system.

On the end of the interaction <*commercii*> *between soul and body,* i.e., on death. It is asked whether the life of the soul is merely an animal or a spiritual life, also whether it is able to think after the death of the human being. All matter is lifeless.[d] (For to be matter means to be composite. Living means being cause of actions through one's own representations. But representations cannot occur in a composite <*composito*>; for here they are divided among several subjects.) One can therefore assume that the separation of a subject from matter is no loss of its life, but rather is a promotion of it. If matter is therefore connected with a principle of life, then the lifelessness of the former must place hindrances in the way of the latter. This seems to be contradicted, in that the body does not always hinder thinking, but rather sometimes is also useful to it. Since both are in interaction <*in commercio*>, so that neither of them is in a position to put aside the other, things stand with them just as with a human being who is welded to a cart. It is certain that the human being goes far better without this than with it; but since he is fastened, then it is a support <*adminiculum*> for his going, if the wheel turns well and there is no friction. Thus as long as the body and soul are also in interaction <*in commercio*>, then the soul must have a support <*subsidium*> of life, but the principle of life still does not, on that account, appear to depend on the lifeless matter.

28:763

A cessation of the whole life is death of the soul. There is not merely the question whether the soul will cease being a substance, but rather whether it will wholly cease to live after the death of the human being. Further, it is asked whether we even have cause to assume that the soul will live in the future, or whether it must live necessarily. The continuation[e] of life after death is not immortality of the soul, i.e., not the impossi-

---

[d] We are adding a period here and at the end of the following parenthetical remark (762_{29, 33}).
[e] *Fortdauer;* this term, whose components mean "further duration," is also translated as "survival."

bility of mortality. Hope of a future life *<spes vitae futurae>* according to a divine decree *<decreto divino>* is not immortality. Immortality is future life *<vita futura>* as necessary from the nature of the soul. The first assumes the system of resurrection, that while it remains as substance, the soul will be awakened out of the state of its death merely by God's will.

Immortality is the necessity of future duration from the nature of the soul. For the hope of future life we have moral ends and grounds. We can attempt to explain the survival of the human soul naturally or supernaturally. The first is *physiological* according to the constitution of its nature, or *hyperphysical* through awakening after death. For the survival of the soul is required the survival of its substance and the identity of its personality, i.e., the consciousness of being the same subject that it was. One attempts to prove the first by the following ground: the soul is simple, thus it is indestructible (incorruptible *<incorruptibilis>* by inner decomposition) and cannot perish in this way. (The parts of matter indeed remain over, but it itself perishes.) Mendelssohn held this proof not to be adequate:[8] he says the substance would perish if it were in one moment and not in the other; between two moments there is always a time. Its being would thus be in the one moment, its non-being in the other; now what is supposed to be between these two moments? This proof is not stringent. The soul cannot perish through division, but clearly through remission, through remission of powers (just as consciousness has various degrees of clarity, which become ever weaker, e.g., in falling asleep). The extinguishing of the human soul until complete evanescence can therefore be quite easily thought. There will also be no leap *<saltus>* here, but rather all can go according to the laws of continuity. With one degree of power the soul is there in one time; between this and the moment where it wholly disappears, there are a multitude of moments where the degrees are various. It seems contradictory to this representation that in all alterations in nature the substance perdures and only the accidents change. But here the talk is merely of bodily substances, which we cognize, but with the human soul we cognize nothing perduring, not even the concept of the I, since consciousness occasionally disappears. A principle of perdurability is in bodily substances, but in the soul everything is in flux. With respect to the identity of the person, intellectual memory *<memoria intellectualis>*, no one comprehends its necessity, and also cannot demonstrate it, although its possibility can be assumed. The survival of life could rest on divine decree, perhaps in order to draw human beings to account, but with that we gain nothing, and we could well assume a future life (perhaps only of some human beings) according to divine decree, but out of this an eternal future life, i.e., immortality, does not follow. One must therefore prove the necessity of this survival from the nature of the soul.

The arguments for the future life can be (1) *psychological*. The psychological grounds are at the same time physiological, but from psychological

28:764

grounds we cannot at all infer to a future life, for we cannot at all have any experiences of what the case is with the soul without a body. In life soul and body are in interaction <*in commercio*> and we would have to be able to isolate both in order to make an experiment whether the soul could think also without body. (2) *Metaphysical.* One can prove this from metaphysical theoretical (from the metaphysics of nature) or metaphysical practical, i.e., moral, grounds (from the metaphysics of morals). The first from the concept of a principle of life in general says nothing more than that our life is not dependent upon a connection of the soul with the body. Whoever assumes that the end of the life of the human being is the end of all life   28:765
assumes that matter contains in it the ground of all life. But all matter is lifeless and thus contains no ground of life in it. Life must depend upon an immaterial, thinking principle; this principle cannot be material, for by the principle of life we always imagine something which determines itself from inner grounds, which matter, which can always be moved only by outer causes, cannot. Hylozoism is the death of all philosophy. – The body as lifeless and yet in interaction <*in commercio*> with the soul will be a hindrance rather than a promotion of life. For outside its life the soul must still animate some matter. The body is, to be sure, a ground of animal but not of spiritual life. Dying is therefore liberation of the principle of life from all hindrances. Survival of the principle of life is to be distinguished from the faculty of life. That the soul lives is more than that the principle of life remains. That the soul lives there must be acts <*actus*> of life, but these happen in no other way than in connection of the body. The soul can in itself perform no acts <*actus*> of life, its actions are accompanied by modifications of the body. Therefore it does not live after death, but its principle of life remains, i.e., as such, which can animate a body.

Theoretical *a priori* grounds will thus settle nothing here. The *teleological* grounds prove from the order of ends. They can be (1) *cosmological-teleological*, (2) *theological-teleological*. Teleology can be (1) of the ends of nature (i.e., cosmological teleology), (2) of the ends of God (i.e., theological teleology). The proof of the immortality of the soul is grounded on the principle of the analogy of nature. Nature has placed in all living organic beings no more predispositions than what they can make use of. The faculties, their organs, are not given any larger than they can make use of. It would be absurd to assume predispositions in nature of which no use can be made. In the animal everything is purposive. With a human being it is otherwise, for he can extend his faculties, raise himself up to the nebulae, feel himself called to ponder over them, but he can make no use of this in life, other than that he knows this. With respect to the faculty of desire there is a predisposition even worthier of admiration in human beings. Namely, a human being damns himself and explains duty as holy, without advantage, indeed even if damage rather arises for him from it. We find in us a   28:766
summons to sacrifice the greatest advantages, without receiving in life the

slightest advantage for it. Here is a predisposition in human nature, and this is just as purposive, according to the analogy of nature, as all predispositions of nature. We thus infer a future life where the use of these predispositions and their end can first be attained. For should a human being sink back into chaos with the other animals, then these predispositions, of which he can make no use in life, would be placed in him wholly without purpose. The proper teleological proof is carried out according to the analogy of organized nature, in which we assume that nothing is in vain and without purpose. We infer that in a human being it must stand with the bodily just as it does with the spiritual organization. If the inner predispositions of the human being go further than can be attained by their end here in this world, then we infer that the human being also will live in the future. The moral predispositions, according to which a human being views even life as nothing if he cannot maintain it without crime, best prove a future existence, for the human being sees by this that he is also determined to develop and to enlarge these predispositions further.

A French philosopher[9] says quite fittingly, if a being came down here from another world wherein the inhabitants, e.g., grew down from the trees, and he saw with penetrating eyes the child in the womb of a dying pregnant woman, with members of a size of which it can make no use there, then he would certainly conclude that it would come into another state in order to make use of them there. Likewise as well would another living being who could look completely through an already living human being, judge that with our predispositions we are determined for another world, because our life in this place is so short that we can make no worthy use of our predispositions here, although we value truth and cognitions so highly that we sacrifice our health for them.

Every organized being attains its predispositions here, but not the human being. Should he thus not attain them in the future? The theo-teleological proof consists in this, that in the future life the human being must give an account of his actions. All actions of a human being are imputable to him; but there is no outer judge who can also judge his inner actions, besides himself. Because his merit and guilt are weighed, he must also obtain what he deserves, so one must therefore assume a future life. This proof maintains neither the necessity nor the universality of the future life, for many human beings have no opportunity at all to extend their moral predispositions, as, e.g., the Pescherae,[10] who in no way emerged from animality, likewise children, who can have no actions imputed to them. Further, concerning the eternity of the future life hereafter, no human being's guilt is so great that he should be eternally punished, and no merit so great that he should be eternally rewarded. Thus the future life cannot on that account be eternal, for if a human being has received the reward or punishment fitting his actions, then he must step aside, for he has received his. The last proof contains the ground for a moral practical hypothesis, to

28:767

assume it namely in a moral respect. The possibility of a future life cannot be cut off from us. But if one actually assumes it, then purposiveness of the moral intentions of God must be presupposed, in order for me to make my existence worthy through actions, to which the prospect of the future life impels me. – The system of resurrection comes rather close to materialism, where one concludes that because the soul cannot think without interaction <*commercium*> of the soul and the body, the soul must be reawakened. The ancients held the body alone as the substance, and the soul as merely that which is blown into it with a breath, as mere modification of it. This is a kind of materialism. Priestley even maintains the immortality of the soul to be opposed to the Christian religion, for in the New Testament only the awakening of the body is mentioned. – If the future life belongs to the nature of the human being, i.e., is necessary, then it follows that he is immortal, i.e., that all human beings will live eternally. I have not the slightest ground for assuming that this natural constitution will ever cease. This proper teleological proof according to the analogy of nature is the most noble, raises the human being the most and teaches us to study our own nature correctly.

THE OPPONENT SAYS HERE:

The human being will be transformed into dust and the whole organization destroyed. So far as we know, without these organs no human being can either live, sense, or think. The cremation of bodies with many peoples, the contingency of the begettings are also instances against it. By impeding weddings, a prince can out of whim enlarge or narrow the number of human beings, here also belongs the Catholic church service, which requires unmarried priests. Since human beings arrive at life through such contingencies, are they supposed to live eternally? 28:768

The best proof would be if we could prove immortality from the nature of the soul. With respect to it one cannot say that a knowledge occurs, but rather only that one can judge. The immortality of the soul is a hypothesis, but not theoretical, rather in a moral-practical respect. With such hypotheses, the constitution of the object is not presupposed, but rather I seek to determine merely the subject.

Rational psychology <*psychologia rationalis*> serves for nothing other than refuting the materialists. The moral proof serves to justify our rational belief in a future life.

STATE OF THE SOUL AFTER DEATH
<*STATUS ANIMAE POST MORTEM*>

This is nothing more than a dream. – The transition into a future life is either a transition to a spiritual or animal life. The first is a transition to another world, the latter not, for there is only one space, and we may be in any location we want, we are still in space and consequently in this bodily world. It can be assumed that our future life is a pure, spiritual life, but then the separation of the soul from the body is not a transfer from one location to another, for the soul has no relation of location to other things. In his *Arcanis Coelestibus*[11] Swedenborg says: his inner soul was opened up, i.e., he has a sense for the intercourse with spirits, and talks with them. He said: each human being is already here in heaven or hell, but in the future he will see himself in the community of the pious and the damned, which here he cannot. The animal life <*vita animalis*> is a life in interaction <*in commercio*> with a body. Separation is the decomposition of the interaction <*commercii*>. In the animal life <*vita animali*> the connection can be (1) with the same body, or (2) with another body. The first is rebirth <*palingenesie*>. But the transition into another animal life is (1) rebirth <*palingenesie*>, (2) metamorphosis. The first is twofold: (1) through evolution, (2) through resurrection. Whoever assumes a rebirth <*palingenesie*> of evolution, assumes a corpuscle <*corpusculum*>, like Leibniz, who says: the soul in human beings is in a small body, which would not be destroyed by death, but rather out of which the soul develops. The Jews say everything in the body perishes except for a small bone in the brain,[12] out of which would arise again the entire body. Rebirth <*palingenesie*> through resurrection is just as if one assumed that a wholly new body would be produced. Those who assume this are materialists, to which class the Apostles also belong, who place personality in matter. The transfigured body is a word without sense. – What is the point of our earthly, calcified body in heaven? And yet it is supposed to be the same. Paul seems to assume the system of rebirth <*palingenesie*> of evolution, but he nonetheless speaks also of the resurrection of the same body. – The system of metamorphosis can be (a) of formal metamorphosis <*metamorphosis formalis*>, (b) of material metamorphosis <*metamorphosis materialis*>. The first is a metamorphosis of transformation, the latter of transmigration (i.e., the migration of the soul <*metempsychosis*>) soul-displacement. According to the first, one assumes that the same body merely assumes another form, according to the latter, that the soul is transplanted into another animal body. In it one assumes the cup of forgetfulness <*letheum poculum*>, where the soul is no longer conscious of its previous state, has lost its previous personality, but has obtained a new one. Here no imputability can occur, but one still assumes that, although in his new state the human being cannot remember the previous one, he will still be rewarded or punished for what he did in the other. It is insipid, because it does not accomplish what it is thought out for; a human being is supposed to be, e.g., punished in a new state for that which he did in another, of which he is not conscious; this is not punishment, but rather only evil. According to it animals can also make themselves deserving that

28:769

they finally come into human bodies. If a human soul comes from an animal again into a human body, then this is called the lama rebirth. If such a human being dies, then he becomes a *burchan*, i.e., a saint.[13] – Some hold souls to be mere parts of a general world soul. This is not possible: for the one is conscious of his subject, the other of a wholly other kind of subject. The Chinese seek to become free of their individuality as much as possible, in order to be swallowed in the general world soul.

The state in transition to another world is (1) *that of a slumbering soul*,   28:770 where the soul is conscious of neither this nor that world. A defender of the sleep of the soul <*hypnopsychita*> is whoever assumes this. A defender of the eternal night <*psychopannychita*> assumes an everlasting slumber of the soul.[14] (b) *A full consciousness of oneself.* The state of the soul in consciousness of survival in another world is (a) that of consciousness in intercourse with the blessed, (b) with the non-blessed. Blessedness is a moral contentment with oneself. Happiness is contentment with the state of the world in which I find myself, in relation to other things outside me.

Heaven and hell. The maximum of everything good, of well-being as well as of the worthiness to be happy, is heaven, it is the love of the highest good. The maximum of evil, i.e., the abhorrence of everything good, is hell. By heaven is understood the infinite progression <*progressus infinitus*> to the good, and so the gradual enlargement of the evil principle is hell. An infinite progression <*progressum infinitum*> in good can easily be thought, but not in evil.

EXAMINATION OF SOME HYPOTHESES ABOUT THE SOUL

The question whether a human being has a body is just as if I were to ask whether he has a soul, soul always presupposes a body. The idealists say: I am nothing more than a thinking principle. Idealism is a merely problematic judgment of which one says that it could never be made assertoric. Idealism is not the claim that there are no bodies outside us, but rather only that we cannot prove it, therefore cannot assume that there are bodies. Egoism maintains that it could not be proved that there are bodies outside us. Everything which is outside us as object of perception is body. Idealism and egoism can be maintained from the same grounds, for we have not been able to perceive souls or spirits; therefore, if we assume (as idealists) no bodily being outside us, then we also assume as egoists no spiritual beings outside us, because we cannot perceive these. Berkeley wanted to say bodies as such are not things in themselves, but he expressed himself wrongly, and therefore he appears to be an idealist. Descartes first brought idealism into fashion. He said: I think therefore I am   28:771 <*cogito ergo sum*>, but he could have said: I think, i.e., I am <*cogito, i.e., sum*>. Descartes held this proposition for the only existential proposition;

we would not be conscious to ourselves of whether there are things outside of us, although we would be conscious of the representations of things. From an effect I can indeed infer to a cause, but not to a determinate cause. A representation of things outside us can have its cause (1) in the imagination, (2) in the presence of the thing. It can no way be ascertained wherein the cause of my representation now lies, therefore idealism is an irrefutable presupposition. Likewise I can assume egoism as an irrefutable hypothesis.

Dualism is the claim that there is something outside me of which I am immediately conscious. Here I must prove that an animal consciousness is possible only when I assume something outside me. The empirical consciousness of my existence is the empirical determination of my existence in time. Since the empirical determination of my existence is not possible other than through this, that something is outside me, then by all means I do assume an existence of a thing of which I have the representation that it is outside me. For I think the thing not as object of the power of imagination, as the idealists maintain, but rather as object of the senses (as the dualist says). Are our intuitions of things representations of the senses or representations of the power of imagination? We cannot immediately decide this, but rather must bring it out through inferences. Even inner intuitions can take place only through this,^{f} that I assume something outside of me. Even the determination of my own existence in time would not be possible if there were not in me representations of something outside of me, and if something were not given outside of me in space. I must thus prove that I have an outer sense. *Proof:* I would have no inner sense if I had no outer sense. There is nothing perduring in inner sense. Time has only one dimension, and the existence of things can be determined according to two dimensions. The perduring is not in us, for all of our representations change. I can never imagine a whole concurrent in time, e.g., a line, but rather only successively, but it still appears that the parts of the line are concurrent, and this rests on that, that the conditions can be reversed, namely, the one part of the line is the condition of the

28:772 other part, and this conditioned part is concurrently again the condition of that part, which was previously condition and now is conditioned. I can begin from one end of the line, from whichever I want. We thus become aware of concurrence only by this, that we can proceed in reverse in the subordination. – If the consciousness of my own existence is possible only through that, that something perduring is outside me, then the existence of this perduring item outside of me is just as necessary as the consciousness of my existence. Now there is nothing perduring in me, but rather everything is in succession, thus something perduring must be outside me. Were this representation of something outside me a mere representa-

---

^{f} We are changing a period to a comma (771$_{26}$).

tion of the power of imagination, then it would rest on inner sense, and since there would again be nothing perduring, the representation must thus be a sensory representation, i.e., of an object outside me or of an object of the outer senses, because this alone can be perduring. Newton took space for the instrument <*organon*> of divine omnipresence and said: space is for all times, and time is everywhere. One cannot say this, otherwise time would be something outside of us, but the first proposition is correct and means: space is perdurable.

If I say space is the representation of something perduring, then I must assume something as perduring; for otherwise I could have no representation and hardly a sensory representation of it. Our inner representations always presuppose the outer ones. In time I determine my representations, which I have from outer senses. If we speak of objects, these are always objects of outer senses. The connection of the representations of outer senses obviously rests on inner sense, but this is a mere synthesis of the already present representations.

But we are acquainted with only the form of the intuitions of outer things (space), but not the things themselves, the intelligibles <*intelligibilia*>. Whether these things outside of me are composite or simple, that I do not know. Extension has its ground in my representation; the thing itself can be simple. Whoever maintains and assumes ideality with respect to the form, that space and time are not properties, but rather are only subjective conditions of our intuition, he is a transcendental idealist. But the psychological idealist assumes that nothing is outside of us, but rather that the perduring is in us, and the representations of something outside us are merely in our power of imagination.

N.B. If idealism cannot be refuted, then egoism also cannot be refuted, 28:773 because we can perceive nothing outside of us other than bodily beings.

ON FATALISM

It is the hypothesis of thoroughgoing natural necessity, i.e., of the necessity of each state occurring in substances insofar as this state is determined by the previous one. It is assumed contrary to freedom. There is then no freedom, because in the previous state the action is already determined, and the previous time is not in my control. That a human being has freedom cannot be proven psychologically, but rather morally. Through morality I consider a human being not as a natural being, as object of the senses, but rather as intelligence, as object of reason. If I wanted to prove freedom psychologically, then I would have to consider a human being according to his nature, i.e., as natural being, and as such he is not free. To be sure no one has maintained in such an easy manner that in the bodily world there is a blind necessity without cause, and if one cites the word fate <*destinée*> as the cause, then one assumes a mere

411

hidden quality *<qualitas occulta>*. – Fatalism is the hypothesis of the human soul as a being of which freedom is not a property. – Is freedom possible (thinkable)? The possibility of the thought, i.e., of thinking the human soul itself as free, can be proved. See the antinomies, above.

We must make a distinction between the human being as noumenon and phenomenon, otherwise we can never prove freedom. As noumenon the determining ground in a human being is an intelligible ground, and not an event, i.e., an empirical ground. Here the ground is necessitated by nothing, but rather pure spontaneity.

I can never give objective reality to the concept of the supersensible, i.e., secure a corresponding intuition. At the same time the supersensible is in theory beyond bounds, i.e., transcendent for our reason. We indeed have ideas of reason, e.g., the idea of the totality of the world, but we can give to them no corresponding intuition. We have something supersensible that is not transcendent, e.g., the moral laws, so far as they determine our own reason by nothing other than the representation of the conformity to law which we take from ourselves. Freedom is here the supersensible, for I do not cognize it through theoretical cognition. The moral laws are immanent, as laws of the practical use of our reason, but they are transcendent as laws of the theoretical use of them, and cannot at all be cognized. No human being can find out through experience that he is free, although before all trials he cognizes it as truth that he is bound to a moral duty, and that he can also actually do this duty (for all idea of obligation falls away if I am not conscious that I can perform that which reason demands, beyond what he is able to do, no man is obliged *<ultra posse nemo obligatur>*). The law necessitates me, and this makes my action necessary, so a stimulus *<stimulus>* still cannot make my action necessary. There can indeed be a reason of obliging *<ratio obligandi>* for the opposite, but not an obliging reason *<ratio obligans>* (not a necessitation *<necessitatio>*). For otherwise both would have to be necessary, the action and its omission; but only one can be necessary, and this one action is necessitated by the moral law of our reason. Through this representation, that the human being is his own lawgiver, he attains to his own high esteem and finds himself ennobled, in that he sees that his reason commands acting well for the sake of the good. But if we still assume the fear of God as a motive, then all worthiness falls away.

Philosophy proper can be classified into transcendental philosophy and metaphysics proper. Transcendental philosophy contains in it the elements of our pure *a priori* cognition. It properly has no *a priori* objects, but rather objects of experience. If we apply our *a priori* concepts to objects, then a doctrine arises. The science which has to do with the limitation of our cognitions is called *discipline,* but that occupied with their amplification is called *doctrine.* If metaphysics is made into a doctrine, i.e., applied to objects that cannot at all be objects of experience (are mere intelligibles *<intelligibilia>*), then this is metaphysics proper. This is the science

28:774

which contains the rules of the supersensible. This supersensible is what drove human beings to metaphysics, without which hope for the cognition of the supersensible human beings would not have undertaken the difficult speculation of metaphysics. No one had devised metaphysics in regard to nature, and one also did not need it. – This metaphysics proper will also contain more discipline than doctrine, but it is still, in the practical respect, amplificatory, although it is merely dogmatic in the theoretical respect.   28:775

There is of this three parts: (1) dogmatic psychology (pneumatology). (2) The metaphysical cosmology (both are occupied with objects of experience). Here an intelligible world <*mundus intelligibilis*> emerges, i.e., a world with pure intelligences, therefore a spiritual world <*mundus pneumaticus*>. (3) The metaphysical theology (considered as dogmatic, theosophy). Here we want to have dogmatic cognitions of God, therefore we seek in theosophy what God's nature is, and not what God can be in us in a practical respect. Here we come to the transcendent[g] ideas, but human beings have a need to climb up from the conditioned to the unconditioned. This unconditioned is always a representation of pure reason, i.e., an idea, i.e., to which no object as corresponding can be given in experience.

Theoretical concepts are immanent if corresponding objects can be given for them in experience; they are transcendent when no corresponding object can be given for them in experience. All concepts in metaphysics are transcendent. Here a human being bounds over his place of residence, to which he otherwise could restrain himself.

---

[g] *überschwenglich;* this is often translated as "beyond bounds," an idea that will be echoed at 775₂₁, where one is said to "bound over," i.e., *schwingt sich über.*

PART VIII
Metaphysik Vigilantius (K₃)

1794–1795 (AK. 29: 943–1040)

[Introduction]   29:945

(1)*[b]* Metaphysics belongs to the material part of philosophy, or rather contains that within itself, and therefore, since it presupposes actual objects, rests on laws, i.e., on grounds of cognition (principles <*principiis*>) of and about that which belongs to the existence of things. From it, therefore, is separated*[c]* the merely formal part of philosophy, or the laws of thinking expounded in logic, since the latter abstracts from the objects themselves. It is thereby already distinguished from mathematics, since this rests not, as philosophy, on laws of the cognition of things, but rather on concepts of things made through construction.

Metaphysical cognitions must therefore be cognitions simply of reason, thus arise *a priori* through pure concepts of reason, i.e., the principles <*principia*> or grounds of cognition are so constituted that one connects the necessity of what one cognizes with the cognition itself, and the concepts are directed at objects that not only are cognized independently of all experience, but that also can never *possibly* become an object of experience. E.g., God, freedom, immortality. They differ thus diametrically <*e diametro*> from all empirical appearances and principles derived therefrom: metaphysics thus has no *a posteriori* principles <*principia*>, but rather only *a priori:* they are given and are cognized through reason alone, but are not made.

---

[a] This title is written directly above the first page of the ms in a continuous line; there is no title page.

[b] A numbering system, beginning here with 1, continues throughout these notes as follows: it proceeds to 25 (at the end of the extant Ontology section), beginning again (after a break in the text) with 68 in the Psychology section, stopping with 70 at another break, beginning again at 82 and proceeding to 87 (at the end of the Psychology). These numbers are occasionally accompanied by a section heading written beside the number in the margin, especially in the early sections of the notes. The numbers (and the accompanying headings) almost certainly did not originate in the lecture hall, and were added at some later date, although presumably not by Reicke, either, whose copy of the original *Vigilantius* (*K₃*) (itself lost) is the ms being translated. Nor do the numbers refer to sections found in Baumgarten. The section heading added in the margin next to this 1 is partially obscured. It seems to read, *Prolegomena* (Introduction). Above this, as is found with most of the marginalia in the first third of the notes, is the prefatory remark (in square brackets), presumably added by Reicke: [*Daneben am Rand:*], that is, "In the margin."

[c] We follow Lehmann in changing *schneiden* (to cut) to *scheiden* (945₅).

Metaphysics is thus generally <*generaliter*> the system of pure philosophy, and thus, in order to express the specific difference from all empirical cognitions, as well as to separate it from pure mathematics, metaphysics is the system of pure cognitions of reason through concepts. Its objects are the material part of philosophy, namely physics and ethics, i.e., the laws of nature and of freedom. Therefore it is divided into

a. metaphysics of nature, i.e., the cognition of the constitution of objects *a priori* from principles <*ex principiis*>. {One also calls it general physics <*physicam generalem*> because it is cognized only from *a priori* principles <*principiis*>. The cognition of nature or doctrine of nature in general is namely either doctrine of body, which is called doctrine of nature specifically <*in specie*>, insofar as it is an object of outer sense, or doctrine of the soul insofar as it is an object of inner sense, and therefore abstracts from all bodily alterations.}*d*

b. Metaphysics of morals, i.e., the cognition of the rules or determining grounds of our actions *a priori* from principles <*ex principiis*>.

29:946   Nonetheless it is thereby wholly different from an empirical doctrine of morals or of nature.

Here the rules of cognition are determined from experience according to the measure of appearances which morals or nature have delivered, in order to derive principles <*principia*> from them: e.g., the laws of the police are moral laws, but these determine pragmatically, or rather practically, the laws of security and of the comfort of life. Similarly the doctrine of nature of the chemists.[1] Their principles <*principia*> obviously are built on experience and cognized from it. Thus the doctrine of nature can also be cognized *a posteriori* from principles <*ex principiis*>. But metaphysical cognition is wholly different from all these kinds of cognitions: it does not at all busy itself with objects as they are, since if metaphysics were built on that, the necessity of experience would not be comprehended thereby. Just as little is it based upon the *a priori* intuitions upon which alone mathematics builds its cognitions of reason: namely on *space and time*. The definition of the author (§1),[2] which is taken from Wolff, is false in that it demands first principles of cognition <*prima principia cognitionis*> for metaphysics, for that can only mean the first concepts in abstraction, therefore in the series of concepts: but thereby metaphysics would busy itself only with the concept *of a thing*, since this is the highest concept of reason, and then would have to descend: but in descending it could not determine beginning and end, and what should be the first or last concept: and then every empirical concept would be connected with it, which however is mistaken because it lies outside the bounds of meta-

---

d Marginalia (946₁₋₆) alongside text printed at 945₃₂–946₉; we insert it after the first sentence of this text. Lehmann does not note that this is marginalia, and he inserts it after this text. Blank lines added by Lehmann have been removed.

physics, e.g., being <*ens*> – substance – composition; body <*corpus*>, on the other hand, is already an empirical concept in space.

It would be as if one cut history according to stretches of time: one could then extend, e.g., ancient history to the first century <*saeculum*> or until the present day.

The concept – first laws – is thus too indeterminate, in that all pure 29:947 cognitions of reason through concepts belong here, although one cannot call them the *first*.

2.' According to the sense of the word, metaphysics is a science of nature which is limited to the rational part, and to that insofar as it can be cognized without experience. Meta-physics is physics beyond the empirical cognition of nature: here one expected a great field, without determining it or being able to determine it according to its boundaries. One came upon three objects here which lay beyond the boundaries of the cognition of nature, and were discovered and cognized merely *a priori* or through human understanding alone. These are

1. God, i.e., the first beginning of all things.
2. Freedom, i.e., a faculty of human beings for acting in accordance with reason, independent of all natural influence, with resistance against all sensible impulses and powers of nature.
3. Immortality, i.e., the object of investigation of the understanding, to what extent the soul, as a being on its own, will survive the physical human being.

All three are pure concepts of reason that simply cannot be exhibited in appearance, which therefore can merely be thought. One can therefore call them supersensible objects, noumena, i.e., objects of the understanding, and oppose them to the phenomena <*phaenomenis*>.

Now the attempt to investigate these objects more closely was the coming about of metaphysics. Chance was thus not the ground of the origin. It is alleged that the founder of metaphysics, Aristotle, did not have the intention to write, nor did he write, a system of pure philosophical cognitions which lie beyond physics, but rather that he ordered something tacked on beyond physics <*meta physicam*>, i.e., after physics <*post physicam*>. This is as empty a story as that of the coming to be of the word <*termini*> philosophy, according to which Pythagoras³ wanted to be called not wise <*sophon*>, but rather only a lover of wisdom <*philosophon*>. It clearly lay in the nature of the things themselves that one concerned oneself with the closer development of these supersensible

---

' Two lines of partially obscured marginalia are to the left of the 2. This is presumably a section heading; the first line is in square brackets and is most likely the copyist's (i.e. Reicke's) note that this is marginalia in the ms being copied. The second line ends with the word *Metaphysik.*

419

objects. Only it is striking that human beings (and this is innate in every human being) found and still find an interest in it. For metaphysics does not contribute to the extension of empirical principles <*principia*>, of the science of empirical physics:⁴ its cognition is wholly unnecessary with respect to physics, where the principles <*principia*> of metaphysics are put wholly to the side, and one starts from settled appearances, and the principles derived from that are adequate to explain everything from them. Experience confirms, e.g., the rational propositions: in all alterations substance never passes away, but rather only the form of the things, or: every alteration has its cause; so much that one simply assumes them without investigating their ground, and through experience one already becomes certain of their truth in all circumstances. On the other hand it is certain that all our sensible cognitions are also only sensibly conditioned, therefore are alterable just as the things themselves, and contingently certain. Therein lies the ground that a human being finds no satisfaction for his reason here except insofar as he exerts himself to cognize and to reach his highest good <*summum bonum*>,⁵ i.e., the highest final end of all his ends, the highest degree of worthiness to be happy connected with the greatest *morality*. This object of his exertion lies beyond nature, he cannot find all his empirical knowledge adequate for this, he must find it simply through reason in its laws: he feels it necessary that this alone is the highest end and vocationᶠ for reason: he may, e.g., direct his investigation toward the determination of duty and justice, toward reward of his actions in that life, toward the determination of himself, etc.; and herein lies the ground that metaphysics absolutely must be cultivated, because otherwise the whole end of all cognitions of theoretical and practical reason cannot be fulfilled. Therefore it is also certain that every man is occupied with his own metaphysics, and of that there is truly no doubt, metaphysics must be explained <*metaphysica enucleanda sit*>; but everything depends on the method by which it is treated. Therefore all despisers of the metaphysical sciences punish themselves in that they despise science itself and yet treasure their own method for thinking about supernatural truths. In short, no human being can be without metaphysics.

3. The critique of pure reason is the propaedeutic to transcendental philosophy.⁶

That is to say, one calls a science which occupies itself with the possibility of comprehending a cognition *a priori* the critique of pure reason. All cognitions of reason, and those that are thought *a priori* independent of all experience, belong here, whether they concern mathematical or philosophical objects, e.g., all alteration must have its cause.

Cognizing reason, as a faculty, stands here as a subject before the testing seat of judgment with respect to how far it can employ itself with

29:948

29:949

ᶠ *Bestimmung* (948₂₁); normally translated as "determination" (as below in this sentence).

respect to its cognitions; the critique of pure reason is to be regarded as a higher logic here, in that it gives reason rules in hand as to how it may cognize objects *a priori*, and these rules are nothing but *a priori* principles; it is thus to be distinguished from logic itself in that the latter abstracts from all objects, and states the rules of thought in general. It is called critique because it proceeds not dogmatically but rather enters into the investigation of errors and testing of our presumed judgments. Thus the critique of pure reason is specifically <*in specie*> that philosophy which employs itself with the possibility of the *a priori* cognitions in our reason; the system of those cognitions themselves, however, which contain the elements of pure reason, is transcendental philosophy, which thus differs from the critique in that the latter investigates the possibility of cognizing *a priori*, transcendental philosophy on the other hand has before its eyes the objective summation of all those cognitions which are cognized *a priori*, and which are viewed as elements <*elementa*> or first principles of our cognition. Transcendental philosophy is also called ontology, and it is the product of the critique of pure reason.

4. All concepts are acquired, but not all from the senses. On the contrary, the faculty for acquiring concepts through the development of features is innate. E.g., the hare seeks to outwit the dog in the chase, the dog learns through practice the artifice of the hare and seeks to surpass him. Of course there are no concepts to assume here, since animals have no faculty of reason, but through many similar cases instinct forms an experience which serves the dog as a guiding thread. Concepts already presuppose representations of objects, and are abstracted from features, thus they cannot be innate, but rather must be acquired or made, but this cannot happen except through the faculty of the soul which operates here.

There was however with all this a great problem:

whether *many* concepts were innate in us, or whether *all* concepts were acquired either <*sive*> *a priori* or <*sive*> *a posteriori*.

Plato assumed the innate ideas <*ideas connatas*>, Aristotle, on the other hand, the principle that nothing is in the intellect which was not first in the senses <*principium nihil est in intellectu, quod antea non fuerit in sensu*>, and according to the sense of this principle upheld that we acquired all concepts through the senses. Of course, Plato also assumed sensible representations, but he separated off as uncertain this source of cognition from the pure concepts of the understanding as the innate ideas <*ideis connatis*>, which he assumed as alone certain. Plato maintained namely that the *a priori* concepts or pure concepts of reason would be produced merely from the fund of reason, and it was not necessary to make use of objects of the senses to be conscious of them, and to presuppose experience in their coming to be. Mathematical truths in particular and their so fruitful consequences and irrefutable certainty amazed him,

29:950

e.g., the propositions which one drew from the figure of the circle in pure mathematics <*in mathesi pura*>.

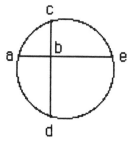

{In the circle all bisecting lines give correct ratios of the lines, angles, triangles, e.g., a:b:c = d:b:e.}[g]

He assumed that the human understanding had not found these concepts and propositions through sensible perception, but rather that there is present in human beings a supersensible cognitive faculty, i.e., a noumenon, which could form for itself cognitions derived purely, without the help of the senses. This faculty and at least the cognition by means of it can be called *supersensible*. But his hypothesis *was mystical*. For he took as the basis a pure intuition of the non-sensible or = a supersensible intuition and assumed that the soul, before it was delivered into a bodily condition, had a faculty for intuiting divinity, and even if it no longer participates in it in this life, nevertheless a consciousness of those ideas of pure understanding could be awakened in human beings, and that this consciousness is the source of *a priori* cognition.

Aristotle assumed, on the other hand, that we cannot obtain any concepts at all through reason alone, denied the innate ideas <*ideas connatas*>, and maintained rather that all our concepts had their source only in sensible reception, and therefore would be acquired through experience, and denied the *a priori* ideas <*ideas*> and affirmed only sensual ones <*sensualia*>; therefore the famous dispute over the certainty of our cognition.

The defenders of the noumenon (or of the pure concepts of the understanding, i.e., that without experience we would be in the position to receive concepts which are called innate through the faculty of pure reason) maintained: *knowledge is not given of phenomena or of sensible things* <*phaenomenorum s. sensibilium non datur scientia*>. {i.e., the senses offer no stuff for the truth or certainty of cognition, that is, all *a priori* cognitions whose object is possible are called phenomena; noumena, on the other hand, [are]

29:951

---

[g] Marginalia (950₁₅₋₁₈); text and figure of the circle are in the left margin of the ms alongside text printed at 950₁₂₋₂₀. We follow Lehmann in inserting it after the first sentence of this text but remove a paragraph break added by him and reverse "b:d."

cognitions, or concepts beyond bounds, which have no object in possible intuition}[h] The defenders of the phenomena <*phaenomenorum*>, on the other hand, declined the pure concepts of the understanding: there is certainty and truth only in outer things.

Epicurus affirmed concepts only insofar as their objects could be visibly exhibited[7] – therefore he also denied straightaway a divinity.

The Skeptics assumed certainty and existence neither with cognitions of the understanding nor empirical cognitions.

With the question of whether innate ideas exist <*ideae connatae existant*> one must distinguish between the manner of acquiring <*modum acquirendi*> and the manner of possessing <*modum habendi*>. All cognition begins from experience, likewise all cognition of reason cannot be obtained otherwise than from experience. But all cognitions that we have do not therefore descend immediately from experience. The manner and way in which cognitions are present in us, or the manner of possessing <*modus habendi*>, can produce cognitions which are grounded only in reason abstracted from all experience. Something similar lies in the derivation of original [and] derived concepts <*conceptus originarii – derivativi*> – ; both are made <*factitii*> according to their nature, just like every concept; but it is true that according to their origin the original ones <*originarii*> are grounded not in experience but rather merely in reason.

In order to determine more closely and to elucidate the preceding, it is certain:

1. with human beings all representations and concepts commence with objects of experience. But this means nothing more than: in order to obtain cognitions, even concepts of the understanding, our faculty of cognition must be awakened by objects of experience, the receptive faculty of the senses must be set into activity.

2. All concepts are acquired, and there cannot be any innate idea <*idea*   29:952 *connata*>. For concepts presuppose a thinking, are made or thought through a comprehension of features and abstraction of the general. *Thoughts* thus arise through a previously undertaken operation of the mind <*operatio mentis*>.

3. In spite of that there are *a priori* concepts, there are *a priori* intuitions <*intuitus*>, there are *a priori* propositions and judgments. Thus the concept of cause and of causality, i.e., of the constitution of an object to be cause, is an *a priori* concept <*conceptus*>, the representation of space is a concept of something that cannot be derived from experience or arise therefrom, rather one must grasp the representation of a space before one thinks of an object within it; this representation is based on an *a priori*

---

[h] Marginalia (951$_{9-12}$) alongside text printed at 951$_{12-17}$. Parenthesis and a period added by Lehmann have been removed. The marginalia appear to be preceded by the copyist's note: "[In the margin]." These marginalia are not noted as such by Lehmann.

intuition <*intuition*> that precedes all experience. The proposition and the judgment: from nothing, nothing comes to be <*ex nihilo nihil fit*> or, in all alterations nothing (substantial) arises and passes away, is an *a priori* judgment. The criterion of all *a priori* concepts on the part of their source lies in this, that they take their origin not from experience but rather from the cognitive faculty of reason itself, therefore our entire attentiveness concerns only this: to investigate in which manner we succeed at and are able to cognize *a priori,* and this the critique of pure reason teaches, as well as the limits of cognition. Moreover, with acquisition <*acquisition*> of *a priori* concepts, it does not matter that we apply our faculty for cognizing to objects of experience: for from this it does not yet necessarily follow that the acquired concepts would also have to descend from experience and not solely from the faculty of reason.

4. The manner of acquiring concepts *a priori* can be thought analogically <*analogice*>, as in natural law, as twofold:[8]

a. *originally* <*originarie*>, i.e., insofar as the *a priori* concepts are taken solely from the nature of the faculty of cognition or from the faculty for thinking. E.g., representation of space. These concepts have arisen so little through experience that they are rather present before all experience, without, however, one being able to call them innate ideas <*ideas connatas*> (perhaps the concept of space in general could belong to the latter).[i]

If besides the ability for cognizing there is still

b. something empirical mixed in, the concept therefore is not pure, so it is derivative <*derivativus*>.

29:953 5. Now just as it is quite certain that no cognition could be present where, although it took its origin from experience, there is nevertheless in the latter no corresponding object present through which the concept can be exhibited, so *a priori* cognitions are distinguished accordingly: (a) into sensible cognitions or <*vel*> *phenomena,* i.e., all *a priori* cognitions that can be exhibited and applied in objects of sense; from these one passes over to the (b) *noumena,* or supersensible cognitions, pure cognitions of understanding the object of which cannot be given in experience and exhibited to the senses.

6. Out of the diversity of the sources from which cognitions are derived originally <*originarie*> the difference arose between:

a. *empiricism,* i.e., the principle of viewing each and every concept, according to its origin, as derived from experience. One accuses Epicurus of this principle, at least to the extent illuminated by the works of his students, since one possesses nothing by him himself. He assumed that one can ascribe certainty to no concept for which an object in experience

---

[i] Parentheses omitted by Lehmann without note have been replaced, and the colon added without note has been removed (952₃₅₋₃₆).

cannot be displayed[j] and thereby certified. It does not strictly follow from this that he contested all *a priori* concepts, because for very many a proof in experience is conceded. A consequence of this principle is that one must reject metaphysics entirely, of which Epicurus is also accused. For metaphysics must rest simply on pure concepts of reason, and therefore can never take them from experience, given their source; the error of empiricism therefore rests on this, that because our faculty of cognition can be set into activity only by objects of experience, it infers from this that also no concept could exist and be made that did not have its origin in experience.

b. *Rationalism*, the principle of the possibility of representing *a priori* cognitions. This principle is the first proposition of all metaphysical truths.

Between both principles, empiricism and rationalism, stood as it were in the middle:[k]

c. *mysticism*, or the presupposition of an intuitive intellect <*intellectus intuitivi*> or intellectual intuition <*intuitus intellectualis*>, i.e., the possibility that purely intellectual *a priori* concepts <*conceptus a priori mere intellectuales*> rest on immediate intuition of the understanding. This mystical hypothesis thus assumed that the understanding could operate like the senses, having pure intuitions <*intuitus puros*>; however the faculty of intuition, which rather applies to the senses alone, cannot be attributed to the understanding, therefore this hypothesis of Plato's collapses by itself. One says indeed that the understanding of God is sheer intuition, nevertheless these are words without a concept, which at least we human beings cannot make of an intuitive understanding, and through which one had wanted merely to place the operation of the divine being in relation to the faculty of thought of human beings; but an analogous thinking in God is in no event to be assumed.

29:954

The principle of Plato, namely, that by virtue of their previously possessed faculty of an intuitive understanding, human beings would now still have the power to remember by their understanding back to previously held concepts, rests clearly on a mistake to which the notable clarity and astonishing fruitfulness of many mathematical propositions, of which he was master, misled him, and consisted in this, that he took pure *a priori* intuition <*intuitus a priori puros*> and *pure a priori* concepts <*conceptus a priori puros*> as the same.

Aristotle improved on him to the extent that he also assumed intellectual things <*intellectualia*>, but at the same time by concepts <*per conceptus*>, and rejected the innate ideas from pure intuition <*ideas connatas ex intuitu puro*>; nonetheless the error is also shown of his basic proposi-

---

[j] We follow Lehmann in adding a *sich* (before *dadurch*) (953₂₀).

[k] We are adding a colon here (953₃₅).

tion: nothing is in the intellect, etc. <*nihil est in intellectu pp.*>, by virtue of which his concepts <*conceptus*> were taken as sensitive things <*sensitivi*> formed through the senses, and not as intellectual ones <*intellectuales*> formed rather through the understanding generally – therefore empirical, e.g., concept of warmth.

4. With respect to supersensible cognitions a closer examination and determination of its powers and boundaries is by all means required of our faculty of cognition. Already in the times of the most ancient philosophy of a Parmenides, Xenocrates, Pythagoras, where concepts were still clothed in a picture language, one thought about the development of the same concepts as now, about freedom of the will in action, about causality, about the beginning of the world, the coming to be and author of which were brooded over by everyone. One viewed these objects as ones that had to have been cognized *a priori*, i.e., through reason; forgot entirely that there was no object in experience that could possibly correspond to the concepts, judgments, and inferences. But one saw the fortunate progress that mathematics made, when by virtue of its *a priori* intuition it advanced itself beyond the boundaries of experience into the field of

29:955 possibility. Since this was a kind of *a priori* cognition, and in mathematics <*mathesi*> one succeeded in extending cognitions beyond sensible objects, one inferred that it could also be attempted with philosophy, and now one abandoned oneself to a free and unconstrained path in the investigations of supersensible objects.

Dogmatism led the investigators, i.e., the principle according to which a critique of reason was not believed to be required with respect[l] to the metaphysical, i.e., the *a priori* cognitions of reason, in order to obtain *a priori* cognitions and to expand one's sensible cognitions beyond the sensible. The mistake of dogmatism here thus lay in that one was not attentive to this, that here one passed over from *physical* objects to *metaphysical ones*[m] {N.B. and indeed from sensible to supersensible objects},[n] that the latter can have no object in experience with which the truth of the obtained representations, concepts, and judgments could be tested, that thus because of a lack of an object in intuition the concepts would have no[o] reality, therefore, if the investigation went further than the *a priori* concepts could lead, empty judgments were possible. One could not appeal to mathematics; for since this *constructs* its concepts from *a priori intuitions* and therefore it must always be possible to exhibit the concepts of the

---

[l] Reading *Ansehnung* as *Ansehung* (955$_8$).
[m] Emphasis is added by Lehmann (955$_{14}$).
[n] Marginalia (955$_{14-15}$) alongside text printed at 955$_{13-16}$. We follow Lehmann in inserting it after the first clause of this text, but parentheses added by him have been removed. The marginalia is prefaced with the copyist's note: "[In the margin.]."
[o] A repeated line (in Lehmann) has been removed (955$_{19}$).

objects in experience or intuition, so it always has a secure guiding thread with which it does not step over the bounds of reason, in making attempts it is certain to discover its mistakes; but not so in philosophy, this has to do here merely with cognitions of reason from pure concepts, and nothing puts chains on the understanding in the progress of the investigation.

Hence also the result that all attempts of the philosophers were thrown overboard by skepticism, which demonstrated the uncertainty of the product of supersensible cognitions, and henceforth for its part declared as uncertain all cognitions which rested on pure concepts of reason.

Therefore dogmatism is the ground of the coming to be of skepticism. The latter also went too far, because actual *a priori* concepts are not to be contested. Before one rejected the possibility of having such cognitions of reason, it was therefore in any event necessary first to test the extent, bounds, and limits of the faculty of the understanding, and to find a standard, or criteria[*p*] of truth according to which one can test the genuineness of such pure concepts to which no object in experience corresponds: then one could rightfully raise doubts. This is now the business of criticism. 29:956

{CLASSIFICATION OF METAPHYSICS}[*q*]

5. Metaphysics or the system of the pure cognitions of reason divides into two main sections:

I. Transcendental metaphysics, or that part of metaphysics which exhibits elementary concepts in order to cognize *a priori* objects which can be given: this system of metaphysical cognitions is called *ontology* and rests on dissection of reason according to all the elementary concepts contained in it, e.g., magnitude, quality, substance, cause, effect, etc.

II. Metaphysics proper <*metaphysica propria*>, as metaphysics is called when it is applied to objects themselves: these objects are

a. either *sensible* and then

1. the system concerns either objects of inner sense or the soul. Therefore doctrine of the soul, rational psychology <*psychologia rationalis*>
2. or objects of outer sense, therefore doctrine of the body, rational physics <*physica rationalis*>

b. or objects of mere reason, i.e., ideas <*ideae*>[*r*] or concepts of mere reason = cognitions whose objects cannot be given by the objects. These are the objects of supersensible cognition, and these are presented in

---

[*p*] Lehmann misprints *Criteria* as *Citeria* (956₂).
[*q*] This heading (956₇) appears in the margin to the left of the 5. The blank lines were added by Lehmann. Above the marginalia is the copyist's note: "[In the margin]."
[*r*] Reading *ideac* (in Lehmann) as *ideae* (956₂₅).

1. rational cosmology <*cosmologia rationalis*>, or cosmology of pure reason and
2. rational or natural theology <*theologia rationalis vel naturalis*>, theology of pure reason.

{HISTORY OF METAPHYSICS}[s]

6. It is striking: nature calls us to investigate cognitions of reason; for human beings there is an especially important interest in becoming more precisely acquainted with the objects of the supernatural, and nevertheless all previous effort has brought little fruit, since at present it is still doubtful what of the metaphysical truths can and should be assumed as certain. Already in the most ancient times of philosophy one busied oneself rather with metaphysics than with physics, and particularly directed one's investigations upon the supersensible rather than upon the sensible. Of course, the doctrinal propositions and theories of Parmenides, Xenocrates, and Pythagoras cannot be stated distinctly since no writings of theirs were left us, but rather only later authors, e.g., Diogenes Laertius and others, portrayed their opinions but did not explain them determinately enough; nonetheless this much is now certain, that they directed investigation to the origin of the world, to the world cause as the highest being, to the constitution of the human soul, to its existence after death, or to the future life.

It is certain that in regard to making good progress in investigation of such *a priori* objects, one was led astray by mathematics and believed that since there was success here in one kind of cognitions of reason, it would also be met with in philosophy, without considering that mathematics, in its investigations, built on intuitions which could be given through the senses, namely space and time; but here with concepts of mere reason, without intuition underlying them, a similar success was not to be expected, at least not from the same grounds.[t]

Plato in particular contributed to this error notably through this, that to the pure concepts of reason, just as to the sensible receptive faculty he attributed a power of intuition, and therefore derived cognitions of reason here through the construction of *a priori* intuitions just like in mathematics.

Now as long as the systems built on this were not impugned, one could build further, but would still not be certain of the truth of one's presuppositions and conclusions, because it was impossible to test the cognitions produced by these attempts against objects, since the latter could not be given, and thus a comparison with them did not take place.

29:957

---

[s] This heading (956₃₅) appears in the margin to the right of the 6. The blank lines were added by Lehmann. Above the marginalia is the copyist's note: "[In the margin]."
[t] To the left and below this (in the bottom left corner of the ms page) is written: *collat. 5/1.83 mit Ida und Hans zusammen* (957₂₄).

All judgments and every whole system were accepted, if one only remained consistent and did not contradict oneself. But there arose a dispute of the philosophers among themselves over the propositions maintained as conclusions of their systems, in that one group believed that they were grounded, and the other group that they were just as clearly refuted, and showed that the opposite could be grounded just as clearly. This dispute in philosophy concerned namely the transcendental propositions or problems that went beyond bounds, e.g., one proved: each space and bodies consists of simple parts of matter – others denied [this and maintained] just as clearly the impossibility of simple parts because all composites <*composita*> consist of parts, and these again consist of parts – the proposition: the world has a beginning, for the absolute cosmos is only an idea of reason, but the world itself is bounded – others denied this and maintained: there cannot be any final boundary of the world, only we cannot determine the boundary – etc. 29:958

Thus as soon as the contradiction*u* and the existence of the wholly conflicting propositions was quite clear, there arose that *party* which doubted the certainty of either; this party took the opportunity thereby to declare all truths of reason as uncertain, and accepted*v* the principle that we lack certainty in all our cognitions; it even contradicted itself, and admitted that even the question whether everything is uncertain is itself uncertain. Now this killed all progress of the investigation because dogmatism was overthrown and skepticism affirmed no principles <*principia*> from which one could proceed. The interest of human beings suffered under this, and neither of the opposites <*opposita*> served any use.

It was necessary, and one should have begun it before one had undertaken investigations into supersensible objects themselves,

> to treat reason, as the investigating subject, as an object that would have to be studied more closely, to investigate its faculty for cognizing *a priori*, and determine its boundary and extent.

One can now classify according to their kind and manner the leading prior principles <*principia*> upon which one built, up until the closer critique of pure reason:

a. Aristotle and later Locke set up a (so-called) physiology of reason, because they viewed *a priori* cognition as something which can be acquired empirically, and which we have elevated by generalization to an *a priori* cognition from the determinations of things drawn from experience. They thus assumed, in view of the origin, all cognition as sensible (nothing is <*nihil est*>, etc.,[9] said Aristotle) and believed that the more a proposition is raised up through abstraction, the more it approaches an *a priori* proposition. Aristotle and Locke thus assumed the system of physi- 29:959

---

u Lehmann misprints *Widerspruch* as *Widerpruch* (958_{13}).

v We follow Lehmann in changing *annehmen* to *nahm . . . an* (958_{16-17}).

cal influence <*systema influens physici*> or the origin of our representations from the senses and their influence, as well as the principle that we arrived" at general *a priori* cognitions only through abstraction. The contradiction is clear. Reason is supposed to deliver up cognition and yet cognition is supposed to be acquired through the senses.

b. Plato and later Leibniz appear to assume a system of preestablished harmony <*systema harmoniae praestabilitae*> with respect to cognitions of reason. That is, they took as a basis innate ideas, which were put in us before we were acquainted with objects themselves, and which agreed with the objects just because the author placed them in us. Now Plato assumed as the source of acquisition of all ideas of pure reason that they descended from the intuition of God; Leibniz modified this in that he supposed certain innate predispositions of reason as existing in us, which had only the use that we, in relying on them, would find the objects themselves in agreement with these ideas.

In order to state such a hypothesis, both were amazed by the conviction that truths often pressed upon them so evidently.

c. Wolff, and in this age his antagonist, Crusius. Crusius indeed contested such a unified effect of the soul on the body, which Leibniz assumed by virtue of the preestablished harmony <*harmonia praestabilita*>, but decreed on the contrary that the criterion of truth is to be sought for only in the ideas which the creator has placed in us, just because he could not trust it to our reason that it would find these ideas itself; he thus assumed an inner revelation with human beings, and with that the necessity of this for bringing one to conviction. Wolff, whom he refuted, had not at all investigated the origin of ideas, but rather acted as a dogmatist. He built his success in philosophy at random on mathematical presuppositions, and by application of the mathematical method confused *a priori* cognitions from pure ideas <*ex puris ideis*> with mathematical cognitions, because he believed himself able to operate with them by the construction of concepts from *a priori* intuition just as in mathematics.

" We follow Lehmann in changing *erlangten* (attained) to *gelangten* (959$_{6-7}$).

7. It is striking to think of *a priori* representations and concepts whose object itself cannot be given through possible intuition. E.g., a spirit is an idea of pure reason whose object absolutely cannot be exhibited: now it is indeed true that taken theoretically this concept and all similar to it are empty, nevertheless the idea is still possible, and is qualified to accomplish practical uses: but these ideas which are beyond bounds, and the elementary principles by which we cognize these *a priori* representations of a supersensible kind, of which however no object can be exhibited in intuition, also do not belong here, but rather the theme of ontology or of transcendental philosophy,[y] to the extent it is treated here, consists only

in those elementary principles of such *a priori* concepts in which the objects themselves can be exhibited or cognized.

They are indeed also called transcendent, but they are at the same time *immanent;* just because they are possible objects of cognition.

{ON AN OBJECT AS HIGHEST CONCEPT}[z]

8. regarding *<ad> Sect. 1. §7–11 of the author <auctoris>*

The highest concept, under which all remaining elementary concepts are ordered, is the

concept of an object in general, which underlies representation.

The author, on the contrary, holds the *concept of possibility* for the first concept,[10] and at the same time opposes it to the concept of *nothing.*[11] But the representation

– of the possible *<possibili>*	impossible *<impossibili>*
– an a	*non*-a
– a something	nothing

---

[x] This heading appears in the margin of the ms, to the right of the "7." Above this is the copyist's note: "[In the margin]." The blank lines were added by Lehmann.

[y] We follow Lehmann in changing *die transcendental Philosophie* to *der transcendental Philosophie* (960$_{13-14}$). Written in the margin of the ms to the left of this: (*Philosophie*).

[z] This heading appears in the margin to the left of the 8; it is prefaced with the standard copyist's note: "[In the margin]." We are inserting it before the 8, as a section heading.

clearly indicates a classification wherein the members must be grounded in a higher concept, and this is the concept of an object in general, which then can be a something or a nothing. It seems striking to think of an object that comprises a nothing: but *a nothing* also *presupposes only a thought which then cancels itself,* {i.e., which contradicts itself}*ᵃ* and therefore never has an existing object as a ground.

29:961

THE NOTHING¹²

is now either {regarding <*ad*> 1 and <*et*> 2 the object, the *nothing*, is thought or matter}*ᵇ*

1. the nothing which is logically such, or the logical nothing, or the negative nothing <*nihilum logice tale s. logicum s. negativum*>, or one to which no *thought* or representation corresponds at all. It is ordinarily so constituted that it involves an inner contradiction in the representation.*ᶜ*

2. the privative nothing <*nihilum privativum*> is one to which *nothing* existent corresponds, although it still can be thought; e.g., the aether in physics is an invented concept that has no reality by intuition of the object <*intuitu objecti*>, but which can be thought without contradiction. Likewise a positive cold, as absolute cause of cold, contains nothing contradictory in thinking it, but it has no existence. All fictions belong here, since they are not met with in nature as an object <*quoad objectum*>, e.g., total contentment, – against its*ᵈ* existence speaks the constant inclination of human beings to elevate themselves above their state and transplant themselves into another that they hold for better. Thus the negative and the privative nothing <*nihil negativum et privativum*> differ among themselves as thought and object: one or the other does not correspond to the representation. Or*ᵉ*

{regarding <*ad*> 3 and <*et*> 4 the object of the nothing is – concept}*ᶠ*

3. A nothing is also an *empty concept* <*conceptus inanis;* G: *leerer Begriff*>, i.e., a concept to which an object cannot correspond or (more properly) = for which one cannot give an object in intuition. One must guard against calling such a concept therefore *false;* one cannot be conscious whether an

---

ᵃ Marginalia (961₁₋₂) alongside text printed at 960₃₇–961₁. We follow Lehmann in inserting it after this text. Parentheses added by Lehmann have been removed. Above the marginalia is the copyist's note: "[In the margin]."

ᵇ Marginalia (printed at Ak. 29: 1178) alongside text printed at 961₅₋₇. We insert it before this text. Above the marginalia is the standard copyist's note: "[In the margin]."

ᶜ We are removing a period following *Vorstellung* (in Lehmann, 961₉).

ᵈ A second *die* added by Lehmann without note has been removed (961₁₈).

ᵉ We are replacing an emphasis omitted by Lehmann without note (961₂₂).

ᶠ Marginalia (printed at Ak. 29: 1178) alongside text printed at 961₂₃. We insert it before this text. Above the marginalia is the standard copyist's note: "[In the margin]."

actual object can correspond to the empty concept, but it can therefore still be thought, i.e., it does not contradict the possibility of its mere representation: between that which is thought and[g] that, the object of which can at the same time be exhibited, i.e., given, there is (according to 1 and <*et*> 2) a difference. Such concepts occur among the supersensible ideas. E.g., the concept of spirit has nothing contradictory in the representation, but whether it is possible that such an immaterial being can exist, this one cannot comprehend. Nothing of contradiction is to be discovered in problematic propositions, but with these one does not make out whether the concept can obtain a corresponding object in intuition, whether an instance can be imputed to it, indicated in existence, and applied. Such empty concepts <*conceptus inanes*> are not useable, but not therefore false. 29:962

4. *A nothing is a merely formal concept*, to the extent that the lack of everything material in intuition is found with it. It is thus only a nothing in the material sense <*nihilum in sensu materiali*>, but by all means a something in the formal sense <*in sensu formali*>, e.g., the concept of space in itself is in its form a concept that can be cognized in intuition, but in the material [sense] <*in materiali*> it has no intuition as long as it is thought without thing or matter; and [is][L] thus relatively a nothing. From this it follows that all concepts belong here for which all empirical intuition is lacking. That is to say, empirical intuiting rests essentially on sensation of the object, and therefore empirical intuition alone gives only empirical concepts.

5. A nothing is called *impossible* because utterly no concept rests on it, not even a thought. This *impossible nothing* is cognized merely in contradiction. – It is a thought that cancels itself, a concept that collapses by inner contradiction. – There can nevertheless be objects impossible in themselves that are assumed as possible because their concept experiences[h] no contradiction (on the other hand, the thought of an actual or possible object cannot be impossible, to the extent that it corresponds to it).

Therefore one can clearly assume as correct:
  everything that contradicts itself is impossible
but cannot[i] deny the reverse:
  everything that does not contradict itself is possible, because otherwise it would have to contradict itself.
Thus impossibility, but not possibility, rests on contradiction.

---

[g] We follow Lehmann in omitting a *zwischen* here (961₃₀).
[h] We follow Lehmann in changing *widerfährt* (occurs) to *erfährt*, but we replace the omitted set of parentheses that follow (962₂₀₋₂₂).
[i] The negative here seems unneeded (962₂₅), i.e., Kant's view is surely that the following proposition *can* be denied.

433

It all depends on whether I comprehend the contradiction, and that which I held as possible will become impossible. Contradiction is only the means for cognizing impossibility. But possibility corresponds to the existence of the object. One can therefore most certainly think of the predicates of a thing without contradiction, but from that the possibility of the thing itself does not yet follow, because the possibility of the thought does not yet involve the possibility of the object in intuition. Therefore an empty concept is also possible, as long as no inner contradiction is there;

29:963 on the other hand if one is acquainted with no object corresponding to it, then the possibility or impossibility of the matter itself does not yet follow from this.

6. *regarding the same §§ <ad eosd. § phos> – The principle of contradiction <principium contradictionis> and the equally prevailing principle of identity <principium identitatis> is the highest principle <principium> with respect to all analytic judgments*, i.e., those judgments where the concept of the predicate and subject can be cognized through dissection; on the other hand it is not sufficient for all and every kind of judgment, e.g., for synthetic judgments, where one goes beyond the concept of the subject and says more through the predicate than was contained in the subject. The formula under which it is grasped is:

no predicate can belong to a subject if the predicate is opposite to the subject itself *<nulli subjecto competit praedicatum sibimet ipsi oppositum>*.[j]

One defines it usually in the manner:

that which at the same time can both be and not be the same thing *<quod idem simul esse et non esse potest>*: i.e., to no thing can a predicate and at the same time (*<eodem tempore;* G: *zugleich>*) its opposite be ascribed.

One easily sees that in this *the determination of [a]*[L] *time relation* {i.e., of the existence of the thing in time}[k] is indicated through the word *at the same time <simul>*. Thus according to this a contradiction between subject and predicate can prevail only under the same condition of time: therefore, if two predicates are attributed to the same subject only not at the same time but rather one after the other, then it is possible that, although they would contradict the subject at the same time *<eodem tempore>*, nevertheless at a different time *<diverso tempore>* each predicate alone could be attributed to it, e.g., a learned man is not learned, in this the contradiction is clear

---

[j] There are two lines of marginalia to the right of this text in the ms. The first line appears to be the standard copyist's note: "[In the margin]." The second line is a single illegible word. Lehmann does not note the marginalia.

[k] Marginalia (963₁₉) appearing alongside text printed at 963₁₈. We follow Lehmann in inserting it after this text. Above the marginalia is the standard copyist's note: "[In the margin]."

because both cannot be at the same time: to be learned and unlearned, therefore the predicate is canceled by the subject and vice versa. But the learned man can forget what he knew, and then later he can thus indeed pass as unlearned. There are thus in the alteration of time two contradictory determinations here: so also in the two concepts of the understanding: resting-moving human being, thought at the same time, contains a contradiction, but not at all with respect to space and time.

This determination of the concept is called *the alterability of the thing:* how this comes about is to be developed below, and here only the consequence will be drawn that the determination of time does not belong to the formula of contradiction.

[In the margin on 23a:]*[l]*   29:964

N.B. With the above formula of the principle of contradiction <*principium contradictionis*>, one must in any event also let the formula hold good: a predicate belongs to a certain subject which is the opposite of a predicate of the subject <*cuidam subjecto competit praedicatum praedicato sui ipsius oppositum*>. For besides the subject and predicate a judgment has also a connective word. If this indicates merely the copula <*copulam*>, then the above formula of the principle of contradiction <*principii contradictionis*> holds good in general: to no subject can [a predicate] belong, etc. <*nulli subjecto competit*>, etc.; because the two concepts cancel themselves directly. But if it also indicates an existence determined in time, then two opposites <*opposita*> can take place according to the second formula. E.g., the learned Cajus *is* unlearned is a contradiction, but not: Cajus, who is learned, is unlearned; for this means: Cajus exists in a time as learned, but exists at another time as unlearned. Therefore it is to be viewed as a mistake that one brought along an existential concept into the concept of the principle of contradiction <*principium contradictionis*>: there is nothing which, at the same time <*nihil est, quod simul*>, etc.]

Besides the introduced negative formula to no <*nulli*>,*[m]* etc., one can also positively determine the principle <*principium*> of analytic judgments: to every subject there belongs a predicate identical to itself <*omni subjecto competit praedicatum ipsi identicum*>. One calls it then the *principle of identity* <*principium identitatis*>. E.g., every scholar has cognitions: it is a contradiction to think the opposite of that, and cognitions lie directly in the concept of the scholar: it is therefore equivalent to the proposition: a scholar is a scholar.

---

[l] This copyist's note appears in square brackets in the ms (Lehmann omits this line without note). It indicates that the following paragraph was originally marginalia and was apparently copied into the main body of the text because of its length. There is also a square bracket at the end of the paragraph, which we add.

[m] See 963₁₃, earlier, for this formula.

The author attempts [in] §11 to prove this principle of identity <*principium identitatis*> through the principle of contradiction <*principium contradictionis*>,¹³ but the proof cannot be carried out for this reason, because the principle of contradiction <*principium contradictionis*>, just as it is supposed to prove the principle of identity <*principium identitatis*>, can also exhibit it, therefore the principle of contradiction <*principium contradictionis*> is being proved through itself.

If one denies that the predicate belongs to the subject, then the opposite <*oppositum*> would belong to it, and this would not contradict" but rather would prove only that the same <*idem*> was not the same <*idem*>: until the contradiction was proved in and for itself: both principles <*principia*> are indemonstrable. One can say: what contradicts itself is nothing; this is an affirmative identical proposition. These are the two highest formal principles <*principia*> of our cognitions, nevertheless the principle of contradiction <*principium contradictionis*> is used more than the principle of identity <*principium identitatis*>. That happens because necessity lies in the principle of contradiction <*principium contradictionis*>, which forces the truth of that which is to be proved. The proof of a truth through this, that its opposite is impossible, is indirect <*indirecte*>, but it is apodictic and connected with the concept of necessity, whereas the mere truth alone does not convey that impression with it, however the principle of identity <*principium identitatis*> is always understood along with it.

29:965

The author defines the impossible <*impossibile*> through the principle of contradiction <*principium contradictionis*>,¹⁴ but this is therefore false because the two concepts lack reciprocity: for were this so, then the proposition: whatever contradicts itself is impossible, would have to be able to be reversed by contraposition <*per contrapositionem*>, therefore the proposition: what is not impossible = is possible, does not contradict itself; there can, as already mentioned, clearly be something possible in the concept, which shows itself as impossible as soon as one has become aware of the contradiction, therefore the definition is incorrect. It is true only that the principle of contradiction <*principium contradictionis*> is necessary in order to cognize impossibility, but impossibility is not refuted through that.

10. *Regarding §12 and §13 of the author* <*ad §12 et 13 autoris*>: if the impossible is posited, contradiction arises <*posito impossibili oritur contradictio*>. It is a contradiction in the predicate <*contradictio in adjecto*> when in one and the same concept two attributed concepts run directly counter to each other, or in one judgment subject and predicate directly contradict each other. A contradiction is apparent <*apparens*>, like e.g., a visible darkness, i.e., approach of light to darkness, as Milton says of hell. – Visible lunar eclipses: the negations of light.

" Lehmann misprints *widerspräche* as *widersrpäche* (964₂₉).

A contradiction is evident <*patens*> (explicit <*explicita*>), and hidden or implicit <*latens sive implicita*>, depending on whether an analysis of the concepts is required in order to cognize it, or it does not need dissection: nevertheless in both cases one must assume with respect to the judge himself that the contradiction was hidden from him, and it must therefore be proved to him.

11. Regarding §10 of the author <*ad §10 autoris*>: there are three *logical principles* <*principia*> *of all judgments* which determine the correctness and certainty of the latter, they are logical formulae of our judgments, but not metaphysical principles <*principia*> of objective cognition. These are

1. the principle of contradiction and identity <*principium contradictionis et identitatis*>
2. logical principle of reason <*principium rationis logicum*>
3. principle of excluded middle between two contradictories or the principle of division or the principle of disjunction <*principium exclusi intermedii inter duo contradictoria sive principium divisionis sive principium disjunctionis*>.

[In the margin:]*

N.B. All analytic judgments are understood under this, because predicates are presupposed that are thought in the concept of the subject, by which its ground of cognition is proved, and its necessary attributes are demonstrated. The principle of contradiction <*principium contradictionis*> and [the principle of] identity <*identitatis*> are the two highest and general principles <*principia*> to which all such judgments are subject, and indeed the *affirmative* to the latter and the *negative* to the former.   29:966

All three principles <*principia*> come down to one concept with the principle of contradiction <*principium contradictionis*>, because one cannot judge without presupposing them, and the principle of contradiction <*principium contradictionis*> contains, so to speak, both the other principles <*principia*>. For

a. the principle of contradiction <*principium contradictionis*> is applied in all problematic judgments. Here all that matters is that the predicate does not contradict the subject in itself, e.g., a divisible soul: an opposite <*oppositum*> lies in the concept of soul, what is presupposed in the judgment or concept cannot be united with the predicate divisible. If this is so, then the judgment is not at all thinkable. Every thought, on the other

---

* This square bracket and copyist's note appears in the ms (Lehmann omits this line without note). It indicates that the following paragraph was originally marginalia and was apparently copied into the main body of the text because of its length. There is also a square bracket at the end of the paragraph, which we add.

hand, that does not collapse itself, is in conformity with this principle <*principio*>, since so far its truth is not yet concerned. This fits

b. with the assertoric judgments or propositions: for in virtue of the principle of reason <*principii rationis*> to be applied here, each proposition must be grounded, but this already presupposes that it is at all thinkable, whereupon then in accordance with this second principle <*principio*> the predicate must be connected with the subject through the ground of the proof.

c. The principle of disjunction <*principium disjunctionis*> can make the judgment only into an apodictic judgment, and give certainty to it through the disjunction of the members of the concept. The latter is achieved through this, that each concept is divided in two opposites <*opposita*>, of which only one member can belong to the subject, and it is proved that the opposite <*oppositum*> cannot belong to it, as well as that beyond both members there can be no third which would at the same time have to be assigned to it. This is therefore the principle of all logical classification of concepts, because these are only dichotomous.

12. All of our cognition consists of concepts, and of intuition.

Intuition *gives* objective reality to the concept, i.e., without intuition each concept falls under the suspicion that it is empty. Therefore if it is indeed thought, but the object cannot be given for it in intuition, then one says of it: it lacks objective reality: here however it does not necessarily matter that the object is sensibly exhibited, but rather only that its exhibition is possible. Intuition allows the object to be cognized, and underlying it is immediate representation of this object; the features which are abstracted by intuition give the representation mediately which the concept includes and through which the object is cognized.

29:967

Through the concept the object is *thought:* now if I could not impute any object to the concept, then I can still think the concept, but this thinking by itself does not yet give any cognition, because it lacks objective reality, it must have intuition added so that the concept would have an object that corresponds to it, and only then does it have objective reality and can be cognized. Cognition is thus as little possible without intuition as it is acquired through mere intuition alone. For this contains only the immediate relation to an object.

Finally, relation to an object is not immediately present with cognition; rather cognition is acquired only on the intuition of the object and in the relation of the concept to the intuition. All intuition is sensible, and to cognize something without it would be, were it possible, supersensible cognition, which would also have to rest on supersensible intuition: all supersensible concepts are of the kind that even if otherwise one may well have grounds for thinking them, no intuitions can be given for them; thus they still lack an objective reality that would be connected directly <*directe*> with the concept, e.g., concept of spirit.

438

13. In order to present the principles <*principia*> themselves of transcendental philosophy, the first thing is the development of the difference between analytic and synthetic judgments.

1. Analytic judgments are those where, when a subject is thought, the predicate can be cognized through the dissection of the concept. The predicate thus lies implicitly <*implicite*> in the subject – or is contained in the subject, the concept of the subject need only be analyzed, i.e., made explicit in order to cognize it, e.g., a body is divisible is cognized through the dissection of extendability. Thus analytic judgments must be able to be thought and cognized in the concept of the subject alone: in this they 29:968 already distinguish themselves essentially from the synthetic. To cognize the latter judgments through the subject alone, without adding a concept *not* lying in it, is impossible. E.g., all mathematical propositions of every kind are synthetic, it is impossible even in algebra to develop even a single proposition through analysis.

The proposition: all bodies are heavy, will not result from the analysis of the concept of body alone, I first must have cognized through experience that it is heavy before I can attribute this predicate to body.

The proposition: 7 + 5 gives the magnitude of 12, is not possible to develop through the development of the concept of the magnitudes 7 + 5 alone. But the magnitude 12 arises very easily out of the other two through synthesis <*per synthesin*>, and is therefore a synthetic proposition: namely through experience I have so arranged the operation for finding 12 with the two magnitudes that to the one magnitude, e.g., 7, I have connected and thus added the other (5) through sensible counting up of the units.

2. Analytic judgments can be called *elucidating judgments*. The judgment serves for the consciousness of the manifold which lies in the concept, and was earlier thought obscurely, but now is developed. On the other hand synthetic judgments are = *amplificatory judgments*. They go beyond the concept of the subject and contain yet a predicate that is not thought in the concept of the subject. One now asks

3. how and which of both kinds of judgment are possible *a priori*? The possibility of *a priori* cognitions is clear in analytic judgments, since here the subject is allowed to be developed only according to the concept, in order to cognize the predicate. Thus no experience is required in order to cognize the predicate contained in it. E.g., in order to cognize the divisibility of body, only the development of the concept of body is necessary, thus one finds its divisibility without it first being necessary to arrange experiments *a posteriori* on it and to search out the product discovered from experience.

Although synthetic judgments can be *a posteriori* judgments, they can also be judgments cognized *a priori*. But even *a priori* reason must always

add something that did not lie in the concept, and this cannot be grounded in experience. Should a synthetic judgment thus be cognized *a*
29:969 *priori*, then this can happen only through an *a priori* intuition *which underlies it* {namely through this that an underlying intuition is provided for the concept which is to be amplified through synthesis <*per synthesin*>. This happens either through empirical intuition of the object that is added to the concept, or through *a priori* intuition, i.e., formal relation to the object and determination of the form, how the subject is affected by the object}[p] and the supplemented object will be taken from this intuition. From this it follows that in general synthetic judgments are possible only by means of the corresponding intuition and the concept formed and added to this, and that this intuition must happen *a priori* if the judgment is to be posited *a priori*.

E.g., the three angles of the triangle are equal to two right angles of 180°, is a synthetic judgment: for this proposition cannot be brought out of the analysis of a figure enclosed by three lines, rather it must be made at least in thought experiments for finding it and through that the proof is thought. But an *a priori* intuition differs from empirical intuition, like form and matter, i.e., namely, if not merely the form, but also the object of sensation underlies the intuition, then the intuition is empirical, but if on the other hand matter, i.e., the object of intuition, is lacking with the intuition and merely the form is present, and the object possible, then the intuition is *pure*. E.g., space in itself is nothing tangible, nothing sensible, is thus merely the form that is intuited: on the other hand something in space which offers resistance, or a filled space which can be sensed sensibly, contains something, and thus contains a sense representation of something *existing*. Thus a synthetic judgment, whose corresponding intuition is an *a priori* intuition, has a pure intuition without being accompanied by an object of the senses.

14. One can assume in advance that (1) all propositions of experience are synthetic judgments and must be cognized through synthesis <*per synthesin*>. For insofar as a judgment is already grounded through analysis, the judgment lay in the concept of the subject, and thus there was needed no amplification of the cognition and the ground of cognition in order to be able to attribute the predicate to it. But if the judgment is grounded in experience, then the predicate can be cognized only through the latter, hence it will be attributed to the subject through synthesis <*per*
29:970 *synthesin*>.[q] (2) But that there are *a priori* propositions that are synthetic *a priori* judgments, hence can be cognized independent of all experience.

[p] Marginalia (969_{2-7}) alongside text printed at 969_{1-14}. We follow Lehmann in inserting it near the beginning of this text. It is prefaced with the standard copyist's note: "[In the margin]."

[q] We are removing a paragraph break here and adding a capital (970_1).

How this is possible, see below <*vide infra*>. – Now the science which one calls metaphysics rests on the latter: it is namely that science or system that sets up all principles of possible synthetic *a priori* judgments. Transcendental philosophy contains the highest principles of this kind, and that science which *determines* the boundaries of the possibility of all synthetic *a priori* cognitions, i.e., not through amplification, but rather limitation of the faculty of cognition to the principles lying in it = is the critique of pure reason.

15. Only through a pure form of sensibility are pure intuitions possible = only through the latter an amplification of our cognition by virtue of synthetic *a priori* judgments, and thus amplifications of our *a priori* cognitions do not take place in any other manner, hence not at all through supersensible intuitions. These propositions are deduced in the following manner: (1) what representation is in itself, is inexplicable. A definition of that cannot be given because a representation can be explained only and in no other way than when one again represents a representation to oneself, hence there is lacking grounds of cognition in the logical sense <*in sensu logico*>. This action of the mind can be described as something in me that refers to something other. Now this relation of this something other in me is representation taken subjectively. The representation is aimed in part *at the object*, to which I am referring, in part *at that action of the mind* through which I compare something in me with the object. {Then one is occupied with the object in itself and its constitution, which must be wholly distinguished from the manner of representation of the subject, which involves the second, the action of the mind.}[r] This latter is called consciousness or the representation of myself insofar as I exhibit the representation of my representation to myself. One is nevertheless not always conscious of the representation, but can nevertheless become conscious of it at any time. Consciousness is also called apperception, which accompanies the represented object. (2) Now representation as a source of cognition can be brought about only by two sources, namely by *intuition and by concepts*.

Both have in themselves a relation to an object, only with the difference that in concepts the object is merely thought, but in the intuition it is given.

Intuition is namely an immediate representation of an object. This latter[s] can thus be only singular. E.g., one sun (for several suns would fall under the concept of a self-luminous body). {I.e., it contains only one

29:971

---

[r] Marginalia (970_{26-29}) alongside text printed at 970_{24-32}. We follow Lehmann in inserting this after the first sentence of the text. It is prefaced with the standard copyist's note: "[In the margin]."

[s] We do not follow Lehmann in changing *letztere* (latter) to *Gegenstand* (object) (971_5), nor in changing a period to a comma (971_2).

object; for were several present at once then they could be represented only together through a feature, i.e., be thought through concepts.}'

Concept is the mediate intuition or exhibition of an object by virtue of a feature common to several objects as a ground of cognition. Thus it always has underlying it a representation that is common to several objects, and thereby the cognition, as a feature, belongs merely to the thinking of the object. The two kinds of representations thus distinguish themselves in that in intuition the object can be represented insofar as it is given, but through the concept the object is representable insofar as it can be thought as given mediately. Thus the concept has reality only insofar as an object can be imputed to it. (3) All human intuition is sensible. But concepts belong merely to the thinking understanding, and sensibility can be mixed in with them only insofar as they rest on intuition, otherwise in and for themselves they can have no sensibility through which they are perceived.

Representing is *sensible* insofar as the object is represented by the subject *as appearance.*

Representing is *intellectual,* on the other hand, insofar as the object is considered through the representation *as it is in itself.*

This is to be understood this way:[15] the faculty of the mind through which the latter is affected by objects so as to be able to obtain a representation is sensibility. Now if an effect on the receptivity (i.e., the noted faculty of sensibility) arises from the object, then a sensation of the object arises, and this brings about a relation to the object, or representation, thus arises the intuition of the object, which now without further closer determination is called appearance. It is thus clear that all intuitions represent the object in *appearance,* i.e., on the part of the subject the intuition is taken in that manner which results from how it is affected by the object. {N.B Appearance can contain truth, and therefore distinguishes itself from *illusion:* i.e., the error from confusing the matter itself with the mere appearance, or the holding as true from subjective representation, which one takes as objectively certain.}" Now if the object is considered merely as phenomenon, i.e., if the representation is merely sensible, then one is looking only at that which is merely subjective in our representation of the object, and this is the manner in which we are affected by the object: in that *manner* the object does *appear* to us: but it is clear that from the manner in which the object appears, and therefore how the subject is affected by it, [it] cannot be inferred, that

29:972

' Marginalia (971₂₋₄) alongside text printed at 971₁₋₉. Lehmann inserts it after the first sentence of this paragraph, whereas we insert it after this paragraph (at 971₇).

" Marginalia (971₃₅₋₃₈) alongside text printed at 972₂₋₆. Lehmann inserts it before this text, whereas we insert it after the first sentence of this text (at 972₄). A blank line and paragraph breaks added by Lehmann have been removed.

the object is also thus in itself; rather it is certain that in itself it is not thus, since sensibility can take regard only of the form of the object in appearance. On the other hand there is no intellectual intuition, the understanding can only think, it does not have the source of sensibility or receptivity, but rather only the ability to represent through concepts, or spontaneity, through which it cognizes, and the latter kind of representations, which apply to objects in themselves, are called noumena. Next is thus

(4) the form of the subject for becoming affected in a certain way by the object, the subjective in representation, through which we are justified in designating the object as appearance; and the form of sensibility for being affected by objects is phenomenon, because the manner in which the subject is affected still rests on the form of this faculty (receptivity), and through that [it] intuits the object as matter. That these can be different one sees already from the difference of the instruments of the outer senses. E.g., the fly has one eye which is a polyhedron (many-sided), the human being a wholly different eye. The human being appears to see simply, and yet perceives the object as double. A jaundiced eye sees in another way than a healthy eye.

(5) Now should we have pure *a priori* intuition, then the specific form of sensibility must underlie it, which we assume with the appearance of the object. But it should be *a priori*, therefore it cannot be determined by the appearance itself. But it is also certain that a specific form of sensibility lies in our inner sense which provides the condition through which the objects of appearance can be cognized by us; this is the pure form of sensibility, which precedes all appearances of things, and thus is present before the objects are cognized through intuition. It is necessary in order to cognize the objects.   29:973

(6) Extensions of our *a priori* cognitions are possible only through synthetic *a priori* judgments. – The possibility of synthetic *a posteriori* judgments occasions no misgivings at all; all synthetic judgments of this kind rest on experience, experiences on appearances, therefore on intuition. Thus a concept which is supposed to be extended, can be extended only through an appearance connected with it. E.g., the concept of body with the intuition and experience abstracted from it of weight: but without any experience how can one attach more to a concept *a priori* than was contained in it? And here there is no answer about the possibility other than that it must happen by virtue of the pure form of sensibility, and that only through this form of sensible intuition can synthetic *a priori* judgments be determined. The actuality of all propositions of mathematics shows the possibility of these. E.g., the greatest chord is the diameter <*cordarum maxima est diameter*>. The judgment cannot be analyzed from the concept of diameter <*diameters*>, rather only through the addition of new appearance. Thus something must be added to it through synthesis <*per*

synthesin> that did not lie in the concept, and this depends not on experience, but rather on the form which the intuition is given.

But synthetic *a priori* propositions can be referred^v to objects only as they exhibit themselves in appearance. For otherwise they would be intellectual, and there would not be any pure intuition. They are therefore possible only if the *a priori* proposition contains nothing else than the *a priori* object insofar as it is appearance; and this applies only this way, that the synthetic judgments should extend our concept, thus should contain more than was thought in it; the concept is posited in connection with pure intuition, and can be cognized by virtue of the pure form of sensibility.

There are only two of these forms of sensible pure intuition, namely

a. space as the form for all outer intuitions,

b. time as the form for all inner intuition.

These forms of pure intuition thus need no object themselves, but rather are representable *a priori*, and are able to determine synthetic *a priori* judgments.

29:974   Consciousness teaches that they are present in us, and they are cognized preexisting before all intuition of sensible objects, therefore present necessarily and generally. Now if synthetic *a priori* judgments are to be brought about, then this is not possible without *a priori* intuition (because no synthetic judgment is possible without intuition). But intuition presupposes an object, therefore the faculty of sensibility underlies it; but this sensibility underlies it *a priori*, and therefore it can be determined in advance through pure intuition how objects will appear before they have come forth, which is possible through the derived principles of the forms of pure intuition. E.g., the different properties of the triangle. The principle: every part of space is again a space, etc. Now if the ground of the possibility of the entirety of synthetic *a priori* intuitions is to be sought only in the inner form of our sensibility, then the latter can be referred to an object only according to the manner that it affects the subject, i.e., insofar as it appears as phenomenon; now from this it follows that since we can extend our cognitions only through synthetic judgments, but these require intuitions, all extension of cognition is grounded in phenomena that must be cognized through the form of sensible intuition. Further, we can therefore not extend our cognition *a priori* insofar as we consider the things in themselves: for since intuitions are needed for that, these would have to be intellectual intuitions, but of these there are none. Therefore with supersensible concepts no extension of cognition takes place.

16. Thus we can have intuitions only in virtue of the form of our sensibility, and the objects will appear according to this form, be it empiri-

---

^{v} We follow Lehmann in changing *gezogen* (drawn) to *bezogen* (973$_{24}$).

cal or *a priori*. The constitution of the objects in appearance thus rests merely on the subjective form of intuition, through which it determines its manner in the mind, and according to the diversity of the relations, how objects are intuited by us and affect the mind. Thus the line of a circle appears even objectively different, even as oblong <*oblongum*> or straight line, according to the diversity of the direction in which we see it. Appearance thus has nothing more in common with the objective constitution of the matter itself, and our cognition is not able to extend itself beyond the boundaries of *appearance* {i.e., its perception and location},*ʷ* rather we are only in the position to transfer the appearance, as it is determined through the pure form of sensibility, to the objects themselves and thus to apply again our perception.

29:975

17. Space and time are thus the only pure forms of sensible intuition, namely space as the form of all outer sensible intuitions and time as the form of all inner sensible intuitions: *therefore they apply a priori only to the subjective manner of representation of things* {i.e., they are the subjective condition for being able to cognize objects through sensible intuition as appearance offers them. For with representation all things in sensible intuition are posited in space and time, and through that it becomes possible that we can represent or intuit the objects in appearance. They are thus the forms*ˣ* of sensibility, that are present in us as the subjective condition of intuition before all experience of an object. They therefore cannot be things in themselves, or coexist with the objects, for were this so, then we would have to cognize space and time, as well as objects, in and for themselves, therefore through the understanding, therefore cognition and extension of it would be possible only *a posteriori*, and could never happen *a priori:* we would thus never be able to judge about representations *a priori* nor comprehend the necessity of the constitution of the things in cognition. They are thus in and for themselves not objective.}*ʸ*

Namely,

(1) both space and time[16] are the forms of sensible intuitions or, what is the same, they are formal sensible intuitions, i.e., they are forms of each single subject, according to which a given object can be represented only under this form and under no other. Also they can be only intuitions, and never concepts: for to this belongs essentially the immediate representa-

---

ʷ Marginalia (974₃₉–975₁) alongside text printed at 974₃₉. We follow Lehmann in inserting it before a comma in the text. Parentheses added by Lehmann have been removed. Lehmann does not note this as marginalia.

ˣ Reading *Form* (form) as *Formen* (forms) (975₁₅).

ʸ Marginalia (975₉₋₂₄) alongside text printed at 975₈–976₇. We follow Lehmann in inserting it at the end of the first paragraph of this text. A *Nehmlich* (namely) omitted by Lehmann, which appears on a separate line in the ms above the text printed at 975₂₅, has been replaced immediately after this marginalia.

tion of objects, and indeed of a single object, and a feature of a concept can never underlie it. –

All spaces, all times are only part of one single space and one time. There is only one space and one time. One can indeed think therefore of parts of one and the same space and time next to and respectively after one another, but these parts cannot be subordinated to a general assumed space or time. Space and time are therefore each representa-

29:976 tions of a single thing <*re singulari*> and not a common [one] <*communi*>: if one says: the world has a beginning and an end, then this can only mean: the object of the world has a time where it*ᶻ* was not, begins to be, and will no longer be, but time itself always remains for itself one unchanging representation.

(2) Space and time are pure sensible *a priori* intuitions and therefore independent of all experience, for, in order to have an experience of that which is in space, this cannot be thought otherwise than by having previously thought a space. All things can be thought as annihilated, and space nevertheless remains. Space and time thus depend not on the things in space and in time as coexistence of things <*coexistentia rerum*> as Wolff believes,[17] but rather are intuitions existent for themselves when one has abstracted from all things. Space thus has in itself essentially only the subjective form of outer – just as time the subjective form of inner intuitions. But one could not assume them as something formal if one holds it necessary first to abstract space and time from things or from matter itself {in order to regard them as something objective};*ᵃ* which would have to be thought of as something outside us coexisting with things; they would then be *a posteriori* concepts; instead of that they are *a priori* intuitions, therefore, in order to think them, one is not permitted first to assume things to which they are supposed to give determination.

(3) Properties of space and of time are of the kind that they must be derived not from any concepts but rather immediately from intuition. Wolff, e.g., derives space and its properties from objective concepts – he says it is the order of simultaneous things insofar as, being supposed to be outside each other, they exist at the same time <*ordo simultaneorum quatenus extra se positae existunt simul*>. But then it cannot be explained why space has three dimensions, namely: length, breadth, and height. These cannot be derived from experience, rather one must already have space with its three dimensions in thought before a body in experience can be represented. They thus lie already as a condition of representation in inner intuition; consciousness is forced to assume them, therefore they exist *a priori* as necessary and abstracted from things, they still cannot be

---

ᶻ We follow Lehmann in changing *sie* to *es* (976₃).

ᵃ Marginalia (976₁₈₋₂₀) alongside text printed at 976₂₁₋₂₃ and inserted into the text with a sign. We follow Lehmann in this insertion.

attributed necessarily to things if they did not preexist, built upon this higher intuition. Through this, the order of things becomes distinct which Wolff in his definition of space determines as obscure when he says that $\quad$ 29:977 space is a confused representation of the order of things[18] insofar as they occur outside each other.

On the contrary there can be no doubt that from the pure intuition of space one can also[b] draw and thereby derive concepts.

(4) Now from this, that space and time are pure *a priori* intuitions and not concepts abstracted from objects, it follows that all propositions of geometry and arithmetic, or that concern numbers and figures, are synthetic judgments, and indeed *a priori* and therefore necessary and apodictically certain, which would not be if they could not be derived from space and time as pure intuitions. E.g., it can be found without experiment that one straight line is perpendicular at a given point.

(5) Space and time are indeed objective with respect to objects, i.e., they represent objects, but only as they are in appearance, but not as they are in themselves.

If one represents the matter in itself, then one considers it as a whole out of many parts; considers all parts in themselves and in their relation among themselves; this happens through the understanding, which thereby forms the concept of the whole, under which the parts are conceived. Now if space and time rested on concepts, then it would be absolutely necessary for one first to represent parts of space and time to oneself {and be able to represent these},[c] before one could think of space and time in the whole; but the parts of these, namely single spaces and times, are of equal standing *in* space and time and are not contained *under* it. No space, no time can be thought without at the same time thinking of a much larger space or time, and through this the representation rises to one single object, and this can be grounded only in intuition. Indeed, were space and time constitutions of the things in themselves, then they would have to be properties of God. For space is unbounded, the duration of time is also without bounds. Space and time agree; both are necessary with respect to the existence of all things. They are all-encompassing in view of all objects that they contain entirely in themselves. They are eternal. Therefore, since the reality of things rests in God as the ground, both would also be able to be attributed to God only, and the hypothesis of Spinozism[19] actually consisted in this, that one took space and time for things in themselves and for properties of God.

---

[b] The ms reads *nicht* (not) and in the margin to the far left stands: *auch?* (also?). We follow Lehmann in replacing *nicht* (at 977₄) with the marginalia.

[c] Marginalia (977₂₃) alongside text printed here, and inserted into the text with a sign. We follow Lehmann in the insertion, but parentheses added by Lehmann have been removed.

29:978   19.^d Now if one passes over to cognition by human beings of things themselves, then the faculty of human beings for cognizing things shows itself as very limited. Only the understanding of God is called intuition: as inexplicable as this kind of understanding is to us human beings, it is still supposed to indicate that God would have the faculty for cognizing things as they are in themselves, which is wholly lacking in human beings. A human being can cognize only through concepts, i.e., through features that he abstracts from the objects sensed through intuition, but in order to comprehend only something of the things much of the things must be set aside by the process of abstraction; therefore, by the features produced and the thinking of the things through these, there is given only a limited cognition which can never go further than the stuff sensibility offers him, therefore he is also able to cognize things only in the manner that they appear to him, but nothing of the things themselves, and how they are in themselves. Thus just as sensibility is the faculty of intuition, so the understanding of human beings is the faculty of concepts. Concepts can also be thought *a priori* if they contain nothing but the concept of synthesis, i.e., of the composition of the manifold in representation in order to constitute a cognition, and this synthesis has unity, i.e., the consciousness of myself of the connection of the manifold in my representation, whether this connection involves negative or affirmative parts of the representation. Under these conditions a concept arises that is thought *a priori* of the object; for the connection of the manifold in the representation and the consciousness of it, or the unity, are not empirical concepts, but rather *a priori*. E.g., that a body is composite, I cannot know from experience, I cannot see the composition. Here there is a mere act <*actus*> of thinking, although at first sight the concept of composition seems to be made *a posteriori*. The understanding alone has connected the manifold in the representation, and the concept arose through the consciousness of the connection. On this rests the pure concept of the understanding: or *a priori* concept. The subject or the understanding maintains the consciousness itself of the connection of the manifold through the pure intuition of space and time. One thus calls the pure concepts of the understanding

29:979   those which contain *synthetic unity* or the consciousness of the connection of the manifold in representation, or concepts of the unity of the manifold in synthetic representation. One predicates the pure concept of understanding as category – therefore this is the consciousness of the synthetic unity of the given manifold in representation. The category in and for

---

^d This ordering seems to be out of place, since a section numbered 18 comes after this section. The following marginalia (printed at Ak. 29: 1179) appears alongside the text printed at 978₁₋₄: "N.B. The following [paragraph] precedes this § *pho* in the connection of the matter, and it is connected with the following *ad §19.*" This note probably originated from Reicke or Arnoldt and was not part of the original ms.

itself leaves unsettled and undetermined whether the concept, i.e., it itself, has objective reality. It is in this like a representation that contains nothing contradictory, thus can be thought, but can be empty. Whether it thus rests on or has sensible synthetic unity – empirical unity – remains undetermined with it. Nevertheless only *at first* is the pure concept of understanding so understood that it is uncertain whether it has reality or not, but *afterwards* there is added through the condition of space and time that I become aware that it means something objective.

E.g., the category of magnitude, as a homogeneous many that together constitutes one: this cannot be grasped without space and time. Besides, what matters here is not the empirical actuality of bodies but, rather, only the possibility of finding what magnitude is according to our understanding, and this possibility is, as said, possible through pure *a priori* intuition.

So it is as well with the concept of cause, insofar as it consists in being the ground of the existence of another according to a standing rule. The category, that B is the effect of A, and the necessity of the cause to be an effect, that an effect <*causatum*> has a cause <*causam*>, is hardly to be conceived if one does not make use of the pure intuition of space and time.

18.' Now on the presupposition that we are only in the position to represent objects in appearance, and not in themselves, Mr. Kant builds

1. the theory of the ideality of space and of time, and rejects
2. the theory of the opposing reality of space and of time.

The theory of the ideality thus assumes that space and time are nothing other than something subjective, or = concerns merely the form of sensible intuition. It thus rests on the principle that space and time are not real determinations of things in themselves, but rather mere forms, which are given merely as conditions lying in the subject for the benefit of the intuition. The possibility for having such sensible forms is already illuminated, e.g., from this, that in the concept of God we can attribute to it not the predicate of thinking, because of the limitedness of this concept, but rather a faculty of intuiting things in themselves, which rests on this principle.

29:980

The defenders of the theory of the reality of space and time assume on the contrary that space and time would be a constitution of things in themselves, and we would have space and time not *a priori* but rather from experience. Mr. Kant refutes this through the existence of *a priori* cognitions of space and time, and that it would be impossible to cognize its constitution synthetic *a priori*, e.g., the three dimensions of space, or to judge of it *a priori*.

' The following marginalia (printed at Ak. 29: 1179) appears to the left of the text printed at 979₂₇: "Goes before the previous number 19."

But Mr. Kant determines

3. more exactly the theory of the ideality of space and time as something merely subjective, such that we would be able to cognize thereby not merely our own subject, but rather could cognize actual objects; for if we once represented objects as phenomena, then all predicates which we had represented and intuited by virtue of the subjective form would actually belong to the objects, but only as mere appearance, and to that extent the objects would have reality for us. Thus since it is accordingly impossible to represent the object in itself, noumena could concern only objects of non-sensible intuition.

Mr. Kant grounds his theory of the ideality of space and of time further through the properties of both.

Namely, if it is necessary that space and time belong to things themselves as properties, and we do not intuit things as appearance through the subjective form of our senses, then we have to cognize space and time from things through the understanding, whose form rests in the formation of concepts, but essentially in this, that it thinks *a many,* i.e., parts, and connects these into a *unity,* i.e., to a whole, i.e., it thinks things through a concept. The object thus has parts essentially: now what is a part of another must also allow of being considered as subsisting for itself, and can be called a part only in relation to the whole. But now a single space can be thought only as a part, i.e., a section of a larger one, and this larger one again as part of a still larger, and this goes forth into infinity, therefore 29:981 infinity must also be predicated of space and time. Thus it can have no boundary like objects, it does not have parts under it that can be connected into a unity, it therefore also cannot be thought of as a whole. It thus has no determination at all that exhibits something objective, is thus no object, and thus cannot be thought through concepts. From this it follows that it is only something singular, therefore the representation of it rests on intuition. It follows from this that this intuition is not empirical, but rather must be *a priori,* since space can be thought before an object in space. Thus the representation lies in the subject alone. Now, since space and time are thought *a priori,* it is necessary to place all objects of sensible intuition in space and time, but they would not be able to be ordered if sensibility were not provided with a form ordered for that, and this form must be sought in space and time. Therefore they are the only sensible forms of our intuition, which are merely subjective. From this it also follows again that since we do intuit the objects themselves only in a certain form, this form lies in our subject and not in the object, and that we can therefore cognize objects only as they appear to us.*ᶠ*

Consequences <consequentiae>. Several synthetic *a priori* propositions now follow from the concept of space and time.

ᶠ A blank line added by Lehmann has been removed (981₂₁).

1. There are not *two times* concurrently, but rather successive, likewise *two spaces* are not successive but rather are concurrent. {intuition <*intuitu*> of space and time}[g]

2. All objects are thought and represented by me *in time*, as they are concurrent or successive, but *in space* objects are represented as they are outside of me, therefore that which exists in me and not outside me cannot be intuited in space. {intuition <*intuitu*> of objects}[h]

3. The representation of time is namely in me, and time belongs thus to inner sense, but the representation of space is outside me and belongs to outer sense. The determinations of representations with respect to time happen therefore all in me, but with respect to space all outside me. Now when Newton says[20] in a scholium <*scholio*> of the *Principles of Natural Philosophy* <*principiorum philosophiae naturalis*>:[i] *time is everywhere and space is in all time*, then this is not to be so understood that time has a location. Time has no location wherein I can posit something in time, and what I think in time is not at all in space. But it can most certainly be said: the time-concept contains all representations, but space only those representations in it insofar as objects are outside me.   29:982

4. Insofar as I pay regard to the relation with other things, I cannot think any things outside me otherwise than in space. I.e., determinations of the relation of the things outside me cannot be assigned otherwise than under the presupposition of their existence in space.

Therefore if Wolff thinks things in space,[21] and posits space in the order of simultaneous things <*ordine simultaneorum*>, then space is cognized through a concept of the understanding, through the relation of things. Likewise if he determines time by the order of successive things, insofar as they are joined one to another (things which would be one *after* another) <*ordinem successivorum, quatenus sunt invicem connexa (quae post invicem essent)*>:[j] but one must already have thought of space and time before one thinks things as concurrent or successive.

NOTE

In the *Critique of Pure Reason*[k] it is deduced through the exhibition of the concept of sensibility (perceptivity) as the faculty for obtaining representa-

---

[g] Marginalia (printed at Ak. 29: 1179) alongside the first line of this paragraph (981$_{23-4}$). We have inserted it after the paragraph.

[h] Marginalia (printed at Ak. 29: 1179) alongside the first line of this paragraph (981$_{25-6}$). We have inserted it after the paragraph.

[i] This is presumably an abbreviation for Newton's *Philosophiae Naturalis Principia Mathematica* (Mathematical Principles of Natural Philosophy) (London, 1687).

[j] Appearing in the margin alongside this (982$_{13-14}$) is the following Latin phrase: *in opp. in simuli – in spatio* (opposed simultaneously – in space).

[k] This is not treated as a title in the ms.

tions according to the manner that the subject is affected, and of the concept of the understanding (faculty to think – spontaneity) as the faculty for cognizing according to these representations, that *the mind appears to itself,* or that the soul can be an object of appearance for itself. It is correct in itself that the subject is affected by itself, and thus can obtain representations through the inner sense of the soul and *from that can cognize, according to how* the mind was *previously* affected by objects, but in order *to avoid ambiguities here,* at this point Mr. Kant proposes instead a definition of *sensibility* as follows: the merely subjective in the representation of things insofar as it contains the formal ground according to which objects present themselves, or also = sensible form of our intuition. For something objective itself cannot lie in it. It determines the appearance according to the form lying in it, i.e., it determines in advance the manner in which the object will appear. It underlies all manners of sensible intuition, and is thus present *a priori* in order to determine these intuitions in space and time, but has no connection at all with the object itself, still less is it a constitution of the object itself, but rather provides merely for its appearance being cognized.

29:983

{*Note.* Here is the location for indicating the distinction of sensibles <*sensibili*> from a representation that is sensitive. With regard to the objects that are represented, the representations are *either:*

sensitive, i.e., sensory,[1] which rest on the form of sensibility alone, without the existence of the matter concurring with it. So space and time are forms of sensibility without an object of sense concurring thereby and being connected with it.

But these can be connected at the same time with the matter or the object of the senses, and then the sensitive ones will become sensibles <*sensibilia^m*; G: *empfindbaren*>, i.e., which contain reality at the same time. So something that is an object of the senses can be in space and time, and this is the sensible that reality provides; therefore the sensible is equivalent to matter, to sensibility. – So all empirical cognitions have not merely the sensitive ground <*sensitive rationem*> of the form, but rather at the same time something sensible, whereas nothing at all empirical, therefore also nothing sensible, is contained in the sensory cognition.

But in contrast <*in opposito*> *to sensory cognition are intellectual* representations, which are thought merely through the understanding. Here also the form of thinking and of matter or reality is similar to the concept of the understanding as the product.}[n]

---

[1] We are translating *sinnlich* in the next few paragraphs as "sensory" (rather than "sensible") in order to avoid confusing it with *"empfindbar,"* which is here translated as "sensible."

[m] The emphasis added by Lehmann has been removed (983₅).

[n] Marginalia (983₄₋₂₄) alongside text printed at 982₂₉–984₃. It begins with *Anmerkung,* which Lehmann omitted and we have replaced. We follow Lehmann in inserting this long marginalia immediately before the paragraph beginning *"ad* §19" – the latter apparently being an addition to the previous §19 (cf. Ak. 29: 978–9, above).

Regarding <*ad*> §19. Everything that was said up until now of the possibility for obtaining *a priori* cognitions through the subjective form of sensible intuition belongs to transcendental aesthetic, i.e., doctrine of the senses, on the other hand transcendental logic, i.e., doctrine of the understanding, furnishes a second source of principles for possibly obtaining pure *a priori* cognitions. This distinguishes itself from general pure logic in this, that the latter occupies itself with the mere form of the use of our understanding, but the former concerns the determination of the pure cognition of objects through the mere understanding.

A pure concept of understanding is a *pure cognition of the object through the mere understanding*, and the full opposite <*oppositum*> of the empirical concept, in that it is entirely thought purely *a priori:* therefore one can also call it *a concept of pure thinking*, in order to distinguish it from sensibility.

The *a priori* concept of the synthetic unity of the manifold in intuition   29:984
is the category. The connection of the manifold and the consciousness of this constitutes what is constitutive of the category.

The consciousness of the unity of the manifold according to concepts is logical function.

All objects (they may occur in appearance or through concepts) can certainly be perceived, but never their composition. This the understanding must add to the representation, and it is thus solely an act <*actus*> of the understanding, namely composition, to represent the composite in such a way that it becomes *one*. – Mr. Kant calls this synthesis, e.g., parts that together constitute a room.

The consciousness of the synthetic unity of the manifold in intuition in general, or (which =) the consciousness of the concept that contains the synthetic unity, is = category.

Aristotle called the pure concepts of understanding thus; the Scholastics called them predicaments <*praedicamenta*> and they were equivalent in number; there are namely twelve altogether, and contain the elements <*elementa*> of *a priori* cognitions through the understanding. Besides these there are yet predicables which are in part composed out of the first ones, e.g., cause connected with magnitude, in part the predicaments <*praedicamenta*> are connected with the concepts of space and time. These also are possible to enumerate, and presumably quite completely. Mr. Kant did not enumerate them.

Taken together categories and predicables constitute the entire elementary principles for cognizing the extent[o] of all *a priori* cognitions.

20. It is quite remarkable, that just as the principles of all sensible cognitions result from the form of space and time it is possible to bring all possible concepts of the understanding into classes, and derive [them] from the faculty of the understanding so that it is thereby exhausted with

---

[o] Lehmann misprints *Umfang* as *Unfang* (984_{27}).

respect to its extent. The understanding is the faculty of concepts. Now in order to bring something under a concept for us, a judgment is necessary each time, therefore all actions of the understanding amount to a *judging*. For thinking is discursive cognition, i.e., cognition through certain features of things. These latter constitute the predicate and are attributed to the representation of the thing as subject, but the judgment lies in this connection. Now as logic contains functions of the understanding,[22] i.e., rules of thinking in general, and without regard to an object, so transcendental logic, which is that general logic applied to objective *a priori* cognition, contains these functions <*functiones*> of thinking or forms of judgment, therefore the four logical functions can here also underlie it, and all possible elementary principles of pure thinking reduce to quantity, quality, relation, and modality. Thus according to this the table of pure concepts of the understanding can be referred back to the table of the four logical functions, thus:

29:985

    (I) According to quantity our logical judgments are *judgments* <*judicia*>
       (a) singular <*singularia;* G: *einzelne*>
       (b) particular <*particularia;* G: *besondere*>
but which one would better call plural <*pluralia*>, since here several objects are always presupposed, but it is still uncertain whether the several are not a totality, yet the latter must be distinguished from these.
       (c) universal <*universalia;* G: *allgemeine*>
   (II) according to quality
       (a) affirmative <*affirmativa*>
       (b) negative <*negativa*>
       (c) infinite <*infinita*>, i.e., affirmative judgments with respect to the copula <*copula*>, or negative with respect to the predicate, e.g., the soul is non-mortal <*anima est non-mortalis*>.
  (III) according to relation (relations)[p]
       (a) categorical in the relation of the predicate to the subject
       (b) hypothetical in the relation of the consequence to the ground
       (c) disjunctive in the relation of a member of the division to the whole sphere of the concept
  (IV) according to modality (relations)
       (a) problematic
       (b) assertoric
       (c) apodictic

These contain the relations of the predicate to the subject, according to differences

---

[p] *der Relation nach (Verhältnisse)* (985₂₆).

regarding $<ad>$ (a) logical possibility
regarding $<ad>$ (b) [logical]^L actuality
regarding $<ad>$ (c) [logical]^L necessity

When the judgment contains a predicate which by reason of its subject $<ratione\ subjecti>$ is thought only under the condition of possibility, then it is thought merely problematically; but it becomes a proposition or assertoric judgment if it is really attributed to the subject, and if this proposition is connected with necessity, then the judgment becomes apodictic.   29:986

Now on this rest just as many categories only with the difference that they are directed at objects; here everything is predicated of objects which with the logical functions would be said of concepts. Thus:

(I) according to quantity
   (1a) unity
   (2a) plurality
   (3c) totality
(II) according to quality
   (4a) reality
   (5b) negation
   (6c) limitation

i.e., according to quality the category rests on the presupposition either of something which contains the concept of being, e.g., light, or the concept of not-being, e.g., contains^q rest, or the concept of being connected concurrently with not-being as limitation. (III) According to relation, where two corresponding concepts always concur

  (7a) substance – accident
  (8b) cause – effect
  (9c) acting $<agens>$ – being acted upon $<patiens>$, or = community
     or = reciprocal influence $<influxus\ mutuus>$
     or = interaction $<commercium>$

{N.B regarding $<ad>$ (9c) the relation of community is different from that of the consequence to the ground in this, that cause and effect are reciprocal here, i.e., there is something in the effect $<causato>$ which is ground of the cause $<causa>$, and something in the cause $<causa>$, which is ground of the effect $<causato>$ = each concurrently.}^{r} (IV) According to modality

---

^{q} An *enthält* (after *Einschränkung*) omitted by Lehmann has been replaced (986_{22}).
^{r} Marginalia (986_{30-34}) alongside text printed at 986_{23-29}. We follow Lehmann in inserting it immediately after this text. A blank line added by Lehmann has been omitted.

(10a) possibility – (impossibility)
       potentiality <*potentialitas*>

29:987   (11b) actuality <*actualitas;* G: *Wirklichkeit*>
       (existence)   (non-existence)

(12c) necessity <*necessitas*> (contingency)

One cannot hereby equate the concept of actuality with the concept of existence, for the existence of a thing comprehends in itself the possibility as well as the actuality, as the necessity of an object, whereby existence is predicated of all three, but actuality of actuality <*actualitas*> alone.

{Comparison of the four logical functions with the twelve categories regarding <*ad*> (A.1) quantity

singular <*singularia*>	particular <*particularia*>	universal <*universalia*>
unity	plurality	totality

(2) quality

affirmative <*affirmativa*>	negative <*negativa*>	infinite <*infinita*>
reality	negation	limitation

regarding <*ad*> (B.1) relation

categorical,	hypothetical,	disjunctive
substance	cause	community
accident	effect	

(2) Modality

problematic	assertoric	apodictic
possibility,	actuality,	necessity}[s]

REMARKS

(1) One can reduce these twelve categories to two classes, of which each again comprehends two classes under it and

(A) call the first six categories of quantity and quality the *mathematical* class.

(B) Call the last six categories of relation and modality from seven to twelve the *dynamic* class.

(2) Aristotle brought out only ten categories: but there was wholly lacking a classification according to the table of logical functions. They were therefore found accidentally, deficiently, and even the forms of space and time among them, notwithstanding these belong in a special class.

29:988   (3) The appearance is always remarkable, that we are in the position to discover completely the functions of the understanding, and that there are just as many pure *a priori* concepts of the understanding as are found logical functions, that the former correspond to the latter, and thus that we are

[s] Marginalia (987₁₀₋₂₃) alongside text printed at 986₁₁₋₂₁. We follow Lehmann in inserting it after the listing and discussion of the categories.

thereby in the position to determine all elements of pure thinking about all objects, namely before all possible experience; nevertheless, as goes without saying, within the boundaries of transcendental philosophy, i.e., that the pure cognitions of reason, whose elements are displayed here, are immanent, i.e., have objective reality, therefore that class of cognitions of reason which have no object of possible experience are excluded here.

(4) From the predicaments <*praedicamenten*>, i.e., these categories so named by the Scholastics, arise the predicables <*praedicabilia*>, i.e., those pure concepts of understanding that either are composed out of two or more categories or arise out of the connection of a predicament <*praedicaments*> with a form of sensibility of space and time.

E.g., in regard to quality the concept of *duration* rests on reality or existence, duration also is the magnitude of an existence with respect to existence in time. For to this extent the duration of a grain of sand is equal to the duration of a sand hill {and this magnitude is different from material quantity}.' Therefore a predicament <*praedicamentum*> concurs with the form of sensibility. The concept of *motion* presupposes existence or quality, and is thought with alteration of existence in opposed determination of time and space, thus existence in successive form after one another in time and space.

(5) In every function the categories are so ordered that the third is composed out of the two preceding ones, e.g., the community of concepts presupposes two substances, with cause and effect, and connects them to a third, namely change – cause and effect. Thus reality, connected with negation, provides limitation.

Thus totality is = a plurality that is concurrently unity.

Thus necessity is a possibility, from which actuality can be inferred.

(6) Now ontology or transcendental philosophy should also be treated according to the standard of the premised classification of the categories, since through this, that the categories are displayed against each other, the 29:989 development of these elements of our *a priori* concepts of the understanding is facilitated, through whose unification is avoided the arbitrariness that is connected with Baumgarten's method, and these *a priori* principles are better encompassed on the whole. The six categories of the mathematical class as well are treated accordingly, and of these follows first:

THE CATEGORY OF MAGNITUDE OR
THE CLASS OF QUANTITY

21. *Quantity – magnitude* is a pure concept of the understanding, whose development rests on this:

' Marginalia (988_{22-23}) alongside text printed here and inserted into the text with a sign. We follow Lehmann in the insertion.

(1) In every magnitude the concept of *many* is contained, which, considered as connected, exhibits itself as a *one*. A homogeneous connected many constitutes quantity as such. The representation of *one* and *many* thus lies in the concept of magnitude.*ᵘ*

(2) One and many are thinkable only as correlates <*correlata*> and can be thought only in opposition <*in opposito*>, but neither of them can be defined, rather they can be thought only through the other. Therefore the definition of the author <*definitio autoris*> S4 §74²³ runs around in circles <*in circulo*>: in the presupposition of many he thinks a one. {that something which is not many}*ᵛ*

(3) Unity can be thought formally <*formaliter*> as well as*ʷ* materially <*materialiter*>.

Formal unity rests on the connection of the manifold under a principle. Material unity is unity of the object itself. Thus formally only *one unity of a thing* is possible (in the singular <*in singulari*>), for each thing has only one concept under which the manifold is brought by the understanding. But materially there are unities of one and the same object, i.e., as many as can be called *one* in each thing. *Therefore plurality in the object* is at all times material. The manifold in the representation of the object is, however, in itself formal plurality.

Therefore a play has plurality of objects, but unity in the representation according to the laws of time, of location, etc., for without this it would be connected for no end.

(4) The Aristotelian school considers formal unity as transcendental, and in a metaphysical sense assumes,*ˣ* as the author also does in Sect. 4, 6, and 7,²⁴ the principle: any being is transcendentally *one, true, good* <*quodlibet ens est transcendentaliter unum, verum bonum*>, and [is] predicated of the object

29:990   (a), *one* <*unum*>, i.e., that one thing is not many things – unity

(b), *truth* <*verum*>, i.e., to each thing is actually applied what is proper to it, or – certain predicates, which belonged to the concept of the thing, actually apply to the thing, therefore the predicates of the thing could be attributed to it according to actuality, not possibility, e.g., every triangle has angles. This is the proposition: every thing *has truth in itself* or in each thing is truth {each thing has nothing in itself that does not agree with itself}.*ʸ*

ᵘ Marginalia (printed at Ak. 29: 1180) alongside the top of this paragraph reads as follows: *viel-mannigfaltiges-multitudo* (many-manifold-multitude). This likely refers to Baumgarten, §74 (see the next paragraph).

ᵛ We are adding this marginalia (printed at Ak. 29: 1180) that appears alongside the bottom of this paragraph.

ʷ Emphasis added by Lehmann has been removed (989₂₁).

ˣ We follow Lehmann in changing *nehmen* to *nimmt* (989₃₀), and we also change *praedicirten* (989₃₉) to the singular.

ʸ Marginalia (990₈₋₉) appearing alongside the bottom of this paragraph. Lehmann does not note that this is marginalia.

(c) *Good* <*bonum*>, i.e., each thing has everything in itself in order to be what it is, or – everything is transcendentally <*transcendentaliter*> perfect.

It clearly shows that here each thing was considered only in relation to its own essence, and to this extent these criteria of the thing are correct, since each thing just is what it is: but in the metaphysical sense, i.e., in the relation of the thing [to what is] outside it, therefore considered against all other possible things, no thing, excluding the most real being <*ens realissimo*>, can be attributed a perfection, rather each has a lack of reality, therefore negative perfection, or is imperfect.

In a metaphysical sense <*in sensu metaphysico*> these criteria are therefore unusable, but as logical prescriptions for the consideration of an object it is important that one must see from its determination whether it has unity, truth, or perfection, e.g., formal unity of a book.

(5) On the other hand transcendental unity is in each thing, insofar as *many* must be thought as *connected*, in order to make a concept of a thing according to a principle. From this arises the formal unity, but formally <*formaliter*> there cannot be unities of one and the same thing. The formal unity belongs essentially to the understanding, as that is the faculty for bringing the manifold of representation under a concept.

The author calls (§74) categorical unity <*unitatem categoricam*> the unity of the object,[25] and he is correct in that. Objectively considered, unity is a thing which is not *many*, which, with respect to that which it contains, is opposed to diversity and to the many, therefore a material unity. But formally <*formaliter*> it is hypothetical. A many thought according to the form can be unity, although materially <*materialiter*> the objects have a plurality.

(6) To magnitude belongs the connection of plurality, and this latter is therefore not adequate to the concept of the quantum <*quanti*>, because with this [plurality] an aggregate of heterogeneous parts is allowed; on the contrary the concept of the composite <*compositi*> is determined thereby. 29:991

A composite is a unit formed from the conjunction of many <*compositum est unum ex conjunctione plurium*>, e.g., a suit of clothes, whatever various parts it also has.

Should the connection involve the concept of magnitude, then the concept of homogeneity underlies it, and the concept of magnitude itself is determined by the word *quantum:* it is the unit conjoined out of many homogeneous things <*est unum ex pluribus homogeneis conjunctum*>. It therefore contains essentially

(1) multitude <*multitudinem*>: thus, what is considered as unity cannot be called quantum.

(2) Homogeneity <*homogeneitatem*>, i.e., things from one and the same sort (<*genus*; G: *Gattung*>), thence <*inde*> composite <*compositum*> differs from quantum <*quanto*>, and the many would in that

case be able to be a variety, every quantum contains a multitude but not every multitude is a quantum <*omne quantum continet multitudinem, sed non omnis multitudo est quantum*>; rather, [it is one] only when the parts are homogeneous.

Now that determination of a thing, through which one cognizes a matter as a quantum, is *quantity* or *magnitude*. Formally <*formaliter*>, quantum is a manifold in representation that is homogeneous, and the determination of the manifold as quantum is quantity. {N.B. Quantity is thus nothing more than determination, *how* large something is: thus something can be thought as quantum, without allowing itself to be determined as quantity, or being determined thereby.}ᶻ

From this follows

(1) there are now several quanta, but not several quantities, since as determination the quantity <*quantitas*> can be only one. Quantity <*quantitas*> as well as quality <*qualitas*> are in general made of a sort of quantum <*quantum qualis*> and in a barbaric manner: one could even say *what quaeddity* <*quaeditas*>, in order to express through all three the familiar question: what, what sort of, how much <*quae, qualis, quanta*>? *Quiddity* <*quidditas*>, if one wants to put it that way,²⁶ would be distinguished from quality as the determination of the genus <*generis*> and the specific difference; e.g., *quiddity* <*quidditas*> the genus <*generis*> *of which:* but whether it is hard or soft, belongs to quality, therefore in regard

29:992   to the species conceived under the genus <*genere*>. {The quaeddity <*quaeditas*> would express the relation; at the least it means that in the interrogative what <*quae?*> where it is supposed to signify the various relations of the concept: categorical, hypothetical, or disjunctive.}ᵃ

(2) Quality <*qualitas*> differs from quantity in that, and to the extent that, the latterᵇ indicates something in the same object which is heterogeneous with regard to other determinations found in it. Therefore quality <*qualitas*> is that determination of a thing according to which whatever is specifically different finds itself under the same genus, and can be distinguished from it. – This is heterogeneous in contrast <*in opposito*> to that which is not specifically different, or to the homogeneous.

(3) Through the comparison of the thing with itself and its parts one can clearly cognize that there is a quantum, but one can never determine, without comparison of a thing with other things, what it would actually have for a magnitude or – *how* large it is. E.g., the earth has 5400 miles –

ᶻ Marginalia (991₁₉₋₂₂) alongside text printed at 991₁₇₋₂₆. We insert it after the paragraph ending at 991₂₅, whereas Lehmann inserts it after the first sentence of this text. Blank lines and a paragraph break added by Lehmann have been removed.

ᵃ Marginalia (992₁₋₃) alongside text printed at 991₃₀₋₂. We follow Lehmann in inserting it after this paragraph.

ᵇ Here, "latter" seems to refer to quality rather than to quantity (992₅).

the mile is 1/15 of a degree – degree 1/360 of the largest meridian. All of this can also be applied to a pea, and it is futile to find the magnitude of the earth without comparison of the measure. Therefore the definition of Wolff and of the author <*autoris*> §69, Sect. 3, quantity is the internal determination of a being which, however, cannot even be given or under-stood without another thing claimed <*quantitas est interna entis de-terminatio, quae dari quidem sine alio assumto autem intelligi nequit*>[27] can never be valid as a definition; however correct and provable the proposi-tion is, it is not a concept equivalent with magnitude, nor can it be brought out in that manner. It is nevertheless

(4) striking: the concept of magnitude or the determination of a thing, that it has magnitude, is given, but the magnitude as magnitude, i.e., how large the object is, is impossible to cognize from the matter itself. Indeed, even more. The concept of magnitude belongs quite properly to the understanding, since it is concerned with the connection of a homoge-neous manifold. Magnitude is employed in mathematics through the help of a pure intuition in sensibility, i.e., through the form of space and time in determination of each figure or number. But in philosophy it cannot be determined from the concept alone whether the category of magnitude has objective reality. I.e., it cannot be cognized that many together consti-tute one.

It is absolutely necessary to make use of *a priori* intuition, as in mathe-matics. All categories are like those of magnitude, of a kind that through their concept itself it cannot be proved to what extent it is possible that the concept also has objective reality. One must search for this proof in the sensible intuition of space and time. Through that alone does *extensive* magnitude also attain reality. {Extension <*extensio*> differs from magni-tude of time, or it is a manifold [of what is] outside one another, e.g., as present time is opposed to future.}[c]

29:993

(5) If one pays special regard to magnitude with numbers one can determine a quantum by positing the same thing several times <*aliquoties facta positio ejusdem*>.

We cognize a multitude successively, we cognize a *multitude* by adding one to one <*unum uni addendo multitudinem cognoscimus*>,[28] i.e., through counting, thus with every number a multitude is present: if this continues into infinity then a multitude greater than any *number* <*multitudo omni numero major*> arises: one can indeed call this an infinite multitude, but not an *infinite number*. For it is just because of its infinity that it cannot be expressed in numbers and the expression thus involves a contradiction in the predicate <*contradictio in adjecto*>. Such an infinite multitude, however,

[c] Marginalia (993₆₋₇) alongside text printed at 993₄₋₈. We follow Lehmann in inserting it after the first paragraph of this text. Blank lines and a paragraph break added by Lehmann have been omitted.

is also a multitude greater than any cognition <*multitudo omni cognitione major*>, for we can have a concept only of a determinate magnitude. {For number <*numerus*> is indeed a *multitude* cognized by counting (by adding one to one) <*multitudo numerando (unum uni addendo) cognita*>, in that counting on into infinity is impossible, since something stops lying within the boundaries of a number as soon as it can no longer be counted.}[d]

(6) Now in order to cognize a magnitude it is necessary that the concept of *measure* be connected with it at the same time: for that something is a quantum merely expresses something that determines the quality of the thing; on the other hand, without measure it is impossible to imagine what *kind of a quantum is produced through the composition*. {i.e. without an object exhibiting it through which its meaning is given, it cannot be cognized with certainty of the category of magnitude that it also has objective reality.}[e] Therefore:

29:994   *measure* <*mensura*> is the unit, which makes quantity knowable by counting <*unum, quod numerando quantitatem reddit cognoscibilem*>.[29] Just as little would one comprehend that there were three kinds of specifically different ways to measure a magnitude, if one did not have an example in the length, height, and depth of space.

Time on the other hand has only one dimension (<*dimensio;* G: *Abmessung*>), and this is represented in length and pictured figuratively through the drawing of a line. The line itself exhibits all points simultaneously, but the drawing of the line expresses the successive sequence or the alterations in time.

(7) Now a magnitude is either

(a) an assignable quantum <*quantum assignabile*>, which one also calls a givable quantum <*quantum dabile*>. This is that magnitude which can be exhibited entirely (in its totality) in intuition; every measure must be so constituted, therefore such a magnitude must also be able to be determined in relation to the measure, or

(b) a quantum greater than any assignation <*quantum omni assignatione majus*>, or

(c) less <*minus*>, i.e., an infinitely large or infinitely small magnitude: therefore they also mean infinite or infinitely small quantum <*quantum infinitum . . . infinito-parvum*>, and thus, since both are respectively larger, respectively smaller than any given magnitude, then both are not assignable quanta <*quanta assignabilia*>, and cannot be given.

---

[d] Marginalia (993₂₁₋₄) alongside text printed at 993₁₄₋₁₈. We follow Lehmann in inserting it after this paragraph. A *Denn* at the beginning of the marginalia and removed by Lehmann has been replaced (993₂₁). Blank lines and a paragraph break added by Lehmann have been removed.
[e] Marginalia (993₃₂₋₄) alongside text printed at 993₂₈–994₂. We follow Lehmann in inserting it after the first paragraph of this text, but an "i.e." opening the marginalia and omitted by Lehmann has been replaced, and blank lines and a paragraph break added by Lehmann have been removed.

(8) The ground why a magnitude is not finite is called a negation; that negation on whose account a quantum is not the greatest <*maximum*>, can be called either *limitation* or *boundedness.*

One calls *limited* only an object of reason, but *bounded* an object of intuition: likewise unlimited and unbounded, according to whether it is an object of mere reason or of the senses.

Limits thus differ from boundaries. A being of the understanding (noumenon) has only limits (<*limites;* G: *Schranken*>), i.e., the negation is thought merely according to the understanding; limitation is therefore here: thus a noumenal quantum <*quantum noumenon*> is magnitude thought through the understanding, and limited insofar as it is not the greatest <*maximum*>, and the negation is called *limit* <*limes; G: Schranken*>, for on its account it is limited. E.g., boundaries or limits of the human understanding, will. –

On the other hand, a phenomenal quantum <*quantum phaenomenon*> is *bounded* if the determination of its magnitude, or the negation, belongs at the same time to the intuition <*intuitus*>, or = if the ground of the limitation at the same time contains something positive in space. 29:995

The positive, through which the limits of the intuition are determined, is called *the boundary* = *The point in space* has for itself no negation, is also not bounded, it is merely positive, and indicates the location wherein something is limited.

The *line* obtains its boundary through the point, the *surface* through the line, and the *body* through the surface. These are also the three dimensions of space, if one thinks it completely as a part for itself of a larger space, and then bodily content, surface, and length each again has its space. Boundedness and boundary are thus always something positive in appearance, but not limitation.

(9) Quantum is *either continuous or discrete* <*quantum est vel continuum vel discretum*>.[30] A continuous magnitude is a continuous quantum <*quantum continuum*> of which all its parts are again quanta, however small or large they may be.

Thus it cannot contain simple parts. Composition, on the other hand, is constituted thus: that there are parts indeterminate through themselves <*quod sunt partes per se indeterminatae*>, i.e., it cannot be determined in itself and from the magnitude itself how many parts one should assume, but rather it remains arbitrary according to our cognition.

Now space and time belong to the continuous quanta <*quantis continuis*>. For each part of space and time cannot be thought otherwise than again as a space or time, and the division continues down to the point and moment: only the latter two are not parts of space and of time.

A point is only the positive, the boundary of a space, and the moment is just the same with respect to time.

From this it follows that space and time do not consist of simple parts.

463

A circumstance that, if the opposite were correct, would prove that space and time would be something objective in *coexistence* and *succession*[f] but, since one cannot meet[g] with any simple part, proves that space and time lie only in the mere subjectivity of the form of intuition.

A point in space is indivisible and it is also not, as thought,[h] a part of space: therefore a space of sheer points would be a space which would consist of sheer boundaries, therefore be a nothing. A point is merely a position in space, but until then space is divisible, just as time down to the moment, therefore it is impossible to assume simple parts in space and time.

29:996

A point cannot be thought before the representation of space, from which follows that space cannot consist of points. Space fills out matter as extension *<extensum>*, but extension *<extensum>* is that *in which* there is space *<id, in quo est spatium>*. The concepts are thus correlates *<correlata>* with matter, space itself makes it that matter is extended: thus matter can consist of no other parts than space itself has, therefore it is impossible that matter could consist of simple parts.

A *discrete quantum <quantum discretum>*,[31] on the other hand, is a quantum that consists of units, i.e., of a determinate multitude of parts which I think as units. This is the concept of number, therefore the magnitude expressed by numbers is a discrete quantum *<quantum discretum>*. E.g., a quantum of gulden: here they cannot be further divided without the unit = gulden, wholly ceasing, therefore the parts do not themselves contain quanta. Just as in general this would be thought of a quantum *<quanto>* of silver in shots, ounces, etc.;[32] the latter can be divided into quanta and is thus a continuous quantum *<quantum continuum>*.

The discrete quantum *<quantum discretum>* can be viewed as discrete *in itself <per se discretum>* because it consists of simple parts, i.e., because its units cannot themselves be considered as quanta, but they must be expressed by a number in order to exhibit their quantity, i.e., in order to know how large the quantum is.

(10) Quantum

Quantity *<quantitas>*

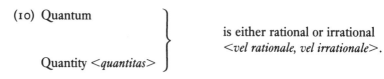

is either rational or irrational *<vel rationale, vel irrationale>*.

A computable quantum *<quantum computabile>* is rational *<rationale>*, i.e., that magnitude which can be calculated or can be expressed in

---

[f] *neben einander und nach einander,* also translated as "[being] next to each other and after one another."

[g] We follow Lehmann in changing *zutreffen* to *treffen* (995₃₃).

[h] We do not follow Lehmann in changing *gedacht* to *gesagt* (said) (995₃₆).

numbers; in contrast, a finite quantum <*quantum finitum*> which is in-commensurable <*incommensurabile*>, i.e., which cannot be calculated or whose relation to a measure cannot be expressed by numbers, is irrational <*irrationale*>. It only nears the determination that the measure gives, e.g., the relation of the roots $\sqrt{1}$ to $\sqrt{2}$ that prevails between the diagonal line and both sides, is immeasurable.

These latter magnitudes in space and time are given to intuition only between the boundaries of space and time.

(II) A greatest quantum <*quantum maximum*>, just like a smallest quantum <*quantum minimum*>, cannot be thought of a phenomenal be-ing <*ente phaenomeno*>, and a representation of it is attributable only to a noumenal being <*ente noumeno*> – God. For a greatest quantum <*quan-tum maximum*> would be totality, magnitude thought without limitation. The like is just as little thinkable for the *human* understanding, as that magnitude whose yet smaller measure would be, as it were, a nothing. E.g., no subjective intuition is capable of a totality of space and of time which was not part of a still larger space and time. The phenomenon can be thought only as a plurality, and under this concept a totality.   29:997

Thus for phenomena there is no absolutely greatest quantum <*quan-tum absolute maximum*>, but rather always only relatively greatest <*relative maximum*>, e.g., the greatest chord in a circle <*chorda maxima in circulo*>, and just as little an absolutely *smallest* quantum <*quantum abso-lute minimum*>. For all parts, even the smallest imaginable, again have quanta, therefore the representation is directed here as well only to a relation.

On the concept of the relation of things, according to which alone we can cognize their magnitude, rests the *concept*, distinct from quantum <*quanto*>, of *largeness, smallness* <*magnitudo, parvitas*>.[33] These involve the determination of the quantum <*quanti*> or of the quantity, according to which one calls something *large* (<*magnum;* G: *gross*>) or *small* (<*parvum;* G: *klein*>).

If one assumes the representation, [that] some things in the universe <*universo*> would become ever smaller and all others in contrast re-mained unaltered, then one imagines a relation in which the smaller remain opposed to the larger, e.g., if our earth, which is called a globe of earth and water <*globum terraquaeum*>, would be so flooded by water that only a magnitude of a pea would remain, then through the comparison the alteration would also be imaginable with respect to magnitude. But if one presupposes that the whole universe has altered, then no comparison is further possible, and thus also no alteration of magnitude is thinkable; the smallest terrestrial globe would be just as large as the largest in regard to our subjective representation, because we could not compare them with a third object.

The concept of magnitude would thus remain in itself the same, therefore this is absolute, but the largeness <*magnitudo*> or smallness <*parvitas*> can never be cognized absolutely, but rather only through *relation*.

Now from that, that we are not in the position to determine the magnitude of things in and for themselves, it follows that we also cannot represent them to ourselves in and for themselves, but rather only as they appear to us. Space and the things which occupy space thus determine themselves merely according to the laws of sensibility, to which they are posited in relation. Space and time are therefore also not thinkable through the understanding and therefore not determinate concepts[i] of the understanding, but rather are merely the subjective form under which things appear to us. They belong not to intuition through sensibility and not to the understanding as concept of the understanding.

29:998

THE CATEGORY OF QUALITY

22. *Quality*,[34] applied also to objects, refers, as does the corresponding logical function of quality, to judgments which contain the condition of the determining quality of a thing. Space and time contain no quality of a thing in itself, i.e., they have no transcendental matter or an object in general in itself; they are only formal conditions of our intuition. A something, on the other hand, such as lies in the concept of being, existence,[j] belongs to the quality of the thing, which therefore presupposes something material. Now quality has as function a threefold object . . . . . . i.e., the representation of a thing . . . . . . involves being[k]

(2) Negation, i.e., the representation of a thing as something that contains a non-being.

(3) Limitation,[35] i.e., the representation of a thing, whose being is affected by its non-being, therefore whose concept contains a being and non-being connected. E.g., light is reality; darkness is negation; shadow is limitation, for it is a darkness which is bounded by light. So also cognition – ignorance – limited knowledge.

It is a positive something, in contrast <*in opposito*> with negation <*negatio*>. *Something or connected.*

(1) Reality of a thing, according to the sense of the word, is the *materiality*[l] of the thing, therefore something positive in itself.

(2) In order to give meaning to the concept of reality, an object of

---

[i] We follow Lehmann in changing *Begriff* (concept) to *Begriffen* (997₃₉–998₁).

[j] *Sein, Dasein, existenz.*

[k] These dots appear to be in the ms (presumably to indicate that the original ms being copied was illegible). We could not verify Lehmann's transcription here. This ms page is in much worse condition than those preceding and succeeding it.

[l] *Sachheit;* this might also be rendered as "thingliness."

sensibility must be put in support of it, so that it can be justified through that, and just as the category of magnitude corresponded to the concept of space and time as a *something in intuition* in order to determine its quantity, so in the representation of quantity, *but only as that which comprehends sensation,* or the real, something sensible in intuition is also necessary, therefore an object of sensation is required in order to represent to one-self the magnitude of the real; not so with quantity, where pure intuition, i.e., without object in space or time, was present. So a thought has, e.g.,   29:999 quantity as intuition in time, but a clear head has reality on account of the subjective sensations of its representations.

(3) The real has a degree of sensation – or in the sensible of sensory representation. Sensation is opposed to the formal in intuition, and the sensible means then the material in the transcendental sense *<in sensu transcendentali>*, therefore the formal intuition in space and time is op-posed here to the real as sensible. Sensation is thus added here to the mere intuition: but an intuition with sensation is perception. But this requires an object of perception. *Perception of an object* is a consciousness of the object through sensation – thus this intuition of the real differs in kind wholly from the *pure.*

One calls this *degree* of sensation *intensive magnitude,* in order to distin-guish it from the extensive magnitude with quantity, and says: everything sensible has intensive magnitude, or = a degree of sensation; that is: it can be represented that from zero = null = which has no sensation at all, the sensation can climb, or again decrease from a certain measure until = o. But it is understood as a magnitude whereby the parts are not cognized previously in order to determine the magnitude, rather they must be cognized as unity, and the parts drawn out from the unity. Thus, e.g., a line, which must be composed, differs from an extinguishing light: with the latter there is only a unity of sensation, but in each following state a different degree of this.

The author calls the *degree of sensation* = the magnitude of the quality;[36] it does express this determination that a something in the thing is thought as posited, but one determines the *degree* better this way: *magnitude of the unity,* i.e., the representation of an object, insofar as I think its magnitude (quantity *<quantitatem>*) as unity, provides the degree of the magnitude. Thus the magnitude is given here not as plurality, but rather as unity and distinguishes itself precisely from extensive magnitude {extensive quantity *<quantitas extensiva>*, and therefore different in consequences from the intensive quantity *<quantitas intensiva>*}.[m] Therefore, e.g., a drop of boil-ing water is indeed *less than* a full kettle, but both are equally hot. The unity, which is perceived here with the sensation of the object, thus shows

---

[m] Marginalia (999$_{35-6}$) alongside text printed at 999$_{36-8}$. We follow Lehmann in inserting it prior to this text. Parentheses added by Lehmann have been removed.

467

29:1000 that it rests on the equality of the ground, and the unity of the ground makes wholly dispensable the multiple homogeneity in consideration of the reality. Thus an angle is equally large, however far the lines or sides may extend: it determines the equality of the inclination, and *only* its difference determines a difference of intensive magnitude, since this reduces merely to the existence of motion in large and small angles. A lively thought that gradually loses its impression has unity however different it is in every step of its waning.

(4) It follows now from this, that the real, since it has its ground in sensation, therefore in the object of the senses, could not have its abode in the merely intellectual, therefore the degree of the real can thus be thought neither as greatest $<maximum>$ nor as smallest $<minimum>$. On the other hand it is certain that the modification of the degree of the intensive magnitude of the real quality must be infinite, even if it can also be unnoticeable. Therefore between the determinate degree A until o = zero there must be found an infinite multitude of qualities of the real, even if in an unnoticeable degree, e.g., knowledge, representations, yes even the consciousness of human beings have many degrees, without one being able to determine the smallest.

(5) One uses the word *reality*[n] in a double sense[37]

(1) adjectivally, and then it means only the form of the object, is therefore applied formally $<formaliter>$, and indeed then it can be used only in the singular $<in\ singulari>$. E.g., representations, concepts have objective reality. Magnitude is here reality and applies to the form of the concept insofar as it has an object;

(2) or substantivally, and then reality refers to the material of the object and is usable only in the plural $<in\ plurali>$, because the reality of the thing in itself is considered.

So the word *unity*[38] is also used differently in the German, Greek, or Latin languages.

Namely adjectivally, e.g., one says: unity of the play, of the lecture, truth of the proposition, of the perfection of the thing. This means the viewpoint that one imputes in regard to the object. Substantivally, on the other hand, or unities of things themselves, i.e., unities quantitatively considered $<unitates\ quantitative\ spectatae>$ are named only in the plural $<in\ plurali>$. So quantity $<quantitas>$ is usable only formally $<formaliter>$ and in the singular $<in\ singulari>$, quanta on the other hand in the plural $<in\ plurali>$, for the latter concern the quality of the object itself, but the former only the form of an object in general.

29:1001 (6) One also calls all realities perfections, i.e., every single perfection in the object itself (therefore this expression also differs from the perfection

---

[n] *Realitaet* is not underlined in the ms, but it is set off on a separate line (1000_{21}).

of things as a species concept in general). Finally reality consists objectively in materiality or something positive – and that which is positive is perfect – and an object *must* have *something* positive, and *can* have many positives or perfections. A merely negative thing <*ens mere negativum*>, i.e., something which would have nothing positive at all, is a direct contradiction, for even the being of the thing already involves something positive, otherwise, if this were also negative, it would be no thing, since here the object is considered only materially. {For formally <*formaliter*> a merely negative thing <*ens mere negativum*> can at least be *thought* without contradiction.}[o] Every thing must thus have reality, and a most real thing <*ens realissimum*>, which one also calls most perfect, highest thing <*ens perfectissimum, summum*>, is that whose determinations <*determinationes*> are all realities, therefore within which nothing is negative.

In the transcendental sense <*in sensu transcendentali*>. Metaphysics [. . .][p]

thus sees that here merely the concept of non-being, therefore an analytic cognition of the thing, underlies it, nevertheless in such a way that the thing still remains thinkable, therefore the principle of contradiction <*principium contradictionis*> is not overthrown; however, real opposites <*realiter opposita*> are contrary opposites <*contrarie opposita*> and must be studied according to the synthetic principles <*principiis*> of ground to consequence, or of the positing [and] not denying ground <*sive rationis ponentis non tollentis*>.

The Wolffian philosophy called negation the formal aspect of things, because reality constitutes the material of the thing.[39] Negation would also constitute nothing more than the formal aspect in the things themselves, whether they arise from a contrary or contradictory opposite <*contrarie . . . contradictorie opposito*>, if one could reduce the opposite realities <*oppositi realitates*> (namely not in the merely logical sense) to a negation. E.g., the Wolffians say sin consists merely in the omission of the *good*, or absence of the good, therefore formally it is the not good, thus they consider it the contrary opposite <*contrarie oppositum*> of the latter as negation. It thus involves the idea of the metaphysical bad <*mali metaphysici*>.[40] [This is] a negation, since with objects of appearance realities <*realia*> and negatives <*negativa*> find themselves mixed, insofar as a being is not the most real being <*quatenus ens non est ens realissimum*>.

---

[o] Marginalia (1001_{11-12}) appearing alongside text printed at 1001_{10-13}. We follow Lehmann in inserting it after the first sentence of this text.

[p] Three ms sheets are apparently missing here. The marginal pagination jumps from 62a to 66b. Lehmann does not note the extent of this break. The text begins again in mid-sentence at the top of the next page.

THE CATEGORY OF THE DYNAMIC CLASS

23. In the logical relation of the category of this class to that of the
29:1002 mathematical class a difference shows up: the categories of relation and
modality carry with them sheer correlates <*correlata*>, which are placed
next to one another such that when one is posited, the other is posited
<*posito uno ponitur est alter*>, e.g., substances are related to accidents
and vice versa <*accidentia et vice versa*> directly <*directe*> to each
other: cause to effect, likewise reciprocal action; with the category of
quantity and quality however the categories were single, subordinated
under one another, and could not be placed next to each other. E.g.,
unity makes no reference to plurality, rather unity lies in plurality, and
together again they constitute totality. Just as little are reality and negation compatible next to each other, just as the modalities are canceled
by each other in their correlates <*correlatis*>: possible – not possible,
actual – not actual, necessary – contingent, contrary opposites <*contrarie*
opposita>.

In their relation to the object, the categories of relation especially
concern the cognition of things themselves, the categories of modality, on
the other hand, concern only the cognition of the concept of the thing [in
relation] to the whole faculty of cognition.

24. Thus especially with the categories of relation realities are considered opposed to one another as relations, i.e., the relations of things with
respect to their existence, because a reality of a thing still always involves
the concept of being, and indeed according to the threefold modes
<*modis*> of existence in the series of logical judgments, namely:

{assertoric	hypothetical	disjunctive
grounds itself on the		
relation of the subject	antecedent <*antecedens*>	relation of the
to the predicate	to the consequent	members of the
		division to the
		divided concept
and yields objective		
substance – accident	cause effect	reciprocal influence
	<*causa causatum*>	<*mutuum influxum*>.}[q]

This way they thus distinguish themselves from the categories of reality
above, where these were compared in diverse ways, but without paying
more regard to the relation.

---

[q] Marginalia (1002₂₃₋₉) alongside text printed at 1002₁₇₋₂₀, and inserted into the text with a
sign. We follow Lehmann in the insertion.

25. The first category is the relation of substance to accident

With respect to substance one calls this relation subsistence <*subsistentia*>, with respect to accident inherence <*inhaerentia*>. Inherence <*inhaerentia*> is a substantivally internal determination <*interna determinatio substantive*>, thus a determination that belongs to <*competirt*>   29:1003
the substance by inhering <*inhaerendo*>, therefore substance is one and the same with that which is inherent to it <*quod ei inhaeret*>. E.g., a human being (substance) thinks, is that which belongs to a human being as if by inhering to his substance <*est id quod homini tamquam substantiae ejus inhaerendo competit*>. The expression dependence which, because there is no better, was used of the effect of a rational cause <*causatis ratione causa*> in the relation of causality, cannot be exchanged with inherence. The latter also depends on substance, but only as necessary inner determination of substance; causality, on the other hand, does not have dependence necessarily in itself. E.g., a thought in human beings is essentially a determination, but the warmth of a stone from sunlight does not inhere in the latter, is also not [in] necessary connection with the stone, but rather exists as something different from the substance. The sound does not inhere substantially <*substantialiter*> in the speaker, also not in the listener, but rather subsists in a manner of its own. So is it likewise with reciprocal action.

There are properly three categories of relation:

1. the relation of inherence to subsistence
2. the relation of causality <*causalitas*> to dependence
3. of community, i.e., that two substances have the determination of cause <*causae*> and effect <*causati*> in themselves at the same time.

Therefore with relation one puts the consideration of a thing in part as subject, and insofar as it cannot be a predicate of another, in part as ground of another thing, [and] in part insofar as it is reciprocally determined by another thing.

The concept of substance requires a prominent discussion, since there lies in this a source of cognition for many metaphysical truths.

Substance is that which can exist without being a predicate of another thing (whatever is able to be, even if it does not exist as the determination of another being <*quod potest esse, etiam si non existit tanquam determinatio alterius*>).

Accident, on the other hand, is that which cannot exist without being a predicate of another thing. Therefore

(1) substance and accident are each something real, since their concept contains a being, and the existence of the thing, be it substance or accident, is necessary for that. Therefore a thing whose concept contains a

non-being (negation) can be neither substance nor accident, just because it lacks reality and existence.

29:1004

E.g.,   Body is real

Motion is real

Rest, on the other hand, is negation,

therefore it cannot be an accident of a body. One therefore calls the existence of substance subsistence, and the existence of its accident <*accidentis*> inherent <*inhaerens*>, i.e., the accident applies to the substance as a positive real predicate in the manner of inhering in it.

SCHOLIUM <*SCHOLION*>

The Scholastics classified the accident or inherent <*accidens sive inhaerens*> into (1) predicables <*praedicabile*>, and understood by that the accident of the essence; therefore [what] was a predicable accident <*accidens praedicabile*> = the contingent. For, essence of a thing is that which belongs necessarily to the concept of a thing: therefore, where the accident was the opposite <*oppositum*>, then it was = apart from the essential <*extraessentiale; G: ausserwesentlichen*>.

(2) Predicaments <*praedicamentale*>, under which they understood accident of the substance, therefore it was something real, positive, inhering in the substance; the two also differ through this, that a predicable accident <*praedicabile accidens*> lies only in the concept and *was there*, but the predicament <*praedicamentale*> exists, and is predicated of a real. E.g., the figure of a place was a predicable accident <*accidens praedicabile*>, it contains no existence, but rather rests only on the mere form or manner of representing the place, while it was wholly indifferent to its matter.

Weight of the body, on the other hand, is predicamental accident <*accidens praedicamentale*>, for it exists by inhering <*inhaerendo*> in the body. Likewise warmth, coldness are also things existing by inhering <*res existentes inhaerendo*> as its accidents, but the body itself exists by subsisting <*subsistendo*> with respect to them.

(2) Substance[41] thought with the omission of all inhering accidents (i.e., their determination) is called the substantial. This remainder is a mere concept that has no determination. It is a something, hence is merely thought or is representable, for the substantial cannot be cognized. Nothing can be cognized if one does not have predicates of the object whereby something is cognized, because all cognitions happen only through judgments. But here only the subject remains without a predicate <*absque praedicato*>, therefore no relation between the two. There thus remains left only a representation of a something, but of which one does not cognize what it is. E.g., if one separates from body

29:1005

all accidents <*accidentia*> like divisibility, impenetrability, extendability, then there remains a figure that is a shape in space, but that does not exist, because a space like that, whatever it is, cannot exist for itself (by subsistence <*subsistendo*>), and since space is thought only as inhering <*inhaerens*> through bodies, there then remains nothing substantial left that exists.

So thinking, willing, feeling of pleasure and displeasure are predicates of the human soul. If these are left away, and the soul is thought without these inhering items <*inhaerentia*>, then something remains left of which one has no concept, a thought without thinking subjects, and this is the substantial. One also calls it the substrate <*substratum*> of all accidents. To cognize objects here is, as said, impossible for the human understanding, and one carries out a needless complaint about its limitedness, by virtue of which the understanding can cognize only through effects, but not the objects in themselves and in their substance. It lies in the quality of the faculty of understanding that we can cognize only through predicates, but these are left aside here, and thus all cognition is impossible without connection of the accidents with the substance.[']

Substantiated phenomena <*phaenomena substantiata*>, an expression of Leibniz's (see author <*ad autorem*>, §193),[42] means nothing more than substance considered as phenomenon, or reality as determination in space and in time. All substances are cognized by us and considered as they can be determined in space and time; we cannot cognize their predicates in themselves, but rather only insofar as they stand in relation with the form of our sensibility. Therefore noumenal substances <*substantiae noumenon*> cannot be cognized, because the concept of the corresponding object is missing in intuition. Therefore, since the substances <*substantialia*> do not exist in themselves, we can cognize the substances not in themselves, but rather only through their inhering accidents; e.g., nothing can be cognized of the subject through the representation of an I without attributing a predicate to it. It serves only as an indication of the representation of a being, which makes itself into an object. Through observation of myself I cognize myself[*] only when I direct my attention to inner sense, which just like outer sense can make itself representable as phenomenon. If one therefore cognizes substances

---

['] The text breaks off here (1005_{19}; cf. Arnoldt, p. 116). Text from the extant ms ends in the middle of the third sentence of this paragraph (after *wie gesagt*), but a copy of the entire paragraph was preserved by Emil Arnoldt (*Gesammelte Schriften*, vol 5, p. 116). The remainder of the Ontology section, and the Cosmology section that follows, was assembled by Lehmann from fragments copied out of the ms by Arnoldt. (The extant ms picks up again in the middle of the section on Empirical Psychology. (See farther on.)

[*] An *erkenne ich mich* (between *selbst* and *nur*) omitted by Lehmann without note has been replaced (1005_{34}). Cf. Arnoldt, p. 117.

according to their determinations in space and in time, and takes these
29:1006 determinations for the matter itself, then with this illusion one mixes up the concept of substances with that of[t] substantiated phenomena <*phaenomenis substantiatis*>.[u]

[t] We follow Lehmann in changing a colon (in Arnoldt) to *der* (of the) (1006₁). Lehmann does not note this change.
[u] The text breaks off here (1006₂; cf. Arnoldt, p. 117).

[Cosmology][v]

[Since the world][L,w] is an aggregate of many substances connected with each other, i.e., a real whole, as soon as one considers it in relation to the senses in space and time, then there can be only one world of the worlds, as phenomenal world <*mundus phaenomenon*>, because of the unity of the unbounded space. [. . .][x] In its form the world is thus a substantial whole which is not a part of another <*totum substantiale quod non est pars alterius*> [. . .][y]

another world than the present cannot in actuality <*actu*> be assumed possible. [. . .][z] Now if one thinks the world as noumenon, then it is nothing further than an absolute whole of substances; but one is also not in the position *a priori* to determine further what it might have as properties or determinations. But if one thinks the world as phenomenon, therefore the things in space and time as their real relations, in which[a] they must stand opposed to each other, then the following four principles can be established, under which the determinations of the world must be thought: [in the world there is no (1) abyss, (2) leap, (3) chance (blind accident), fate (blind necessity) <*in mundo non datur* (1) *abyssus*, (2) *saltus*, (3) *casus* (. . .), *fatum* (. . .)>.][b]
This was also the opinion of Wolff and Leibniz. One easily sees that this idea, thought through the mere understanding, can hold as correct in itself, and to this extent can be thought: a substantial composite is made up of simple things <*compositum substantiale consistit ex simplicibus*>. But here as phenomenon there is an extended substance, a perdurable in

---

[v] The following few pages of fragments come from the otherwise lost section on cosmology, and were preserved by Arnoldt.
[w] This addition is from Arnoldt's introduction to the passage (cf. Arnoldt, p. 121). Lehmann treats it as though it were part of the ms text (1006₃).
[x] Arnoldt omits text here (1006₇; cf. Arnoldt, p. 121).
[y] The text breaks off here (1006₈; cf. Arnoldt, p. 121).
[z] Arnoldt omits text here (1006₁₀; cf. Arnoldt, p. 122).
[a] We do not follow Lehmann's changing *worin* (in Arnoldt) to *wozu* (to which). Lehmann does not note the change (1006₁₅). There is also a break in the quotation of the text (in Arnoldt) at this point.
[b] This is part of Arnoldt's summary, although Lehmann treats it as part of the ms text (1006₁₇₋₁₉; cf. Arnoldt, p. 122).

space that cannot be thought without parts and without division into infinity. But the monads can constitute in space no parts of a body, but rather must be mere points, for otherwise they would be parts of a space. [. . .]*c*

The substances in the world must have a reciprocal influence on each other, i.e., stand in real connection <*in nexu reali*>, which can take place only through a reciprocal action on each other. This real connection through interaction <*nexus realis per commercium*>43 would not be possible to assume among the things if one thinks them through the understanding as existing in themselves. The substances would exist each for themselves without any relation and connection among one another. Therefore a real whole <*totum reale*> of necessary substances cannot be thought at all. For then none is dependent on another with respect to its being, each exists for itself because each has its necessary adequate ground of its existence in itself: many necessary substances would thus have no connection among themselves, each can be only a world for itself and the basic cause of a world, but it could not stand in the slightest connection with another world and the things in it, e.g., many gods. All such substances would thus be unconditioned and determined by themselves, but each isolated by its absolute necessity. Since accordingly their connection among themselves cannot be assumed directly, and without hindering their necessity, then one can do nothing else, in order to think this, than to derive their existence from a general communal primordial source, which is the general power for the general effecting of all things. But through this the latter become dependent on it, and contingent in themselves, they are connected with each other by this general cause, and therefore there arises a reciprocal connection and community with each other through the communal cause, since an action of a united being was necessary in order to produce them all, and in this manner the real connection <*nexus realis*> arises.

29:1007

Newton called *space* the instrument <*organon*> of the divine omnipresence.44 But this idea is incorrect since space is nothing in itself, and cannot be thought as something in itself actually existent through the connection of things. On the contrary, if one thinks of space as symbol <*symbolum*>, i.e., in the place of all relations and reciprocal action itself, then one thinks under this the summation of all phenomena, and indeed as co-presences <*compraesentia*>, i.e., as present to one another, and reciprocally acting on each other, and the being which contains them, as symbol. [. . .]*d*

Physical influence <*influxus physicus*>45 is (a) original <*originarius*>, i.e., by their existence substances are already assumed to be in interaction

---

c The text breaks off here (1006₂₈; Arnoldt, p. 124).
d The text breaks off here (1007₃₀; Arnoldt, p. 126).

<in commercio> without a ground, (b) derivative (of reason) *<derivativus (rationalis)>*. All physical influence *<influxus physicus>* presupposes a derivative *<derivativum>* [influence], for this is the only true one. – It is not immediately understandable in itself that substances are in interaction *<in commercio>*, for substances are precisely things that exist alone for themselves, without depending on another. With the phenomenal world *<mundo phaenomeno>* (which is in space and time) it is just space which connects the substances, through which they are in interaction *<in commercio>*. But how are the substances in interaction in the noumenal world *<in mundo noumeno in commercio>*? – The harmony of the sub-   29:1008
stances is to consist in this, that their state agrees with each other, i.e., according to general laws. The world is considered either as an ideal whole *<totum ideale>*, and then a harmony without interaction *<harmonia absque commercio>* is here; or the world is real whole *<totum reale>* and a harmony of substances in interaction *<harmonia substantiarum in commercio>* is here. This latter system is called the system of physical influence *<systema influxus physici>*. But the system of the harmony of substances without interaction *<systema harmoniae substantiarum absque commercio>* is the system of hyperphysical influence *<systema influxus hyperphysici>*, i.e., the world arises from an extramundane cause *<causa extramundana>*, i.e., from God.

Now this latter can be: (1) system of assisting *<systema adsistentiae>* – (2) system of pre-established harmony *<systema harmoniae praestabilitae>*. Leibniz wanted to explain through this not the interaction *<commercium>* of substances, but rather only the interaction *<commercium>* between soul and body, because this is a pair of such heterogeneous substances. But cause and effect can be really *<realiter>* distinct; thus I can suppose that something depends on something else entirely heterogeneous, e.g., motion of the body on the representation of the soul, as effect on cause. But this cannot be further explained, rather we assume such propositions because experience is possible through them. The system of physical influence *<systema influxus physici>* has again a twofold manner of representation for thinking this to be possible: (1) original interaction *<commercii originarii>*, when substances are in interaction *<in commercio>* through this, that they exist; (2) derivative *<derivativi>*, when something else must still be added in order to bring about this interaction *<commercium>*. An original interaction *<commercium originarium>* is a hidden quality *<qualitas occulta>*; it is assumed as its own ground of explanation. Thus nothing remains but the system of physical influence *<systema influxus physici>* and indeed in derivative interaction *<in commercio derivativo>*, where I assume that all substances exist through a causality through which they are all in interaction *<in commercio>*. This idea has something sublime. If I assume all substances as absolutely necessary, then they cannot stand in the slightest community. But if I assume the substances as existing in community, then I assume that they all exist through a causality, for only through that can their community be explained. – Space itself is the form of the divine omnipresence, i.e., the omnipresence of God is expressed in the form of a phenomenon, and through this omnipresence of God all substances are in harmony. But here our reason can comprehend nothing more. –

29:1009 Those who assume space as a matter in itself or as a constitution of things in themselves, are required to be Spinozists, i.e., they assume the world to be a summation of the determinations of a united necessary substance, thus only one substance. Space as something necessary would then also be a property of God, and all things exist in space, thus in God.

[Psychology]

[EMPIRICAL PSYCHOLOGY]

... it displeases.^{e} If the *ground of pleasure* or displeasure is to be found merely in *sensation through sense,* or *sense*-sensation^f (not sensible, because to that the here unsuitable power of imagination also belongs), then it is not the object that pleases, but rather there is a state that pleases me by virtue of the sensation excited in me through sense. This merely <*mere*> subjectively referred constitution of the influence of the object, which expresses the state of the subject excited through inner or outer sense is, however, that of which one must say: it gratifies, it hurts.

Therefore gratification and pain come about merely through the immediate sense-sensation of the subject: what is *characteristic of it lies in the interest in the existence of the object,* or its non-existence; and *gratification* is therefore the satisfaction and interest in the existence of the matter. What gratifies us is also agreeable to us, and we take an interest in that existence each and every time because this [interest] and the gratification with it take place only to the degree that and as long as the existence of the object pleases us, or (properly) is agreeable; because it depends on maintaining us longer in the subjective state in which we are placed. It is likewise in the contrary case <*in casu contrario*> with pain. But there is also a state of pleasure {and non-pleasure}^{g} that depends not on the immediate influence of the sense-sensation, but rather *on the reflection about the object* and arises out of that. Gratification, or pain, or an interest in the existence of the object and maintenance of our subjective state is not present here: rather indifference with regard to the existence of the object is present, it is indifferent whether the state of my sensation should be gratification or

^{e} This selection from the section on Empirical Psychology begins in mid-sentence (1009$_5$) at the top of a right-hand page (in the middle of 161a of the original ms). The preceding ms page (which is part of the Ontology section) has 70a as marginal pagination; thus approximately 90 sheets of the ms are missing here (this includes the end of the Ontology section, the entire Cosmology section, and the first part of the section on Empirical Psychology).
^{f} *Sinnen = Empfindung* (1009$_6$). As below (1009$_{15}$: *Sinnen Empfindung*), Kant is contrasting mere sense sensation and sensible (*sinnliche*) experience, the latter requiring a higher element, e.g., imagination.
^{g} Marginalia (1009$_{25}$) alongside text printed here, and inserted with a sign. We follow Lehmann in the insertion.

pain, from that side *no* particularly decisive influence is indicated. Out of this arises what is called *pleasure,* i.e., that satisfaction in the object through the mere intuition of it, with complete indifference (without regard) to its existence. – It can be based on pure or sensible intuition. E.g., a beautifully built house pleases me with its form: it is possible that its existence pains me on some wholly other grounds, which the understanding presents, and which can concur accidentally with the gratification and pain.

29:1010

That which pleases through mere intuition is *beautiful,* that which leaves me indifferent in intuition, although it can please or displease, is *not-beautiful;* that which displeases me in intuition is ugly. Now on this pleasure rests the *concept of taste.* That is, much can please in representation through the senses, with which the understanding can connect in its operation, and gratification arises; but insofar as the *power of judgment* connects itself with the feeling of pleasure or displeasure, and it accompanies and determines the former in the intuition of an object of the senses, or even its impression of it, there arises thus taste, which then resting on the aesthetic power of judgment determines aesthetic (from perception of the senses <*aistho*>,^h to taste through the sense-organs <*per organa sensum*>, sense as source of sensible representations) representation according to the laws of sensibility. *Aesthetic power of judgment* is therefore that power of judgment which is aimed at satisfaction or dissatisfaction in objects, insofar as these are objects of my sensible intuition, just as the logical power of judgment judges the object not as such in intuition but rather through reason alone.

All objects of sense-intuition or of the power of imagination are also objects of the aesthetic power of judgment – and this is entirely the same with the concept of taste. It is thus occupied with the satisfaction in the beautiful, which it is to determine whether it is beautiful or not, and therefore whether it should build its operation on a principle of the beautiful.

Now were the matter of the object, i.e., that which affects the mind through its immediate sensation, the object of judgment, then gratification and pain would be the same to it. These sensations of the senses, however, which here would be aesthetic sensations, do not allow themselves to be determined and judged according to rules since they are merely subjective. Satisfaction or dissatisfaction in an object therefore, whereby the aesthetic power of judgment considers the feeling of pleasure or displeasure, concerns *merely the form of the object,* which is subject to sensible or pure intuition, and of which it determines only whether it is beautiful or not beautiful.

29:1011

A peculiar phenomenon manifests itself in judging of the beautiful. One demands and presupposes that what we find beautiful as an object of

---

^h This is written with Greek letters in Lehmann (1010₁₅).

taste, everyone else who has taste will, like us, also find beautiful; and it is just as peculiar that a judging person absolutely cannot determine whether something is beautiful otherwise than through his own judgment; else he would want to imitate another's judgment without himself judging, from which one can then also easily assume that that which does not obtain approval according to the judgment of all other similarly cultivated persons, may in the end also not be beautiful: and there arises therefore a peculiar antinomy, which at this time cannot be developed very distinctly with respect to its ground. One assumes that the other must find something beautiful, at the same time one fears his dissatisfaction, because one has no grounds to force his approval.

For, what is supposed to please the other absolutely must be able to be cognized *a priori* by him, thus there must be a rule present which is prescribed to him, by virtue of which he is determined to approval or dissatisfaction: therefore only when a principle of the beautiful exists can the necessity and universal validity of the beautiful be demonstrated. But now a demonstration of the beautiful is impossible; it is only abstracted from the sensible according to laws of the understanding, without one being able to declare universally valid these laws which are found thereby, precisely on account of the subjective in the feeling. – Even the Greeks had models, e.g., their Doriphoron of Polycleitus, which in sculpture they called the rule of a beautifully built young human being. Therefore the judgment of the beautiful, likewise the ground and the source of taste in general, which the soul takes as a basis so much, remains an object of the most difficult investigation.

Beautiful[46] in aesthetic judging is only that which pleases without any interest in the existence of the object itself, merely in the intuition of it, and indeed in the form of it, and pleases because here a free play of the power of imagination is effected in agreement with the lawfulness of the understanding.

From this it thus follows:

(a) that everything that is to be beautiful must at least have a similarity with concepts, or with the laws of the understanding. Nevertheless, it is in no way necessary to be conscious of the rules or of these laws of taste, rather their existence in the subject is required only to the extent that it can serve for the support and guidance of the power of imagination: therefore these concepts of the understanding may also not be present in its determination;

29:1012

(b) that the power of imagination concern itself only with the form of the object and not with its bodily existence, so that it is not pulled back by the deficiencies of these limits, but rather is to maintain within itself an unconstrained flight for developing the form; but in such a way that it does not follow its laws alone and become extravagant over the immeasurableness of the object, but rather merely provides for understanding a whole from the manifold of the object.

(c) The understanding again refers it back to order each time, holds it in limits, according to which then

(d) both powers reciprocally support each other, carry out a free play, and thus concern themselves with satisfaction. An object of this kind is found tasteful.

From that which gratifies and pleases is yet distinguished that which is approved. This is the good, i.e., what pleases in the representation of reason.*ⁱ*

Note. One can compare the threefold kinds of faculties of the soul with the three operations of the understanding, according to which the cognitive faculty displays concepts in which pleasure and displeasure is subsumed under concepts through the power of judgment, and the faculty of desire is determined through reason, thereby concluding to what extent pleasure or displeasure takes place in the representation.

§68 Faculty of desire

All representations refer to the object as object of cognition, but they can also be considered as actions, and then the ground of producing the object lies in the representation of it. With this corresponds then *the faculty of the soul for becoming cause of the actuality of the object through the representation of an object itself,* = and this is the *faculty of desire,* which one can just as validly also

29:1013   determine as *causality of the representation with respect to its object.* That action of the soul in general, through which the representation seeks to attain the actuality of its object, is in general desire or desiring,ʲ which is sensible or intellectual. One expresses *the feeling of pleasure and displeasure* <G: *Lust und Unlust*> by pleasure and displeasure <*voluptas et taedium*>. Both are however merely sensible: according to Mr. Kant it can be determined more generally by

> satisfaction and dissatisfaction <*complacentia et displicentia;* G: *Wohlgefallen und Missfallen*>

and on this ground the concept of *desiring* can be grounded, namely as

> satisfaction with respect to the actuality of the object <*complacentia respective actualitatis objecti*>, i.e., the representation of the object, which is connected with satisfaction in its actuality, and which is the ground of producing it.

Satisfaction in the intuition of the object is thus distinguished from the desiring for it in this, that the latter concerns that relation of the representation to the object insofar as it can be cause of its actuality.

A doubt would seem to militate against this concept in that one quite

---

ⁱ A blank line added by Lehmann has been removed (1012₂₀₋₂₁).
ʲ *die Begierde und Begehren* (1013₃₋₄). Kant shifts between the two expressions here, but the general "faculty of desire" here is called the *Begehrungs-Vermögen.*

often desires something whose actuality is impossible to produce. There are namely two kinds of desire: *a practical desire* <*appetitio practica*>, i.e., the representation of the possibility of making it actual, therefore a desire according to which the representation is qualified so that the object can become actual, *and a less practical desire* <*appetitio minus practica*>, which one calls *wish* <*optare; G: Wunsch*>, a desire connected with the consciousness that it does not stand in our control to be able actually to produce the object. Nevertheless, the two kinds of desires still agree in that they aim at a representation of the object, by virtue of which they posit in themselves the ground of the possibility for producing the object, only with the difference that in the first case the ground of determination is sufficient, but in the latter case the causality is insufficient. This latter is called *wishing* <*conatum; G: Wünschen*> with respect to the desire, which then degenerates into *yearning* when the wishing turns into a violent mental motion, until exhaustion, in order to make actual often wholly unnatural or physically impossible representations, to which belong, e.g., this: oh if only Jupiter would return past years to me <*o mihi prateritos referat si Jupiter annos*>. The cause of this property of human nature lies in this, that one often harbors and attempts to realize wishes whose possible causality one cognizes as insufficient in oneself. But if, instead of risking attempts, a human being wanted first to test whether his powers sufficed with certainty to attain his end, then he would abstain from much, and attempt to save himself the trouble. But there lies in him the challenge of his nature to apply his exertions so that he tests his powers; he is at peace with the possibility of being able to attain his end, although now he feels insufficient before himself, and it is fully uncertain whether he can succeed; and with great exertion a human being often develops powers that were previously unknown to him, but now convince him even more of the possibility; he no longer has cause to place mistrust in himself, and he will have adequate powers to attain his end.[k] Of course, if the wishes are unnatural, then there comes about that useless sinking back that is expressed in females by weakness in weeping, and in the male sex by mere futile attempts. Now the desire with respect to such objects of which we are conscious of having adequate powers for producing, is an *act* <*actus*> *of the power of choice, and the faculty that corresponds to this desire is the power of choice* <*arbitrium; G: Willkür*>, which thus involves not only determination to causality, but rather also sufficient power to make the object actual: but where the faculty of choice with respect to the production of the object is, there must also always be in accompaniment the faculty for abandoning the production, or omitting it. Power of choice <*arbitrium; G: Willkür*> is therefore in the proper sense a faculty of

29:1014

---

[k] We do not follow Lehmann in changing a period to a comma (1014_{15}). Lehmann does not note the change.

desiring or shunning an object, i.e., by omitting or committing <*facultas appetendi vel aversandi objectum, i.e., omittendo vel committendo*>.

The power of choice <*arbitrium*> has in it a double side in regard to the ground of determination. There lie in human beings, namely, incentives of the soul <*elateres animi*> or grounds of determination, sources of the possibility for producing the represented, determining or impelling causes <*causae determinantes sive impulsivae*>, and these *lie either in the understanding as in the law of action, or in the sensibility, namely, in the feeling of pleasure and displeasure,* and are therefore either sensitive causes and incentives or intellectual causes and incentives <*vel sensitivae causae sive elateres vel intellectuales causae sive elateres*> – the former are called stimuli <*stimuli*>, the latter motives <*motiva*>. Thus arises the division of the concept into *the higher or rational power of choice* <*arbitrium intellectuale sive superius;* G: *obere oder vernünftige Willkür*>, i.e., the faculty of desiring through motives <*facultas appetendi per motiva*>, or will or the power of choosing from an impelling intellectual cause <*voluntas sive arbitrium ex causa impulsiva intellectuali*>, and sensitive power of choice, the faculty of desiring through stimuli <*arbitrium sensitivum, facultas appetendi per stimulos*>.

The rational power of choice is again either pure or affected <*vel purum vel affectum*>, according to whether no stimuli <*stimuli*> at all concur as coeffecting causes with the power of choice, or sensible impulses of this kind affect the mind at the same time and determine it to action.

But in appearance, it can never be assumed that human choice is determined without being affected by stimuli <*stimulis*>, *and just as little that it can be determined by stimuli* <*per stimulos*> *alone.*

Animals have a merely sensitive power of choice <*arbitrium mere sensitivum*>, e.g., in choosing food – thus they are determined by stimuli <*per stimulos*> alone, therefore one can call a sensitive power of choice <*arbitrium sensitivum*> also *brute* <*brutum*>: *human power of choice* <*arbitrium humanum*>, on the other hand, is never pure <*purum*>, *but rather always affected* <*semper affectum*>. But the coeffecting stimuli <*stimuli*> can never determine it, but rather merely affect it sensibly, and in order to determine it there remains necessary the concurrence of the understanding: but one can never say that stimuli <*stimuli*> should not have affected it, e.g., with the giving of alms stimuli <*stimuli*> would already be there[47] if he gives the alms away for the sake of the comfort that he draws from it, or from love of honor not to be harshly reprimanded in the eyes of his neighbors, or from compassion toward the tattered needy one, or toward his pleas touching the weakness of the giver, or also for an expected reward from God: the stimuli <*stimuli*> are often so hidden that one must examine oneself closely, whether merely the love of following the law brings me to the action, and I thus act from pure power of choice <*arbitrio puro*>: but it is likewise just as true that it is never stimuli <*stimuli*> alone that determine me to the action: a representation, even if unclear, of the law of duty is always concurring alongside, and one must on that account already assume this, because otherwise one would make a human being equal to cattle or the devil, if one could presuppose he can be doing everything from self-interest etc.; otherwise it is quite possible that stimuli <*stimuli*> can stimulate one to good as well as to evil.

Now the *concept of freedom* rests on this: *namely the faculty of a human being for determining oneself to action through motives, independently of the sensible impulses affecting him,* therefore the power of choice is free only insofar as it is not determined by stimuli <*per stimulos*>: which in the human power of choice is accomplished by the overcoming of the stimuli <*stimulorum*>. Therefore the free power of choice, or freedom, is the *independence of the power of choice from determination through stimuli* <*a determinatione per stimulos*>. – So stimuli <*stimuli*> will and must not be excluded from the human power of choice, for otherwise it would be a pure power of choice <*arbitrium purum*>, a pure self-dependent being, which can determine itself only according to the laws, not against them. A human being has lower faculties <*facultates inferiores*> that work for him as sensible impulses, and in any event become impelling causes <*causae impulsivae*>, but only affect him, [and] can never determine him, neither to good nor to evil: his power of choice is thus in part sensual, in part intellectual <*partim sensualis, partim intellectualis*>, where the effecting stimuli <*stimuli*> are indeed to be viewed also as a ground for action, but only as an insufficient ground, the motives, on the other hand, contain that ground of determination which makes the action necessary.

29:1016

§69. *All objectively necessary rules and determinations of the power of choice, insofar as they are subjectively contingent, are called imperatives.*

(a) They are *objective* in general, because they express what must be done.

(b) Every imperative is *objectively necessary*, i.e., it contains *a ground of determination* with respect to the action *that makes the action necessary according to a rule;* but at the same time

(c) every imperative is *subjectively contingent*, i.e., it is connected in its determination with the *possibility for the subject to deviate from the rule and to do the opposite.* Therefore with a being that acts according to imperatives arranged according to both conditions of the imperative, there arises *the necessitation of action:* for it is subjected to commands which are such that an objectively necessary rule, as well as a possibility for the subject to deviate from the rule, is present; and therefore an imperative is for him an *objective rule insofar as it is necessitating with respect to the subject,* and with him both conditions are connected, if he is to act according to imperatives. Such a being is also the only one of which an ought can be predicated, i.e., a necessity for acting according to a rule whose transgression remains subjectively possible. Therefore neither a god nor an animal can act

29:1017

according to imperatives. God is not capable of a deviation from the law, he determines himself only by the law, i.e., by himself, with him there takes place no necessitation, no ought. He thus also has no duties, since these actions[l] rest on an ought or a necessitation. He has only rights against human beings, just as these can have only duties toward him, but never rights. Animals, on the other hand, do not act according to rules because due to a lack of understanding they do not know them, but rather have only sensible impulses; therefore they also cannot observe imperatives and determine themselves thereby to an action, i.e., allow themselves to be necessitated.

Imperatives thus have actions as an end, and hence are called practical imperatives, i.e., practical rules that indicate what should be done. – The opposite <*oppositum*> are physical rules according to which something is supposed to happen, but *practical imperatives* can be either

    technical practical imperatives

i.e., they can offer *hypothetically* the means for attaining an end, they are therefore rules that demand conditioned observance. That is where all *mechanical rules* belong for an art or skill through which one observes the rules in order to attain an end. – [Or] *rules of cleverness* with respect to the action of other human beings to one's end, the latter however are called *pragmatic. In both cases it still depends primarily on the will of the agent, whether he wants the end.* If he has no interest for it, then no one can force him to observe the rule; thus they both command only conditionally, for the sake of the end; or as

    moral practical imperatives.

{Note. One could also quite easily assume a disjunctive imperative which would consist in this, that the choice of the subject with respect to several disjunctively commanded determinations would indeed be permitted, but the transgression and contravention of every condition of the law be disallowed, e.g., in a civil war remaining neutral would be disallowed, rather one would have to attack one or the other party.}[m]48

29:1018   Moral practical rules are by their nature *categorical* because they command *absolutely* immediately through reason and without any regard to the existence of other determining or motive grounds: they are unconditioned and immediate determining grounds of actions; every other assumed motive ground other than that which reason gives to itself would be only a hypothetical condition and command. E.g., if a witness wanted to speak the truth only because he fears earthly or divine punishment, because his friend has an advantage in it, then this and other grounds could be easily

---

[l] We follow Lehmann in replacing *handeln, wenn die Ursache des handelns* (= act, if the cause of the acting) with *Handlungen* (actions)(1017₇).

[m] Marginalia (1017₃₂₋₈) alongside text printed at 1017₃₀–1018₇. We follow Lehmann in inserting it after the first sentence of this text.

eluded, and the duty to truth would no longer occur at all if it depended only on conditioned circumstances, since the opposite is just as easily possible. Reason alone is the lawgiver, and its law should also be observed by the subject. If the subject should do this in spite of its preference for sensible impulses, then it must be capable *of being able to do this, it must be possible for it to carry out what reason commands.* The categorical imperative thus presupposes with human beings a subjective possibility for observing the law as well as transgressing it, or, what is the same thing, an independence from determination by stimuli <*a determinationibus per stimulos*>, therefore freedom; a human being must thus be free if he is supposed to observe absolute commands, simply and only because reason commands them.

{Theoretical deduction of freedom}[n]

For were this not the case, then all actions of human beings would have to be determined merely by laws of nature, or by natural necessity, and therefore all imputability would fall away. For freedom is contradistinguished to natural necessity. Actions that happen according to laws of freedom must be exercised so that they are not determined by the previous state of the world, actions according to natural necessity,[o] on the contrary <*in contrario*> cannot be considered otherwise than that they are previously determined in the series of effects and causes[p] as necessary. But if they are this, then they are also determined in the previous (past) time, and [for] actions considered as determined in a previous time, omitting the action also does not stand under my control. Thus the opposite cannot happen, because they are determined according to unalterable laws of causality in the previous time, and thus appear as mere effects of which the cause is present in the previous time, therefore they are not in my control because   29:1019
in general previous time is not in my control.

Thus a power of choice <*arbitrium*> that would be determined by natural laws as predetermining causes would be a *servile power of choice* <*arbitrium servum*>, and the opposite of the predetermined effect could not possibly be done by it. But this is contrary to the nature of a command of reason, which permits and presupposes possibility of fulfillment, not necessity, therefore also possibility for the opposite. The determination of the observance thus lies in the free power of choice of the subject. Free power of choice is therefore accompanied by a will that does not draw its determining, and indeed adequate, grounds (intellectual) from states and conditions of the previous time but, rather, performs the action by self-determination (spontaneity) and without being necessitated by any cause of the previous time.

---

[n] Marginalia (printed at Ak. 29: 1183) alongside the top of the following paragraph (1018$_{23}$).
[o] *Natur* = *Notwendigkeit* (1018$_{30}$).
[p] We follow Lehmann in changing *Ursache* to *Ursachen* (1018$_{32}$).

It becomes clear from this that that system or principle which previously was called determinism, must properly be called *predeterminism.* For since it is absolutely necessary that every action must be determined by a ground, even that which a divinity performs, then determinism does not express what is of concern here, namely the principle according to which every action, even of a free being, is thought of as determined by its determining grounds in the previous time, and thus as not given in the control of the agent. According to Mr. Kant, one should call this predeterminism.

But now the striking phenomenon with a human being is that freedom united with natural necessity is found in him. Both occur in him, so that one can say that with a human being everything happens according to laws of natural necessity, and also everything happens according to the principle of freedom.

As a natural being (phenomenon), every new action can be explained as determined according to laws of natural necessity. One also does this often in criminal cases. E.g., with the criminal one takes into consideration his education, external circumstances, inclinations or other motive grounds that are merely subjective, in order to derive from this the determination to the crime. As intelligence (rational being) that nevertheless must not be thought of as determined purely by reason itself (or as noumenon),*q* a human being is self-determining, independent of all laws of nature, takes from himself the ground for omitting the action that he can do, or should, which he would not be capable of [if] determined according to natural laws. We are thus forced to assume, in his *selfhood,* an agreement of two, apparently wholly contradictory beings present in him by virtue of which he is namely a person who is affected by lower powers but determines himself by the independence of reason, and so he appears as ordered under reason and nature not successively, but rather at the same time. In consideration of his actions one can therefore also designate *freedom* (nominal definition):

29:1020

the imputability of human beings.

Considered merely as intelligence, a human being is an imputable subject in which, of course, at the same time is united a natural being that subjects it to natural laws; [a being] nevertheless, whose determination depends upon intelligence, insofar as the possibility to act is granted him; therefore it is only to be derived how far a human being can be called cause of his actions and these can be imputed to him; and [it is] just as certain that, if he were led merely by natural laws, it would be impossible to impute to him any action, since the ground of action then would never lie in his control, but rather would be determined in the previous time.

A human being thus has as noumenon the faculty to determine himself

---

q We are replacing a period with a comma here (1019₃₈).

to action notwithstanding his natural necessity. From this it follows that *freedom is thinkable without contradiction of concept, and thus logically possible.*

But we can cognize things not in themselves, what and how they are in themselves, but rather only in appearance, therefore we also know a human being only as he is exhibited to us in the form of sensibility as phenomenon, therefore his actions, but not his determining grounds: *it is thus impossible to prove the real possibility of the absolute self-determination of a human being, or how a human being freely determines himself and nevertheless at the same time is subjected to natural laws,* for that would necessarily require that freedom would be an object of possible intuition. Freedom is so far from being this that all actions of a human being appear rather as determined according to the law of causality or according to their ground in the previous time, thus that a human being does not have in his control how he should act, thus that he must be subjected to natural necessity. But precisely because of this, because a human being exhibits himself in the manner of the form of sensibility, a possible inference to the supersensible can be made, as something present that could be counted on with the determining grounds of his actions. A supersensible source can perhaps be sought for in him where he no longer appears as object of the senses, although indeed we are not able to determine *a priori* how he is there. This source would be the power of choice of the human being as noumenon, i.e., the independent, but to us unknown, ground of all appearances of the sensible human being. To that extent one can presuppose him as his very own independent ground of all his actions, and assume with him that he now begins a series of actions by the ground of determination present in him, and thus consider him as if he were not in time: in this respect one could determine *freedom as the faculty of a human being for beginning from himself a series of consequences.* 29:1021

One says in this regard quite correctly of him that his actions are subjected to determinism for, since he cannot act without the action being determined by some ground, there is here only the presupposition that he determines himself to action, but not [that] the action is predetermined by a previous determining time, i.e., by the law of causality. This confusion of concepts made it that the concept of freedom became the true cross of philosophers <*vera crux philosophorum*>.[49] How is one supposed to reconcile that a human being is subject to the law of natural necessity and to that extent is already predetermined to his actions as effects by a previous determining time as cause, and that notwithstanding this the human being is supposedly able to act freely? Of course, as a natural being he stands only under predeterminism <*praedeterminismo*>, and thus should the power of choice of the human being be able to be assumed as determined merely in the previous time then no freedom at all would be possible: but if one is allowed to presuppose a noumenon in the human being, if one is therefore allowed to assume that the actions flow from independent determinations of the powers of this being in him; then the concept of freedom is possible and thinkable without contradiction. The reality of this is of course impossible to prove since it is a pure *a priori* concept of reason which cannot be grounded by the moral actions that are exercised in virtue of the determination of reason, and that are the only thing through which it reveals itself in appearance. Suppose, e.g., a witness represents to himself with the rendering of his testimony the importance of his duty for speaking the truth, and for arranging his actions lawfully, in accord with it, without any other accompanying motive grounds, and he acted without concurrence of any natural cause; yet this would prove nothing more in him than the existence of the consciousness of the moral law that commands him to observe the law, passing over all natural causes. From this example it immediately follows that there is present in us a consciousness of a moral law by which we are required to act because it absolutely commands us, and by virtue of the existence of this law we can infer the freedom of our actions, that we are duty-bound or required to act according to the law with every sensible sacrifice. Wholly incorrect, however, is the idea of some *philosophers* {e.g., Rehberg}ʳ⁵⁰ here, as if one could directly and immediately be conscious of absolute spontaneity or of the effectiveness of the law of freedom in our actions, i.e., we can cognize that the law alone would determine us, and no prior determining ground in that sense would be connected with it. But this is impossible, we can indeed be aware that sensible impulses concur with the determination to act dutifully, but from that, that we are not conscious of their existence in a special case <*in casu speciali*>, we can in no way infer that they were also not at all present in us and did not show themselves effective, for how is one supposed to be aware of their nonexistence? This is in itself immediately impossible; that it provides no sign and that it does not take place mediately is clarified by this: insofar as sensible affecting concurs, action from duty rests on necessitation, no free power of choice is thinkable without necessitation; now how can one cognize whether the determination to an action has its ground in the sensible impulses or in spontaneity alone, or in both? E.g., one leaves someone the choice between two {things}ˢ that are in themselves wholly equal. It is false to assure that he can choose in no other way than by a free self-determination of his own reason without concurrence of any natural causes: one can assume that previously he certainly inspects both {things}ᵗ often and frequently, be it from mistrust, or because he expects an advantage with one, finally after fruitless bother, impatience overcomes him and he grabs one: is the latter

29:1022

29:1023

ʳ Marginalia (1022₁₈) alongside the text printed at 1022₁₇₋₁₈. We follow Lehmann in the insertion, but have removed parentheses added by him.

ˢ Marginalia (1022₃₅) with a question mark and an insertion sign. We follow Lehmann in the insertion.

ᵗ Marginalia (1022₃₉) with a question mark and insertion sign. We follow Lehmann in the insertion.

not a determining ground that influences his reason, so that this finally decides for that which it demands of him? So it is undecided whether the witness was determined to the deposition of the truth more from a feeling of his moral conscience or from rules of cleverness. Thus one cannot become aware of freedom, and that this offers the determining grounds of our moral actions, but rather must infer to the existence of that only from the consciousness of the laws of reason. From this it follows that we cognize the laws of morality indeed *a priori,* but as dogmatic, practical laws, to be distinguished from the dogmatic, theoretical *a priori* propositions that we can have only of objects of possible experience. *Now these moral laws are also something that properly belongs to a human being as noumenon, and constitutes the character of the latter; as which it exhibits itself in a human being as the subjective principle of lawgiving.* This, to us unknown, essence in us is the most sublime thought, which is quite fruitful in consequences for our moral existence. One finds thereby that all these laws are placed in us plain and clear, and that it is so unremarkable to see them observed that one must rather wonder that so often they are not observed; that on their ground every common human understanding decides at once about the legitimacy of actions, and that we alone are ourselves guilty for each case of transgression. Now if one finds in the examination of this essence ruling in us that it commands beyond our whole sensible nature, therefore must itself be something supersensible, now if its actual nature and constitution remains unknown to us, then this circumstance puts us into a deep admiration: we do not know, is a productive being in us that represents to us these laws as effects, or do we possess this productive faculty? In short, we cannot explain what is working in us. Nevertheless its effects over sensible nature are astonishing. Nothing is to be done against its commandments. Torment and bodily suffering, indeed even suffering death does not outweigh it: though Phalaris should command <*Phalaris licet compert*>, says Juvenal,[51] and other poets attribute to it the most sublime properties. But precisely this deep admiration of the sublime properties of an unknown essence present in us is what constitutes its excellence and should be used above all for religion and instruction.

29:1024

§70. *The consideration of the sensibility of a human being* indicates a noteworthy difference with respect to the power of choice <*arbitrio*> and especially the morality of a human being, namely, between the representation of a sensibility that includes merely sensible feeling, or [one] that offers intellectual feeling, through which arises the diversity in determining grounds for our moral actions.

That is, sensibility affects either our sensible feeling alone, or at the same time with this our faculty of desire. In the latter case it becomes at the same time determining ground of our actions, in the first not, because the power of choice cannot be brought to action without previous determination of the faculty of desire. Therefore are distinguished:

(a) *sensible pleasure and displeasure* {or sensible feeling},ᵘ i.e., when the produced representation or the action itself had its ground in a faculty of desire determined by pleasure or displeasure. Therefore every circumstance situated outside me, every gratification or pain, advantages or representations of happiness, if these become the ground of the action or representation in such a way that the feeling of pleasure or displeasure in the representation precedes the faculty of desire, and acts upon that as determining ground, then pleasure and displeasure, which is at the same time determining ground of the faculty of desire, is *sensible feeling;* which is at all times empirical and determines the faculty of desire in that manner, or

(b) *intellectual feeling,* i.e., insofar as the representation of the law precedes and from that first arises the determination of the feeling of pleasure and pain effected in the faculty of desire. The determining ground lies here in the law and its consciousness, reason determines it according to the power of choice, and from that follows the pleasure in my representation or action, because the claim of reason is satisfied by my observance of its prescription, and therefore gives birth inevitably to an inner pleasure of the soul. This pleasure is rational, which [has] its source always in the moral determinationsᵛ

29:1025

[RATIONAL PSYCHOLOGY]

First of all it must (a) be maintained against the materialists that the soul can hardly be in and for itself material, or a simple part of matter. The soul is rather a simple being (in the negative concept), therefore also: the soul is immaterial and non-bodily. Now here matter is called not only what is itself throughout matter, but rather what can also be only a part of a matter, thus an extended, impenetrable being.

But first of all it cannot be simple and nevertheless a part of matter. For as (an also simple) part of matter it must occupy a space with the latter; but space consists again of spaces, therefore this simple would again have parts; but every part of matter is again matter, therefore the soul must be either <*vel*> material (wholly) or immaterial (for itself). But to assume a thinking matter <*materie cogitans*> is something impossible; rather the soul is simple and in no case composite.ʷ *This simplicity rests on the unity of*

ᵘ Marginalia (1024₁₆) alongside text printed here. We follow Lehmann in inserting it after the first clause of this text. Parentheses added by Lehmann have been removed.

ᵛ The ms breaks off here (1024₃₇); the last marginal pagination of the ms (at 1024₃₅) is 180a, and the next (at 1025₂₈) is 203b, so approximately 23 sheets are missing here from the ms copy (there is a close approximation in the page lengths between the original ms and the ms copy). The text begins again in the middle of the section on rational psychology.

ʷ The preceding paragraph, as well as the present paragraph up to this point, are missing from the *Vigilantius* (K₃) ms. Lehmann copies this material from a passage copied in Arnoldt (pp. 147–8) that overlaps slightly with the following text. Lehmann does not note this use of Arnoldt.

consciousness in thinking or on the unity of the manifold in representation in general. All representations refer to an object by virtue of the determination in the mind, by virtue of which alone we are at all capable of representing something to ourselves. But the object to which the consciousness of the manifold is connected must be an absolute unity, for otherwise the sentence, e.g., (a) to have learned (b) faithfully (c) arts (d) softens (f) customs <(a) *didicisse* (b) *fideliter* (c) *artes* (d) *mollit* (f) *mores*>, etc., would have to be able to be thought in its entirety in such a way that diverse powers: a, b, c, d, e, f, etc., would each have thought one concept, and nevertheless have been able to be collectively conscious of the whole sentence. – Since this is impossible, there can arise no representation of an object without an absolute unity of the representing subject being present, and it is impossible to let the consciousness of the representation arise through a bodily divisibility, as though there were diverse subjects there who divided the representation among themselves, because it would then be impossible that these parts, which would be known only to each subject himself, could be connected to a whole, i.e., to a whole without an^*x* intermediate means. Now if one assumes that the thinking matter <*materia cogitans*> is an aggregate of substances, then the representation attributed to it would also have to contain an aggregate of representations, namely its parts, which would be separated from one another, whereby from one part of this, one part would be conceived, by the other another would be thought, and a unity would not be attained thereby. But in order for it still to be brought to a whole, it remains always necessary to assume   29:1026
a unifying subject which again connects all of these parts under itself and with each other. Thus a composite representation cannot be attributed to the thinking subject, but rather only a simple representation: i.e., it connects the representation to a simple principle or is simple.

{The materialists are refuted}^*y* Through this it is now indeed proven *that the subject can think without* its principle being bodily, but from this it follows

(b) not yet *that the soul can think without being connected to the body, and this is what pneumatology teaches,* whose possibility, however, can never be proven.

We are not in a position to investigate the causality of such a self-subsistent principle, to determine the effects and the constitution which could arise from it as cause, and thus do not know *a priori* whether such a thinking principle is present, separated from the body. We could not experience it otherwise than empirically by observing a soul separated from the body. But this does not work in life because of the connection with the body, and

---

^*x* We follow Lehmann in changing *einem* to *ein* (1025_{32}).
^*y* Marginalia (1026_{8-9}) alongside text printed at 1026_{7-8}. We insert this at the beginning of the text, while Lehmann inserts it after this text.

apart from this state we are aware of nothing of the soul, and what the soul will be after death is for the same reason just as impossible for us to know: therefore, since we cannot obtain any object of representation here through experience, it is *also impossible to arrive at pneumatology, and to cognize whether there is any spirit, even a god, in the universe <universo>*.

We know nothing more than that the soul is an immaterial substance, and that it cannot be cognized as the predicate of another being, because I cannot think a composite <*compositum*> out of many substances, rather the unity of the subject is absolutely presupposed for that, therefore materialism contradicts itself in the idea, and nothing can be explained from it; but whether the soul is a spirit (<*spiritus;* G: *Geist*>), as a thinking being, as the author §742 suggests, does not follow from the latter concept. Animals also have souls, but they are not on that account spirits. *Spirits are specifically <specifice> thinking immaterial substances that also can think without connection with the material;* were it only the case that the body is an indispensable support <*adminiculum*> and a condition for the thinking of the soul, then it would exist as soul, but not as spirit, since the former, but not the latter, stands in a necessary connection with the body in order to bring about acts <*actus*> of the substance.

29:1027

§82. In case one now considers this immaterial being in the body, what we call *soul, in relation to matter,* one has endeavored to find out *the seat of the soul, or the location where the seat of the senses <sensorium commune> is situated,* i.e., in part the location where the soul obtains all impressions from objects, i.e., sensation from them, in part the location corresponding to this sensation; this can be called the prime moving power <*primum movens*> of the animal, i.e., from which the whole body can be brought into motion.

One calls this faculty of the soul the *locomotive faculty <facultatem locomotivam>*[52] to distinguish it from the faculty of thinking <*facultate cogitandi*>; both faculties, namely for sensing and for imparting motion, are put in the seat of the senses <*sensorio communi*>, from which both of them supposedly proceed.

Now some have taken the pineal gland <*glandulam pinealem;* G: *Zirbeldrüse*> as the location of the seat of the senses <*sensorii communis*>. There is to be sure only one isolated nerve in the human brain, the pineal gland, which lies in the middle of the brain where the points of the nerves going to the brain at first strike, which are effected in turn by the soul when the body is to be moved. There is only one such gland in the entire body, and since the simplicity of the soul does not allow permitting it more than one location, this nerve has been assumed as the communal seat; this was particularly the opinion of Descartes. Meanwhile it is still in itself always possible that there could be still other living principles in other parts of the body which are not soul or highest principle of all; and then one has recently discovered that the pineal gland is most of the time filled with sand.

Others, especially Bonnet, have therefore given *the corpus callosum* <*corpus callosum; G: Gehirnschwiele*> as the seat of the senses <*sensorium commune*>, to which place the sensation, or from which the movement, is supposed to press forth. But if one considers the *question metaphysically, whether the soul can perceive itself and determine the location of its residence in the body, then one must declare the solution to be impossible.*

An immaterial being cannot be assigned a location anywhere in space because that which is an object in space absolutely must be matter if all 29:1028 relations of a local presence are not to be lacking in it. One can therefore attribute to the soul only a dynamic relation, a virtuality, toward the body, and only by virtue of this dynamic connection <*nexus dynamici*> does it stand in connection with it, and produce its alterations through it and after excited sensation, but how this occurs is not to be determined. For one can never think first of the location from where the soul effects the body, but rather one must think first of the sensation, and then, with the location, that which immediately produces the sensation. In general, what is object of outer sense cannot be thought in any relation with the object of inner sense; the soul is indeed conscious of the objects of outer sense, but as little as they are present in the soul, as little does their influence on the soul determine the location where they are produced. It is impossible to perceive the soul externally, as well as not possible to perceive the location of another soul. Just as little can the soul itself determine its location immediately in the body, also not immediately in the world, for it cannot be aware of itself as object of outer sense. For that it would have to determine outer things in their relation to the soul and would have to perceive their presence according to a location, therefore become thus aware of itself through its outer sense. But perceiving oneself belongs to inner sense, perceiving oneself through a location belongs to outer sense. Thus it would have to perceive itself as an object of inner sense at the same time through outer sense: but both senses have absolutely no relation at all that would be local. – Thus the soul cannot become conscious of all this because it lacks an outer perception of itself, and it cannot be aware of itself and its relations to itself outside itself, thus the soul cannot determine a location. Now it is asked how then should one understand it when one maintains an actual perception of the soul? The community of the soul with the body cannot be thought at all, as long as that which is phenomenon in each is taken: for, e.g., in regard to pleasure and displeasure, also in regard to the power of imagination, how can something bodily be made noticeable? Should a human being have representations of outer objects, they still are not formed in him as though enclosed in space. He does not cognize the objects in material figure, i.e., the outer material does not flow over into the soul. *But an unknown something, which is not* 29:1029 *appearance, is what influences the soul, and so we obtain in us a homogeneity with things. Herein lies the representation* that is produced in us not by the phenomenon itself of the body but, rather, by the substrate *<substratum>* of matter, the noumenon. The representation is distinguished from the object; the noumenon in the body stands in agreement with that noumenon of the soul, and this unity is the determining ground of both for representing the object, and on this rests the interaction of the body and soul *<commercium corporis et animae>*. So one must also explain the assumed physical influence *<influxum physicum>*. First of all one must think it real, i.e., that the substances outside each other somehow can be an influence on one another by their existence (therefore apart from space, for in space the influence *<influxus>* has no problem); nonetheless, to think this influence *<influxus>* on one another between soul and body materially, and yet so that both would be outside each other, and each for itself, is something in itself impossible: and if one assumes it ideally, then this would be nothing but the preestablished harmony *<harmonia praestabilita>*, and would no longer be influence *<influxus>*. It *must thus be thought as the immaterial effect of the noumenon of each*, whereupon then this means nothing more than that something influences the soul, and then no heterogeneity remains that could raise doubts here, since nothing further can be said about the constitution of this influence. Thus one can only say the soul is in connection with the body, and where the body is, there is the soul, but one cannot indicate a place in the body for the soul.

One says further against this: the brain feels the thinking. It is true that the nerves are the instruments whereby according to its deportment *<déportement>* the soul exercises its influence through excited stimulations and that, vice versa, feelings are propagated through the nerves to the soul. *One can assume that the soul is in the brain virtually <virtualiter>, but it cannot be concluded from this* that [it is] locally *<localiter>*. The ancients rather said: the soul is whole in the whole body and whole in any part *<anima est tota in toto corpore et tota in quavis parte>*. But to assume that it can be whole and undivided, but also in two particular locations, is not possible, because otherwise it would also be possible that it could also be outside me, and I would then observe myself as an object outside of myself, which is impossible. We cognize merely the effect of the reciprocal influence of the soul on the body, e.g., we feel a pain whose effect comes from the finger, and reduce it finally to the finger. But how sensibility and locomotion hang together in their effects, or [how] to determine the kind of effect, is no more possible than determining the location of the reacting soul. The soul has no determinate location or local relation to the body; for this would be a mathematical relation that we absolutely do not grasp, but rather we can make for ourselves a concept only of the dynamic relation of the soul.

§83. The object regarding *<ad>* (b) rational psychology *<psychologia rationalis>*: *namely what the soul was before the birth of the human being, or*

29:1030

the question on the origin of the soul <de origine animae>,[53] on which human beings divide themselves thus,

1. that one allows it to arise *through physical origin <per ortum physicum>* either as educt or as product of an older soul, or

2. that one represents it as produced by God at birth, which one calls the *hyperphysical origin <ortum hyperphysicum>*. The latter is the *system of creations* to which one should not take refuge, however, as long as one could make do with the physical origin *<orto physico>*. {The system of creation, where the soul is assumed to be the product of the parents, and the parents are assigned a creative power}[z]

The physical origin *<ortus physicus>*, on the other hand, indicates two systems, namely

a. one assumes the soul *as an educt*, i.e., that the human soul or the animating principle, the animal, was already present in the body before its birth (perhaps as raw substance, which was inanimate), and now is brought to life by the powers of nature. This is the *system of preexistence <systema praeexistentiae>*, because it must have already existed previously in the body of the parents {to the extent it exists freely in the body, and from this is carried over in the descendents, or if it is placed in the soul of the parents as a germ of the soul, and goes out from it as a part of the parents' soul separated from it. This latter is the system through transference *<systema per traducem>*, which nevertheless also includes the former under it, since it always comes from the body of the parents no matter what germs could also have come from the air, etc., through nutrition.}[a]

b. or one assumes it as educt, yet in such a manner that it was produced from the parents by mixing with other materials, and thus proceeded from the soul of the parents, thus where parent souls bear children souls. Now this latter is obviously contrary to the simplicity of the soul's substance, because it would be presupposed here that the parents' souls must be composite in order to deliver the children's souls as parts.

29:1031

Basically, insofar as they take into consideration the physical origin *<ortum physicum>*, these systems are formed and thought by analogy with the animal procreation of human beings, where likewise the diverse systems amount to

1. the *system of preformation <systema praeformationis>*, which either assumed like Leeuwenhoek, according to his *theory of involution <theoria involutionis>* (the system of encasement), that in the entire animal and plant kingdom of creation, the germ for all future generations was placed in the seed of each kind, so that one germ would be placed in the other as

---

[z] Marginalia (1030₁₇₋₁₉) alongside text printed at 1030₁₅₋₂₀. We are inserting it at the end of this paragraph, while Lehmann inserts it after *Creationen*.

[a] Marginalia (1030₂₉₋₃₆) alongside text printed at 1030₂₈–1031₃. We follow Lehmann in inserting it after the first paragraph of this text.

dead matter, and would become animate only singly. Thus the little animal seeds <*animalcula spermatica*> of animals; or, as others assume, that providence had previously created single germs, lying free and next to one another {e.g., if they are suspended in the air, are free in the body, and are educed from these.}[b]

The system of free preexistence <systema praeexistentiae liberae>

One has now rejected this system rather generally because, in order to maintain a kind, an infinite sum of germs would have to be assumed in each individual, and with the consumption of one seed nucleus millions would immediately have to be lost, but this useless sacrifice would not at all be arranged in conformity with the ends of nature.

2. Therefore the *system of epigenesis* <*systema epigenesis*>[54] is now generally assumed, according to which the parents are the productive causes of the conception, and the young animal thus arises from the mixture of both sexes as a product. This is more likely, as already indicated by the mating of related kinds, e.g., donkey and horse, black and white human beings, the similarities of variations, in mules and mulattos, etc., etc., and so likewise the bastard plants produced by related pollen.

Now if one wants to apply these theories to the origination of an infinite soul, it appears that, taken as educt, the system of propagation through transference or of preexistence <*systema propagationis per traducem vel praeexistentiae*> must be correct, nevertheless one would also 29:1032 have to presuppose that the souls of the children and their descendants were present in the body of the parents, but then the parent souls would be composite, which is impossible. And, as product in a way similar to epigenesis, one would have to grant to the parents a generative power of the soul; but then the soul could not previously have been an accident in the body of the parents. For the soul is substance and thus as simple substance cannot have existed at the same time as accident, therefore the parents would have had to undertake a creation, and the begetting consist in that, but this would thus be production from nothing <*productio ex nihilo*>, which belongs to creative power. But now this power cannot be thought in any being that is itself created; it can clearly alter, separate, connect the form and shape of created beings, but not produce anything new: the faculty for that can be only in the primordial being of all creatures.

One could thus infer that since the soul can be neither educt nor product, thus neither system of transference <*systema per traducem*> nor of creation <*creationis*> occurs, hence the soul must be preformed as a

---

[b] Marginalia (1031₁₇₋₁₈) alongside text printed at 1031₁₇₋₂₀. We follow Lehmann in inserting it at the end of the section. Lehmann does not note this as marginalia.

simple being, but properly we have no proper representation of that, however it may relate to the origin of the soul.

One could also maintain as hypothesis, that perhaps the *noumenon,* the substrate of matter *<substratum materiae>* that underlies all appearances of the material, *in addition to manifesting itself as body, at the same time also produces another appearance that we call soul,* i.e., that this substrate of matter *<substratum materiae>* at the same time also represents the place of the soul, though of course without being able to produce a soul.

§84. The unity of monads

Leibniz, after him Wolff and others, assumed *that all matter is an aggregate of monads,*[55] *and these [are] in themselves simple substances,* propositions that were already negated above, since it [is]^L impossible that matter can consist of simple parts, rather [it is] divisible to infinity *<in infinitum>*, while remaining matter.

Now externally these unities should have all the relations that belong to things in space in their composition, therefore composites *<composita>*, and as such composed substances have contact, motion, etc.

But Leibniz attributed to the monads above all a power of representation *<vis repraesentativa>*, and to each monad as substantial its own power of representation. Of course, since we are not in a position to observe what is inner of other things, and can observe only ourselves, but then are aware of nothing but that we have representations, it was to that extent correctly inferred that the inner powers of the monads consisted in the power of representation and the consequences of the representation of pleasure = desire; nevertheless substance and power do not mean the same thing, but rather substance only has powers, it is not at all a necessary consequence that insofar as they are substance *<quoad substantiam>* the monads could have no other powers than the power of representation; we are only not acquainted with them. Now on account of the interaction *<commercii>* of the things in the world, Leibniz assumed further that all monads stood in connection with each other, and each monad is conscious of all other monads in the universe *<universo>*. He called this the mirror of the universe *<speculum universi>*, nevertheless decreed that although all monads live and had a power of representation *<vim repraesentativam>*, still some were to be considered *as slumbering <sopita; G: schlummernd>*, i.e., either having no current consciousness at all of their representations, or at least not a consciousness of the manifold in things, therefore not being able to produce any cognition for themselves then because they were not in the condition to separate, to connect, to compare representations, and [he] dismissed them as brute *<bruta>*. Mr. Kant calls this division [of beings] brute mirrors *<specula bruta>* in contrast to the rational mirrors, rational beings *<rationalia>*. Now with the latter he decreed degrees and a progres-

29:1033

499

sion of representative powers <*veribus repraesentativis*>, namely obscure, clear, distinct <*obscuris, claris, distinctis*>, and so on in all degrees up until the highest perfection of God. This is a continuation of the continuum of forms <*continuum formarum*>, which Bonnet's[56] order of physics <*ratione physicorum*> in particular brought together, where he passed from the minerals to the fungi, mushrooms, lichens, from here {to the plants, from here}ᶜ to the zoophytes, to the animals, human beings, and finally over to God, who as the source of all included all things in himself, and from which one later assumed an emanation. Leibniz likewise assumed that matter contained in itself the stuff for all souls, and then built all things up to the levels of divinity.

So little can be said as to the justification of this hypothesis of Leibniz, that Bonnet is rather already very well refuted by Blumenbach.

§85. According to what has been noted above, we thus know nothing about the origin of the soul, and even if we also assume the life of the soul as immaterial substance (and not predicate of another matter) and as created (only not by generative power of the human being and his soul), then it is nevertheless impossible for us to experience whether the state of life can be animal or [rather] spiritual life <*vita animalis vel spiritualis*>. In life we know nothing other than that, in thinking, the soul is in connection with the body, and if we went with the soul beyond the body, it is just as impossible to experience something of the state of the thinking being that would then be, or how it is now constituted.

Nonetheless it still seems allowed to maintain that one can assume a spiritual life, i.e., an animating principle without connection to the body. For

a. *all matter is lifeless. A proposition* that indeed contradicts the animated monads of Leibniz but that one must assume because to be matter means to be composite, but to live [means] to be the cause of the representation of the actuality of an action. Representing requires a thinking principle; but a composite as such <*compositum qua tale*> simply cannot think, because this manifold of representation must be unified into a unity of the subject: thus a living principle should be present for thinking, so it must be simple.

b. *From that one can conclude that a separation from matter is possible of the living principle in the subject*, that this separation hinders life so little that since matter is rather lifeless, it can therefore only burden and hinder the thinking of the living principle; thinking will be facilitated and promoted by the separation and an unhindered life will be produced. Thus according to this

c. the connection with matter is not the ground of life and necessary for it. On the other hand

d. it does seem to be opposed to this, that the body is a support

29:1034

ᶜ The text is extended in the margin here (1033₂₈).

<*adminiculum*> for thinking, as one must assume according to experience; but the question is whether it is absolutely necessary that the body remain in connection with the soul in order to be able to think. It is impossible for us to think the effect that each separated substance (body and soul) would have, we assume that in the connection the body is a support <*adminiculum*> as well as a hindrance with respect to thinking; nevertheless it still can be assumed that in spite of it there would lie in matter

e. *a predominant hindrance* that would fall away after the separation, and the soul would work all the more freely. But its connection with the body   29:1035 cannot be necessary, because matter, as remarked, is lifeless, and the support <*adminiculum*> as well as the hindrance that the body effects with respect to the soul can be contingent. Nonetheless about this question as well nothing can be decided with certainty.

§86. Now regarding <*ad*> (c) the third section of the rational psychology <*psychologia rationalis*>.

namely, what the soul will be after death,

^deverything rests on the question whether death (separation of the soul and body) will consist in a dissolution of the entire life of the human being, namely of the soul and of the body, or whether the life of the human being can continue even after the separation from the body. Now in deciding this the essential difference of the *theories* deserves consideration:

    a. *concerning the hope of a future life* <*spem vitae futurae concernens*>
    b. *on the immortality of the soul* <*de immortalitate animae*>.

Both presuppose a future life, only *immortality* involves *the assumption that it is viewed as necessary from the nature of the soul that a human being cannot at all die, therefore a future life after death is also necessary.*

With respect to its source, immortality is by all means still to be distinguished from *resurrection, according to their sources:* for this latter consists in the substance of the human being (not the connection of the accidents of the body with the appearance as well as the spiritual breath) *remaining, to be sure, also after death, but its animation being dependent solely on the divine choice, and thus the body will be reawakened with the soul only in consequence of its decision.*

In relation to the hope of a future life <*spes vitae futurae*> immortality also distinguishes itself as something that follows according to order = according to the laws of the nature of the soul. One assumes the future life from moral grounds for the sake of general purposiveness, which then has its ground either in general natural ends or in divine ends, and the future life is considered accordingly in conformity with teleology or theology. Now from the purposiveness in nature one can say no more that it is a

---

^d We follow Lehmann in omitting an *anbetrifft* (concerning) here (before *so beruhet*)(1035_{11}).

29:1036 natural law of the soul to be immortal than that it would be in conformity with divine intention that a future life should be. That would require that the nature of the human soul would make this necessary, since immortality is the impossibility of dying, and being unable to die can lie as a condition in the nature of the soul only if it should be necessary to assume a future life. On the other hand the determination of the divine will to a future life can be regarded only as a supernatural cause of immortality. Therefore immortality and resurrection also rest on the difference, either

a. that the life of the soul after death is thought and assumed according to *natural causes*, i.e., according to the constitution of its nature, or from *physiological grounds*, or

b. that it is assumed from *supernatural, i.e., hyperphysical* causes.

In the former case *immortality*, in the latter *resurrection*. On the other hand if one derives it from the purposiveness in nature, or from the moral end of the highest being, then one cannot infer to any necessity of the future life, but rather only that we have cause from moral grounds to expect a future life, which is hope of a future life very greatly different <*spes vitae futurae quam maxime different*> from the immortality of the soul <*immortalitate animae*>.

§87. Now should one be able to assume a life of the soul after death, then this requires

1. *survival of its substance after death.*
2. *survival of its person*, i.e., identity of its personality, i.e., that in the state after death it is conscious of being just the same subject as it was previously. {N.B. The consciousness of oneself is intellectual memory in the psychological sense <*memoria intellectualis in sensu psychologico*>, of others in the moral sense <*in sensu morali*>, where it consists in the ground of imputation or imputability.}*ᵉ*

Both must be proved. {from *physiological grounds*}*ᶠ*

a. Now regarding <*ad*> (1) one draws up the proof for it usually this way: *the soul is simple, thus indivisible*, or whatever = the soul is incorruptible <*anima est incorruptibilis*>; it is subjected to no decay, i.e., no disintegration by dissolution of its parts, thus it cannot pass away. *This is inferred by analogy with the body.* Wood, e.g., indeed decays although it is still also true that diverse constituents of the wood remain which themselves are 29:1037 not chemically dissolvable, but still make the disintegration possible. But the soul, as a non-bodily substance, hence simple, is therefore not subject to the presupposition of corruption <*corruption*>. Mendelssohn (in his

---

ᵉ Marginalia (1036₂₇₋₂₉) alongside text printed at 1036₂₄₋₂₆. We follow Lehmann in inserting it after this passage but omit the blank lines added by him.

ᶠ Marginalia (1036₃₀) alongside text printed at 1036₃₁₋₃₂. We follow Lehmann in inserting it before this passage.

Phaedon)[57] recognized entirely correctly this proof to be insufficient, because no necessity lay in assuming that because the soul is not corruptible <*corruptibilis*> then it cannot pass away, because without disintegration it could still pass away by vanishing. But on the other hand, from the assumption that he took its substance *to be imperishable*, he concluded nevertheless too much: he inferred this way: were it not this, then it would be present in one point in time but no longer in the following. But since between two moments there absolutely must be a time through which the one can pass over into the other; then if it is supposed to be no more in the next moment, a being and a non-being must[g] follow one another, without there being determined an intermediate time of a not-wholly being and a not-fully non-being; therefore the transition would be thought through a leap, but a simple substance could not be transformed into nothing through any leap, or be annihilated, therefore the soul is immortal. {N.B. He presupposed that a simple being could not pass away like a body through successive diminishing of its parts, but rather it would either wholly have to be or stop at once having been at all.}[h]

It is correct, there is no time between which there is not always again an infinite series of times, there is no state [where] between this and another yet another would not be, through which the transition happens: but from that one cannot declare it to be impossible that the soul cannot pass away after death. Since it is simple, parts of the soul can indeed not pass away by disintegration in it, but [the soul can pass away] through an *evanescence, i.e., a gradual remission of its powers.* {an intension of the powers is opposed}[i] Just as the clarity of a representation can gradually become obscure so that finally the soul slumbers in it and thus its consciousness is lost little by little, so can all degrees of the powers of the human soul give way little by little, and when they have been diminished through all degrees, finally pass over into a nothing. Here is no leap <*saltus*>, but rather it observes the laws of continuity by descending through ever smaller degrees, between which there is always again a time.   29:1038

Of a bodily thing one says indeed correctly in the cosmological sense <*in sensu cosmologico*>: *substance is perduring, while its accidents change,* but it is also only with bodily things that the perdurability of the substance can be noticed, e.g., in weight, impenetrability, etc. But with a simple being we are not in a position to cognize perdurability, for even the I – self-consciousness of the human being – vanishes. Therefore one can apply the principle of perdurability to a body, but not to a simple being, and one

---

[g] We follow Lehmann in changing *müsste* to *müssten* (1037_{13}).

[h] Marginalia (1037_{20-23}) alongside text printed at 1037_{8-13}. We follow Lehmann in inserting it at the end of the sentence but are omitting blank lines added by him.

[i] Marginalia (1037_{31-32}) alongside text printed at 1037_{30-31}. We follow Lehmann in inserting it after the text.

cannot infer from that something about the soul, where everything is in flux, and everything can pass away.

What concerns <*ad*> (2) the identity of the person of the soul, this would be the intellectual memory <*memoria intellectualis*>. To what extent this should belong to it after death, the necessity of that one cannot comprehend at all: one can, of course, assume the possibility, but not prove it, therefore one cannot infer it *a priori*. Psychologically we rather find that the human being forgets what he previously was.

Since it is drawn from the life of the human being in experience, it is thus not feasible to ground on psychology the state of the soul after death and its existence in general, and it is also self-evident that from the interaction <*commercio*> of the soul with the body, from the consciousness of both in their connection, and with the impossibility of an attempt at even a momentary separation, with continuation of consciousness, absolutely nothing can be cognized of what our soul will be after the suspension of this connection. Now besides the psychological proof from the nature of the soul, one has still further an *a priori* proof, and indeed metaphysical, drawn from (b), the concept of *a principle of life in general.*[58]

It is demonstrated that our life (as a principle <*quoad principium*>) does not depend on a connection of the soul with matter, that it thus exists without it, and death must be viewed as a continuation of life. That is, since matter is lifeless, there is no reason to assume that life can be dependent on a connection with it, i.e., that matter is a ground of the possibility of the principle of life, rather, the connection with matter could make a hindrance in life for the latter, because besides its own life the soul is necessitated to animate matter also, or to produce an animal life.

29:1039

But one must *distinguish the survival of the principle of life, or the faculty for living, from the act <actu> of life itself.* The first can in some possible way also survive more freely and unhindered after the separation from the body, but in order to assume the actuality of life itself an experience is still required of whether the human being or his soul can exercise acts <*actus*> of life without connection to the body. The experience that we have of our state teaches us rather the opposite here, that we can think, will, desire, etc., in no other way than in connection with the body, because the cooperation of the body visibly manifests itself through sensation as the consequence of these actions of life, e.g., in every sacrifice of powers; in thinking we sense fatigue, etc., and precisely its cooperation thus appears to betray a condition that underlies the exercise of life. Thus it is not proven that the soul lives in actuality <*actu*> after death, if the principle of life survives after death. One thus sees that metaphysically as well, from the nature of the soul nothing can be proved regarding immortality, therefore all physiological arguments about this make nothing provable. Besides that, one has *sought* for the proof of the immortality of the soul *in the order of ends,*[j] *or drawn from purposiveness,* and indeed

a. either derived from *the ends of nature* according to laws of nature. This is the *teleological proof;*
b. or derived from the divine end according to moral (considered as divine) laws. This is the *theological proof.*

The teleological proof is taken from this: {N.B. it is still the only one that grounds a possibility of the future life and deserves approval in metaphysical consideration}[k]

a. *There is no organic being in nature whose existence can possibly be thought other* than through *and by virtue of an end* to be effected by it. One must connect this absolutely immediately with the idea of a being that has created the organic creature for some end or other. One takes into consideration, e.g., the circulation of the saps in trees, bushes and plants and the connection of the parts of flowers with the manner of their fertilization, etc.   29:1040

b. *There are in nature no superfluous predispositions.* With minerals the purposiveness is indeed not yet[l]

To make possible the communication of an appropriate happiness for the whole human race, and to bring into agreement the well-being of human beings with their good conduct: only we do not know how God brings this about, but rather assume this presupposition only because, on the one hand, the moral good conduct of the human race is made a duty, but it lies outside its powers to procure happiness for itself. Indeed laws of nature already indicate that observation of the moral laws in our conduct secures a contentment with ourselves, as well as the approval of others, but it cannot secure from itself satisfaction with respect to sensible good. One sees very easily from this how much the assumption of divine unconditional decrees or of the absolute divine decree <*decreti divini absoluti*>[59] is opposed to all concepts. This is an act of the consequent will of God <*actus voluntatis consequentis dei*> by virtue of which indeed God wanted to have all human beings blessed through his antecedent will, i.e., by

---

[j] Marginalia (printed at Ak. 29: 1185) alongside the text at 1029_{23-24} reads: *Aus der Zweckmässigkeit* (From purposiveness).

[k] Marginalia (1039_{30-32}) alongside text printed at 1039_{30-34}. We are inserting it after the first clause of this text, while Lehmann inserts it within this clause, and parentheses added by Lehmann have been removed.

[l] The manuscript breaks off here (1040_4). The marginal pagination (alongside the penultimate line of the ms page) is 220a. The pagination on the following ms page (about three-quarters down the page) is 279b, so approximately 59 sheets of the ms are missing here. The final ms sheet that follows (which closes with: "*finitum* – 2ond Febr. 95") is most likely the end of a discussion on natural theology. See §§976–81 of Baumgarten on divine decrees.

chance the impelling cause was general and rather common to all subjects of the human race <*per voluntatem antecedentem,* i.e., *casu causa impulsiva erat generalis atqui omnibus subjectis generis humani communis*>, but through his consequent will <*per voluntatem consequentem*> determined with the creation of the world blessedness for one class, for the other damnation, and consequently imparted to the former their necessary means of grace, but simply withdrew from the latter; therefore, since man is evil by nature, some expect blessedness absolutely, others on the contrary shall be subjected absolutely to damnation. This is the doctrine of predestination, which is distinguished entirely from the hypothetical divine decree <*decretum divinum*>, according to which a blessedness or damnation by God is previously determined depending on whether the subject has made himself worthy or unworthy of it by his moral conduct.

end <*finitum*> – 20th February 1795.

English-German glossary

ability – *Fähigkeit*
absurdity – *Ungereimtheit, Wahnwitz*
abyss – *Abgrund*
accident – *Ungefähr*
account – *Rechenschaft*
acquaintance – *Kenntnis*
acquainted with (to be) – *kennen*
act (to) – *handeln*
action – *Handlung, Wirkung*
active (to be) – *wirken*
activity – *Tätigkeit*
actual – *wirklich*
actuality – *Wirklichkeit, Actualitaet*
acumen – *Scharfsinn*
acute – *scharfsinnig*
adequate – *hinreichend, zulänglich*
affect (to) – *afficiren, wirken*
affection – *Affect*
agreeable – *angenehm*
alteration – *Veränderung*
amplificatory judgment –
   Erweiterungsurteil
amplify (to) – *erweitern*
animate (to) – *beleben*
annihilation – *Vernichtung*
anticipation – *Erwartung*
anticipatory faculty –
   Erwartungsvermögen
anticipatory power – *Vorbildungskraft*
appearance – *Erscheinung*
application – *Anwendung*
applied – *angewandt*
arbitrary – *beliebig, willkürlich*
archetype – *Urbild*
argue (to) – *streiten*

argument – *Argument*
arise (to) – *entspringen, entstehen*
arise [from] (to) – *herkommen*
ascription – *Zurechnung*
assessment – *Beurteilung*
association – *Vergesellschaftung*
attentiveness – *Aufmerksamkeit*
attraction – *Anziehung*
attractive power – *anziehende Kraft*
attribute (to) – *beilegen*

basic proposition – *Grundsatz*
being – *Sein, Wesen*
being (primordial) – *Urwesen*
beneficial – *zuträglich*
beyond bounds – *überschwenglich*
blessed – *selig*
blessedness – *Seligkeit*
bodily – *körperlich*
body – *Körper*
body (mundane) – *Weltkörper*
body (human) – *Leib*
bound (to) – *begrenzen*
boundary – *Grenze*
bounded – *begrenzt*

causal law – *Wirkungs Gesetz*
cause – *Ursache*
caused – *Verursachten*
chance – *Zufall*
change (to) – *ändern*
change – *Wechseln*
choice – *Wahl*
choice (power of) – *Willkür*
choose (to) – *wählen*

507

circumstance – *Umstand*
cleverness – *Klugheit*
coexistent – *nebeneinander*
cognition – *Erkenntnis*
cognize (to) – *erkennen*
cohere (to) – *zusammenhängen*
come about (to) – *entstehen*
comfort – *Annehmlichkeit*
coming about – *Entstehen*
communal – *gemeinschaftlich*
community – *Gemeinschaft*
complete – *vollständig*
composite – *zusammengesetzt*
composition – *Zusammensetzung*
comprehend (to) – *auffassen, einsehen*
comprehension – *Auffassung*
compulsion – *Nötigung, Zwang*
conceive (to) – *begreifen, concipiren*
conceive (to) [biological] – *zeugen*
concept – *Begriff*
conclusion – *Folgerung*
concurrent – *zugleich*
condition – *Bedingung, Bewandtnis*
conduct – *Betragen, Verhalten*
conflict – *Widerstreit*
conflict with (to) – *widerstreiten*
conformity to the law –
  Gesetzmässigkeit
conjoin (to) – *zusammenhängen*
connect (to) – *verbinden*
connection – *Verbindung, Verknüpfung,*
  Zusammenhang
conscience – *Gewissen*
consciousness – *Bewusstsein*
consequence – *Folge*
conservation – *Erhaltung*
constant – *stetig, beständig*
constitution [of a thing] –
  Beschaffenheit
contact – *Berührung*
contentment – *Zufriedenheit*
contingency – *Zufälligkeit*
contingent – *zufällig*
continuation – *Fortgang, Fortsetzung*

continue (to) – *fortfahren, fortgehen*
contrary to nature – *widernatürlich*
corporeal – *körperlich*
corpus callosum – *Gehirnschwiele,*
  Hirnschwiele
correlate – *Gegenbild*
cosmos – *Weltall, Weltganze, Weltraum*
counteraction – *Gegenwirkung*
creation – *Schöpfung*

debate (to) – *disputiren*
deceit – *Trug*
deception – *Betrug, Täuschung*
decompose (to) – *auflösen*
decomposition – *Auflösung*
delight – *Wollust*
delusion – *Blendwerk, Wahn*
desire (to) – *begehren*
desire – *Begehrung, Begierde*
destiny – *Schicksal*
determinate – *bestimmt, determinirt*
determination – *Bestimmung*
determine (to) – *bestimmen,*
  determiniren
difference – *Unterschied*
different – *verschieden*
differentiate (to) – *unterscheiden*
dignity – *Würde*
discipline – *Disciplin, Zucht, Fach*
discretion – *Belieben*
discriminate (to) – *unterscheiden*
discrimination – *Unterscheidung*
disintegration – *Zerteilung*
displeasure – *Sinnenunlust, Unlust*
disposition – *Denkungsart, Gesinnung,*
  Gemütsart
dispute – *Streit, Streitigkeit*
dispute (to) – *streiten*
dissatisfaction – *Missfallen*
dissected – *zergliedert*
dissecting judgment –
  Zergliederungsurteil
distribute (to) – *austeilen, verteilen*
diverse – *mancherlei, verschieden*

diversity – *Verschiedenheit*
doctrine – *Lehre*
doctrine of nature – *Naturlehre*
duration – *Dauer*

effect – *Einwirkung, Wirkung*
effective – *wirksam*
effectiveness – *Wirksamkeit*
efficient – *wirkend*
elucidating judgment –
 Erläuterungsurteil
elucidation – *Erläuterung*
end – *Zweck*
endeavor – *Bestrebung*
endure (to) – *dauern*
enjoy (to) – *geniessen*
enjoyment – *Genuß*
equality – *Gleichheit*
equilibrium – *Gleichgewicht*
essence – *Wesen*
event – *Begebenheit*
exhibit (to) – *darstellen*
existence – *Dasein, Existenz*
existent (to be) – *vorhanden*
experience – *Erfahrung*
explanation – *Erklärung*
extend (to) – *erweitern*
extended – *ausgedehnt*
extension – *Ausbreitung, Ausdehnung,*
 Erweiterung
external – *äusser, äusserlich*

fabricate (to) – *erdichten*
fabrication – *Erdichtung*
faculty – *Vermögen, Facultät*
faculty of assessment –
 Schätzungsvermögen
faculty of correlation –
 Gegenbildungsvermögen
faculty of cultivation –
 Ausbildungsvermögen
faculty of memory –
 Erinnerungsvermögen

faculty of sensation –
 Empfindungsvermögen
fantasy (wild) – *Schwärmerei*
fate – *Verhängnis*
feature – *Merkmal*
feel (to) – *empfinden*
feeling – *Fuhlen, Gefuhl, Empfinden*
fiction – *Erdichtung*
fictive faculty – *Dichtungsvermögen,*
 Erdichtungsvermögen
fictive power – *Dichtungskraft*
final end – *Endzweck*
force – *Kraft*
formative – *bildend*
formative faculty – *bildende Vermögen,*
 Bildungsvermögen
formative power – *bildende Kraft*

general – *allgemein*
generate (to) – *zeugen, erzeugen*
generation – *Zeugung, Erzeugung*
genus – *Gattung*
germ – *Keim*
ghost – *Gespenst*
gratification – *Vergnügen, Vergnügung*
ground – *Grund*
ground of explanation –
 Erklärungsgrund
groundlessness – *Ungrund*

habit – *Gewohnheit*
happen (to) – *geschehen*
happiness – *Glückseligkeit*
harmony – *Zusammenstimmung,*
 Harmonie
hindrance – *Hinderniss*
holiness – *Heiligkeit*
homogeneous – *gleichartig, homogen*
human being – *Mensch*

illusion – *Schein, Täuschung, Illusion*
illustrative power – *Abbildungskraft*
image – *Bild*

509

imagination – *Einbildung,*
   Einbildungskraft
imaginative faculty –
   Einbildungsvermögen
imagine (to) – *einbilden, sich vorstellen*
imitation – *Nachahmung, Nachbildung*
imitative power – *Nachbildungskraft*
impenetrability – *Undurchdringlichkeit*
impression – *Eindruck*
impulse – *Antrieb*
imputability – *Zurechnungsfähigkeit,*
   Imputabilitaet
imputation – *Zurechnung*
inadequacy – *Unzulänglichkeit*
incentive – *Triebfeder*
inclination – *Neigung, Belieben*
indifference – *Gleichgültigkeit*
inertia – *Trägheit*
inference – *Schluss*
infinity – *Unendlichkeit*
influence – *Einfluss*
innate – *anerschaffen, angeboren*
insanity – *Wahnsinn*
insight – *Einsicht*
intention – *Absicht*
interaction – *Gemeinschaft*
intuition – *Anschauung*
invent (to) – *dichten, erfinden, fingiren*

judge (to) – *urteilen*
judgment – *Urteil, Beurteilung*
justice – *Recht*

kind – *Art, Gattung*
kingdom – *Reich*
know (to) – *kennen*
knowledge – *Kenntnis, Wissen*

law – *Gesetz*
limit – *Grenze, Schranke*
limitation – *Einschränkung*
limited – *beschränkt, eingeschränkt*
location – *Ort*
lust – *Wollust*

madness – *Wahnwitz*
magnitude – *Grösse*
manifold – *Mannigfaltigkeit*
matter – *Materie, Sache*
mean (to) – *bedeuten*
meaning – *Bedeutung*
measure – *Mass, Massgabe*
memory – *Gedächtnis,*
   Erinnerungsvermögen
mind – *Gemüt, Geist*
miracle – *Wunder*
mode of explanation – *Erklärungsart*
modification – *Abänderung*
moral philosophy – *Moral*
morality – *Moral, Moralität, Sittlichkeit*
morals – *Sitte(n)*
motion – *Bewegung*
motive – *Bewegungsgrund, Motive*
motive cause – *Bewegungsursache*
motive ground – *Bewegungsgrund*
mutual – *gegenseitig*

necessitate (to) – *nötigen*
necessitation – *Nötigung, Necessitation*
necessity – *Notwendigkeit*
non-being – *Nichtsein*
nonsensical – *widersinnig, widersinnisch*
nothing – *Nichts*

object – *Gegenstand, Objekt, Sache*
obligation – *Verbindlichkeit, Obligation*
observe [a law] (to) – *folgen*
obstruction – *Behinderung*
occasion – *Gelegenheit*
oneness – *Unität*
opposed – *entgegengesetze, opponierte,*
   wider
origination – *Entstehen*
ought [noun] – *Sollen*
outer – *äusser*

particular [noun] – *Besondere, Einzelne*
pass away (to) – *vergehen*
passion – *Leidenschaft*

passive – *leidend*
passivity – *Leiden, Passivitaet*
perceive (to) – *warhnehmen, vernehmen*
perception – *Wahrnehmung*
perdurability – *Beharrlichkeit*
perdure (to) – *beharren*
perfect – *vollkommen*
perish (to) – *vergehen*
persist (to) – *beharren, bestehen*
phantom of the brain – *Hirngespenst*
place – *Platz, Stelle, Ort*
pleasant – *angenehm*
please (to) – *gefallen*
pleasure – *Gefallen, Lust*
plurality – *Vielheit*
position – *Ort, Stelle*
possibility – *Möglichkeit*
power – *Kraft*
power of imagination –
  Einbildungskraft
power of judgment – *Beurteilungskraft,*
  Urteilskraft
predisposition – *Anlage*
preservation – *Erhaltung*
pretend (to) – *fingiren*
principle – *Grundsatz, Satz*
production – *Erzeugung*
proficiency – *Fertigkeit*
progress – *Fortschritt*
propensity – *Hang*
proper – *eigentlich*
proposition – *Satz*
providence – *Vorsehung*
purpose – *Absicht*
purposiveness – *Zweckmässigkeit*

quantity – *Menge, Grösse, Quantitaet*

reaction – *Rückwirkung*
reason (contrary to) – *vernunftwidrig*
reason – *Vernunft*
receptivity – *Empfänglichkeit*
reciprocal – *wechselseitig*
reciprocal action – *Wechselwirkung*

reciprocally – *wechselweise*
recognize (to) – *erkennen*
reference – *Beziehung*
relation – *Beziehung, Verhältnis,*
  Relation
represent (to) – *vorstellen*
representation – *Vorstellung*
resistance – *Widerstand*
resisting – *widerstehende, widerstrebende*
restricted – *eingeschränkt*
rule – *Regel*

sameness – *Einerleiheit, Gleichheit*
satisfaction – *Wohlgefallen, Befriedigung,*
  Genugtuung
seeming – *Schein*
sensation – *Empfindung*
sense (to) – *empfinden*
sense – *Sinn*
sense (common) – *gemeinen*
  Menschenverstand
senseless – *sinnlos*
sensibility – *Sinnlichkeit*
sensible – *empfindbar, sinnlich*
sensitive – *empfindlich*
sensory – *sinnlich*
sensuous – *sensuell*
separate (to) – *abscheiden, absondern,*
  trennen
sequence – *Folgerung, Folge*
series – *Reihe*
shape – *Gestalt*
signifying faculty –
  Bezeichnungsvermögen
simultaneous – *gleichzeitig*
singular – *einzelne*
singularity – *Einzelheit*
skill – *Geschicklichkeit*
sort – *Gattung*
soul – *Seele*
source – *Ursprung*
space – *Raum*
specific – *bestimmt*
specious – *vernünftelnde*

spirit – *Geist*
spiritual – *geistig, geistlich*
spontaneity – *Selbsttätigkeit,*
   Spontaneitaet
standard – *Masstab*
state – *Zustand*
stimulus – *Anreiz, Bewegungsursache,*
   Reiz
subsist (to) – *bestehen*
subsistent – *bestehende*
substance – *Substanz*
substantiate (to) – *dartun*
succession – *Succession, Folge*
successive – *aufeinander, nacheinander*
suffer (to) – *leiden*
suffering – *Leiden*
sufficient – *zureichend, genugsam,*
   hinreichend
suitability – *Geschicklichkeit*
supernatural – *übernatürlich*
supersensible – *übersinnlich*
survival – *Fortdauer*
survive (to) – *fortdauern*
suspend (to) – *aufheben*

temptation – *Lockung*
thing – *Ding*
thought – *Gedanke*
time – *Zeit*
totality – *Allheit, Totalität*
touch (to) – *berühren*
transform (to) – *verwandeln*
transformation – *Verwandelung*
transition – *Übergang, Überschritt*

transitoriness – *Vergänglichkeit*
truth – *Wahrheit*

understanding – *Verstand*
unification – *Vereinigung*
union – *Vereinigung*
unit – *Einheit*
united – *einig*
unity – *Einheit, Unität*
universal – *allgemein*
universe – *All*
unlimited – *uneingeschränkt*
use – *Gebrauch, Nutzen*
useful – *nützlich*
usefulness – *Nützlichkeit*

virtue – *Tugend*
vocation – *Bestimmung*
voluntarily – *willkürlich*
voluntary – *willkürlich*

whole – *Ganze*
will – *Wille*
willing – *Wollen*
wish – *Wunsch*
wit – *Witz*
work – *Werk*
world – *Welt*
world (of the understanding) –
   Verstandes Welt
world (sensible) – *Sinnen Welt*
worth – *Werth, Würde*

yearning – *Sehnsucht*

German-English glossary

Abänderung – modification
Abbildungskraft – illustrative power
Abgrund – abyss
abscheiden – to separate
Absicht – purpose, intention
absondern – to separate
Actualitaet – actuality
Affect – affection
afficiren – to affect
All – universe
allgemein – general, universal
Allheit – totality
ändern – to change
anerschaffen – innate
angeboren – innate
angenehm – agreeable, pleasant
angewandt – applied
Anlage – predisposition
Annehmlichkeit – comfort
Anreiz – stimulus
Anschauung – intuition
Antrieb – impulse
Anwendung – application
Anziehung – attraction
Art – kind
aufeinander – successive
auffassen – to comprehend
Auffassung – comprehension
aufheben – to suspend
Auflösung – decomposition
Aufmerksamkeit – attentiveness
Ausbildungsvermögen – faculty of
  cultivation
Ausbreitung – extension
Ausdehnung – extension

äußer – outer, external
äußerlich – external

bedeuten – to mean
Bedeutung – meaning
Bedingung – condition
Befriedigung – satisfaction
Begebenheit – event
Begehrung – desire
Begierde – desire
begreifen – to conceive
begrenzt – bounded
Begriff – concept
Beharrlichkeit – perdurability
Behinderung – obstruction
beilegen – to attribute
beleben – to animate
Belieben – discretion, inclination
beliebig – arbitrary
berühren – to touch
Berührung – contact
Beschaffenheit – constitution of a thing
beschränkt – limited
Besondere – particular
beständig – constant
bestehen – to subsist, to persist
bestehende – subsistent
bestimmen – to determine
bestimmt – determinate, specific
Bestimmung – determination, vocation
Bestrebung – endeavor
Betragen – conduct
Betrug – deception
Beurteilung – judgment, assessment
Beurteilungskraft – power of judgment

Bewandtnis – condition
Bewegung – motion
Bewegungsgrund – motive ground, motive
Bewegungsursache – motive cause, stimulus
Bewusstsein – consciousness
Bezeichnungsvermögen – signifying faculty
Beziehung – relation, reference
Bild – image
bildend – formative
bildende Vermögen – formative faculty
Bildungsvermögen – formative faculty
Blendwerk – delusion

darstellen – to exhibit
Dasein – existence
Dauer – duration
dauern – to endure
Denkungsart – disposition
determinirt – determinate
dichten – to invent
Dichtungskraft – fictive power
Dichtungsvermögen – fictive faculty
Ding – thing
Disciplin – discipline
disputiren – to debate

eigentlich – proper
Einbildung – imagination, imaginative faculty
Einbildungskraft – power of imagination, imaginative faculty
Eindruck – impression
Einerleiheit – sameness
Einfluss – influence
eingeschränkt – limited, restricted
Einheit – unity, unit
einig – united
Einschränkung – limitation
einsehen – to comprehend
Einsicht – insight

Einwirkung – effect
Einzelheit – singularity
einzelne – singular
Einzelne – particular [noun]
Empfänglichkeit – receptivity
empfindbar – sensible
empfinden – to sense, to feel
Empfinden – feeling
empfindlich – sensitive
Empfindung – sensation
Empfindungsvermögen – faculty of sensation
Endzweck – final end
entgegengesetze – opposed
entspringen – to arise
entstehen – to arise, to come about
Entstehen – coming about, origination
erdichten – to fabricate
Erdichtung – fabrication, fiction
Erdichtungsvermögen – fictive faculty
Erfahrung – experience
erfinden – to invent
Erhaltung – conservation, preservation
Erinnerungsvermögen – faculty of memory, memory
erkennen – to cognize, to recognize
Erkenntnis – cognition
Erklärung – explanation
Erklärungsart – mode of explanation
Erklärungsgrund – ground of explanation
Erläuterung – elucidation
Erläuterungsurteil – elucidating judgment
Erscheinung – appearance
Erwartung – anticipation
Erwartungsvermögen – anticipatory faculty
erweitern – to extend, to amplify
Erweiterung – extension
Erweiterungsurteil – amplificatory judgment
erzeugen – to generate
Erzeugung – production, generation

Existenz – existence

Facultät – faculty
Fähigkeit – ability
Fertigkeit – proficiency
fingiren – to invent, to pretend
Folge – consequence, sequence, succession
Folgerung – conclusion, sequence
Fortdauer – survival
fortfahren – to continue
Fortgang – continuation
Fortschritt – progress
Fortsetzung – continuation
Fuhlen – feeling

Ganze – whole
Gattung – genus, kind, sort
Gebrauch – use
Gedächtnis – memory
Gedanke – thought
Gefallen – pleasure
Gefuhl – feeling
Gegenbild – correlate
Gegenbildungsvermögen – faculty of correlation
gegenseitig – mutual
Gegenstand – object
Gegenwirkung – counteraction
Gehirnschwiele – corpus callosum
Geist – spirit, mind
Gelegenheit – occasion
Gemeinschaft – interaction, community
gemeinschaftlich – communal
Gemüt – mind
Gemütsart – disposition
geniessen – to enjoy
genugsam – sufficient
Genugtuung – satisfaction
Genuss – enjoyment
geschehen – to happen
Geschicklichkeit – skill, suitability
Gesetz – law

Gesetzmässigkeit – conformity to the law
Gesinnung – disposition
Gespenst – ghost
Gestalt – shape
Gewissen – conscience
Gewohnheit – habit
gleichartig – homogeneous
Gleichgewicht – equilibrium
Gleichgültigkeit – indifference
Gleichheit – sameness, equality
gleichzeitig – simultaneous
Glückseligkeit – happiness
Grenze – boundary, limit
Grösse – quantity, magnitude
Grund – ground
Grundsatz – principle, basic proposition

handeln – to act
Handlung – action
Hang – propensity
Harmonie – harmony
Heiligkeit – holiness
herkommen – to arise from
Hinderniss – hindrance
hinreichend – adequate, sufficient
Hirngespenst – phantom of the brain
Hirnschwiele – corpus callosum
homogen – homogeneous

Illusion – illusion
Imputabilitaet – imputability

Keim – germ
kennen – to be acquainted with, to know
Kenntnis – acquaintance, knowledge
Klugheit – cleverness
Körper – body
körperlich – bodily, corporeal
Kraft – power, force

Leib – human body
leiden – to suffer

515

Leiden – passivity, suffering
leidend – passive
Leidenschaft – passion
Lehre – doctrine
Lockung – temptation
Lust – pleasure

mancherlei – diverse
Mannigfaltigkeit – manifold
Mass – measure
Massgabe – measure
Massstab – standard
Materie – matter
Menge – quantity
Mensch – human being
Menschenverstand (gemeinen) – common
  sense
Merkmal – feature
Missfallen – dissatisfaction
Möglichkeit – possibility
Moral – moral philosophy, morality
Moralität – morality
Motive – motive

Nachahmung – imitation
Nachbildung – imitation
nacheinander – successive
Naturlehre – doctrine of nature
nebeneinander – coexistent
Neigung – inclination
Nichts – nothing
Nichtsein – non-being
nötigen – to necessitate
Nötigung – necessitation, compulsion
Notwendigkeit – necessity
Nutzen – use
Nützlichkeit – usefulness

Objekt – object
Ort – location, place, position

Platz – place

Raum – space
Rechenschaft – account

Recht – justice
Regel – rule
Reich – kingdom
Reihe – series
Reiz – stimulus
Rückwirkung – reaction

Sache – matter, object
Satz – proposition, principle
Scharfsinn – acumen
scharfsinnig – acute
Schätzungsvermögen – faculty of
  assessment
Schein – seeming, illusion
Schicksal – destiny
Schluss – inference
Schöpfung – creation
Schranke – limit
Schwärmerei – wild fantasy
Seele – soul
Sehnsucht – yearning
Sein – being
Selbsttätigkeit – spontaneity
Seligkeit – blessedness
sensuell – sensuous
Sinn – sense
Sinnenunlust – displeasure
sinnlich – sensible, sensory
Sinnlichkeit – sensibility
sinnlos – senseless
Sitte – morals
Sittlichkeit – morality
Sollen – ought [noun]
Stelle – place, position
stetig – constant
Streit – dispute
streiten – to dispute, to argue
Streitigkeit – dispute
Substanz – substance

Tätigkeit – activity
Täuschung – deception, illusion
Trägheit – inertia
trennen – to separate

516

Triebfeder – incentive
Trug – deceit
Tugend – virtue

Übergang – transition
übernatürlich – supernatural
Überschritt – transition
überschwenglich – beyond bounds
übersinnlich – supersensible
Umstand – circumstance
Undurchdringlichkeit – impenetrability
uneingeschränkt – unlimited
Unendlichkeit – infinity
Ungefähr – accident
Ungereimtheit – absurdity
Ungrund – groundlessness
Unität – unity, oneness
Unlust – displeasure
Unterschied – difference
unterscheiden – to differentiate, to
  discriminate
Unterscheidung – discrimination
Unzulänglichkeit – inadequacy
Urbild – archetype
Ursache – cause
Ursprung – source
Urteil – judgment
Urteilskraft – power of judgment
Urwesen – primordial being

veränderung – alteration
verbinden – to connect
Verbindlichkeit – obligation
Verbindung – connection
Vereinigung – unification, union
Vergänglichkeit – transitoriness
vergehen – to pass away, to perish
Vergesellschaftung – association
Vergnügen – gratification
Vergnügung – gratification
Verhalten – conduct
Verhältnis – relation
Verhängnis – fate
Verknüpfung – connection

Vermögen – faculty
vernehmen – to perceive
Vernichtung – annihilation
Vernunft – reason
vernünftelnde – specious
vernunftwidrig – contrary to reason
verschieden – diverse, different
Verschiedenheit – diversity
Verstand – understanding
Verursachten – caused
verwandeln – to transform
Verwandelung – transformation
Vielheit – plurality
vollkommen – perfect
vollständig – complete
Vorbildungskraft – anticipatory power
vorhanden – to be existent
Vorsehung – providence
vorstellen (sich) – to represent (to
  imagine)
Vorstellung – representation

Wahl – choice
wählen – to choose
Wahn – delusion
Wahnsinn – insanity
Wahnwitz – absurdity, madness
Wahrheit – truth
wahrnehmen – to perceive
Wahrnehmung – perception
Wechseln – change
wechselseitig – reciprocal
wechselweise – reciprocally
Wechselwirkung – reciprocal action
Welt – world
Weltall – cosmos
Weltganze – cosmos
Weltkörper – mundane body
Weltraum – cosmos
Werk – work
Werth – worth
Wesen – being, essence
wider – opposed
widernatürlich – contrary to nature

517

widersinnig – nonsensical
Widerstand – resistance
widerstehende – resisting
widerstrebende – resisting
Widerstreit – conflict
Wille – will
Willkür – choice (power of)
willkürlich – arbitrary, voluntary, voluntarily
wirken – to be active, to affect
wirkend – efficient
wirklich – actual
Wirklichkeit – actuality
Wirksamkeit – effectiveness
Wirkung – action, effect
Wirkungs Gesetz – causal law
Wissen – knowledge
Witz – wit
wohlgefallen – satisfaction
Wohllust – delight, lust
Wollen – willing
Wunder – miracle
Wunsch – wish
Würde – worth, dignity

Zeit – time

zergliedert – dissected
Zergliederungsurteil – dissecting judgment
Zerteilung – disintegration
Zeugung – generation
Zucht – discipline
Zufall – chance
zufällig – contingent
Zufälligkeit – contingency
Zufriedenheit – contentment
zugleich – concurrent
zulänglich – adequate
Zurechnung – imputation, ascription
Zurechnungsfähigkeit – imputability
zureichend – sufficient
zusammengesetzt – composite
Zusammenhang – connection
zusammenhängen – to conjoin, to cohere
Zusammensetzung – composition
Zusammenstimmung – harmony
Zustand – state
zuträglich – beneficial
Zwang – compulsion
Zweck – end
Zweckmässigkeit – purposiveness

Latin-German equivalents
occurring in the text

absque ratione intermedia; G: *Grunde ohne Zwischengrund* (28: 662)/ grounds without intermediate ground

abyssus; G: *Abgrund* (28: 661)/ abyss

actio immanens; G: *innere Handlung* (28: 565)/ inner action

actualitas; G: *Wirklichkeit* (28: 987)/ actuality

actuare; G: *wirklich machen* (29: 823)/ to make actual

acumen; G: *Scharfsinn/* acumen (cf. Baumgarten, §573: Scharfsinnigkeit)

aequilibrium; G: *Gleichheit* (29: 901)/ equality

agere; G: *handeln* (28: 565)/ acting

agirt; G: *handelt* (29: 772)/ acts

animalia; G: *lebende Wesen* (28: 594)/ animals/living beings

apperceptio; G: *Bewusstsein* (28: 584)/ apperception

appetitio per motiva; G: *intellectuellen Begierden* (29: 895)/ desire aroused by motives

– per stimulos; G: *sinnliche Begierde* (29: 895)/ desire aroused by stimuli

arbitrium; G: *Willkür* (28: 255, 587, 676; 29: 896, 1014)/ power of choice

– intellectuale sive superius; G: *die obere oder vernünftige Willkür* (29: 1015)/ the higher or rational power of choice

– liberum; G: *freie Willkühr* (28: 254)/ power of free choice

association; G: *Vergesellschaftung* (29: 883)/ association

casus; G: *Ungefähr* (29: 924)/ chance; G: *blindes Ungefähr* (29: 1006)/ blind accident

circumstantia; G: *Umstand* (29: 573)/ circumstance

coactio; G: *Zwang* (29: 897)/ compulsion

complacentia; G: *Wohlgefallen* (29: 1013)/ satisfaction

completudo; G: *Totalität* (28: 195)/ completeness

conatum; G: *Wünschen* (29: 1013)/ wishing

conatus; G: *Bestrebung* (28: 565; 17: 73)/ endeavor

conceptus; G: *Begriff* (29: 888)/ concept

conceptus inanis; G: *leerer Begriff* (29: 961)/ empty concept

consensus; G: *Übereinstimmung* (28: 549)/ agreement

consequens; G: *Folge* (29: 818)/ consequence

corpus callosum; G: *Hirnschwiele* (28: 756; 29: 909, 1027)/ corpus callosum

corpuscula; G: *Unsichtbaren Teilen* (29: 932)/ corpuscles

519

datum; G: *was gegeben ist* (28: 575)/ the given

decomposition; G: *Auflösung* (29: 852)/ decomposition

dignitas; G: *Würde* (29: 846)/ worth

dimensio; G: *Abmessung* (29: 994)/ dimension

displicentia; G: *Missfallen* (29: 1013)/ dissatisfaction

efficax; G: *wirksam* (28: 676)/ effective

efficiens; G: *wirkend* (28: 676)/ efficient

ens singulare; G: *Individuum* (28: 560)/ singular thing

entia rationis ratiocinantis; G: *Hirngespenst* (29: 852)/ beings of the reasoning reason

eodem tempore; G: *zugleich* (29: 963)/ at the same time

essentia; G: *Wesen* (28: 553)/ essence

exspectationis casuum similium; G: *Erwartung ähnlicher Fälle* (28: 674)/ expectation of similar cases

extraessentiale; G: *ausserwentlichen* (29: 1004)/ beyond the essential

facere; G: *tun* (28: 565)/ doing

facultas; G: Vermögen
 – *appetitionum practicarum;* G: *Vermögen, practisch zu begehren* (29: 896)/ faculty of practical desires
 – *appetitiva;* G: *Begehrungsvermögen* (28: 676)/ faculty of desire
 – *characteristica;* G: *Gegenbildungs vermögen* (28: 238)/ faculty of characterization
 – *fingendi;* G: *Dichtungsvermögen* (28: 585)/ fictive faculty
 – *formandi;* G: *Abbildungskraft* (28: 231)/ illustrative power; *Vermögen der Abbildung* (28: 235)/ faculty of illustration
 – *imaginandi;* G: *Nachbildungskraft* (28: 231)/ imitative power; *Vermögen der*

Nachbildung (28: 235)/ faculty of imitation
 – *praevidendi;* G: *Vorbildungskraft* (28: 231)/ anticipatory power; *Vermögen der Vorbildung* (28: 235)/ faculty of anticipation

fatum; G: *Verhängnis* (28: 663)/ fate; G: *blinde Notwendigkeit*/ blind necessity

genus; G: *Gattung* (29: 991)/ sort

glandula pinealis; G: *Zirbeldrüse* (28: 686, 755; 29: 1027)/ pineal gland

glandulum pinealem; G: *Zirbeldrüse* (29: 1027)/ pineal gland

habitus; G: *Fertigkeit* (28: 565)/ aptitude; *Denkungsart* (28: 678)/ disposition

homogeneitatem; G: *Dinge von einer und derselben Gattung* (29: 991)/ homogeneous things

hyperphysicus; G: *Supernaturalist* (28: 684)/ supernaturalist

immutabilien; G: *Unveränderlichen* (28: 558)/ the unalterable

in commercio; G: *in Gemeinschaft* (28: 591)/ in interaction

inclinatio; G: *Neigung* (28: 588)/ inclination

indoles; G: *Gemütsart* (28: 258)/ character (cf. Baumgarten, §538)
 – *abjecta;* G: *unedle Gemütsart* (28: 258)/ humble character
 – *erecta;* G: *edle Gemütsart* (28: 258)/ lofty character

influxum mutuum; G: *wechselseitigen Einfluss* (28: 590)/ reciprocal influence

influxus; G: *Einfluss* (28: 565)/ influence

ingenium; G: *Witz* (28: 244)/ wit

isola; G: *Insel* (29: 807)/ island

judicium determinandi; G: *bestimmende Urteilskraft* (28: 675)/ determining power of judgment

letheum poculum; G: *Becher der Vergessenheit* (28: 689)/ cup of forgetfulness

lex associationis idearum; G: *Gesetz der Vergesellschaftung* (28: 674)/ law of the association of ideas

lex exspectationis casuum similium; G: *das Gesetz der Erwartung ähnlicher Fälle* (28: 585)/ the law of expectation of similar cases

limes; G: *Schranken* (29: 994)/ limits (cf. 28: 644)

limites; G: *Schranken* (29: 994)/ limits

magnum; G: *gross* (29: 997)/ large

maxime; G: *Maximen* (28: 678)/ maxims

meta [Greek]; G: *jenseit* (29: 773)/ beyond

metempsychosis [Greek]; G: *Seelenwanderung* (28: 593)/ migration of the soul; G: *Seelenversetzung* (28: 769)/ migration of the soul

motive; G: *Bewegungsgründe* (28: 254)/ motives

motivum; G: *Bewegungsgrund* (28: 587)/ motive; G: *Bewegungs-Ursache* (28: 589)/ motive

mutabilien; G: *Veränderlichen* (28: 558)/ the alterable

nexus; G: *Verknüpfung* (28: 549)/ connection (cf. *CrPR*, B 201n)

notiones connatae; G: *angebornen Begriffe* (28: 542)/ innate concepts

omnitudo; G: *die Allheit* (28: 196)/ totality

oppositum; G: *das Gegenteil* (28: 558)/ the opposite

optare; G: *der Wunsch* (29: 1013)/ wish

organon [Greek]; G: *Instrument* (28: 286)/ instrument

originarius; G: *ursprünglich* (28: 666)/ original

otiosae; G: *müssige* (29: 895)/ idle

papillon [French]; G: *Schmetterling* (29: 876)/ butterfly

particularia; G: *besondere* (29: 985)/ particular

parvum; G: *klein* (29: 997)/ small

passio; G: *das Leiden* (29: 772)/ suffering

per se; G: *an sich selbst* (28: 561)/ in itself

perduratio; G: *Beharrlichkeit* (28: 564)/ perdurability

plica; G: *Falte* (29: 758)/ fold

porticus; G: *Spaziergang* (28: 538)/ walkway

potentialitas; G: *Möglichkeit* (29: 986)/ potentiality

praejudicium; G: *Fascination, Behexung* (28: 673)/ prejudgment

praeternaturale; G: *widernatürlich* (28: 667; 29: 869)/ contrary to nature

principia; G: *Erkenntnis Gründen* (29: 945)/ principles

principium contradictionis; G: *Satz des Widerspruchs* (28: 549)/ principle of contradiction

principium rationis sufficientis; G: *Satz des zureichendes Grundes* (28: 551)/ principle of sufficient reason

propensio; G: *Hang* (28: 588)/ propensity; G: *Neigung* (28: 679)/ inclination

quantitas extensiva; G: *extensiven Grösse* (29: 999)/ extensive quantity

quantitatas; G: *Grösse* (29: 999)/ quantity

quantitates; G: *Grössen* (28: 562)/ quantities

quantum; G: *Menge* (28: 568)/ the how much

ratio logica; G: *logische Grund* (28: 549)/ logical ground

– *prima;* G: *oberste Grund* (28: 552)/ highest ground

rationis; G: *Grunds* (29: 834)/ of the ground

reactio; G: *Ruckwirkung* (28: 208)/ reaction

repraesentatio communis; G: *Merkmal das mehreren gemein* (28: 672)/ common representation

resistentia; G: *Gegenwirkung* (28: 208)/ resistance

resistenz; G: *Wiederstand* (29: 825)/ resistance

respectus; G: *Beziehung* (28: 549, 564)/ relation

secundum quid; G: *respective* (28: 589)/ in some respect

sensibilia; G: *empfindbaren* (29: 983)/ sensibles

sensitivus; G: *sinnlich* (29: 983)/ sensory

simplicitas; G: *Einfachheit* (28: 683)/ simplicity

simul; G: *zu gleicher Zeit* (28: 543)/ at the same time

singularia; G: *einzelne* (29: 985)/ singular

sopita; G: *schlummernd* (29: 929, 1029, 1033)/ slumbering

spiritus; G: *Geist* (29: 1026)/ spirit

stabilitas; G: *Beharrlichkeit* (28: 564)/ perdurability

stimulus; G: *Anreizung* (28: 587)/ stimulus

stimuli; G: *Bewegursachen* (28: 254)/ stimuli

stoa [Greek]; G: *Spaziergang* (28: 538)/ walkway

sub conditione restrictiva; G: *unter gewissen Bedingungen* (29: 550)/ under certain conditions

sub nulla hypothesis; G: *unter gar keinen Bedingungen* (29: 550)/ under no conditions

substantiare; G: *zur Substanz machen* (28: 682)/ to make into a substance

supernaturale; G: *übernatürlich* (28: 667; 29: 869)/ supernatural

taedium; G: *Unlust* (29: 1013), *Sinnenunlust* (28: 675)/ displeasure

tertium datur; G: *giebt es ein Drittes* (29: 549)/ there is a third

tertium non datur; G: *giebt's kein Drittes* (29: 549)/ there is no third

totus; G: *Ganzen* (28: 568)/ whole

transmigration; G: *Seelenversetzung* (28: 769)/ transmigration

unicitas; G: *Ein(zeln)heit* (28: 683)/ singul(arity)

universaliis; G: *allgemeine* (29: 985)/ universal

unum idemque; G: *eben dasselbe Ding* (29: 839)/ one and the same thing

vacuum extra mundanum; G: *leerer Raum ausserhalb der Welt* (29: 922)/ extramundane vacuum

vicissitudo; G: *Veränderung* (28: 564)/ vicissitude

vitium subreptionis; G: *Fehler des Erschleichens* (28: 673)/ fallacy of subreption

voluptas; G: *Lust* (29: 1013), *Sinnenlust* (28: 675)/ pleasure

Concordance of Baumgarten's Metaphysics
and Kant's Metaphysics lectures

Concordance of Kant's Lectures on Metaphysics	Baumgarten §§1–1000 1757	Herder 28: 1–166, 869–962 1762–64	anon-L₁ 28: 167–350 mid-1770s?	Mrongovius 29: 747–940 1782/83
I. INTRODUCTION	1–3	(5–7)	(171–7)	747–84
Overview of metaphysics		x	(172–5)	747–57
Cognitions . . .				
. . . aggregate & systematic			(186)	747, 785
. . . coordinate & subordinate			(171–2)	747–8
. . . rational & historical			(172–3)	748–50
. . . mathematical & philosophical			x	749–52
. . . dogmatic & critical				753
Philosophy/metaphysics . . .				
. . . definition & term	1		(172, 174)	749–50, 773
. . . pure & applied			(172–5)	750–5, 775
. . . other areas of	2–3		(172–5)	753–7
. . . transcendental			x	750–6
Learning philosophy		(7)	x	x
History of metaphysics	x	x	(175–7)	757–64
studied prior to physics				757
language and philosophy			x	757–8
intelligibles & sensibles			(175)	759
reason: concrete & abstract				782–3
appearance & illusion				758–9
dogmatism & skepticism			(176)	x
concepts: innate & acquired			232–4	760–3
intuition: sensible & intellectual			206–7, 241	759–61, 888
physiology of pure reason			x	763–4, 781
The use of metaphysics	x	x	x	766–82, 937–40
transcendent & immanent				767–8
negative & positive				773–6, 937–9
interest: speculative & practical				774
morality: its nature				776–8
need for a critical metaphysics				764, 779–84
II. ONTOLOGY	4–350	(7–39, 843–9)	(177–91)	784–848
Introduction	4–6	(7)	(185–8)	784–7
definition	4			752, 784
transcendental philosophy	x			748–8
Analytic & synthetic judgments	x		(186–7)	787, 793–4
criteria of truth	x		(186–7)	788–92, 806
synthetic *a priori* judgments	x		(187)	788, 794–5
Intuitions and concepts	x		(177–86)	795–806
forms of intuition (space & time)	x		(177–81)	797–800, 829–34
forms of intuition as ideal	x		x	799–800
intuitive intellect	x		(179)	796–7
judgments (logical functions)	x		(186)	801
categories (forms of understanding)	x		(186)	802
Aristotle's categories	x		(186)	801–3

x = topic is neither mentioned nor discussed.   () = passages not included in this translation.

Baumgarten 1757	Volckmann 28:351–459 1784/85	von Schön I 28:461–524 1780s?	anon-L₂ 28:531–610 1790/91?	Dohna 28:615–702 1792/93	anon-K₂ 28:705–816 early 1790s	Vigilantius (K₃) 29:943–1040 1794/95
1–3	(355–90)	(463–9)	531–42	(615–22)	(709–10)	945–59
	(355–67)	(463–6)	531–5	(615–18)	(709)	945–56
	(355)	(463)	534–5	(622, 628)	x	x
	x	(463–4)	x	(628)	x	
	(356–7)	(463)	531–5	x	x	945
	x	(464)	531–4	(616)	x	945–7, 957
	x	(464–6)	x	x	775	949
1	(357–8, 381–2)	(464, 468)	532–3, 540–2	(615–16)	(709)	946–7, 970
	(359–60)	x	539–40	(616)		x
2–3	(364–7)	(470–1)	533–4, 541–2	(617, 656)	(709)	945, 956
	(359–4)	(470)	576–7	(651–6)		948–9, 956
	x	x	531–4	x		x
x	(367–80)	(466–8)	535–40	(618–20)	(709–10)	956–9
	(367–8)	x	x			
	(369–70)	x	536	x		954
	(370)	(466)	536–7	(618–19)		x
	x	x	535	x		x
	(370)	x	536, 539	(654)	(710)	971–2
		x	538–40	(619–20)		951, 955–6
	(372–5)	(466–8)	542	(619)	(709)	949–51, 954
	(371–2)			(619)		953–4
	(376–7)		540			958–9
x	(380–90)	x	x	x		x
	x			(617)		
	(381–4)					
	(380–1)		536	(618)		
	(383–7)					948
	(388–9)		540	(621)		948–9
4–350	(390–440)	(469–524)	542–77	(622–56)	(710–27)	960–1006
4–6	(390–2)	(469–71)	542	(622–3)	(711)	960
4	(390–1)	(474)	541–2	(622)	(711)	960
x	(391–2)	(470)	576–7		774–5	960, 967, 970
x	(392–5)	(473–7)	544–6	(622–3)	(711)	967–70
x	(392–3)	(476–7)	543–4	(622–3)	(711)	963–6
x	(393–5)	(475)	545, 549–50	(654–5)	(711)	968–70, 973–4
x	(395–9)	(471–4)	546–8	x	(712–714)	966–71
x	(395)	(474, 482–4)	546	(652–4)	(712)	969–79
x	x	(477)	x	x	x	979–82
x	x	x	x	x	x	972, 978
x	(395–8)	(472, 480–1)	547	(626–27)	(713–14)	981–5, 987
x	(396–8)	(479–82)	547	(626, 652)	(713–14)	984–7
x	x	(481)	548	(634, 652)	x	984, 987

x = topic is neither mentioned nor discussed.   () = passages not included in this translation.

Concordance of Kant's Lectures on Metaphysics	Baumgarten §§1–1000 1757	Herder 28: 1–166, 869–962 1762–64	anon-L$_I$ 28: 167–350 mid-1770s?	Mrongovius 29: 747–940 1782/83
A. INTERNAL UNIVERSAL PREDICATES				
1. Possibility and impossibility	7–18	(7–13, 53–4)	x	789–93, 811
... not highest concept	x			811
... real (metaphysical) & logical	x			811–14
principle of contradiction	7–9			791–3, 810–13
principle of excluded middle	10			791, 793, 810
principle of identity	11			789, 791, 807
contradiction: actual & apparent	12			792–3, 833
contradiction: obvious & hidden	13			793
ground and consequence	14			806–8
possibility: internal & external	15–18			790, 813
2. Connection	19–33	(13–14, 54–5)	x	807–10, 813–18
ground: real & logical	x			807–10
connected & unconnected	19			x
principle of ground (reason)	20			813–17
ground: sufficient & insufficient	21			817
principle of sufficient reason	22			813–15
nothing is without a consequence	23			813, 817
reciprocal connection	24			817
transitivity of grounding	25–6			x
ground: mediate & immediate	27			817
ground: subordinate & coordinate	28			817
modus ponens & tollens	29–32			808, 818
connection: transitivity	33			x
3. Being and essence	34–71	(14–15, 54)	x	818–22
determinate/determinable	34–5			818–19
reality & negation	36			770
determination: internal & external	37			819–20
same & different	38			820
essence & essential parts	39–40			820
essence: logical & real (nature)	x	49		820–1
affections (attributes & modes)	41–52			820
essence = internal possibility	53			821
actuality and possibility	54–60			820–2
possible & actual not predicates	x			822
something: logical & metaphysical	x			x
thing (*ens*)	61			x
non-thing/fictional thing	62			x
thing, essence, & essential parts	63–4			x
mode undetermined by essence	65			x
actuality compossible with essence	66			x
discrimination of things	67–8			x
quality and quantity	69			x
similar, equal, & congruent	70–1			x
4. Unity	72–7	(15–16)	x	x
separate and separable	72			
transcendental unity	73			
multitude and categorical unity	74			
determinations in each thing	75			
unity: absolute & hypothetical	76			
the single (*unicum*)	77			

x = topic is neither mentioned nor discussed.   () = passages not included in this translation.

Baumgarten 1757	Volckmann 28:351–459 1784/85	von Schön I 28:461–524 1780s?	anon-L₂ 28:531–610 1790/91?	Dohna 28:615–702 1792/93	anon-K₂ 28:705–816 early 1790s	Vigilantius (K₃) 29:943–1040 1794/95
7–18	(406–7)	(488)	524–4	(623–7)	x	960–6
x	x	x	543, 552	(628)		960
x	x	x	544, 547, 554	658		985–ú, 1020
7–9	(406)	(487–8)	543–4	(623–4)		960–4, 965
10	(410)	x	544–5, 549	(624)		965–6
11	x	x	544–5	x		964–5
12	x	(479)	544–5	(624)		965
13	x	(479)	544	(624)		965
14	(399)	(485–6)	548–50	(624–5, 627)		x
15–18	(406–7)	(488)	550	(627)		x
19–33	(407–10)	(489–92)	551–2	(627–8)	x	x
x	x	(486–8)	548–9	(625)		
19	(407)	(489)	x	x		
20	(407–8)	(489)	551	(625, 627)		
21	(409)	(490)	552–3	x		
22	(407–9)	(489)	546, 551–2	x		
23	(409)	x	x	(625, 627)		
24	(409)	(489–90)	x	x		
25–6	x	x	x	x		
27	(409)	(490)	552	(628)		
28	(410)	(490–1)	549, 552	(628)		
29–32	x	(486–7, 491)	549, 552	(628)		
33	x	x	x	x		
34–71	(410–14)	(491–5)	552–5	(628–31)	(723–4)	
34–5	(410)	(491)	552	(628)		
36	(410–11)	(491–2)	552	x		
37	(411)	(492)	552	(629)	992, 1003	
38	x	x	x	x		
39–40	(411)	(492–3)	553	(629)		
x	(411)	(492–3)	552–53, 559	(629)		
41–52	(411)	(493)	x	(629)		
53	x	x	x	x		
54–60	(412–14)	(493–4)	554–5	(630)	(724)	
x	(412–13)	(494)	554	(630)	(723)	
x	(414)	x	544, 552, 555	x		
61	(414)	(494)	555	(628)		
62	(414)	(494–5)	555–6	(630)		
63–4	(414)	x	x	x		
65	(414)	x	x	(630)		
66	x	x	x	x		
67–8	x	(495)	x	(630)		
69	(414)	(495)	x	(630–1)		991–2, 998
70–1	(414)	(495)	x	(631)		
72–7	(414–6)	(495–8)	555–6	(631–2)	(714)	989–90
72				(631)		
73			562			989–90
74		(497)		(631)		989–90
75						
76						989
77						

x = topic is neither mentioned nor discussed. () = passages not included in this translation.

Concordance of Kant's Lectures on Metaphysics	Baumgarten §§1–1000 1757	*Herder* 28: 1–166, 869–962 1762–64	*anon-L$_I$* 28: 167–350 mid-1770s?	*Mrongovius* 29: 747–940 1782/83
5a. Order	78–88	(16)	x	x
order & disorder	78–9			
ground: suitable & deficient	80–2			
prescriptions in orders	83–8			
5b. Truth	89–93	(16–17)	x	x
. . . metaphysical & transcendental	89			
. . . and grounds of cognition	90			
dreaming	91			
universal principles	92			
objective certainty	93			
6. Perfection	94–100	(17–18)	x	766–7
harmony & order	94–5			x
. . . simple & composite	96			x
exceptions: true & apparent	97			x
. . . transcendental & accidental	98–9			766, 936–7
the perfect is the good	100			865

B. INTERNAL DISJUNCTIVE PREDICATES

1. Necessary and contingent	101–23	(18)	x	x
necessity & contingency	101			
. . . absolute & hypothetical	102–5			
. . . & essence/affections	106–12			
. . . & unity/order/truth	113–19			
fictions and non-things	120			
perfection & necessity	121–3			
necessity: logical & real	x			
2. Alterable and unalterable	124–34	(18–19)	x	x
. . . and succession	124–5			
. . . internal & external	126			
. . . absolute & hypothetical	127–8			
. . . and the necessary	129–34			808
essence: logical & real	x			
3. Real and negative	135–47	(19–20)	x	x
opposition: logical & real	x			807, 810
real and negative (partly real)	135–8			
ground requires reality	139–40			
harmony & reality	141–2			
perfection: essential & accidental	143–5			
good & bad: metaphysical	146–7			
4. Particular and universal	148–54	(21)	x	x
thing: singular & universal	148			
universal: concrete & abstract	149			
species, genus, & difference	150–1			
singulars are actual	152			
genus in species & individual	153–4			

x = topic is neither mentioned nor discussed.　　　　() = passages not included in this translation.

Baumgarten 1757	Volckmann 28:351–459 1784/85	von Schön I 28:461–524 1780s?	anon-L₂ 28:531–610 1790/91?	Dohna 28:615–702 1792/93	anon-K₂ 28:705–816 early 1790s	Vigilantius (K₃) 29:943–1040 1794/95
78–88	x	(497)	x	(632)		
78–9						
80–2						
83–8				(632)		
89–93	(414–16)	(495–7)	555–6	(631–2)	(714)	990
89	(415)		556, 562	(632)		989–90
90	x					
91	x			(632)		
92	x			(643)		
93	x					
94–100	(414–16)	(495–7)	555–66	(631–3)	(714)	990
94–5	x			(632–3)		
96	x					
97	x			(633)		
98–9	(415–16)		555–6, 560	(632)		990, 1001
100	(416)			676		990
101–23	(416–19)	(498–500)	556–8	(633–4)	(722–4)	x
101	(418)	(498)	557	(633)		
102–5	(417–18)	(498–500)	557–8	(633–4)	(722)	
106–12	(417)	(499–500)	x	(633)		
113–19	x	x	x	x		
120	x	x	x	x		
121–3	x	x	x	x		
x	(418–19)	(498)	557–8	(633–4)		985–6
124–34	(419–20)	(500–1)	558–9	(634)	(720–1)	x
124–5	(419)	(500)	558	(634)	(721)	
126	x	x	x	x	x	
127–8						
129–34	(419–20)	(501)	559	(634)	x	
x	x	x	559	(634)	x	
135–47	(420–1)	(501–3)	559–60	(634–6)	(715–17)	998–1001
x	(420–1)	(502)	549, 558–60	(635)	(716–17)	1001
135–8	(420)	(501–3)	559–60	(635–6)	(715–17)	998
139–40	x	x	x	(635–6)	(717)	x
141–2	(421)	x	560	x	x	x
143–5	(421)	x	560	(635)	(716)	1001
146–7	(421)	x	555	(634–5)	(716)	1001
148–54	(421–2)	(503–4)	560	(636)	x	x
148	(421–2)	(503)	560	x		
149	(422)	(503)	560	(636)		
150–1	(422)	(504)	560	x		
152	x	(503–4)	560	x		
153–4	x	x	x	x		

x = topic is neither mentioned nor discussed.   () = passages not included in this translation.

Concordance of Kant's Lectures on Metaphysics	Baumgarten §§1–1000 1757	*Herder* 28: 1–166, 869–962 1762–64	anon-L*1* 28: 167–350 mid-1770s?	*Mrongovius* 29: 747–940 1782/83
5a. Whole and part	155–64	(21–2)	x	x
whole, part, & complement	155			
part: actual & possible	156–7			
thing: complete & incomplete	158			
magnitude & number	159			
more & less	160–1			
increased & decreased	162–4			
5b. First principles of the science of intensity	165–90	(22–3, 843)	x	766–7
Intensive magnitude of . . .				
. . . possibility	165			x
. . . ground (fruitfulness)	166			x
. . . connection (harmony)	167			766
. . . hypothetical possibility	168			x
. . . sufficient & ultimate ground	169–70			
. . . essence	171			
. . . universal connection	172			
. . . unity	173			x
. . . identity	174			
. . . order	175			766
. . . agreement with grounds	176–9			x
. . . conformity to law	180	(843)		x
law: higher & lower	181–2			x
. . . order	183			
. . . truth	184			x
. . . perfection	185			766
exceptions to laws	186			x
worst and best (*optimum*)	187			x
. . . contingency	188–89			x
. . . alteration	190	(843)		767
6a. Substance and accident	191–204	(23–5, 843–5)	x	769–72
substance & accident	191–2			769–70
apparent substances	193			771, 827–8
accidents require substances	194–5			769
the substantial	196			771
power & substance	197–9			770–1
apparent accidents	200			771
power & accidents	201			770
substance: necessary & contingent	202			x
intensive magnitude of inherence	203			x
dynamics: science of power	204			x
power: primitive & derived	x			770–3, 822
hidden qualities	x			x
6b. State	205–23	(25–8, 845–7)	x	772–3, 822–5
. . . internal & external	206–7			772
. . . modification & variation	208–9			772
acting & suffering	210			772–3, 822–3
influence	211			823
acting & suffering: real & ideal	212			823
reaction & conflict	213–14			824
action: simple & composite	215			823, 845
faculty & receptivity	216–19			772, 823–4
power: living & dead	220			824–5
hindrance & resistance	221–2			824–5
presence & contact	223			824–5

x = topic is neither mentioned nor discussed. () = passages not included in this translation.

Baumgarten 1757	Volckmann 28:351–459 1784/85	von Schön I 28:461–524 1780s?	anon-L₂ 28:531–610 1790/91?	Dohna 28:615–702 1792/93	anon-K₂ 28:705–816 early 1790s	Vigilantius (K₃) 29:943–1040 1794/95
155–64	(422–4)	(504–6)	560–1	(636–7)		
155	(422)	(504–5)	560	(636)		
156–7	(423)	(505)	x	x		
158	(422)	(505)	561	(636)		
159	(422–4, 437)	(505–6)	561	(636–7)	(715)	993, 995–6
160–1	(424)	(506)	561	(637)		997
162–4	(424)	(506)	561	x		
165–90	(424–8)	(506–10)	562	(637–8)	(716)	999–1000
165	(426)	(508)	562	(637)		
166	x	x	562	(638)		
167	x	x	x	x		
168	x	(508)	562	(637)		
169–70			562			
171						
172						
173	(426–7)	x	562	(638)		
174						
175	x	(509)	x	x		
176–9	(427)	x	562	(638)		
180	(427)	x	x	x		
181–2	x	x	x	x		
183						
184	(426–7)	(509)	562	x		
185	(426–7)	(509)	562	(638)		
186	(427)	(509)	x	x		
187	(427–8)	x	x	(638)	(716)	
188–89	x	x	x	x		
190		(509)	x	x		
191–204	(428–32)	(510–12)	562–4	(638–9)	(718)	1002–6
191–2	(428–32)	(510)	563	(638)	(718)	1002–4
193	x	x	x	(639)	x	1005–6
194–5	(428)	x	564	x	x	x
196	(429)	(511)	563	(639)	(718)	1004
197–9	(431)	(511–12)	564–5	(639)	(718)	1033
200	x	x	x	x	x	x
201	x	x	x	x	x	x
202	x	x	x	x	x	x
203			x			
204	x	(512)	x	(639)	x	x
x	(431–2)	(512, 515)	564	x	x	x
x	(432)	(512)	564	x	x	1008
205–23	(432–5)	(512–15)	564–5	(639–41)	(718–19)	x
206–7	(432–3)	(512)	564	(639)	x	
208–9	x	(512)	x	(639)	(718)	
210	(433)	(512)	564–5	(639), 657	(718)	
211	(433)	(513)	565	(640)	(720)	
212	(433–4)	(513–14)	x	(640), 684	(718–19), 759	x
213–14	(433–5)	(514)	x	(640)	x	
215	x	x	x	x	x	
216–19	(434–5)	(514–15)	565	(640)	x	
220	(434)	(515)	565	(640–1)	(718)	
221–2	(434–5)	(515)	565	x	(718)	
223	(435)	x	x	(641)	(720)	

x = topic is neither mentioned nor discussed.   () = passages not included in this translation.

Concordance of Kant's Lectures on Metaphysics	Baumgarten §§1–1000 1757	*Herder* 28: 1–166, 869–962 1762–64	*anon-L_I* 28: 167–350 mid-1770s?	*Mrongovius* 29: 747–940 1782/83
7a. Simples and composites	224–9	(28, 847)	x	825–7
composition: real & ideal	224–5			825–8
composition & essence	226			826
origin & death . . .	227			826–7
. . . *ex nihilo*	228			826
. . . & contingency	229			832–3
7b. Monads	230–45	(28–31, 847–9)	(177–81)	827–34
monad is a simple substance	230		x	827
composites . . .	231–2		x	827
. . . are phenomenal substances	233–4		x	827–8
. . . consist of monads	235		x	827–8
monads arise *ex nihilo*	236–7		x	832–3
space and time	238–40		(177–81)	830–1, 833
extension & physical division	241–4		(181)	x
composites imply monads	245		x	x
8. Finite and infinite	246–64	(31–2)	x	834–8
degree & intensity	246–7			834
. . . & indefinite	248–9			834–7
. . . & contingent/necessary	250–60			
. . . & degree of reality	261			835
. . . & alteration	262			x
. . . & good/bad	263–64			x

C. RELATIVE PREDICATES

	Baumgarten	*Herder*	*anon-L_I*	*Mrongovius*
1. Agreement and diversity	265–79	(32–3)	x	838–9
all things partly similar	265			838
similar, equal, & congruent	266–7			838–9
indiscernibility of identicals	268–73			838–9
transitivity, etc., of agreement	274–8			x
harmony among all actuals	279			x
2a. Simultaneous things	280–96	(33–5)	x	840
extension & figure	280			x
position: location & age	281–2			840
motion & rest	283			840
action at a distance impossible	284–5			x
point, line, surface, & solid	286–89			840
dimensions & measurement	290–2			841
parts of space	293			x
motive power, matter, & body	294–6			840–1
2b. Successive things	297–306	(35–6)	x	841–3
time: past/present/future	297–8			841
duration/perdurable/instantaneous	299			841–2
moment; beginning & end	300–1			840, 842
eternity & sempiternity	302–3			842–3
potency: proximate & remote	304			
necessity of actual things	305			x
all connected in space/time	306			x

x = topic is neither mentioned nor discussed.   () = passages not included in this translation.

Baumgarten 1757	*Volckmann* 28:351–459 1784/85	*von Schön I* 28:461–524 1780s?	*anon-L$_2$* 28:531–610 1790/91?	*Dohna* 28:615–702 1792/93	*anon-K$_2$* 28:705–816 early 1790s	*Vigilantius (K$_3$)* 29:943–1040 1794/95
224–9	(435–6)	(516)	565–6	(641–2)	x	x
224–5	(435–6)	(516)	565	(641)		995–6
226	(436)	(516)	x	(641)		
227	(436)	(516)	566	(641)	(721–2)	
228	(436)	x	x	(641–2)	(721–2)	
229	x	x	x	x		
230–45	(436–8)	(517–18)	566–8	(642–3)	(726–7)	x
230	(436)	(517)	x	(642)	(726)	
231–2	(436)	x	x	x		
233–4	(436)	(517)	x	(642)	(727)	
235	(436–7)	(517–18)	566	(642)		
236–7	x	x	566	(642)	(726)	
238–40		(467)	567–8			995–6
241–4	(436)	x	567–8	(643)		
245	x	x	x	x		
246–64	(438–40)	(518–19)	568–9	(643–5)		994–5
246–7	(425n, 438)	(507, 519)	568	(643)		999
248–9	(439–40)	(518)	568–9	(643–5)	(715)	
250–60		x	x	x		
261		(518–19)	x	x		
262	x	x	x	x		
263–64	x	x	x	x		
265–79	x	(519–20)	569–70	(645)	x	x
265		x	x	x		
266–7		x	x	(645)		
268–73		(519–20)	569–70	(645)	(726)	
274–8		x	x	x		
279		x	x	x		
280–96	x	(520)	570	(645–6)	x	
280		(520)	x	(645–6)		996
281–2		x	570	(646)		
283		x	x ·	x		
284–5		x	x	(646)		
286–89		x	570	x		
290–2		(520)	570	(646)		994–5
293			x			995
294–6		x	x	x		
297–306	x	(521–2)	570	(646)	x	994
297–8		(521)	570	(646)		
299		(521–2)	570	(646)		
300–1		(522)	570	x		
302–3		(522)	570	x		
304		(521	x	(646)		
305		x	x	x		
306		x	x	x		

x = topic is neither mentioned nor discussed.   () = passages not included in this translation.

Concordance of Kant's Lectures on Metaphysics	Baumgarten §§1–1000 1757	*Herder* 28: 1–166, 869–962 1762–64	*anon-L₁* 28: 167–350 mid-1770s?	*Mrongovius* 29: 747–940 1782/83
3a. Cause and effect	307–18	(36–8)	x	843–5
contingency not cognizable	x			843–4
cause & effect	307			843
causation & contingency	308–10			843–4
principles: *essendi, fiendi, cognoscendi*	311			748, 809, 844
cause . . .				
. . . & relation	312–13			844
. . . concurrent/single/main	314			844–5
. . . coordinate & subordinate	315			844–5, 859
. . . essential & accidental	316–17			844, 45
sufficient & insufficient	318			x
3b₁. Efficient cause	319–35	(38–9)	(190)	845–6
cause . . .				
. . . efficient & deficient	319			845
. . . associated & auxiliary	320–1			845
. . . instrumental	322			x
. . . occasional	323			845
circumstance & alteration	324–5			845
cause/effect: positing & canceling	326–28			x
effect . . .				
. . . univocal & equivocal	329			845–6
. . . mediate & immediate	330–1			846
. . . shows worth of cause	332–3			846
finite thing	334			x
efficient connection	335			846–7
3b₂. Usefulness	336–40	(39)	x	846–7
useful, useless, & noxious	336			846
worth & value	337			846
use, misuse, & consumption	338			846–7
utility: connection of	339–40			847
3b₃. Other kinds of causes	341–6	x	(190–1)	847–8
final cause: ends & intentions	341		(190–1)	845, 847
motive cause	342			847
ends: mediate & ultimate	343			847
matter and form	344–5		195–6	845, 847–8
example & archetype	346			847–8
4. Sign and signified	347–50	x	x	848
sign & signified	347			881
signified: past/present/future	348			x
science of signs	349			x
signs & language	350			881, 887

x = topic is neither mentioned nor discussed.   () = passages not included in this translation.

Baumgarten 1757	Volckmann 28:351–459 1784/85	von Schön I 28:461–524 1780s?	anon-L_2 28:531–610 1790/91?	Dohna 28:615–702 1792/93	anon-K_2 28:705–816 early 1790s	Vigilantius (K_3) 29:943–1040 1794/95
307–18	x	(522–4)	571–2	(647–9)		x
x		(523)	571–2	x		
307		(522)	571	(647)		
308–10		x	571	x		
311		(523)	571, 572	(648)	(724)	
312–13		x	x	(648)		
314			572–3	(648)	(720)	
315		x	572	(648)		
316–17		x	x	(648–9)		
318		x	x	(648)		
319–35	x	(523–4)	572–4	(649)		
319		(524)	572	(649)	(719)	
320–1		x	572–3	(649)		
322		x	572	(649)		
323		x	573	(649)	(720)	
324–5		x	573	(649)		
326–28		x	573	(649)		
329		x	573	(649)		
330–1		x	573–4	(649)		931–2
332–3		x	573–4	(649)		
334		x	x	x		
335		x	574–5	x		
336–40	x	x	x	(649–50)		x
336				(650)		
337				(650)		
338				x		
339–40				(649)	(720)	
341–6	x	x	574–7	(649–50)		x
341			574–5	(649–50)	(719)	
342			x	(650)		
343			x	(650)		
344–5			575–6	(650)		969
346			577	(650)	(719–20)	
347–50	x	x	x	(650)	x	x
347				x		
348				x		
349				x		
350				x		

x = topic is neither mentioned nor discussed.   () = passages not included in this translation.

Concordance of Kant's Lectures on Metaphysics	Baumgarten §§1–1000 1757	*Herder* 28: 1–166, 869–962 1762–64	*anon-L₁* 28: 167–350 mid-1770s?	*Mrongovius* 29: 747–940 1782/83
III. COSMOLOGY	351–500	42–53	195–221	848–75, 921–37
Introduction to cosmology	351–3	x	195	848–9

A. CONCEPTS OF THE WORLD

1. Positive concept of the world	354–79	39–40	195–7	849–54
World = series of finite things	354–5	39	196	849–52
all parts in real connection	356–7	39	195–6	851, 852–3
kinds of connection	358			
every world is good, ordered, true, perfect, alterable	359–67	40	x	x
the least world	368		x	x
state of the world	369		x	x
origin/death *ex nihilo*	370–1			
only one actual world	372–9	40	196–7	853–4
2. Negative concept of the world	380–91	40–2	197	854–64, 921–7
infinite progression & regression	380	40–1	197–9	854–61
synthesis: mathematical	x		x	854–9
synthesis: dynamical	x		x	859–61
freedom & nature	x		200	861–2, 924
first cause required	381		197–9	861
events: ordinary & extraordinary	384–5	41	x	x
Four negative principles			199–205	862–4, 921–6
. . . *non datur fatum* (no fate)	382	41	199–200	925–6
. . . *non datur casus* (no chance)	383	41	199–200	923–6
. . . *non datur saltus* (no leap)	386–7	41	200–5	862–4, 921–2
Law of continuity . . .	x	41–42	200–5	863–4, 921–2
. . . and Leibniz	x	41	202	x
. . . and quanta	x	x	200–4	862
. . . and drawing an angle	x		203–4	864
. . . and velocity	x	41–42	203–4	863, 921
. . . and light ray	x	42	204	921
. . . and representations	x		202, 208	x
. . . and species	x	42	205	921–2
. . . *non datur hiatus/abyssus* (no gap)	x		x	922
God as extramundane	388	42	205	861, 924–7
against Spinoza	389–91	42	x	x

B. PARTS OF THE WORLD

1. Simples				
1a. Simple parts in general	392–401	42–4	205–8	927–30
egoism	392	42	205–7	851, 927–8
world made of finite substances	393–4	x	208	929–30
materialism	395	43	261	929–30
nature of monads	396–7	x	x	x
monads are impenetrable	398	43	208	929
monads are physical points	399	43	208	930
monads as microcosms	400	43–4	208	929
sleeping monads	401	x	x	929–30
1b. Spiritual monads/idealism	402–5	42, 44, 50	206–7	928

x = topic is neither mentioned nor discussed.   () = passages not included in this translation.

Baumgarten 1757	Volckmann 28:351–459 1784/85	von Schön I 28:461–524 1780s?	anon-L_2 28:531–610 1790/91?	Dohna 28:615–702 1792/93	anon-K_2 28:705–816 early 1790s	Vigilantius (K_3) 29:943–1040 1794/95
351–500	x	x	581–3	656–70	(727–35)	1006–9
351–53			541–2	656	x	x
354–79	x	x	581–2	657–8	(728)	x
354–5			581	657	(728; Ar126)	1006
356–7			581	657–8	(Ar127)	1006–7
358						
359–67			x	x	x	x
368			x	x	x	x
369			x	x	x	x
370–1						
372–9			581	658	(728; Ar128–9)	1006
380–91	x	x	581–2	658–63	(728–31)	x
380			569, 583	658–61	(729)	
x			x	658–60	(729)	
x			x	660–1	(729)	
x			582–3	660–1, 663	(729)	
381			x	x	x	
384–5			x	x	x	
382			x	661–3	(729–31)	1006
383			x	663	(731)	
386–7			x	662–3	(730–1)	
x			x	662–3	(730)	1038
x			x	x	762	
x			x	662	(730)	994–6
x			x	662	x	
x			x	662–3	(730)	
x			x	x	(730)	
x			x		(730)	
x			x	662–3	(730–1)	1033
x			x	661–2	(730)	
388			x	661, 667	x	996, 1008
389–91			x	x	x	
392–401	x	x	x	663	(731; Ar129–30)	1006
392	x	x	x	657, 680–1	(731; Ar126–27)	x
393–4				657	(731)	1006
395				663	(731)	x
396–7				x	x	x
398				x	x	x
399				x	x	1006
400				x	x	1032–3
401				x	x	1033
402–5	x	x	x	663	(731), 770	

x = topic is neither mentioned nor discussed.   () = passages not included in this translation.

537

Concordance of Kant's Lectures on Metaphysics	Baumgarten §§1–1000 1757	*Herder* 28: 1–166, 869–962 1762–64	anon-L₁ 28: 167–350 mid-1770s?	*Mrongovius* 29: 747–940 1782/83
2. Composites				
2a. The first origin of bodies	406–29	44–9	208–11	931–2
world as monadatum	406	44	x	929, 931
extended things	407	44	x	793, 929
location mutually determined	408	44–5	x	931
action & reaction	409–12	45–6	208	852, 931–2
cohesion & contact	413–14	46–7	x	931–32
motion & inertia	415–18	45–6, 47	x	931
elements: primary & secondary	419–21	47	209	931
monads are immaterial	422	47	x	x
philosophy of the lazy	423	48		932
atoms (primary elements)	424	48	209	931–2
corpuscular philosophy	425–6	48	209–210	932
divisibility of matter	427–8	48	204–5	x
atomic philosophy as false	429	49	x	932
2b. The nature of bodies	430–5	49–50	211	933–6
nature of a body	430–1	49	211	933–5
laws of motion	432	46, 49–50	x	924, 934–6
every body a machine	433	49	x	935
mechanical connection	434	50	x	935
mechanical philosophy	435	50	210–11	935
dynamical philosophy	x	x	210	935–6
C. PERFECTION				
1. The idea				
1a. The best world . . .	436–47	50–1	211–12	936–7, 864–5
. . . has the most reality	436–7	50	211	936–7
. . . & egoism/idealism	438	50	x	x
. . . & materialism	439	51	x	x
. . . is finite	440	51	x	x
. . . has the greatest harmony	441–2	x	x	936–7, 864
. . . is not the best possible thing	443	x	211	x
. . . has the most rules of order	444	x	x	x
. . . and thus many exceptions	445–6	x	x	x
. . . need is not fatalistic	447	x	x	x
1b. Interaction (*commercium*)	448–65	51–53	212–15	865–8
interaction: original & derivative	x	x	213	867–8
space as God's omnipresence	x	x	214	866
Systems of explanation . . .	448			
. . . preestablished harmony	449	52–53	214–15	866–7
. . . physical influence	450–1	53	214	866–8
. . . occasionalism	452–3	x	214–15	866–7
comparison of the systems	454–6	x	x	x
only three systems	457–8	x	x	x
best world has preestablished harmony	459–64	x	215	x
best world is dualistic	465	x	x	x
2. The means				
2a. Natural	466–73	x	215–16	868–9
nature of the world . . .				
. . . is the sum of natures of the parts	466–7		215–16	868–9
. . . is contingent	468		x	x
natural: absolute and relative	469–70		x	869
course of nature	471		216	869
order & rules of nature	472		216	869
natural is mechanically explicable	473		x	x

x = topic is neither mentioned nor discussed.   () = passages not included in this translation.

Baumgarten 1757	Volckmann 28:351–459 1784/85	von Schön I 28:461–524 1780s?	anon-L₂ 28:531–610 1790/91?	Dohna 28:615–702 1792/93	anon-K₂ 28:705–816 early 1790s	Vigilantius (K₃) 29:943–1040 1794/95
406–29	x	x	x	663–5	(731)	1006
406				663–4	(731; Ar129)	
407				x		
408				664		
409–12				664		
413–14				664	(Ar130)	
415–18				x		
419–21				664		
422				664		
423						
424				664–5		
425–6				664–5		
427–8				664		
429				x		
430–5	x	x	x	665	(731)	x
430–1				665		
432				662, 664		
433				x		
434				x		
435				664		
x				664		
436–47	x	x	x	665	(731)	x
436–7				665	(731)	
438				x		
439				x		
440				x		
441–2				x		
443				665	(731)	
444				x		
445–6				x		
447				x		
448–65	x	x	x	665–6	(731–2)	1006–8
x				665–6	(732)	1007–8
x				666	(732), 772	1007–8
448						
449				665–6	(731–2)	1008
450–1				665–6	(731–2)	1007–8
452–3				665–6	(732)	1008
454–6				x	x	
457–8				x	x	
459–64				x	x	
465				x	x	
466–73	x	x	x	x	(732)	x
466–7					x	
468					x	
469–70					x	
471				669	x	
472				668–9	x	
473					x	

x = topic is neither mentioned nor discussed.   () = passages not included in this translation.

Concordance of Kant's Lectures on Metaphysics	Baumgarten §§1–1000 1757	*Herder* 28: 1–166, 869–962 1762–64	*anon-L₁* 28: 167–350 mid-1770s?	*Mrongovius* 29: 747–940 1782/83
2b₁. Supernatural and miracles	474–81	x	216–21	869–75
supernatural & unnatural	474–76		216–17	869–70
miracles ...				
... comparative & strict	477		219	870, 874–5
... formal & material	x		217–18	870
... occasional & preestablished	x		218	870–4
... frequency	x		218–20	871–2
... reasons for belief	x		218–21	871–4
... ancient & recent	x		220–1	874–5
... & signs	478		x	x
supernatural & contrary to nature	479–81		216–17	x
2b₂. Miracles and the best world	482–500	x	x	871–2
IV. PSYCHOLOGY	501–799	(59–122, 850–906, 924–31)	221–301	875–920
A. EMPIRICAL PSYCHOLOGY	504–739	(59–102, 850–87, 924–31)	221–62	875–903
Introduction	501–3		221–4	875–6, 877
empirical & rational psychology	503		222–4	875–6
status of empirical psychology	x		223–4	750, 756–7, 876
1. Existence of the soul	504–18	(924)	224–8	876–880
my soul exists (*cogito sum*)	504		224–7	877
soul as "inner"	x		225	876–7
I = human being/soul/spirit	x		224–5	878
soul as a power of representation	505–7		261	906
my body	508–9		224–5	879
representations: clear & obscure	510–14		227–8	878–80
kinds of cognition & representation	515–17		x	x
kingdoms of darkness & light	518		x	x
2. Faculties of the soul				
Overview of the faculties	x	x	228–30	877–8
2a. Cognitive				
2a₁ Lower cognitive faculties (in general)	519–33	(59, 850, 924–6)	228–30	880–2
my soul has a cognitive faculty	519		228	x
sensible/intelligible representation	520–1		229–30	880–1
kinds of features	522–6		x	x
easy & difficult	527		x	x
least clear/least obscure	528		x	x
abstraction & attention	529		x	878
kinds of representations	530		x	x
aspects of clarity	531–2		x	878
aesthetics	533		x	880

x = topic is neither mentioned nor discussed.   () = passages not included in this translation.

Baumgarten 1757	Volckmann 28:351–459 1784/85	von Schön I 28:461–524 1780s?	anon-L₂ 28:531–610 1790/91?	Dohna 28:615–702 1792/93	anon-K₂ 28:705–816 early 1790s	Vigilantius (K₃) 29:943–1040 1794/95
474–81	x	x	x	667–70	(732–5)	x
474–76				667	(733)	
477				667–8	(733)	
x				668–9	(733)	
x				668–9	x	
x				669	(733–4)	
x				668–9	(734–35)	
x				668	(734)	
478				x	x	
479–81				x	(732)	
482–500	x	x	x	669–70	(734–5)	x
501–799	440–50	x	583–94	670–90	(735–75)	1009–40
504–739	x	x	583–90	670–79	(735–50)	1009–24
501–3			584	670	(735)	x
503			584	670	x	
x	(367)	(470)	541, 584	679	(735, 750)	
504–18	x	x	584	670–2	(735–7)	x
504			590	670–1, 680	(735–6), 770–1	
x			583–4	x	753	
x			583–4	671	(736)	
505–7			x	671–2, 680	(736–7)	
508–9			x	671	x	
510–14			x	x	x	
515–17			x	x	x	
518			x	x	x	
x	x	x	584	672	(737)	x
519–33	x	x	584	x	(737)	
519			x			983
520–1			584			
522–6			x			
527			x			
528			x			
529			x			
530			x			
531–2			x			
533			x			

x = topic is neither mentioned nor discussed.   () = passages not included in this translation.

Concordance of Kant's Lectures on Metaphysics	Baumgarten §§1–1000 1757	Herder 28: 1–166, 869–962 1762–64	anon-L₁ 28: 167–350 mid-1770s?	Mrongovius 29: 747–94• 1782/83
2a₂ Lower cognitive faculties (in kind)				
Sense (*sensus*)	534–56	(59–64, 850–6, 926–8)	230–5	882–3
=to represent a present state	534		x	881
sense: inner & outer	535		224–5	882
sense organs	536		231	882
sphere & point of sensation	537		x	883
distance of object & sensation	538		x	x
intensive magnitude of sense	539			
vital sense	x		x	882
sense: objective & subjective	x		231	882–3
sense: coarse & fine	540		231–2	x
law of sensation	541		x	x
aids/hindrances to sensation	542–3		x	x
obscurity of relations	544		x	x
sense deception & illusion	545–7		234–5	x
fallacies of the senses	548		232	x
representations: varying strength	549–51		x	x
waking, sleep, etc.	552–6		x	885–6
Fantasy (*phantasia*)	557–71	(64–6, 855–6)	235–6	883–6
=to represent a past state	557–9		236	883
material ideas	560		259–60	908
law of association	561		236	883
. . . clarity & obscurity	562–6		x	x
imaginings versus sensations	567		x	x
. . . aiding & hindering	568–9		x	x
science of fantasy	570		x	x
. . . well-ordered & unruly	571		235–7	885
Wit (*perspicacia*)	572–8	(66–7, 857–8)	244–5	884
=skill in noting agreement	572		244–5	881, 884
acumen = skill in noting differences	572–3		244–5	881, 884
law of wit & acumen	574		x	x
wit: sensible & intellectual	575–6		245	x
aptitude & its lack; errors	577–8		x	x
Memory (*memoria*)	579–88	(67–9, 858–9)	237	881
=to represent a past state as past	579		x	881, 884
law of memory	580		x	x
remembering & forgetting	581–3		x	x
kinds of memory	584–6		x	x
mnemonics	587		x	x
error	588		x	x
Fictive faculty (*facultas fingendi*)	589–94	(69–70, 86–7, 143–4, 859–62, 928–9)	230–1, 237	881, 883, 884–
=to separate/unite imaginings	589		x	884
law of fictive faculty	590		x	883
kinds of chimeras	591		x	x
kinds of fictive faculties	592		x	x
dreams & sleepwalking	593–4		x	885–6

x = topic is neither mentioned nor discussed.   () = passages not included in this translation

Baumgarten 1757	Volckmann 28:351–459 1784/85	von Schön I 28:461–524 1780s?	anon-L₂ 28:531–610 1790/91?	Dohna 28:615–702 1792/93	anon-K₂ 28:705–816 early 1790s	Vigilantius (K₃) 29:943–1040 1794/95
534–6	x	x	585	672–3	(737–9)	x
534			585	672	x	
535			583, 585	672–3	(738)	
536			585	673	(738)	
537			x	x	x	
538			x	x	x	
539						
x			585	x	x	
x			585	673	x	
540			x	x	x	
541			585	x	x	
542–3			x	x	x	
544			x	x	x	
545–7			x	x	(738)	
548			x	673	(738–9)	
549–51			x	x		
552–6			x	x	764	
557–71	x	x	585	673	(739)	x
557–9			585	673	x	
560			x	x	x	
561			585	674	(739)	
562–6			x	x	x	
567	449		x	672	x	
568–9			x	x	x	
570			x	x	x	
571			x	673	x	
572–8	x	x	x	x	(739)	x
572					(739)	
572–3					x	
574					x	
575–6					x	
577–8					x	
579–88	x	x	x	674	(739)	x
579				x		
580				x		
581–3				x		
584–6				x		
587				x		
588				x		
589–94	x	x	585	674	(739)	x
589			585	x		
590			585	674		
591			x	x		
592			x	x		
593–4			x	x	(740)	

x = topic is neither mentioned nor discussed.   () = passages not included in this translation.

Concordance of Kant's Lectures on Metaphysics	Baumgarten §§1–1000 1757	Herder 28: 1–166, 869–962 1762–64	anon-L$_1$ 28: 167–350 mid-1770s?	Mrongovius 29: 747–940 1782/83
Anticipation (*praevisio*)	595–605	(72–3, 87, 862–3, 930)	236	881, 883–4
=to represent a future state	595		236	884
law of anticipation	596		x	884
. . . strength & clarity	597–600		x	x
. . . sense & imagination	601		x	x
. . . aiding & hindering	602–3		x	x
. . . sensible only	604		x	x
. . . true & false	605		x	x
Judgment (*judicium*)	606–9	(73–5, 863–5)	242–3	888–90
=to represent the perfections and imperfections of things	606		246	x
judgment & kinds of taste	607–9		249	x
Expectation (*praesagitio*)	610–18	(76–7, 866)	x	884
=to represent an anticipated representation as one to occur in the future	610			884
prediction & its laws	611–13			883
intensive quantity of prediction	614–15			x
prediction & prophecy	616			x
errors of prediction	617–18			x
Characterization (*facultas characteristica*)	619–23	(77–8, 866–7)	237–38	881, 887
=to represent signs and signified things	619		x	887
cognition: symbolic & intuitive	620		238	x
errors of signifying	621		x	x
science of signs	622		x	x
dream interpretation	623		x	886–7
2a$_3$. Higher cognitive faculties				
Understanding (*intellectus*)	624–39	(78–82, 868–71)	238–44	888–90
=to cognize distinctly	624		x	x
attention & abstraction	625		x	x
reflection & comparison	626–30		240	888
law of understanding	631		239	x
conceive = understand the essence	632–3		241	x
purity of representations	634–6		x	x
kinds of understanding	637–8		243	x
aptitude in understanding	639		242–4	890
Reason (*ratio*)	640–50	(83–5, 88, 872–4, 931)	242–4	889–90
=to cognize distinctly the connections of things	640–1		x	x
analogon rationis = indistinct cognition of connections	640		276	x
personality	641		x	x
law of reason	642		x	x
rational & irrational	643		x	x
the sphere of reason	644		x	x
foundation & sagacity of reason	645		x	x
healthy & corrupt reason	646–7		243–4	x
kinds of minds	648–50		244	x
improving the mind	650		x	x

x = topic is neither mentioned nor discussed. () = passages not included in this translation.

Baumgarten 1757	Volckmann 28:351–459 1784/85	von Schön I 28:461–524 1780s?	anon-L₂ 28:531–610 1790/91?	Dohna 28:615–702 1792/93	anon-K₂ 28:705–816 early 1790s	Vigilantius (K₃) 29:943–1040 1794/95
595–605	x	x	585	x	(739)	x
595			585			
596			585	674		
597–600			x			
601			x			
602–3			x			
604			x			
605			x			
606–9	x	x	x	x	x	x
606						
607–9				675		
610–18	x	x	x	x	x	x
610						
611–13			585	674	(740)	
614–15						
616						
617–18						
619–23	x	x	585	674	(739)	x
619			585	x		
620			x	674		
621			x	x		
622			x	x		
623	448		594	x		
624–39	x	x	x	674	(740)	x
624					x	
625					(740)	
626–30					(740)	
631					x	
632–3					x	
634–6					x	
637–8					(740)	
639					x	
640–50	x	x	x	674	(739–40)	x
640–1				x	x	
640	450		594	690	(740)	
641				x	(739–40)	1036
642				x	x	
643				x	x	
644				x	x	
645				x	x	
646–7				x	x	
648–50				x	x	
650				x	x	

x = topic is neither mentioned nor discussed.   () = passages not included in this translation.

Concordance of Kant's Lectures on Metaphysics	Baumgarten §§1–1000 1757	*Herder* 28: 1–166, 869–962 1762–64	*anon-L₁* 28: 167–350 mid-1770s?	*Mrongovius* 29: 747–940 1782/83
2b. Appetitive				
2b₁. . . . in general				
Indifference and equilibrium	651–4	x	253	901–3
. . . intuitive & symbolic	651		253–4	901–2
. . . total & partial	652–3		253	x
. . . subjective & objective	654		x	x
Pleasure and displeasure	655–62	x	245–53	890–3
. . . & indifference	655		247	890–1
kinds of pleasure	656–7		247–8	891
sources of pleasure	658–9		248–50	x
good & bad: internal/external	660–1		249–50	892–3
beauty & ugliness; taste	662		245–53	832, 892–3
the pleasant promotes life	x		247–8	891, 894
Faculty of desire	663–75	x	253–4	893–6
=to attempt to produce a representation	663–8		253–4	893–4
incentives of the mind	669		x	895, 898
equilibrium of incentives	670		x	901–2
kinds of desire/aversion	671		x	x
self-deception	672		254	895
equilibrium & predominance	673–4		x	x
desire: efficient & inefficient	675		x	x
desire & living beings	x		253–4	893–4
2b₂. . . . kinds				
Lower faculty of desire	676–88	(88–91, 875–8)	254–6	895–6
desire of a sensible representation	676		x	895
stimulus & instincts	677		254–6	895
passion	678–81		256	895–6
passion taxonomy	682–8		x	x
Higher faculty of desire	689–99	(92–4, 878–80)	254–6	895–6
desire of a distinct representation	689		x	895
motives: rational incentives	690–1		254–5	895
desire: mixed & pure	692		x	x
conflict: stimuli & motives	693–4		256	895–6
decide, deliberate, & estimate	695–7		x	x
kinds of minds	698–9		x	x
Presuppositions of freedom				
i. Spontaneity	700–7	(96, 882)	x	x
no state is absolutely necessary	700			
necessitation	701–2			
contingency of most actions great	703			
spontaneous actions	704–6	(96, 882)	269	902–3
necessitation: external & internal	707		256–7	903
ii. Power of choice (*arbitrium*)	708–18	(96–7, 882)	254–9	896–901
actions under my control	708–9		x	x
internal necessitation	710–11		256	x
=to desire at one's discretion	712	(882)	x	896
discretionary action	713–16	(96, 882)	x	897
intensive magnitude of choice	717–18	(882)		
power of choice: human & brute	x		255	896–7, 902

x = topic is neither mentioned nor discussed.   () = passages not included in this translation.

Baumgarten 1757	Volckmann 28:351–459 1784/85	von Schön I 28:461–524 1780s?	anon-L₂ 28:531–610 1790/91?	Dohna 28:615–702 1792/93	anon-K₂ 28:705–816 early 1790s	Vigilantius (K₃) 29:943–1040 1794/95
651–4	x	x	x	676	(743, 747)	x
651				x	x	
652–3				676	(743)	
654				676	x	
655–62	x	x	586–7	674–5	(741–3)	1009–13
655			586	676	(743)	x
656–7			586–7	675	(742)	x
658–9			586	x	x	x
660–1			586–7	676	(742)	1012
662			586–8	672, 675–6	(741–3)	1009–12
x			586	x	x	x
663–75	x	x	587–8	676–7	(743–4)	1012–14
663–8			587	x	(743)	1012–13
669			587	677	(744)	1014
670			x	678	x	x
671			x	x	x	x
672			x	676	(743)	1013–14
673–4			x	x	x	x
675			x	676	x	x
x			587	x	x	x
676–88	x	x	587–8	678	(744–6)	x
676			x	x	x	x
677			587, 589	677	(744, 749)	1014–15
678–81			588	679	(746)	x
682–8			x	x	(746)	x
689–99	x	x	587–8	678	(744–6)	x
689			x	x	x	
690–1			587, 589	677		1014–15
692			x	x	x	
693–4			x	678	x	
695–7			x	x	(746)	
698–9				x	x	
700–7	x	x	x	x	x	x
700						
701–2						
703						
704–6				660, 677, 682		1019, 1022
707						1019
708–18	x	x	587–90	676–9	(746–8)	1014–16
708–9			x	677	(747)	x
710–11			x	x	x	x
712			589	677	x	1014
713–16			589–90	678	(746–7)	x
717–18						
x			588	677, 683		1015–16

x = topic is neither mentioned nor discussed.   () = passages not included in this translation.

Concordance of Kant's Lectures on Metaphysics	Baumgarten §§1–1000 1757	Herder 28: 1–166, 869–962 1762–64	anon-L₁ 28: 167–350 mid-1770s?	Mrongovius 29: 747–940 1782/83
Nature of freedom				
Freedom (*libertas*)	719–32	(97–100, 882–6)	259–6, 267–71	896–903
=intellectual power of choice	719–20		256	896, 898
voluntary action	721–2		270–1	896–7, 901
freedom & morality	723–5	(882–5)	255, 257	899–900
law of choice & freedom	726	(885)	257	812, 862, 911
self-compelled acts are free	727	(885)	x	x
enticements, threats, etc.	728–9		x	897
self-mastery & servility	730		256	x
freedom: direct & indirect	731		x	x
qualities of mind	732	(885–86)	258	x
arts: free & liberal	x		258–9	x
transcendental freedom	x		255–7, 264–70	861, 900, 903
practical freedom	x		257, 269–70	901
against fatalism	x		270	x
argument for freedom	x		x	897
freedom of equilibrium	x		x	901–3
3. Interaction between body and soul	733–9	x	259–61, 273–4	x
voluntary motions	733		x	x
proof of influence	734–5		x	x
mutual influence	736		x	x
various fallacies	737–9		x	x
B. RATIONAL PSYCHOLOGY	740–799	(102–22, 887–906)	262–301	903–20
Classification	x	x	262–5	903–4
1. The human soul	740–60	(144–7)	265–71, 280–2	904–6
. . . represents world via the body	740–1	(145)	224–5	906
anima, animus & spiritus	742	(144–5)	224–6, 273–4	878
matter does not think	742	44	x	904
. . . is singular/simple	742	47	226, 266–7	905
. . . is substantial	742		225–6, 266	904–5
. . . is finite	743		x	x
faculties based on representation	744		x	x
seat of the soul	745	(144)	225, 280–2	879, 907–9
. . . is incorruptible/perduring	746		x	903–6, 912
anthropology	747		x	x
apotheosis is impossible	748		x	x
no two souls are identical	749		261	x
. . . has power of locomotion	750		280	x
. . . represents the world	751–2		227–8	x
. . . and its faculties	753–6		x	x
. . . is immaterial	757		226, 271–3	904–6, 929–30
natural & unnatural	758–9		x	x
. . . connected with others	760		x	x
. . . is an object of inner sense	x		224–26, 265	876, 904
2. Soul/body interaction	761–9	(101–5, 886–9)	279–80	907–9
special explanatory systems	761–2	(103–4, 886)	279	907
. . . of physical influence	763–6	(101–3, 886–7)	279–80	907–9
. . . of occasionalism	767	(102–4, 887–9)	280	x
. . . of preestablished harmony	768–9	(102–4, 887–9)	280	x

x = topic is neither mentioned nor discussed. () = passages not included in this translation.

Baumgarten 1757	Volckmann 28:351–459 1784/85	von Schön I 28:461–524 1780s?	anon-L₂ 28:531–610 1790/91?	Dohna 28:615–702 1792/93	anon-K₂ 28:705–816 early 1790s	Vigilantius (K₃) 29:943–1040 1794/95
719–32	x	x	588–90	x	(713, 729)	1015–25
719–20			588	677		1015–16
721–2			589	678, 682	(747)	1018, 1021–22
723–5			x	677–8, 682–3	x	1016–18
726			x	x	x	945, 1018, 1022
727			x	x	x	x
728–9			589	x	(748)	x
730			589	679	(748)	x
731			x	x	x	x
732			588, 590	678–9	(748), 774	x
x			588	679	(748–9)	x
x			x	x	x	x
x			x	x	x	x
x			x	682–3	773–4	1019
x			x	x	x	1018–20
x			x	678	(747)	1022–3
733–9	x	x	590–1	679	(749–50)	x
733			x	x	x	
734–5			x	x	x	
736			590	x	x	
737–9			x	x	x	
740–799	440–50	x	590–4	679–90	753–75	1025–40
x	x	x	x	680	x	x
740–60	x	x	590–1	679–84	753–7	1025–30
740–1			x	x	x	x
742			x	680, 683–4	753, 755	1026–7
742	449		x	681–2	753–60	1025
742	443		590–1	664, 684	753–5	1025–7
742	443		590	680	755	x
743			x	x	x	x
744			x	x	x	x
745	445		x	685–6	755–7	1027–30
746	440–3		590–1	681, 683, 688	763–4	1036–8
747			x	x	x	x
748			x	x	x	x
749			x	x	x	x
750			x	x	755	1027
751–2			x	x	x	x
753–6			x	x	x	x
757	443		591	680, 682	754–5, 759	1025–6
758–9			x	x	x	x
760			x	x	x	x
x			590–1	x	756	x
761–9	x	x	591	684–5	757–60	1028–30
761–2			x	684–5	x	x
763–6			591	684–5	757–60	1028–30
767			x	685	757–60	x
768–9			x	685	757–60	1029–30

x = topic is neither mentioned nor discussed.   () = passages not included in this translation.

Concordance of Kant's Lectures on Metaphysics	Baumgarten §§1–1000 1757	*Herder* 28: 1–166, 869–962 1762–64	*anon-L₁* 28: 167–350 mid-1770s?	*Mrongovius* 29: 747–940 1782/83
3. Origin of the human soul	770–5	(105, 889)	282–83	909–10
Pre-existentialism	770	(105, 889)	x	910
Traducianism	771–2	(105)	x	910
Inducianism/creationism	771–2	x	x	910
Concreationism/epigenesis	773	x	x	910
Preformationism/involution	774	x	x	x
origin vs. transference	775	x	x	x
4. Immortality of the human soul	776–81	(105–6, 889–90)	283–95	910–19
requirements for survival	x	x	296	911, 912
death of the body	776–7	(105, 889)	283–4	913
death: absolute & relative	778–9	(106, 889–90)	x	910–11
death of the soul	780	x	296	x
mortal & immortal	781	(106, 890)	x	x
contingency of generation	x	(109, 111, 893, 895)	295	918
PROOFS of immortality:	x	(107–11, 891–5)	284–95	911–19
empirical/physiological		x	291	911–12
simplicity of soul/Mendelssohn		x	x	905, 912–13
theoretical: life & spontaneity		x	285–7	913–14
practical: analogy with nature		(107–10, 891–3)	292–5	911–12, 914–17
moral-theological (moral incentive)		x	288–9	917–18
theological-moral (reward virtue)		(110–11, 894–5)	287–91	775–6, 917
5. State of the soul after death	782–91	(108–15, 892–9)	295–301	919–20
sleep of the soul (*hypnopsychita*)	782	(107, 890–1)	296	913, 919
eternal sleep (*psychopannychita*)	782	x	x	913
cup of forgetfulness	783	x	x	x
rebirth (*palingenesis*)	784		296	919
soul migration (*metempsychosis*)	784	(112–13, 896–7)	296	913, 918
evolution (from indestructible part)	x	x	x	920
resurrection	x		x	913
Swedenborg	x	(113–14, 897–8)	298–300	x
bodies: old & new	785–6	x	x	x
blessedness/damnation	787–91	(115, 899)	297–9	919–20
6. The soul & other beings	792–9	(115–22, 148–50, 899–906)	273–8	906–7
6a. Brute souls	792–5	(115–17, 899)	274–7	878–9, 906–7
brutes have only sensible souls	792		274–7	878–9, 906
brute souls have faculties	793		277	x
brute souls: three questions	794		x	x
brute souls are not spirits	795		x	x
6b. Other finite spirits	796–9	(118–22, 148–50, 902)	277–8, 300	907
. . . are higher/lower; good/evil	796			
. . . have some body	797			
. . . have a lower cognitive faculty	798			
. . . are immortal	799			

x = topic is neither mentioned nor discussed.   () = passages not included in this translation.

Baumgarten 1757	Volckmann 28:351–459 1784/85	von Schön I 28:461–524 1780s?	anon-L₂ 28:531–610 1790/91?	Dohna 28:615–702 1792/93	anon-K₂ 28:705–816 early 1790s	Vigilantius (K₃) 29:943–1040 1794/95
770–5	x	x	x	684	760–2	1030–2
770				684	760–1	1030–2
771–2				684	761	1030
771–2				684	760	1030
773				684	760–1	1030–2
774				684	760–1	1030–1
775				x	x	x
776–81	440–5	x	591–2	686–90	762–8	1036–40
x	440–1		x	688	763	1036
776–7	x		x	686	762	x
778–9	x		x	x	x	x
780	x		x	x	763	x
781	x		x	x	x	x
x	x		x	688	768	x
x	441–5	x	591–2	686–8	762–8	1036–40
	441		591	686	763–4	1036, 1038–9
	x		591	x	763–4	1036–8
	441–2		591–2	687	762, 764–5	1034–5, 1038–9
	442–3		592	687–8	765–6	1039–40
	x		x	x	x	x
	442–3		x	687	766–7	x
782–91	445–7	x	555, 592–3	689	768–70	1035–6
782	445		593	689	770	x
782	445		593	x	770	x
783	x		x	689	769	x
784	x		x	689	768–9	x
784	445		593	689	769	x
x	445		x	689	760, 769	x
x	x		x	689	763, 767, 769	1035–6
x	447		593	689	768	x
785–6	x		x	x	x	x
787–91	446–7		593	689	770	1040
792–9	447–50	x	593–4	689–90	x	x
792–5	448–50	x	594	689–90	x	x
792	449–50		594	689–90		
793	449		x	x		
794	x		x	x		
795	x		x	x		1026
796–9	447–8	x	555, 593–4	x	x	x
796				667–8		
797						
798						
799						

x = topic is neither mentioned nor discussed.   () = passages not included in this translation.

Explanatory notes

These explanatory notes are ordered by the chronological placement of the lecture notes (viz., *Herder*, *L₁*, *Mrongovius*, *Volckmann*, *L₂*, *Dohna*, *K₂*, and *Vigilantius* (*K₃*)), and within any given set of lectures they are ordered by their occurrence in the translated text. Because of pagination errors when the *Metaphysik Mrongovius* was being transcribed for the Academy edition, it will appear as though many of these notes are out of place; our translation follows the order of the manuscript, not the Academy edition, and the notes are ordered by their appearance in the translation.

Many of these explanatory notes are paraphrased – and occasionally abridged – translations of notes provided by Gerhard Lehmann (the late editor of the Academy edition of Kant's Metaphysics lectures); these are all indicated as such, with the location in the Academy edition (page and line number) of the text being discussed also provided. We have altered without comment Lehmann's notes whenever this improved the clarity or uniformity of style, while significant additions to his notes are indicated with square brackets. Where possible, Lehmann's references have been updated to more recent (or English) editions. All works cited without an author are Kant's; these titles are abbreviated, with a full citation provided in the bibliography immediately following the notes. N.B. Readers referring to Lehmann's original notes in the Academy edition should be forewarned that he occasionally prints the wrong page and/or line number in citing his notes; these and various other errors have been silently corrected.

The many references to "Baumgarten" are to Alexander Baumgarten's *Metaphysica*, 4th edition (Halle: Carl Hermann Hemmerde, 1757), the textbook used by Kant for nearly all of his courses on metaphysics, and reprinted in vols. 15 and 17 of the Academy edition.

Metaphysik Herder (Ak. 28: 39–53)

1 [Lehmann note to Ak. 28: 41₃] In §380 (Ak. 17: 107), Baumgarten distinguishes progression and regression to infinity, progression in a circle and linear progression and regression. On the Platonic year, see Johann Heinrich Zedler, *Grosses vollständiges Universal Lexicon* (Large and Complete Universal Encyclopedia), 64 vols. (Halle and Leipzig: 1732–50), vol. 2 (1732), column 426 ("The Great Platonic Year" <*Annus magnus sive Platonicus*>): "For one had demonstrated in our time that the fixed stars advanced 50″ within a year, and thus one degree within 72 years; the entire circumference contains 360, and thus the Platonic year cannot be greater than 25,920 solar years. . . . Now since after the expiration of that same year the heavenly bodies come again to stand with respect to each other as they did in the beginning, it thus

appears believable to some that the end of such a year would also put the bodies in the same state as they were at its beginning. . . ." – See also Refl. #3733 (Ak. 17: 275$_3$): "infinite circular regression <*regressus in infinitum curvilineus*>."

2   Lehmann (noting Ak. 28: 41$_8$) refers here to Spinoza, *Ethica, ordine geometrico demonstrata* (*Ethics Demonstrated in Geometrical Order*), Pt. 1, Prop. 33, Schol. 2: "This is indeed nothing else than to subject God to fate <*Quod profecto nihil aliud est, quam Deum fato subjicere*>" [tr. by James Gutmann (New York: Hafner, 1949), p. 71].

3   [Lehmann note to Ak. 28: 41$_{30}$] Cf. note to Ak. 1: 37$_3$ (*Thoughts on the True Estimation of Living Forces*). On this, see especially the letter from Leibniz to Varignon (Feb. 2, 1702), which played a role in the conflict between Maupertuis and König [in *Gottfried Wilhelm Leibniz: Philosophical Papers and Letters*, by Leroy Loemker, 2nd ed. (Reidel, 1970), pp. 542–4].

4   [Lehmann note to Ak. 28: 42$_{22-3}$] Berkeley's late work *Siris: A Chain of Philosophical Reflexions and Inquiries Concerning the Virtues of Tar-Water, and divers other Subjects connected together and arising one from another* appeared in 1744 and was translated in excerpts in the next year as: George Berkeley, *Siris. Gründliche Historische Nachricht vom Theer-Wasser, dessen herrlichen Medicinischen Tugenden, Zubereitung und Gebrauch* . . . , compiled and edited from the original English by Diederich Wessel Linden (Amsterdam and Leipzig: Peter Mortier, 1745). See also the bibliography in H. M. Bracken, *The Early Reception of Berkeley's Immaterialism 1710–1733* (The Hague: Nijhoff, 1959), pp. 121–8. Among the earliest articles on Berkeley's *Siris*, six from the years 1744 to 1746 are cited here.

5   Lehmann (noting Ak. 28: 42$_{24-5}$) refers to Berkeley, *Siris*, §251: ". . . for all phenomena are, to speak truly, appearances in the soul or mind; and it hath never been explained, nor can it be explained, how external bodies, figures, and motions should produce an appearance in the mind."

6   Lehmann (noting Ak. 28: 43$_{3-5}$) refers us to his note to Ak. 28: 71$_{34-5}$ (*Metaphysik Herder*): See Locke's *An Essay Concerning Human Understanding*, Bk. 2, Ch. 27 ("Of Identity and Diversity"), §14: "as I once met with one, who was persuaded his had been the soul of Socrates . . . – would any one say, that he, being not conscious of any of Socrates's actions or thoughts, could be the same person with Socrates?"

7   Baumgarten discusses impenetrability at §398, arguing that no two monads can occupy the same space (Ak. 17: 110): "An *impenetrable substance* is a substance *such that no other substance supposed to be outside of it can occupy its location* <*Substantia, in cuius loco nequit esse alia extra eam posita, est impenetrabilis*>."

8   [Lehmann note to Ak. 28: 43$_{33}$] In §400 (Ak. 17: 111), Baumgarten evaluates the "properties" of monads: that they represent the universe, are active mirrors of the universe, indivisible, microcosms, worlds in miniature, condensations of their own worlds <*microcosmi, mundi in compendio, suique mundi concentrationes*>. In the next paragraphs, he goes on to the slumbering monads, and in §402 (Ak. 17: 111) he comes to spirit, or intellectual substance <*substantia intellectualis*>. Cf. the later "Note to the Amphiboly of the Concepts of Reflection" in *CrPR* (A 274/B 330).

9   Baumgarten discusses spiritual monads and idealism at §§402–5, a topic that Kant suggests is more appropropriately treated in the Psychology. See note 19 (to Ak. 28: 51₁), below.

10   Baumgarten, §414 (Ak. 17: 113): "Things *cohere* when they touch each other in such a way that they cannot be separated except by some third force <*Ita se mutuo contingentia, ut non nisi per vim tertiam separari possint, cohaerent*>."

11   Baumgarten, §414 (Ak. 17: 113): "No alteration occurs in a composite world without motion. For, suppose A is to be altered from B to non-B. It had coexisted with its simultaneous things supposed to be outside it, as B. Now it will coexist as non-B. Hence, it will acquire a different relation to its simultaneous things, a different position, and a different location, and motion will occur. Whenever such alteration, such motion, happens in a composite world, the state of the altered thing, and the state of the universe of which the thing is a part, is partly the same as the preceding states, partly different. Hence, there was some certain motion, inasmuch as the new state differs from the original state; so, inasmuch as the state remained the same, this duration of state, in a composite world, is at the same time a duration of location, an absence of a certain motion, rest, was an obstacle of a certain motion, and a resistance <*Nulla mutatio fit in mundo composito sine motu. Sit enim A mutandum ex B in non-B. Coexstiterat cum simultaneis suis extra illud positis, ut B, nunc coexsistet, ut non-B, hinc diversam ad ea relationem, positum, et locum nanciscetur, et fiet motus. Quoties talis mutatio, talis in mundo composito motus fit, status mutati, et universi, cuius pars est, partim idem est cum praecedentibus, partim diversus. Hinc sicuti certus aliquis motus fuit, quatenus status novus a pristino differt; ita, quatenus status idem mansit, haec duratio status, est in mundo composito simul duratio loci, certi motus absentia, quies, certique motus impedimentum fuit, et resistentia*>."

12   Baumgarten, §416 (Ak. 17: 113): "Monads which constitute an extended thing in the universe always act by their own power – representing each of the states of their universe, and their own, even future states, by a power impeding some motion, or resisting some motion, inasmuch as these monads are the same, perduring with antecedent states; and by a power effecting some other certain motion, or a moving power, inasmuch as they are different from antecedent states <*Monades in universo constituentes extensum, semper agunt, vi, sua, repraesentantes universi sui singulos status, et suos, etiam futuros, quatenus hi iidem sunt cum antecedentibus perdurantes, certum motum impedient resistente, certo motui resistente, quatenus autem hi diversi sumt ab antecedentibus, certum alium motum efficiente, s. movente*>."

13   Baumgarten, §422: "The absolutely elementary parts of bodies are immaterial <*Elementa corporum absolute talia sunt immaterialia*>."

14   [Lehmann note to Ak. 28: 48₈] Aqua regia consists of hydrochloric and nitric acid in a water solution; it forms gold chloride. As to how laborious the production of this "gold-dissolving water" was in Kant's time, see the recipes given in Johann Heinrich Zedler, *Grosses vollständiges Universal Lexicon* (Large and Complete Universal Encyclopedia), 64 vols. (Halle and Leipzig: 1732–50), vol. 2 (1732), columns 1035f.

15   Baumgarten, §430 (Ak. 17: 116): "The *nature of a thing* is the sum of those of its internal determinations which are the principles of its alterations, or, in

general, of the accidents which inhere in it <*Natura entis est complexus earum eius determinationum internarum, quae mutationum eius, aut in genere accidentium ipsi inhaerentium sunt principia*>."

16 In this reference to a "single thing" (*singula res*), Kant appears to be amending Baumgarten's definition of machine in §433 (Ak. 17: 116–17): "A MACHINE is a composite strictly speaking which is movable according to the laws of motion. Therefore *every body* in the world *is a machine* <MACHINA *est compositum stricte dictum secundum leges motus mobile. Ergo omne corpus in mundo est machina*>." Precisely this point is repeated at *Metaphysik Mrongovius* (Ak. 29: 935$_{14}$).

17 [Lehmann note to Ak. 28: 50$_4$] See Pierre Louis Moreau de Maupertuis, *Vénus Physique* in vol. 2 of his *Oeuvres* (Works) (Lyon, 1768), pp. 67f, 85 (a polemic against Descartes), also pp. 83f., 88, etc.

18 Baumgarten, §436 (Ak. 17: 117): "The most perfect world is that in which the most and the greatest parts compossible in a world agree to the extent that is possible in a world. Hence, the most perfect world has the most greatly composite perfection, and a world is not the most perfect if the only perfection which belongs to it is simple perfection <*Mundus perfectissimus est, in quo plurimarum partium maximae, et maximarum plurimae partes in mundo compossibiles tantum ad unum consentiunt, quantum in mundo fieri potest. Hinc mundus perfectissimus habet perfectionem maxime compositam, cuique mundo non nisi simplex convenit perfectio, non est perfectissimus*>."

19 Since Baumgarten in §439 defines materialism as involving the rejection of monads, Kant seems to be suggesting here that this issue is more appropriately discussed in the Rational Psychology; see, for example, Kant's discussion at the beginning of the Rational Psychology in *Metaphysik Vigilantius* (*K$_3$*) (Ak. 29: 1025). See also note 9 (to Ak. 28: 44$_{26}$), above.

20 Kant is referring (at Ak. 28: 51$_{14}$) to Baumgarten, §440 (Ak. 17: 118), which refers back to the definition of "indefinite" given at §248 (Ak. 17: 81).

Metaphysik L$_1$ (Ak. 28: 195–301)

1 [Lehmann note to Ak. 28: 205$_{23–30}$] Voltaire, *Dictionnaire Philosophique* (1764), translated as *Philosophical Dictionary*, 10 vols., edited by William Fleming (New York: E. R. DuMont, 1901), vol. 3, pp. 55-8 ("Chain of Created Beings").

2 [Lehmann note to Ak. 28: 205$_{34–5}$] Heinze adds here, from *Metaphysik K$_1$*: "We indeed find gradations; there are human beings who come very close to kinds of animals, but still there is no infinite quantity of intermediate kinds. Thus it is possible only in the idea in the logical sense, but not in reality" (Max Heinze, *Vorlesungen Kants über Metaphysik aus drei Semestern* (Kant's Lectures on Metaphysics from Three Semesters) (Leipzig: S. Hirzel, 1894), p. 533n).

3 [Lehmann note to Ak. 28: 206$_{19}$] Heinze reports that, according to *Metaphysik K$_2$*, "the egoist is defined as one who considers himself, as thinking being, as the only mundane being. But the egoistic world <*mundus egoisticus*> should be a contradiction because only diverse substances constitute a world" (Max Heinze, *Vorlesungen Kants über Metaphysik aus drei Semestern*

(Kant's Lectures on Metaphysics from Three Semesters) (Leipzig: S. Hirzel, 1894), p. 534n).

4 [Lehmann note to Ak. 28: 207$_{18-19}$] See here Refl. #3803 (Ak. 17: 297$_{21}$): "Every Spinozist is an egoist <*Omnis spinozista est egoista*>."

5 Lehmann (noting Ak. 28: 209$_{29}$) refers us here to a note added in Karl Pölitz's anonymous edition of *Immanuel Kants Vorlesungen über die Metaphysik* (Immanuel Kant's Lectures on Metaphysics) (Erfurt: Kaisers, 1821), p. 345: "According to the new chemistry, *water* can actually be separated into two sorts of gases, and thus Kant's example borrowed from water loses its validity; so these lectures probably fall in the time before that new discovery had come to Kant's attention." Cf. Arnoldt's remarks on this note in Emil Arnoldt, *Gesammelte Schriften* (Collected Writings), ed. by Otto Schöndörffer, 11 vols. (Berlin: B. Cassirer, 1906–11), vol. 5 ("*Kritische Exkurse im Gebiete der Kantforschung*," 1909), pp. 60–1, as well as Adickes's note to Refl. #5300 (Ak. 18: 148$_{20-4}$). See also *Metaphysik Dohna* (Ak. 28: 664$_{14-15}$), below.

6 [Lehmann note to Ak. 28: 210$_{10-11}$] Crab stones or crab eyes are calcium deposits on the stomach walls of the river crab (*Astacus fluvialis*), according to Johann Heinrich Zedler, *Grosses vollständiges Universal Lexicon* (Large and Complete Universal Encyclopedia) 64 vols. (Halle and Leipzig: 1732–50), vol. 15 (1737), columns 1822–4: "Crab eyes, or better, crab stones, are those round stones which at certain times, namely during molting, are found inside on the head, or more often in the stomach, of the crab. But they are not always met with in crabs, at least not in any perceivable size, but rather only when crabs are molting, that is, when they cast off the shell and receive a new one.... These crab stones have been much used in medicine, mostly since the time of Paracelsus..., as one of the most common daily home remedies for heartburn, colic, gallstones, stabbing pains, high and changing fever, with or without the addition of other things...."

7 [Lehmann note to Ak. 28: 212$_{26-9}$] Cf. Refl. #3730 (Ak. 17: 272).

8 [Lehmann note to Ak. 28: 213$_{12-14}$] Cf. Christian Wolff, *Ausführliches Nachricht von seinen eigenen Schriften in deutscher Sprache* (Complete Account of his own Writings in the German Language), 3rd ed. (1757), p. 279: "... In the explanation of the community between body and soul I have preferred the system of preestablished harmony <*systema harmoniae praestabilitae*>.... But I have never maintained that it is contrary to the nature of a spirit to have an effect in a body...."

9 [Lehmann note to Ak. 28: 218$_4$] Cf. Max Heinze, *Vorlesungen Kants über Metaphysik aus drei Semestern* (Kant's Lectures on Metaphysics from Three Semesters) (Leipzig: S. Hirzel, 1894), pp. 510–11, where he discusses the use of this example in *Metaphysik K$_2$* (at Ak. 28: 733$_{27-35}$). See also Kant's note in *The Only Possible Argument in Support of a Demonstration of the Existence of God:*

In those cases where revelation tells us that something which has happened in the world is an extraordinary and divinely instituted event, it is to be desired that the eagerness of the philosophers to make a public show of their physical speculations should be restrained. They do religion no service. On the contrary, their speculations simply arouse the suspicion that the event which they have sought to explain by natural causes may, indeed, be a natural accident. Such is the case where the destruction of Sennacherib's army is attributed to the wind Samyel. In such instances, philosophy frequently finds itself in difficulties, as happens in Whiston's theory, where astronomical knowledge of the comets is employed to explain the Bible. (Ak. 2: 120_{30-6}; Walford translation)

[Walford glosses "Whiston's theory" as a reference to his *A New Theory of the Earth* (1696). On the wind of Samuel, cf. I Samuel 12: 17–18, but Kant doesn't seem to be referring to this passage in Samuel, as there is no reference there to Sennacherib. And at II Kings, 19: 35, where Sennacherib is mentioned, there is no reference to wind. Perhaps this "Samyel wind" is a product of later commentators, postulated as the cause of the destruction of Sennacherib's troops during the night.]

10   Lehmann refers to a note to *Metaphysik K_2* (Ak. 28: 735_{14-20}), which we include in part here: See Heinze's comments at Ak. 28: 740_{10-17} (*Metaphysik K_2*), as well as Lehmann's "Introduction" (Ak. 28: 1353). In the *Anthropologie Philippi* (1772), Kant answers the question as to why

> ... a connected science of man [was not made] from the great supply of observations by English writers. It appears to be because one has viewed the science of man as a part attached to metaphysics. ... This mistake perhaps arose from the error that, because in metaphysics one must take everything out of oneself, one viewed all parts of metaphysics as consequences of the doctrine of the soul. But metaphysics has nothing to do with experiential cognitions. (ms p. 1)

11   The following terms (at Ak. 28: 230_{28}) do not come from Baumgarten, except for *facultas praevidendi* (faculty of anticipation). *Facultas signandi* (faculty of signifying) is likely Kant's counterpart to Baumgarten's *facultas characteristica* (faculty of characterization) (§§619–23). Also, *componendi* (composing) might be a variant of *comparandi* (comparing), a faculty that Baumgarten discusses at §626; *facultas imaginandi* (faculty of imagining) corresponds to Baumgarten's *phantasia* (fantasy) (§§557–71), and *facultas praevidendi* (faculty of anticipation) corresponds to Baumgarten's *praevisio* (anticipation) (§§595–605) or *praesagitio* (prediction) (§§610–18). The subgroupings under *facultas fingendi* (fictive faculty) is a departure from Baumgarten, and *facultas formandi* (faculty of illustration) has no counterpart in Baumgarten.

    Makkreel discusses Kant's terminology of imagination at some length, offering the following interpretations of *Bildung: Abbildung* (direct image formation), *Nachbildung* (reproductive image formation); *Vorbildung* (anticipatory image formation). Two other modes are temporally definable: *Ausbildung* (that mode of formation which completes images) and *Gegenbildung* (that which allows images to serve as linguistic signifiers or symbolic analogues of something else). See Ch. 1 of Rudolf Makkreel, *Imagination and Interpretation in Kant: The Hermeneutical Import of the Critique of Judgment* (Chicago: University of Chicago Press, 1990). See also the entry for *facultas* in the list of Latin-German equivalents in the present volume and note 13 (to Ak. 28: 237_{10}), below.

12   [Lehmann note to Ak. 28: 233_{28}] See Christian August Crusius, *Weg zur Gewissheit und Zuverlässigkeit der menschlichen Erkenntnis* (Road to Certainty and Reliability of Human Cognition) (Leipzig, 1747), §432 (p. 768): "But ultimately one will cognize that the source of all truth and certainty must lie

in a necessary understanding, namely in the divine. . . ." Cf. *Metaphysik von Schön* (Ak. 28: 467$_{20}$–468$_{17}$). Still sharper is Kant's judgment about Crusius in the *Logik Philippi* (Ak. 24: 335$_{27-30}$): "Crusius has an anti-philosophical method which undermines all philosophy. He advances things as subjective laws which are often only the effects of the understanding and not laws. He has sheer phantoms of the brain. He casts aside all means of proof."

13 What is here (at Ak. 28: 237$_{10}$) called "the faculty of reproductive imagination" (*imagination; facultas imaginandi*) or "imitation" (*Nachbildung*) parallels what in Baumgarten is called *phantasia* (fantasy) (§§557–71). What is here called "the faculty of imagination" or "fantasy" (*Vermögen der Einbildung; Phantasie*) seems to parallel Baumgarten's *facultas fingendi* (fictive faculty) (§§589–94). See note 11 (to Ak. 28: 230$_{28}$), above.

14 Lehmann quotes (at Ak. 28: 1471) a parallel passage from *Metaphysik K$_1$* (as preserved in Benno Erdmann, "*Eine unbeachtet gebliebene Quelle zur Entwicklungsgeschichte Kants*" (An Unnoticed Source on Kant's Developmental History) in *Philosophische Monatshefte*, 1883, p. 133n):

Of the faculty of contrast or faculty of characterization <*facultate characteristica*> we must say something in more detail: a representation which serves as a means of reproduction through association is a character; but a representation which serves intellectuality as [a] means is a symbol <*symbolum*>. In themselves, words have no sense, but rather serve only to produce other representations through association and these are *characters*. On the other hand, there are means of intellection, and these are symbols <*symbola*>. Most of the symbolic representations occur with the cognition of God. These are all by analogy <*per analogiam*>, i.e., by an agreement of relation, e.g., with all peoples the sun was a symbol <*symbolum*>, a representation of divine perfection, in that it is present everywhere in the great cosmic system, contains much, has light and warmth without receiving any.

15 This (Ak. 28: 246$_{20}$) is a reference to Alexander Baumgarten, *Aesthetica* (Aesthetics), 2 vols. (Frankfurt an der Oder, 1750–8).

16 [Lehmann note to Ak. 28: 248$_3$] Cf. Refl. #4237 (Ak. 17: 472$_{2-7}$): "A human being has two sorts of life: (1) *animal*, (2) *spiritual*." But we later read: "In the existence of the human soul (1) the existence of substance is to be considered; (2) life in general (animal) as a soul; (3) personality, i.e., life as a human spirit. . . ."

17 Lehmann refers (at Ak. 28: 253$_{17}$) to the "Introduction" to the *Metaphysic of Morals* (Ak. 6: 223$_{5-10}$): "An action that is neither commanded nor prohibited . . . is called morally indifferent (a thing which may but need not be done <*indifferens, adiaphoron, res merae facultatis*>). One can ask whether there are such. . . ."

18 [Lehmann note to Ak. 28: 258$_{1-5}$] Cf. Paul Menzer, *Eine Vorlesung Kants über Ethik* (Berlin, 1924), p. 45 [English translation: Louis Infield, *Kant's Lectures on Ethics*, p. 37]: "the principle <*principium*> of morality is not pathological; it would be pathological if it were derived from subjective grounds, from our inclinations, from our feeling . . . ," as well as *Groundwork to a Metaphysic of Morals* (1785; Ak. 4: 442).

19 [Lehmann note to Ak. 28: 261$_{14-15}$] On Georg Ernst Stahl (1660–1734), cf. Paul Menzer's note to Ak. 2: 331$_{29}$ (*Dreams of a Spirit-Seer*), as well as Hans Driesch, *Geschichte des Vitalismus* (Leipzig, 1922), pp. 27ff. Stahl's formative

power <*vis plastica*> was often criticized by Kant – see Refl. #3160 (Ak. 16: 688) and Adickes's note to this. See also Lehmann's note to Ak. 28: 432$_{25}$ (*Metaphysik Volckmann*): "In the animism (vilalism) of Stahl, the formative power (the power of the generative spirit) <*vis plastica (spiritus genitalis)*> is the procreative power." Cf. Adickes's notes to Ak. 15: 943$_{15-22}$ ("On Philosophers' Medicine of the Body"). Similar, and also without reference to Stahl, is a passage in the *Logik Blomberg* (Ak. 24: 81$_{32-7}$): "If one were to ask about the cause of the propagation and increase of the human and animal understanding . . . the ancients said with an affected, learned mien: the cause of the propagation of human beings and animals is the formative power <*vis plastica*>, power of propagation" [*Lectures on Logic*, p. 62, translated by J. Michael Young, slightly modified].

20 [Lehmann note to Ak. 28: 263$_{16}$] On the following classification, cf. Refl. #4230 (Ak. 17: 467–8).

21 Lehmann refers (at Ak. 28: 274$_{35}$) to a note to Ak. 28: 116$_{9-10}$ (*Metaphysik Herder*) that speaks of Descartes's "paradoxical" opinion of animal machines. In *The Passions of the Soul* we read, e.g., in Art. 50:

> For although they lack reason, and perhaps even thought, all the movements of the spirits and of the gland which produce passions in us are nevertheless present in them too, though in them they serve to maintain and strengthen only the movements of the nerves and muscles which usually accompany the passions and not, as in us, the passions themselves. (Translation by Robert Stoothof in *The Philosophical Writings of Descartes*, tr. John Cottingham, Robert Stoothof, and Dugald Murdoch, Cambridge University Press, 1985, vol. 1, p. 348)

Cf. Hermann Samuel Reimarus, *Allgemeine Betrachtungen über die Triebe der Thiere hauptsächlich über ihre Kunsttriebe: zum Erkenntniss des Zusammenhanges der Welt, des Schöpfers und unser selbst* (General Observations on the Drives of Animals, especially their Artificial Drives; on the Cognition of the Connection of the World, the Creator, and Our Self), 2nd edition, enlarged with an appendix (Hamburg: Carl Holm, 1762), pp. 211f. (§109). According to Kant (*Philosophische Enzyklopädie*, Ak. 29: 44$_{34-6}$): "the main and nearly the only difference between animals and human beings is consciousness, but this is also so large that it cannot be replaced by anything . . ." Cf. the note to Ak. 28: 96$_{19}$ (*Metaphysik Herder*), which refers to Baumgarten, §705 (Ak. 17: 131), Leibniz's *Systéme nouveau de la nature et de la communication des substances aussi bien que de l'union qu'il y a entre l'âme et le corps* (*New System of the Nature and Communication of Substances*), §15 [in *G. W. Leibniz: Philosophical Essays*, tr. by Roger Ariew and Daniel Garber (Indianapolis: Hackett, 1989), p. 144], and Refl. #3855 (Ak. 17: 313–14).

22 [Lehmann note to Ak. 28: 280$_{16}$] Cf. Kant's discussion in *CrPR* (A 649f/B 677f) in the appendix to the "Transcendental Dialectic" and in his essay "On the Use of Teleological Principles in Philosophy" (Ak. 8: 180$_{18-30}$). See also Heinz Heimsoeth, *Transzendentale Dialektik* (Transcendental Dialectic) (Berlin, 1966–71), vol. 4, p. 837, for more references on the idea of a basic power (*Grundkraft*).

23 Lehmann notes (Ak. 28: 284$_{26}$): Adickes connects this text to the following distinction drawn in Refl. #4239 (Ak. 17: 473$_{12-15}$): "The surviving life of the soul is distinguished from its immortality. The first means that it will not

die . . . ; the second that it *cannot die* in a natural manner." See also Refl.
#4342 (Ak. 17: 512$_{13f}$): "That the principle <*principium*> of life cannot
die. . . ."

24 Lehmann refers (noting Ak. 28: 285$_7$) to his note to Ak. 28: 284$_{26}$ (note 23
above), and to Refl. #4342 (Ak. 17: 512).

25 [Lehmann note to Ak. 28: 285$_{24}$] Cf. Refl. #4240 (Ak. 17: 474–5): "Matter
is lifeless. . . ." Cf. also Adickes's note to this at Ak. 17: 474$_{30f}$.

26 [Lehmann note to Ak. 28: 286$_{30}$] Max Heinze, *Vorlesungen Kants über
Metaphysik aus drei Semestern* (Kant's Lectures on Metaphysics from Three
Semesters) (Leipzig: S. Hirzel, 1894), p. 548 discusses this passage.

27 [Lehmann note to Ak. 28: 289$_{30}$] Cf. here Refl. #4106 (Ak. 17: 417$_{9–12}$).

28 [Lehmann note to Ak. 28: 298$_{37}$] Cf. note 11 to *Metaphysik K*$_2$ (Ak. 28: 768$_{28}$),
below. The (contemporaneous) remarks of the *Logik Philippi* (Ak. 24: 448$_{31–7}$)
also appear to belong to the context of the discussions here and on the next
page: "But there are things, the certainty of which one is led to only by special
persons. They require a degree of personal credibility which only a special
character of person warrants. E.g., if we are informed of divining rods or
ghosts by persons of credible character, then we begin to believe it." [On Kant
and Swedenborg, see Kant's letter to Charlotte von Knobloch (Aug. 10, 1763)
and Kant's *Dreams of a Spirit-Seer,* as well as Lehmann's note to Ak. 28: 897$_{37}$
(*Nachträge Herder*).]

Metaphysik Mrongovius (Ak. 29: 747–940)

1 [Lehmann note to Ak. 29: 747$_1$] Cf. Refl. #3709 (Ak. 17: 249–50): "Introduction to Metaphysics" <*Prolegomena Metaphysicorum*>.

2 See Baumgarten's list of topics at §§7f. (Ak. 17: 24f).

3 [Lehmann note to Ak. 29: 749$_{33}$] Baumgarten, "Introduction <*Prolegomena*>," §1 (Ak. 17: 23): "METAPHYSICS is the science of the first principles
in human cognition <METAPHYSICA *est scientia primorum in humana cognitione
principiorum*>." Cf. the *Metaphysik K*$_2$ (Ak. 28: 709$_{7–11}$; Heinze excerpt).

4 Cf. Baumgarten, §28 (Ak. 17: 32): "A ground which has yet a further ground is
called A GROUND IN SOME RESPECT (intermediate), a ground which does not is
called A GROUND WITHOUT QUALIFICATION (ultimate) <*RATIO SECUNDUM
QUID* (G: *der Zwischen-Grund*) (*intermedia*) *dicitur, quae habet adhuc ulteriorem,
quae non habet,* SIMPLICITER TALIS (G: *der letzte Grund*) (*ultima*)>." See also
Kant's Refl. #3519 (Ak. 17: 33): "A ground either suffices for the thing
grounded [only], or it suffices for itself as well; in the first case, it is sufficient
in a certain respect, whereas in the second, it is sufficient without qualification
<*ratio vel sufficit rationato vel etiam sibimet ipsi; si prior: est secundum quid
sufficiens, si posterior: est simpliciter*>."

5 [Lehmann note to Ak. 29: 750$_{10–13}$] On that see the explanations in the
Danziger Physik (Ak. 29: 97–8), and the note to Ak. 29: 98$_{15–18}$.

6 Cf. *CrPR*, A xii, A 57/B 81, A 154/B 193, A 235/B 294; and see Locke's
proposal "to enquire into the Original, Certainty, and Extent of humane
knowledge" (*An Essay Concerning Human Understanding*, 2 vols. (1690), Bk. 2,
Ch. 1, §2). See also Ak. 29: 756$_{5–7}$, below. And see the "Subject Index"
under "Reason, limit, extent, and scope of."

7 [Lehmann note to Ak. 29: 752$_{19}$] See Christian Wolff, *Ontologia*, §495: "Truth, which is called transcendental and is understood to be in things themselves, is the order within the diversity of things [that exist at the same time and mutually condition each other; or, if you prefer, the order of those things] that are appropriate to a being <*veritas adeo, quae transcendentalis appellatur et rebus ipsis inesse intelligitur, est ordo in varietate eorum, [quae simul sunt ac se invicem consequuntur, aut, si mavis, ordo eorum,] quae enti conveniunt*>." See Norbert Hinske, *Kants Weg zur Transzendentalphilosophie* (Kant's Route to Transcendental Philosophy) (Stuttgart, 1970); Hinske, "*Kants neue Terminologie und ihre alten Quellen*" (Kant's New Terminology and Its Old Sources) in *Akten des 4. Internationalen Kant Kongresses* (Proceedings of the 4th International Kant Congress) (Berlin: de Gruyter, 1974), vol. 1, pp. 68–85; also K. Bärthlein, *Die Transzendentalienlehre der alten Ontologie I* (The Doctrine of Transcendentals of the Old Ontology I) (Berlin: de Gruyter, 1972). See also Ak. 29: 784–6, below.

8 [Lehmann note to Ak. 29: 755$_{30}$] Cf. *Metaphysik Vigilantius (K$_3$)* (Ak. 29: 955$_{1-4}$): "Since this was a kind of *a priori* cognition, and in mathematics <*mathesi*> one succeeded in extending cognitions beyond sensible objects, one inferred that it could also be attempted with philosophy. . . ." One can clearly relate metaphysics "brought about" mathematically to the *Metaphysical First Principles of Natural Science* (1786), especially to its Preface (Ak. 4: 470$_{30-2}$): a "pure doctrine of nature about determinate natural things is possible only by means of mathematics."

9 [Lehmann note to Ak. 29: 754$_{21}$] See note 30 (to Ak. 29: 785$_{25}$), below.

10 [Lehmann note to Ak. 29: 757$_{1-2}$] The question of the relation of empirical psychology to anthropology is complicated because in the Physical Geography lectures Kant also treats "of human begins" (Ak. 9: 311–20). This connection is stressed by Benno Erdmann, *Reflexionen Kants zu Kritische Philosophie* (Kant's Reflections on Critical Philosophy), vol. 1 (Leipzig, 1882), p. 46, whose "developmental history" is rejected by Emil Arnoldt, *Gesammelte Schriften* (Collected Writings), ed. by Otto Schöndörffer, 11 vols. (Berlin: B. Cassirer, 1906–11), vol. 4 ("Kritische Exkurse im Gebiete der Kantforschung" (1908–9), p. 335f). Regarding text, see the contemporaneous *Anthropologie Mrongovius* (1785), which is set aside for vol. 26 of the Academy edition: "The study of human beings in general is called by another name, anthropology; but it is again of two sorts, either (1) pragmatic anthropology <*anthropologia pragmatica*> if the study of human beings is considered as it is useful in society in general or (2) scholastic anthropology <*anthropologia scholastica*> if one considers (treats) it more as a school subject, the former is the application of the latter in a society" (ms, p. 3). Moral philosophy also serves pragmatic anthropology, because without it "moral philosophy [would be] scholastic and wholly inapplicable to the world. Anthropology is related to moral philosophy as pure geometry is to geodesy" (*Anthropologie Mrongovius*, ms, p. 4). See the same formulation further below (Ak. 29: 877$_{4-5}$), and see the note to Ak. 28: 735$_{14-20}$ (*Metaphysik K$_2$*) [included in note 10 to *Metaphysik L$_1$*, Ak. 28: 223$_{2f}$), above].

11 [Lehmann note to Ak. 29: 758$_5$] Cf. Diogenes Laertius, *De vitis philosophorum* (Lives of Eminent Philosophers), Bk. 1, pp. 116–22. Pherecydes was, as

Theopompus reported, the first to provide writings to the Greeks about nature and the gods. Kant referred often to Pherecydes, who was counted among the seven sages in the wider sense. E.g., in the historical overviews at Refl. #1635 (Ak. 16: 59) and Refl. #5660 (Ak. 18: 318). The anecdote that he recounts of him at Refl. #2660 (Ak. 16: 457) and in the *Logik Blomberg* refers, however, not to Pherecydes but rather to Lacydes (see Adickes's note to Refl. #2660 at Ak. 16: 456).

12   [Lehmann note to Ak. 29: 758₁₀] This oft-cited sentence of Socrates is found in Diogenes Laertius, *De vitis philosophorum* (Lives of Eminent Philosophers), Bk. 2, p. 22. [R. D. Hicks translation: "They relate that Euripides gave him the treatise of Heraclitus and asked his opinion upon it, and that his reply was, 'The part I understand is excellent, and so too is, I dare say, the part I do not understand; but it needs a Delian diver to get to the bottom of it' " (Harvard University Press: Cambridge, Mass., 1942). Note also the parallel passage in *Metaphysik Volckmann* (Ak. 28: 369₁₄₋₁₆).]

13   [Lehmann note to Ak. 29: 758₁₃] I.e., *impossibile* does not belong to classical Latin, but rather only to later Latin.

14   [Lehmann note to Ak. 29: 758₁₇] Cf. the notes to Ak. 29: 107₂₇, 149₂₄₋₇ (*Danziger Physik*); Refl. #4449 (Ak. 17: 555₁₈₋₂₀): "Plato . . . and Pythagoras made the intellectual things <*intellectualia*> into special objects of possible intuition"; note to Ak. 27: 212₃₄f (*Praktische Philosophie Powalski*).

15   [Lehmann note to Ak. 29: 758₃₇] Refl. #1635 (Ak. 16: 59): "Eleatics, Xenophanes. Parmenides. Zeno of Elea" <*Elaetici, Xenophanes, Parmenides, Zeno eleates*>; Refl. #1636 (Ak. 16: 60): "From purely rational principles, after the Ionian school under Anaxagoras, the Eleatic under Melissus and Parmenides, [and] the Italian under Pythagoras. Great defender: Plato. The intelligible is opposed to the sensible <*ex principiis pure rationalibus post scholam Ionicam sub Anaxagora, Eleaticam sub Melisso et Parmenide, Italicam sub Pythagora. Magnus defensor: Plato. Intelligibile oppositum sensibili*>."

16   [Lehmann note to Ak. 29: 759₁₋₇] Namely, Kant himself in his inaugural dissertation: *On the Form and Principles of the Sensible and the Intelligible World* (Ak. 2: 392f). In part four (Natural Theology <*theologia naturalis*>) of his *Metaphysics*, Baumgarten distinguishes "the world as a drama of sensibility (sensible world <*mundus sensibilis*>) [and] the world as an object of the understanding (intelligible world <*mundus intelligibilis*>)" (§869; Ak. 17: 169). "Phenomena" is (in Baumgarten's Cosmology, §425; Ak. 17: 115) the term for perceivables <*observabilia; G: das wahrzunehmende*>.

17   [Lehmann note to Ak. 29: 760₄] See *On the Form and Principles of the Sensible and the Intelligible World*, §10 (Ak. 2: 396₁₉₋₂₀): "An *intuition* of intellectual [objects] is not given to man, but only a *symbolic cognition*. . . . <*intellectualium non datur (homini) intuitus, sed nonnisi cognitio symbolica* . . . .>." Compare Refl. #4451 (Ak. 17: 556₁₈₋₂₁): "Theosophical and mystical principles. Pythagoras, the Eleatic school: Parmenides, Plato wrote of intellectual things <*intellectualia*>; Plato through innate and intuitive ideas <*plato per ideas connatas et intuitivas*>, the others through discursive [ideas] <*per discursivas*>, but the objects of sense <*sensitiva*> only as appearances <*apparentias*>."

18   [Lehmann note to Ak. 29: 761₂₅] As Swedenborg taught and also Kant, in a tone of irony, in the *Dreams of a Spirit-Seer* (Ak. 2: 327).

19 [Lehmann note to Ak. 29: 763$_{15}$] Cf. note to Ak. 28: 1275$_{18f}$ (*Danziger Rationaltheologie*), as well as note 7 to *Metaphysik Vigilantius* (*K$_3$*) (Ak. 29: 951$_{15}$), below.

20 [Lehmann note to Ak. 29: 764$_1$] According to *CrPR* (A 845/B 873), transcendental philosophy and the physiology of pure reason are coordinated in so far as the former considers the concepts of understanding and reason as such, whereas the latter considers nature. Immanent physiology is distinguished into physics and psychology, the "objects" of outer and inner sense (A 846/B 874). Here one should no doubt abstract from this questionable division and think only of the Preface to *CrPR* (A ix): "In more recent times, it once seemed as if an end might be put to all these controversies and the claims of metaphysics receive final judgment, through a certain physiology of the human understanding – that of the celebrated Locke." Cf. now, R. Brandt, "Materialen zur Entstehung der *Kritik der reinen Vernunft* (John Locke und Johann Schultz)" (Materials on the Emergence of the *Critique of Pure Reason* [John Locke and Johann Schultz]) in *Beiträge zur Kritik der reinen Vernunft, 1781–1981* (Contributions on the *Critique of Pure Reason, 1781–1981*), ed. by I. Heidemann and W. Ritzel (Berlin: de Gruyter, 1981), pp. 37–68.

21 [Lehmann note to Ak. 29: 764$_{11}$] This is a questionable "condensed proposition," probably by a copyist. Locke's *An Essay Concerning Human Understanding* appeared in 1690 (2 vols.), a Latin translation (*Johannis Lockii Libri IV de Intellectu Humano* by G. H. Thiele) in one volume in 1741 in Leipzig. Leibniz's *Nouveaux Essais sur l'entendement humain* (New Essays in Human Understanding) were published only in 1765 (Leibniz died in 1716) by R. E. Raspe. The same mistake occurs in the *Metaphysik von Schön* (Ak. 28: 466$_{29-30}$).

22 [Lehmann note to Ak. 29: 764$_{20}$] Cf. *Metaphysik Volckmann* (Ak. 28: 377$_{20-2}$): "Wolff does not investigate how we are to attain a concept; instead he propounds a system of reason that he called metaphysics." Cf. Ak. 28: 467$_{16-18}$ (*Metaphysik von Schön*), as well as Heinz Heimsoeth, *Studien zur Philosophie Immanuel Kants* (Studies on Immanuel Kant's Philosophy) (Köln: Kölner Universitäts-Verlag, 1956; Kant-Studien Ergänzungsheft #71), Sect. 1: "Chr. Wolffs Ontologie und die Prinzipienforschung I. Kants" (Christian Wolff's Ontology and the Research of Principles of Immanuel Kant), pp. 1–92.

23 [Lehmann note to Ak. 29: 765$_{12}$] Cf. the note to Ak. 29: 10$_{25}$ (*Philosophische Enzyklopädie*).

24 [Lehmann note to Ak. 29: 766$_{10}$] Cf. Heinz Heimsoeth, *Studien zur Philosophie Immanuel Kants* (Studies on Immanuel Kant's Philosophy) (Bonn, 1970; Kant-Studien Ergänzungsheft #100), Ch. 3, "Experimentelle Physik" (Experimental Physics) (pp. 49–58), and Ch. 4, "Chemie" (Chemistry) (pp. 58–66). [See also note 5 (to Ak. 29: 750$_{10-13}$), above, and note 1 to *Metaphysik Vigilantius K$_3$* (Ak. 29: 946$_{14}$).]

25 [Lehmann note to Ak. 29: 776$_{32}$] *CrPR* (A 840/B 868) says, "The former [ultimate end] is no other than the entire vocation of human beings, and the philosophy concerning this is called moral philosophy"; in the *Moral Mrongovius* itself (Ak. 27: 1398$_{3-7}$): "Morality attempts to bring its [i.e. human] good behavior under rules, namely what should happen. That something should be means a possible action can be good. Moral philosophy contains rules of the good use of the will. . . ."

26 [Lehmann note to Ak. 29: 778₁₆] On this reference to Hutcheson, see note to Ak. 27: 4₂₅ (*Praktische Philosophie Herder*).

27 [Lehmann note to Ak. 29: 781₃₅] It is difficult to say whether this expectoration stems from Kant or from the notetaker. The *Prolegomena*, which appeared in 1783, describes Hume's attempt to think the connection of cause and effect as necessary (Ak. 4: 257f), and at Ak. 4: 260₆₋₉ breaks out into the famous call: the recollection of David Hume "was just that which many years ago first aroused me from a dogmatic slumber . . ."

28 The first edition of Kant's *Critique of Pure Reason* was published shortly before this lecture in 1781 by Johann Friedrich Hartknoch in Riga.

29 [Lehmann note to Ak. 29: 783₅] After Aquapendente [Harvey's Paduan teacher] discovered the venous valves, William Harvey (1578–1657), the personal physician to Charles I, succeeded in correctly understanding and describing the circulation of the blood (*De motu cordis et sanguinis* (On the Motion of the Heart and Blood),1628). He was at first strongly attacked and ridiculed (*De circulatione sanguinis ad Riolanum* (On the Circulation of Blood, Reply to Riolan), 1649). See his *Opera omnia* (Complete Works) (London, 1766), in which there is also a work on spontaneous generation <*generatio aequivoca*> (see note 109 to Ak. 29: 845₃₇₋₈, below).

30 [Lehmann note to Ak. 29: 785₂₅] Metaphysic of morals, "as Mr. Kant calls it," was contrasted in *CrPR* (A 841/B 869) with the metaphysics of nature, and is supposed to be "properly the pure moral philosophy" in the *Groundwork to a Metaphysic of Morals* (Ak. 4: 410) where Kant "passes over" to the metaphysics of morals. It should be distinguished as "pure philosophy of morals" from the applied. This entire "architectonic" is altered in the *Metaphysic of Morals* itself by inclusion of the "Doctrine of Justice." See above (Ak. 29: 754₂₃₋₄): metaphysic of morals contains the principles of the practical use of reason.

31 [Lehmann note to Ak. 29: 785₂₇f] Cf. the well-known note from the *CrPR* (A 21/B 35): Baumgarten, "the splendid analyst"; see also the "Announcement of the Programme of his Lectures for the Winter Semester 1765–6" (Ak. 2: 308₃₃₋₄): "the author, A. G. Baumgarten, whose textbook I have chosen primarily because of the richness and the precision of its method, . . ."; and the *Menschenkunde* (vol. 1, p. 9): Baumgarten, a man "who is very rich in material and very brief in exposition."

32 [Lehmann note to Ak. 29: 785₃₆–786₁] Cf. Baumgarten's introduction to the Ontology (§4–6), especially §6 (Ak. 17: 24): "Ontology contains the predicates of a thing, (I) internal, (1) universal, which are in individual things, (2) disjunctive, of which one is in individual things; (II) relative <*ontologia continet praedicata entis*, (I) *interna*, (1) *universalia, quae sunt in singulis*, (2) *disiunctiva, quorum alterutrum est in singulis*; (II) *relativa*>." Wolff, as is known, determines ontology or first philosophy <*philosophia prima*> as the science of a being in general, or as far as a being is a being <*scientia entis in genere, seu quatenus ens est*> (*Ontologia*, §1).

33 [Lehmann note to Ak. 29: 788₃₀] Christian Wolff, *Ontologia*, §70, "Proof of the principle of sufficient reason: Nothing exists without a sufficient reason for why it exists rather than does not exist. That is, if something is posited to exist, something must also be posited that explains why the first thing exists

rather than does not exist. For either (i) nothing exists without a sufficient reason for why it exists rather than does not exist, or else (ii) something can exist without a sufficient reason for why it exists rather than does not exist (§53). Let us assume that some A exists without a sufficient reason for why it exists rather than does not exist. (§56). Therefore nothing is to be posited that explains why A exists. What is more, A is admitted to exist because nothing is assumed to exist: since this is absurd (§69), nothing exists without a sufficient reason; and if something is posited to exist, something else must be assumed that explains why that thing exists <*Principium rationis sufficientis probatur: Nihil est sine ratione sufficiente, cur potius sit, quam non sit, hoc est, si aliquid esse ponitur, ponendum etiam est aliquid, unde intelligitur, cur idem potius sit, quam non sit. Aut enim nihil est sine ratione sufficiente, cur potius sit, quam non sit; aut aliquid esse potest absque ratione sufficiente, cur sit potius, quam non sit (§53). Ponamus esse A sine ratione sufficiente, cur potius sit, quam non sit. Ergo nihil ponendum est, unde intelligitur, cur A sit (§56). Admittitur adeo A esse, propterea quod nihil esse sumitur: quod cum sit absurdum (§69), absque ratione sufficiente nihil est, seu, si quid esse ponitur, admittendum etiam est aliquid, unde intelligitur, cur sit>.*"

34   [Lehmann note to Ak. 29: 789₁₂] See Baumgarten, Ch. 3 ("Relative Predicates of a Thing" <*Praedicata entis relativa*>), Sect. 1 ("Same and Different" <*Idem et diversum*>), §267 (Ak. 17: 84): "SAMENESS and DIVERSITY, as a single predicate is TOTAL, as a specific predicate is PARTIAL. Therefore likeness, equality, congruence are either total or partial <*IDENTITAS et DIVERSITAS, qua singula predicata, est TOTALIS* (G: *völlig, gänzlich*), *qua quaedam, PARTIALIS* (G: *zum Theil statt findend*). *Ergo similitudo, aequalitas, congruentia, sunt vel totales, vel partiales*>."

35   [Lehmann note to Ak. 29: 790₂₈] Baumgarten begins with the principle of contradiction <*principium contradictionis*>, §7 (Ak. 17: 24): "The A and the non-A is the negative nothing – the unrepresentable, the impossible, the repugnant (the absurd), that which involves a contradiction, that which implies the contradictory; or nothing is the subject of contradictory predicates; or nothing both is and is not. o = A + non-A. *This principle* is called *the principle of contradiction,* and is *absolutely first* <*nihil negativum, irrepraesentabile, impossibile, repugnans, (absurdum) contradictionem involvens, implicans, contradictorium, est A et non-A, seu, praedicatorum contradictoriorum nullum est subiectum, seu, nihil est, et non est. o = A + non-A. Haec propositio dicitur principium contradictionis, et absolute primum*>." Cf. *Metaphysik Vigilantius (K₃)* (Ak. 29: 963₄ₗ), below. Cf. also *Metaphysik von Schön* (Ak. 28: 478f).

36   [Lehmann note to Ak. 29: 790₃₂] Baumgarten, §15 (Ak. 17: 29): "Indeed, that which regarded in itself is not even representable, is IMPOSSIBLE IN ITSELF <*quod nec in se quidem spectandum repraesentatibile est, est IMPOSSIBLE IN SE* (G: *an und vor sich, innerlich, schlecterdings unmöglich*)>."

37   [Lehmann note to Ak. 29: 791₁₈ₗ] Baumgarten, §11 (Ak. 17: 25), "Every possible A is A, or, *whatever is, is that,* or, every subject is a predicate to itself. . . . *This proposition* is called *the principle of positing, or of identity* <*omne possibile A est A, seu, quicquid est, illud est, seu, omne subiectum est praedicatum sui. . . . Haec propositio dicitur principium positionis, seu, identitatis*>."

38   [Lehmann note to Ak. 29: 791₂₆ₗ] Baumgarten, §10 (Ak. 17: 24–5): "Every

565

possible thing is either A or not-A or neither, now the neither is nothing, because it would be both. Therefore *everything possible is A or not-A*, or, one of all contradictory predicates agrees with every subject. *This proposition is called the principle of the excluded third, or of the middle, between two contradictories <omne possibile est aut A, aut non-A, aut neutrum, iam neutrum est nihilum, quia esset utrumque. Ergo omne possibile aut est A, aut non-A, seu, omni subiecto ex omnibus praedicatis contradictoriis alterutrum convenit. Haec praepositio dicitur principium exclusi tertii, seu medii, inter duo contradictoria>.*"

39 [Lehmann note to Ak. 29: 792₂₅] Baumgarten, §7 (Ak. 17: 24): "The negative *nothing*, the unrepresentable, the impossible, the repugnant (the absurd) <*Nihil negativum, irrepraesentabile, impossibile, repugnans, (absurdum)*>." On clear darkness (Ak. 29: 792₂₈), see Refl. #3491 (Ak. 17: 25): "visible darkness."

40 Cf. Refl. #3496 (Ak. 17: 26), which Kant wrote alongside §13 of his copy of Baumgarten: "hidden <*latens*> is pious fraud <*pia fraus*>."

41 The moments listed under (1) and (2) differ from those given in the list at *CrPR* (A 70/B 95) and *Prolegomena* (Ak. 4: 302–3).

42 The terms in (1), (3), and (4) differ from those used in the *CrPR* and *Prolegomena*. *Limitation* is used in (2) and *Einschränkung* in the *Prolegomena*.

43 Passion <*passio*> is traditionally a separate category, but it is listed here with action <*actio*>, and Kant apparently viewed them as falling under a single category. After a listing of Aristotle's ten categories in the *Metaphysik von Schön* (Ak. 28: 481), we read: "Action <*actio*> and passion <*passio*> constitute only one category."

44 Note that there are five (not four) *postpraedicamenta* listed here. In the *Metaphysik von Schön* (Ak. 28: 481), these are called *praedicamenta*, while the *postpraedicamenta* are listed as follows: homonyms <*homonymia*>, synonyms <*synonymia*>, paranyms <*paranymia*>, paranyms with a conclusion <*paranymia cum complexione*> and without a conclusion <*absque complexione*>.

45 [Lehmann note to Ak. 29: 803₁₁] Baumgarten begins naturally not with the category of modality, but rather with "the possible" as an ontological predicate (see Sect. 1: "Possible" <*possibile*>; Ak. 17: 24–30).

46 [Lehmann note to Ak. 29: 806₂₈f] Christian Wolff, *Ontologia*, Sect. 1, On the Principles of First Philosophy <*De principiis philosophiae primae*>, Ch. 1: On the Principle of Contradiction <*De principio contradictionis*> (§§27–55), Ch. 2: On the Principle of Sufficient Reason <*De principio rationis sufficientis*> (§§56–78).

47 [Lehmann note to Ak. 29: 806₃₅] Baumgarten, §37 (Ak. 17: 35): "Relative determinations of possible things are RELATIONS <*determinationes possibilium respectivae sunt* RESPECTUS (G: *Beziehungen*)>."

48 [Lehmann note to Ak. 29: 807₃₄] Baumgarten, §81 (Ak. 17: 45): "If when A is posited B is denied, A and B are OPPOSITES <*si posito A tollitur B, A et B* OPPOSITA *sunt* (G: *entgegen gesetzt, mit einander streitend*)>." From this logical opposition Kant distinguishes the real (in his "Attempt to Introduce the Concept of Negative Magnitudes into Philosophy," Ak. 2: 171₁₅₋₁₇): "here two predicates of a thing are opposed, but not through the principle of contradiction."

49 [Lehmann note to Ak. 29: 807₃₈] Baumgarten, §§14, 33 (Ak. 17: 27, 33).

And Refl. #3501 (Ak. 17: 28): "Things are connected of which [it is true that] when one is posited the other is posited <*connexa sunt, quorum uno posito ponitur aliud*>." Likewise Baumgarten, Sect. 2 ("Connection" <*Connexum*>), §19 (Ak. 17: 30): "The possible in connection – that is, that in which there is a connection, that with which a connection agrees – is the CONNECTED (the rational); the impossible in a connection is the IRRATIONAL (the unconnected, the incoherent). Therefore irrationals are either things impossible in themselves or things impossible hypothetically <*possibile in nexu i.e. in quo nexus est, cui nexus convenit,* CONNEXUM (G: *zusammenhängend, verknüpft*) (*rationale*) *est, in nexu impossibile est* IRRATIONALE (G: *ungereimt*) (*inconnexum, incohaerens*). *Hinc irrationalia vel sunt in se, vel hypothetice impossibilia*>."

50 [Lehmann note to Ak. 29: 811$_2$] Baumgarten, Sect. 1 ("Possible" <*Possibile*>), §7f (Ak. 17: 24f).

51 [Lehmann note to Ak. 29: 813$_6$] Baumgarten, §15 (Ak. 17: 29): "Whatever is regarded, but is not regarded in connection with those things which are posited outside of it, is REGARDED IN ITSELF <*quod spectatur, sed non in nexu cum iis, quae extra illud ponuntur,* SPECTATUR IN SE (G: *wird an und vor sich betrachtet*)>."

52 [Lehmann note to Ak. 29: 813$_{31}$] Baumgarten, Sect. 2 ("Connection" <*Connexum*>), §20 (Ak. 17: 31): "Therefore the ground of every possible thing either is nothing or is something . . . something is the ground of every possible thing or every possible thing is a consequence, or *nothing is without a ground* <*ergo omnis possibilis ratio aut nihil est, aut aliquid. . . . omnis possibilis aliquid est ratio, s. omne possibile est rationatum, s. nihil est sine ratione . . .* >."

53 [Lehmann note to Ak. 29: 815$_{32}$] Baumgarten, §23 (Ak. 17: 31): "Every possible thing is a ground, or *nothing is without a consequence,* . . . the consequence of every possible thing would be either nothing or something. If nothing were the consequence of some possible thing, it would be understood from this . . . <*omne possibile est ratio, seu nihil est sine rationato,* . . . *omnis possibilis rationatum aut nihil est, aut aliquid. Si nihil esset rationatum possibilis alicuius, posset ex hoc cognosci . . .* >."

54 [Lehmann note to Ak. 29: 817$_1$] Baumgarten, §24 (Ak. 17: 31): "Connected and rational, knowable both *a priori* and *a posteriori*. *This proposition* is called *the principle of things connected on both sides* (from the previous part and from the later part) <*connexum et rationale, tam a priori quam a posteriori cognoscibile. Haec propositio dicitur principium utrimque connexorum* (*a parte ante, et a parte post*)>."

55 [Lehmann note to Ak. 29: 817$_{17f}$] Cf. Baumgarten, §23 (Ak. 17: 31): principle of consequence <*principium rationati*>.

56 [Lehmann note to Ak. 29: 818$_{13}$] This refers to Baumgarten, §29 (Ak. 17: 33): "When the consequence has been posited, the ground is posited <*posito rationato, ponitur ratio*>," and §30 (Ak. 17: 33): "When the ground has been posited, the consequence is posited <*posita ratione, ponitur rationatum*>."

57 This parenthetical remark probably belongs to the discussion of Baumgarten, §§31–2 (Ak. 17: 33), and thus was likely marginalia (in an earlier copy) to the preceding paragraph, later being copied into the wrong paragraph.

58 [Lehmann note to Ak. 29: 819$_{34}$] See Baumgarten, §37 (Ak. 17: 35): "Relative

determinations of possible things are RELATIONS <*determinationes possibilium respectivae sunt* RESPECTUS (G: *Beziehungen*)>."

59 [Lehmann note to Ak. 29: 820$_{1-2}$] Baumgarten, §38 (Ak. 17: 36): "If those things are in A which are in B, A and B are THE SAME. Things which are not the same are DIVERSE (different) <*si in A sunt, quae in B, A et B sunt* EADEM (G: *einerlei*). *Non eadem sunt* DIVERSA (G: *verschieden*) (*alia*)>." Also Refl. #3527 (Ak. 17: 36): "This is a logical relation <*respectus*>."

60 [Lehmann note to Ak. 29: 820$_8$] Baumgarten, §50 (Ak. 17: 37): "Affections have their ground in the essence, which may be either a sufficient ground or less than sufficient. In the former case, the affections are ATTRIBUTES; in the latter case, they are MODES (predicable accidents or adjuncts from a logical point of view, secondary predicates) <*affectiones habent rationem in essentia, hinc aut sufficientem, aut minus. Illae sunt* ATTRIBUTA (G: *Eigenschaften*), hae MODI (G: *Zufälligkeiten*) (*accidentia praedicabilia, s. logica adiuncta, praedicata secundaria*)>."

61 [Lehmann note to Ak. 29: 820$_{21-3}$] See Baumgarten, §40 (Ak. 17: 36): "The complex of essentials in a possible thing, or its internal possibility, is the essence <*complexus essentialium in possibili, seu possibilitas eius interna est* ESSENTIA (G: *das Wesen*)>." *Metaphysik von Schön* (Ak. 28: 492$_{13-22}$): "Essence is the complex <*complexus*> of the inner grounds of all predicates that belong to a something. . . . The essential properties <*essentialia*> constitute the matter of the essence. But a certain form also is needed for that, for constructing the essence. . . ."

62 Cf. Ak. 29: 802$_{14-16}$, above, where the Latin terms were used, viz., *possibilitas, existentia, necessitas.*

63 See *The Only Possible Argument in Support of a Demonstration of the Existence of God* (Ak. 2: 73), Sect. 1, First Reflection, §2: "Existence is the absolute positing of a thing. Existence is thereby also distinguished from every predicate; the latter is, as such, always posited only relative to some other thing" (Ak. 2: 73; Walford translation).

64 [Lehmann note to Ak. 29: 766$_{31}$] Baumgarten, §98 (Ak. 17: 47): "The harmony of the things belonging to an essence is (*essential*) TRANSCENDENTAL PERFECTION <*Consensus essentialium est* PERFECTIO (*essentialis*) TRANSCENDENTALIS (G: *wesentliche*)>." [See also Baumgarten, §185 (Ak. 17: 65).]

65 [Lehmann note to Ak. 29: 767$_1$] On the degree of reality and limits, cf. Baumgarten, §247f (Ak. 17: 80f). On sameness, see Refl. #3599 (Ak. 17: 83): "Sameness and diversity belong to the relation of comparison." [See also Baumgarten's discussion of the degrees of alteration at §190 (Ak. 17: 66).]

66 [Lehmann note to Ak. 29: 769$_{23}$] Cf. *CrPR*, "First Analogy" (B 225): "But the substrate of everything real, i.e., that belongs to the existence of things, a *substance*, of which everything that belongs to existence can be thought only as determination."

67 [Lehmann note to Ak. 29: 769$_{31}$] See note 60 (to Ak. 29: 820$_8$).

68 [Lehmann note to Ak. 29: 770$_{20}$] Baumgarten, §36 (Ak. 17: 34): "Those things which, by determining, are posited in something (notes and predicates) are DETERMINATIONS: one positive and affirmative, which, if it truly exists, is REALITY; the other negative, which, if it truly exists, is NEGATION.

Apparent negation is CRYPTIC REALITY; apparent reality is IDLE REALITY <*Quae determinando ponuntur in aliquo (notae et praedicata), sunt DETERMINA-TIONES* (G: *Bestimmungen*), *altera positiva, et affirmativa, quae si vere sit, est* REALITAS, *altera negativa, quae si vere sit, est* NEGATIO (G: *Verneinungen*). *Negatio apparens est* REALITAS CRYPTICA, *realitas apparens est* VANITAS (G: *Eitelkeit*)>."

69 [Lehmann note to Ak. 29: 771₅f] Baumgarten, §197 (Ak. 17: 68): "If accidents inhere in a substance, then something is the ground of the inherence <*si substantiae inhaerent accidentia, est aliquid inhaerentiae ratio*>...." He then distinguishes power broadly speaking <*vis latius dicta*> and strictly speaking (sufficient) <*strictius dicta (sufficiens)*>.

70 [Lehmann note to Ak. 29: 771₃₀] Baumgarten, §193 (Ak. 17: 67): "Accidents, if they seem to subsist through themselves, are SUBSTANTIATED PHENOMENA (that which appears to subsist for itself) <*accidentia si videntur per se subsistentia, sunt* PHAENOMENA SUBSTANTIATA (G: *das vor sich zu bestehn scheinende*)>." On the example of the rainbow, see *CrPR* (A 45–46/B 62–3).

71 [Lehmann note to Ak. 29: 771₃₄] Baumgarten, §196 (Ak. 17: 67): "That in substance in which accidents are able to inhere, or substance insofar as it is a subject in which accidents are able to inhere, is called SUBSTANTIAL, nor do accidents exist outside of the substantial <*Id in substantia, cui inhaerere possunt accidentia, s. substantia, quatenus est subiectum id, cui accidentia inhaerere possunt,* SUBSTANTIALE *vocatur, nec accidentia existunt extra substantiale*>." Christian Wolff, *Ontologia*, §792: "The substantial [is] in a composite <*substantiale in composito*>."

72 [Lehmann note to Ak. 29: 772₁₇] See *CrPR* (A 649/B 677): "The logical principle of reason requires bringing about this unity insofar as it is possible ..." See also the note to Ak. 29: 82₁₂ (*Berliner Physik*), and *Metaphysical First Principles of Natural Science* (Ak. 4: 513). On Newton, cf. note 155 (to Ak. 29: 936₉, below).

73 [Lehmann note to Ak. 29: 772₂₀₋₁] Baumgarten, §206 (Ak. 17: 69): "The coexistence of modes with stable [affections] is THE INNER STATE <*coexistentia modorum cum fixis est* STATUS INTERNUS (G: *der innre Zustand*).>" Also Refl. #3577 (Ak. 17: 69); Refl. #4313 (Ak. 17: 503₉₋₁₁): "The existence of a thing, insofar as it is determined in time, is its state; the state is either the coexisting or the successive determinations. A primal being is in no state." Wolff gives this definition in his *Ontologia*, §705: "The state of a thing arises from the determination of what is changeable <*mutabilium determinatione enascitur status rei*>."

74 [Lehmann note to Ak. 29: 772₃₄] Action <*actio;* G: *Handlung*> and passion <*passio;* G: *Leiden*> are defined by Baumgarten at §210 (Ak. 17: 70): "... the substance whose state is changed ... SUFFERS. For this reason, ACTION (act, operation) is a change of state through one's own power: PASSION ... through a power not one's own <*substantia, cuius status mutatur ...* PATITUR. *Hinc* ACTIO (*actus, operatio*) *est mutatio status ... per vim ipsius:* PASSIO ... *per vim alienam*>." It is likewise in Christian Wolff, *Ontologia*, §713: "Action is a change of state whose ground is contained in the subject which changes the state <*actio est mutatio status, cujus ratio continetur in subjecto, quod eundem mutat*>." Correspondingly, passion <*passio*> (§714) is defined as a change of

state <*mutatio status*>, whose ground is contained outside of the subject <*extra subjectum continetur*>.

75 [Lehmann note to Ak. 29: 823₂₃] Baumgarten, §211 (Ak. 17: 71): "A substance acting on a substance outside of itself INFLUENCES it. Therefore INFLUENCE (transeunt action) is the action of a substance on a substance outside of itself. ACTION which is not influencing, is IMMANENT <*substantia in substantiam extra se agens in eam INFLUIT, adeo INFLUXUS* (G: *Einfluß*) (*actio transiens*) *est actio substantiae in substantiam extra se. ACT* 10, *quae non est influens, est IMMANENS*>." See note 159 (to Ak. 29: 866₄) and note 45 to *Metaphysik Vigilantius* (*K₃*) (Ak. 29: 1007₃₀), below.

76 Lehmann refers to *Metaphysik Volckmann* (Ak. 28: 433₁₆₋₁₈): "Passion <*passio*> means the inherence of an accident <*accidentis*> of a substance through the power which is outside it. . . ." See also note 74 (to Ak. 29: 772₃₄, above).

77 [Lehmann note to Ak. 29: 824₁₂₋₁₃] Baumgarten defines in §221 (Ak. 17: 75): "AN IMPEDIMENT (an obstacle) is what is opposed to the inherence of an accident; hence an impediment is also what is opposed to changes <IMPEDI-MENTUM (G: *Hinderniss*) (*obstaculum*) *est oppositum accidentis inhaerentiae, hinc et oppositum mutationibus est impedimentum*>." In the same place, Refl. #3586 (Ak. 17: 75): "The opposite ground is impediment <*impedimentum*>; if it is another substance: resistance <*resistentia*>." Cf. also Ak. 29: 825₂₋₃.

78 [Lehmann note to Ak. 29: 824₁₈] Baumgarten gives verbal definitions in §223 (Ak. 17: 76) of "presence" <*praesentia;* G: *Gegenwart*>, "to come in contact with" <*contingere;* G: *sich einander berühren*>, "contact" <*contactus;* G: *Berührung*>, "being absent" <*absens;* G: *abwesend*>. Cf. *Metaphysical First Principles of Natural Science* (Ak. 4: 485₂): "perduring presence" <*praesentia perdurabilis*>.

79 [Lehmann note to Ak. 29: 825₂f] In Baumgarten, §222 (Ak. 17: 75): "RESISTANCE is the impediment of an action. . . . When an impediment has been posited, an impeding power is posited; when resistance has been posited, a resisting power is posited <RESISTENTIA (G: *Wiederstand*) *est impedimentum actionis. . . . Posito impedimento ponitur vis impediens: posita resistentia ponitur vis resistens*>." Also Refl. #3589 (Ak. 17: 76): "Where power is, there is also action (in lifeless beings), but not on that account also effect, because an inner or outer resistance . . . is the reaction of a power which cancels the effect of the previous one. . . ."

80 [Lehmann note to Ak. 29: 825₁₀] See note 78 (to Ak. 29: 824₁₈, above).

81 This possibly refers to a section missing from the ms, such as a discussion of the sections on "Unity" (§§72–7; Ak. 17: 43–4) or "Whole and Part" (§§155–64; Ak. 17: 58–61).

82 [Lehmann note to Ak. 29: 825₂₅₋₇] Cf. Baumgarten, Sect. 5 ("Whole and Part" <*Totale et Partiale*>), §§155–64, as well as Sect. 9 ("Simple and Composite" <*Simplex et Compositum*>), §§224–9. In §224 (Ak. 17: 76–77), Baumgarten characterizes the composite thing, strictly speaking <*ens compositum stricte dictum*>, as a whole of parts outside of parts <*totum partium extra partes*>, the non-composite thing <*ens non compositum*> as "simple (in a more precise meaning)"; the composite thing in the broad sense <*ens compositum latius dictum*> has parts, the less composite <*minus compositum*> is simple by comparison <*simplex comparative;* G: *einfach in Vergleichung*>.

83 [Lehmann note to Ak. 29: 826₄] This commonly occurring phrase in Kant, especially in the *Opus postumum*, is taken over from Christian Wolff (*Ontologia*, §§945–46) and is found first in Petrus Hispanus – according to Hans Graubner, *Form und Wesen; ein Beitrag zur Deutung des Formbegriffs in Kants Kritik der reinen Vernunft* (Form and Essence: A Contribution to the Interpretation of the Concept of Form in Kant's *Critique of Pure Reason*) (Bonn: Bouvier Verlag H. Grundmann, 1972) (*Kantstudien-Ergänzungshefte*, vol. 104), p. 40n. Cf. Baumgarten, §§344–5 (Ak. 17: 101). See also further below at Ak. 29: 870₃₁.

84 [Lehmann note to Ak. 29: 826₂₃] Baumgarten, §227 (Ak. 17: 77): "ORIGINA-TION is a change from non-existing into existing. The change from existing into non-existing is DEATH <*ORTUS* (G: *das Entstehn*) *est mutatio ex non exsistente in exsistens. Mutatio ex exsistenti in non exsistens est* INTERITUS (G: *der Untergang*)>"; §228: "ORIGINATION OUT OF NOTHING is the origination of that of which no part exists before itself, and ANNIHILATION is the death of that of which no part remains in existence. The origination from nothing and annihilation of a necessary being and substance is absolutely impossible <*ORTUS EX NIHILO* (G: *das aus nichts entstehn*) *est ortus eius, cuius nulla pars ipsi praeexsistit et* ANNIHILATIO (G: *Vernichtung*) *interitus eius, cuius nulla pars exsistit superstes. Entis et substantiae necessariae ortus ex nihilo et annihilatio est absolute impossibilis*>." See *Metaphysik von Schön* (Ak. 28: 516₂₆): "On Origination and Death" <*De Ortu et Interitu*>.

85 [Lehmann note to Ak. 29: 829₁] Cf. Max Heinze, *Vorlesungen Kants über Metaphysik aus drei Semestern* (Kant's Lectures on Metaphysics from Three Semesters) (Leipzig: S. Hirzel, 1894), Appendix 2: "*Begriff vom Raum und Zeit*" (Concept of Space and Time), pp. 670–74 (reprinted at Ak. 28: 177–81). See also *Metaphysik L₁* (Ak. 28: 188–190; Heinze excerpt); *Metaphysik von Schön* (Ak. 28: 520–2), separated and much shorter than in ms H (the *Metaphysik Rosenhagen*).

86 Lehmann notes (Ak. 29: 830₂₅): Baumgarten, §239 (Ak. 17: 79): "The order of simultaneous things posited outside of each other is SPACE, the [order] of successive things is TIME <*ordo simultaneorum extra se invicem positorum est* SPATIUM, *successivorum* TEMPUS>." See *Metaphysik von Schön* (Ak. 28: 521–2): "On Time."

87 [Lehmann note to Ak. 29: 830₃₇] See note 86 (to Ak. 29: 830₂₅).

88 [Lehmann note to Ak. 29: 833₁₉] See Christian August Crusius, *Entwurf der nothwendigen Vernunft-Wahrheiten, wiefern sie den zufälligen entgegen gesetzet werden* (Sketch of the Necessary Truths of Reason, so far as They are Opposed to the Contingent),1st ed.(Leipzig, 1745), §46: "If we represent to ourselves something as existing: then the essence of our understanding requires us, apart from that through which we think it and distinguish it from others, to think also this in addition, that it is somewhere and sometime." See note 12 to *Metaphysik L₁* (Ak. 28: 233₂₈).

89 [Lehmann note to Ak. 29: 833₃₀] Baumgarten, §12 (Ak. 17: 25): "That which not only seems to be, but also is, is called the TRUE, that which only seems to be, but is not, is called the [MERELY] APPARENT <*Quod non tantum videtur, sed et est,* VERUM (G: *wahr*), *quod tantum videtur, non est,* APPARENS (G: *nur scheinend*) *dicitur*>."

90 [Lehmann note to Ak. 29: 834₁₉] Baumgarten, Sect. 11 ("Finite and Infinite" <*Finitum et Infinitum*>), §246 (Ak. 17: 80): "The quantity of quality is the DEGREE (the quantity of strength). Hence we are unable to understand degree unless another has been assumed <*quantitas qualitatis est* GRADUS (G: *eine Stufe, Staffel*) (*quantitas virtutis*). *Hinc gradum non nisi alio assumpto intelligere possumus*>." Christian Wolff, *Ontologia*, §746: "Degree is an intrinsic difference of the same qualities, that is, a difference that occurs only when the qualities are identical <*gradus est discrimen internum qualitatum earundem, scilicet quod solum salva identitate in easdem cadit*>." Cf. also *Metaphysik Volckmann* (Ak. 28: 425n): "The author calls intensive magnitude the quantity of a quality <*quantitas qualitatis*>, which however does not explain the matter, for if I view something as a quantity then I must also represent it as a magnitude"; *Metaphysik von Schön* (Ak. 28: 507).

91 [Lehmann note to Ak. 29: 838₆] Namely, in Ch. 3 ("The Relative Predicates of a Thing" <*Praedicata entis relativa*>), §§265–350 (Ak. 17: 83–103). Also cf. Refl. #3599 (Ak. 17: 83): "Sameness and diversity belong to the relation of comparison." The concepts of comparison <*conceptus comparationis*> are first treated in detail in the "Amphiboly of the Concepts of Reflection" (*CrPR*, A 262f/B 318f), and are related to Leibniz. The "General Note to the System of Principles" (*CrPR*, B 288–94), which is missing in the first edition, presupposes Refl. #141f (Ak. 23: 37).

92 [Lehmann note to Ak. 29: 838₁₁] Baumgarten, Ch. 3, Sect. 1 ("The Same and the Different" <*Idem et Diversum*>), §265 (Ak. 17: 83): "all beings are similar to each other in some degree. . . . The least equality is in two beings in which the smallest single quantity is common <*omnia entia sibi sunt in aliquo gradu similia. . . . Aequalitas minima est in duobus, in quibus unica minima quantitas est communis . . .* >." §266 (Ak. 17: 83): "IDENTITY, LIKENESS, EQUALITY, CONGRUENCE are said to be essential to ESSENTIAL PROPERTIES, NECESSARY to attributes and essentials, CONTINGENT to modes, [and] ACCIDENTAL to affections <*IDENTITAS, SIMILITUDO, AEQUALITAS, CONGRUENTIA essentialium ESSENTIALES* (G: *wesentliche*), *essentialium et attributorum NECESSARIAE* (G: *nothwendige*), *modorum CONTINGENTES*, affectionum *ACCIDENTALES* (G: *zufällige*) *vocantur*>." Christian Wolff, *Ontologia*, §452: "Every intrinsic determination of a thing, which is able to be understood without assuming another, is called quality <*omnis determinatio rei intrinseca, quae sine alio assumto intelligi potest, dicitur Qualitas*>."

93 [Lehmann note to Ak. 29: 838₂₆] Baumgarten, §270 (Ak. 17: 85): "Totally congruent things in which all differences are internal, are the same <*totaliter congruentia, qua omnia discrimina interna, sunt eadem*>."

94 [Lehmann note to Ak. 29: 839₄] Baumgarten, §269 (Ak. 17: 84–5): "The complete IDENTITY of singular things is NUMERICAL. *It is impossible for two distinct singulars to be absolutely or totally the same.* For when one posits two things, one posits more than one thing, hence [things which are] partly the same and partly diverse. Therefore the two things are not totally the same. Singulars that are totally the same are numerically the same, not partly the same and partly different. Hence they are not more than one thing, and they are not two things. *This proposition* is called *the principle* (of the identity) *of*

indiscernibles, broadly construed, or *of the denial of complete identity* <IDENTITAS *totalis singularium est* NUMERICA. *Impossibilia sunt duo extra se singularia prorsus seu totaliter eadem. Cum enim ponantur duo, ponuntur multa, hinc partim eadem, partim diversa. Ergo non sunt totaliter eadem. Quae sunt totaliter eadem singularia, sunt eadem numero, nec partim eadem, par*·*tim diversa. Hinc non sunt multa, nec duo. Haec propositio dicitur principium (identitatis) indiscernibilium late sumptum, aut negatae totalis identitatis>.*"

95 [Lehmann note to Ak. 29: 839$_{16}$] The distinguishing principle of Leibnizian individualism, the principle of indiscernibles <*principium indiscernibilium*>: ". . . there are never two beings in nature which are perfectly alike and in which it is impossible to find a difference that is internal or founded on an intrinsic denomination" (*Monadology*, §9, in *G. W. Leibniz: Philosophical Essays*, tr. by Roger Ariew and Daniel Garber (Indianapolis: Hackett, 1989), p. 214), is debated with respect to space and time in Leibniz's confrontation with Locke – although not in Kant's formulation: "it can be added that it is by means of things that we must distinguish one time or place from another, rather than vice versa, for times and places are in themselves perfectly alike, and in any case they are not substances or complete realities" [*Nouveaux Essais sur l'entendement humain* (New Essays on the Human Understanding), Bk. 2, Ch. 27, tr. by J. Bennett and P. Remnant (Cambridge, 1981), p. 230]. The principle of indiscernibles, which Kant rejects in the "Amphiboly of the Concepts of Reflection" (*CrPR*, A 281/B 337), is formulated differently by Leibniz, e.g., in his dialogue with Locke (*New Essays*, p. 230); here one also finds the example of the vain attempt to find two perfectly similar leaves of a tree (*New Essays*, p. 231).

96 [Lehmann note to Ak. 29: 840$_1$] Cf. Baumgarten, Sect. 2 ("Simultaneous things" <*simultanea*>), §28of (Ak. 17: 86f). Also Refl. #3606, 3608 (Ak. 17: 89, 90).

97 [Lehmann note to Ak. 29: 841$_{21}$] In Baumgarten, Sect. 3 ("Successive things" <*successiva*>), §§297–306 (Ak. 17: 92–4); cf. Ak. 29: 833$_{2f}$ above.

98 [Lehmann note to Ak. 29: 842$_{13}$] Baumgarten, §299 (Ak. 17: 92–3): "The continuation of existence is DURATION. In whatever thing duration is possible, that thing is called PERDURABLE. The actual but not perdurable is the INSTANTANEOUS (the momentary) <*existentiae continuatio est* DURATIO (G: *die Dauer*). *In quo possibilis est duratio,* PERDURABILE (G: *eine Dauer fähig*) *dicitur. Actuale vero non perdurabile* INSTANTANEUM (G: *keiner Dauer fähig*) (*momentaneum*)>." Christian Wolff, *Ontologia*, §578: "If being A coexists with successive things in a continuous series a, b, c, etc., it is said to endure: so, for this reason, duration is the existence A insofar as something coexists with several successive things, or existence simultaneous with several successive things <*si ens A coexistit successivis in continua serie a, b, c, etc. durare dicitur: ut adeo Duratio sit A existentia, qua rebus pluribus successivis quid coexistit, seu existentia simultanea cum rebus pluribus successivis*>." Cf. *Metaphysik von Schön* (Ak. 28: 521$_{25-6}$): "Existence observed as quantity is called duration <*existentia spectata ut quantitas dicitur Duratio*>."

99 This refers to Baumgarten, Sect. 3 ("Successive things" <*successiva*>), §301 (Ak. 17: 93).

100 [Lehmann note to Ak. 29: 842₃₂] Baumgarten, §302 (Ak. 17: 93): "ETER-NITY (strictly speaking) is duration without beginning and without end. Duration without end only is ABETERNITY, and *duration simultaneous with all time* is SEMPITERNITY <*AETERNITAS* (G: *die Ewigkeit*) (*rigorose dicta*) *est duratio sine initio et fine. Duratio sine fine tantum est* AEVITERNITAS (G: *das nur ohne Ende*), *et omni tempori simultanea* SEMPITERNITAS (G: *das zu aller Zeit sein*)>."

101 [Lehmann note to Ak. 29: 843₉] The reference is to Baumgarten, §307 (Ak. 17: 94): "Whatever contains the ground of another is its PRINCIPLE <*quod continet rationem alterius, eius est* PRINCIPIUM (G: *die Quelle*)>."

102 [Lehmann note to Ak. 29: 843₁₂] Baumgarten, §844 (Ak. 17: 164): "MANICHEANISM is the view that an author of evil exists which is equally powerful as God, and it is an error <*MANICHAEISMUS est sententia aeque potentem deo auctorem mali ponens existere, et error est*>." On Kant, who was frequently preoccupied with Mani and Manicheanism, see note to Ak. 28: 137₁₃f (*Metaphysik Herder*).

103 [Lehmann note to Ak. 29: 843₂₅] Baumgarten treats in Ch. 2, Sect. 1 ("The Necessary and The Contingent" <*necessarium et contingens*>), §101 (Ak. 17: 48): "That thing is NECESSARY whose opposite is impossible, what is not necessary is CONTINGENT <*NECESSARIUM est, cuius oppositum impossibile, non necessarium est* CONTINGENS>"; §108 (Ak. 17: 49): ". . . no relations of a thing are absolutely necessary, all are contingent <*nullae relationes entis sunt absolute necessariae, omnes contingentes*>"; §307 (Ak. 17: 94): "Whatever is not able to exist except as the effect of another posited outside of itself is A THING DERIVED FROM ANOTHER (dependent), whatever is able to exist even though it is not the effect of another thing posited outside of itself, is A THING BY MEANS OF ITSELF (independent) <*quod non potest exsistere, nisi ut causatum alterius extra se positi, est* ENS AB ALIO (G: *abhängend*) (*dependens*), *quod potest etiam exsistere, licet non sit causatum alterius extra se positi, est* ENS A SE (G: *selbstständig*) (*independens*)>." Also Refl. #3615 (Ak. 17: 94): "a thing by means of itself is not changed <*ens a se, non mutatur*>. For in no determination is it through another, thus is not [changed] to something other." Wolff gives a review of the Scholastics up to Clauberg (§169) in *Ontologia*, Pt. 1, Sect. 2, Ch. 3: "The Concept of a Being" <*De Notione Entis*> (§§132–78): "That which can exist is said to be a being <*Ens dicitur, quod existere potest*> . . ." (§134).

104 [Lehmann note to Ak. 29: 845₁] Baumgarten in Sect. 4 ("Cause and Effect" <*Causa et Causatum*>), §314 (Ak. 17: 95): "The various causes of one and the same effect are CO-CAUSES and they are said TO COME TOGETHER for that effect <*causae plures unius eiusdemque causati sunt* CONCAUSAE (G: *Mitursachen*) *et ad causatum* CONCURRERE (G: *zusammenkommen*) *dicuntur*>." Cf. *Vernunfttheologie Magath*, §954 (ms, p. 115): "The causality of the causes <*causarum*> is called concurrence <*concursus*>. That is, several causes can unite in order to produce one effect. If this happens: several co-causes <*concausae*> concur in such a case. Of these contributing causes, one must not be sufficient by itself for the production of the effect; for otherwise the uniting with another which is to give it the complement to sufficiency <*complementum ad sufficientiam*> would be unnecessary. . . ."

105 [Lehmann note to Ak. 29: 845$_{16-17}$] Baumgarten, §320 (Ak. 17: 97): "AUXIL-
IARY CAUSE <*CAUSA AUXILIARIS*; G: *eine helfende Ursach*>." Christian Wolff,
Ontologia, §921: "An associate cause is called auxiliary <*Causa socia dicitur
auxiliaris*>."

106 [Lehmann note to Ak. 29: 845$_{22-4}$] Baumgarten, §323 (Ak. 17: 97): "A single
action with its own effect is called an EVENT. The relation of an event is its
CIRCUMSTANCE <*actio singularis cum effectu suo* EVENTUS (G: *ein Vorfall, eine
Begebenheit*) *dicitur. Relatio eventus est* CIRCUMSTANTIA (G: *ein Umstand*)>."

107 [Lehmann note to Ak. 29: 845$_{29}$] Baumgarten, §323 (Ak. 17: 97): "An
occasion greater in respect to place is OPPORTUNITY, its opposite is
INOPPORTUNITY, (greater) in respect to its time is TIMELINESS, its opposite
is UNTIMELINESS <*occasio maior respectu loci* OPPORTUNITAS, *eiusque oppositum* INOPPORTUNITAS, *respectu temporis* TEMPESTIVITAS, *eiusque oppositum* INTEMPESTIVITAS *est* (G: *bequemre und unbequemre Zeiten und
Orte*)>."

108 [Lehmann note to Ak. 29: 845$_{34}$] Cf. Baumgarten, §329 (Ak. 17: 98).

109 [Lehmann note to Ak. 29: 845$_{37-8}$] It is not especially remarkable that Kant,
with equivocal effect <*effectus aequivocus*>, is thinking of spontaneous generation <*generatio aequivoca*; G: *Urzeugung*>, "by which is understood the
production of an organic being through the mechanism of raw, unorganic
matter" (*Critique of Judgment*, Kant's note at Ak. 5: 419$_{29-30}$). Already during
the time that Herder was a student [i.e. 1762–4] (see the notes to Ak. 28:
944$_{23}$ (*Nachträge Herder*) and Ak. 28: 163$_8$ (*Metaphysik Herder*)) Kant had
taken a lively interest in the discoveries of the "infusion researchers" and in
the conflict between Leeuwenhoeck and Buffon, and he still finds himself
here in opposition to the panvitalism of Leibniz, whose *Monadology* (§74)
included spermatazoa and (microscopic) knowledge about them.

110 [Lehmann note to Ak. 29: 846$_1$] Baumgarten, §329 (Ak. 17: 98): "Every
effect is like its deficient or efficient cause, that is, *whatever sort of cause, the
same sort of effect*. The effect is either similar to the efficient cause as the
specific difference of both, or less similar. The former effect is called
UNIVOCAL, the latter is called EQUIVOCAL <*omnis effectus causae deficienti vel
efficienti similis est, i.e. qualis causa, talis effectus. Effectus causae efficienti vel
similis, qua differentiam utriusque specificam, vel minus. Prior* EFFECTUS
UNIVOCUS (G: *eine Wirkung von einerlei*), *posterior* AEQUIVOCUS (G: *von
verschiedener Art*) *dicitur*>."

111 [Lehmann note to Ak. 29: 846$_{17}$] Baumgarten, §331 (Ak. 17: 98): "For this
reason *the full effect is equal* (proportionate) *to the living powers of the efficient
cause* <*hinc effectus plenus aequalis (proportionatus) est viribus causae efficientis
vivis*>."

112 This is probably an abbreviated section heading. Lehmann refers us
to Baumgarten, Sect. 6 ("Usefulness" <*utilitas*>), §§336–40 (Ak. 17:
99–100).

113 [Lehmann note to Ak. 29: 847$_4$] See note 83 (to Ak. 29: 826$_4$), above.

114 Cf. Baumgarten, §§347–50 (Ak. 17: 102–3).

115 [Lehmann note to Ak. 29: 849$_{20}$] Baumgarten, "Cosmology," Ch. 1, Sect. 1,
§354 (Ak. 17: 103): "The world (the universe, the all) is a series (multitude,
whole) of actual finite things, which is not part of another <*MUNDUS* (G: *die*

ganze Welt) (*universum, παν*) *est series (multitudo, totum) actualium finitorum, quae non est pars alterius*>." Cf. *Metaphysik L₁* (Ak. 28: 195₂₄₋₅): "The world is a substantial whole <*totum substantiale*> ...."

116 This refers to Kant's Inaugural Dissertation, *On the Form and Principles of the Sensible and the Intelligible World*. Lehmann reports that he is unable to identify the "foreigner" (perhaps a reviewer of the dissertation), and refers us to a discussion of other reviews in Karl Vorländer, *Immanuel Kant, der Mann und das Werk* (Immanuel Kant, the Man and His Work), 2 vols. (Leipzig, 1924), vol. 1, p. 254.

117 [Lehmann note to Ak. 29: 850₂₉] See the definition at §254 in note 115 (to Ak. 29: 849₂₀), above.

118 [Lehmann note to Ak. 29: 851₂₋₃] Baumgarten, §392 (Ak. 17: 109): since the world is composite, it cannot be a simple thing <*ens simplex*>. "Whoever thinks that this world is a simple thing is AN EGOIST <*qui hunc mundum se putat ens simplex est EGOISTA*>." The world of the egoist <*mundus egoisticus*> also would not be the most perfect world (§438, Ak. 17: 118).

119 Cf. note 115 (to Ak. 29: 849₂₀), above.

120 Baumgarten, §357 (Ak. 17: 104): "In every world there are actual parts. These each are connected with the whole. Hence, they are each connected with each other. Therefore, in every world there is connection of parts and universal harmony <*In omni mundo sunt partes actuales, hae singulae connectuntur cum toto, hinc singulae connectuntur cum singulis. Ergo in omni mundo nexus est partium et harmonia universalis*>."

121 [Lehmann note to Ak. 29: 853₁₇] Baumgarten, §362 (Ak. 17: 104): "Every world is one <*Omnis mundus est unum*>." In all the paragraphs which treat the positive concept of the world, the scholastic transcendentals are recapitulated; see also Ak. 28: 495f (*Metaphysik von Schön*).

122 See Wolff, *Ontologia*, §572.

123 [Lehmann note to Ak. 29: 857₂₅] Cf. Lehmann's note to *Metaphysik Herder* (Ak. 28: 102₃₃f), and also Leibniz, *Remarques sur le sentiment du P. Malebranche, qui poste que nous voyens en Dieu, concernant l'examen que Mr. Locke on fait* (Remarks on the View of Father Malebranche who posits that we see in God, concerning the examination which Mr. Locke makes of it) (1708), *Opera Philosophica* (Philosophical Works), ed. by J. E. Erdmann (Berlin, 1890), pp. 450ff and 690ff. Cf. Nicholas Malebranche, *Entretiens métaphysiques II: Que nous pouvons voir en Dieu toutes choses et que rien de fini ne peut le représenter. De sorte qu'il suffit de penser à lui pour savoir ce qu'il est* (Dialogue on Metaphysics, II: That we can see all things in God, and that nothing finite can represent him. It suffices to think of him to know he is) (1688). *De la recherche de la vérité* (Search after Truth) (1674), Bk. 3, Pt. 2, Ch. 6: "That we see all things in God."

124 [Lehmann note to Ak. 29: 861₂₀] Baumgarten distinguishes (in Sect. 21: "Freedom" <*Libertas*>) freedom <*libertas*> and pure freedom <*libertas pura*; G: *reine Freiheit*>, cf. §719 (Ak. 17: 136): "ACTIONS in which it is supposed to be in the power of some substance to determine itself through freedom are FREE, and the SUBSTANCE itself, insofar as it is able to perform free actions, is FREE <*ACTIONES, ad quas per libertatem se determinare est in potestate alicuius substantiae positum, LIBERAE* (G: *das sinnliche Willkür*) *sunt, et*

ipsa SUBSTANTIA, quae et quatenus actiones liberas patrare potest, est LIBERA (G:
Freiheit)>." Lehmann also cites the contemporaneous *Naturrecht Feyerabend*
(1784) (Ak. 27: 1320$_{2-3}$): "The freedom of the human being is the condition
under which the human being can be his own end . . ."

125 [Lehmann note to Ak. 29: 862$_{32}$] See Baumgarten, Sect. 2 ("Negative
Concept of the World" <*Notio mundi negativa*>", §382 ("fate" <*fatum*>,
with a reference to Spinozism), §383 ("chance" <*casus*>), §386 ("leap"
<*saltus*>), §380f ("infinite progression" <*progressus in infinitum*>). Also
Refl. #3853 (Ak. 17: 312$_{21-3}$): "For otherwise all members of the series
would be effects <*causata*> of one other member of the series. Thus one
member of the series would be something which would be other than all
members of it."

126 [Lehmann note to Ak. 29: 921$_2$] Abraham Gotthelf Kaestner, *Anfangsgründe
der höhern Mechanik, welche von der Bewegung fester Körper besonders die
praktischen Lehre enthalten* (First Principles of Advanced Mechanics, Containing in Particular the Practical Doctrine of the Motion of Solid Bodies)
(Göttingen, 1766). See the note to Ak. 2: 400$_{3f}$ (*On the Form and Principles of
the Sensible and the Intelligible World*).

127 [Lehmann note to Ak. 29: 921$_6$] See also *Metaphysik K$_2$* (Ak. 28: 730$_{26-9}$;
Heinze excerpt): "So no ray of light reflects from the mirror in an acute
angle, for otherwise two directions would have to follow one upon the other
immediately, but rather [it reflects] from the previous direction through an
infinite multitude of small deviations from the prior direction."

128 [Lehmann note to Ak. 29: 922$_4$] See note 1 to *Metaphysik L$_1$* (Ak. 28:
205$_{23-30}$), above.

129 [Lehmann note to Ak. 29: 922$_{12}$] On gap <*hiatus*> or leap <*saltus*>, see
Baumgarten, §386 (Ak. 17: 108): "An event without any proximate sufficient ground would be AN ABSOLUTE LEAP. An event without any ordinary
proximate sufficient ground is A RELATIVE LEAP <*eventus sine ulla ratione
sufficiente proxima esset SALTUS ABSOLUTUS* (G: *das völlig durch einen Sprung
geschähe*). *Eventus sine ratione sufficiente proxima ordinaria est SALTUS RE-
SPECTIVUS* (G: *wobei gewisser maassen ein Sprung statt hat*)>." [. . .] Kant
fully unfolded (thematized) the problem of transition only in the *Opus
postumum*, where the opposition between transition <*transitus*> and leap
<*saltus*> is also always emphasized (Ak. 21: 387$_{1-2}$): "The transition (<*tran-
situs;* G: *Übergang*) from one kind of cognition to another must be only a
step (*passus;* G: *Schritt*), no leap (*saltus;* G; *Sprung*)." The elephant example
is also here!

130 [Lehmann note to Ak. 29: 925$_{35}$] Baumgarten, §382 (Ak. 17: 107): "FATE is
the necessity of events in the world <*FATUM* (G: *das Schicksal, Verhängniss*)
est necessitas eventuum in mundo>" and is to be assumed neither in this nor in
any other world. Leibniz distinguishes the Mohammedan fate <*fatum
Mohametanum*> from the Christian, and rejects the former (*Essais de
théodicée sur la bonté de Dieu, la liberté de l'homme et l'origine du mal*
(Theodicy: Essays on the Goodness of God, the Freedom of Man, and the
Origin of Evil) (Amsterdam, 1710), §§106, 107).

131 [Lehmann note to Ak. 29: 926$_{22}$] Baumgarten, §388 (Ak. 17: 108): "Hence
every world must be posited outside the infinite substance, and so this

world also exists outside the infinite being which therefore is called THE EXTRAMUNDANE BEING, the actual being outside this world <*Hinc omnis mundus extra substantiam infinitam ponendus est, adeoque hic etiam mundus exsistit extra ens infinitum, quod ideo vocatur* ENS EXTRAMUNDANUM (G: *das Wesen ausser der Welt*), *ens extra hunc mundum actuale*>."

132 See note 118 (to Ak. 29: 851_{2-3}), above. Lehmann also notes that, in the *Anthropologie Mrongovius*, Kant distinguishes the "egoist of sensibility and egoist of the power of judgment" (ms, p. 113f).

133 [Lehmann note to Ak. 29: 928_3] Baumgarten defines, in §465 (Ak. 17: 123): "THE DUALIST is one who posits that this world stands firm with spirits and bodies outside of each other <*DUALISTA est, qui ponit hunc mundum constare spiritibus et corporibus extra se*>." The term is found in Kant at *CrPR* (A 367): in comparison with idealism, dualism is called "the assertion of a possible certainty of objects of outer sense."

134 [Lehmann note to Ak. 29: 928_8] In Baumgarten, who of course presupposes Leibnizian idealism, it reads only (§402, Ak. 17: 111): "He who admits only spirits in this world is an IDEALIST <*Solos in hoc mundo spiritus admittens est IDEALISTA*>." See also the well-known passages from the Paralogisms (*CrPR*, A 368): "Thus I cannot actually perceive outer things, but rather can only infer their existence from my inner perception . . ." and: "Thus by *idealist* one must not understand someone who denies the existence of outer objects of the senses. . . ."

135 [Lehmann note to Ak. 29: 928_{23}] The copyist simply did not know that after 1734 Berkeley was Bishop of Cloyne. Kant possessed a German translation of Berkeley's works (Part 1, 1781) – see Arthur Warda, *Immanuel Kants Bücher* (Immanuel Kant's Books) (Berlin: Martin Breslauer, 1922), p. 46 – and had indeed occupied himself with Berkeley, but only sporadically. Cf. note 13 to *Metaphysik Dohna* (Ak. 28: 680_{26}), below, and note 4 to *Metaphysik Herder* (Ak. 28: 42_{22-3}), above. Lehmann also refers to Kant's judgment of Berkeley in the *Prolegomena* (Ak. 4: 374_{18-20}): "All cognition through sense and experience is nothing other than sheer illusion, and only in the ideas of pure understanding and reason is there truth."

136 [Lehmann note to Ak. 29: 929_1] On the other hand, see Baumgarten's definition (§395, Ak. 17: 110): whoever denies the existence of monads "is A UNIVERSAL MATERIALIST. Whoever denies the existence of the monads of the universe . . . is A COSMOLOGICAL MATERIALIST <*est MATERIALISTA UNIVERSALIS. Qui negat exsistentiam monadum universi . . . est MATERIALISTA COSMOLOGICUS*>." Also §439 (Ak. 17: 118): ". . . therefore there is neither any WORLD nor the most perfect world <*ergo MUNDUS nec ullus, nec perfectissimus est*>."

137 [Lehmann note to Ak. 29: 929_{12}] See, e.g., Leibniz, *Considerations sur la doctrine d'un esprit universel* (Reflections on the Doctrine of a Single Universal Spirit) (1702): "For why cannot the soul always retain a subtle body organized after its own manner, which could even some day reassume the form of its visible body in the resurrection, since a glorified body is ascribed to the blessed . . ." [in *Gottfried Wilhelm Leibniz: Philosophical Papers and Letters*, tr. by Leroy Loemker, 2nd ed. (Reidel, 1970), pp. 556–7]. A whole consisting of monads <*monadatum*> is discussed in Baumgarten, §406

("First Origin of Bodies" *<Prima corporum genesis>*; Ak. 17: 112). On Leibniz's corpuscle *<corpusculum>*, see note 4 to *Metaphysik Volckmann* (Ak. 28: 445$_{21}$), below.

138 [Lehmann note to Ak. 29: 929$_{39}$] Cf. Baumgarten, §401 (Ak. 17: 111): "... They are NAKED MONADS (sound asleep) *<Illae sunt MONADES NUDAE (sopitae)* (G: *im tiefen Schlaf liegende Monaden)>*." Cf. the so-called – not by Leibniz – *Monadology*, §20: "For we experience in ourselves a state in which we remember nothing and have no distinct perception; this is similar to when we faint or when we are overwhelmed by a deep, dreamless sleep" [in *G. W. Leibniz: Philosophical Essays*, tr. by Roger Ariew and Daniel Garber (Indianapolis: Hackett, 1989), p. 215].

139 [Lehmann note to Ak. 29: 930$_{5-7}$] Cf. this with the criticism of Leibniz in the "Note to the Amphiboly of Concepts of Reflection" (*CrPR*, A 270f/B 326f) and in the treatise against Eberhard, which presents itself as "actually a defense of Leibniz himself against his ... disciples" ("On a Discovery, according to which any new Critique of Pure Reason is made Dispensable through an Older," Ak. 8: 250$_{35-7}$).

140 [Lehmann note to Ak. 29: 930$_{32}$] Baumgarten, §399 (Ak. 17: 110): "Monads ... are POINTS, but in no way MATHEMATICAL.... A mathematical point, an abstract possibility, if it is imagined to exist, is a ZENONICAL POINT, a fiction. If by a PHYSICAL POINT you mean an actual thing that is completely determined beyond its simplicity, then some monads of this universe are physical points, a collection of which constitutes extension *<Monades ... sunt PUNCTA, sed neutiquam MATHEMATICA. ... Punctum mathematicum, abstractum possibile, si fingatur exsistere, ZENONICUM est PUNCTUM, ens fictum. PUNCTUM PHYSICUM si dicas actuale et praeter simplicitatem omnimode determinatum, quaedam monades huius universi sunt puncta physica, nempe quarum ex aggregato extensum>*." For Leibniz, see, among others, the fourth letter to Des Bosses (Feb. 5, 1712) [in *Gottfried Wilhelm Leibniz: Philosophical Papers and Letters*, tr. by Leroy Loemker, 2nd ed. (Reidel, 1970), pp. 600–1]. Wolff, who of course rejects the doctrine of monads, provides a plenum of points in the *Mathematisches Lexicon* (Mathematical Lexicon) (Leipzig, 1716) in *Gesammelte Werke* (Collected Works), edited by Jean Ecole, et al. (Hildesheim and New York: Olms, 1962), vol. I.11. At column 1116, he defines a mathematical point *<punctum mathematicum>* (distinguished from an accidental point *<punctum accidentale>*) as "something so small that it has no parts at all. The point is in fact nothing other than the goal which one posits in thought, where a line should begin and where it should stop."

141 [Lehmann note to Ak. 29: 931$_2$] Baumgarten, Sect. 2 ("The First Origin of Bodies" *<Prima corporum genesis>*), §406f (Ak. 17: 112f). That is, he treats the monads as productive of extension and matter – in the Leibnizian sense.

142 [Lehmann note to Ak. 29: 931$_5$] On this, and especially on the relation of motion, Baumgarten §417 (Ak. 17: 113): "If one part of this world were to move, its relation to the remaining single things which occur at the same time would be changed *<Si moveatur una pars huius mundi, mutatur eius relatio ad reliquas simultaneas singulas>*." For Kant, cf. *CrPR* (A 192/B 237) and *Metaphysical First Principles of Natural Science* (Ak. 4: 487; the "Principle").

143 [Lehmann note to Ak. 29: 931$_{7-9}$] Cf. *CrPR* (A 192/B 237): "I see, e.g., a ship driven downstream" – the example for the Second Analogy.

144 [Lehmann note to Ak. 29: 931$_{11}$] Baumgarten, §415 (Ak. 17: 113): "In a composite world, no change happens without motion <*Nulla mutatio fit in mundo composito sine motu*>." §416 (Ak. 17: 113): "The monads that constitute extension in a universe are always acting ... representing their universe ... by impeding a certain motion, by opposing a certain motion, ... by causing a certain other motion or moving <*Monades in universo constituentes extensum semper agunt ... repraesentantes universi ... certum motum impediente, certo motui resistente ... certum alium motum efficiente, s. movente*>."

145 [Lehmann note to Ak. 29: 931$_{29}$] Baumgarten, §408 (Ak. 17: 112): "Therefore there is in this world universal influence and universal conflict (*the war of all against all, discordant harmony, harmonious discord*) <*Ergo est in hoc mundo influxus et conflictus universalis (bellum omnium contra omnia, concordia discors, discordia concors)*>."

146 [Lehmann note to Ak. 29: 932$_{10}$] Baumgarten equates atom and monad, and "proves" this at §424 (Ak. 17: 115): "A thing in itself indivisible is said to be AN ATOM. Every monad is indivisible through itself. It follows that every monad is an atom. Therefore the elements are atoms; hence they are called atoms of nature <*ATOMUS* (G: *das an und vor sich untheilbare) dicitur ens per se indivisibile. Omnis monas est indivisibilis per se. Hinc omnis monas est atomus. Ergo elementa sunt atomi, hinc atomi naturae dicuntur*>." Wolff, who replaced Leibnizian pluralism by his own doctrine of "simple things" – of which he said that they have no figure, magnitude, and take up no space – argues no less simply: there must be simple things, "for if everything were composed from parts, then one would have to admit things which had a figure and magnitude, without a reason being present why . . ." (*Vernünftige Gedancken von Gott, der Welt und der Seele des Menschen, auch allen Dingen überhaupt* (Rational Thoughts on God, the World and the Soul of Man, and on All Things in General), 1st edition (Halle, 1719) in *Gesammelte Werke* (Collected Works), vol. I.2 (Hildesheim, 1962), §§81 and 77, respectively.

147 [Lehmann note to Ak. 29: 932$_{25}$] Cf. Descartes, *Principia philosophiae* (Principles of Philosophy) (Amsterdam: Louis Elzivir, 1644), Pt. 4, §§201–2: "Yet who can doubt that these are many bodies, so minute that we do not detect them by any of our senses? . . . [§202] It is true that Democritus also imagined certain small bodies having various sizes, shapes, and motions, and supposed that all bodies that can be perceived by the senses arose from the conglomeration and mutual interaction of these corpuscles" [*The Philosophical Writings of Descartes*, 2 vols., tr. John Cottingham, Robert Stoothof, and Dugald Murdoch (Cambridge University Press, 1985), vol. 1, pp. 286–7] – Baumgarten (§425; Ak. 17: 115) wants to call bodies which are not perceivable through the senses, i.e., which are only confusedly cognizable, corpuscles <*corpuscula*>, and a philosophy that explains the phenomena of bodies from corpuscles, corpuscular philosophy. Cf. also note 4 to *Metaphysik Volckmann* (Ak. 28: 445$_{21}$), below.

148 [Lehmann note to Ak. 29: 932$_{30}$] On Peter Gassendi, the mention of whose corpuscular philosophy did not appear in Kant's published writings, see the

note to Ak. 28: 1275$_{18f}$ (*Danziger Rationaltheologie*). [See also note 4 to *Metaphysik L$_2$* (Ak. 28: 536$_{6-8}$), below.]

149   [Lehmann note to Ak. 29: 933$_{19}$] Cf. here, apart from the Analogies in the *CrPR*, Refl. #66 (Ak. 23: 28): "One must subsume the perceptions under the categories. But from the categories for themselves nothing at all can be inferred, but rather from the possibility of perception, which can happen only through determination of time and in time, in which the act <*actus*>, which determines the intuition, is possible only according to a category."

150   [Lehmann note to Ak. 29: 933$_{24}$] Essence <*Essentia*; G: *das Wesen*> and nature <*natura*> are, on the contrary, equated by Baumgarten (§40; Ak. 17: 36). Cf. Ak. 29: 868$_{31}$, below [in our repagination of the lecture notes, the text of Ak. 29: 868 comes *below* the text of Ak. 29: 933].

151   [Lehmann note to Ak. 29: 934$_{3-4}$] Hermann Samuel Reimarus, *Allgemeine Betrachtungen über die Triebe der Thiere hauptsächlich über ihre Kunsttriebe: zum Erkenntniss des Zusammenhanges der Welt, des Schöpfers und unser selbst* (General Observations on the Drives of Animals, especially their Artificial Drives; on the Cognition of the Connection of the World, the Creator, and Our Self), 2nd edition (Hamburg: Carl Holm, 1762), §164: "Therefore one would hold entirely different things as the same and group them together if one did not attend to the essential determination of the powers and the essential levels of their determination." – See the notes to Ak. 28: 116$_{25}$ and Ak. 28: 116$_{36}$ (*Metaphysik Herder*).

152   [Lehmann note to Ak. 29: 935$_{10}$] Baumgarten, §430 (Ak. 17: 116): "The beginning of nature is BIRTH, the duration LIFE, the end DEATH <*Initium naturae est* ORIGO (G: *Erzeugung*), *duratio* VITA (G: *Leben*), *finis* MORS (G: *Tod*)>."

153   [Lehmann note to Ak. 29: 935$_{14}$] Baumgarten, §433 (Ak. 17: 116): "A MACHINE is a composite strictly speaking which is movable according to the laws of motion. Therefore *every body* in the world *is a machine* <MACHINA *est compositum stricte dictum secundum leges motus mobile. Ergo omne corpus in mundo est machina*>."

154   [Lehmann note to Ak. 29: 936$_5$] Cf. note 1 to *Metaphysik Vigilantius (K$_3$)* (Ak. 29: 946$_{14}$), below.

155   [Lehmann note to Ak. 29: 936$_9$] On Newton's "explanation" of attraction, see his *Opticks* (1704), 1st edition, p. 242f: "What I call attraction, may be performed by Impulse, or by some other means unknown to me, I use that word here to signify only in general any force by which bodies tend toward one another, whatsoever be the cause. For we must learn, from the phaenomena of Nature, what bodies attract one another, and what are the laws and properties of the attraction, before we enquire the cause by which the attraction is performed."

156   [Lehmann note to Ak. 29: 936$_{32}$] Baumgarten, §437 (Ak. 17: 117): "For this reason *the most perfect world is* also *the best* of all possible worlds <*Hinc mundus perfectissimus est etiam mundorum possibilium omnium optimus*>." On this question, see Kant's "Attempt at Some Reflections on Optimism" (Ak. 2: 31–5).

157   Cf. note 215 (to Ak. 29: 901$_{12}$).

158   [Lehmann note to Ak. 29: 865$_{27-8}$] Leibniz asks about the connection of the

soul and the body in the *Système nouveau de la nature et de la communication des substances aussi bien que de l'union qu'il y a entre l'âme et le corps* (New System of the Nature and Communication of Substances and of the Union of the Soul and Body) (1695), §12f [in *G. W. Leibniz: Philosophical Essays*, tr. by Roger Ariew and Daniel Garber (Indianapolis: Hackett, 1989), p. 142f]; Baumgarten treats the interaction of worldly substances *<commercium mundanarum substantiarum>* in §§448–65, and develops here "opinions of the manner and sort of such connection" (§448; Ak. 17: 119–20), in particular the systems of physical influence and of occasional causes *<systema influxus physici et causarum occasionalium>*, and preestablished harmony (§§452ff) – wherein he discusses Descartes and Malebranche (§452; Ak. 17: 121). Wolff, who rejects monads and replaces them with "simple things," reduces the Leibnizian harmony to the "dualism of body and soul by which sensations have their ground in the body on account of the harmony with the body" (*Vernünfftige Gedancken von Gott, der Welt und der Seele des Menschen, auch allen Dingen überhaupt* (Rational Thoughts about God, the World and the Human Soul, and on All Things in General) ["German Metaphysics"], 1st edition (Halle, 1719) in *Gesammelte Werke* (Collected Works), I.2 (Hildesheim, 1962), §818); empirical psychology *<psychologia empirica>* is defined as "the science of establishing principles through experience, whence the ground of those things which are in the human soul is derived *<scientia stabiliendi principia per experientiam, unde ratio redditur eorum, quae in anima humana sunt>*" – thus with a view to rational psychology (as "the science of those things which are possible through the human soul *<scientia eorum, quae per animan humanam possibilia sunt>*") [Christian Wolff, *Psychologia empirica methodo scientifica pertractata, qua ea, quae de anima humana indubia experientiae fide constant, continentur,* new edition (Frankfurt and Leipzig, 1738), §1]. See also note 225 (to Ak. 29: 907$_9$), below.

159 [Lehmann note to Ak. 29: 866$_4$] On this, Baumgarten, §§450ff. In §450 (Ak. 17: 120): "The real INFLUENCE of a substance of part of the world on another part of the world is PHYSICAL. Hence, UNIVERSAL PHYSICAL INFLUENCE is the universal harmony of substances in the world, insofar as one really influences another, and one who posits it as happening in this world is a UNIVERSAL INFLUXIONIST. This system is THE SYSTEM OF UNIVERSAL PHYSICAL INFLUENCE *<INFLUXUS realis substantiae mundi partis in aliam mundi partem est PHYSICUS. Hinc INFLUXUS PHYSICUS UNIVERSALIS est universalis substantiarum in mundo harmonia, qua una in alteram realiter influit, eumque ponens in hoc mundo est INFLUXIONISTA UNIVERSALIS. Huius systema est SYSTEMA INFLUXUS PHYSICI UNIVERSALIS>*." Cf. note 75 (to Ak. 29: 823$_{23}$), above.

160 Lehmann refers to his note to Ak. 28: 1108$_{12}$ (*Philosophische Religionslehre Pölitz*): On this often cited passage from Newton's *Optick* (in the Latin translation by Clarke, 1740, p. 298), see the dismissive criticism that is raised by Johann August Eberhard (in §17 of his *Vorbereitung zur natürlichen Theologie* (Preparation for Natural Theology) (Halle, 1781), reprinted at Ak. 18: 552) against space as "being next to one another," not as the seat of the senses *<sensorium>*, and the answer that Kant gives in Refl. #6285 (Ak. 18: 552–3).

161 [Lehmann note to Ak. 29: 866$_{35}$] The parable of the watch is found in Leibniz in the Postscript of a Letter to Basnage de Beauval (1696): "Consider two clocks or watches in perfect agreement. Now this can happen in *three ways:* the *first* is that of a natural influence. . . . *The second way* to make two faulty clocks always agree would be to have them watched over by a competent workman, who would adjust them and get them to agree at every moment. *The third way* is to construct these two clocks from the start with so much skill and accuracy that one can be certain of their subsequent agreement. Let us now put the soul and the body in place of these two watches; their agreement or sympathy will also come about in one of these three ways. *The way of influence* is that of the common philosophy; but since we can conceive neither material particles nor immaterial qualities or species that can pass from one of these substances to the other, we must reject this opinion. *The way of assistance* is that of the system of occasional causes. But, I hold, that is to appeal to a *Deus ex machina* in a natural and ordinary matter, where, according to reason, God should intervene only in the sense that he concurs with all other natural things. Thus there remains only my hypothesis, that is, *the way of preestablished harmony*" [*G. W. Leibniz: Philosophical Essays*, tr. by Roger Ariew and Daniel Garber (Indianapolis: Hackett, 1989), pp. 147–8].

162 [Lehmann note to Ak. 29: 868$_{31}$] In Ch. 2, Sect. 3 ("The Nature of Bodies" <*Natura corporum*>, Ak. 17: 116–17), Baumgarten goes from the nature of a thing <*natura entis*> as a complex of its determinations (§430) to the nature of bodies (nature simply speaking) <*natura corporum (natura simpliciter dicitur)*> (§431) and to the laws of motion (§432), i.e., mechanism and mechanical philosophy <*Philosophia mechanica*> (§434f). In Ch. 3, Sect. 3 ("Natural" <*Naturale*>, Ak. 17: 123–5), he speaks of universal nature <*natura universa*> (§466) as a contingent thing <*ens contingens*>, of the course of nature <*cursus naturae*> (§471), of the natural order (§472) – all found in Leibniz.

163 [Lehmann note to Ak. 29: 869$_{36}$] Baumgarten, Sect. 4 ("Supernatural" <*Supernaturale*>), §474 (Ak. 17: 125): "A mundane EVENT that does not arise from the nature of a contingent being is SUPERNATURAL. An event not arising from the determinate nature of a certain contingent being in which [the event] occurs is PRETERNATURAL. . . . A supernatural event insofar as it is regarded as extraordinary is a MIRACLE <*EVENTUS mundi a nullius entis contingentis natura actuatus SUPERNATURALIS est. Eventus a determinata certi entis contingentis, in quo evenit, natura non actuatus, respectu illius entis PRAETERNATURALIS est. . . . Eventus supernaturalis, qua spectatur ut extraordinarius, est MIRACULUM* (G: *ein Wunder, Wunderwerk*).*" Cf. *Religionslehre Pölitz* (Ak. 28: 1106f) as well as *Vernunfttheologie Magath* (ms, p. 116): "For we call that a miracle if the cause of an event is supernatural, as it would then be if God himself as co-cause <*concausa*> took part in producing this effect."

164 [Lehmann note to Ak. 29: 870$_9$] Baumgarten naturally reckoned miracles to the supernatural (Sect. 4 of Ch. 3: "The Perfection of the World" <*Perfectio Universi*>), which he (§477; Ak. 17: 126) distinguished into comparative and strict miracles <*miracula comparativa . . . rigorosa;* G: *Vergleichungs-Weise und nach der Strenge sogenannte Wunder*>.

165 [Lehmann note to Ak. 29: 870$_{36}$] William Whiston (1667–1752), English mathematician and divine, philosopher disciple of Newton's, and his successor at Cambridge, became a Unitarian around 1710 after initial doubts about the trinity. As such he had to leave the university and went to London, where he recruited for his congregation (Whistonites). – Kant refers to the German translation of the *Neuen Betrachtung der Erde nach ihrem Ursprunge und Fortgange bis zur Hervorbringung aller Dinge* (Frankfurt a. M., 1715). [English edition: *A new theory of the earth, from its original, to the consummation of all things: wherein the creation of the world in six days, the universal deluge, and the general conflagration, as laid down in the Holy Scriptures, are shewn to be perfectly agreeable to reason and philosophy: with a large introductory discourse concerning the genuine nature, stile, and extent of the mosaick history of the creation* (London: Printed by R. Roberts for Benj. Tooke, 1696).]

166 [Lehmann note to Ak. 29: 871$_3$] This problem concerns Hermann Friedrich Teichmeyer (1685–1744), who was a professor of physics and medicine in Jena, a physician in Weimar, the discoverer of cobalt ink, and the author of many compendiums. The passage cited by Kant could not be ascertained. On Teichmeyer, see Johann Heinrich Zedler, *Grosses vollständiges Universal Lexicon* (Large and Complete Universal Encyclopedia), 64 vols. (Halle and Leipzig: 1732–50), vol. 42 (1744), columns 504–11. According to Arthur Warda, *Immanuel Kants Bücher* (Immanuel Kant's Books) (Berlin: Martin Breslauer, 1927), p. 35, Kant owned a copy of Teichmeyer's *Institutiones chemiae dogmaticae et experimentalis, in quibus chemicorum principia, instrumenta, operationes et producta, simulque analyses trium regnorum succincta methodo traduntur, in usum auditorii sui cum figuris aeneis et indicibus* (Instructions in dogmatic and experimental chemistry, in which are succinctly treated the principles, instruments, operations and products of chemists, along with analyses of the three realms [of chemicals], in use in their lecture hall, with engravings and indices) (Jena, 1729).

167 [Lehmann note to Ak. 29: 871$_6$] "And Isaiah the prophet cried unto the Lord: and he brought the shadow ten degrees backward, by which it had gone down in the dial of Ahaz" (II Kings 20: 11, King James version).

168 [Lehmann note to Ak. 29: 876$_{14}$] Baumgarten, §504 (Ak. 15: 5), with which the Empirical Psychology begins, treats of the existence of the soul: "If there is anything in a being which can be conscious of something, that is a SOUL. In me there exists that which can be conscious of something. Therefore, in me there exists a soul (I exist as a soul) <*si quid in ente est, quod sibi alicuius potest esse conscium, illud est* ANIMA (G: *eine Seele*). *In me exsistit quod sibi alicuius potest esse conscium. Ergo in me exsistit anima (ego anima exsisto)*>." The published *Anthropology from a Pragmatic Point of View* also begins with the consciousness of the self (§1; Ak. 7: 127); the *Anthropologie Mrongovius*, on the other hand, does not – here it is first treated in the second chapter ("On the Investigation of the I," ms, p. 6'), and a reference is there made to Baumgarten.

169 The cavity of a gun, the inner strand of a cable, the sound post of stringed instruments, etc., are in German all called a *Seele* (soul).

170 [Lehmann note to Ak. 29: 877$_{7-9}$] Cf. Baumgarten, §505 (Ak. 15: 6): "I think, my soul is changed. Therefore thoughts are accidents of my soul, of which some, at least, have a sufficient ground in my soul. Therefore my soul is a power <*cogito, mutatur anima mea. Ergo cogitationes sunt accidentia animae meae, quarum aliquae saltim rationem sufficientem habent in anima mea. Ergo anima mea est vis*>."

171 [Lehmann note to Ak. 29: 877$_{10}$] Descartes, *Principia philosophiae* (Principles of Philosophy) (Amsterdam: Louis Elzivir, 1644), Pt. 1, §9: "By the term 'thought', I understand everything which we are aware of as happening within us, insofar as we have awareness of it" [*The Philosophical Writings of Descartes*, 2 vols., tr. John Cottingham, Robert Stoothof, and Dugald Murdoch (Cambridge University Press, 1985), vol. 1, p. 195].

172 These are the divisions of Baumgarten's Empirical Psychology.

173 On the distinction between desire and pleasure, see Kant's "Preface" to the *Critique of Practical Reason* (Ak. 5: 9).

174 [Lehmann note to Ak. 29: 879$_{6f}$] See Baumgarten §512 (Ak. 15: 6): my representations direct themselves according to the position of my body. See also Refl. #111 (Ak. 15: 5), which is not entirely in order, according to Adickes [the editor of the Reflections]. – By AFFECTIONS <*AFFECTIONES*> Baumgarten understands internal determinations of a possible thing <*determinationes possibilis internae;* G: *innere folgende Bestimmungen*> (§41; Ak. 17: 36).

175 [Lehmann note to Ak. 29: 879$_{20-3}$] Here too Kant cites according to Leibniz's *Nouveaux Essais sur l'entendement humain* (New Essays on the Human Understanding) (R. E. Raspe, 1765), Bk. 1, Ch. 1, §5: "I am surprised by what you say about potential knowledge and about these inner suppressions. For it seems 'to me near a contradiction, to say, that there are truths imprinted on the soul, which it perceives … not' " [translation by Peter Remnant and Jonathan Bennett (Cambridge University Press, 1981), p. 76].

176 [Lehmann note to Ak. 29: 880$_8$] See Baumgarten's Empirical Psychology, Sect. 2 ("The Lower Cognitive Faculty" <*Facultas Cognoscitiva Inferior*>). My soul has "the faculty for cognizing" (§519) both clear and confused (§520); the "REPRESENTATION which is not distinct is called SENSITIVE <*REPRAESENTATIO non distincta SENSITIVA* (G: *eine sinnliche Vorstellung*) *vocatur*>" (§521; Ak. 15: 9).

177 [Lehmann note to Ak. 29: 880$_{28-30}$] Baumgarten, §533 (Ak. 15: 13): "The science of knowing and setting forth in the manner of the senses is AESTHETICS (the science of the beautiful) (the logic of the lower cognitive faculty, the philosophy of the Graces and Muses, the lower gnoseology, the art of thinking beautifully, the art of the analogue of reason) <*Scientia sensitive cognoscendi et proponendi est AESTHETICA* (G: *die Wissenschaft des Schönen*) (*logica facultatis cognoscitivae inferioris, philosophia gratiarum et musarum, gnoseologia inferior, ars pulcre cogitandi, ars analogi rationis*)>." See also Baumgarten, *Aesthetica* (Aesthetics), 2 vols. (Frankfurt an der Oder: 1750–8), §1: "Aesthetics (the theory of the liberal arts, the lower gnoseology, the art of thinking beautifully, the art of the analogue of reason) is the science of sensitive cognition <*Aesthetica (theoria liberalium artium, gnoseologia inferior, ars pulchre cogitandi, ars analogi rationis) est scientia cognitionis sensitivae*>."

178 [Lehmann note to Ak. 29: 881₁₀] Baumgarten's Empirical Psychology, Sect. 8 (§§595–605; Ak. 15: 27–9): "A representation of the future state of the world, and hence of my future state, is ANTICIPATION <*Repraesentatio status mundi, hinc status mei, futuri est* PRAEVISIO (G: *die Vorhersehung, das Vorhersehen, vorausbemerken*>)" (§595). Cf. *Anthropology from a Pragmatic Point of View*, §35 (Ak. 7: 185–7): "On the Faculty of Foresight (*Praevisio*)."

179 [Lehmann note to Ak. 29: 881₁₀₋₁₂] See Baumgarten's Empirical Psychology, Sect. 6 ("Memory" <*Memoria*>), §§579–88 (Ak. 15: 24–5). Cf. *Anthropology from a Pragmatic Point of View*, §34: "On the Faculty of Making Present the Past and Future through the Power of Imagination: A. On Memory" (Ak. 7: 182–5).

180 [Lehmann note to Ak. 29: 881₂₀] Baumgarten's Empirical Psychology, Sect. 12 ("Understanding" <*Intellectus*>), §626 (Ak. 15: 34): "Attention to the whole perception after reflection is COMPARISON. I reflect. I compare. Therefore, I have the faculty of reflecting and comparing <*Attentio ad totam perceptionem post reflexionem est* COMPARATIO (G: *Vergleichung, das Zusammenhalten*). *Reflecto. Comparo. Ergo habeo facultatem reflectendi comparandique*>."

181 In Baumgarten, this faculty is called acumen <*acumen*> (§573; Ak. 15: 22–3).

182 [Lehmann note to Ak. 29: 881₂₂] Cf. Baumgarten's Empirical Psychology, Sect. 7 ("The Fictive Faculty" <*Facultas Fingendi*>), §589 (Ak. 15: 26): "By combining and DIVIDING phantasms, i.e., by attending only to part of some perception, I INVENT <*Combinando phantasmata et* PRAESCINDENDO (G: *durch Trennen und Absondern*), *i.e. attendendo ad partem alicuius perceptionis tantum,* FINGO (G: *dichte ich*)>." Cf. *Anthropology from a Pragmatic Point of View*, §33 (Ak. 7: 180): "inventive power of imagination." – Cf. Baumgarten, *Meditationes philosophicae de nonnullis ad poema pertinentibus*, §28, tr. by Karl Aschenbrenner and William B. Holther, *Reflections on Poetry: Alexander Gottlieb Baumgarten's* Meditationes Philosophicae de nonnullis ad poema pertinentibus (Berkeley: University of California Press, 1954), with a facsimile of the 1st ed. (Halle: Joh. Hen. Grunerti, 1735).

183 On sign <*signum*> and signified <*signatum*>, see Baumgarten, §347 (Ak. 17: 102), §619 (Ak. 15: 32), and also *Anthropology from a Pragmatic Point of View*: "On the Signifying Faculty (*facultas signatrix*)" (Ak. 7: 191).

184 [Lehmann note to Ak. 29: 882₂f] Baumgarten, in Sect. 3 ("Sense" <*Sensus*>; Ak. 15: 13–19) of the Empirical Psychology, distinguishes inner and outer sense (§535); the five senses: touch, sight, hearing, smell, taste (§536); perceptual areas and points (§537), acuity and dullness of the senses (§540), and then gives as the rule of internal sensation <*sensationis internae*>: As the states of my soul succeed each other, so the representations of the same presences follow each other in turn <*ut sibi succedunt status animae meae, sic se sequantur invicem repraesentationes eorundum praesentium*> (§541) – but this "state" of my soul is not the object of a special vital sense. In the *Anthropology from a Pragmatic Point of View* (Ak. 7: 154), vital sensation <*sensus vagus;* G: *Vitalempfindung*> is distinguished from the sensation of the sense organs (*sensus fixus;* G: *Organempfindung*), and the sensation of warm and cold is reckoned to the "vital sense." The *Anthropologie Mrongovius* (with the same distinction) says: "I perceive

through the vital sense my entire life" (ms, p. 23). Thus Refl. #202 (Ak. 15: 78): "All self-activity promotes the consciousness of life." – Cf. Ak. 28: 850f (*Nachträge Herder*).

185 [Lehmann note to Ak. 29: 882$_{22}$f] *Physische Geographie* (lecture notes from 1792): "Live turtles were brought to England, where they are eaten with much pleasure. The turtles move from Yucatan to an island lying south of Cuba, easily 150 miles distant, without ever erring. What special instinct could be guiding them?" (ms, p. 147f). See the *Physische Geographie Powalski*, ms, p. 41 (Adickes F, p. 89), and the published *Physical Geography* (Ak. 9: 340$_{18-24}$).

186 [Lehmann note to Ak. 29: 883$_{1-2}$] Although Diderot is not mentioned in Kant's published writings, perhaps here and in the following Kant had Diderot's *Lettre sur les aveugles* (Letter on the Blind) (1760) in mind: "when she heard singing, she distinguished *dark* and *fair* voices . . ." [*Diderot's Early Philosophical Works*, tr. and ed. by Margaret Jourdain (Chicago and London: Open Court, 1916), p. 146]. In any event the problem of the congenitally blind (*aveugle-nés*), or those operated upon, was discussed so frequently at the time (Berkeley, Voltaire, Condillac, Smith/Kästner, etc.; see Adickes's note to Ak. 15: 802$_{21}$), that Kant must have taken a lively interest in it. Above all, the blind mathematician N. Saunderson gained a general interest. His *Elements of Algebra* (1740) is also treated by Diderot (op. cit., p. 90: "Wonderful stories are told of him, and yet there is not one to which, from his attainments in literature and his skill in mathematics, we may not safely give credit"). Diderot cites Saunderson's biography, *The Life and Character of Dr. Nicholas Saunderson*, late Lucarien Professor of the Mathematicks in the University of Cambridge; by his disciple and friend William Inchliff, Esq. (Dublin, 1747). Kant concerned himself with Saunderson in the (contemporaneous) *Danziger Physik* (Ak. 29: 148$_{2-4}$): "Saunderson, professor of optics, called out in an empty room and then knew at once through his hearing how long and large the room was. . . ." See also Lehmann's note to Ak. 29: 148$_2$. And see also the *Menschenkunde* (vol. 1, p. 64). Kant already reported on W. Cheselden's (1688–1752) cataract operations in the *Metaphysik Herder* (Ak. 28: 61$_{9-12}$, 852$_{8-10}$, 902$_{36-7}$).

187 [Lehmann note to Ak. 29: 883$_{26}$] Cf. Baumgarten's Empirical Psychology, Sect. 4 ("Fantasy" <*Phantasia*>), §§557–71 (Ak. 15: 19–22): fantasy <*phantasia*> is the faculty of imagining <*facultas imaginandi*>. As the law of imagination <*lex imaginationis*> (§561; Ak. 15: 20): "an idea perceived in part returns in its totality. This proposition is also called *the association of ideas* <*percepta idea partiali recurrit eius totalis. Haec propositio etiam associatio idearum dicitur*>." In *Anthropology from a Pragmatic Point of View*, §§31–3 (Ak. 7: 174–82), Kant distinguishes and discusses plastic imagination, associating imagination, and affinity <*imaginatio plastica, imaginatio associans, affinitas*>.

188 This law is included in Baumgarten's discussion of expectation <*praesagitio*> (§§610–18; Ak. 15: 30–2), rather than that of anticipation <*praevisio*> (§§595–605; Ak. 15: 27–9).

189 [Lehmann note to Ak. 29: 884$_{25}$] Conjunction <*coniunctio*> belongs to the concept of order (§§78–88; Ak. 17: 44–5): "The conjunction of insepara-

bles is unity <*coniunctio inseparabilium est unitio*>" (§79). – Comparison <*comparatio*> is treated in the Psychology, and the rule of comparison <*regula comparationis*> is: "Perceiving by turning back to the many parts of the whole perception and its clearer notes, I pay more attention to it afterwards <*reflectendo ad partes totius perceptionis plures et clariores notas eius percipiens ad eam postea magis attendo*>" (§627; Ak. 15: 35).

190 [Lehmann note to Ak. 29: 884₂₉] This well-known pair of concepts from the *Anthropology from a Pragmatic Point of View* (§44, Ak. 7: 201): "*Faculty* of acumen (<*acumen;* G: *Scharfsinnigkeit*>), to think out the general in the particular" – thus the reflecting power of judgment ("First Introduction to the *Critique of Judgment*," Ak. 20: 211–16), which leads into the "technique of nature" (Ak. 20: 215) as discussed in the *Opus postumum* – is treated and classified in detail by Baumgarten. Also rooted here is the likewise important concept for Kant of genius (*Critique of Judgment*, Ak. 5: 307₁₄₋₁₅: "The condition of the mind *through which* the nature of art gives the rule"). The relevant lecture material here is in Schlapp, *Kants Lehre vom Genie und die Entstehung der Kritik der Urteilskraft* (Kant's Doctrine of Genius and the Origin of the Critique of Judgment) (Göttingen, 1901). In Wolff, acumen <*acumen*> is the faculty for discerning the abstract in the concrete and the faculty of expressing it with clear words <*ad pervidendum in concreto abstractum idque verbis perspicuis enunciandi*> (*Ontologia*, §490). Baumgarten, §578 (Ak. 15: 23–4). See also *Metaphysik Herder* (Ak. 28: 67).

191 [Lehmann note to Ak. 29: 885₆₋₉] Baumgarten (§571; Ak. 15: 22) translates *Phantasia effrenis* as *auschweifende* (unbridled), and *phantasia subacta* as *wohlgeordnete* (well-ordered) power of imagination. Cf. Refl. #314 (Ak. 15: 124), *Metaphysik Herder* (Ak. 28: 66₅₋₁₀), and *Anthropology from a Pragmatic Point of View* (Ak. 7: 178₂₀–79₇).

192 [Lehmann note to Ak. 29: 885₂₁₋₃] Cf. *Anthropology from a Pragmatic Point of View:* "With respect to the sense representation a mental disturbance is either *senselessness* <G: *Unsinnigkeit*> or *insanity* <G: *Wahnsinn*>. As perversion of the power of judgment and reason it is called *madness* <G: *Wahnwitz*> or *conceit* <G: *Aberwitz*>" (Ak. 7: 202₁₈₋₂₀). – Cf. also Kant's pre-critical essay "Essay on the Maladies of the Mind" (Ak. 2: 268), where he orders the "infirmities of the disturbed mind" according to three concepts: *craziness* <G: *Verrückung*> as a perversion of the concepts of experience, *insanity* <G: *Wahnsinn*> as a disorderly use of the power of judgment, and *madness* <G: *Wahnwitz*> as a perverted reason. Cf. Refl. #1486 (Ak. 15: 706), where Kant similarly distinguishes insanity <G: *Wahnsinn*>, imbecility <G: *Blödsinn*>, and madness <G: *Wahnwitz*>. – See also *Metaphysik Herder* (Ak. 28: 67₃₀₋₅): "Mental diseases are all so different that a name for distinguishing [them] takes trouble." More details in *Anthropologie Mrongovius* (ms, pp. 112f). [Mary Gregor, in her translation of *Anthropology from a Pragmatic Point of View* (The Hague: Martinus Nijhoff, 1974), offers the following German/Latin equivalents of terms for mental illness, as found in Kant's various notes: *Unsinnigkeit/ amentia, Wahnsinn/dementia, Wahnwitz/insania, Aberwitz/vesania* (p. 74).]

193 Kant is probably referring to the natural illusion of the moon's size at the horizon, but see also *Anthropology from a Pragmatic Point of View,* §33 (Ak. 7: 180).

194 [Lehmann note to Ak. 29: 885₃₂] Baumgarten treats the dream taken subjectively <subiective sumpta> in §593f under "The Fictive Faculty" <Facultas fingendi>. In §594 (Ak. 15: 27), the sleepwalker and other "crazy people" are discussed. – On Kant, for whom the topic of dreams lies close to the heart, see Anthropology from a Pragmatic Point of View, §37 (Ak. 7: 189–90), The Conflict of the Faculties (Ak. 7: 105), Metaphysik Herder (Ak. 28: 71₂₂₋₃). Here the saying: we never forget anything, but circumstances for remembering are required when awake. Similarly, Kant's note at Ak. 2: 338 (Dreams of a Spirit-Seer), where he accepts that dreams that were quite lively during sleep do indeed disappear upon awakening.

195 [Lehmann note to Ak. 29: 886₂₈] Baumgarten, §556 (Ak. 15: 19): "SLEEP is the state of obscure external sensations in which the vital motions of the body, so far as we can tell, remain almost the same as they are in the state of being awake; one who is in this state SLEEPS <status obscurarum sensationum externarum, in quo motus corporis vitales, quantum observatur, fere iidem manent, qui sunt in statu vigiliarum, SOMNUS (G: Schlaf) est, in eoque constitutus DORMIT (G: schlafen)>." – Cf. The Conflict of the Faculties (Ak. 7: 104f); Menschenkunde (vol 1, p. 164): "A sound sleep is a series of representations displacing one another, which happens so quickly that one has no impression of it upon waking."

196 [Lehmann note to Ak. 29: 886₃₃] Baumgarten speaks of mantic art in general (§349; Ak. 17: 102) as "the art of prophecy," the faculty of prophecy <facultas divinatrix; G: Wahrsagergabe> (§616; Ak. 15: 31) – and negatively as empty expectations and presentiments (§617; Ak. 15: 32). – Cf. Anthropology from a Pragmatic Point of View (Ak. 7: 187–9).

197 [Lehmann note to Ak. 29: 887₂₄] See Ak. 29: 881₂₅, above.

198 [Lehmann note to Ak. 29: 888₃₇] Baumgarten, Sect. 12 ("Understanding" <intellectus>), §625f (Ak. 15: 34f), distinguishes: the faculty of attending <facultas attendendi>, of abstracting <abstrahendi>, of prescinding (of abstracting a part from a whole) <praescindendi (abstrahendi partem a toto)> (§625). Reflection <reflexio> and comparison <comparatio> belong to attention <attentio> and abstraction <abstractio> (§626; Ak. 15: 34).

199 [Lehmann note to Ak. 29: 889₁₀] Baumgarten, §86 (Ak. 17: 45): "common rules are in order <in ordine sunt regulae communes>."

200 [Lehmann note to Ak. 29: 889₃₇] Cf. CrPR (A 646/B 674): "If reason is a faculty for deriving the particular from the general. . . ." Baumgarten distinguishes "the lower cognitive faculty . . . the faculty of learning anything obscurely and confusedly or in separate groups <facultas cognoscitiva inferior . . . facultas obscure confuseque seu indistincte aliquid cognoscendi>," whose representation <repreaesentatio> is called sensitive <sensitiva; G: eine sinnliche Vorstellung> (§519–20; Ak. 15: 9), and the higher cognitive faculty <facultas cognoscitiva superior>, mind <mens> or understanding <intellectus> (§624; Ak. 15: 34). Reflection <reflexio> and comparison <comparatio> belong here (§626; Ak. 15: 34). Reason <ratio; G: Vernunft> is, on the other hand, that faculty of distinctly perceiving the identities and diversities of things <distincte identitates diversitatesque rerum perspiciendi> (§641; Ak. 15: 38) – the rational perceptions <perceptiones rationis> are then inferences of reason (<ratiocinia; G: Vernunft-Schlüsse>) (§646; Ak. 15: 39).

201 [Lehmann note to Ak. 29: 890₂₈] Baumgarten, Sect. 15 ("Pleasure and Displeasure" <*Voluptas et Taedium*>), §655–62 (Ak. 15: 41–5). Baumgarten translates *voluptas* as *Lust, Gefallen, Vergnügen* (pleasure, gratification) and *taedium* as *Unlust, Missfallen, Missvergnügen* (displeasure, non-gratification). See also Baumgarten (§655) on the state of indifference <*status indifferentiae*; G: *Stand der Gleichgültigkeit*>, and *Anthropology from a Pragmatic Point of View*, §60 (Ak. 7: 230f).

202 [Lehmann note to Ak. 29: 890₃₁] In Baumgarten, the concepts satisfaction <*complacentia*> and dissatisfaction <*displacentia*> (for pleasure <*voluptas*> and displeasure <*taedium*>) enter right in the first lines of §655 (Ak. 17: 41). Baumgarten translates *complacentia* as *Gefallen*, Kant translates it as *Wohlgefallen* (satisfaction) in the *Anthropology from a Pragmatic Point of View*, §69 (Ak. 7: 244₆). [This is similar to *Metaphysik Vigilantius* (*K₃*) (Ak. 29: 1013₇₋₈), below. *Voluptas*, on the other hand, is translated as *Lust* (pleasure; *Metaphysik Vigilantius* (*K₃*), Ak. 29: 1013₅) and *Sinnenlust* (sense-pleasure; *Metaphysik Dohna*, Ak. 28: 675₁₃₋₁₄).]

203 [Lehmann note to Ak. 29: 891₁₇] Cf. *Anthropology from a Pragmatic Point of View*, §72 (Ak. 7: 249–50): "On Luxury"; *Menschenkunde* (vol. 1, p. 122): "When a miser collects money without thereby having a further intent, then nothing attracts him but the pleasure of these riches in his fantasy. . . . This condition has many advantages for the miser; he has his money in his pocket, and sees all this pleasure still before him."

204 [Lehmann note to Ak. 29: 892₁₄] In Sect. 15 ("Pleasure and Displeasure" <*voluptas et taedium*>), §§655–62 (Ak. 15: 41–45), Baumgarten defines "beauty" (<*pulcritudo;* G: *Schönheit*>) as "perfection of appearance, or [perfection] observable to taste, in the broader sense <*perfectio phaenomenon, s. gustui latius dicto observabilis*>" (§662; Ak. 15: 45). On the more extended explanation by Kant on taste, see the reflections on aesthetics compiled by Adickes (Refl. #618–996; Ak. 15: 265–440). In the *Anthropology from a Pragmatic Point of View* itself, see Ak. 7: 239–50. In the *Critique of Judgment*, see the analysis of the judgment of taste (§§1–22; Ak. 5: 203–44).

205 [Lehmann note to Ak. 29: 893₁₃₋₁₅] "Beauty" (<*pulcritudo;* G: *Schönheit*>) is defined by Baumgarten as perfection of appearance <*perfectio phaenomenon*>, its opposite is ugliness <*deformitas*> (§662; Ak. 15: 45). – Baumgarten's *Aesthetica* (Aesthetics), 2 vols. (Frankfurt an der Oder: 1750–8) begins with the concept of beautiful cognition <*pulchritudo cognitionis*> (§14f).

206 [Lehmann note to Ak. 29: 893₂₆] This is Kant's reinterpretation of Augustine's city of God <*civitas dei*> in Leibniz and Baumgarten. Cf. Baumgarten, §974 (Ak. 17: 199): "the greatest is the despotic monarchy, of whom all created spirits are subjects <*maxima monarchia despotica, cuius omnes spiritus creati sunt subditi*>." Leibniz, "*Causa Dei*," §144 (in *Opera Philosophica* (Philosophical Works), ed. by J. E. Erdmann (Berlin, 1890), p. 663); on Baumgarten's determination of God as "despot": "The despot wants blind obedience, but God wants that we obey him because we comprehend that it is right and good" (*Danziger Rationaltheologie*, Ak. 28: 1314₂₁₋₃). Or the *Vernunfttheologie Magath*: "A general system of ends is possible only according to a doctrine of morality" (ms, p. 107). – See also the third part of

Religion within the Bounds of Unaided Reason: ethical state, "kingdom of virtue" (Ak. 6: 94f).

207 [Lehmann note to Ak. 29: 894₃] Baumgarten, Sect. 16 ("The Faculty of Desire" <*facultas appetitiva*>), §663 (Ak. 15: 45): "if I determine the power of my mind or myself for producing a certain idea, I DESIRE. I SHUN that thing whose opposite I desire <*si vim animae meae seu me determino ad certam perceptionem producendam, APPETO* (G: *se begehre ich). Cuius oppositum appeto, illud AVERSO* (G: *davon bin ich abgeneigt*)>."

208 [Lehmann note to Ak. 29: 895₃₈] Baumgarten, §679 (Ak. 15: 49): "Affections, which are stronger desires, since they arise from a stronger sensory pleasure, will increase the associated pleasure, whence affections of this sort are called PLEASANT; and insofar as the pleasure from which they arise hides the associated displeasure, they are called GRATIFYING <*affectus, qui appetitiones fortiores sunt, cum ex fortiori voluptate sensitiva oriantur, haec voluptatem sociam augebit, unde eiusmodi AFFECTUS IUCUNDI* (G: *angenehme*) *dicuntur, et quatenus voluptas, ex qua oriuntur, taedium socium obscurat GRATI* (G: *nicht unangenehme) appellantur*>."

209 [Lehmann note to Ak. 29: 896₆] Baumgarten, §712 (Ak. 17: 134): "Therefore I have the faculty of desiring and of shunning as I please, that is, [I have] the POWER OF CHOICE <*ergo habeo facultatem appetendi et aversandi pro lubitu meo, i.e. ARBITRIUM* (G: *Willkür*)>." Cf. Ak. 29: 862₉₋₂₁.

210 On animal and human will, see: *CrPR* (A 533–4, 802/B 561–2, 830), *Lectures on Ethics* (tr. by Louis Infeld (New York: 1963), pp. 28, 121–2), *Metaphysic of Morals* (Ak. 6: 213₂₉₋₃₅; 442₃₀₋₁), F. C. Starke, *Menschkunde* (vol. 1, p. 370), *Groundwork to a Metaphysic of Morals* (Ak. 4: 445–6, 459n).

211 Cf. note 124 (to Ak. 29: 861₂₀), above.

212 [Lehmann note to Ak. 29: 897₁₈] Baumgarten, §701 (Ak. 17: 131): "NECESSITY (compulsion) is the change of some thing from contingency into necessity; hence it is either ACTIVE [necessity], of what is necessitating, or PASSIVE [necessity], of what is necessitated <*NECESSITATIO (coactio)* (G: *die Nöthigung) est mutatio alicuius ex contingenti in necessarium, hinc est vel ACTIVA* (G: *die vorgenommene) necessitantis, . . . vel PASSIVA* (G: *die gelittene) necessitati*>." See also the practical philosophy: Alexander Gottlieb Baumgarten, *Initia philosophia practicae primae* (Elements of Practical First Philosophy), §§50–9 (Ak. 19: 27–31); *Moralphilosophie Collins* (Ak. 27: 268₉₋₁₃): "Not all necessitation is pathological, but rather also practical. Practical necessitation is not subjective, but rather objective. . . . No other necessitation agrees with freedom except practical necessitation by motives <*per motiva*>." See also the lectures on "Natural Right" from the same time (1784/85): "Necessitation <*necessitatio*> of an action contingent in itself through objective grounds is practical necessitation <*necessitatio*>, that is different from practical necessity" (*Naturrecht Feyerabend;* Ak. 27: 1323₁₄₋₁₆). [See also *Lectures on Ethics,* tr. by Louis Infeld (New York: 1963), pp. 27–33.]

213 [Lehmann note to Ak. 29: 897₂₆₋₉] Baumgarten, Sect. 18 ("The Higher Faculty of Desire" <*facultas appetitiva superior*>), §690 (Ak. 15: 51): ". . . there is either desire or desire-that-not. Representations [that are] impelling causes of desiring and of desiring-that-not are MOTIVES. The incentives of the soul are either stimuli or motives <*est vel voluntas, vel noluntas.*

Repraesentationes volitionis nolitionisque causae impulsivae sunt MOTIVA (G: *Bewegungsgründe*). *Elateres animi, vel sunt stimuli, vel motiva>*." Cf. note to Ak. 27: 112₈ (*Practische Philosophie Powalski*).

214 Cf. *Metaphysik Herder* (Ak. 28: 99₉₉₋₆): "The less one is conscious, the smaller is one's freedom"; *Lectures on Ethics*, tr. by Louis Infeld (New York: 1963), p. 28.

215 [Lehmann note to Ak. 29: 901₁₂] According to Baumgarten (§190; Ak. 17: 66), the highest good is the metaphysically best <*optimum metaphysicum*>, which contains in itself the CONTINGENT HIGHEST GOOD <*SUMMUM BONUM CONTINGENS;* G: *das zufällige höchste Gut*> (physical in the broad sense <*physicum late dictum*>).

216 [Lehmann note to Ak. 29: 901₂₄] On the indifferent <*adiaphoron*> in Baumgarten's Empirical Psychology, see Sect. 15 ("Indifference" <*Indifferentia*>), §§651–4 (Ak. 15: 40–1); see also Refl. #150 (Ak. 15: 41): "whoever has no choice at all cannot be entirely insensitive. But he only cannot judge." Cf. the note to Ak. 27: 522₃₇f (*Metaphysik der Sitten Vigilantius*).

217 [Lehmann note to Ak. 29: 902₂₆] Baumgarten, Sect. 21 ("Freedom" <*libertas*>), §719 (Ak. 17: 135–6): "Freedom purely from desire and desire-that-not is PURE FREEDOM <*libertas pure volendi nolendive est* LIBERTAS PURA (G: *reine Freiheit*)>."

218 [Lehmann note to Ak. 29: 902₂₇] Baumgarten, §342 (Ak. 17: 101): "The grounds of intention in the one intending are called THE IMPELLING CAUSES (drive or motive causes) <*intentionis rationes in intendente vocantur* CAUSAE IMPULSIVAE (G: *Trieb oder bewegende Ursachen*)>." Christian Wolff, *Ontologia*, §940.

219 [Lehmann note to Ak. 29: 902₃₆] Cf. Ak. 29: 897₃₆f.

220 [Lehmann note to Ak. 29: 904₁₇] Baumgarten, §505 (Ak. 15: 6): "I think; my soul is changed. Therefore thoughts are accidents of my soul, some of which at least have their sufficient ground in my soul. Therefore my soul is a power <*cogito, mutatur anima mea. Ergo cogitationes sunt accidentia animae meae, quarum aliquae saltim rationem sufficientem habent in anima mea. Ergo anima mea est vis*>." This is in the Empirical Psychology; in the Rational Psychology, the human soul is designated as a soul which is in closest interaction with a human body <*anima, quae cum corpore humano in artissimo est commercio*> (§740; Ak. 17: 140). Only in §742 (Ak. 17: 141) is there discussion of thinking substance: "Whatever can think is either a substance, a monad; or else a whole of which a part is a substance that can think. Therefore every soul is a substance, a monad <*quicquid cogitare potest, aut est substantia, monas, aut totum, cuius substantia, quae cogitare potest, pars sit. Ergo omnis anima est substantia, monas*>."

221 See Baumgarten, §741 (Ak. 17: 141).

222 See Baumgarten's Rational Psychology, Sect. 6 ("The Souls of Brutes" <*animae brutorum*>), §§792–5 (Ak. 17: 155–6).

223 See *Metaphysik Herder* (Ak. 28: 116₂₄₋₅): "If this [animal behavior] can all be explained without consciousness then one will prefer to explain it *from a simple power*"; *CrPR* (A 546/B 574): "In lifeless, or merely animal, nature, we find no ground for thinking that any faculty is conditioned otherwise than in a merely sensible manner"; "Reviews of Herder" (Ak. 8: 57): that

human reason is possible in another organic form "can be as little proved as the notion that reason is possible only in the present form."

224 [Lehmann note to Ak. 29: 906₃₆] Georg Friedrich Meier (1718–77), upon whose *Auszug aus der Vernunftlehre* (Extract from the Doctrine of Reason) (Halle, 1752) Kant based his logic course, wrote in 1749 the *Versuch eines neuen Lehrgebäudes von den Seelen der Thiere* (Essay on a New System of the Souls of Animals) (Halle, 1749). See also "Announcement of the Programme of his Lectures for the Winter Semester 1765-6" (Ak. 2: 310₃₆–311₉) for Kant's judgment of Meier. [Meier had studied under Baumgarten and succeeded Wolff at Halle. He used the Wolffian philosophy to argue for animal souls, attributing simple reasoning powers to brutes and a development similar to that described by Bonnet. He argues that the ability for abstract thought is all that separates humans from brutes. On Kant's belief in the animals' inability to attain reason or understanding, see also Kant's "Idea for a Universal History with a Cosmopolitan Purpose" (1784) (Ak. 8: 17), *Metaphysik Dohna* (Ak. 28: 689–90), *Metaphysik L₁* (Ak. 28: 276), *Metaphysik Volckmann* (Ak. 28: 450).]

225 [Lehmann note to Ak. 29: 907₉] Cf. Baumgarten's Rational Psychology, Sect. 2 ("Psychological Systems" <*systemata psychologica*>), §§761-9 (Ak. 17: 145-8), esp. §761 (Ak. 17: 145): "PSYCHOLOGICAL SYSTEMS are views which seem fit to explain the interaction of the soul and body in men. . . . None of them is possible, except the system of preestablished harmony, of physical influence, and of occasional, perhaps psychological, causes <*SYS-TEMATA PSYCHOLOGICA sunt sententiae, quae videntur ad explicandum animae et corporis in homine commercium aptae. . . . Illorum nullum possibile, praeter systema harmoniae praestabilitae, influxus physici, et causarum occasionalium forsitan psychologicum*>." See also *Metaphysik Herder* (Ak. 28: 102-5).

226 Charles Bonnet (1720–93), a Swiss scientist and philosopher born in Geneva. His works include *Contemplation de la Nature* (Contemplation of Nature) (1764-5). He attempted to reconcile naturalism and the doctrine of resurrection.

227 [Lehmann note to Ak. 29: 909₆₋₇] See note 17 to *Metaphysik Dohna* (Ak. 28: 686₁), below.

228 [Lehmann note to Ak. 29: 910₆] Baumgarten, Sect. 3 ("The Origin of the Human Soul" <*origo animae humanae*>), §772 (Ak. 17: 148): "The soul is not able to come into being, unless out of nothing. Therefore it does not arise from parents <*anima non potest oriri, nisi ex nihilo. Ergo non oritur ex parentibus*>." See also §926 (Ak. 17: 190): "To bring about something from nothing is TO CREATE <*actuare quid ex nihilo est CREARE* (G: *erschaffen*)>."

229 [Lehmann note to Ak. 29: 910₁₇] Baumgarten, §771 (Ak. 17: 148): ". . . or they want the soul to arise from parents, and they are called TRADUCIANS (a friend of origin through transition) . . . <*aut eam ex parentibus oriri volunt et TRADUCIANI* (G: *ein Freund des Ursprungs durch den Übergang*) *vocantur*>"; §772 (Ak. 17: 148): "Traducians or out of the soul of parents, as a little flame out of a little flame . . . <*Traduciani sive ex parentum anima, ut flammulam ex flammula*>."

230 See note 1 to *Metaphysik Volckmann* (Ak. 28: 440₃₃).

231 On the teleological proof, see Ak. 29: 915-16.

232 [Lehmann note to Ak. 29: 912_8] See the parallel passage in *Metaphysik Volckmann* (Ak. 28: 441_{15-20}).

233 [Lehmann note to Ak. 29: 912_{34}] Moses Mendelssohn discusses the simplicity of the soul and the soul as substance in the second talk of his *Phädon, oder über die Unsterblichkeit der Seele* (Phaedo, or On the Immortality of the Soul) (Berlin: F. Nicolai, 1767), and discusses its immortality in the third talk. [Cf. *CrPR*, B 413f.]

234 [Lehmann note to Ak. 29: 913_{16}] In the *Menschenkunde* (vol. 1, pp. 245–6), Kant reflects: "Nelli [the text wrongly has "Kelli"] in Florence remarks that there is a metempsychosis of genius. He remarks on it above of all of three persons, that the birthday of the one was the death day of the other. On the death day of Michelangelo, Galileo was born, and on his death day Newton [was born]. But when Newton's mother was pregnant, Galileo was still alive, and the child in the womb surely must have already had a soul."

235 [Lehmann note to Ak. 29: 914_{34}] Baumgarten acknowledges a hypothetical immortality at §781 (Ak. 17: 151): "No substance of this world is annihilated. Therefore, when a body such as the one men have on this earth dies, the surviving human soul lives immortally <*nulla substantia huius mundi annihilatur. Ergo anima humana moriente corpore, quale in his terris homines habent, superstes vivit immortaliter*>."

236 [Lehmann note to Ak. 29: 915_{13}] Cf. *Danziger Physik* (Ak. 29: 155).

237 Lehmann refers to the note to Ak. 29: 84_{25} (*Berliner Physik*), which quotes from Leonhard Euler, *Briefe an eine deutsche Prinzessin über verschiedene Gegenstände aus der Physik und Philosophie* (Letters to a German Princess concerning Various Items from Physics and Philosophy) (Leipzig, 1773).

238 [Lehmann note to Ak. 29: 915_{18}] John Dollond (Dolland) (1706–61), an optician in business with his father, acquired as an autodidact a comprehensive education, wrote in 1758 an *Account of some experiments concerning the different refrangibility of light* wherein he describes the Dolland Telescope that he constructed (with lenses from three glasses). – Cf. *Danziger Physik* (Ak. 29: 150–4): "On Light and Color."

239 Lehmann refers to a parallel passage in *Metaphysik L_1* (Ak. 28: 294_{10}).

240 [Lehmann note to Ak. 29: 916_{30}] David Fordyce (1711–51), Scottish philosopher, wrote *The Elements of Moral Philosophy* (1754; German translation: 1757). Cf. the *Metaphysik Dohna* (Ak. 28: 688_{1-2}).

241 See note 5 to *Metaphysik Volckmann* (Ak. 28: 445_{34}), below.

242 [Lehmann note to Ak. 29: 918_{31}] Baumgarten (§14; Ak. 17: 27) equates ground <*ratio;* G: *Grund*> with hypothesis <*condicio*>, thus defines hypothesis as that from which it is knowable why something is <*ex quo cognoscibile est, cur aliquid sit*>. – For Kant, see the Doctrine of Method (*CrPR*, A 769–82/B 797–810): "The Discipline of Pure Reason with respect to Hypotheses"; at A 776–7/B 804–5 it is suggested that reason has a "right" with respect to the *practical* use which it does not have in the field of mere speculation. This is the *doctrine of postulates*, although the term was already employed elsewhere (see the "Postulates of Empirical Thought," A 218f/B 265f), and in any event Kant is not at all meaning to draw upon analogies and arguments of probability, e.g., for immortality. Cf. Ak. 29: 914_{34}, above.

243 [Lehmann note to Ak. 29: 919₅] Baumgarten, Sect. 5 ("State after Death" <*status post mortem*>), §§782–91 (Ak. 17: 151–5).

244 [Lehmann note to Ak. 29: 920₅] The substantial vehicle <*vehiculum substantiale*> refers to composite substances, in particular living beings – denoted as "divine machines" in Leibniz's *Monadology* – to whom it gives a special binding, "a new substantiality <*novam substantialitatem*>," as "a principle of the action of a composite <*principium actionis compositi*>." This doctrine, developed in Leibniz's letters to Des Bosses (1712–13), is contested because of its contradiction to the monadology and its theological accommodation.

Metaphysik Volckmann (Ak. 28: 440–450)

1 [Lehmann note to Ak. 28: 440₃₃] Joseph Priestley (1733–1804), English physicist and theologian, discoverer of hydrogen and other gases, is often mentioned by Kant. In the *CrPR* (A 745/B 773) he says of Priestley "the hope of the future life is with him only the expectation of a miracle of being reawakened." Cf. Kant's "Review of Johann Heinrich Schulz" (Ak. 8: 12–13); the note to Ak. 24: 749₁₃₋₁₄ (*Logik Dohna-Wundlacken*) and *Metaphysik K₂* (Ak. 28: 767₂₆₋₈): "Priestley even maintained the immortality of the soul is opposed to the Christian religion, for in the New Testament only the awakening of the body is mentioned."

2 [Lehmann note to Ak. 28: 443₂₇] Kant understands by the inhabitants of Tierra del Fuego (archipelago of Tierra del Fuego) essentially the so-called Pescherae or Ona [a group of people indigenous to the region]. See *Metaphysik K₂* (Ak. 28: 767₆).

3 [Lehmann note to Ak. 28: 443₂₇₋₈] Old designation for Australia. Cf. also the *Reflexionen zur physischen Geographie* (Adickes's notes to Refl. #90–2; Ak. 14: 553).

4 [Lehmann note to Ak. 28: 445₂₁] Cf. *Metaphysik K₂* (Ak. 28: 769₂₋₃): "Whoever assumes a rebirth <*palingenesie*> of evolution, assumes a corpuscle <*corpusculum*>, like Leibniz. . . ." For Leibniz, see especially his *Système nouveau de la nature et de la communication des substances aussi bien que de l'union qu'il y a entre l'âme et le corps* (New System of the Nature and Communication of Substances) (1695), §§4–11 [in *G. W. Leibniz: Philosophical Essays*, tr. by Roger Ariew and Daniel Garber (Indianapolis: Hackett, 1989), pp. 139–42].

5 [Lehmann note to Ak. 28: 445₃₄] Cf. Kant's note in *Religion within the Bounds of Unaided Reason* (Ak. 6: 73₃₈–74₃₂₋₃): "With the *Hindus* human beings are nothing more then spirits (called *devas*) imprisoned in animal bodies as punishment for past crimes." Cf. Helmuth von Glasenapp, *Kant und die Religionen des Ostens* (Kant and the Religions of the East), Beihefte zum Jahrbuch der Albertus-Universität (Köngisberg/Pregel: Kitzingen-Main, 1954), pp. 40–1.

6 [Lehmann note to Ak. 28: 445₃₇] *Burham* is a miswrite of *Burchan*. See note 13 to *Metaphysik K₂* (Ak. 28: 769₃₄).

7 [Lehmann note to Ak. 28: 446₁₈] Cf. Baumgarten, §791 (Ak. 17: 155): "Therefore a human SOUL surviving after the death of the body either enjoys greater happiness than in this life, and is BLESSED, or it is inflicted

with greater misery, and is DAMNED <*Ergo* ANIMA *humana durans post mortem corporis, aut maiori fruetur, quam in hac vita, felicitate, et est* BEATA (G: *eine seliger), aut maiori laborabit infelicitate, et est* DAMNATA (G: *verdammte Seele*)>."

8   See "What Is Orientation in Thinking?" (Ak. 8: 302n; Reiss, 247n): "The Neo-Platonists who called themselves Eclectics because they managed to find their own conceits throughout the works of earlier authors after they had themselves imported them into these. . . ." Cf. *Metaphysik L₂* (Ak. 28: 539–94), below.

Metaphysik L₂ (Ak. 28: 531–594)

1   The following pages (Ak. 28: 531–40) are actually from a set of lecture notes on logic; see the discussion of this manuscript in the Translators' Introduction above.

2   Lehmann refers here to his note to Ak. 28: 367_{35} (*Metaphysik Volckmann*): On this "history" of metaphysics (Ak. 28: 367–80) see the shorter and/or fragmentary essay at Ak. 28: 466–8 (*Metaphysik von Schön*) and Ak. 28: 535–40 (*Metaphysik L₂*). Compare that with the history of philosophy components of the *CrPR*, especially A 852–6/B 880–4, as well as the *What Real Progress Has Metaphysics Made in Germany Since the Time of Leibniz and Wolff?* (Ak. 20: 253–329), and Refl. #4446 (Ak. 17: 553–4). On *verbatim* repetition in the sketches of the history of philosophy, e.g., in the *Jäsche Logik* (Ak. 9: 27–33) and metaphysics, see Max Heinze, *Vorlesungen Kants über Metaphysik aus drei Semestern* (Kant's Lectures on Metaphysics from Three Semesters) (Leipzig: S. Hirzel, 1894), pp. 566–8. – That Kant could, however, arrange the "history of philosophy" also in a wholly different way, see *Logik Blomberg* (Ak. 24: 31–7). Cf. also the *Religionslehre Pölitz* (Ak. 28: 1122–6).

3   [Lehmann note to Ak. 28: 536_{1-2}] Cf. the note to Ak. 24: 325_{4-6} (*Logik Philippi*).

4   Lehmann refers here to his note to Ak. 28: 1275_{18f} (*Danziger Rationaltheologie*): That Kant would have taken the theology of Epicurus seriously is hardly believable; already in the *Universal Natural History and Theory of the Heavens* (Ak. 1: 227_{6-7}) he spoke of his philosophy (and that of Leucippus and Democritus) as a "scholarly doctrine which in the ancient world was the veritable theory of the rejection of God . . ." (see also Kant's notes for this essay at Ak. 23: 12_{2f}). In Refl. #4591 (Ak. 17: 603_{28-9}), he put Epicurus at the apex of atheism: "There is no primal being at all." On the other hand, he was full of sympathy for Epicurus and his sensual system, and he occasionally also touched on its theological representations: cf. Refl. #3705 (Ak. 17: 238_{21f}), Refl. #4554 (Ak. 17: 592_{11f}), as well as *Metaphysik Volckmann* (Ak. 28: $375_{39}–376_{16}$). Also, the formulation of the *Marburger Anthropologie* (ms, pp. 251–2): "Epicurus said: one must appeal to neither the gods nor spirits nor anything else. With that he did not mean to say that he rejected these, but rather that, if one supposed them, one would then take a step over the boundaries of the use of reason." That Kant does not want to judge Epicurus according to Lucretius is indicated by the detailed presentation in the *Logik Philippi* (Ak. 24: 328–9). – See also Christoph Meiners, *Vermischte philosophische Schriften* (Assorted Philosophical Writings) (Leipzig, 1775–6),

vol. 2: *Abhandlung über Epikurs Charakter und dessen Widersprüche in der Lehre von Gott* (Essay on Epicurus's Character and his Contradictions in the Theory of God). Kant's familiarity with Gassendi – who renewed the doctrine of Epicurus in 1647 and 1649 and made an appearance in Descartes *(Meditations)* as well as in Leibniz *(Theodicy)* – cannot be doubted from material grounds, even though Gassendi is not named in Kant's philosophical writings, and is mentioned only in the *Metaphysik Herder* (at Ak. 28: 48$_{10}$ and 71$_6$). [As it turns out, Kant also mentions Gassendi in his early "Further Reflections on Earthquakes" (1756; Ak. 1: 469$_{21}$).]

5 [Lehmann note to Ak. 28: 536$_{23}$] Similarly, *Jäsche Logik* (Ak. 9: 28$_{13-14}$): "*Pherecydes* was supposedly the first author of prose." See also the overview in Refl. #1635 (Ak. 16: 59$_1$).

6 [Lehmann note to Ak. 28: 537$_{10}$] Carneades of Cyrene, founder of the new Academy, belonged to the emissary of philosophers that visited Rome in 156/55 B.C. Cicero often mentioned him. The given passage is *De Oratore* (On Oratory), II, 38, 161. – On Carneades's skepticism, see Ak. 28: 538$_{23-4}$, below, as well as Refl. #1648 (Ak. 16: 65$_{3-5}$): "Carneades made them – the Pyrrhonists – into the new Academy. The academicians <*academici*> did not dispute the reality of our cognition, but rather its general validity."

7 [Lehmann note to Ak. 28: 537$_{13-14}$] Perhaps what is meant here is the well-known passage in Plutarch – *Cato maior* (Cato the Elder), 22 – that Carneades "had the power to convince" the young Romans "of everything easily." But that would not fit the sense of the above principle. Professor Schottlaender (Berlin) proposes going back to Cicero's *Academica*, II (Lucullus), 45 – where to be sure Cato does not appear, but rather *Clitomachus* is cited. The latter professed he was never able to make out rightly with his teacher Carneades what his own opinion was of the matter he was defending. ("Clitomachus used to assert that he was never able to understand what was made plausible by Carneades <*Clitomachus affirmabat numquam se intellegere potuisse, quid Carneadi probaretur*>.") Here the double meaning of *probare* comes into play: (1) to make plausible, (2) to hold as true. Carneades is strongest when he *probat* (makes plausible) something, but what he *probat* (holds to be true) one never knows.

8 [Lehmann note to Ak. 28: 538$_{26}$] Cf. *Jäsche Logik* (Ak. 9: 31$_{1-10}$): "If we begin the epoch of skepticism with Pyrrho, then we get a whole school of skeptics, who ... made it the first maxim for all philosophizing use of reason *to withhold one's judgment even when the semblance of truth is greatest;* and they advanced the principle: *philosophy consists in the equilibrium of judgment and teaches us to uncover false semblance*" (Young translation, pp. 542–3). Cf. also *Logik Blomberg* (Ak. 24: 83$_{17-22}$). – See also the overview of the history of philosophy at Refl. #1635 (Ak. 16: 57$_{14}$, 58$_{11}$), Refl. #1648 (Ak. 16: 64$_{18}$).

9 [Lehmann note to Ak. 28: 538$_{28}$] Cf. *Wiener Logik* (Ak. 24: 803$_{13-14}$).

10 See note 8 to *Metaphysik Volckmann* (Ak. 28: 448$_{23}$), above.

11 [Lehmann note to Ak. 28: 549$_{16-20}$] Cf. Kant's 1763 "Attempt to Introduce the Concept of Negative Magnitudes into Philosophy" (Ak. 2: 202$_{13-18}$): "The first kind of ground I call the logical ground, for the relation of the ground to its consequence can be understood logically. In other words, it can be clearly understood according to the law of identity. The second kind of ground,

however, I call the real ground, for this relation belongs, presumably, to my true concepts, but the manner of its relating can in no wise be judged" (Walford translation, p. 229). On the development of this distinction in the *CrPR* see Heinz Heimsoeth, *Transzendentale Dialektik. Ein Kommentar zu Kants Kritik der reinen Vernunft* (Transcendental Dialectic. A Commentary on Kant's *Critique of Pure Reason*), Teil I–IV (Berlin: de Gruyter, 1966–71), vol. 4, index, p. 839. On p. 732, Heimsoeth also quotes from Kant's 1790 essay against Eberhard ("On a Discovery, according to which any new Critique of Pure Reason is made Dispensable through an Older," Ak. 8: 195_{12-14}): Eberhard had to set up the concept of the ground so "that, although in fact it had a merely logical meaning, it appeared still to contain real grounds (therefore causality) under it."

12   See, e.g., Wolff, *Ontologia*, §§56–78.

13   While proving the principle of sufficient reason is characterized as "the philosopher's cross" here, in *Metaphysik Vigilantius (K_3)* it becomes the concept of freedom (Ak. 29: 1021_{26}).

14   [Lehmann note to Ak. 28: 552_{37}] Cf. here – materially and for dating – Kant's explanations in the letter to Reinhold, May 12, 1789 (Ak. 11: 36_{28f}), which is especially important for the confrontation with the philosophy of the schools (Eberhard): "For in general the entire chapter on *essence, attributes,* etc., simply does not belong in metaphysics (where Baumgarten and several others have put it), but rather merely in logic."

15   [Lehmann note to Ak. 28: 555_{14}] Cf. the note to Ak. 24: 822_{32-4} (*Wiener Logik*), which cites the *Anthropologie Parow* (ms, p. 61): "Lavater's *Views into Eternity* are good to read, but he admits himself that in falling asleep he has noticed the body to be as if separated from the soul, which is already quite a wild fantasy." Cf. also Adickes's notes to Ak. 15: 664_9 (*Entwürfe zu dem Colleg über Anthropologie aus den 70er Jahren*) and Ak. 15: 952_{23} ("On Philosophers' Medicine of the Body"). Johann Kaspar Lavater's *Aussichten in die Ewigkeit* (Views into Eternity) in *Briefen an Dr. Zimmermann* (Letters to Dr. Zimmerman), 4 vols., appeared in 1768.

16   [Lehmann note to Ak. 28: 563_{10-12}] See John Locke, *An Essay Concerning Human Understanding*, 2 vols. (1690), Bk. 2, Ch. 23, §2: "So that if any one will examine himself concerning his notion of pure substance in general, he will find he has no other idea of it at all, but only a supposition of he knows not what *support* of such qualities which are capable of producing simple ideas in us; which qualities are commonly called accidents."

17   [Lehmann note to Ak. 28: 576_{35}] Cf. Refl. #4160 (Ak. 17: 438–9); *Logik Blomberg* (Ak. 24: 300_{19-20}): "Locke, whose book can be seen as a grammar of the understanding," and the note to this; *Metaphysik K_2* (Ak. 28: 775_{29-30}), as well as a fragment of *Metaphysik K_1* as copied by Erdmann (reprinted at Ak. 28: 1521). In connection with Refl. #1574 (Ak. 16: 14): "Healthy reason grounds itself not on logic, but rather this serves it like (arises from it like) grammar, for correction," Adickes refers to Johann Georg Sulzer, *Kurzer Begriff aller Wissenschaften und andern Theile der Gelehrsamkeit* ... (Short Conception of all Sciences and other Parts of Learnedness), 2nd edition (1759), p. 147: "Logic is with respect to philosophy approximately that which grammar is to language."

18 [Lehmann note to Ak. 28: 577$_{12}$.] Cf. here the more detailed confrontation with Plato in *CrPR* (A 313f/B 370f). See Heinz Heimsoeth, *Transzendentale Dialektik. Ein Kommentar zu Kants Kritik der reinen Vernunft* (Transcendental Dialectic. A Commentary on Kant's *Critique of Pure Reason*), Teil I–IV (Berlin: de Gruyter, 1966–71), vol. 4, Index, p. 832, as well as *Metaphysik Dohna* (Ak. 28: 618–19) and the corresponding explanations in the Rational Theology. [On the latter, see *Lectures on Philosophical Theology*, p. 94.]

19 Cf. Baumgarten, §379 (Ak. 17: 107).

20 These notes stop far short of the end of the Cosmology section in Baumgarten, as well as of the Cosmology sections in the other sets of notes.

21 [Lehmann note to Ak. 28: 588$_{22-3}$] Erasmus, *Diatribe de libero arbitrio* (Discourse on Free Will) appeared in Basel in 1524; Luther, *De servo arbitrio* (Bondage of the Will) (Wittenberg, 1525) appeared in a German translation in 1528 by J. Jonas.

22 See note 8 to *Metaphysik Volckmann* (Ak. 28: 448$_{23}$), above.

Metaphysik Dohna (Ak. 28: 656–690)

1 This number refers apparently to the class session (classes for this set of lectures met from 7 to 8 A.M. each Monday, Tuesday, Thursday, and Friday during the winter semester of 1792/93, beginning October 15 and ending March 15); this and other numbers in this series all appear to be added to the ms later, being written in the margin. The blank lines separating these sections are added by Lehmann, as are the corresponding paragraph breaks.

2 Lehmann refers here to his note to Ak. 28: 729$_{37f}$ (*Metaphysik K$_2$*): See, above all, *CrPR* (A 229–30/B 282): "These four propositions (in the world there is no gap, there is no leap, there is no chance, there is no fate <*in mundo non datur hiatus, non datur saltus, non datur casus, non datur fatum*>) . . . they are all unified solely in this, to admit nothing in empirical synthesis that could disrupt the understanding and the continuous connection of all appearances." – Max Heinze, *Vorlesungen Kants über Metaphysik aus drei Semestern* (Kant's Lectures on Metaphysics from Three Semesters) (Leipzig: S. Hirzel, 1894), p. 619n, refers to *Metaphysik L$_1$* (Ak. 28: 199), to Baumgarten (§§380–91; Ak. 17: 107–9), to eleven Reflections collected by Erdmann: #5377 (Ak. 18: 166), #5610 (Ak. 18: 251–2), #5954, 5955 (Ak. 18: 398), #5957, 5959 (Ak. 18: 399), #5970 (Ak. 19: 408–9), #5973 (Ak. 18: 410–11), #5975 (Ak. 18: 411–12), #5979 (Ak. 18: 413–14), #6423 (Ak. 18: 711), and to a passage from Emil Arnoldt, *Gesammelte Schriften*, ed. by Otto Schöndörffer, 11 vols. (Berlin: B. Cassirer, 1906–11), vol. 5 ("Kritische Exkurse im Gebiete der Kantforschung," 1909), pp. 122–3.

3 Cf. Baumgarten, §§406–16 (Ak. 17: 112–13).

4 Cf. Baumgarten, §§408 (Ak. 17: 112): "There is in this world a universal reciprocal influence of monads on each other and a universal conflict among them."

5 [Lehmann note to Ak. 28: 664$_{15}$] On oxygen and hydrogen, see Refl. #71–3 (Ak. 14: 502–16). Cf. also note 5 to *Metaphysik L$_1$* (Ak. 28: 209$_{20}$).

6 [Lehmann note to Ak. 28: 666$_{17-20}$] Cf. here Refl. #6006 (Ak. 18: 421),

dated by Adickes to the period 1785–8, in which Kant makes an effort to clarify the presuppositions of Leibniz's preestablished harmony.

7 [Lehmann note to Ak. 28: 666$_{20}$] Cf. Baumgarten, §448 (Ak. 17: 119–20). Cf. also Ak. 28: 732$_{13-14}$ (*Metaphysik K$_2$*).

8 [Lehmann note to Ak. 28: 667$_{2-3}$] Cf. Ak. 28: 732$_{37f}$ (*Metaphysik K$_2$*). Here, as also with the following discussions of miracles, there appears to exist a complete doctrinal agreement between the *Metaphysik Dohna* and the *Metaphysik K$_2$*.

9 [Lehmann note to Ak. 28: 669$_3$] Cf. Ak. 28: 733$_{31}$ (*Metaphysik K$_2$*).

10 Baumgarten, §504 (Ak. 15: 5): "If there is anything in a being which can be conscious of something, that is a SOUL <*Si quid in ente est, quod sibi alicuius potest esse conscium, illud est ANIMA*>" and §506 (Ak. 15: 6): "Thoughts are representations. Thus my soul is a power of representation <*Cogitationes sunt repraesentationes. Ergo anima mea est vis repraesentativa*>.*"

11 See *Metaphysik Dohna* (Ak. 28: 638$_{34}$): "Spinoza's system derives from a false definition of substance: that whose existence (concept) requires no other thing." Cf. the discussion of soul, representation, and substance at 671$_{21}$, above. Wolff defines the souls as a power of representation in §66 of his *Psychologia rationalis, methodo scientifica pertractata, qua ea, quae de anima humana indubia experientiae fide innotescunt, per essentiam et naturam animae explicantur* (Rational Psychology treated scientifically, in which those things about the human soul which become known with the undoubting confidence of experience are explained by means of the essence and nature of the souls, and are set forth for the more intimate knowledge of nature and of its creator) (Frankfurt and Leipzig, 1740) (in *Gesammelte Werke* (Collected Works) (Hildesheim, 1972), II.6). He defends the doctrine that the soul has one power (representation) underlying all its different faculties, in §§745–6 of his *Vernünfftige Gedancken von Gott, der Welt und der Seele des Menschen, auch allen Dingen überhaupt* (Rational Thought about God, the World and the Human Soul, and on all Things in General) ["German Metaphysics"], 1st edition (Halle, 1719) in *Gesammelte Werke* (Collected Works), I.2 (Hildesheim, 1962) and §265 of *Anmerkungen zur Deutschen Metaphysik* (Remarks on the German Metaphysics) in *Gesammelte Werke* (Collected Works) (Hildesheim, 1962), I.3. A detailed synopsis of Wolff's system is provided in J. N. Findlay, *Kant and the Transcendental Object* (Oxford: Clarendon Press, 1981), pp. 38–57.

12 [Lehmann note to Ak. 28: 679$_8$] This could refer to the disputation of J. H. Dietz, *Commercium mentis et corporis* (Interaction between the mind and body) (Giessen, 1724). Contents given in G. Fabian, *Beitrag zur Geschichte des Leib-Seele-Problem* (Contribution to the History of the Body-Soul Problem) (Langensalza, 1925), pp. 176f. The work of Dietz was not available. [See also the parallel passage in *Metaphysik K$_2$*, as paraphrased by Heinze (Ak. 28: 749$_{36-7}$): "Gaubius wrote a useful work: *On the Direction of the Mind, which is the Task of Physicians <de regimine mentis, quod medicorum est>*." The letter in the ms is likely a *D*, as Lehmann has it, and is clearly not a *G*; but the parallel suggests the possibility of a miswrite.]

13 [Lehmann note to Ak. 28: 680$_{26}$] Berkeley, *Principles of Human Knowledge* (1710), Pt. 1, §18: "Hence it is evident the supposition of external bodies is not necessary for the producing [*sic*] our ideas." Cf. Kant's judgment of Berkeley

in the *Prolegomena* (Ak. 4: 293$_{18-20}$) and *CrPR* (B 71): "So one cannot blame the good *Berkeley* if he degraded bodies to mere illusion," as well as (B 274): "*Berkeley*, who explains space along with all things . . . as something which is impossible in itself, and therefore also the things in space as mere imagining . . ." See notes 4 and 5 to *Metaphysik Herder* (Ak. 28: 42$_{22-5}$), above.

14 [Lehmann note to Ak. 28: 683$_9$] Cf. *Religion within the Bounds of Unaided Reason* (Ak. 6: 49$_{27}$): "Though Phalaris himself should command you to be false and should bring up his bull and dictate perjuries <*Phalaris licet imperet, ut sis falsus, et admoto dictet periuria tauro*>" (Juvenal, *Satirae* (Satires), Bk, 8, l. 81–2) and Georg Wobbermin's note to this (Ak. 6: 502).

15 [Lehmann note to Ak. 28: 683$_{24}$] Intended is presumably Ch. 27 of the second book of John Locke's *An Essay Concerning Human Understanding*, 2 vols. (1690): "Of Identity and Diversity," to which Kant also refers elsewhere (cf. *Metaphysik Herder*, Ak. 28: 71$_{34-6}$).

16 [Lehmann note to Ak. 28: 684$_4$] Potash is calcium carbonate (K_2CO_3) and is obtained from glowing ashes (from wood, coal, etc.) that contain calcium. Therefore it is called ash salt <G: *Aschensalz*>. Since oxygen is added, this naturally does not concern an *educt* (Ak. 28: 684$_{20}$), in the sense of evolution – this could hold only from the standpoint of the then-current phlogiston theory.

17 [Lehmann note to Ak. 28: 686$_1$] Descartes posits the pineal gland as the seat of the soul for various reasons, above all because it is unpaired. Cf. *Passions de l'âme* (Passions of the Soul) (Amsterdam: Louis Elzevir, 1649), Articles 32 and 34f.

18 [Lehmann note to Ak. 28: 687$_{6-7}$] Cf. *Metaphysical First Principles of Natural Science* (Ak. 4: 544$_{25-6}$): "The opposite of the former [i.e., the law of inertia] and therefore also the death of all natural philosophy, would be hylozoism." Cf. also *Critique of Judgment* (Ak. 5: 392$_{10}$).

19 [Lehmann note to Ak. 28: 689$_{9-10}$] Cf. Ak. 28: 298$_{37f}$ (*Metaphysik L$_1$*) and Ak. 28: 593$_{34}$ (*Metaphysik L$_2$*).

20 Lehmann refers to the *Metaphysik K$_2$* (Ak. 28: 770$_{3-4}$) and to his note to Ak. 28: 891$_1$ (*Nachträge Herder*).

Metaphysik K$_2$ (Ak. 28: 753–75)

1 [Lehmann note to Ak. 28: 753$_{29}$] See Johann Heinrich Zedler, *Grosses vollständiges Universal Lexicon* (Large and Complete Universal Encyclopedia), 64 vols. (Halle and Leipzig: 1732–50), vol. 8, column 1567: "Jo. Andr. Agricol, in his first Attempt at Universal Propagation, called the land crab that harmful insect which is called *Werre* (mole-warp) in Lausitz, Curland, and other locations. . . ." He then refers to *Reitwurm* (mole-cricket); both designations still apply today for the mole-cricket (*Gryllotalpa vulgaris*).

2 [Lehmann note to Ak. 28: 754$_{21}$] Baumgarten, §742 (Ak. 17: 141): "Thinking matter is impossible in the world <*materia cogitans est in mundo impossibilis*>."

3 This is not a quote, but rather a summing up of Baumgarten, §§755–7 (Ak. 17: 144).

4 [Lehmann note to Ak. 28: 756$_4$] Samuel Thomas Sömmering, *Über das*

Organ der Seele. Mit Kupfern (On the Organ of the Soul, with Illustrations) (Königsberg: Friedrich Nicolovius, 1796), p. 31, refers to Charles Bonnet, *Oeuvres d'histoire naturelle et de philosophie de Charles Bonnet* (Works on Natural History and Philosophy by Charles Bonnet) (Neuchâtel: S. Fauche, 1779–83), vol. 5, p. 2, noting on p. 33: "For, notwithstanding that Descartes considered the pineal gland <*glandula pinealis;* G: *Zirbel*> for that [i.e., the seat of the soul]; . . . Bonnet, the corpus callosum <*corpus callosum;* G: *Balkan*> . . . ; the great distance of these given places from one another, and the striking differences of these places themselves, already betrayed that no anatomical certainty could take place here. . . ."

5 [Lehmann note to Ak. 28: 756₆] Cf. here Kant's contribution to Sömmering, "On the Organ of the Soul" (Ak. 12: 31–5).

6 [Lehmann note to Ak. 28: 759₃₋₄] Baumgarten, §211 (Ak. 17: 71): "A substance acting on a substance outside of itself INFLUENCES IT, therefore INFLUENCE (transeunt action) is the action of a substance on a substance outside of itself <*substantia in substantiam extra se agens in eam INFLUIT, adeo INFLUXUS (actio transiens) est actio substantiae in substantiam extra se . . .* >," and §212 (Ak. 17: 71): "If the passivity of that substance which another influences is at the same time the action of the one who is being acted upon, the PASSIVITY and INFLUENCE are said to be IDEAL. If, however, the passivity is not the action of the one being acted upon, the PASSIVITY and INFLUENCE are said to be REAL <*si passio illius substantiae, in quam altera influit, simul est ipsius patientis actio, PASSIO et INFLUXUS dicuntur IDEALES. Si vero passio non est patientis actio, PASSIO et INFLUXUS dicuntur REALES*>." Cf. *Metaphysik Dohna* (Ak. 28: 684₃₆f), above.

7 [Lehmann note to Ak. 28: 762₁₇₋₂₁] Friedrich Blumenbach (1752–1840), a natural scientist in Göttingen, whose writing *Über den Bildungstrieb* (On the Formative Drive) (1789) Kant praised in the *Critique of Judgment* (Ak. 5: 424₂₂ and the note to this), polemicized in the *Handbuch der Naturgeschichte* (Handbook of Natural History) (Göttingen, 1780) and in his *Beiträgen zur Naturgeschichte* (Contributions to Natural History) (1790) against the "prized metaphor of the gradation of creatures: all the beloved images of a chain, ladder, net, etc., in nature indeed have their unmistakeable use for methodology," but now to put them into the plan of creation, "and to want to seek the perfection and connection of this [creation] in that, that nature . . . makes no leaps, because with respect to their outer form, creatures follow one another in such fine steps – this would already be in itself an arrogant weakness, even if it were not, which indeed is the case, refuted upon serious examination" (*Handbuch der Naturgeschichte*, 10th ed. (Göttingen, 1821), pp. 8f). Kant refers to Blumenbach's *Handbuch* also in the *Opus postumum* (Ak. 21: 180₂₇, and see Lehmann's note to this at Ak. 22: 804–5). Cf. further *The Conflict of the Faculties* (Ak. 7: 89f).

8 Cf. *CrPR* (B 413f) and Moses Mendelssohn, *Phädon oder über die Unsterblichkeit der Seele* (Phaedo; or, On the Immortality of the Soul) (1767) in his *Gesammelte Schriften* (Collected Writings) (1843), p. 131f.

9 Lehmann suggests in his note to Ak. 28: 688₁f (*Metaphysik Dohna*) that Maupertuis may be intended here, but that this cannot be confirmed.

10 See note 3 to *Metaphysik Volckmann* (Ak. 28: 443₂₇).

11 [Lehmann note to Ak. 28: 768₂₈] Swedenborg's *Arcana coelestia, quae in scriptura sacra seu verbo domini sunt, detecta* (Heavenly sacred mysteries, which are in sacred scripture or in the word of the Lord, uncovered) appeared in eight volumes (London, 1749–56). [. . .] It is this great work of which Kant says in *Dreams of a Spirit-Seer* (1766) that it contains "eight quarto volumes full of nonsense" (Ak. 2: 360₁₄₋₁₅), and of which he confesses to have not only bought, but "which is much worse, to have read" (Ak. 2: 318₂₁). Cf. the note to Ak. 2: 360₁₅ (*Dreams of a Spirit-Seer*) and Herder's anonymous review of Kant's book in the *Königsbergschen Gelehrten und Politischen Zeitungen* (Königsberg Intellectual and Political Newspaper) (1766; reprinted in *Herders Sämmtliche Werke* (Herder's Collected Works) edited by Bernard Suphan, vol. 1, pp. 125–30). See also *Metaphysik Herder* (Ak. 28: 122₉ᵣ, 113₃₅) and *Metaphysik* L₁ (Ak. 28: 298₃₇ᵣ). As a summary, see E. Meyer, "Kant und der Occultismus" (Kant and the Occult) in *Immanuel Kant, Festschrift zur zweiten Jahrhundertfeier seines Geburtstages* (Immanuel Kant, Festschrift Celebrating the Second Centenary of his Birth) published by the Albertus-Universität Königsberg in Preussen (Leipzig, 1924), pp. 115–28.

12 [Lehmann note to Ak. 28: 769₅₋₆] The passage reads in Max Heinze, *Vorlesungen Kants über Metaphysik aus drei Semestern* (Kant's Lectures on Metaphysics from Three Semesters) (Leipzig: S. Hirzel, 1894), p. 692: "The Jews say that everything in the body passes away, except for a small bone in the brain *Lutz* <G: *Knöchelchen im Gehirn Lutz*> – ." Since the text appeared corrupt, the word *Lutz* was replaced (by Lehmann) with *nicht* (not). Nevertheless Ms. Quadt succeeded in finding *Knöchelchen Lutz* in the *Jewish Encyclopedia* (New York and London, 1901), vol. 8. There we find under *Luz:* "Aramaic name for the os coccyx, the 'nut' of the spinal column. The belief was that, being undestructible, it will form the nucleus for the resurrection of the body. The Talmud narrates that the emperor Hadrian, when told by R. Joshua that the revival of the body at the resurrection will take its start with the 'almond' or the 'nut' of the spinal column, had investigations made and found that water could not soften, nor the pestle and mortar crush it (*Leviticus*, R. XVIII, *Ecclesiastes*, R. XII). The legend of the 'resurrection bone,' connected with Psalm XXXIV 21 (A. V. 20: 'one of those bones will not be broken <*unum ex illis ossibus non confringetur*>') and identified with the horse's tailbone <*cauda equina*> . . . was accepted as an axiomatic truth by the Christian and Mohammedan theologians and anatomists, and in the Middle Ages the bone received the name 'little bone of the Jews <G: *Juden Knöchlein*>.' " – Since the coccyx does not lie in the brain, the passage still remains corrupt.

13 [Lehmann note to Ak. 28: 769₃₄] *Burchan* is the Tibetan designation for Buddha. Cf. Helmuth von Glasenapp, *Kant und die Religionen des Ostens* (Kant and the Religions of the East), Beihefte zum Jahrbuch der Albertus-Universität (Königsberg/Pregel: Kitzingen-Main, 1954), pp. 59 and 76f. – In the *Physischen Geographie Dohna* (ms, p. 215) we read: "The Dalai Lama is the living Foë. It is maintained that this Foë is supposed to have come down from heaven with the name Buddha. . . . His spirit later entered into a child. . . . They call that the lamaistic rebirth. – The migration of the soul is the purgatory of the Tibetans. If, according to their opinion, the soul finally

enters again into a human being, then he is called Burchan, object of worship." – On Foë, see also the notes to Ak. 28: 897_3 (*Metaphysik Herder*) and Ak. 28: 1252_{16-18} (*Danziger Rationaltheologie*), as well as Leibniz's introductions on the "quietism of the Foë, originator of a large sect in China" (*Essais de théodicée sur la bonté de Dieu, la liberté de l'homme et l'origine du mal* (Theodicy: Essays on the Goodness of God, the Freedom of Man, and the Origin of Evil) (Amsterdam, 1710), §10).

14 [Lehmann note to Ak. 28: 770_{3-4}] Max Heinze, *Vorlesungen Kants über Metaphysik aus drei Semestern* (Kant's Lectures on Metaphysics from Three Semesters) (Leipzig: S. Hirzel, 1894) prints *Panochita* and remarks, "The notetaker did not hear correctly; it should read *psychopannychita.*" See Baumgarten, §782 (Ak. 17: 151–2): here the *hypnopsychita* are the "defenders of the sleep of the soul," *psychopannychita,* the (defenders) "of the eternal night." Cf. the note to Ak. 28: 891_1 (*Metaphysik Herder*).

Metaphysik Vigilantius (K₃) (Ak. 29: 943–1040)

1 [Lehmann note to Ak. 29: 946_{14}] Cf. *Danziger Physik* (Ak. 29: 97_{30-3}): "In recent times, chemistry has raised itself to the greatest perfection; it also deserves with every right a claim on the entire doctrine of nature: for only the fewest appearances of nature can be explained mathematically." On this see Ak. 29: 98, and Lehmann's note to Ak. 29: 98_{15-18}, which mentions J. Christian Erxleben's *Anfangsgründe der Naturlehre* (Foundations of the Doctrine of Nature) (1771), which was Kant's physics compendium along with W. J. G. Karsten's *Anleitung zur gemeinnützlichen Kenntniss der Nature* (Introduction into the Practical Knowledge of Nature) (Halle, 1783), and Johann Peter Eberhard, *Erste Gründe der Naturlehre* (First Principles of the Doctrine of Nature) (Halle, 1753). – Cf. Lehmann's "Introduction" (Ak. 29: 655); Heinz Heimsoeth, *Studien zur Philosophie Immanuel Kants* (Studies on Immanuel Kant's Philosophy) (Bonn, 1970; Kant-Studien Ergänzungsheft #100), vol. 2: *Methodenbegriffe der Erfahrungswissenschaften und Gegensätzlichkeiten spekulativer Weltkonzeption* (Methodological Concepts of the Empirical Sciences and Contradictions in the Speculative Conception of the World), Ch. 4: "Chemie" (Chemistry) (pp. 58–66).

2 [Lehmann note to Ak. 29: 946_{23}] Cf. note 3 to *Metaphysik Mrongovius* (Ak. 29: 749_{33}), above.

3 [Lehmann note to Ak. 29: 947_{33}] Diogenes Laertius, *De vitis philosophorum* (Lives of Eminent Philosophers), Bk. 8, p. 8.

4 Lehmann refers here to the *Danziger Physik* (Ak. 29: 97f) and the note to Ak. 29: 98_{15-18}.

5 Lehmann refers here to the *Critique of Practical Reason* (Ak. 5: 112–13) and the *Moral Mrongovius II* (Ak. 29: 600_{1-3}): "The greatest worth of one's state is happiness. Thus virtue connected with happiness is the highest good. Virtue is the condition under which I am worthy of happiness: but that is not yet the highest good."

6 Lehmann refers here to *CrPR* (A 841/B 869) and to the *Jäsche Logik* (Ak. 9: 13).

7 [Lehmann note to Ak. 29: 951_{15}] On Kant's judgment of Epicurus, see the

note to Ak. 29: 9_{20} (*Philosophische Enzyklopädie*) and the note to Ak. 29: 107_{27-8} (*Danziger Physik*), and also *Metaphysik L₁* (Ak. 28: 176; Heinze excerpt): "he believed that we have no certainty of things themselves, but rather that only such knowledge of them is in us as accords with the impressions that they make on our senses . . . ," as well as the not very friendly Refl. #5637 (Ak. 18: 274_{16-18}): "For nature is our task, the text of our interpretation. Who knows what Epicurus thought of that, and also what his gibberish explanations of nature are supposed to be." [See also note 4 to *Metaphysik L₂* (Ak. 28: 536_{6-8}).]

8   [Lehmann note to Ak. 29: 952_{28}] See here the *Naturrecht Feyerabend* (1784) (Ak. 27: 1343_{12-15}): "The manner of acquiring a thing belonging to someone else is derivative; [the manner of acquiring] a thing which belongs to nobody, original <*Modus acquirendi rem alienam est derivativus, rem nullius, originaria*>. I acquire by derivation <*derivatione*> when I derive my right from another right."

9   For a fuller mention of this principle, cf. Ak. 29: 950_{1-2}, above.

10   [Lehmann note to Ak. 29: 960_{27}] Baumgarten, Sect. 1 ("The Possible" <*Possibile*>), §7 (Ak. 17: 24): "The A and not-A is the negative *nothing* . . . not representable . . . involving a contradiction. . . . *This proposition* is called *the principle of contradiction,* and is *the absolutely first principle* <*Nihil negativum, irrepraesentabile . . . contradictionem involvens . . . est A et non A. . . . Haec propositio dicitur principium contradictionis, et absolute primum*>." Contrary to this, Christian Wolff (*Ontologia*, §§28–9) immediately adds "at the same time" <*simul*>. See *Metaphysik Dohna* (Ak. 28: 623_{19-20}): "the formula it is impossible that something at the same time be and not be <*impossibile est aliquid simul esse ac non esse*> is not good."

11   [Lehmann note to Ak. 29: 960_{28}] Baumgarten, §9 (Ak. 17: 24): "whatever is and is not, is nothing. A + non-A = 0 <*quicquid est et non est, nihil est. A + non-A = o*>."

12   Lehmann refers here to *CrPR* (A 290/B 347f).

13   [Lehmann note to Ak. 29: 964_{23}] Baumgarten, §11 (Ak. 17: 25): "Every possible A is A; or, *whatever is, is that;* or, every subject is its own predicate. If you deny this, some possible A if not-A; hence, both A and not-A, or nothing, which is impossible <*Omne possibile A est A, seu, quicquid est, illud est, seu, omne subiectum est praedicatum sui. Si negas: quoddam possibile A est non-A, hinc A et non A, seu nihil, quod impossibile*>."

14   Cf. note 10 (to Ak. 29: 960_{27}).

15   [Lehmann note to Ak. 29: 971_{27-34}]Printed at Ak. 28: 824_{25-32} (*Metaphysik Vigilantius* (*K₃*), Arnoldt selections).

16   Lehmann refers here to *CrPR* (A 318f/B 375f), *Philosophische Enzyklopädie* (Ak. 29: 39), and *Metaphysik Herder* (Ak. 28: 848f).

17   [Lehmann note to Ak. 29: 976_{25}] Christian Wolff, *Ontologia*, §589: "Space is the order of simultaneous things, that is to say, insofar as they coexist <*Spatium est ordo simultaneorum, quatenus scilicet coexistunt*>"; §572: "Time . . . is the order of successive things in a continuous series <*Tempus . . . est ordo successivorum in serie continua*>." Cf. Baumgarten, §239 (Ak. 17: 79): "The order of simultaneous things posited outside of each other is SPACE, the [order] of successive things is TIME <*Ordo simultaneorum extra se invicem positorum est SPATIUM* (G: *Raum*), *successivorum TEMPUS* (G: *Zeit*)>."

18 [Lehmann note to Ak. 29: 977₁] In the "Note to the Amphiboly of the Concepts of Reflection" it reads, "Thus Leibniz thought of space as a certain order in the community of substances, . . . But [its character] proper and independent of things . . . he ascribed to the confusion" of this concept (*CrPR*, A 275f/B 331f). Cf. Baumgarten, §510 (Ak. 15: 6): "Certain things I think distinctly, certain things confusedly. He who thinks something confusedly does not distinguish its marks, yet he represents or perceives them. . . . Therefore he who is thinking something confusedly represents certain things obscurely *<Quaedam distincte, quaedam confuse cogito. Confuse aliquid cogitans eius notas non distinguit, repraesentat tamen, seu percipit. . . . Ergo confuse quid cogitans quaedam obscure repraesentat>.*"

19 [Lehmann note to Ak. 29: 977₃₇] For Baumgarten (§855; Ak. 17: 166), "THEOLOGICAL SPINOZISM is the belief denying that God is an extramundane being, and it is error *<SPINOZISMUS THEOLOGICUS est sententia tollens deum ens extramundanum, et error est>*," to which Kant remarks (Refl. #3639; Ak. 17: 166): "Because things subsist through God, it appears as though they subsist in him. There is not a world-soul *<Non est anima mundi>.*" Cf. the notes to Ak. 28: 511₄₋₅ (*Metaphysik von Schön*), Ak. 28: 1193₂₀f (*Natürliche Theologie Volckmann*), and Ak. 28: 1297₃₃ (*Danziger Rationaltheologie*).

20 Lehmann cites the following passage from Newton: "Although each particle of space may always be, and every indivisible moment of duration may be everywhere *<Cum unaquaeque spatii particula sit semper, et unumquodque durationis indivisibile momentum ubique>* . . . ,*" Philosophiae Naturalis Principia Mathematica* (Mathematical Principles of Natural Philosophy) (London, 1687), vol. 3, p. 172.

21 [Lehmann note to Ak. 29: 982₁₀] See note 17 (to Ak. 29: 976₁₂).

22 Lehmann refers here to *CrPR* (A 69/B 93) and *Philosophische Enzyklopädie* (Ak. 29: 36₂₁₋₂).

23 [Lehmann note to Ak. 29: 989₁₈] Baumgarten, Sect. 4 ("Unity" *<unum>*), §74 (Ak. 17: 43): "One A and one B and others, partly the same, partly different, are MANY. Whatever we might think, either there are many things, or there are not many things. The prior determination is MULTITUDE (plurality), the latter is CATEGORIAL UNITY *<A unum et B unum e.c. partim eadem, partim diversa sunt MULTA* (G: *Viele*). *Quicquid cogitemus, aut sunt multa aut non multa. Prior determinatio est MULTITUDO (pluralitas)* (G: *die Vielheit, Mehrheit*), *posterior UNITAS CATEGORICA* (G: *die Einheit*)>." See also Refl. #3543 (Ak. 17: 43).

24 [Lehmann note to Ak. 29: 989₃₆] Baumgarten, Sect. 4 ("Unity" *<unum>*), Sect. 6 ("Truth" *<verum>*), Sect. 7 ("Perfection" *<perfectum>*).

25 [Lehmann note to Ak. 29: 990₃₁] Cf. note 23 (to Ak. 29: 989₁₈), above.

26 [Lehmann note to Ak. 29: 991₃₂] On the enumeration by Baumgarten (§40; Ak. 17: 36), see Christian Wolff, *Ontologia*, §243: "Whatever is, or is thought to be able to be, is called a thing, insofar as it is something. . . . For this reason, both reality and quiddity are synonyms among the Scholastics *<Quicquid est vel esse posse concipitur, dicitur Res, quatenus est aliquid. . . . Unde et realitas et quidditas apud scholasticos synonyma sunt>.*"

27 [Lehmann note to Ak. 29: 992₁₉] Baumgarten, Sect. 3, §69 (Ak. 17: 41): "Internal differences can be represented in a being regarded in itself; hence

they can in some way be comprehended or BE GIVEN (is given). Either we are able also to conceive and understand what is given (without its co-presence) without assuming another thing, without a relation to another thing – that is we are able TO COMPREHEND it distinctly – or we are not able to. In the first case, what is given are QUALITIES; in the second case, what is given are QUANTITIES (magnitudes) <*Discrimina interna possunt repraesentari in ente in se spectato, hinc quomodocumque cognosci, seu DARI* (G: *angegeben werden*). *Data vel possumus etiam (sine compraesentia) sine assumpto alio, sine relatione ad aliud,* CONCIPERE (G: *begreifen und verstehn*) *et intelligere, i.e. distincte cognoscere, vel non possumus. Illa sunt* QUALITATES (G: *Beschaffenheiten*), *haec* QUANTITATES (G: *Grössen*)>." Cf. Christian Wolff, *Ontologia*, §348 (the definition for quantities <*Quantitates definitio*> quoted in Ak. 29: 995$_{14}$, below) and §452 (here Wolff defines quality as "every intrinsic determination of a thing, which is able to be understood without first assuming another <*omnis determinatio rei intrinseca, quae sine alio assumto intelligi potest*>").

28   [Lehmann note to Ak. 29: 993$_{11}$] Cf. note to Ak. 29: 989$_{18f}$ above. Cf. Christian Wolff, *Mathematisches Lexicon* (Mathematical Lexicon) (Leipzig, 1716) in *Gesammelte Werke* (Collected Works) (Hildesheim: Georg Olms, 1965), vol. I.11, columns 938–67 (in general), columns 944f: "Number <*Numerus;* G: *eine Zahl*> is called in agreement with Euclid a quantity of unities: that is, one says, a number arises if one takes together many things of the same kind, as, e.g., stone balls. But Euclid explained only the whole rational numbers, . . ." See also the overview in *Mathematik Herder* (Ak. 29: 49–50).

29   [Lehmann note to Ak. 29: 994$_1$] Baumgarten, §291 (Ak. 17: 90): "If by means of some quantity used as a unit we understand another commensurable or similar quantity, we MEASURE this MEASURED [quantity] by THE MEASURE, and this action itself is called MEASURING <*Si ex quantitate pro una assumpta aliam homogeneam, seu similem, intelligimus, hanc* MENSURATAM (G: *das gemessene*) *ex illa* MENSURA (G: *das Maass*) METIMUR (G: *messen*) *et ipsa haec actio dicitur* DIMENSIO (G: *Ausmessung*)>." – Wolff's definition (*Ontologia*, §438): "If we take some magnitude as a unit and determine the ratio of another magnitude to it, we are said to measure the latter [magnitude]. But the magnitude that we use as the unit is called the measure and the other magnitude, whose ratio to the measure is under investigation, is called the thing measured <*Si magnitudinem aliquam pro unitate assumimus et alterius ad eam rationem determinamus, eam metiri dicimur. Vocatur autem magnitudo, quae pro unitate assumitur, mensura et magnitudo altera, cujus ad mensuram ratio investigatur, mensuratum*>." – On this, see Christian Wolff, *Mathematisches Lexicon* (Mathematical Lexicon) (Leipzig, 1716) in *Gesammelte Werke* (Collected Works) (Hildesheim: Georg Olms, 1965), vol. I.11, columns 881–4.

30   [Lehmann note to Ak. 29: 995$_{14}$] Baumgarten, §159 (Ak. 17: 59): "A multitude of parts is (absolute) MAGNITUDE or continuous quantity. A multitude of wholes is (absolute) NUMBER or discrete quantity. If the wholes that constitute a number are in turn regarded as parts, the NUMBER is a FRACTION (a fraction, a particle); if not, the NUMBER is an INTEGER <*Multitudo partium est* MAGNITUDO (G: *die Grösse des Ganzen*) *(absoluta) seu quantitas continua. Multitudo totorum est* NUMERUS (G: *eine Zahl*) *(absolutus) seu quantitas discreta.*

Si tota, quorum est numerus, iterum spectentur, ut partes, NUMERUS est FRACTUS (G: *ein Bruch*) *(fractio, minutia), sin minus, NUMERUS est INTEGER* (G: *eine ganze Zahl*)>." See also Refl. #3566 (Ak. 17: 59–60). Christian Wolff, *Ontologia*, §348: "Quantity in general can be defined as the internal difference of like things, that is, that by which similar things can be intrinsically distinguished, their similarity being preserved <*Quantitas in genere definiri potest, quod sit discrimen internum similium, hoc est, illud, quo similia salva similitudine intrinse differre possunt*>."

31 [Lehmann note to Ak. 29: 996₁₁] Baumgarten, §159 (Ak. 17: 59). See also *Metaphysik Volckmann* (Ak. 28: 423₁₈₋₂₂): "We can also consider a continuum <*continuum*> as discrete <*discretum*>, if we view it first as unity and then also as multitude, e.g., I can consider minutes as units of the hour, but also again as a multitude itself containing units, namely sixty seconds. . . ."

32 Lehmann explains that these are jewelry weights, like carats (144 carats = one ounce).

33 [Lehmann note to Ak. 29: 997₁₅] Baumgarten, §161 (Ak. 17: 60): "A greater magnitude is A COMPARATIVE MAGNITUDE, a lesser is SMALLNESS <*Magnitudo maior est MAGNITUDO COMPARATIVA* (G: *eine Grösse des Ganzen und Zahl, auch in der Vergleichung*), *minor, PARVITAS* (G: *Kleinigkeit*)>." Christian Wolff, *Ontologia*, §432: "A small quantity is great, relatively speaking, when it is compared to another commensurable quantity and found to be greater than it; but it is truly small when it is compared to another commensurable quantity and found to be less than it <*Parvum, consequenter magnum est, quod ad aliud homogeneum relatum eodem majus deprehenditur; parvum vero est, quod ad aliud homogeneum relatum eodem minus deprehenditur*>." Cf. *Metaphysik von Schön* (Ak. 28: 505–6).

34 See notes 27 (to Ak. 29: 992₁₉) and 30 (to Ak. 29: 995₁₄), above.

35 [Lehmann note to Ak. 29: 998₁₈] Baumgarten, §248 (Ak. 17: 81): what has boundaries is finite <*finitum*> or limited <*limitatum*>, what has no boundary is infinite <*infinitum*> or unlimited <*illimitatum*>, thus the mathematical finite and imaginary infinite <*infinitum imaginarium*>. – Cf. *Metaphysik Volckmann* (Ak. 28: 439₁₀₋₂₃): "All negations are limitations, if we think all reality belonging to a thing, then that is an unlimited thing <*ens illimitatum*>. . . . A quantum which in comparison with its measure as a unity is larger than all number, is called mathematically infinite."

36 [Lehmann note to Ak. 29: 999₂₈] Baumgarten, §248 (Ak. 17: 81): "every being has a certain degree of reality <*omne ens habet certum realitatis gradum*>." – Christian Wolff, *Ontologia*, §746: "That by which identical qualities can differ, we call degree. . . . Degree is an intrinsic difference of the same qualities, that is, a difference that occurs only in the same [qualities], their identity being preserved <*Gradum apellamus id, quo qualitates eaedem salva identitate differre possunt. . . . Gradus est discrimen internum qualitatum earundem, scilicet quod solum salva identitate in easdem cadit*>."

37 [Lehmann note to Ak. 29: 1000₂₁] Baumgarten, §36 (Ak. 17: 34): "Those things which are posited in something in determining [the thing] (marks and predicates) are DETERMINATIONS, some positive and affirmative, which if it exists in fact is REALITY, others negative, which if it exists in fact is NEGATION <*Quae determinando ponuntur in aliquo (notae et praedicata), sunt DETERMINA-*

TIONES (G: *Bestimmungen*), *altera positiva, et affirmativa, quae si vere sit, est* REALITAS, *altera negativa, quae si vere sit, est* NEGATIO (G: *Verneinungen*)>." – Wolff, *Ontologia*, §243: "Whatever is, or is thought to be able to be, is called a thing, insofar as it is something <*quicquid est vel esse posse concipitur, dicitur Res, quatenus est aliquid*>."

38 Cf. note 23 (to Ak. 29: 989₁₈). Lehmann notes (Ak. 29: 1003₃₁): Christian Wolff, *Ontologia*, §361: "unity is some part of any common number or of any rational integer <*unitas est pars aliquota cujuslibet numeri vulgaris seu rationalis integri*>."

39 [Lehmann note to Ak. 29: 1001₂₃] Baumgarten, §807 (Ak. 17: 158): "All realities are indeed positive, nor is any negation a reality <*Omnes realitates sunt vere positiva, nec ulla negatio est realitas*>." Negation in the strictest sense is privation (<*privatio;* G: *Beraubung*>) (§137; Ak. 17: 55).

40 [Lehmann note to Ak. 29: 1001₃₂] Baumgarten, §146 (Ak. 17: 56): "That by which, when it is posited, the imperfect is posited, is BAD, hence negations are bad: either negation strictly so called, in which case they are METAPHYSICALLY BAD – that by which, when it is posited, the absolute, necessarily imperfect is posited – or privations <*Quo posito ponitur imperfectio,* MALUM (G: *Das Übel, Böse*) *est, hinc negationes sunt malum, eaeque vel stricte dictae,* MALUM METAPHYSICUM (G: *das schlechterdings nothwendige*), *quo posito ponitur imperfectio absoluta necessaria, vel privationes*>." – The question of the metaphysically bad belongs to the fundamental questions of Leibniz's *Essais de théodicée sur la bonté de Dieu, la liberté de l'homme et l'origine du mal* (Theodicy: Essays on the Goodness of God, the Freedom of Man, and the Origin of Evil) (Amsterdam, 1710); it consists in imperfection: "It can be that all evils are merely nothing in comparison to the goods that are in the universe" (*Opera Philosophica* (Philosophical Works), ed. by J. E. Erdmann (Berlin, 1890); reprint: Aalen, 1974, p. 509). Kant later dismissed this Leibnizian "optimism" in his "On the Failure of all Philosophical Attempts in Theodicy." – Cf. a sketch of Kant's toward answering the Berlin Academy "prize essay" question on optimism for the year 1755, printed as Refls. #3703–5 (Ak. 17: 229–39); the note to Ak. 28: 1076₂₂₋₃ (*Religionlehre Pölitz*).

41 [Lehmann note to Ak. 29: 1004₂₇₋₃₆] Printed from *Metaphysik Vigilantius (K₃)* (Ak. 28: 824₃₃–825₈; Arnoldt selections).

42 [Lehmann note to Ak. 29: 1005₂₀f] Baumgarten, §193 (Ak. 17: 67): "Accidents if they seem to subsist through their own power are SUBSTANTIATED PHENOMENA (that appearing to subsist by itself) <*Accidentia si videntur per se subsistentia, sunt* PHAENOMENA SUBTANTIATA (G: *das vor sich zu bestehn scheinende*)>."

43 [Lehmann note to Ak. 29: 1006₃₁] Baumgarten, §358 (Ak. 17: 104): "In this world there exists effective connection (the rule of power), the connection of usefulness, the connection of uses, final connection (the rule of wisdom), subjective and formal connection, exemplary connection, signifying connection. Hence, connections of this sort are possible in the world <*In hoc mundo exsistit nexus effectivus (regnum potentiae), utilitatis, usuum, finalis (regnum sapientiae), subiectivus et formalis, exemplaris, significativus. Hinc nexus eiusmodi sunt in mundo possibiles*>."

44 [Lehmann note to Ak. 29: 1007₂₁] Cf. the *Metaphysik Mrongovius* (Ak. 29:

866_{10}), as well as the notes to Ak. 28: 326_{1of} (*Metaphysik L,*) and Ak. 28: 1108_{12f} (*Religionslehre Pölitz*).

45 [Lehmann note to Ak. 29: 1007_{30}] See the *Metaphysik Mrongovius* (Ak. 29: 823_{23f}), also note 6 to *Metaphysik K$_2$* (Ak. 28: 759_{3-4}), above. Baumgarten defines in Sect. 2 ("Interaction of Worldly Substances" <*substantiarum mundanarum commercium*>) §450 (Ak. 17: 120), physical influence <*influxus physicus*> as "the real INFLUENCE of a substance of a part of the world on another part of the world <*INFLUXUS realis substantiae mundi partis in aliam mundi partem*>." – §451 (Ak. 17: 120): "The system of universal physical influence does not deny the reciprocal harmony of the substances of the world . . . but [denies] preestablished [harmony] <*systema influxus physici universalis non tollit harmoniam substantiarum mundi mutuam . . . sed praestabilitam*>." The system of "so-called only occasional causes" is then referred to Descartes (and Malebranche), but occasionalism proper (Geulincx) is not named (§452). On the "psychological theory of physical influence" <*systema influxus physici psychologicum*> as Baumgarten developed it in the Rational Psychology (§§761ff; Ak. 17: 145f), cf. Karl Spazier, *Antiphädon, oder Prüfung einiger Hauptbeweise für die Ewigkeit und Sterblichkeit der menschlichen Seele in Briefen* (Anti-Phaedo, or Examination of Some Main Arguments for the Eternity and Mortality of the Human Soul, in Letters) (Berlin, 1783), pp. 111f.

46 [Lehmann note to Ak. 29: $1011_{30}-1012_{16}$] Printed in *Metaphysik Vigilantius* (*K,*) (Ak. 28: 837_{9-33}; Schlapp excerpt).

47 [Lehmann note to Ak. 29: 1015_{21}] Cf. the (contemporaneous, and stemming from Vigilantius – i.e., the presumed author of these notes) *Metaphysik der Sitten Vigilantius*, §132 (AK. 27: 706_{15-20}): "The duty to give *alms to the poor* and *support to the needy* differ in this: from the side of the poor the former is a begged assistance and is based on distress . . . the latter, on the other hand, presupposes an extended state or certain situation that makes someone needy of help, to be saved from this situation. . . ." Like here, Kant also requires in the *Doctrine of Justice* (Ak. 6: 326) to insure the care of the poor through continuing contributions by the state.

48 [Lehmann note to Ak. 29: 1017_{36}] Cf. Kant's remarks in his essays "On the Common Saying: 'This may be true in theory, but it does not apply in practice' " (Ak. 8: 302) and "Perpetual Peace" (Ak. 8: 372_{33-4}): "through the turbulence of a revolution created by a bad constitution."

49 In *Metaphysik L$_2$* the "philosopher's cross" is characterized as the proof of the principle of sufficient reason (Ak. 28: 551_{26}).

50 [Lehmann note to Ak. 29: 1022_{18}] On August Wilhelm Rehburg (1757–1836), see Kant's *Briefwechsel* (Correspondence) (Ak. 13: 220). Rehburg was a politician, bureaucrat, philosopher, and studied in Göttingen, where he also died. In 1786 he became an adviser in state affairs in the ministry at Hanover, and took leave of his post in 1820. Of his numerous writings and reviews (e.g., on Kant's *CrPR*), the most important is: *Über das Verhältnis der Metaphysik zu den Religionen* (On the Relation of Metaphysics to the Religions) (1787). [Given Rehberg's determinism, the marginal reference (perhaps added by Reicke or Arnoldt, and thus not necessarily stemming from the lecture) is likely meant to indicate difficulties, rather than support, for the argument for freedom in the text.]

51 [Lehmann note to Ak. 29: 1023_{36}] Cf. note 14 *Metaphysik Dohna* (Ak. 28: 683_9), above.

52 [Lehmann note to Ak. 29: 1027_{13}] Baumgarten, §750 (Ak. 17: 143): "The human soul moves its own body. Therefore it has THE FACULTY of moving something posited outside of itself, i.e. [the] LOCOMOTIVE [faculty] <*Anima humana corpus suum movet. Ergo habet FACULTATEM movendi quid extra se positum, i.e. LOCOMOTIVAM*>."

53 [Lehmann note to Ak. 29: 1030_{12}] Baumgarten's Rational Psychology, Sect. 3 ("Origin of the Human Soul" <*origo animae humanae*>), §§770–5 (Ak. 17: 148–9). [See notes 228 and 229 to *Metaphysik Mrongovius* (Ak. 29: 910_6 and Ak. 29: 910_{17}, respectively), above.]

54 [Lehmann note to Ak. 29: 1031_{26}] "now generally assumed" – namely, after the discovery of spermatozoa and Blumenbach's "formative drive." Cf. *Critique of Judgment* (Ak. 5: 424).

55 [Lehmann note to Ak. 29: 1032_{28f}] As spiritualism and phenomenalism, the Leibnizian philosophy – in contrast to the immaterialism of Berkeley – is ambiguous with respect to matter: there is primary and secondary matter (<*materia prima . . . secunda*>), neither of which is substance: "*matter*, primary and pure, taken without the souls and lives which are united to it, is purely passive . . . *secondary matter* as, for example, body, is not a substance, but for another reason, which is that it is merely a collection of several substances . . . an accidental unity <*Unum per accidens*>, in a word, a phenomenon" (Leibniz to Remond, 1715, *Opera Philosophica* (Philosophical Works), ed. by J. Erdmann (Aalen, 1974), vol. 3, p. 736; tr. in *Leibniz Selections*, ed. by Philip P. Wiener (New York: Scribner's, 1951), p. 554). Christian Wolff (*Ontologia*, §949) distinguishes matter from which <*materia ex qua*>, in which <*in qua*>, and around which <*circa quam*>. Thus also Baumgarten, §295 (Ak. 17: 92): "MATTER to which this power alone is attributed, is PRIMARY <*MATERIA, cui haec sola vis tribuitur, est PRIMA*>"; §296 (Ak. 17: 92): "that to which a motive power is attributed is a physical BODY (secondary matter) and a substantiated phenomenon <*cui vis motrix tribuitur, est CORPUS physicum (materia secunda) et phaenomenon substantiatum*>."

56 [Lehmann note to Ak. 29: 1033_{26}] See *CrPR* (A 668/B 696): "Similar observations are relevant in regard to the assertion or denial of the widely discussed law of the *continuous gradation* of creatures, which was brought into fashion by Leibniz, and admirably supported by Bonnet. It is simply the following out of the principle of affinity which rests on the interest of reason."

57 Moses Mendelssohn, *Phädon, oder über die Unsterblichkeit der Seele* (Phaedo, or On the Immortality of the Soul) (Berlin: F. Nicolai, 1767).

58 [Lehmann note to Ak. 29: 1038_{28}] Cf. *Critique of Judgment* (Ak. 5: 278_{3-4}): "because the mind for itself alone is entirely life (the principle of life itself)."

59 [Lehmann note to Ak. 29: 1040_{16}] Baumgarten, Sect. 4 ("Divine Decrees" <*decreta divina*>), §980 (Ak. 17: 202–3): "A DECREE OF GOD is said to be ABSOLUTE if its *motive was neither the foreseen perfection of the object nor its [foreseen] imperfection;* on the other hand, [a decree of God] which is a consequence of the foreseen perfection or imperfection of the object [is said to be] HYPOTHETICAL; no decrees of God concerning contingencies are absolute, all are hypothetical <*DECRETUM DEI ABSOLUTUM* (G: *der unbedingte*) *si dicitur,*

cuius motivum nec praevisa obiecti perfectio, nec imperfectio fuit, HYPOTHETICUM (G: *der bedingte Rathschluss Gottes) contra, quod praevisam obiecti perfectionem imperfectionemve sequitur; nulla dei de contingentibus decreta sunt absoluta, omnia hypothetica*>." Also, Refl. #3700 (Ak. 17: 202): "Whether the divine will is determined in itself by motives, or is merely thought by us according to this analogy?" – Cf. *Danziger Rationaltheologie* (Ak. 28: 1315$_{37-9}$): "Speculative minds are to be forgiven the concepts of predestination <*praedestinationi*> and absolute decree <*absoluto decreto*>; but how theologians, whose end is moral, could cherish them is incomprehensible."

Bibliography of Kant's works cited in the explanatory notes

"Announcement of the Programme of his Lectures for the Winter Semester 1765–6" ("*Nachricht von der Einrichtung seiner Vorlesungen in dem Winterhalbenjahr von 1765– 1766*" [Ak. 2: 303–13]) (1765). Translated by David Walford in Immanuel Kant, *Theoretical Philosophy 1755–1770*, edited by David Walford (Cambridge: Cambridge University Press, 1992), pp. 287–300.

Anthropologie Mrongovius (1785).

Anthropologie Parow (c. 1772/73).

Anthropologie Philippi (1772).

Anthropology from a Pragmatic Point of View (Anthropologie in pragmatischer Hinsicht [Ak. 7: 117–334]) (Königsberg: Friedrich Nicolovius, 1798; 2nd ed., 1800). Translated by Mary J. Gregor (The Hague: Martinus Nijhoff, 1974).

Anweisung zur Menschen- und Weltkenntniss, from the lectures of winter semester 1790–1, edited by Friedrich Christian Starke [pseudonym of Johann Adam Bergk] (Leipzig: Expedition des europäischen Aufsehers, 1831). New ed. (Quedlinburg: Ernst, 1838).

"An Attempt at Some Reflections on Optimism by Immanuel Kant, also containing an announcement of his lectures for the coming semester. 7th October 1759" ("*Versuch einiger Betrachtungen über den Optimismus von M. Immanuel Kant, wodurch er zugleich seine Vorlesungen auf das bevorstehende halbe Jahr ankündigt. Den 7. October 1759*" [Ak. 2: 27– 36]) (Königsberg: J. F. Driest, 1759). Translated by David Walford in Immanuel Kant, *Theoretical Philosophy 1755–1770*, edited by David Walford (Cambridge: Cambridge University Press, 1992), pp. 67–83.

"Attempt to Introduce the Concept of Negative Magnitudes into Philosophy" ("*Versuch den Begriff der negativen Grössen in die Weltweisheit einzuführen*" [Ak. 2: 165–204]) (Königsberg: Johann Jakob Kanter, 1763). Translated by David Walford in Immanuel Kant, *Theoretical Philosophy 1755–1770*, edited by David Walford (Cambridge: Cambridge University Press, 1992), pp. 203–41.

Berliner Physik [Ak. 29: 73–92] (1776?).

The Conflict of the Faculties (Der Streit der Fakultäten [Ak. 7: 1–116]) (Königsberg: Friedrich Nicolovius, 1798). Translated by Mary J. Gregor (New York: Abaris Books, 1979).

Critique of Judgment (Kritik der Urteilskraft [Ak. 5: 165–486]) (Berlin and Libau: Lagarde and Friederich, 1790; 2nd ed., 1793). Translated by James Creed Meredith (Oxford: Clarendon Press, 1952) and Werner S. Pluhar (Indianapolis: Hackett Press, 1987).

Critique of Practical Reason (Kritik der praktischen Vernunft [Ak. 5: 1–164]) (Riga: Johann Friedrich Hartknoch, 1788). Translated by Lewis White Beck (Indianapolis: Bobbs-Merrill, 1956).

Critique of Pure Reason [CrPR] (*Kritik der reinen Vernunft* [Ak. 3: 1–552; Ak. 4: 1–252]) (Riga:

J. F. Hartknoch, 1781 ["A"-edition] ["B"-edition, 1787]). Translated by Norman Kemp Smith (London: Macmillan, 1933).

Danziger Physik [Ak. 29: 93–169; "Mrongovius"] (1785).

Danziger Rationaltheologie [Ak. 28: 1227–1319; "Mrongovius"] (1784).

Dreams of a Spirit-Seer Elucidated by Dreams of Metaphysics (*Träume eines Geistersehers, erläutert durch Träume der Metaphysik* [Ak. 2: 315–73]) (Königsberg: Johann Jacob Kanter, 1766). Translated by David Walford in Immanuel Kant, *Theoretical Philosophy 1755–1770*, edited by David Walford (Cambridge: Cambridge University Press, 1992), pp. 301–59.

Entwürfe zu dem Colleg über Anthropologie aus den 70er Jahren [Ak. 15: 657–798].

"Essay on the Maladies of the Mind" (*"Versuch über die Krankheiten des Kopfes"* [Ak. 2: 257–72]) (1764).

"The False Subtlety of the Four Syllogistic Figures Demonstrated by M. Immanuel Kant" (*"Die falsche Spitzfindigkeit der vier syllogistischen Figuren erwiesen von M. Immanuel Kant"* [Ak. 2: 45–62]) (Königsberg: Johann Jacob Kanter, 1762). Translated by David Walford in Immanuel Kant, *Theoretical Philosophy 1755–1770*, edited by David Walford (Cambridge: Cambridge University Press, 1992), pp. 85–105.

"First Introduction to the *Critique of Judgment*" [Ak. 20: 193–251] (1790, unpubl.). Translated by James Haden (Indianapolis: Bobbs-Merrill, 1965).

"Further Reflections on Earthquakes" (*"Fortgesetzte Betrachtung der seit einiger Zeit wahrgenommenen Erderschütterungen"* [Ak. 1: 463–72]) (1756).

Groundwork to a Metaphysic of Morals (*Grundlegung zur Metaphysik der Sitten* [Ak. 4: 385–464]) (Riga: Johann Friedrich Hartknoch, 1785; 2nd ed., 1786). Translated by H. J. Paton (London: Hutchinson, 1949) and Lewis White Beck as *Foundations of the Metaphysics of Morals* (Indianapolis: Bobbs-Merrill, 1959).

"Idea for a Universal History with a Cosmopolitan Purpose" (*"Idee zu einer allgemeinen Geschichte in weltbürgerlicher Absicht"* [Ak. 8: 15–32]) (in *Berlinischen Monatsschrift*, pp. 385–411, November 1784). Translated by H. B. Nisbet in Immanuel Kant, *Political Writings*, edited by Hans Reiss, 2nd ed. (Cambridge: Cambridge University Press, 1991), pp. 41–53.

Lectures on Philosophical Theology, translated by Allen W. Wood and Gertrude M. Clark (Cornell University Press, 1978). Translation based on 2nd ed. of *Immanuel Kants Vorlesungen über die philosophische Religionslehre*, edited by Pölitz (1830; 1st ed., 1817).

Logik Blomberg [Ak. 24: 7–302]. Translated by J. Michael Young in Immanuel Kant, *Lectures on Logic* (Cambridge: Cambridge University Press, 1992), pp. 5–246.

Logik Dohna-Wundlacken [Ak. 24: 687–784]. Translated by J. Michael Young in Immanuel Kant, *Lectures on Logic* (Cambridge: Cambridge University Press, 1992), pp. 425–516.

Logik Jäsche (*Immanuel Kants Logik, ein Handbuch zu Vorlesungen*, edited by Gottlob Benjamin Jäsche [Ak. 9: 1–150]) (Königsberg: Friedrich Nicolovius, 1800). Translated by J. Michael Young in Immanuel Kant, *Lectures on Logic* (Cambridge: Cambridge University Press, 1992), pp. 517–640.

Logik Mrongovius [Ak. 29: 1043–7] (1784).

Logik Philippi [Ak. 24: 303–496] (1772).

Marburger Anthropologie (ms).

Menschenkunde oder philosophische Anthropologie. Nach handschriftlichen Vorlesungen, edited by Fr. Ch. Starke [pseudonym for Johann Adam Bergk] (Leipzig: 1831). Stemming from anthropology lectures of 1778/79 or 1787/88.

Metaphysic of Morals (*Die Metaphysik der Sitten* [Ak. 6: 203–494]) (Königsberg: Friedrich

Nicolovius, 1797; 2nd ed.: 1798). Edited and introduced by Roger Sullivan, translated by Mary J. Gregor, 2nd ed. (Cambridge: Cambridge University Press, 1995).

Metaphysical First Principles of Natural Science (*Metaphysische Anfangsgründe der Naturwissenschaft* [Ak. 4: 465–566]) (Riga: Johann Friedrich Hartknoch, 1786). Translated by James Ellington as *Metaphysical Foundations of Natural Science* (Indianapolis: Bobbs-Merrill, 1970).

Metaphysik Vigilantius (*K₃*) [Ak. 29: 941–1040] (1794/95). Translated in this volume. Excerpts from Emil Arnoldt (1909) and Otto Schlapp (1901) reprinted at Ak. 28: 817–38.

Metaphysik der Sitten Vigilantius [Ak. 27: 475–732] (1793/94).

Metaphysik Dohna [Ak. 28: 613–702] (1792/93). Selection translated in this volume.

Metaphysik Herder [Ak. 28: 1–166] (1762–64). Selection translated in this volume.

Metaphysik K₂ [Ak. 28: 705–816] (early 1790s?). Selection translated in this volume.

Metaphysik L₁ [Ak. 28: 167–350] (mid 1770s?). Selection translated in this volume.

Metaphysik L₂ [Ak. 28:: 525–610] (1790/91?). Selection translated in this volume.

Metaphysik Mrongovius [Ak. 29: 743–940] (1782/83). Translated in this volume.

Metaphysik Rosenhagen (not extant; mid 1770s?).

Metaphysik Volckmann [Ak. 28: 351–459] (1784/85). Selection translated in this volume.

Metaphysik von Schön [Ak. 28: 461–524] (late 1780s?).

Moral Mrongovius [Ak. 27: 1395–1581] (late 1770s?).

Moral Mrongovius II [Ak. 29: 593–642] (1784/85).

Moralphilosophie Collins [Ak. 27: 237–473] (1784/85).

Nachträge Herder [Ak. 28: 839–962] (1762–4).

Natürliche Theologie Volckmann [ak. 28: 1127–1226] (1783).

Naturrecht Feyerabend [Ak. 27: 1317–94] (1784/85).

A New Elucidation of the First Principles of Metaphysical Cognition (*Principiorum primorum cognitionis metaphysicae nova dilucidatio* [Ak. 1: 385–416]) (Königsberg: J. H. Hartung, 1755). Translated by David Walford in Immanuel Kant, *Theoretical Philosophy 1755–1770*, edited by David Walford (Cambridge: Cambridge University Press, 1992), pp. 1–45.

"On the Common Saying: 'This may be true in theory, but it does not apply in practice' " (*"Über den Gemeinspruch: Das mag in der Theorie richtig sein, taugt aber nicht für die Praxis"* [Ak. 8: 273–314]) in *Berlinischen Monatsschrift*, pp. 201–84, September 1793. Translated by H. B. Nisbet in Immanuel Kant, *Political Writings*, edited by Hans Reiss, 2nd ed. (Cambridge: Cambridge University Press, 1991), pp. 61–92.

"On a Discovery, according to which any new Critique of Pure Reason is made Dispensable through an Older" [Essay against Eberhard] (*"Über eine Entdeckung, nach der alle neue Kritik der reinen Vernunft durch eine ältere entbehrlich gemacht werden soll"* [Ak. 8: 185–252]) (1793). Translated by Henry E. Allison in *The Kant-Eberhard Controversy* (Baltimore: The Johns Hopkins University Press, 1973).

"On the Failure of all Philosophical Attempts in Theodicy" (*"Über das Misslingen aller philosophischen Versuche in der Theodicee"* [Ak. 8: 253–72]) (1791). Translated by Michel Despland as "On the Failure of All Attempted Philosophical Theodicies" in Despland, *Kant on History and Religion* (Montreal: McGill University Press, 1973).

On the Form and Principles of the Sensible and the Intelligible World [Inaugural Dissertation] (*De mundi sensibilis atque intelligibilis forma et principiis* [Ak. 2: 385–420]) (Königsberg: Johann Jakob Kanter, 1770). Translated by David Walford in Immanuel Kant, *Theoretical Philosophy 1755–1770*, edited by David Walford (Cambridge: Cambridge University Press, 1992), pp. 373–416.

"On the Organ of the Soul" (*"Aus Sömmering über das Organ der Seele"* [Ak. 12: 30–5, a letter to Sömmering, Aug. 10, 1795]) in Samuel Thomas Sömmering, *Über das Organ der Seele, nebst einen Schreiben von Imm. Kant* (Königsberg: Friedrich Nicolovius, 1796), pp. 81–6.

"On Philosophers' Medicine of the Body" ("*De medicina corporis, quae philosophorum est*") [Ak. 15: 939–53] (1788?). Translated by Mary J. Gregor in *Kant's Latin Writings: Translations, Commentaries, and Notes,* edited by Lewis White Beck (New York: Peter Lang Publ., 1986), pp. 228–43.

"On the use of Teleological Principles in Philosophy" ("*Über den Gebrauch teleologischer Principien in der Philosophie*" [Ak. 7: 157–84]) (in *Teutscher Merkur,* Jan./Feb. 1788).

The Only Possible Argument in Support of a Demonstration of the Existence of God (Der einzig mögliche Beweisgrund zu einer Demonstration des Daseyns Gottes [Ak. 2: 63–164]) (Königsberg: Johann Jakob Kanter, 1763). Translated by David Walford in Immanuel Kant, *Theoretical Philosophy 1755–1770,* edited by David Walford (Cambridge: Cambridge University Press, 1992), pp. 107–201.

Opus postumum [Ak. 21 and 22] (written c. 1790–1801). Translated by Eckart Förster and Michael Rosen, edited by Eckart Förster (Cambridge: Cambridge University Press, 1993).

"Perpetual Peace: A Philosophical Sketch" ("*Zum ewigen Frieden. Ein philosophischer Entwurf.*" [Ak. 8: 341–86]) (Königsberg: Friedrich Nicolovius, 1795). Translated by H. B. Nisbet in Immanuel Kant, *Political Writings,* edited by Hans Reiss, 2nd ed. (Cambridge: Cambridge University Press, 1991), pp. 93–130.

Philosophische Enzyklopädie [Ak. 29: 1–45] (late 1770s).

Philosophische Religionslehre Pölitz [Ak. 28: 989–1126]. First published as *Immanuel Kants Vorlesungen über die philosophische Religionslehre,* anonymously edited by Karl H. Ludwig Pölitz (Leipzig: Carl Friedrich Franz, 1817). 2nd ed. (Leipzig: Taubert, 1830). Translated by Allen W. Wood and Gertrude M. Clark as *Lectures on Philosophical Theology* (Cornell University Press, 1978).

Physical Geography (Physische Geographie [Ak. 9: 151–436]), "edited and in part revised at the author's request, from his own manuscript, by Fr. Th. Rink" (Königsberg: Göbbels and Unzer, 1802), 1st vol.: xvi, 312 pp. 2nd vol.: 248 pp.

Physische Geographie Powalski (1777).

Physischen Geographie Dohna (1792).

Praktische Philosophie Herder [Ak. 27: 1–89] (early 1760s).

Praktische Philosophie Powalski [Ak. 27: 93–235] (late 1770s?).

Prolegomena to any Future Metaphysics that will be able to present itself as a Science (Prolegomena zu einer jeden künftigen Metaphysik, die als Wissenschaft wird auftreten können [Ak. 4: 253–384]) (Riga: J. F. Hartknoch, 1783). Translated by Lewis White Beck (Indianapolis: Bobbs-Merrill, 1950).

Reflexionen zur physischen Geographie [Ak. 14: 539–635].

Religion within the Bounds of Unaided Reason (Die Religion innerhalb der Grenzen der blossen Vernunft [Ak. 6: 1–202]) (Königsberg, 1793; 2nd ed., 1794). Translated by Theodore M. Greene and Hoyt H. Hudson as *Religion within the Limits of Reason Alone* (New York: Harper & Row, 1960).

"Review of Herder Ideas" ("*Recension von J. G. Herders Ideen zur Philosophie der Geschichte der Menschheit*" [Ak. 8: 43–66]) (printed in three parts in the *Jenaier Allgemeinen Literatur-Zeitung:* January 6 (pp. 17–20); Appendix to the March issue; November 15 (pp. 153–6), 1785). Translated by H. B. Nisbet in Immanuel Kant, *Political Writings,* edited by Hans Reiss, 2nd ed. (Cambridge: Cambridge University Press, 1991), pp. 201–20.

"Review of Johann Heinrich Schulz" (*"Rezension von [Johann Heinrich] Schulz's Versuch einer Anleitung zur Sittenlehre für alle Menschen, ohne Unterschied der Religion, nebst einem Anhang von den Todesstrafen"* [Ak. 8: 9–14]) in *Räsonnirendes Bücherverzeichnis* (Königsberg, 1783).

Thoughts on the True Estimation of Living Forces (*Gedanken von der wahren Schätzung der lebendigen Kräfte und Beurtheilung der Beweise, deren sich Herr von Leibniz und andere Mechaniker in dieser Streitsache bedient haben, nebst einigen vorhergehenden Betrachtungen, welche die Kraft der Körper überhaupt betreffen* [Ak. 1: 1–182]) (1747).

Universal Natural History and Theory of the Heavens, or Essay on the Constitution and Mechanical Origin of the Entire Universe, treated in accordance with Newtonian Principles (*Allgemeine Naturgeschichte und Theorie des Himmels oder Versuch von der Verfassung und dem mechanischen Ursprunge des ganzen Weltgebäudes, nach Newtonischen Grundsätzen abgehandelt* [Ak. 1: 215–368]) (Königsberg and Leipzig: Johann Friederich Petersen, 1755). Translated by W. Hastie (Glasgow: J. Maclehose, 1900). Revised and edited by Willey Ley (New York: Greenwood Publ. Co., 1968).

Vernunfttheologie Magath [Ak. 29: 1049–77].

Eine Vorlesung Kants über Ethik, edited by Paul Menzer (Berlin, 1924). Translated by Louis Infeld as *Lectures on Ethics* (London, 1930; reprint: New York, 1963).

"What Is Orientation in Thinking?" (*Was heißt: Sich im Denken orientiren?* [Ak. 8: 131–46] in *Berlinische Monatsschrift*, 8: 304–30, October 1786. Translated by H. B. Nisbet in Immanuel Kant, *Political Writings*, edited by Hans Reiss, 2nd ed. (Cambridge: Cambridge University Press, 1991), pp. 237–49.

What Real Progress Has Metaphysics Made in Germany since the Time of Leibniz and Wolff? (*Welches sind die wirklichen Fortschritte, die die Metaphysik seit Leibnizens und Wolfs Zeiten in Deutschland gemacht hat?* [Ak. 20: 253–332]) (1804). Translated by Ted Humphrey (New York: Abaris Books, 1983).

Wiener Logik [Ak. 24: 785–940] (early 1780s). Translated by J. Michael Young in Immanuel Kant, *Lectures on Logic* (Cambridge: Cambridge University Press, 1992), pp. 247–377.

Name index

617

Subject index

Two sets of numbers are used in this index. Section-numbers – for example, §369 – refer to the Concordance, which is arranged by the sections of Baumgarten's *Metaphysics*. All other numbers refer to pages in this volume. This index includes all topics listed in the Concordance (except for certain redundant subtopics) as well as many other topics. Where all the relevant passages are cited in the Concordance under a section number of Baumgarten, we simply refer to the relevant section.

Science (*cont.*)
  classification of, 119, 245, 281, 307–8,
    337, 381, 413 (*see also* Metaphysics,
    kinds of)
  discipline & doctrine, 381, 413
  natural, 113, 125, 130, 135–6, 142, 284,
    295, 305, 354, 361, 373 (*see also*
    Physics)
  & philosophy/metaphysics, 43, 111–13,
    117, 130, 134, 136–41, 267, 286,
    300–1, 419–20, 441
  & system, 111, 125, 300
  treatment of, dogmatic & critical, 134–5,
    285
  worth of, 44, 100–1, 300
Self, §§672, 727, 730, 742 (*see also* Consciousness, self-; Soul)
  concept of I, 44–6, 79, 84–7, 350–1,
    404
  as human being, soul, & spirit, §742;
    175, 343–4, 372
Sempiternity (*see* Eternity)
Sensation (*sensatio; Empfindung*), §§537–8,
  541–3, 567; 150, 154, 187, 219, 279,
  296, 314, 338, 373–4, 466–8, 480 (*see
  also* Illusion; Perception)
  & brain/nerves, 74, 91, 386–7, 398,
    494–6
  & cognition, 152–3, 249–50, 314, 345
  degree of, 192, 218, 467
  faculty of, 53, 88, 250 (*see also* Sensibil-
    ity)
  & impression, 52, 154, 187, 494–5
  & intuition, 157–8, 250, 314, 374, 433,
    440, 442, 467
  & perception, 149, 250, 467
  privacy/subjectivity of, 52, 66–7, 149,
    159, 374, 467
  sense- (= aesthetic), 479–80
Sense (*sensus; Sinn*), §§534–56; 374
  common (*sensu commu; gesunde Verstand*),
    27, 129
  inner & outer, §535; 25–7, 43–6, 78–9,
    83–91, 103, 118, 152, 154, 187, 190–
    1, 228–9, 245–8, 250–2, 270, 275,
    344–5, 350–1, 357, 371–5, 382–3,
    397, 410–11, 418, 427, 443, 450–1,
    473, 479, 495 (*see also* Hearing; Sight;
    Smell; Taste; Touch)
  objective & subjective, 50, 345, 374–5
  private & universal, 64–7
  vital, 251, 345
Sensibility (*Sinnlichkeit*), 48–50, 53, 58, 73,
  151–2, 169, 247, 249–50, 331, 344–
  5, 373–4, 444, 448, 451–2
  a priori, 153, 339, 444
  & *a priori* conditions, 153, 371
  & beautiful, 66–8, 259–60, 377

faculty of, 67, 442, 444
form of, 151–4, 189–91, 206, 441–44,
  450–2, 457, 473, 489
law/rule of, 68, 87, 152, 259–60, 268–9,
  346, 362, 480
outer, 87
Sensibles (*sensibilia; Empfindbaren*) (*see* Intelligibles, & sensibles)
Separate & separable, §72
Sight, 7, 27, 45, 47–50, 54, 67, 70, 86,
  101, 124, 152–4, 157, 190, 198, 213–
  14, 222, 226, 247–8, 251–2, 256,
  262, 274, 279, 375, 397, 400, 443,
  445, 498 (*see also* Color; Hearing;
  Smell; Taste; Touch)
Sign & signified, §§347–50
Signifying, faculty of (*facultas signandi;
  Bezeichnungsvermögen*), 49, 250, 255
  (*see also* Characterization, faculty of)
Similar, equal, & congruent, §§70–1,
  265–7
Simples, §§224–45, 392–405 (*see also* Com-
  posites; Matter, & divisibility; Mo-
  nads)
Simultaneous (*simultanea; gleichzeitig*),
  §§280–96
Single (*unicum*), §77
Singulars (*singularia; Einzelne*), are actual,
  §152
Skepticism (*see* Dogmatism, & skepticism)
Sleep, §§555–6, 782 (*see also* Dreams)
Smell, 50, 67, 251–2 (*see also* Hearing;
  Sight; Taste; Touch)
Solipsism (*see* Egoism)
Somatology, 357–8, 371 (*see also* Cosmology)
Soul (*anima; Seele*), §§504–18, 700, 740–
  60, 770–5, 780, 782–99; 78–81, 86,
  95, 118, 247–8, 272, 278–9, 290,
  354, 372, 381, 383, 395, 496–7 (*see
  also* Body, & soul; Explanation, of
  soul; Immortality of soul; Material
  ideas; Mind; Perception, of self; Psychology; Self; Spirit; Thought)
  actions of, 75–6, 86–4, 90–1, 95, 223,
    254, 272, 273–4, 405, 504
  cognition/knowledge of, 75–6, 96, 277,
    290, 381, 452
  concept of, 76–8, 83–9, 94, 105, 118,
    438
  incentives of (*elateres animi*), 262, 265,
    347, 379, 484
  is singular/simple, §742; 75, 84, 227,
    275, 437, 502
  & matter, 271–2, 383, 400
  migration of (*metempsychosis;
    Seelenwanderung, Seelenversetzung*),
    §784